Table of Contents

Foreword by Muhammad Yunus

Unit One: Introduction to the Field of Development

Chapter One: Introduction	p. 3
Chapter Two: The Realities of Poverty in the LDCs	p. 9
Chapter Three: The Challenges of Conceptualizing World Poverty	p. 41
Chapter Four: Toward an Understanding of the Concept of Development	p. 65

Unit Two: The Concept of Rural Development — p. 101

Chapter Five: Concept of Rural Development	p. 103
Case One: The Y. C. James Yen Story	p. 125
Case Two: The Village Bank System of Egypt	p. 135
Case Three: Sarvodaya: A New Form of Development	p. 147
Case Four: The Grameen Bank	p. 160
Case Five: ACCORD Organization	p. 168
Lessons Learned From the Case Studies	p. 175

Unit Three: Becoming an RDF, Challenges of Training — p. 181

Chapter Six: Is A Career in Development for You?	p. 183
Chapter Seven: Getting the Most From RDF Education and Training	p. 203
Chapter Eight: Stage One of Rural Development: The Process of Trust Building and Cultural Awareness	p. 237
Chapter Nine: Stage Two of Rural Development: The Process of Problem-Solving in Village Development	p. 267
Chapter Ten: Stage Three of Rural Development: The Process of Local Institution Building, Empowerment, Networking and Coalition Building:	p. 299

Unit Four: Five Dimensions of Rural Development — p. 323

Chapter Eleven: First Dimension: Non Formal Education and Grassroots Literacy Programs	p. 327
Chapter Twelve: Second Dimension: Primary Health Care in the Village	p. 349
Chapter Thirteen: Third Dimension: The Role of Agriculture and Small Scale Enterprise in Village Development	p. 389
Chapter Fourteen: Fourth Dimension: A Concern and an Appreciation for the Local Environment.	p. 417
Chapter Fifteen: Fifth Dimension: Local Culture Enhancement: A Key to Long-Term Sustainable Development	p. 447
Chapter Sixteen: Reflections On Foreign Aid and Technical Assistance: The Role of NGNOs	p. 473

ONE CAN MAKE A DIFFERENCE

The Challenges and Opportunities of Dealing with World Poverty

The Role of Rural Development Facilitators (RDFs) in the Process of Rural Development

James B. Mayfield

University Press of America, Inc.
Lanham • New York • Oxford

Copyright © 1997 by
University Press of America,® Inc.
4720 Boston Way
Lanham, Maryland 20706

12 Hid's Copse Rd.
Cummor Hill, Oxford OX2 9JJ

All rights reserved
Printed in the United States of America
British Library Cataloguing in Publication Information Available

Library of Congress Cataloging-in-Publication Data

Mayfield, James B.
One can make a difference : the challenges and opportunities of dealing
with world poverty : the role of rural development facilitators (RDFs)
in the process of rural development / James B. Mayfield
p. cm.
Includes index.
1. Rural development--Developing countries. 2. Rural development
personnel--Developing countries. 3. Poverty--Developing countries.
I. Title.
HN981.C6M39 1997 307.1'412'091724--dc21 97-5519 CIP

ISBN 0-7618-0714-4 (cloth: alk. ppr.)
ISBN 0-7618-0715-2 (pbk: alk. ppr.)

∞™ The paper used in this publication meets the minimum
requirements of American National Standard for information
Sciences—Permanence of Paper for Printed Library Materials,
ANSI Z39.48—1984

Foreword

In an age when centralized bureaucracies, large-scale donor agencies, and well funded Non Government Organizations (NGOs) seem to dominate the process of development, it is appropriate to reflect on the hundreds, perhaps thousands, of individuals who have dedicated their lives to living and working among the poorest of the poor, those nearly two billion who often live in the more isolated and disadvantaged villages of the world. Professor Mayfield has sought to outline the processes of rural development, seeking to emphasize the various programs, strategies and interventions that have been successul in confronting the tragedies of world poverty.

It is refreshing to find a book that approaches the challenge of poverty alleviation with some sense of optimism. Professor Mayfield has done the discpline a great service in outlining the many examples of success that are available in the literature. It is easy to criticize the many efforts that have tended to fail, to dwell on the blunders and mistakes that have been made in the past. What we need are models of success, approaches that have worked, interventions that appear to produce sustainable long-term development.

For many of the general public and even a significant number of experts in development, there is not much good that can be said for foreign aid, technical assistance, and the past efforts to help the disadvantaged of this planet. While it is easy to see failure and misuse of funds, a more objective assessment of the past four decades, suggests in a most profound way that there has been far more progress than might be believed in general, that the real test of success, may not be in the budgetary allocations of the larger government programs or in the well-funded international donor agencies, but more in the lives and in the work of the many community development workers, rural development facilitators, village school teachers, primary health care workers, agricultural extension workers, micro-credit workers, and others who are willing to live and work out among the poor, experiencing the heat, the dust, and the misery on a day to day basis -- these are the real heroes of development.

This book has been dedicated to the proposition that *One Person Can Make A Difference.* Over the past several decades we have learned a lot about what works and what does not work in a village setting, what is more apt to be sustainable and what is less likely to be sustainable, and why a sensitivity and an appreciation for the local knowledge, culture and spiritual values of the rural areas of this world may well be far more important than the complicated administration systems, the large budget allocations or the costly technologies that have characterized so much of development work in the past and in the present.

I agree with the notion, that rural development is best defined as "people development," that what is needed is a greater commitment to recruiting and training people to live and work in the rural areas of the world. This is a book that takes us in that direction, that demonstrates a number of successful approaches and interventions, and thereby helps to document that *One Can Make A Difference.*

Muhammad Yunus
Grameen Bank

Unit One
An Introduction to the Field of Rural Development Administration

An Assessment of the Realities of World Poverty
An Attempt at Understanding the Concepts, Theories and Processes of Rural Development

Chapter 1

Introduction

Since time immemorial, Africa, Asia, and Latin America have been, still continue to be, and will remain in the foreseeable future, to be areas of village communities. The predominant poverty found in most of the less developed countries (LDCs) tends to reflect the very high proportion of the population living in rural areas: over 80 percent in Africa, roughly 70 percent in Asia, and nearly 65 percent in Latin America. The fact that there is today nearly three billion people living in rural villages and towns and most of them lack adequate food, medical care, schools and employment opportunities suggest that something needs to be done. Mahatma Gandhi, in describing his own country had this to say: "India is to be found not in its few cities but in its 700,000 villages. But we town dwellers have believed that India is to be found in its towns and the villages were created to minister to our needs. We have hardly paused to inquire if those poor folk get sufficient to eat and clothe themselves with and whether they have a roof to shelter themselves from sun and rain."

This is a book about the challenges of Rural Development which I define as a strategy to enable a specific group of people, the poor men and women of rural areas, to gain for themselves and their children more of what they want and need. It involves helping the poorest among those who seek a livelihood in the rural areas to demand and control more of the benefits of this life.

This book has been some 30 years in the making. It all started in a small village in the Delta region of Egypt. As a young graduate student, I was seeking to understand the process by which the Nasser regime was attempting to introduce change and development into the villages of rural Egypt. I was intrigued by the challenge of such an undertaking, the seemingly impossible task of changing these unchanging peasants. Equally significant, were the contrasting levels of commitment and desire of the young Egyptian professionals working in the village where I was living. First was the young physician reluctantly arrived after being assigned to the village by the Ministry of Health. He was there only because all graduating physicians had to spend at least two years in a village as part of their training in medical school. He admitted to me a desire to help these peasants who suffered so much from disease, poverty, illiteracy and exploitation. Yet one evening as we were discussing the challenge of helping peasants to improve their miserable existence, he shared with me his frustration, even his anger, at being unable to bring about any kind of meaningful change. He saw their resistance to change as the key obstacle. He lamented the superstition, the closed-mindedness, the apathy and fatalistic attitudes that appeared to be so prevalent among these villagers. For this young educated urban-based physician, there seemed to be little hope for these rural people.

A few months later I observed another Egyptian working in the nearby rural community of Mit Ghamr. His name was Ahmad al-Nagger and he was engaged in a project to introduce a simple village banking system into rural Egypt. He too acknowledged the challenge of bringing change to these peasants, but his perception of these peasants was quite different from the young physician. He saw the obstacle not in the peasants themselves but in the system of constraints that characterized their lives. He argued that what they needed was an opportunity, that given some help they were quite capable of improving their own lives. His optimism was contagious and in the community where he was working, he helped establish a functional banking system and provided micro-credit for peasants willing to develop small scale income projects. Later he encouraged the villagers to complete a community school and then helped established a health clinic where mothers sought prenatal care and family planning advice.

Some thirty years later as I now reflect on those two individuals I am struck by the contrast. The physician had been assigned to the village, was there reluctantly in the beginning, yet after living in the village for while, came to see the pathetic conditions of these peasants and therefore had a keen desire to help. After working with them for nearly two years, he had given up. For him there was little hope. In contrast, the bank worker voluntarily went to the village, learned to see the peasants not as they were, but as they could become. He learned to listen to them, to see the world through their eyes and to understand their motivations, their fears and the constraints that characterized their world. These two men represent the contrasting way in which people might approach the tragedy of world poverty. For some there appears little that can be done for the millions of village people living in the squalor of poverty. Yet the proposition that I seek to present for your consideration is that people are making a difference in these rural communities, that problems are being confronted, that village development strategies are available, and that meaningful change is possible.

This book seeks to define rural development as a process that is about people, about their strengthens, weaknesses, about their feelings, hopes and dreams. One cannot travel to the rural areas of Africa, Asia, or Latin America without having feelings of despair and frustration. Experiencing the realities of extreme poverty, illiteracy, disease and social apathy for the first time often evokes feelings of depression. Many will lament the expanding systems of elite exploitation, the mindless examples of human degradation, violence and human rights violations that characterize much of the less developed world. While such structural constraints of exploiting local elites, dominating regional middlemen, and powerful national and international economic interests, often appear determining in most local settings, such predictions, such dominating systems of exploitation, greed, and violence, are not inevitable nor impervious to human will, agency and reflective thought. A model of development that ignores this capacity in the human spirit to reflect, to challenge, to organize, to change such structures overtime is incapable of reflecting the realities of world history. Progress requires more awareness of the ways that our Western-oriented theories of development will often distort what we experience and understand, filtering out potentially important factors that cannot be comfortably accommodated in most Western systems of development thought. The time has come to consider alternative systems of development, structured to reflect both the realities, but also the opportunities that presently exist.

Time for a New Perspective in Rural Development

The experiences of the past 20-30 years demonstrate that solutions to development problems are available, but in order for them to be effective, they must reflect the historical, social, political and economic realities of the areas in question. The context of development continually creates both new obstacles and new opportunities for variation in approach and strategy. Accordingly, it is impossible to draw conclusions from the experiences of one area or situation and expect these findings to be necessarily valid for all other cases. No one set of development interventions or approaches will be capable of accommodating this geographical, cultural and historical diversity.

Development strategists of the past have generally worked within two almost mutually exclusive mind-sets: (1) the top down, highly centralized model seeks to help the disadvantaged of the world by offering them pre-determined, outside funded plans and programs that reflect what the outsider considers to be appropriate. The outsider is the helper, the local people are the beneficiaries, the outsiders, because of their training and experience, often assume that they know what is best for the villagers. The villagers who have so many problems and disadvantages often appear to be very grateful for whatever the outsider might give them. (2) Another mind-set emphasizes the grassroots approach or the single village approach, insisting that villagers must be protected from the harmful influences of the outside world, must be given limited resources that are needed to solve their most pressing problems. This approach tends to reject central government help, insisting that government-support seldom benefits the poor, and often causes more problems that it solves. Interestingly, both approaches are widely used in the business of development and technical assistance and both of them are based upon a common set of assumptions: (1) The outsiders really know best how to help the local communities, (2) the local communities are too poor to mobilize any of their own resources and thus they must rely on outside resources if they are to be helped, and (3) local communities need outsiders to define their problems, identify solutions, and fund the projects to solve these problems.

Between these two approaches is a middle ground approach that emphasizes a different set of assumptions: (1) the disadvantaged communities of the world have been surviving without outsider help for centuries, and thus know a great deal about survival and self-reliance. Their local knowledge, experience, traditions and indigenous institutions are a resource that needs to be developed and supported. (2) few outsiders are aware of the amount of local resources that are actually available in these communities, that can be mobilized once the community is committed to a course of action that is meaningful, meets clearly understood needs and reflects traditional ways of doing things, and (3) long-term sustainability does require that local communities are gradually integrated into the broader society through institutional linkages that strengthen individual competencies, enhance community capacities, and promote mutually beneficial contacts, relationships and associations. Many government and non government agencies that work at the national level often fail to implement programs that penetrate down to the village level. Too many organizations that focus on the village level often introduce programs that are ostensibly for the benefit of the peasants, (marketing and consumer activities) that in reality drain resources from these areas and reinforce elite-dominated systems of exploitation and inequality. Such systems are counter to the interests of the poor, almost never provide long-term benefits, and even when services are provided they are seldom sustainable over time.

While both national-focused and village-focused organizations do have a role to play in development programs, I am suggesting that a more appropriate focus is at the sub national level, where clusters of villages linked to district level political and economic systems have a greater probability of strengthening local leadership, stimulating local resource mobilization, and eventually being linked and integrated into local government systems and national and international support systems in ways that are mutually beneficial. Such a process requires networking, coalition building, even the establishment of mass movements, that unite people in common undertakings. This book acknowledges that such grandiose schemes of mutually beneficial relationships will not be easy, nor implemented without some conflict and serious confrontation. Yet if such processes are to improve the quality of life of the poor, the poor themselves must be intimately involved. The gradual empowerment of such people requires opportunities for them to solve their own problems, to develop confidence and self-esteem, and to learn through day-to-day experiences, the skills needed to organize, manage and confront the constraints they face. The sub-national approach advocated in this book, reflects this basic premise that local participation and involvement is absolutely crucial if the programs and projects implemented are truly to benefit the poor of these planet.

Such processes of local participation and empowerment are seldom initiated without some outside help. This book documents a number of people, individuals I am calling rural development facilitators (RDFs), who have dedicated their lives to improving the quality of life in rural areas, and who have been willing to help in confronting the systems of exploitation and inequality. It appears that such people who can make a difference are most apt to be effective not by working at the national or provincial capital level or contrarily in some isolated village, but better, by developing their skills and capacity for intervention at the district level, at the level where clusters of villages can be integrated and linked to the broader system without destroying their own autonomy, their own sense of community, initiative and innovation. At this level, innovators and risk-takers are more apt to emerge as they work at a level that is generally freer from the demands of the central bureaucracy and the machinations of national politics, but also are broad enough to provide for some economies of scale for program development and also diverse enough to field test a number of different strategies and models of intervention in a variety of different communities.

A General Outline

This book will be divided into four units. The First Unit will seek to describe in some detail the realities of world poverty, to make concrete what is now generally abstract, to bring these realities of sickness and disease, illiteracy and fatalism, malnutrition and passivity to your consciousness. In introducing the statistics of such poverty, it is not easy to make such information real in the sense that we might see what such poverty does to an individual peasant.

Few of us can truly imagine the misery that such people must bear, the mother who weeps over her third child that has died of dehydration, the teenager that walks four kilometers along a dusty road two and three times a day to bring water to her home, the farmer who cultivates his half acre knowing that it will hardly supply the food that his family needs, the young girl who is unable to attend a nearby school because her family needs her to help in the weeding or in the meager harvest of their farm, or the landless peasant who simply cannot find enough work to feed his five children who are all undernourished and sickly.

In this First Unit we shall seek to outline various explanations often given to explain why there is world poverty, to consider various approaches, theories and strategies that have been used over the past fifty years or so and to suggest a process of rural development that might be appropriate for our day and age.

In the Second Unit of this book, a series of case studies is presented to help identify the ways in which one might make a difference. These case studies suggest in specific terms how one individual with energy and commitment was able to introduce interventions that were both sensitive and efficacious in introducing change and improvement. Each case study takes place in a less developed country, each individual approaches the problem of village development from a slightly different perspective, and each one had to confront a very different set of social, political, economic and cultural conditions. Yet it will be the contention of this section, that there are some common principles that characterized all of these efforts at village development and that anyone seeking to make a difference must be aware of and willing to consider these principles.

The Third Unit seeks to introduce to the reader the process by which one might become a rural development facilitator (RDF). Within the broader field of Development there is a sub field that focuses on the processes by which village communities can be energized and organized to confront the challenges of poverty, illiteracy and disease. This new sub-discipline requires special skills and awareness that are not readily developed simply through the reading of a book, or the completion of a university degree. In fact, one of the challenges of this new field of activity is the observation that the work of an RDF requires considerable time in the field, time to live and work with peasants, to appreciate the constraints of their lives. Also in the Third Unit, the three stages of rural development will be defined in some detail, and the processes of empowerment at the individual and at the local community levels are outlined, including a description of how and why the processes of networking and coalition building are so crucial for any long-term process of rural development

The Fourth Unit will present field-tested programs, strategies, approaches and action step interventions in various activities in what I am calling the five dimensions of rural development: literacy, health, income generation, environment protection, and local culture enhancement. In writing this book *One Can Make A Difference*, I am very much aware of the fact that rural development facilitators that will make a difference must have the commitment, the cultural sensitivity, the social awareness, and field experience needed to help people help themselves, but also they will need specific information, knowledge, and competency in areas of interest and relevancy to villagers themselves. One of the interesting dilemmas of this work of village development facilitation is the seemingly contradiction that the more effective the RDF might be, for example, the more technically trained and the more competent the RDF might be in programs related to rural health, village literacy, small-scale enterprises, village credit systems, or in organic agriculture, the greater the danger that the villagers will remain dependent upon that RDF and thus will fail to generate their own sense of responsibility and as a consequence, will be unwilling or unable to take initiative in their own development. Clearly, there are certain skills, competencies, and technical abilities that an RDF needs to be aware of in order to work in a village setting. However, experience also suggests that there needs to be a balance between what the RDF does for the villagers and the extent to which such an RDF is willing to let villagers make mistakes and learn for themselves. In the final analysis, RDFs must continually support local people to take responsibility for their own development, to let the villagers develop a sense of self-esteem and self-reliance, quite independent and often in spite of the RDF's efforts. Finding this balance and conceptualizing this process is the purpose of this book.

Chapter 2

The Realities of Poverty in Less Developed Countries (LDCs)

The challenge of this chapter will be to make concrete what is generally perceived as abstract, to increase your level of consciousness to the realities of what it means to be poor, and to sensitize you to the profound consequences for the poor of this world, when little or nothing is done to solve these problems.

Today, even as you read, an unprecedented outpouring of public sentiment, concern, and commitment is gathering. Quietly and without fanfare, individuals throughout the planet are declaring their personal commitment to a world without severe malnutrition, debilitating illiteracy and preventable diseases, a world in which the rain forests, the grasslands and wetlands will be protected, and era in which cultural diversity, human rights and democratization will be encouraged. One by one, as individuals, not necessarily a part of any formal movement, men and women in North and South America, Europe, Asia, Africa and elsewhere, are looking into their lives and their communities, and are choosing to include these world-problems as directly related to their own life concerns and as part of their own personal commitments. Thus while an earlier generation struggled with the fear of insecurity and communist expansion, a new generation is waking up to the fact that world poverty and ecological degradation will be the challenge of the next century.

This book, *One Can Make a Difference*, was created to respond to that challenge. It is intended as a tribute to those men and women for whom world poverty and ecological degradation is a personal and daily concern -- not because they themselves are hungry or involved in this damage to the environment, but because they are committed to doing something to confront these problems.

Section One
What are the Basic Problems?

Much of the literature suggests there are five major problems associated with world poverty especially found within the Less Developed Countries (LDCs). These include: (A) the problems of public health associated with disease, poor sanitation and malnutrition, (B) the problems of public education and cultural enhancement associated with illiteracy and cultural stagnation, (C) the technical and economic problems associated with low income, lack of entrepreneurial, technological and management skills; (D) the ecological problems associated with environmental degradation and resource depletion, and (E) the political and governmental problems associated with political authoritarianism, human rights violations, highly centralized bureaucracies, communal violence, and systems of exploitation.

A more detailed analysis suggests there are at least ten basic tragedies associated with these five groups of problems generally outlined as follows:

A. Health and Sanitation: (1) widespread hunger and malnutrition due to the lack of proper diet and poor distribution of nutritious foods, (2) high levels of infant mortality and low life expectancy due to the lack of potable water and the existence of poor housing and unacceptable sanitary conditions (3) high levels of sickness and poor health due to lack of health facilities and health personnel;

B. Education and Culture: (4) high levels of illiteracy and low technical knowledge base, (5) low levels of cultural identity, self esteem and community cooperation;

C. Economy and Technology: (6) very low levels of income and high levels of unemployment and underemployment, (7) low productivity, lack of credit systems and marketing opportunities, (8) low levels of entrepreneurial skills, unavailability of appropriate technology and proper tools;

D. Ecology and Environmental Protection: (9) high levels of environmental degradation and local natural resource depletion.

E. Politics and Government: (10) high levels of political authoritarianism, inefficiency, high levels of communal violence and political instability.

Let us reflect on these five sets of problems and these ten tragedies by considering the ways in which the More Developed Countries (MDCs) are different from the LDCs of the world. If the distinction is simply based upon income or the amount of wealth available to people in a given society, then we may conclude that we of the MDCs are superior, better, certainly more fortunate than those of the less developed countries. Looking at the data provided by Lester Brown in the *State of the World 1995*, one finds that in 1960, the richest 20 percent of the world's people absorbed 70 percent of global income; by 1989, the wealthy's share had climbed to nearly 83 percent.[1] The poorest 20 percent, meanwhile, saw their share of global income drop from an already meager 2.3 percent to just 1.4 percent. The MDCs with roughly 22 percent of the world's population have access to nearly 70 percent of world's goods and services. The bottom 40 percent of the world's population has access to less than 15 percent of world's wealth and even worse, the bottom twenty percent (roughly one billion people) has access to less than 3 percent of the world's wealth, measured in Gross National Product (GNP) terms. The low-income countries contain nearly all of the world's chronic poor people. Throughout the world, according to the World Bank, more than 1.1 billion people live in chronic poverty, and of those, 630 million are "extremely poor," having an average annual per capita income of less than $275 (roughly $23 per month). Other estimates put the number of poor at 2 billion or more, especially if you use the criteria of the MDCs as the basis for measuring poverty. It is also estimated that at least 2 billion adults are for most purposes functionally illiterate, over 1.5 billion people are without safe drinking water, 1 billion people suffer from hunger, 150 million children under age of five (one in three) are malnourished, about 100 million people are completely homeless, and 12.9 million children each year die before their fifth birthday. Let us review some of these statistics in greater detail.

Section Two:
The Basic Problems of Poverty in the LDCs

A. The Challenges of Health
Hunger and malnutrition in the world today.

All of us have been "hungry" at some time or other. This usually means simply that we have an appetite. The hunger experienced by hundreds of millions of people on our planet is not an appetite that comes and goes; it is a consuming, debilitating, minute-by-minute, day-after-day experience. Hunger and chronic malnutrition -- the persistent, relentless condition -- keep millions of men, women, and children from working productively and thinking clearly. It decreases their resistance to disease. It can be intensely painful. Prolonged hunger can result in permanent damage to body and mind. Ultimately, if hunger goes on long enough, it kills.

This intensely dehumanizing and debilitating hunger and malnutrition are experienced by one out of every five people on the planet. Estimates range from 750,000 to two billion, depending upon how an adequate diet is defined. Every year 20-25 million people die as a result of hunger and starvation. More people died from hunger in the past three years than were killed in World War I, World II and the Vietnam Wars combined.

A full 50 percent of the hungry people are located in just five countries: India, Bangladesh, Nigeria, Pakistan, and Indonesia. The vast majority of the countries in Latin America, Africa and Asia have large populations that go to bed each night with less calories than are needed for a healthy, productive life.

In areas where food supply is limited three manifestations of hunger are often found in combination (under-nourishment, lack of specific vitamins and minerals, and seasonal hunger). In children, a chronic deficiency of calories causes listlessness, muscle wastage, and failure to grow. In adults it leads to a loss of weight and a reduced inclination toward and capacity for productive activity. Undernourished people of all ages are more vulnerable to infection and other illness, and recover more slowly and with much greater difficulty. One of every four children in the less developed countries (LDCs) will die before the age of five of diseases related to malnutrition. They die very quietly; one hears very little about them; they come from the world's poorest families, who themselves are the weakest and most powerless members of these powerless families.

Chronic Under Nutrition

The most widespread manifestation of hunger today -- and the least recognized -- is chronic under nutrition. To suffer hunger in the form of chronic under nutrition means that over a long period of time an individual consumes fewer calories and less protein than the body needs. Ultimately, the person is too weakened to resist diseases, work productively, or think clearly. Yet because the condition is chronic, it is often unobserved, undramatic, and continuous. In fact, the lethargy and ill health that result from under nutrition often seem the normal state of life in areas where hunger persists.

Chronic under nutrition has particularly severe effects in children. Diseases that a healthy, well-nourished body would quickly throw off -- such as measles, diphtheria, diarrhea, and respiratory problems -- often mean death for children whose bodies are under nourished. In fact, many children who are thought to have died from diseases such as these were actually victims of under nutrition.

Malnutrition

Another "invisible" form that hunger can take is malnutrition, a condition that occurs when an individual's diet has a relative deficiency of specific nutrients vital to good health. Malnutrition may not cause death, but it can cripple, maim, and deform. Lack of vitamin C can lead to scurvy, loss of teeth, and an inability to fight infection. Lack of iron can produce anemia and loss of energy. As a result of iodine deficiency, a public health problem in 118 countries, at least 30,000 babies are stillborn each year and over 120,000 are born mentally retarded, physically stunted, deaf-mute or paralyzed. Lack of vitamin A can cause blindness; and some 250,000 children become blind every year as a result of this insufficiency. Nutritional anemia's are found in developing countries among 20 to 25 percent of children, 20 to 40 percent of women and up to 10 percent of adult males. Mricronutrient malnutrition is estimated to affect at least 2000 million people of all ages, but children are particularly vulnerable

Seasonal Hunger

In some parts of the world, seasonal hunger occurs annually before each harvest, when the food from the last harvest runs out. Until the new crop comes in, people may be hungry for weeks or even months at a time. As a result of this seasonal hunger, people often enter a harvest season too weak to cope with its heavy physical-work demand. Over many of the vast savanna areas of Africa, the main staple foods are cereals and legumes. In the late Spring or the "hungry months," the millet crop slowly ripens and the rural people, especially children, wait patiently for the harvest. It is in these months that many children, weakened by malnutrition, can die of illnesses which would hardly affect normal children. It is, perhaps, not by chance, that in the language of the Iteso people of Uganda, that the month of May is called the "month when the children wait for food."

Who are the Hungry?

Behind these grim statistics are real people. They are men, women, and children, with hopes and dreams, loves and hates, strengths and weaknesses, who find themselves caught in the circumstances of hunger. They are African refugees, Peruvian peasants, beggars in the streets of Calcutta, barrio dwellers in Mexico City, subsistence farmers in Indonesia, women who tend herds of livestock in Kenya. About 40 percent of the world's hungry are children; most of the rest are women. The majority of hungry people live and work in rural areas. Many are landless laborers or tenant farmers who do not own their land. If they do, their land is a small plot, and they lack access to the credit and technical support needed to make the land productive.

The Brandt Commission describes the condition of poverty with these words: "Few people in the North have any detailed conception of the extent of poverty in the less developed countries (LDCs) or of the forms it takes. Many hundreds of millions of people in the poorer countries are preoccupied solely with survival and elementary needs. For them work is frequently not available or, when it is, pay is very low and conditions often barely tolerable. Homes are constructed of impermanent materials and have neither piped water nor sanitation. Electricity is a luxury. Health services are thinly spread and in rural areas only rarely within walking distance. . . Permanent insecurity is the condition of the poor. There are no public systems of social security in the event of unemployment, sickness or death of a wage-earner in the family. Flood, drought or disease affecting people or livestock can destroy livelihoods with no hope of compensation. . . . It is a condition of life so limited as to be, in the words of the President of the World Bank 'below any rational definition of human decency.'"

Infant Mortality Rates in the LDCs.

The 2.3 billion children under age 19 who inhabit the earth today represent 40 percent of the planet's population; 82 percent of these children live in LDCs. The conditions in which these children live pose a serious threat to their current health and future prospects. At the World Summit for Children, held at the United Nations in September 1990, leaders from 71 countries committed themselves to: "promoting the survival, protection, and development of the present generation of children and all generations to come." Despite this kind of rhetoric, the economic, social, and environmental conditions in which many children live put them at serious risk for ill health, malnutrition, life-long disability and early death.

Moreover, during the 1990s, the largest generation ever will be born with nearly 90 percent of the expected 1.5 billion births to occur in the LDCs. These are the same countries in which large numbers of children still die needlessly from malnutrition and disease caused by inadequate drinking water, poor sanitation, and other environmental ills. Nearly all deaths of children under age 5 (97%) and maternal deaths (99%) are in developing countries.[2]

Table 2-1
Decline in Infant Morality Rates

	1950	1970	1990
MDCs	28	22	10
LDCs	125	105	78
Africa	165	137	100
Asia	122	99	64

Progress has been made. Worldwide, the annual number of deaths of children under 5 declined by 4.7 million between 1970 and 1990. Developing countries have improved their children's health considerably. Between 1970 and 1990, infant mortality rates declined by 33 percent in the LDCs, from 116 per 1,000 live births to 78. From these statistics it easy to see why a child born in a less developed country (LDC) is seven times more like to die before its first birthday than a child born in a more developed country (MDC). Also, even though some progress has been made, the gap between the MDCs and LDCs is actually growing. In the early 1960s the disparities between the rich nations and the poor nations was 1 to 7; by the early 1980s, they had increased to 1 to 15 and today, the ratio is nearly 1 to 20.3

The estimated global figure for mortality among children under 5 years in 1993 was 87 per 1000 births, an encouraging fall from rates of 215 during the period 1950-55 and of 115 in 1980. Yet in parts of the developed world only 6 out of 1000 liveborns die before age 5, whereas in 16 of the least developed countries the rate is over 200 per 1000 and in one country it is 320 per 1000.

The Level of Sickness and Disease in the LDCs.
Statistics on causes of death in LDCs in 1985 provided by the World Health Organization(WHO) suggest that nearly 37 million people (23.3 million adults and 13.5 million children) died unnecessarily: 6.5 million adults died of infectious and parasitic diseases, 4.3 million from acute respiratory diseases, 3.2 million from diarrhea diseases, 3.0 million from tuberculosis, 1.5 million from viral Hepatitis B, 1.0 million from malaria in some 100 different countries, 880,000 from measles, 550,000 from AIDS and 200,000 from schistosomiasis which is endemic in 76 countries where 200 million are infected and about 600 million are at risk and another 6.5 million from other degenerative diseases.

The World Health Organization in 1995 estimated that about 12 million children under age 5 (roughly 35,000 a day) were dying annually in the LDCs. Infectious and parasitic diseases in 1990 killed about 9.8 million children before their fifth birthday. The most common causes of death in the LDCs are respiratory infections, neonatal and perinatal complications, and diarrhea.

Respiratory infections are responsible for 4.3 million childhood deaths annually. About 17 percent of these deaths are a consequence of pertussis (whooping cough) and measles and thus are preventable through immunization; the vast majority -- roughly 75 percent -- are caused by pneumonia. In the MDCs, most children recover from pneumonia; in the LDCs, they often do not. In Guatemala, the mortality rate among infants due to influenza and pneumonia is estimated to be 1,000 per 100,000 live births; this is 8 times higher than Argentina (120 percent 100,000) ten times higher than Cuba (97 per 100,000) and 125 times higher than Canada (8 per 100,000). One important contributing cause to acute respiratory infections in children is the particulates released when wood and animal dung are used to fuel traditional stoves. WHO estimates that 400-500 million people are affected worldwide, with rural homes having levels of particulate pollution ranging from 300 to 14,000 micrograms per cubic meter. The WHO maximum recommends level is 100 to 150 micrograms, an amount possible simply by introducing an inexpensive lorena stove and chimney system into their homes.[4]

Diarrhea is the second major cause of death among children in most LDCs, causing about 3.2 million deaths annually. The most serious consequence of diarrhea is extreme dehydration -- a condition that can be prevented if parents and health care workers have access to, and know how to use, oral rehydration therapy In this simple technique, vital fluids and ions lost during diarrhea episodes are restored through the administration of either a prepared packet of oral rehydration salts (ORS) or a home prepared solution which costs roughly 7 cents on average. Promoted by WHO since 1978, oral rehydration is now theoretically accessible to about 60 percent of the children in the LDCs, but is actually used to treat less than 30 percent of the children who contract diarrhea simply because there are no health workers or Rural Development Facilitators (RDFs) available to teach this simple technique to the people. According to UNICEF, this simple treatment saves approximately 1 million young lives a year.

Even more important than treatment of diarrhea, however, is its prevention. Most diarrhea is caused by bacterial, viral, and parasitic infestations transmitted through water, food, and contact with fecal matter. Preventing diarrhea requires better sanitation and more abundant, cleaner water supplies, as well as health education aimed at promoting breast feeding, immunization, improved personal hygiene and food handling practices, and the penning of farm animals such as chickens and cattle.

Vaccine-Preventable Diseases

At the end of the 1970s, the international community made a major commitment to immunize the world's children against six major childhood diseases -- measles, diphtheria, pertussis (whooping cough) tetanus, polio, and tuberculosis. Today, average immunization levels of children in LDCs are at least 80 percent for all vaccine-preventable diseases except measles (78%). UNICEF estimates that these successes are preventing at least 2.5 million child deaths each year. Despite this progress, more than 2.4 million children died of vaccine-preventable diseases in 1993 mostly in the more isolated rural areas, again emphasizing the importance of placing RDFs in the more isolated areas of the LDCs.

Malnutrition

Although data are incomplete, a 1990 UNICEF survey suggests that more than one-third of the LDCs children under 5 years of age are malnourished. Of these 150 million children, at least one in six, 25 million, is severely malnourished. Most of the world's malnourished children reside in Asia -- 80 percent. How frequently malnutrition is an immediate cause of death is unknown. UNICEF, however, estimates that it is a contributing cause in approximately one third of child deaths. In Latin America, malnutrition is the underlying or related cause in more than half of all childhood deaths.[5]

Malnutrition can lower a child's immunity, making the child more susceptible to diseases such as diarrhea, measles, and respiratory infections. These in turn reduce appetite, cause nutrient loss, inhibit absorption, and alter the body's metabolism, thereby resulting in inadequate dietary intake and further malnutrition. This vicious cycle of malnutrition and infection has been termed the "most prevalent public health problem in the world today."[6] Often the cycle begins even earlier when malnourished women give birth to babies with low birth weight (2,500 grams or less). Some 350 million women are estimated to have nutritional anemia. These women are more likely to die in childbirth and to have babies too small to thrive. Low weight babies are seven times more likely than other babies to die of respiratory infections and three times more likely to die of diarrhea.

The international community has committed itself to halving the incidence of severe and moderate malnutrition among children by the year 2000. If that target is to be met, parents and community workers (RDFs) must be given basic nutrition information and trained to monitor children's growth. For example, exclusive breast feeding for the first few months of life can improve a child's health significantly. As noted before, it reduces diarrhea morbidity and provides newborns with the best possible nourishment as well as antibodies against common infections. UNICEF estimates breast feeding could save 1.5 million lives a year. Because breast feeding acts as a natural contraceptive by inhibiting ovulation, it lowers fertility rates and helps lengthen birth spacing, thus improving the health of both the mother and the child.

Water and Sanitation

Universal access to safe drinking water and to sanitary disposal of excreta are two of the major international targets for improving the health and well-being of people in the LDCs. As of 1990, 81 percent of urban areas, but only 58 percent of rural areas had access to safe water supplies; 71 percent of urban areas but only 48 percent of rural areas had access to sanitation. A 1990 review of 144 community-level studies concluded that when water and sanitation are made available to people, substantial health impacts can be achieved. In particular, the review found that water and sanitation were associated with a median reduction in child mortality of 55 percent. These community studies also suggest those, particularly for diarrhea disease, improvements in excreta disposal and water quantity, have even greater health impacts than improvement in water quality.[7]

The gains to be made from improving water supplies (both quantity and quality) and sanitation is not automatic, however. Simply installing water taps, pit latrines, hand pumps, and other hardware is not enough; their success depends as well on community participation and changes in behavior. Studies have found, for example, when hand washing is taught in a given family that it can reduce the incidence of diarrhea disease by as much as 50 percent.[8]

Health Care

The technologies associated with health care in the LDCs, such as immunization and oral rehydration therapy, have made a significant difference in child health when well-informed parents are supported by an accessible health worker. The parent, usually the mother, must recognize the initial symptoms in time to provide home care or seek outside assistance. She must also be able to turn to someone who can immunize children, take other steps to prevent illness, and treat children who do fall ill. This person need not be an expensively educated physician or nurse; a well-trained village health worker, preferably one with roots in the community and opportunities for both further education and support through a Rural Development Facilitator (RDF), can handle most situations.

Primary health care, consisting of a network of community health clinics and community-based health workers providing basic preventive care and health education as well as treatment for the most common illnesses, offers an effective, quick, and relatively inexpensive way of improving the health of the majority of the population in the LDCs. The UNDP estimates that it costs between $200 and $300 to save each additional life through a village-level preventive health care system, compared with $2,000 and $3,000 for a more formal curative care system requiring modern medical personnel.[9]

Almost three quarters of the health expenditures of developing countries are devoted to urban hospitals that provide expensive Western-style curative care to a minority of the population. UNICEF estimates that reducing LDC government spending on urban hospitals by 45 percent would release enough funds to train 1 million village health workers needed to provide health services to the poorest 1 billion people in the more isolated rural areas of these countries.[10] Many of the poorest countries spend as much as 80-90 percent of their health budgets on hospitals and, at the same time, have some of the highest infant mortality rates in the world. Restructuring these health expenditures offers significant opportunities for improving a population's health. Bangladesh, for example, redirects its health care spending from a largely urban and curative focus toward grassroots health services to the poor throughout the country. Between 1978 and 1988, the share for rural health clinics in the budget rose from 10 percent to 60 percent; in the same time period (1981 through 1989), the proportion of 1-year olds immunized against the major causes of death in childhood increased from one percent to 60 percent.

Switching to lower-cost drugs (e.g., generic rather than name-brands), buying them more efficiently (e.g., by purchasing through competitive bidding), choosing more appropriate therapies, (e.g., oral rehydration therapy rather than intravenous feeding for diarrhea), employing traditional healers and other personnel with fewer formal qualifications, and involving communities in building or paying for health clinics all offer the potential for savings in health expenditures which would enable far more people to be reached.

The Challenge of World Wide Plague

For years, various scientists have warned that humanity was becoming too confident that medicine's powerful weaponry would forever maintain its mastery over the microbial world. By 1988, some of the world's leading biologists were declaring the sudden appearance and subsequent global spread of the AIDS virus, far from being an aberration, was a harbinger of things to come. Far from having been vanquished by the great medical advances of the 20th century, the bacteria, virus and parasites are now claiming record numbers. The global rises in tuberculosis (up from 7 million active cases in 1990 to over 10 million predicted for 2000, with increasing percentages having fatal outcomes due to drug-resistance mutations), HIV/AIDS (up from virtually zero cases in 1980 to a predicted 120 million cumulatively by 2000), and malaria (close to eradication in 1965, now claiming over a million lives annually) have taken particularly acute tolls among young, productive-aged adults. We in the more developed countries (MDCs) are much more vulnerable to disease from the LDCs than in any other period in our history. The recent outbreak of Ebola in Zaire, suggests how quickly these serious diseases can be transmitted. The earth has truly become a global village. For example, infection can be passed on through increased air travel. Between 1950 and 1990, passengers on international commercial flights increased from 2 million to 280 million. A recent study suggests that a number of serious diseases are re-emerging as serious threats to world health: yellow-fever, dengue hemorrhagic fever, anti-microbial resistant organisms including malaria and TB, measles, polio, cholera and other food and water-borne diseases, viral hemorrhagic fevers, plague and rabies. Again what is happening in the LDCs will increasingly become relevant to the MDCs. Concern for world health must be a significant emphasis in the field of development over the next decade.

B. The Challenge of World Illiteracy

Below are statistics that reflect the level of literacy in many typical LDCs. While progress has been made, there is still much to do.

Table 2-2
Levels of Literacy in Less Developed Countries

Country	Female		Male	
	1970	1990	1970	1990
Afghanistan		14		44
Bangladesh		24		45
Bolivia	46	71	68	85
Chad		18		42
Egypt	20	34	50	63
Ghana	18	51	43	70
India	20	39	47	64
Indonesia	42	68	66	84
Iran		43		64
Kenya	19	59	44	80
Mali	4	24	11	41
Mexico	69	83	78	88
Nepal		23		52

One must not be too optimistic by such figures on literacy. First, many countries define literacy as anyone who can sign their names and read common signs, or who have finished 4-6 years of education. More telling is the number of individuals who have finished primary and even middle school but who when they are tested -- are found to be functionally illiterate. Finally, international data document that while national figures can be quite low, the rural areas consistently have percentages of illiteracy 40 and 50 percent higher than in urban areas of the country. Perhaps most important from these statistics is the tendency for women to be consistently under-educated in most of these countries. Obviously, much still needs to be done

There are today about 100 million children of primary school age in the LDCs not attending school. Nearly 900 million adults in the LDCs are illiterate, two-thirds of whom are women. Over 85 percent of the primary children (480 million) of the world are found in the LDCs generally with inadequate facilities and untrained teachers. Thus, in contrasting schooling opportunities, the children of Africa and Latin America spend 500 hours a year in school, while European and American children spend nearly 1000 hours a year. The governments of the Africa and Asia spend, on average, roughly $2.00 per child, while the United States and Western Europe spend over $50.00 per child per year. Teachers in Africa and

Asia receive less than 10 years of training and generally have over 55 children per class, while in the US and Europe, teachers receive roughly 16 years of training and generally have less than 30 children per class room.

In both education and health, the most urgent priority is to provide basic services for the poor majority. In many poor countries, the economic returns from primary education for both the individual and the society are almost twice as high as those from higher education. Moreover, spending on primary education is one means of specifically providing resources to the poor. Many poor countries, however, spend more on higher education than on primary education; over 100 million children receive no primary education at all.

C. Unemployment and Low Economic Opportunities

About 1,500 million jobs must be created in the world between now and the year 2025, according to a recent ILO study.[11] It predicts that by the year 2000, the world's active population will reach 2.7 billion and 25 years later will be 3.6 billion and that up to one-third of these will be unable to find work. Compared with an estimated 2.1 billion workers in 1985, this growth would represent increases of 600 million by the year 2000 and 1.5 billion by 2025. To deal with this massive increase in the workforce on the one hand, and to absorb an estimated 90 million unemployed and provide more equitable conditions of work for about 300 million under employed on the other, the world will find itself faced with the formidable task of creating more than 1.9 billion new jobs in the space of 40 years -- an average of 47 million new jobs a year.

The backlog of the millions of unemployed and under employed is a legacy from the 35-year period between 1950 and 1985 when the world's active population grew by 975 million workers -- an average of 28 million a year -- but the world's economy was unable to create enough jobs to absorb this growth. Ninety percent of this need for new jobs will take place in the LDCs. Unfortunately, the majority of these developing countries have experienced growing difficulties in recent years in assuring their economic development and creating enough jobs to absorb their constantly expanding labor force.

Women and Children: The Forgotten Group in Development

There are two groups of people, comprising well over half of humanity, for whom the three imperatives of human development -- fulfillment, productivity, and justice -- are regularly denied. They are the great majority of the world's women and children. It has been suggested that women do roughly 65 percent of the work, earn 20 percent of the income and own less than 1 percent of the productive assets of this world

During the Summit For Children in New York 1990 (71 presidents and prime ministers), 159 countries pledged to the children of the 21st Century that the 40,000 deaths each day from ordinary malnutrition and controllable diseases, the 150 million children who live with poor health, and the 100 million 6-11 year olds who are not in school, will by then have been brought to an end. The cost of achieving this goal is roughly $20 billion a year over the present decade. This is equivalent to just ten days' military expenditures throughout the world per year.

The Role of Women

Much has been learned recently about which factors help or hinder women in improving their children's health. Such factors as women's level of income and education are closely related to child health, whether health is measured in terms of infant and child mortality or children's nutritional status. Detailed studies in 28 countries show a nearly consistent inverse relationship between child mortality and mothers' education and level of income. An estimated three quarters of all health care takes place at home, where women, particularly in their role as mothers, generally have responsibility for promoting their families' health and nutrition.

Helping women to increase their income and their levels of education can improve children's health through a variety of mechanisms: increased use of health services and better knowledge of nutrition; more decision making power within the family and the community; and greater earning power. Women with higher levels of education are more likely to plan their families and thus to increase birth spacing, thus reducing a major mortality risk factor.[12] Lack of education is not the only problem constraining mothers from protecting their children's health. Poor rural women in LDCs often work 60-90 hours per week gathering wood, collecting water, growing and cooking food, contributing to the family income, and caring for their children. For these women, steps to make immunization more accessible and the administration of oral rehydration therapy easier may be key to their ability to raise healthy children. Today it is widely recognized that if you help a man increase his income and employment opportunities, you tend to help one individual, for his surplus tends to go for drinking, gambling and his own personal pleasures; if you help a women increase his employment opportunities and her income you tend to help the whole family, for she is much more apt to use her surplus for the needs of her children.

D. Challenge of the Environment and Natural Resource Depletion

The evidence of human poverty and deprivation in the world is unmistakable. In many poor countries, rapid population growth, agricultural modernization, and inequalities in land tenure are creating increasingly large populations with little or no access to productive land. Without jobs and without productive land, poor people are forced onto marginal lands in search of subsistence food production and fuelwood, or they move to the cities. Those who stay on the land are forced to graze livestock herds where vegetation is sparse or soils and shrubs are easily damaged and to create agricultural plots on arid or semiarid lands, on hillsides, in tropical forests, or in other ecological sensitive areas. It has been estimated that 60 percent of the LDCs people live in areas that are ecologically vulnerable. As more and more people exploit open-access resources in an often desperate struggle to provide for themselves and their families, the further their environment is degraded.

The toll on natural resources takes many forms, including soil erosion, loss of soil fertility, desertification, deforestation, depleted game and fish stocks from over hunting and over fishing, loss of natural habitats and of species, depletion of ground water resources, and pollution of rivers and other water bodies. The result is to reduce the carrying capacity and productivity of the land and its biological resources. This degradation further exacerbates poverty and threatens not only the economic prospects of future generations, but also the livelihoods, health, and well-being of current populations, both in LDCs and MDCs.

The first systematic index to include ecological factors in the study of world poverty is the Daly and Cobb's Index of Sustainable Economic Welfare (ISEW), which combines a figure of personal consumption with statistics on income distribution, capital growth, value of the household labor, and others, including a number of environmental indicators. A monitoring of ISEW since the mid 1970s suggests a gradual decline since its peak in 1979, providing confirmation of the way in which the welfare benefits of increasing GNP are now being offset by a variety of other factors. As Daly and Cobb say: "Economic welfare has been deteriorating for a decade, largely as a result of growing income inequality, the exhaustion of resources and the failure to invest adequately to sustain the economy of the future."[13]

World Food Production

Global food production has increased substantially over the past two decades, but factors such as population pressures and environmental degradation are undermining agriculture's future prospects. Measured in absolute terms, global production increases have been impressive. Nevertheless, prospects for global food and agriculture are at once promising and troubling. On the one hand, global food production has increased significantly since 1970 and has generally been able to meet the demands of a growing world population. In addition, bumper harvests in the 1990-91 crop year exceeded global consumption and helped reverse a three-year decline in world cereal stocks. Estimates of the number of people in the world who are undernourished range from about 500 million to about 1 billion. Thus the absolute number of undernourished people may be increasing slightly, although the proportion of the population that is undernourished appears to be declining in all regions except Africa.

In Africa, production increases have not kept up with population growth, and famine continues to be a serious problem in some areas. Wars which can disrupt food production, markets, and relief efforts have contributed heavily to famine in many African countries in recent years. Drought, poor distribution and marketing, and ineffective government policies also have been important factors.

Sudan, Rwanda, Somalia, Ethiopia are in a particularly perilous conditions; famine threatens millions of people in these countries. The problem is wider than that: for example, per capita cereal consumption in some 55 low-income countries, based on the 1980-89 levels, would have required an estimated 16 million tons of food aid in 1990-91, yet only about 10 million tons were actually available.[14]

Per Capita Production Trends in Agriculture

Agriculture production increases in the developing countries since 1970 are much less dramatic when population growth is taken into consideration. For example, food production per capita has managed to increase fast enough to stay well ahead of population growth in the MDCs. In Latin America and the Near East. however, production barely managed to stay even with population, and in Africa, population growth has generally outstripped production increases. The index of per capita production compiled by the Food and Agriculture Organization of the UN (FAO) using the 1979-81 period as a baseline of 100, shows that 35 of 47 countries dropped below 100 in 1989, with the worst declines in countries such as Angola, Botswana, Gabon, Mozambique, and Rwanda.

Largely because of population growth, per capita cropland has declined in all regions. If current population projects are accurate, the world average of 0.28 hectares of cropland per capita is expected to decline to 0.17 hectares by the year 2025. In Asia, cropland per capita is expected to decline to 0.09 hectares. There are large areas of uncultivated land in sub-Saharan African and Latin America, but in much of this area the soil is marginal or rainfall is unreliable.

Soil Degradation

Increased farming activities are major contributors to soil erosion, salinization, and loss of nutrients. A global assessment of human-induced soil degradation, prepared by the International Soil Reference and Information Center in the Netherlands, found that 1.96 billion hectares of soils were degraded to some degree, and that 300 million hectares of this total have suffered strong to extreme degradation. Agriculture activities accounted for 28 percent of this degradation, overgrazing about 34 percent, and deforestation another 29 percent. Most of the damage has been done by wind and water erosion; other forms of degradation include salinization, loss of nutrients, compaction, and water logging. Most of the land damaged by agriculture and overgrazing is in Asia and Africa. All of this demonstrates the importance of considering the long-term consequences of modern agriculture and the importance of finding alternative systems of agricultural production.

In the 1960s the Green Revolution using heavy doses of fertilizers and insecticides greatly increased yields. However, the impact of this conventional system on the health of the ecosystem is now being documented. Soils under intensive monoculture tend to lose organic matter and their ability to retain moisture, thus becoming more susceptible to erosion and ultimately losing their fertility and productivity. Growing the same crop year after year also allows the pests and diseases that attack that crop to prosper. Local farmers are then forced to use heavy doses of insecticides. Many conventional practices -- growing shallow-rooted crops, using heavy machinery, or removing organic matter from the soil -- encourage soil compaction, which restricts root growth, water retention, and air exchange all dramatically reducing yields per hectare. Soil salinization, which is primarily caused by faulty irrigation, can lower crop yields and ultimately make land unsuitable for cultivation. Declines in soil productivity caused by erosion can be reduced with alternative systems of agriculture which will be described in some detail in a later section of this book.

Forest and Rangelands

Tropical deforestation is currently a significant environmental and development issue. The FAO's second report on deforestation in the world concludes that deforestation to be almost 17 million hectares per year compared to an early 1980s estimate of 12 million -- an increase of 50 percent. Loss of tropical forests diminishes biodiversity, contributes to climate change by releasing stored carbon into the atmosphere, and often results in serious soil degradation, sometimes rendering the land unfit for future agriculture. Yet poor farmers in many tropical countries have no choice but to clear forests to grow crops. Some countries offer economic incentives for establishing large ranches on tropical forestland.

Local forest dwellers are most vulnerable to the impacts of forest destruction. These people are typically unrepresented when land-use decisions are made regarding their homelands, although the results of those decisions frequently jeopardize their cultural and economic survival. In Altamira, Brazil, for example, some 600 people representing indigenous groups rallied to block the Xingu River dam construction and in Malaysia, native Penan have erected more than three dozen blockades in the past several years to protect their ancestral lands from logging. The message from these actions is clear: local peoples must be a part of any attempt to manage their forests.

E. Political Instability and Human Rights Violations

As the gap between the MDCs and the LDCs, rich and poor, haves and have-nots grows, frustrations and resentments among the less fortunate tend to increase and often find expression through the reassertion of traditional ethnic, national, religious, and tribal identities. The end of the Cold War and the erosion of central Soviet power (and central Yugoslav power) allowed the ethnic antagonisms that have simmered beneath the surface to erupt with extra vigor. It is a mistake, however, to view these explosions as a result of the Cold War's end; rather, they should be seen as a consequence of the central authorities' failure to address existing ethnic and national aspirations in an honest and constructive way.

This political instability in the LDCs affects world peace and security at three levels. It is increasing tensions between the North (MDCs) and the South (LDCs); it is fueling interstate rivalries in the Third and Fourth World; and it is exacerbating ethnic, tribal, and religious antagonisms within LDCs.

Arms' races and hostilities are growing between competing regional powers of the LDCs, as in the Iran-Iraq war, the Arab-Israeli conflicts, the India-Pakistan conflict, and the conflict between the Koreans. An especially dangerous aspect of such rivalries is the tendency of nations on one side of such disputes to foment or support internal ethnic or tribal disorders within the territory of their rivals. More recently, efforts by ethno-nationalist groups within multi-ethnic states, seek to secede and establish their own nation-states, along with efforts by central government authorities to suppress such drives (as, for instance, in Croatia, Eritrea, Kashmir, Iraqi Kurdistan, the southern Sudan, and the Tamil-populated parts of Sri Lanka). Equally common in the LDCs are the violent struggles between authoritarian governments and popular forces seeking social and political change, as in Algeria, Burma, El Salvador, and Haiti. The persistence of revolutionary movements employing guerrilla strategy, as in Colombia, Peru, and the Philippines, is still common.

In many LDCs, competing factions often have such divergent outlooks that they are unwilling to work with one another toward some mutually satisfactory compromise. This conflict undercuts the ability of governments to function and reflects the absence of political consensus so vital to effective conflict resolution. Often such governments are not worthy of support because of corruption, human rights violation, malfeasance, or worse. Military dictators often emerged in these kinds of situations, who then become more concerned with remaining in power than in dealing with the problems of disease, illiteracy and poverty. The tragedy of authoritarian governments is clearly an added burden to those already suffering from disease, illiteracy and poverty.

Section Three
How is Population Related
to the Challenges of Poverty

We in the United States are a blessed people overall. Few understand the contrast between us and the LDCs of the world. Americans are 3 percent of the worlds population, but consume 23 percent of the energy, 27 percent of its aluminum and more than 30 percent of its tin. The average American uses as much energy as six Mexicans, 153 Bangladeshis, or 499 Ethiopians.

In the US in 1990 there were 2 million more births than deaths. Immigration added at least another 600,000 inhabitants. The US population, nearly 250 million now, is growing faster than any other industrialized nation. An yet, more than 90 percent of the world's population growth is taking place in the less developed countries (LDCs). And while millions of acres of cropland are lost annually to soil degradation and erosion and to sprawling urbanization and modernization, statistics indicate global population is galloping ahead at the rate of 100 million new mouths to feed each year.

Population Trends.

The different prospects for the industrialized and developing countries are nowhere more evident than in their respective populations. In 1950, nearly one third of all people lived in the MDCs of the world, by the late 1990s they will make up only about 20 percent. By 1990, of the world's 5.3 billion people, 4.2 billion -- 77 percent -- lived in the LDCs. Population growth in the MDCs has been relatively modest, rising about 1.3 percent over the 1970-90 period. In those same two decades, the population of the LDCs grew by almost 5.5 percent, from 2.65 billion to 4.1 billion. By the year 2025, the disparity in the number will widen where the LDCs will have nearly 85 percent of the world's population or nearly 7.15 billion people to take care of.

It is a common assumption that the issue of poverty is largely a question of the relationship of people to resources available. To put it in its simplest terms, are there too many people on this planet given the land and resources presently available? A review of history suggests it took 100 years to go from 1 billion to 2 billion, 45 years to go from 2 billion to 4 billion, and probably less than 38 years to go from 3 billion to 6 billion. At the time of Christ, the world's population is estimated to have been 250 million. Note how population has grown over the past 100 years:

Table 2-3
History of Growth of the World's Population

1830	1 billion people on the earth
1930	2 billion took 100 years to reach the second billion
1960	3 billion took 30 years
1975	4 billion took 15 years
1987	5 billion took 12 years
1998	6 billion (estimated) will take 11 years
2008	7 billion (estimated) will take 10 years
2015	8 billion (estimated will take 7 years

At midyear 1994 world population stood at 5,600,000,000, according to estimates prepared by the Population Reference Bureau. This represented an increase of about 95 million over the previous year. Currently, the number of Earth's inhabitants was rising by nearly one billion each decade. This rise was all the more remarkable in view of the fact that world population numbered only 2.5 billion in 1950, a sum that had taken all of human history to accumulate. In 1994, 386,00 babies were born very day and 137,500 persons died, leading to a daily increase of 245,090. Since the mid-1970s, the world-wide birth rate increase has been steadily dropping from nearly 2.1% in 1975 down to 1.6% in 1994. However, the population growth rate of the LDCs remains at 2.3%. Thus at today's birthrate, the world is gaining almost 90 million newcomers each year, more than 85 million of them coming from the LDCs.

Today the world's population is growing by 170 people a minute, so fast that the number of people on this already crowded planet could more than double from 5.6 billion in 1994 to as many as 12.5 billion by 2050. These mind boggling numbers are at the heart of a problem so pervasive that -- even though most in the USA do not directly see it -- it affects everything from the quality of air we breathe and the water we drink, to worldwide resources and stability. Nobel Prize winner, Henry Kendall of the Union of Concerned Scientists argues: "If we do not stabilize population with justice, humanity and mercy . . . it will be done for us by nature, and it will be done brutally. Much of the tragedy of Rwanda reflects the kind of instability and brutality that often overcomes societies confronted with extreme poverty ,ethnic conflict, and limited resources.

In the MDCs (US, West Europe, Japan) the total fertility rate (TFR) was roughly 1.6 meaning that the average woman had 1.6 children during her child-bearing years. In sub-Saharan Africa, the TFR has tended to remain above 6.4 (over 7.3 in Mali), while in both Southeast Asia and Latin America, the TFR was 3.5. South Asia's TFR stood at 4.3, ranging from 2.5 in Sri Lanka and 3.6 in India to 6.1 in Iran, Nepal, and Pakistan. Of the 23 nations having 5 million or more people and the highest birth rates, 18 were LDCs that had per capita incomes of less than $1000. Bisi Ogunleye, president of a Nigerian women's association, who attended the International Conference on Population and Development in Cairo, 1994, stated: "Those who are rich, it is time for you to share your riches. If you don't, the poor will share their poverty."

The ten largest countries are: China 1.1 billion, India has 889 million, United States 255 million; Indonesia 184 million, Brazil 151 million, Russia 149 million, Pakistan 130 million, Japan 124 million, Bangladesh 110 million, Nigeria 89 million,

Note that eight of the top ten countries are LDCs

The next countries are: Mexico 84 million, Germany 79 million, Vietnam 69 million, Philippines 63 million, Iran 59 million, Turkey 58 million, France 57 million, Thailand 56 million, Egypt has 55 million, Ukraine 52 million. Thus 16 of the top twenty or 80 percent are among the nations categorized as LDCs.

Before we are too quick to judge these LDCs and the massive increases in population, we must understand this issue from their perspective. The agrarian nature of LDCs encourages large families. In agrarian societies, children represent productive assets. They provide low-cost labor to the farm and may earn income from nonfarm employment. With the historical (and sometimes persistent) high infant mortality rates, only a large number of live births could ensure an adequate number of living offspring. Further, since most LDCs cannot provide public care for their elderly, having a large number of children is a sort of old-age security system for parents. The pattern is perpetuated when parents in rural and disadvantaged urban families discourage their children from attending school. Time in school limits time for farm or other work and can require money for books and clothes that the parents cannot afford.

American who grew up during the nation's rural, agrarian period will readily empathize with this type of value system. It was only after economic development occurred and the role of children was redefined that people in the United States (and in other MDCs as well) found reasons to limit family size voluntarily. A better quality of life replaced subsistence as the family goal. Higher incomes and improved education among rural families tend to promote changes in value systems. Voluntary control of population would then be more likely, based on evidence from around the world. Unfortunately, not enough people in enough LDCs have been exposed to these kinds of changes to produce widespread voluntary reductions in population growth.

The problem of population growth cannot be wished away. Even moderate success of some control programs offers no solution. Unless a better approach is initiated, the areas of the world, least able to do so, will be dealing with the desperate problems of hunger and starvation for the foreseeable future. The growth rate in First World is averaging less than 2 percent per year, while the Third World averages 2.5 percent and the Fourth World is averaging nearly 4 percent. LDCs are now nearly 80 percent of the world population and will be 85-90 percent by the year 2010. More than 55 percent of the world's population is in Asia. Education and increased income do lead to lower birth rates -- but such education and income trends generally are only found in the more developed countries (MDCs) found in North America and Western Europe. For example in Bangladesh in 1981 some 20 percent of the adult women used birth control methods, by 1990 it was 30 percent, but it will need to be 65 percent before population will stabilize in most LDCs.

Contrasting Views on Population Growth

Thomas Robert Malthus, an English clergyman in the 18th century, argued: "that the power of population is indefinitely greater than the power of the earth to produce subsistence for man. Population, when unchecked, increases in a geometrical ratio. Subsistence increases only in a arithmetical ration. . . . thus the period when the number of men surpass their means of subsistence has long since arrived, and that this necessary oscillation, this constantly subsisting cause of periodical misery, has existed even sincere have had any histories of mankind, does exist at present, and will for ever continue to exist, unless some undecided change takes place in the physical constitution of our nature."[15]

Paul Ehrlich, a Stanford University biology professor, is a widely read contemporary advocate of population control. His book, *The Population Bomb*, combines hard scientific data with passionate advocacy for population control. Ehrlich candidly admits his intention to raise public consciousness and concern about the population problem. His vivid description of Delhi, India dramatized his concerns: "The temperature was well over 100, and the air was a haze of dust and smoke. The streets seemed alive with people. People eating, people washing, people sleeping. People visiting, arguing, and screaming. People thrusting their hands through the taxi window, begging. People defecating and urinating. People clinging to buses. People herding animals. People, people, people, people.[16]

Most advocates of population control highlight two themes: First, resources are, ultimately, limited. The human population must divide a finite stock of resources; more people mean less for each person. Second, there is something called "quality of life," which should take precedence over most other values.[17] Critics of population planning order these values differently. They see quality of life as less important than the right to human life and, in some cases, than the right of individuals to make their own reproductive decisions.

Many are concerned that the increase in people who must be fed, clothed, educated, and employed will constantly undercut progress in all kinds of human endeavors. They point to Mexico: Every 50 minutes the government builds a new classroom; but the needs of the children who would benefit from these classrooms cannot be met, because 240 children are born during the same period. Just to keep even with population increases, India each day would have to build 1,000 new classrooms, 1,000 hospital wards, and 10,000 new houses. Thus at current rates of population growth, most countries will have to double their economic output by the year 2000 just to stay even with population growth, let alone trying to improve living conditions.[18]

U Thant, former Secretary-General of the United Nations, expressed the viewpoint that population growth was a major deterrent to economic growth and increased quality of life in the LDCs: "There is an ever-increasing realization that too rapid population growth constitutes a major obstacle to education and the promotion of the welfare of the young in general, the attainment of adequate standards of health, the chance of earning a decent living, and in many cases even the availability of food at subsistence level. The task of providing opportunities for the world's as yet unborn children and developing their talents and their capabilities to the full appears in a number of countries well-nigh insuperable, unless action is taken to moderate the population growth rate."[19]

In contrast to these rather pessimistic views on population growth, Julian Simon, professor of economics at the University of Illinois, has used a fairly persuasive mathematical-based model with carefully collected empirical data to bring an anti-Malthusian view to the public's attention. He argues as follows: "Why is the standard of living so much higher in the United States or Sweden than in India or Mali? And why is our standard of living so much higher now than it was 200 years ago? The all-important difference is that there is a much greater stock of technological know-how available, and people are educated to learn and use that knowledge."[20] Later he challenges the Malthusian argument that the world has only so much resource by suggesting: "Sound appraisal of the impact of additional people upon the scarcity (cost) of a natural resource must take into account the feedback from increased demand to the discovery of new deposits, new ways of extracting the resource, and new substitutes for the resource. And we must take into account the relationship between demand now and supply in various future years, rather than consider only the effect on supply now of greater or lesser demand now. The more people, the more minds there are to discover new deposits, increase productivity, and improved technology, all else equal."

This point of view is not limited to economists. One technologist writing on minerals put it this way: "In effect, technology keeps creating resources. So the major constraint upon the human capacity to enjoy unlimited minerals, energy, and other raw materials at acceptable prices is knowledge. Ultimately, then, the key constraint is human imagination acting together with educated skills. This is why an increase of human beings, along with causing an additional consumption of resources, constitutes a crucial addition to the stock of natural resources."[21]

In an attempt to consider the implications of this pro-growth approach to population, let us consider the following:

1. Both the US and Ethiopia have the same number of people per square mile roughly, 61 and 65 respectively. Yet the US population has a per capita GNP of $21,700 and Ethiopia has $120.

2. Singapore has the same number of people per square mile as Calcutta, but has 35 times the per capita income. It obviously is not simply the number or density of population that determines the standard of living in a given situation.

3. Japan has more people per square mile than nearly any Third World country and is essentially devoid of local natural resources, yet has learned to provide its people with a very high standard of living. Obviously it is not simply the lack of resources that determine quality of life in a given country.

4. Mexico and Brazil with great sources of oil, iron, soil and rivers still have one/tenth the per capita income of Japan which has almost no natural resources within its own borders.

Apparently, it is not the availability of resources that necessarily determines poverty, nor the number of people in a given area that determines wealth in a given society. The MDCs have simply developed higher levels of education, technical skills, discipline and organizational capability. For those who challenge the Malthusian Thesis, the material just presented seems to suggest that population is not the problem, nor is the lack of scarce resources necessarily the problem. What is needed is quality human resources if a country's quality of life is to be improved. Foreign observers of Japan at the beginning of the 20th century argued that Japan could never become an industrialized nation for it had neither the resources nor the educated population needed for industrialization and furthermore, so it was argued, the Japanese culture was based upon a set of traditional values which belittled commercial and business activities and was simply not conducive for the development of the social and economic relations needed for economic growth. Therefore, while we must recognize that development will not come easily to most LDCs, history suggests that with appropriate development of human resources, utilizing the human, institutional and technological dimensions of that process, we may find solutions to these problems.

Some General Conclusions on Population and World Hunger

World hunger is not caused by a lack of food. The problem of world hunger is characterized by an unequal and inadequate distribution of people and food. Instances of hunger and malnutrition occur when people are unable to obtain an adequate share of the world's supply of food. The Food and Agriculture Organization (FAO) estimates there are 500-700 million people who presently suffer from hunger and the effects of malnutrition. Roughly 10-20 million people die each year from hunger and malnutrition. Probably 800-1000 million people live in absolute poverty.

Periodically, conditions worsen dramatically and people in famine-affected regions are thrown into a food crisis that subject them to starvation. These short-term crises are usually precipitated by political unrest, droughts and floods. It is important to remember those food shortages and inadequate food distribution are merely symptomatic expressions of more fundamental causes of world hunger, the principal one of which is poverty. Combine aggregate poverty with low productive agriculture; soaring population growth; poor income distribution; and inadequate social, political, and economic systems and policies, and the result is a dilemma of staggering complexity. The widespread presence of poverty in LDCs creates a gap between demand for food and the capacity of agriculture to supply adequate amounts of food.

It is clear that the number of people the Earth can sustainably support has a limit and that, in a situation where people's lifestyles are damaging the environment, more people with similar lifestyles will increase the damage. However, there is much evidence that it is the industrialized countries, with less than a quarter of the world's population, that are responsible for more than 75 percent of global waste, a major cause of environmental degradation, while polluting technology used in most manufacturing processes have more than twice the negative environmental impact of a growing population. UN studies suggest that the problems of poverty and population growth, found mostly in the LDCs accounts for less than 10 percent of environmental degradation found in the world.

While the statistics provided above will obviously generate some alarm and should give us some cause for concern, still the major thesis of this book is that while such problems are serious, things are not hopeless. The lessons learned of the past three decades suggest that solutions are available, that successes can be found and have been documented, and that effective confrontation of these problems will require much greater political leadership and vision, much greater economic sharing and resource distribution and finally a growing popular commitment in more developed countries (MDCs) to continue their efforts to help others in the LDCs to help themselves.

Section Four
The Tragedy of Low Income and Economic Inequality

The economic value of a country is often defined as the sum of all-money based goods and services produced by the domestic economy in a year and calculated as the Gross National Product (GNP). GNP is calculated, with a few adjustments, from the market prices for which goods and services are sold. But it fails to measure the total output of the economy for several reasons. For example, non marketed goods and services produced in the home, have no price and thus are excluded from GNP. Other activities often ignored include "moonlighting", and informal trading, in which cash transactions are undeclared. A different type of error is where GNP is widely used as a measure of economic welfare. This is a double mistake: firstly because welfare depends on factors other than production and, secondly, there are many costs -- pollution, traffic accidents, commuting -- associated with production of GNP goods and services that are generally excluded from GNP. Thus GNP systematically overstates the benefits of market-based production.

The World Bank identifies low-income countries as those having an average annual per capita gross nation product (GNP) of less than $580 in 1989. Among the 41 countries meeting this criterion, a dozen have an average per capital GNP of less than $250. Per capita GNP is one measure of development but by no means the only appropriate one. According to the United Nations Development Program (UNDP), the quality of life as measured by longevity and literacy is also of critical importance in the development process. Today, a significant number of nations have per capita GNPs of $300 or less per year. All such nations are in Africa and Asia. Countries like Somalia or Bangladesh are the countries most often cited for low average incomes. Yet in reality there are nearly 50 nations where the average per-capita income is less than $40 per month (less than $500 per year). Among nations having per capita GNPs above $300 but below $1000 annually, most, again, are in Africa and Asia but several are also in Latin America. In Chart 2-4 is a list of countries of the world which distinguishes the MDCs from the LDCs in terms of their annual per capita income. Many scholars have distinguished between the Fourth, the Third, the Second, and the First worlds.

Table 2-4
(1) Less Developed Countries (LDCs)
A. Fourth World Economies (1992)

Lower Low Income (the lowest 25 are under $300 per capita GNP)

Mozambique	$60	Tanzania	$110
Ethiopia	$110	Nepal	$170
Cambodia	$280	Vietnam	$220
Bangladesh	$220	Afghanistan	$200
Mali	$300	Niger	$300

Middle Low Income (next 36 are between $300-$600 per capita GNP)

Nigeria	$320	Kenya	$330
India	$310	**China**	$380
Pakistan	$410	Ghana	$450
Nicaragua	$410	Honduras	$580

***61 countries are under $600 per capita GNP ($50 per month)

B. Third World Countries

Upper Low Income : (**Next 55 nations** are between $600 and $2,000)

Burma(Myanmar)	$660	Indonesia	$670
Egypt	$630	Bolivia	$680
Philippines	$770	Mongolia	$900
Guatemala	$980	Dominican Rep	$1,040
Ecuador	$1,070	Syria	$1,370
Congo	$1,030	Paraguay	$1,340
Colombia	$1,290	Lebanon	$1,400
Ukraine	$1,670	Thailand	$1,840

Thus, there some 116 nations which are called the Third and Fourth World Countries and all have per capita GNP below $2000 ($160 or less per month)

(2) More Developed Countries (MDCs)
C. Second World Countries (Mostly in Latin America and the former Soviet Union and East Europe)

Lower Middle Income: (Next 36 nations between $2,000 and $5,000)

Chile	$2,730	Brazil	$2,770
Malaysia	$2,790	Russia	$2,680
Venezuela	$2,900	Yugoslavia	$3,000
Belarus	$2,910	Mexico	$3,470
Trinidad	$3,940	Gabon	$4,450

Upper Middle Income: (Next 18 nations between $5,000 and $10,000)

Libya	$5,350	Croatia	$5,600
Slovenia	$6,330	South Korea	$6,790
Greece	$7,180	Malta	$7,240
Argentina	$6,050	Saudi Arabia	$7,940

D. First World Countries (Industrialized Market Economies) The **top 40 nations** (the top 23% of the nations) all have a per capita income above $10,000.

Lower Upper Income Next 11 nations between $10,000 and $16,000

Taiwan	$10,180	Kuwait	$10,680
New Zealand	$12,060	Israel	$13,230
Spain	$14,020	Hong Kong	$15,380

Upper Upper Income the next 29 nations are all above $16,000

Monaco	$16000	Qatar	$16,240
Great Britain	$17,760	Italy	$20,510
France	$22,300	Finland	$22,980
USA	$23,110	Germany	$23,030
Norway	$25,80	Sweden	$26,780
Japan	$28,220	Switzerland	$36,230

From this table, it is clear there are at least three readily distinguishable groups of nations: first are those 40 nations that have an average per capita income (in 1991) of $16,000, comprising one-fifth of the world's people; another group comprising 54 nations with per capita income averaging $3000, comprising 18 percent of the world's people; and the one hundred plus countries at the bottom of the global class system with per capita incomes averaging less than $600, where the remaining 62 percent of the earth's population lives. In terms of shares of the world's economic pie, the poorest 62 percent of humankind earn only 7 percent of its income, while the richest 20 percent earn 82 percent. For many people this kind of inequality is not only immoral, but extremely dangerous and may well someday come back to haunt the rich nations of the world if something is not done.

Even more depressing is the fact that this gap is widening. Thirty years ago the ratio of incomes between the more developed countries (MDCs) and the less developed countries (LDCs) was somewhat less than 40 to 1. The UN Development Program calculates that as of 1988, the top one fifth of nations in terms of income, some 38 countries ranging from Switzerland to the former USSR, laid claim to 65 times as much in per capita income as the poorest one fifth, or the 30 nations ranging from Mozambique to India. In table 2-5 below note how the ratio between the richest 20 percent of the world's population and the poorest 20 percent of the world's population is a huge 140 to 1. However, in the United

States the ratio between the richest 20 percent and the poorest 20 percent is only 12 to 1. We all acknowledge that there is poverty in the United States, but compared to the rest of the world, poverty in the LDCs is almost unbelievable.

Dissatisfaction with GNP as a single measure of development has led to suggestions for an alternative. Several scholars in the 1960s and 1970s argued that increased GNP is not only an inadequate measure of progress, but in many LDCs such increased GNP has often been closely associated with an increase in poverty, misery and inequality. Such economic inequalities have led to dissatisfaction, unrest and even violence as disadvantaged people are organized and motivated to engage in rebellion, terrorism and revolution. Are there only two options? (1) acceptance of the status quo in which the bottom 40 percent remain in the squalor of poverty and (2) instigation of a some type of revolutionary process to forcibly take from the rich and give to the poor. The whole focus of this book is to suggest that there are other alternatives.

The Great Question of Inequality in this World

Many philosophers and humanitarians believe that substantial inequalities among incomes are unfair, and that development must reduce or eliminate this unfair situation. To them, disparities among incomes pose a simple problem of inequity to be remedied by transfers of income from the richer to the poorer nations. Moderates argue for gradual transfers through peaceful, political processes, while radicals call for the immediate transfer of such wealth through some type of violent revolution. Not only are such transfers seen to be desirable primarily as a means of equalizing incomes, but for many, less unequal incomes are believed to foster development.

These beliefs have often been the basis for much of the socialist and communist approaches to development. While they have been used by leaders to justify confiscation of wealth from the rich to be distributed to the poor, the long-term consequences of these approaches have not been that successful as the history of East Europe and the Soviet Union seem to demonstrate. Thus, it is now argued that such beliefs cannot lead to effective public policies. Indeed, a policy of forced income equality, has seldom been associated with long term processes of sustainable development and growth.

Development and disparities between incomes are distinct phenomena, interrelated in complex ways. One basic principle is that inequalities among the incomes of individuals are best seen as a reflection of the differences in their contribution to the production of goods and services needed in a given society. By bringing forth incentives and rewards to productive effort, savings and investment, they foster economic growth. Logic and history demonstrate the truth of this proposition in both capitalist and non-capitalist societies. Of course, inequalities that are extreme and rigid and markedly exceed differences in productivity and personal physical effort can so offend the popular sense of justice as to generate political instability and civil unrest and thereby impede development. At the other extreme, efforts of the low-income countries to equalize incomes by confiscator taxes can so blunt incentives to productive effort as also to impede development. There is an appropriate distribution of incomes between these extremes that is optimal for development, and public policy must be structured to seek some balanced perspective.

It is important to understand that equality of incomes is neither a desideratum nor a necessary consequence of development. The central problem of development is not maldistribution of incomes, it is low productivity of workers. In developing, as in advanced countries, the majority has more to gain in the end from increases in the size of the national income (in the size of the pie) than from any feasible changes in its distribution (how the pie might be divided). The world's poverty cannot be erased by taking from the rich to give to the poor. It can only be ended by helping the poor to become more productive and by creating systems of social and political interaction where the productive are able to share fairly in the wealth produced.

Inequality in society

Economists like to point to improvements in average per capita income as indications of increased consumption and progress in achieving economic development. Such changes, however, do not guarantee that the welfare of all people is improving. The truism, "the rich get richer and the poor get poorer," still holds in most LDCs. The reason for this in most LDCs is that as development occurs, incomes rise at different rates within different groups in society, which can aggravate existing inequalities. Well into the 1970s, it was being argued that the benefits of general economic improvements would eventually expand to all parts of the economy and "trickle down" even to the poorer segments. Beginning in the early 1970s, however, it became apparent that this process was far from automatic. The poor segments of populations were not participating equally (if at all) in economic development. Inequalities were in fact, being enlarged in most LDCs. A common way to measure the level of inequality is a given society is the Gini Coefficient: a measure of relative household incomes. If the Gini coefficient is 0, income is evenly distributed (10% of the population receive 10% of the income, 20% receive 20%, and so forth. If the Gini coefficient is close to 1, a tiny proportion of the population are receiving most of the income.

There must be a subtle balance between the need to distribute wealth more equitably through the public sector and the need to provide incentives to the private sector. In Chart 2-6 below, note how the Gini coefficient in Brazil is .51 quite similar to most LDCs. However, South Korea has been able to reduce its Gini coefficient to .36, a level of income distribution similar to much of Western Europe. Note also, although in 1965, both countries had rather similar debt service ratios (percentage of interest due for foreign debt to the level of GNP --

roughly 21.8% and 20.4% respectively), by 1988 South Korea's had been cut almost by half to 11.5 percent, while that of Brazil had almost doubled to 42 percent. Brazil has also suffered from far more serious inflationary problems than South Korea, particularly in the 1980s. The experiences of South Korea and Brazil also suggest that a more balanced gini index can impact on other aspects of the economy. As well as out performing Brazil in terms of some economic indicators, South Korea has also done much better in terms of the major social indicators of development. In the 1960's life expectancy was 54 years for both countries. By the 1980s life expectancy in South Korea had jumped to 70 years but only to 65 in Brazil. Also literacy went from 61 percent to 77 percent in Brazil, but from 71 percent to 93 percent in South Korea.

Equally interesting is the tendency for many East European countries with a communist government background to have extremely low Gini coefficients, suggesting lower levels of inequality. An assessment of their economies would raise questions as to their ability to provide meaningful incentives for greater economic growth and increased productivity. Thus nations are continually struggling to balance the need for a fair distribution of resources and the need to provide reasonable incentives for productive activity within the society.

Chart 2-6
Levels of Inequality Found in Different Countries

Country	Lowest 20%	Lowest 40%	Highest 20%	Highest 40%	Gini
Peru	4.4	13.5	60.0	35.8	.56
Kenya	2.6	13.8	68.0	45.8	.55
Mexico	2.9	14.0	64.0	40.6	.52
Brazil	2.4	8.1	62.2	46.2	.51
Columbia	4.0	17.5	59.4	37.1	.51
Philippines	5.5	15.4	55.4	32.1	.46
Egypt	5.8	10.2	--	33.2	.45
Sri Lanka	--	13.0	46.0	--	.37
South Korea	--	17.0	45.0	--	.36
Great Britain	7.2	16.0	39.2	19.1	.32
United States	4.7	16.7	38.8	25.0	.31
Sweden	5.3	24.3	--	18.6	.29
Hungary	10.9	26.5	33.5	18.7	.24

Questions about income distribution weigh heavily on issues of overall economic development and a nation's ability to share its wealth equitably among all its people. Studies of these very complicated issues have produced no pronouncements of what distribution of income would be best for each nation. Those who favor increases in GNP as the best indicator of economic growth, generally favor a more capitalist free enterprise system which, so it argued, is more apt to provide appropriate economic incentives for increased productivity and expanded businesses which provide jobs and increased income for the masses. Those who favor economic equity as the key indicator of growth, tend to emphasize fairness, a greater role for government in the distribution of wealth through government programs in health, education and welfare.

Many nations, including LDCs, have adopted extensive public policies aimed at redistribution of income among their people. Welfare payments, land reform, and graduated income tax systems are techniques that have been used by some developing nations. LDCs, however, generally lack the administrative structures or resources needed to implement such basic needs programs. Instead of trying to redistribute income in the manner of most MDCs, they often opt for cheap-food policies. These involve combinations of subsidies and price controls that are supposed to make basic food items available to large segments of the population at a low cost.

Such policies are frequently counterproductive. Artificial control of consumer prices can increase the amount demanded. At the lower prices, people demand more food and greater supplies are needed. Simultaneously, the low prices penalize the farm producers who then grow less. Resultant food shortfalls may have to be offset by food aid or increase imports of grains from the MDCs. Such imports increase national debt that often simulates greater inflation and thus weakens their economy. This is one of great dilemmas facing LDCs. In addition, administering these programs requires large amounts of budgetary support that generally increases government deficit spending which in turn tends to increase the burden of foreign debt and to stimulate increased inflation.

Today, achieving a fair income distribution is given attention comparable to that assigned to improving per capita income in earlier decades. In other words, not only is it considered important to increase the size of the economic pie, but its distribution must also be improved. In most nations, an unregulated distribution of income will favor the already rich. In LDCs, the distortion often is magnified. Most of their populations typically receive a small share of the nation's income. Mexico is an example of the distorted distribution of income that can occur in LDCs. In the early 1970s, 40 percent of the people who had the lowest incomes received only 4 percent of the nation's income, while 64 percent of the income went to the top 20 percent of the population who had the highest incomes. Such disparity is often overlooked when one simply evaluates the process of growth in GNP terms. More alarming is the fact that between 1950 and 1975 the Gini index of income distribution worsened at a time when economic growth was booming. Thus the bottom 20 percent suffered an absolute decline in real income during this period of economic growth.

In 1979 the Mexican Nutrition Institute published their major survey of under nutrition. They concluded that 52 percent of the population existed on diets that did not meet the minimum standard of 2750 calories established as necessary for normal life in Mexico. The average Mexican consumed only one-third of the recommended protein level, set at 80 grams per day. They estimated that 28 percent of the population (or 19 million) suffered from "serious malnutrition." The tragedy of these statistics is that such levels of malnutrition are even worse in other LDCs where their levels of growth are far lower.

Economic growth rates in LDCs averaged around 4-5 percent per year throughout the 1960s. Over the decade of the 1970s, the economic growth rates were almost as high. Generally, these rates were above the historic growth rates of the MDCs. Unfortunately, while many western economists were extremely pleased with these growth rates, a number of studies revealed that inequalities of income were not only persisting but in many cases were actually increasing. The poor clearly were getting poorer inspite of some rather spectacular economic growth defined in GNP aggregate terms. During the early 1970s the World Bank began to study the problem of the "forgotten poor," the "bottom 40%" of the population in the underdeveloped countries. Subsequent independent studies confirmed the phenomena of high economic growth and rising inequality.[22]

Dudley Seers, a leading scholar in the field of development, challenges the notion that increased GNP by itself means a society is developing -- with these words. "The questions to ask about a country's development are threefold: What has been happening to poverty? What has been happening to unemployment? What has been happening to inequality? If all three of these have declined from high levels, then beyond doubt this has been a period of development for the country concerned. If one of two of these central problems have been growing worse, especially if all three have, it would be strange to call the result 'development' even if per capital income doubled."[23] Unfortunately, inspite of the growth of GNP in many LDCs, most rural areas of the LDCs have in fact been plagued with increased levels of poverty, unemployment and inequality.

---

[1] Lester Brown, State of the World, (New York: Watch Institute, 1995).
[2] UN, *Mortality of Children Under Age 5: World Estimates and Projections 1950-2025* (NY; United Nations, 1988)
[3] Kenneth Hill and Anne R. Pebley, "Child Mortality in the Developing World, "*Population and Development Review*, 15:4 (December, 1989), p. 680.
[4] Global Environment Monitoring Service, Assessment of Urban Air Quality (New York: WHO, 1988)pp. pp. 86-88
[5] Pan American Health Organization, *Health Conditions in Americas:* 1990 (Washington DC: PAHO, 1990)
[6] Andrew Tomkins and Fiona Watson, "Malnutrition and Infection: A Review," (New York: United Nations Subcommittee on Nutrition, 1989), p.1.

[7] Steven A. Esrey, James B. Potash, Leslie Roberts, *et al.*, "Effects of Improved Water Supply and Sanitation on Ascariasis, Diarrhea, Dracunculiasis, Hookworm, Infection, Schistosomiasis, and Trachoma, *Bulletin of the World Health Organization*, 69:5 (1993).

[8] Richard G. Feachem, "Interventions for the Control of Diarrhoeal Diseases Among Young Children: Promotion of Personal and Domestic Hygiene, *Bulletin of the World Health Organization*, 62:3 (Geneva: WHO, 1984)

[9] *Ibid.*, pp. 50-51.

[10] State of World's Children 1990, *op cit.*, pp. 43-44.

[11] ILO, *Economically Active Population Estimates and Projects*, 1950-2025 (Geneva, 1990)

[12] Joanne Leslie, Margaret Lycette, and Mayra Buvinic, "Weathering Economic Crisis: The Crucial Role of Women in Health," in David E. Bell and Michael R. Reach, *Health, Nutrition, and Economic Crises: Approaches to Policy in the Third World* (Dover, Mass: Auburn House, 1986), p. 313.

[13] H. Daly and J. Cobb, *For the Common Good* (Boston: Beacon Press, 1989

[14] US Department of Agriculture (USDA), *Global Food Assessment: Situation and Outlook Report* (Washington DC: Economic Research Service, USDA, 1990), p. 4.

[15] Thomas R. Malthus, *An Essay on the Principle of Population*, ed. Philip Appleman (New York: W. W. Norton, 1976), pp. 59-60

[16] Paul R. Ehrlich, *The Population Bomb*, (New York: Ballantine, 1968), p. 1.

[17] Paul f. McCleary and J. Philip Wogaman, *Quality of Life in a Global Society* (New York: Friendship Press, 1978), p. 25

[18] Cynthia P. Green, *People: An Endangered Species*: rev. (Washington, DC: National Wildlife Federation, 1980), p. 6.

[19] United Nations, Secretariat, Text of Statement by Secretary-General, U Thant, at Opening of Orientation Course for Population Program Officers (Press Release SG/SM/1055, SOC/3624), 14 January 1969), n.p.

[20] Julian L. Simon, "The Case for More People," *American Demographics* 1 (10) (November-December, 1979): pp. 26, 28.

[21] Julian Simon, *The Ultimate Resource*, (Princeton, NJ: Princeton University Press, 1981)

[22] Irma Adelman and Cynthia Taft Morris, *Economic Growth and Social Equity in Developing Countries* (Stanford: Stanford University Press, 1974) and Keith Griffin, *International Inequality and National Poverty (London: Macmillan, 1978)*

[23] Dudley Seers, "What are We Trying to Measure?" *Journal of Development Studies*, 8 (1972).

Chapter 3

The Challenges of Conceptualizing and Measuring the Reality of World Poverty

This chapter will seek to define poverty, identify some of the common ways poverty is measured and considered and outline some of the causes, seeking to distinguish between symptoms and causes. Poverty is often defined in terms of some level of income. Defining poverty in terms of income suggests that in a given society, the poverty level is best defined as not having the financial resources needed to purchase the basic needs of food and water, shelter and clothing, opportunities for education and access to primary health care services.

When we define poverty in monetary terms, we may both overestimate and underestimate the consequences of poverty in a given area. In many LDCs, especially in the rural areas, monetary income often represents a small faction of the resources available to a given family. Through systems of barter and reciprocal helping, many villagers can meet their basic needs without using cash, yet this ability is gradually disappearing as a money economy comes more and more to dominate in the LDCs. Yet equally prevalent is the tendency to assume that things are reasonably good if their basic needs of food and shelter are being provided. Questions as to whether the family's diet is balanced and nutritious for a productive life, whether they have access to clean water and appropriate facilities for sanitation, whether the environment provides clean air and productive agricultural lands, and finally whether life is meaningful with significant opportunities for cultural, emotional and spiritual development, are all issues that need attention as we seek to define poverty.

When poverty is defined in these kinds of terms, income is not necessarily the best criteria. Poverty, for me, dramatizes the lack of options, the lack of choice in a given situation. Poverty is a condition where people have no opportunities, no ways of changing that which they would like to change, with environmental (economic, political, and social), physical (productive stamina and freedom from disease) and mental (educational, emotional and intellectual) constraints blocking these people from improving their way of life.

At this point it is important to distinguish between long-term and short-term forms of poverty. In this book, when we speak of poverty we will be emphasizing those forms of poverty that are long-term and seldom easily dealt with. For example, certain forms of poverty relate to the short-term consequences of periodic draughts, floods, hurricanes and earthquakes which can bring devastating famine and starvation, but of a temporary type. Humanitarian relief, while clearly needed in times of disaster, are short term, tend to provide the immediate help needed for survival with no intention that such help will continue after the immediate question of survival has been addressed. While some forms of disaster relief will always be needed, one must be careful that such "good intentions" do not foster greater dependency, welfarism and social entropy. For example, some have argued that such humanitarian effort may be counter-productive even when the intentions were good, especially if the "free food" distributed to the poor interferes with the local farmers' efforts to grow and market their own crops in that area.

Section One
How Do We Define Poverty

Poverty can be defined in relative or absolute terms. Most of us are relatively poorer than the Rockefellers, "poor" people in Los Angeles drive five-year old cars; unemployed people in Britain live at a state-defined subsistence level, but they are much richer than the unemployed in Calcutta, India or the landless farmers in the Alti Plano of central Bolivia. Clearly, relative poverty can only be defined in terms of the society or class to which it refers -- that is, in relation to a general standard of living and an accepted quality of life. Others have suggested that any analysis of poverty especially in the poorer areas of the LDCs requires that a distinction be made between absolute poverty and the less severe levels of poverty that characterized much of these countries. In the extreme forms of poverty which generally includes the bottom 10 to 20 percent of society spend more than 80 percent of their income on food, experience acute forms of malnutrition, and are especially vulnerable to the hazards of poor health and unemployment. Moderate forms of poverty which generally include the next 15 to 35 percent of society, are still apt to suffer from malnutrition but not in its chronic or acute forms. While they generally use upwards of 60 to 70 percent of their income for food, their major problem is generally less apt to be keeping healthy, and more concerned with finding adequate employment, land for the production of food and other types of assets which can be used to generate needed income. Note the factors which distinguish absolute from moderate forms of poverty.

Absolute poverty is a condition of failure to meet the basic essentials of physical existence with almost no income for housing, medicine, clothing, transportation, or even necessary tools to obtain needed income. At rock bottom this means only having enough food to keep yourself alive over time. Therefore, a measure of absolute poverty is almost entirely a measurement of subsistence nutrition. Yet the more moderate forms of poverty must still be seen as essentially a very devastating way of life with little hope for any improvement from the day-to-day drudgery that characterizes this form of life.

Table 3-1
Factors Which Distinguish Absolute and Moderate Forms of Poverty

Key Factors	Moderate Forms	Extreme Forms
1. Percentage of household budget required for food	60-70%	80-90+%
2. Percentage of the total population	15-35%	10-20%
3. Spatial concentration	Both rural and urban areas	Mostly rural areas
4. Household size	5-8 children	3-5 children
5. Malnutrition	Moderate	Acute
6. Basic Needs	Assets/employment	Food/health

The minimum needs approach is a rather cold-hearted one. It appraises man as a machine-like organism, capable only of function, fit only to work, eat and sleep. Many people involved in the measurement of poverty object to this approach. Rowntree, one of the first to attempt to quantify poverty in Britain, used it when designing a minimum budget. He noted that the very poor "...must never spend a penny on railway fare or omnibus. They must never go into the country unless they walk. They must never purchase a half penny newspaper or spend a penny to buy a ticket for a popular concert. They must write no letters to absent children, for they cannot afford to pay the postage... the children must have no pocket money for dolls, marbles, or sweets... The father must smoke no tobacco, and must drink no beer. Nothing must be bought but that which is absolutely necessary for the maintenance of physical health, and what is bought must be of the plainest and most economical description ..."[1]

According to Rowntree, anyone whose income fell below his estimated minimum requirement was suffering from "primary poverty". In the early 1970s, Robert McNamara described people on or below the poverty-line adopted by the World Bank as living "below any rational level of human decency". He pointed out that four-fifths of their income is spent for food. Their diet is monotonous, limited to cereals, yams or cassavas, a few vegetables, and in many regions, only limited fish or meat. All, at this level, are undernourished, many millions are severely undernourished. Energy and motivation are reduced, performance in school and at work is undermined; resistance to illness is low; and the physical and mental development of children is often impaired. Two of every 10 children born die within the first year; and another dies before the age of five; and only five reach the age of 40. People are many times more apt to die from diseases like measles, diphtheria, whooping cough, and average life expectancy is often twenty, even thirty, years less than in the MDCs.[2]

Of course, poverty can be defined as more than just a set of minimum requirements for physical efficiency. It may also be defined with reference to the norms of society, and conceived of as a set of "basic needs" rather than "minimum needs." Basic needs would include those material comforts that will give people an element of choice, have enough resources to have options in the way they would live. There are many layers of "perceived poverty" and they change for individuals and groups over time. In visiting a village on the island of Cebu in the Philippines, I was surprised to note how people that I would have judged to be extremely poor were quick to suggest that the "really poor" people on this island lived in the next village over. Nobody in the United States today expects to see a child without shoes on its feet, as a consequence of poverty -- even in summer. Yet such a sight is commonplace, if regrettable, in most LDCs.

Another issue in measuring poverty in a given society is concerned with determining a precise definition of the nutritional minimum needed for a healthy productive life. In attempting to assess the minimum nutritional needs of people, there has been some debate concerning whether caloric intake is enough or whether the amount of protein eaten must also be considered. For this reason, it is now accepted practice to refer to protein and caloric deficiencies as related, under the general term "protein-energy malnutrition" (PEM).

PEM is not as easy to define as might be assumed. The minimum needed will depend upon the nature of work that a person does; his physical condition, sex, age; the climate he is working under, etc. Most researcher today acknowledge that somewhere between 2200 and 3000 calories are needed depending on age, sex and type of work. One significant attempt to determine the extent of poverty in India during the 1950s and 1960s used a fairly sophisticated measure of poverty, using two indicators, one expressed in money terms and the other as a caloric minimum. The later was considered more realistic because it could be translated into a money value in each year and thus used to measure trends over time. The poverty line in India was taken as Rs 15 per capita per month at 1960-61 prices. This gave an estimate of 38 percent of rural people living below the poverty line in 1960-61, rising to 53 percent by 1967-68. Prices had doubled over the decade, while real incomes had fallen, leading to one-third increase in absolute poverty.

When a dietary minimum is used to measure poverty, a conservative estimate of the minimum energy intake necessary for moderate physical labor was assumed to be 2700 calories. Using this level of food intake, the cost of such a minimum diet in 1960-61 was Rs 12, rising to Rs 30 in 1967-68. Based upon these figures, some 18 percent of rural people were assumed to be below the minimum in 1960-61, rising to a colossal 63 percent in 1967-68. Either method gives a final calculation of poverty in excess of 50 percent by the late 1960s.

Recent studies suggest that the percentage of those in the LDCs living at below these minimum levels of income and caloric intake did drop significantly in the 1970s and early 1980s, but has been rising in recent years to roughly 30-40 percent among Third World countries and to roughly 40-50 percent among Fourth World countries.

In a more socially oriented definition of poverty, people are defined as poor based upon social comparison to others in their society who are not poor. Poverty is then a product of social organization, and in particular, reflective of the unequal structures of society. When we say that people are poor, deprived, suffering from hardships, or in need, we usually have a fairly good idea of what we mean. Yet such perceptions will clearly differ from country to country. Poverty in the United States among the welfare recipients of a major city are not the same as the poor in rural Somalia or urban Calcutta.

So when is one poor? Poverty as was suggested, is sometimes related to a "poverty line", so that everyone whose income is below a certain level is considered to be "poor", and everyone above the line is not. But this kind of approach leads to obvious problems -- because some people do have a low income without being thought of as poor -- college students in a mid-western college may be poor but not in poverty as one would find in Bangladesh. Readers who hope to find an authoritative "scientific" definition of poverty in this book will be disappointed. The use of the term varies from society to society, from situation to situation, the concept is liable to be contested, and the issues cannot be resolved beyond dispute. "Poverty" does not describe a particular kind of attribute which people do or do not have; the term is used to describe a range or cluster of conditions. A person starving in Ethiopia, an Indonesian hill farmer with less than two acres, or a Bolivian pensioner unable to afford heating, might all be said to be "poor" in some sense; but it is not necessary to suppose that they are all poor in exactly the same sense. The problems they face, the reasons for these problems, and the sorts of response which have to be made, are clearly going to be different.

Poverty is not only a descriptive category; it is also a moral one. The term "poverty" carries with it an implication and morale imperative that something should be done about it. Its definition is a value judgment and should be clearly seen to be so. A wide range of factors are suggested in the literature[3], which is not to say that these factors define people as being poor, but only that they are likely to occur in the circumstances where people are poor. They include: living conditions which do not provide adequate protection from the elements, is poorly lighted or heated. overcrowded or filthy, people who are malnourished and chronically hungry, clothing which does not provide adequate protection from the elements, high probability of short life-span, frequent and often chronic illnesses, permanent physical or mental disability, polluted water, lack of protection against major loss of assets, lack of good quality education, inability to perform a socially valued function in society, low aspirations and a sense of hopelessness, severe restrictions on economic and social opportunity and activity (especially discrimination), exclusion from participation in the political process, victim of injustice in the law enforcement process, experienced exploitation from elites, and generally lack of any symbols of social status or dignity.

All the factors one might list could be conceptualized as potential consequences of being poor, but some might also be seen as factors which lead to poverty, and others -- like hunger, lack of clothing and inadequate housing -- as factors which are virtually descriptive of poverty; that is, they are the kinds of things by which poverty is identified. Poverty is sometimes defined in terms of deprivation. People experience many different kinds of deprivation: Material deprivation is perhaps the most important in relation to poverty because most indicators of poverty emphasize lack of food, clothing or shelter all defined as material. Certainly, aspects of ill health -- like malnutrition, infant mortality, early death, or chronic disability -- constitute some of the common physical factors by which poverty is identified, being at the same time a cause of poverty, an aspect of deprivation and a potential consequence of poverty. Recently, people have come to recognize the psychological and social implications of poverty in which a weak sense of self-esteem, feelings of powerlessness and a general social alienation are both cause and consequence of extreme poverty.

Following this line of thinking, Runciman argues for a concept of "relative deprivation" based upon a set of socially established norms. People in a given community determine the standards which are appropriate by a comparison of their circumstances with the circumstances of other people in that community. When they do not have things that they can reasonably expect or believe they need to have, they may consider themselves deprived. Runciman's arguments seem, at first sight, to be based on subjective impressions, but that is misleading; the views which are formed are actually inter-subjective, formed through an interactive process, rather than by individuals in isolation. The process produces social norms of what constitutes poverty and what does not.[4] I find this approach most useful, especially when seeking to identify who is poor in a given community and what constitute appropriate strategies and resources to alleviate poverty in a given society. The concept of poverty defined inter-subjectively, that is socially, is obviously more difficult to operationalize, but it probably provides a more accurate description of the way in which poverty is conceived in a given village or community.

Section Two
How Do We Define Those Who Live in Poverty?

Because the task of finding an appropriate definition of poverty is so difficult, and so frustrating, many experts and academics and practitioners often simply use a specific income level and declare all people below that income level as being in poverty. In most studies such a poverty line is derived from an estimate of the **level of income necessary to ensure a minimum diet**, although the studies analyzed differ widely as to what should be the contents of a minimum diet. Although most knowledgeable observers see such a definition as inadequate, misleading and sometimes even contradictory, still there are some advantages to such a definition: **First** it is convenient, for it allows one to identify a large number of people as poor without having to justify your categorization through extensive and expensive research. **Second**, it is conventional, and as such gives a fairly constant reference point, making it possible to discuss other issues about poverty, like why are people poor or what sort of people become poor, without going through the process of defining the problem and identifying the people concerned.

One of the unsatisfactory things about "poverty lines" is that it is impossible to tell from them what has happened to the distribution of income among those below the line. Recent studies suggest that even among the poorest of the poor, the bottom 30-40 percent, there is considerable variations concerning the extent to which different groups have access to food and shelter. For example, a minimum level of income, a minimum amount of food (or even foods with basic nutritional values), standards of health, education, all can provide criteria against which communities, regions and even countries could be measured. The World Bank, while recognizing the arbitrariness of the definition, using 1985 data treats people as extremely poor if they have a purchasing power of less than $275 a year, and poor if they have less than $370 a year. This is useful as a rule of thumb; they supplement the material with other information about public services, health, education and so forth, because the availability of such services affects the basic standard of living for people who are poorest. Using this type of figure, it is possible to suggest that as much as 50 to 60 percent of the populations in many LDCs are below such a poverty line.

Measurements of Poverty: A Global Perspective

One of the most widely used attempts to measure the existence of poverty beyond GNP was the Overseas Development Council's Physical Quality of Life Index (PQLI), which combined infant mortality, life expectancy, and literacy, with equal weights, into a single number.[5]

As would be expected, rich nations do tend to have high PQLIs and poor nations have low PQLIs. Yet within the LDCs there are significant differences in their quality of life measurements, with some countries achieving very superior results relative to their per capita income levels requiring some explanation of this "greater social efficiency." Among a number of nations such as in the Middle East, several have high incomes from oil and yet have very low PQLIs. One dramatic example in the late 1970s was in Iran, where per capita GNP was more than nine times greater than in India ($1260 vs. $133) but whose PQLI (+43) was exactly the same. If nothing else, such observations show that "money is not everything." This observation may not be surprising but policy makers and government leaders have tended to ignore its implication. While many governments appear to have some commitment to achieve a higher PQLI for their people, some governments have been much more sensitive and responsive to the needs of their people than others. Governments willing to allocate significant resources to the reduction of poverty, illiteracy and sickness can make a difference.

Table 3-2
Comparing Per Capita GNP and the PQLI (the early 1970s)

Country	Per Capita GNP	PQLI	Life Expectancy at Age One	Infant Mortality (per 1000)
Nations Under $700				
Mali	90	15	45	188
Bangladesh	92	35	53	132
Ethiopia	97	20	50	181
Nepal	102	25	51	169
India	133	43	55	122
Sri Lanka	**179**	**82**	**70**	**45**
Samoa	**300**	**84**	**64**	**40**
Bolivia	332	43	51	108
Philippines	342	71	61	74
Ghana	595	35	55	156
Cuba	**640**	**84**	**71**	**29**
Costa Rica	700	85	69	38

Table 3-2 above lists countries with 1970-75 per capita GNPs under $700 and PQLIs that vary from as low as 15 in Mali and as high as 85 in Costa Rica (remember that a PQLI of 70 suggests a literacy rate of at least 70%, an infant mortality rate no higher than 55 per thousand, and a life expectancy at age one of 62.4 years). The realization that growth has been uneven and has, in some cases, contributed little to the alleviation of the misery of the masses of poor people has led many to consider alternative strategies for development not just based upon increased GNP.

In recent years the United Nations Development Program's Human Development Index (HDI) seeks to adjust GNP to better reflect the different levels of purchasing power that can exist from a given level of per capita income. This new focus reflects the reality that a dollar converted into a local currency varies considerably from nation to nation in terms of what that dollar can purchase. A UNDP team, under a Pakistani economist, Mahboub ul-Haq, offers an alternative guide to measuring development. In a study called *Human Development 1990* a new human development index (HDI) is presented which combines the factor of purchasing power, along with life expectancy and literacy rates of some 130 countries.

Table 3-3
The Human Development Index: Mid-1980s

Country	Life Expectancy	Literacy % of Adults	GNP Ranking	HDI Ranking	Real GDP ($) Per Head
Niger	45	14	20	1	452
Mali	45	17	15	2	543
Sudan	51	23	32	14	750
*Bangladesh	52	33	6	23	837
Ghana	55	54	37	30	481
*Pakistan	58	30	33	36	1585
*India	59	43	25	37	1,053
*Kenya	59	60	30	42	794
Egypt	62	45	49	45	1,357
Bolivia	54	75	44	49	1,380
*Indonesia	57	74	41	54	1,160
Guatemala	63	55	63	55	1,957
*Algeria	63	50	91	92	2,633
Syria	66	60	79	62	3,250
Saudi Arabia	64	55	107	64	8,320
*Philippines	64	86	46	65	1,878
*China	70	69	22	66	2,124
*Turkey	65	74	71	72	3,716
Nigeria	57	52	52	44	1,860
*Thailand	66	91	55	78	2,576
*Sri Lanka	71	87	38	83	2,053
Brazil	65	78	85	80	4,307
Malaysia	70	74	80	85	3,849
Mexico	69	90	81	91	4,624
USA	76	96	129	112	17,615
Japan	78	99	126	130	13,135

A review of this study provides some interesting food for thought. For example Sri Lanka, if you can accept the validity of the data, has an official GNP of $400 per head giving them a GNP ranking of only 38 among the 130 countries listed. However, with purchasing power of roughly $2,000 per head because goods are relatively cheap; a life expectancy of 71 years; and a 87 percent literacy rate, Sri Lanka has a Human Development Index (HDI) score of .78 that means they are ranked as high as 83rd among the 130 countries listed. At the other extreme is Mauritania with a GNP ranking of 40 but an abysmal ranking of 8 in human development terms because of a life expectancy of only 46 and a literacy rate of only 17 percent. This puts Mauritania in terms of quality of life roughly equal to such nations as Mali, Chad, Somalia and Niger who have much lower levels of GNP. Note for example a comparison of Sri Lanka and Brazil. At an average annual per capita income of only $430, Sri Lanka has one of the lowest child mortality rates of all developing countries (36 per 1,000). Brazil, with an average per capital income five times higher than Sri Lanka's ($2550), has a child mortality rate twice as large (77 per 1,000). With an average annual per capita income of $182, the state of Kerala in India is poorer than India as a whole; yet in 1986, the state had an infant mortality rate of 27 per 1,000 much lower than India as a whole.

The strength of the HDI like the PQLI is in reminding those who cannot see beyond the end of their statistics that there is more to life than GNP. Its big weakness, inevitably, is that it is still rather subjective and that quality and accuracy of the data used to determine the ranking is always suspect.

From my perspective, this type of analysis can be useful in sensitizing policy makers to the importance of considering how they allocate scarce resources in their societies. Such assessments require some consideration as to how much is spent on education, health and other human resource development activities, and how much goes for defense, for example. There is another dimension of these rankings that invites discussion. As one compares various countries on their GNP rankings and on the Human Development Index rankings, an interesting question emerges. Even a rough review of these rankings cries for answers: To what extent is such differences attributable to policy makers and their commitment to human development programs? Does democratic representation somehow stimulate a greater concern for such issues as literacy, health and greater economic equity? Do the differences in rankings have any thing to do with the quality and effectiveness of social institutions in implementing and providing social services? To what extent do effective managerial and organizational capacities have anything to do with a society's ability to transfer fewer resources into a higher standard of living for its people?

When one observes a number of nations with lower economic resources able to provide a higher quality of life than other nations with higher economic resources, one is tempted, if one has a management training or development administration background, to consider ways by which a society might seek to measure its own organizational and managerial abilities and capacities, to implement some type of Institutional Assessment/Development program to determine the ways in which that society might improve its relative position. In Table 3-3 above, an * is place by the countries that appear to be more effective in using their scarce resource, i.e., have a lower GNP ranking than their HDI ranking. Whenever the GNP rank and the HDI rank is more than 10 points apart that country is in bold type. Note for example that while Bangladesh is the sixth poorest country in the world in terms of real GDP per head adjusted for purchasing power, she has a HDI ranking of 23 suggesting a better allocation of resources for health and education than would be expected given her level of income. Some of this effective use of resources in Bangladesh is attributed to Sri Lanka's commitment to a grassroots approach to rural development.

The index reveals that some countries -- Sri Lanka, Chile, Costa Rica, Jamaica, Tanzania, and Thailand, among others -- seem to have been far more successful than others in translating economic progress into broad welfare gains for their people. The 1991 report came to several conclusions: (1) The most effective means of sustaining human development are economic growth accompanied by an equitable distribution of income (as in South Korea). (2) Even in the absence of rapid growth or equitable income distribution, countries can make significant improvements in human development through well-structured social spending utilizing grassroots strategies and rural development programs (Botswana, Malaysia, and Sri Lanka). (3) Well-structured government social spending, especially when such programs are decentralized, can generate dramatic improvements in a relatively short period, not only for countries starting from a low level of human development, but also for those starting at a moderate level (Chile and Costa Rica). (4) Setbacks in economic growth caused by political instability or social violence can seriously disrupt human development (Chile, Zimbabwe, and Botswana). (5)In countries experiencing economic growth, human development may not improve if income distribution is uneven and social expenditures are low (Nigeria and Pakistan) or most of the wealth is appropriated by those who are better off (Brazil).

Another approach to measuring progress in the world is one developed by UNICEF that provides a more detailed picture through an array of indicators without seeking to aggregate them into a single index. This approach is adopted by UNICEF in its annual State of the World's Children reports and includes the following types of social indicators: morality rates (under 5 and under 1 year of age) number of births to number of child deaths, life expectancy, adult literacy rates, primary school enrollment, share of income of the poorest 40% and richest 20%, population, per capita GNP, various measures of nutrition, health, education, and income for both women and children. Gradually, development specialists are beginning to recognize the need to raise production of the poor by improving their quality of life, by raising demand for their goods and services, by improving their skills, and by raising their productivity. First, it must be recognized that this also will not be enough as long as the present levels of income distribution and opportunities for upward mobility remain in their present inequitable form. Second, with some exceptions, most countries have failed to provide critical social services for the poor, and few resources have been consistently allocated to provide basic services to the bottom 40 percent of society.

Section Three
How Does One Explain Poverty?

One common way to explain poverty is to attribute it to the culture of the people involved. The best known expressions of poverty as a "subculture" have been Oscar Lewis's anthropological studies of poor people in Mexico, Puerto Rico and New York. Lewis summarizes some of the major characteristics as follows: "On the family level, the major traits of the culture of poverty are the absence of childhood as a specially prolonged and protected stage in the life cycle, early initiation into sex, free unions or consensual marriages, a relatively high incidence of the abandonment of wives and children, a trend toward female- or mother-centered families. . .a strong disposition to authoritarianism, lack of privacy, real emphasis on family solidarity which is only rarely achieved because of sibling rivalry, and competition for limited goods and maternal affection.

On the level of the individual, the major characteristics are a strong feeling of marginality, of helplessness, of dependence and inferiority. Other traits include a high incidence of maternal depravation, or immorality, or weak ego structure, confusion of sexual identification, a lack of impulse control, a strong present-time orientation with relatively little ability to defer gratification and to plan for the future, a sense of resignation and fatalism, a widespread belief in male superiority, and high tolerance for psychological pathology of all sorts."[6]

Valentine attacks the characterization of Lewis on the basis that it is not really about a "culture" at all[7] -- it has far more to do with the supposed effect of poverty on personality. One of Lewis's principal faults is that he mixes psychological characteristics with social relationships, and then compounds them with other factors (like unemployment, lack of savings and lack of privacy) which are aspects of poverty itself, rather than any culture.[8] Ultimately, Lewis's description can be seen -- like many others in the field -- as a "middle class rationale for blaming poverty on the poor".[9]

A more common way of explaining poverty is to refer to the structure of society as the major cause. Structural explanations are those which attribute poverty in one sense or another to the structure of society, including both the national and international dimensions as the major cause. One common technique for measuring the causes of poverty is to define poverty in social structural terms. Many structural explanations for poverty are generally conceived in terms of power relationships. The argument is that poor people do not simply find themselves at the bottom, but that they are put there and kept there by a repressive social structure. This is taken to support a view of society which is based on the dominance of an elite, or of a class in whose interests rules are made. Explanations which are based on interpreting gender relationships and the feminization of poverty may base the analysis on the understanding of patriarchy, or male dominance.

According this approach, it is not possible to get very far in understanding the problems of poverty in the LDCs until one understands that there are groups of people with different levels of power and influence and that the interests of these various groups (big landowners, small landowners, landless laborers, village artisans, etc.) are often in conflict. Posing the issue in this way forces one to examine the distribution of wealth in a given society (a variable neglected in many models dealing with poverty) and then to view the distribution of income as closely related to the underlying distribution of assets. A chain of association is thereby established between such groups defined in structural terms, including the ownership of wealth and the distribution of income.

The main implication of an argument based on such social relationships are two fold. The first is that, if poverty is produced as a result of deliberate action of those with power, or even of knowing indifference, there is unlikely to be an acceptance of measures to alleviate poverty, and the best which can be hoped for will be minor ameliorative measures which do not conflict too far with the interests of those who have power. The second is that this situation can ultimately be addressed only through seeking to redress the structure of power in society either through some form violence and revolution, or through some forms of empowerment and coalition-building, a point which will be discussed in chapter 10 of this book.

Policy Implications of the Causes of Poverty

Attempts to link the relief of poverty to a causal analysis reflect a set of moral positions that have been taken about the condition of people who are poor. Those who attribute poverty to the fault, laziness or immorality of the poor are likely to argue that they deserve their fate and that attempts to improve their situation without addressing the root problems are doomed to failure. Those who view poverty as the product of an unequal society in which people are disadvantaged in economic, political and social terms suggest that, since no amount of individual effort can redress the balance, it is inappropriate to structure the relief of poverty through a system which requires them to lift themselves by their own bootstraps. Neither of these positions is set and immutable. Even if poverty is seen as the result of individual fault, it is possible to argue that in a well-ordered society, individuals and their dependents, can and should be protected from the consequences of individual failure. Equally, it can be argued that even if there are structural problems or constraints to poverty alleviation, people can overcome the disadvantages imposed on them through the implementation of gradual reforms.

Structural explanations for poverty imply that some change in social structure is not only desirable but a basic requirement if poverty is to be reduced. The problem with this proposition is not that it is self-evidently wrong or unreasonable, but that it difficult to translate into operational terms outside of some type of revolutionary or violent form of change. The question about how one reduces or eliminates poverty in a given society has confronted scholars and officials for decades and will be considered in detail in later chapters.

Section Four
Understanding the Causes of World Poverty

Much of Political Science theory is compartmentalized into competing levels of analysis: some focusing on the international determinants of world poverty, some on the national and some on the local or societal determinants of this phenomenon called world poverty. The issue of poverty in a given country is not which level is determinate or which approach is "right" but, rather at what level is the realities and consequences of poverty best to be explained. The properties of the international system, as described in dependency theory, for example, force one to concentrate on some specific variables that often lead to the exclusion of other variables at the national or the local levels.

When one focuses on the central administrative system of a country, emphasizing the internal workings of the national bureaucracy and the structural constraints observed, without considering the impact of Western imperialism/colonialism and the exploitative relationships that have tended to characterize most more-developed and less-developed nations over the past several centuries, then much of the explanatory power of such an approach will be lost. The same is also true if one looks at the local culture and the basic societal factors (cultural traditions, social associations, patron-client relationships) but ignores the impact of international trade relations and the demands of national policy-making. The need to consider all three levels of analysis reflect the importance of seeking to conceptualize poverty not only as a national issue, but the ways in which international and local forces also impact on the causes and consequences of poverty. In Chapter 4, below, a fairly in-depth discussion will be presented on the various theories and approaches that have been developed both to explain the causes and to suggest solutions to the problems of world poverty and underdevelopment

At the local level, in talking to peasants, farmers, students, and bureaucrats, the simple explanation for underdevelopment will be presented as ignorance, disease and poverty -- implying that solutions are simple: just provide education, health services and money. Most lists of causes fail to distinguish between causes, symptoms and consequences. Do people have poor health because they are poor or are people poor because they are sick. Is idleness a cause of poverty, or are people apparently idle because they have nothing productive to do with their time? We obviously need to separate the symptoms from the real causes. Many scholars have described these problems as a consequence of the vicious cycle of poverty

Vicious Cycle of Poverty

Anyone who considers the causes of poverty acknowledges that some things are causes of poverty while others are better seen as consequences or symptoms of poverty. Is ill health a cause or consequence of poverty? In some sense, poor health reduces the amount of time one can work and the level of strength one needs to work in the fields and factories of a society and thus causes one to have less income. Yet, when you are poor you do not have the resources needed to purchase medicine or see a doctor and thus poverty may better be seen as the cause of poor health.

Note this causal sequence: Disease and malnutrition lead to poor health, which leads to lower production, which leads to lower income, which leads to lower surplus that means less taxes collected, which means less health facilities which means less treatment available which means more disease and sickness which leads to poor health etc., etc., etc. In reality, this rather simple cycle of poverty fails to capture the complexity of most LDC settings. After all, poor health is not simply caused by the lack of health facilities. There are many other factors including: lack of potable water (clean drinking water), lack of toilets and prevalence of unsanitary conditions, poor housing that does not provide protection from the elements, the use of open-pit fires with poor ventilation.

For example, in trying to understand why a poor person would not build an inexpensive stove which would reduce the smoke in the house as a way of improving the health of his family, a number of possibilities come to mind. Many villagers do have the income needed to buy the materials for a stove. However, many lack the knowledge to see the connection between health and the existence of smoke their family has to breath, others would rather spend their scarce resources for other things -- perhaps a farm implement or a simple radio. Some people are uncomfortable using a stove -- forcing people to behave in ways that seem strange or unnecessary. Some would argue from experience that the existence of smoke in the house keeps termites away and thus preserves their wooden houses for a longer period of time. Often, such people have very good reasons for the things they do that only make sense when we see reality from their perspective.

It is often said that peasants are lazy and illiterate and therefore refuse to increase their production. On closer look, in many countries, marketing boards are set up that pay farmers a fixed price for their crops, usually far below the world market price in order to maximize the country's export income or to provide cheap food prices for the urban masses. What is depicted as laziness, may, in fact, be the cunning awareness that hard work and efforts to increase production will never be rewarded, as long as the government pays a subsistence price for the crops the peasants produce.

The complexity of poverty should be apparent. Many might argue that lack of education would be a good first place to start: Low levels of education are often associated with lack of knowledge, lack of certain skills, awareness, self-confidence and motivation, innovation and creative problem solving. All of these consequences of lack of education do lead to lower levels of production and lower levels of productivity that will lead to lower income that ensure lower levels of surplus in society and thus lower levels of taxation, with the consequence of fewer schools and teachers in a given society.

Others might argue that the causes of poverty are ultimately related to economics and access to resources. Lack of income means lack of savings and capital and the concomitant lack of collateral or assets, which means no access to bank credit. Lack of credit and capital ensure low levels of investment, lack of access to fertilizers, insecticides, and other equipment needed to increase production. Also, without access to reasonable credit, many farmers must rely on moneylenders who charge such high rates of interest that much of the surplus earned must be used to pay off the debt. Also, the lack of education often means lack of knowledge about more productive forms of agriculture, the lack of modern skills ensures lower levels of productivity, less profit, inability to compete with larger farmers, often forcing smaller farmers to sell their land. Loss of land forces such farmers to seek employment usually at even lower wages, thus the cycle of poverty often spirals ever downward.

The more one studies poverty in the LDCs of the world, the more one sees the multiplicity of causes and the many interrelationships between and among such causes. Often development specialists tend to focus on symptoms without going back to the more basic causes of poverty. It is easy to assume that poor health is a cause of poverty, without considering the macro-political and economic factors that creates the environment where poor health can thrive. Stan Burkey presents an illuminating list that seeks to identify the cause of poverty at each of the three levels of analysis within some four categories of causes related to poverty:[10]

(1) Physical Causes of Poverty:
Local: Poor soils, unreliable rainfall, lack of surface water, lack of natural resources, unfavorable marginal terrain.
National: Land destruction: Deforestation, Erosion, Overgrazing, Lack of energy sources
International: Tropical disease Vectors, Land-locked nation, land and resource exploitation's from past colonial regimes.

The placement of a particular cause under the category of local, national, or international will always be a bit arbitrary in as much as land destruction and tropical disease vectors can also be defined as local problems. Nevertheless, such an issue as land destruction is probably best confronted through some type of national policy perspective and the problem of disease vectors is generally better confronted through some process of cooperation among nations. Equally significant is the tendency for large landowners to cut down forest areas to provide for greater beef production, stimulated by developed country demand. It is also important to acknowledge that land destruction through erosion and deforestation could be included under social causes, since much of this destruction is reflective of family decisions at the local level. Many families, seeing their forest disappear, are forced to use animal dung and crop residue for their cooking and heating, instead of putting such natural fertilizers on their farms, thus creating a downward spiral in land productivity. Others might want to argue that such destruction of the forests and lands, for example, like in Brazil, might best be understood as a problem of public policy, political corruption and the inability of government agencies to implement the policies created to deal with these kinds of problems. As will emphasized in chapter 14 below, the gradual destruction of the local environment is one of the major causes of poverty in many parts of the world.

(2) Political Causes of Poverty

Local: lack of local government institutions; sectarianism, nepotism and favoritism, lack of law and order; corruption; lack of local participation; and lack of political education.

National: political instability, civil war, lack of democratic decision-making; lack of interest in poor people, legacies of colonialism, corruption and nepotism, lack of good administration; breakdown of the legal system

International: Neo-colonialism, National rivalries, refugees

Many students of development have been quick to blame the problems of the LDCs on the often inexperienced, generally corrupt and usually unstable regimes found in many LDCs. Government change through incessant *coup d'etats*, political leaders stashing huge amounts of money in Swiss banks, greedy elites more interested in the business opportunities that political office provides, and the political unrest and frustrations of the masses are all related to the spread and constancy of poverty in many of these countries. Perpetual in-fighting among military leaders, tragic human rights violations, and the lack of any system of rule by law make consistent programs of development and poverty alleviation very difficult.

Many of these problems, however, can also be seen as the consequences of colonialism. Overemphasis on centralized government structures; lack of genuine local government participation and accountability; imposition of external law and foreign constitutions; inappropriate educational systems and curricula; the exacerbation of ethnic and religious conflict; acceptance of European values as better than local cultural values; class conflict and prejudice; regional favoritism based on the colonial power's interest rather than the country's interests; creation and perpetuation of dependency thinking and a lack of democratic processes are all consequences of this tradition. It is amazing how many of these political factors still dominate in LDCs. It is easy to see that these legacies of colonialism are still in place both because of the mind-set of the country's ruling elites and the feelings of inferiority and dependency among the people at large. No analysis of world poverty is complete without some understanding of these political factors and their inter-relationships.

(3) Economic Causes of Poverty

Local: lack of capital, savings, credit, skilled labor, management skills, entrepreneurs, storage facilities, tools and equipment, and exploitation of traders.

National: Inflation, central marketing, lack of crop finance, late payments to producers, low producer prices for export crops, inefficient parastatal industries, lack of effective demand, lack of transport and communication.

International: neo-colonialism, fluctuating commodity prices, tariffs and quotas, unfair trade practices; external debt. structural adjustment requirements.

While the political legacy of colonialism is fairly easy to identify, the economic consequences of colonialism and western imperialism are often even more apparent. Centuries of natural and human resource exploitation have impoverished many regions of the LDCs. The emphasis on cash crops for export; the often short-sighted exploitation of natural resources, especially minerals, for export; the confiscation and expropriation of native lands; discouragement of local manufacturing; centralized and monopolistic control of export marketing; centralized and bureaucratic domestic pricing policies; export oriented communications and transport are all part of this historical process of resource transfer from the colonies to the mother country. One should not ignore these centuries of occupation, control and exploitation as a primary cause of much of the poverty seen in the world today.

Yet equally significant are the economic causes related to a set of centralized marketing systems instituted in the wake of political independence. Basing economic planning on the dictates of a Socialist ideology, many of the most productive assets of society were nationalized, central government bureaucrats were given the power to allocate resource, quite independent of market forces and economies of scale, and unfortunately the needs of the military generally took precedent over economic or social concerns and needs of the society.

(3) Social Causes of Poverty

Local: lack of knowledge, skills, awareness, cooperation, misdirected priorities: unnecessary consumption, drinking/smoking, laziness and apathy, dependency thinking (waiting for the government to take care of us), lack of initiative, resistance to change, traditional beliefs, religious beliefs, mistrust, corruption, jealousy and fear, division of labor, large families.

National: Ethnic differences, social classes, corruption, mismanagement, legacies of colonialism, land destruction: deforestation, erosion, overgrazing, lack of family planning programs, inappropriate school curriculum, poor social services
International: Neo-Colonialism, racial prejudice, and ethnic conflicts across borders

It is easy to blame poverty on the poor themselves. It is easy to argue that they are poor because they are lazy, drink too much, lack initiative, are resistant to change, have large families, and lack any spirit of social cooperation. Far more difficult is the need to assess the social and historical factors that have created these conditions. Centuries of exploitation, occupation, slavery and systems of colonial control, we are now beginning to understand, have had devastating consequences for family unity, social pride and dignity, processes of communal cooperation and self-help. Deep feelings of social inferiority, fear and submission are the direct results of the legacy of colonialism and western imperialism: social, cultural and commercial.

In chapter 15 below, we shall argue that while political and economic factors are crucial in our understanding of world poverty, it may well be that the social factors related to feelings of pride and dignity, a recognition of the importance of cultural identity and social energy may, in fact, be even more crucial in understanding not only the causes, but perhaps more important, the development and implementation of possible solutions.

Primary and Secondary Causes

Up to this point, we have sought to understand some of the causes of poverty. If we are to be effective in alleviating the problems of world poverty, it will be important to distinguish between the symptoms of poverty as opposed to primary or secondary causes. Only when we can deal directly with the cycles of poverty, documenting the complex inter-relationships among a number of causes and effects, will we be in a position to develop appropriate interventions. Since this is a book about rural development with an emphasis on the local village community, we will seek to identify and better understand specific strategies appropriate for the local level of analysis. Later in chapter 10, we will be talking specifically on the types of interventions that might be useful in approaching problems at the national and even the international level through a process of networking and coalition building through systems of linkage and empowerment.

Professor Burkey argues that "local initiatives cannot attempt to alleviate all of the local causes of poverty at once. Trying to alleviate the symptoms without first identifying the real underlying causes will not lead to sustainable results. For example, building a health clinic may not significantly reduce the burden of illness if the people being served cannot afford treatment or if there is no local governmental body able to manage and fund the continued operation of the clinic... This further analysis involves identifying symptoms, secondary causes and primary causes. A secondary cause is one that, at first glance, appears to be the immediate cause of the symptom. A primary cause is one that, on deeper analysis, turns out to be the real origin of the secondary cause and, more importantly, is an entry point for breaking a vicious circle. Once we have identified the entry points, we can begin to promote local initiatives for breaking the vicious circles."[11]

Let us review a set of local problems that are common in many LDC villages: malnutrition, low income, lack of clean water, low agriculture productivity. Each of these are better seen as symptoms of poverty, rather than causes. In attempting to distinguish the secondary and primary causes, it will be necessary to reflect on prior conditions that are most apt to be associated with the symptoms identified. Let us review each of the symptoms mentioned above and attempt to identify secondary and primary causes: Below, we can see how such an in-depth analysis would be helpful in determining the appropriate entry points and the approaches that might be most useful.

A. **Malnutrition**: most villagers experiencing malnutrition suffer from a lack of food. The obvious reasons for this problems is the lack of food, the lack of resources to buy food, the unavailability of the right kinds of food. In a more in-depth review of the situation, we often find that such people lack land to grow food on, or they lack the tools and skills to grow the food they need. Still an understanding of these secondary causes, may force us to consider the more basic causes, such as a land ownership system that denies peasants access to land. Obviously a lack of knowledge and understanding about the nutritional value of different kinds of food is a basic cause. Appropriate interventions might include some type of training in nutrition and organic gardening, or perhaps the establishment of some type of income generating project that would help the local villager to supplement his or her income.

B. **Low Income**: many outsiders when they see poor people with very low incomes, often assume that they must be lazy or too fatalistic to take responsibility for their own lives. Others, with more experience in rural development would recognize that such poverty is often related to various secondary causes like the lack of work opportunities, no access to credit, low productivity because of inadequate tools or skills. Again a more in-depth look at the situation would suggest that such low income is basically related to the lack of marketable skills, perhaps an economic system tightly controlled by the elites of the area, or a bank system that refuses to provide credit to people with no collateral, or even a money lender who charges exorbitant interests which keep peasants perpetually in debt.

C. **Lack of Clean Water**: A number of secondary causes can be identified for the lack of potable water. First, many peasants are accustomed to drinking canal water or other sources of polluted water, insisting that it tastes better, it has supernatural powers, etc. Most peasants are ignorant of microbes that bring sickness and even death to these people. Often peasants lack the technology, the resources to dig deep wells or to store clean water. Beyond these kinds of causes are again the more basic causes related to systems of tradition and illiteracy, the lack of community awareness and cooperation concerning ways to provide a community drinking system.

D. **Low Agricultural Productivity**: The obvious reasons why peasants have low productivity include the lack of good tools, no access to insecticides and fertilizers, the poor soils they have to work with, the lack of adequate irrigation water, etc. Much more basic to this kind of problem, are the land tenure systems that do not encourage farmers to invest in modern approaches to agriculture, the reality that most peasants lack the resources/income needed to purchase the high yield varieties of seeds, the chemical fertilizers and insecticides needed to increase yields. In many countries, the government pricing and marketing systems keep farmers at a subsistence level regardless of the hours worked or the skills that might be developed. Again the most basic causes of these kinds of problems are beyond the control of the peasant-farmer, for they relate to the structural constraints imposed upon many of these farmers by those who have power and influence in the community. As you reflect on ways to intervene into these kinds of problems, obviously, local systems of agricultural extension would be helpful, but only if the more structural constraints related to land reform and a more liberal marketing system would be implemented.

Such examples demonstrate the utility of approaching problems of rural poverty from a more systematic and analytical way. Too many development strategies tend to deal with the symptoms rather than the causes. By seeking some understanding of how political, social, economic and cultural factors can impact on rural areas, and as one seeks to "peel" away the secondary causes searching for the basic root causes, the connecting processes of village development become apparent and the ability to develop strategies and approaches that will be more relevant, efficacious and sustainable will be enhanced.

The Root Causes

A careful analysis of secondary and primary causes of underdevelopment and poverty will help identify those few crucial factors that keep coming up over and over again. Such factors should be carefully analyzed as they must be dealt with before sustainable development will be possible.[12]

1. Lack of capital and resources. There appears to be at least four sources of capital for a given community: savings, credit, grants and plundering. Plundering (banditry, local money-lending, exploitative taxation, etc.) is no long-term solution not even for Robin Hood. While donor agencies may be available to provide financial and technical assistance, aid and grants, still such sources are not sustainable, generally have disagreeable conditions attached and often force unwanted and inappropriate technology on to nations and communities.

Significant progress has been made in the development of local credit systems which reward local savings, provide reasonable credit when needed, and ensure that needed capital is available at rates of interest and collateral requirements that are both appropriate and acceptable to the local community. Equally important are the lack of good soil, lack of water, and other resources needed to provide for a sustainable living.

2. Lack of Community Unity. A common root causes of poverty is often related to the lack of cooperation and community unity, lack of solidarity, social energy, and a willingness to work together in a common activity, a tradition of mistrust and disunity, jealousy and fear, or the destructive conflicts of sectarianism, blood feuds and patron-client exploitation. In recent years there has been an increase in national fragmentation, ethnic divisions, and religious conflicts. No approach to community development that does not consider such factors will ever be successful.

3. Misdirected priorities, Many problems are related to past traditions, superstition, drunkenness, demand for prestige (e.g. keeping large numbers of unproductive cattle), family pressures, unessential expenditures on items of consumption (e.g. beer, tobacco), many children, expensive weddings and funerals. Of course anyone sensitive to the local culture and the important role many of these traditions play might question this as a necessary cause of poverty. While one might see such cultural priorities as obstacles to change, there is a need to consider the possible role that such practices play in the community. Some development specialist might argue that such cultural obstacle should be eliminated as soon as possible. Others, with a more anthropological orientation, might argue that such traditions are the very essence of the local culture and must not be tampered with. In chapter 15, we suggest a third alternative that merely allows the local community to consider both advantages and disadvantages of these traditional activities, ceremonies, patterns of behavior. What is needed is the development of some level of consciousness in which local people can consider a variety of options, a level of understanding where the consequences of present behaviors are considered in terms of other choices that might be made that would have different consequences.

4. Dependency thinking: This type of thinking has been in the making for centuries in many countries, through systems of colonial control and local elite exploitation. People have come to expect government to solve their problems, to take care of them, to provide the services and resources needed to improve their situation. This type of thinking, unfortunately has been reinforced in recent decades and may in fact be very difficult to eliminate. Past patron-client systems in which local elites exploit the poor for their own benefit, also keep people at the subsistence level. On every hand they are cheated and taken advantage of. Not only do they pay high prices for their purchases of agricultural inputs, food and supplies, but these essential supplies are often short-weighted, diluted, impure and of inferior quality. Observers, in their indignation, maintain that the poor are never visited by the government extension agents, they cannot get bank credit, and they have no say in cooperative decisions. Their children are discriminated against at school, as are the women in local health clinics. They cannot draw water at the wells controlled by the wealthy and the high caste. They are always at the tail-end of irrigation systems and never receive their rightful share of the precious water. The list of oppressions is endless.

These patron-client relationships, however are not as irrational as they might look. If something goes wrong -- a poor harvest, an illness or death in the family -- the patron can be relied upon to provide a loan or give help. Obliged by circumstances, the poor peasant is forced to adopt a short-term strategy to solving problems which inevitably leads to greater debt and dependency. Organizing to break out of these exploitative relationships carries a high risk of violent repression by the patrons. Any strategy of development, if it is to be successful, must act upon the factors that create dependency without creating a new and unbearable high-risk situation.[13]

5. Lack of awareness: people have no conception concerning the alternatives services that can be available, the significant economic opportunities waiting to be developed, the many organizational and community development options that are, in fact, available to them. Most rural people, in particular have little understanding concerning their rights and protections available from their own government against illegal exploitation and control by local elites. Much of this lack of awareness is due to centuries of illiteracy and lack of education.

6. Lack of skills and knowledge: Most people recognize that villagers generally lack the skills and knowledge needed to improve their standards of living. Many lack an understanding of modern methods of agriculture and fishing, lack an understanding as to how disease can be prevented and how the health of their families can be enhanced. It is not surprising that local cooperatives and income generating projects often fail when the participants lack book-keeping and management skills. The lack of adult education and opportunities for training are key factors in explaining world poverty.

7. Political Instability: Even a cursory review of the nations of Africa, Asia, and Latin American will demonstrate the tendency for political unrest and social insecurity caused by civil war/banditry, military dominance, conflicts from sectarianism, and the ever frustrating challenge of ethnic nationalism (tribalism). No system of development will be implemented as long as war and political instability dominate in these societies.

8. Over-centralized Authoritarian Government Systems: Unfortunately most LDCs lack the democratic institutions of national and local government systems. Governments are generally over involved in production, marketing and control of the economy. Most of these central administrative systems are fraught with corruption, non-accountability and total lack of concern for the masses of people in their country. .

In reviewing these root causes of poverty, one is tempted to throw one's hands in the air in despair, perhaps believing that there is little hope for these kinds of problems. In Unit Two of this book, we shall be reviewing a series of case studies that demonstrate that change is possible, that even with the many constraints and obstacles that do exist, progress can be made. While this first unit has been structured to generate a certain amount of pessimism, my real purpose was to stimulate in the reader some sense of realism, some awareness of the realities of the less developed countries of the world. Before we go to Unit Two, let us first review the ways in which scholars and practitioners have sought to develop conceptual frameworks, strategies, and approaches that were assumed to be efficacious in solving the problems thus defined. In my opinion we have learned a great deal in the past forty or fifty years about the processes of development. But there is still much to learn. Our priority for the next chapter is to ensure that you are aware of what we think we have learned and that based upon this learning we might be able to develop strategies and approaches better suited to the realities and challenges that presently exist.

---

[1] B.S. Rowntree, *Poverty: A Study of Town Life* (London: Macmillan, 1901)
[2] Robert S. McNamara, "Presidential Address", in the World Bank, *World Development Report, 1980*, (New York: Oxford University Press, 1980), p. 30.
[3] One of the early attempts to define the factors related to poverty was developed by M.S. Baratz and W. G. Grigsby, "Thoughts on Poverty and Its Elimination", *Journal of Social Policy*, 1 (2) (1971), pp. 119-34
[4] W. G. Runciman, *Relative Deprivation and Social Justice* (London: Routledge and Kegan Paul, 1966)
[5] M. D. Morris, *Measuring the Condition of the World's Poor: The PQLI*, (New York: Pergamon, 1979). The PQLI does rank nations somewhat differently than GNP but not in any significant way. Each of the three variables used in this index are too highly correlated to provide any significant new insights.
[6] Oscar Lewis, *La Vida*, (London: Panther, 1968), p. 53.
[7] C. Valentine, *Culture and Poverty*, (Chicago: University of Chicago Press, 1968
[8] A. Leeds "The Concept of the Culture of Poverty" in E.B. Leacock (ed.) *The Culture of Poverty: A Critique* (New York: Simon and Schuster, 1971.
[9] Valentine, *op cit.*, p. 144.
[10] Stan Burkey, *People First: A Guide to Self-Reliant, Participatory Rural Development* (London: Zed Books, 1993), pp. 17-20
[11] *Ibid.*, p. 21-22
[12] *Ibid.*, pp. 24-25. I am indebted to professor Burkey for his very insightful analysis of poverty in the LDCs I have found his eight root causes of poverty to be especially useful.
[13] *Ibid.*, p.11.

Chapter 4

Toward an Understanding of the Concept of Development

Thoughtful people everywhere are distressed by the deprivation in which most of the human community continues to exist. Famine and epidemic diseases stalk a significant portion of this planet's people. Their babies die with a frequency many times that suffered by infants born in the more developed countries (MDCs) of the world. Those who survive receive little or no formal education and exist in a mental and spiritual poverty that matches their physical destitution. Many of the adults lack sufficient energy to fulfill their economic needs, are subject to chronic infections, and anticipate a span of life little more than half that of Americans or Western Europeans.

During the past four decades, a rising consciousness of this human waste has caused the enlightened leadership of the world to seek a reversal of these somber conditions. Some progress has been made but the pace has been too slow to satisfy the rising expectations of either the leaders or the restless peoples of the less developed countries (LDCs). In recent decades a population explosion has canceled out much of the anticipated gains in human welfare. The wars and civil strife which scar this period have thwarted the progress of orderly economic growth. Errors of conception, design and implementation have marred the proper utilization of both external and internal resources. Among the advanced nations, balance-of-payments problems and the struggle to eliminate domestic poverty have limited resources which might otherwise have been channeled into foreign aid. And, perhaps most dispiriting of all, both the more advanced countries (MDCs) and the less developed countries (LDCs) have grossly underestimated the span of years required for traditional societies to move into the contemporary world.

For some, the sheer enormity of the problem and a new awareness of its complexities have bred a sense of despair about its solution. Hope for the future has diminished as powerful voices from both the political Left and Right counsel a retreat, if not a withdrawal, from the effort to deal with world poverty. Not surprisingly, advanced nations have sharply reduced their economic aid and will continued to do so unless a new approach can be found. Even though aid from the United States did increase from $9.6 billion in 1980 to $19.5 billion in 1985, it has gradually declined back down to $9.7 billion in 1994 (including both military and economic aid). Equally disturbing is the tendency for the vast majority of this aid to go for military expenditures (46% in 1980, 68% in 1985 and 66% in 1987) rather than for economic development. Are we giving enough to deal with these tragedies of poverty? First, as a percentage of our national budget, foreign aid has consistently been less than one percent of all federal spending. Even more disturbing is the fact that we are 18th in per capita income giving among all the MDCs of the world. In 1965 we gave 0.58 percent of GNP, in 1970, it was down to 0.32 percent, in 1980, it was 0.27 percent and in 1991 it was down to 0.20 percent. We are clearly much less generous than many other countries: Norway at 1.14 percent, Netherlands at 0.88 percent, France at 0.62 percent and Germany at 0.41 percent.[1]

Thus, it is urgent that a fresh review of the problem of development of the world's poor people be undertaken. The **issue and the problem of world poverty** demands a global perspective, in which both the more developed and less developed countries of the world create a partnership of commitment to deal with this issue. Some scholars are arguing for the creation of a general theory of development, insisting that such an effort would be prerequisite for the determination of policies and strategies to enable the peoples of the world to make faster progress toward a better and more humane existence. Others with a more practitioner perspective would argue that much has been learned in the past several decades about what works and what does not work, the problem is not theory, the problem is commitment and a willingness to get on with the challenge.

The reality of development and underdevelopment is an extremely complex phenomenon, which each specialist views from his own point of vantage. Economists lay stress upon the expansion of savings and investment, capital formation, and instruction of people in new technology. Management theorists see the primary obstacle as a shortage of organizational and administrative talent. Political Scientists emphasize shifts in the distribution of economic and political power among groups and classes in the state. Sociologists analyze the process in terms of changes in the basic values, attitudes, and goals of society. Theologians and philosophers see development as a problem of morality and justice. Historians are more apt to see development as simply the manifestation of the processes of history with no pre-determined goal. Anthropologists are torn between their desire to protect traditional societies from the ravages of modernity and their desire to help improve the ability of these societies to find appropriate solutions to their own problems.

All of these aspects are pertinent, and none should be neglected. For our purposes development may simply be defined as a complex socio-economic process whereby the people of a country progress from a static mode of life with few options available to solve their individual and collective needs toward a more dynamic mode of life in which greater options and opportunities are available. The emphasis is upon changes that enhance the physical, material, social and cultural welfare of people. For them we assert the simple moral principle that development is good if it results from their own free choice of values.

In our effort to understand the concept of development, a concept that students of development studies must understand, let us suggest three different ways in which this idea of development might be conceptualized: (1) Development is best understood as the consequence of fairly random historical factors generally defined in political and economic terms and which are best seen as a reflection of both international and national macro-factors for analysis, (2) Development is best understood in terms of some paradigmatic conceptual framework which seeks to explain why there is underdevelopment and development in the world. Development as a paradigm for analysis seeks to provide a theoretical justification for a certain strategy or approach being suggested utilizing both macro and micro factors in the analysis, (3) Development is best understood as a people-oriented process which requires specific allocations of resources, certain configurations of human energy, technology and organization, and a focus of effort which reflects the needs and aspirations of the people involved, thus suggesting that development is best seen as "people development" which emphasizes individual knowledge, will and purpose -- mostly micro factors for analysis. In this chapter and the next we shall confront the concept of development from these three different approaches -- recognizing that each has something to tell us about development.

Section One
Development as Political Economic History

When one approaches the concept of development as history-shaped and influenced by both economic and political forces, one tends to see development and underdevelopment as the consequence of the events, ideas and personalities that shape history. Economic history, for example, shows that a country can develop without resort to external assistance by consuming less and investing increasing amounts of savings in more efficient technology and other physical capital, together with investments in better education, skills in technical knowledge, and other human capital. Great Britain during the nineteenth century, Russia after the Bolshevik revolution, and later Communist China illustrate such self-sufficient development. However, the appalling deprivation of laborers in British mines and factories, the starvation of millions of Russian peasants who were forced to contribute food for industrial workers in the cities, and the highly structured society of China built upon a system of human rights violations were the heavy costs of such capital formation. Few countries, having some awareness of these historical realities, are prepared to pay such costs today.

From the perspective of political-economy, the development of the United States and most other advanced nations, while largely self-sufficient, was greatly accelerated by foreign private investments made by the older industrialized countries of Europe. Today, in the majority of poor countries, sustained and substantial increases in national production will probably still depend upon the availability of external resources both private and public. However as we shall see in the next section, such external resources only come with a price, a price that may include greater dependency and even debilitating debt and inflation -- factors that may hinder development much more than facilitate such needed development. Let us now review the historical factors that appear to have influenced the success and failure of many of these LDCs.

The 1930s and 1940s: An Era of New Economic Thinking and International Cooperation

At the end of the Second World War, most world leaders saw this as a unique opportunity to reshape the world's international system both politically and economically. The new system which was eventually established at Bretton Woods and in the United Nations reflected both the optimism of the period but also a set of assumptions that were not clearly understood.

First, there was the perceived need to avoid the disastrous economic policies of the 1920s and 1930s, when countries, dominated by a set of traditional and classical economic doctrines which had insisted on the "equilibrating" mechanisms of an open market, found themselves falling deeper and deeper into competitive devaluations, rising unemployment, and trade protectionism, with their terrible social and political consequences associated with the "Great Depression." Second, the belief in classical economic policies had come under sharp attack by a group of British economists led by John Maynard Keynes who insisted on active macroeconomics management by governments, with full employment set as the primary objective.[2] In the international field, the conclusion drawn was that nationalist policies must be replaced by international rules of conduct which would be controlled by international institutions, later to be known as the Bretton Woods system.

When the Point Four Program, or Marshall Plan, was initiated in the late 1940s, the intention of aid-giving nations was to rebuild the physical and industrial structure of countries that had attained relatively high levels of productive capacity prior to the Second World War. American aid was primarily aimed at rehabilitating physical infrastructure and industrial plant, at temporarily feeding large numbers of people displaced from their livelihoods by the war, and at reestablishing market mechanisms in European economies. Other international funding organizations, established in the wake of the Marshall Plan, had similar objectives. The World Bank's mission, for instance, was clearly reflected in the bank's formal title -- the International Bank for Reconstruction and Development -- and in the order in which the elements of the title appear. Concern for promoting development in poor countries was subordinate to reconstructing productive capacity in more economically advanced nations that had suffered devastation in a long and intense global conflict. The governments receiving aid were generally experienced in industrial development, had well-trained professionals and skilled workers, high levels of planning and managerial capability and a strong motivation to recover as quickly as possible.[3] And success there was, when in much of

Europe and Japan annual growth rates consistently reached five percent and more over the next decade.

The success of this effort was not entirely due to its intrinsic value. The Marshall Plan funded by the United States (1948-1952) had a great deal to do with stimulating a decade of nearly full employment, with little inflation or balances of payments problems in either Europe or Japan. With strong US investments followed later by a strong recovery of exports and the emerging balance of payments surpluses developing in Europe and Japan, the more developed countries (MDCs) provided a firm foundation (or "engine") for growth of production and exports in the less developed countries (LDCs), enabling some of them to maintain aggregate growth rates similar to or even higher than those of the industrial countries (although not on a per capita basis). World trade expanded even faster than GNP during this period, and protectionist incentives were minimized.

The 1950s and 1960s: The Boom Years of the Post World War II Era

The 1950s and 1960s were a period of global expansion of production and trade, one of the longest and most pronounced booms in world history, with full employment and little inflation in the More Developed Countries (MDCs) of North America, Western Europe and Japan. By this time, the Keynesian model of government intervention into fiscal policy ruled supreme, and the Harrod-Domar formula, which emphasized capital accumulation as the source of growth with an emphasis on industrialization was touted as the most appropriate strategy.[4] This **emphasis on capital accumulation for investment** was almost universally shared at this time.[5]

Based upon the success of the Marshal Plan era, development activists in the UN and elsewhere began to think in terms of large scale aid of the Marshal type for less developing countries. Unfortunately, little attention was given during the 1950s to the differences in the conditions and needs which existed in the LDCs until these conditions appeared to create obstacles to achieving high levels of industrial output. While it was recognized and admitted from the beginning that development problems would be more difficult and longer term than the reconstruction of Europe and Japan, this was assumed to be offset by the strengthening of those economies which had benefited by the earlier Marshal Plan. Thus Europe itself would now begin to provide some of the capital investments needed by the LDCs in their efforts to industrialize.

The industrialization policies prescribed by macro-economic development theorists during the 1950s and 1960s sought high levels of economic growth and rapid increases in gross national product (GNP). The only real debate over these policies concerned the means by which the goals would be achieved. Some theorists argued that the most effective way of attaining high levels of economic growth was through heavy investment in capital-intensive industry as a "leading sector." Others contended that a "big push" was needed in all sectors at the same time to increase output and demand for industrial sector production. But many economists, such as Albert Hirschman, argued that it really did not matter which sector was emphasized. Hirschman maintained that heavy public investments in either directly productive or social overhead activities would lower costs, and through complementarities in the economy, create increased demand and pressures for mobilization and investment of private capital. The ripple effect from this initial stimulation would generate growth throughout the economy. The mechanisms by which growth would spread were thought to be largely automatic once investment began. "If such a chain of unbalanced growth sequences could be set up," Hirschman predicted, "the economic policy makers could just watch the proceedings from the sidelines."[6] Of course, these kinds of theories were modeled on processes of economic growth that occurred in Western Europe and North America during the second half of the nineteenth and first half of the twentieth centuries.[7]

The question of how massive poverty -- a major factor limiting the size of markets in the LDCs -- would be alleviated was rarely asked by development theorists or directly addressed in the development strategies of this period. The problem of reducing the large gaps in income and wealth between rich and poor nations would be solved, Rosenstein-Rodan argued in the 1940s, by achieving "a more equal distribution of income between different areas of the world by raising incomes in depressed areas at a higher rate than in the rich areas."[8] This would occur internationally through the same automatic mechanisms that Hirschman relied upon in national economies. As industrial production increased in developing countries new jobs would be created, demand for new products would be expanded, and through forward, backward and lateral linkages new investments would be made. This would create additional employment opportunities and raise overall levels of income.

Increasing employment would not only draw larger numbers of people into the productive system, but the resulting demand for labor, goods and services would spread from the major urban centers where large-scale industries were located, into smaller towns and rural areas. Increasing incomes would create higher demand for agriculture goods and the application of new technology by farmers would make agriculture more productive and less labor-intensive and the surplus agricultural labor would be absorbed in the expanding industrial sector. Walt Rostow confidently talked about the ways in which the LDCs, adopting the strategies of the MDCs, would predictably follow in their path. Once the economy reached the **"take-off" stage**, more of the poor would begin to benefit and a growth cycle would generate higher levels of output, create incentives for diversification and ensure long-term sustainable growth.[9]

Many economists believed, along with Kuznets who formalized the idea theoretically, that in the initial stages of growth the largest share of income would go to higher income groups, but as growth continued over time, the poor's relative share of income would gradually increase. Thus, in the initial stages the income of the poorer sectors of society would inevitably drop. But following the Kuznets "Inverted U Curve," income for the poor would eventually begin to rise. When growth was rapid enough to change the dualistic structure (i.e., a society in which both a dynamic modern sector and a more passive traditional sector existed at the same time) of the economy, a more equitable distribution of benefits would naturally occur and excessive poverty would gradually be eliminated through what came to be called the "trickle down" effect. Many economists of that period argued that any reallocation of investments to generate a wider distribution of income by channeling aid to poor groups in developing societies would slow the overall rate of economic growth and thus delay the time at which the poor's share of income would begin to rise on the "Kuznets Inverted U curve."[10]

By the early 1960s, it became increasingly apparent that in most LDCs a strategy of rapid growth through capital intensive industrialization was not working. Growth occurred in some Third World nations during the 1950s and early 1960s, but at rates well below those sought in national development plans. Studies found that foreign aid had little direct impact on increasing the levels of GNP in LDCs. Griffen and Enos discovered, for instance, that the correlation between foreign aid and increases in GNP during the 1950s was weak or insignificant for most of the poor nations in Africa and Asia. Aid and growth were negatively correlated for many Latin American countries, where they found that "the greater the inflow of capital from abroad, the lower the rate of growth of the receiving nation."[11]

Gradually the experts began to see that development was also governed by "human" factors such as education, skill training, health, nutrition and so on, not explicit in the Harrod-Domar model. Much of the physical capital investments available in the LDCs, at least in the earlier stages, were used to develop the infrastructure requirements of these societies, which simply did not generate economic returns as quickly and as efficiently as such investments had produced in Europe under the Marshal Plan. Moreover, contrary to the optimistic belief so characteristic of the period, increased investments tended to outrun the technical and administrative capacity of most of the LDCs to design, implement and operate efficient development projects.

As was mentioned before, the emphasis on physical capital accumulation as the "crux" of development also led during the 1950s and 1960s to a tolerance for income inequalities and the persistence of poverty. This took the form of either a belief that growth was sooner or later bound to "trickle down" and spread to the poor, or even more strongly, that increased income inequalities were a necessary price to pay for the time being, until the luxury of welfare could be afforded from an enlarged economy.

The Arthur Lewis model[12] was also indicative of another weakness in the type of development suggested during these early two decades, **namely a**

comparative neglect of agriculture. In this model and much related thinking, the main function of agriculture was to provide rural surplus labor as the cannon fodder of industrialization (reminiscent of what happened in the pioneer days of the Industrial Revolution in Great Britain), to provide a market for industrial goods and to provide the raw materials for processing by prominent textile, leather and other industries. This passive or negative role ascribed to agriculture was never very convincing: how could agriculture provide a market for industrial goods unless rural incomes were raised? How could agriculture release surplus labor unless productivity was increased? How could growth trickle down to the poor when the great mass of the poor lived in rural areas? These and similar questions were not clearly faced, let alone answered. Such optimistic projections of a turning point gradually faced the reality that poverty was not going away and that in fact by the end of the 1960s, in aggregate terms the number of people living below the poverty line was actually greater than had been the case before the twenty years of seeking to emphasize industrialization and increased GNP.

There were several reasons for this blind spot in the early industrialization drive. One was the justified pessimism about relative prices of primary and agricultural products, which was perhaps too unthinkingly extended from the international to the domestic arena. There was also a strong belief (derived from classical assumptions) that technical progress in agriculture would always be much slower and more difficult than in industry. This belief has proved unjustified, as shown by the tremendous increases in agriculture productivity in North America, Europe and the Far East, where technical progress in agriculture proved to be at least as fast as in industry, a process aptly called the "green revolution" in some parts of the LDCs.

Another reason was more political: an "urban bias"[13] injected into development policies by the disproportionate political influence of the urban minority compared with the rural majority. The opposite "rural bias" in the agricultural policies followed in North America, Europe and Japan provided another reason for comparative neglect of agriculture in developing countries: it reduced international food prices, making imports easier and more tempting. It also made available during this period of surplus, massive US food aid, enabling governments so inclined to justify low investment priorities for national food production. However, all the very large recipients of food aid during the 1950s and early 1960s, such as India, South Korea, Israel and Greece, eventually managed to use the resources provided by massive aid, including food aid, to provide the infrastructure investment for their own green revolutions. In this they followed in the footsteps of Western Europe and Japan, who also very quickly graduated out of the massive food aid provided by the Marshall Plan into becoming substantial surplus producers with strong "rural bias" policies.

A third trend of this period which proved to be very disconcerting was the gradual awareness that growth was distinctly faster and easier among the middle-income countries than among the low-income countries. Thus, during the last five years of the period (1965-1970), the per capita income of middle-income countries, growing at nearly four per cent per annum, increased almost twice as fast as the low-income countries, at roughly two percent.[14] In fact, the middle-income developing countries grew slightly faster than the industrial market economies, even in per capita terms. Thus the gap opening up during that period was not so much between the MDCs and the LDCs, but rather between the upper- and middle-income countries on the one hand, and the low-income countries on the other. This group of "least developed countries" gradually emerged as the Fourth World, with significantly lower levels of growth and development.

In assessing the two decades of 1950s and the 1960s, two contradictory trends can be identified. First, the favorable growth experience, particularly for the middle-income countries, had certainly demonstrated the possibility of economic growth for the LDCs. It was especially important to note that progress was made not only in increased physical investment rates, but also in such indicators of human capital formation as spreading literacy and education, elimination of a number of diseases, and reduced mortality rates, including infant mortality rates. This progress in human indicators could be shown to be only tenuously related to GNP growth, illustrating both the limitations of the "trickle down" approach and the possibility of development along alternative routes.

A more puzzling trend of this period was the realization that most of this encouraging progress was made at a time of rapid growth in the industrial (MDCs) countries. The situation in these countries, as a result of full employment and increased demand for commodity purchases, was extremely favorable to trade liberalization. It was not clear during these two decades to what extent the growth achieved was dependent on the existence of an "engine of growth" outside the control of the developing countries themselves. Only as we moved into the 1970s and the 1980s with threatening recession and greater inflation in the MDCs did we begin to realize how salutary the events of the 1950s and 1960s in the MDCs had been for the LDCs. It was then that the lack of an internal dynamism in many LDCs, due often to the neglect of agriculture and the weaknesses of indigenous managerial and technological capacity, became painfully apparent.

The Decade of the 1970s

The decade of the 1970s saw the breakdown and disintegration of the Bretton Woods system. The best date to attach to the end of the Bretton Woods is probably 15 August 1971 when President Nixon suspended the free convertibility of the US dollar into gold at the fixed rate agreed at Bretton Woods. The breakdown of the system with an end to fixed exchange rates, was immediately connected with increasing concerns with the "overheating" of their economies and a consequent displacement of full employment with a need for control of inflation as a priority objective.

Probably the event which most marked the 1970s and gave the international system its final ominous push was the assertion of oil power by OPEC in 1973-74, with the decade inevitably ending with a second assertion of oil power in 1979-80. Yet, inspite of these trends, growth rates among LDCs did continue to rise, demonstrating that such growth was possible even in the face of reduced growth and serious recessions in the MDCs (the industrial West). In fact, contrary to what happened during the preceding two decades, the gap in per capita income between the developing countries and the industrial market economies narrowed rather than widened during 1970-1981, at least in relative terms.

Yet this growth had its down side that must be understood. The growth rate of GNP for all LDCs, excepting the high-income oil exporters, receded from the high of 5-6 percent per annum which it had reached during 1965-1970 to just somewhere around 4-5 percent in 1971-1980, although this was still higher than the average figure for the preceding two decades. The serious exception was sub-Saharan African, where the 1971-80 growth not only fell much more heavily (from 4.8 to 3.3 percent), but was lower than at any period during the 1950-70 era. At the other extreme, the Middle East and North Africa, benefiting directly or indirectly from higher oil prices, achieved new growth records, well beyond the level of the two preceding decades, and the East Asia and Pacific region maintained the very high growth rate of 7-8 percent which it had achieved in the preceding five years. But Latin America and South Asia shared the African decline, although less drastically: both these regions, accounting for most of the population of developing countries (outside China), more or less returned to the growth rates of the earlier part of the 1950s.[15]

This growth, however, is very misleading, because most of the growth came not from domestic industrialization but from the investments and operations of multi-national corporations. As a result, by the mid-1970s in Latin America and Africa, typically 40-50 percent of manufacturing industry was controlled by foreign firms (in some countries 60-70 percent). In Asia this share was typically lower (India and South Korea 10-15 percent). Many of these multi-national corporations had sales valued equal to or higher than the GNP of many LDCs. For example, Exxon had sales value equivalent to the GNP of Argentina or Nigeria, close to South Korea, more than twice the GNP of Egypt or Pakistan, and almost four time that of Chile or Peru.[16]

Equally important for our understanding of development theory during this period, was the gradual realization, actually a disillusionment, that rapid growth of GNP was often combined with growing unemployment and under-employment, increasing poverty, and often also greater inequality of income distribution as the rich got richer and the poor got poorer. At the same time many industrialized countries also became disillusioned with growth, although for rather different reasons, since in their experience growth led to inflationary pressures, balance of payments trouble and often led to disastrous consequences for the environment.

Understanding the Concept of Development 75

For the less developed countries the shift in objectives from simple growth initially took two forms: one was the establishment of employment as an overriding objective; the other was a shift to redistribution and greater equity.

In a significant article written in the late 1960s, Dudley Seers argued that a new definition of development was needed not just based on an increase in GNP.[17] He argued persuasively that countries with increasing GNP could not be considered developing if at the same time, unemployment, numbers under the poverty level, and the extent of inequality was also growing at the same time. Unfortunately, most of the LDCs were experiencing that kind of growth in which GNP was increasing while the masses of these countries were experiencing ever greater levels of poverty and human degradation. Thus, while growth continued to be regarded as a necessary condition for development, it was no longer accepted as a sufficient condition. Employment became more and more not an alternative to growth, but as a proper instrument of growth which would produce not only growth in itself but also a pattern of growth conducive to more equal income distribution, less poverty, more social contentment and less political unrest.

In development analysis, this shift to employment objectives was typified by the move from the **Arthur Lewis model**, in which the surplus labor released from agriculture was assumed to be more or less fully absorbed by the growing urban industries, to the **Harris-Todaro model**. Under the Harris-Todaro model the drift to the towns would be far in excess of available employment opportunities; the gap between rural subsistence incomes and wages in the modern industrial urban sector would attract job seekers from the rural areas. The model suggests that if modern urban sector wages are three times rural incomes, one-third of the chance of a job would be sufficient to attract a migrant from the rural areas; hence there would three job seekers for each available job and two-thirds of them would remain unemployed or condemned to make a living as well as they could in the informal sector. This model seemed to correspond much better to reality than the Arthur Lewis model.[18]

The shift to employment as a main objective was quite logically accompanied by a particular emphasis on the need for employment-intensive technologies; so this also became the era of a search for and an emphasis on "appropriate" technologies. Moreover, since small-scale production was emphasized, it also became the era of "small is beautiful". Equally logically, with employment moving to the center as the crux of development, such "human capital" aspects as training, skills, health and other factors in productivity were now given increased weight, compared with the simple notion of physical capital accumulation.[19]

In institutional terms, the new emphasis on employment placed the International Labor Organization (ILO) in the center of development policy, particularly through its newly organized World Employment Program. The ILO employment missions, first with "pilot missions" to Colombia, Sri Lanka and

Kenya and subsequently many other countries, had a considerable impact on policy and thinking. This was true in particular of the Kenya Employment Mission, which also marked the transition from an emphasis on employment to an emphasis on the need for a more direct attack on poverty, by pointing out that the so-called unemployment or underemployment in developing countries was a misnomer. In fact, most of the so-called unemployed or under employed were working quite hard to earn a living; the real problem was their low income levels. They were the "working poor" rather than the "unemployed."

The new "employment-oriented strategy" had some obvious limitations. First, the creation of more employment would only intensify the urban unemployment problem, since for every new job there would be several new migrants seeking jobs in the urban areas as long as rural surplus labor was available. Also, employment could not deal with the poverty groups not capable of employment: those too old to work, too ill, crippled, broken families, orphaned children, and so on. Employment to provide an income does not solve the problem of access to health, education, clean water, sanitation, and so on -- all services which related to public action rather than employment.

Yet in spite of such limitations, the employment orientation had a valid and lasting impact. It emphasized not only the contribution to production which employment could provide, but also the sense of participation and self-respect which improved earning capacity from employment could bring: the issue of human rights as a development object emerged at this stage. Employment emphasis was especially useful in the agricultural sector, where the basis for an appropriate technology already existed, and it became increasingly realized that the small-scale farmer was more productive in terms of output per acre than the large farmer, and also was quite capable of responding to economic incentives.[20]

Employment creation in the rural sector also became the key to agricultural improvement through public works schemes, particularly during the slack agricultural seasons, and in times of drought or other emergencies It was discovered that not only emergencies but also persistent poverty were due not so much to a lack of food available, but rather to a breakdown in the "entitlement" mechanism for obtaining access to food and other essentials of life. Employment, either for an income or directly paid in food, was perhaps the most obvious way of creating such entitlements.

An employment-oriented development policy also provided an essential bridge between the growth-oriented strategy emphasizing "productive" investment, and a subsequent poverty orientation which could be accused of shifting to "unproductive" activities such as redistribution, provision of social services subsidies and direct income support. Employment creation was at the same time clearly productive and yet naturally targeted so as to achieve greater equality of income distribution and better able to produce a trickle-down effect on the poor than mere growth by itself.

The other shift in development strategy during the earlier part of the 1970s, apart from the emphasis on employment objectives, was greater concern with income distribution, or "redistribution with growth" (RWG). Redistribution from growth put growth first and then suggested the use of the resources created by growth for deliberate distributive measures, rather than waiting for "trickle down". Yet for many observers, who emphasized a Basic Needs strategy, the proper sequence was better seen as redistribution before growth. Japanese and Korean growth, for example, owed both its intensity and egalitarian character to the fact that through land reform, heavy investment in education and health, and so on, physical and human capital assets were fairly equally distributed before the growth process started. It was argued that in this way growth not only had a more solid and sustainable foundation, but would also assume a pattern which was favorable for sustained equality and poverty reduction.[21]

The World Bank, under the leadership of Robert McNamara, became a lead agency in advocating RWG strategies, emphasizing the importance of human capital investment and helping to promote directly poverty-oriented "basic needs strategies." This new strategy, emphasizing an appropriate redistribution in the form of greater government services in health and education, still rested on the earlier notions of a centralized government system. Here the emphasis was on strengthening the governmental bureaucracy to provide these basic services through well organized and financed centralized ministries.

The crucial issue for the 1970s was still the problem of finding adequate funding to pay for these services deemed necessary for long-term growth. If such services are to come before growth, then the surplus needed to pay for such services would need to come from outside the country, either in the form of aid and grants, or in the form of private bank loans. The lower growth rate and re-emergence of unemployment in the industrial countries almost inevitably meant an increase in their protectionism. These barriers, while hurting trade in general, were applied with greater severity to the LDCs, often affecting upwards of a quarter of their total exports. The long term consequences of such restrictions stimulated a lot of doubt concerning the utility of an export-oriented strategy especially as the world would be flooded with manufactured goods from more and more LDCs.[22]

Lessons To Be Learned

The nature of the 1970s as a period of illusionary debt-led growth raises a number of issues which contain important lessons for the future. The initial collapse of the Bretton Woods system in 1971 and the subsequent failure of the MDCs to coordinate their own exchange rate and other policies, together with the shock in 1973-74 of the first large rise in oil prices, clearly led to quite different perceptions on the part of the MDCs and the LDCs respectively. The MDCs at first assumed that the crisis was merely a temporary phenomenon, no doubt a serious hiccup in the progress of the two previous decades but one that could be dealt with through existing institutions, largely by way of normal lending operations of their own commercial banks recycling OPEC surpluses, etc. Meanwhile, the rapid growth with full employment of the 1950s and 1960s might have to be abandoned in favor of slower growth, unemployment and recessionary periods. But at a time when prevailing politics and ideologies were beginning to swing to the right, and the fight against inflation became a chief objective, this price seemed worth paying. It took the second big rise in oil prices in 1979-80 to shake these perceptions of optimism.

On the part of the developing countries there was a different perception. It was felt that the shift in financial power and the successful assertion of commodity power represented a permanent and fundamental break with the past, both necessitating and making possible a new international economic order. The LDCs felt strong enough to confront the MDCs with programs and demands for such an order. They underestimated the ability of the industrial countries to absorb such economic shocks by adjusting to a slower rate of growth, using new technologies to reduce the impact of high oil prices by energy substitution and by changing the volume and pattern of their production, stepping up exploration and new supplies, and so on. In many ways, the LDCs were once again prematurely optimistic that the terms of trade were finally shifting to the commodity producing countries of the world.

Decade of the Eighties: Lost Opportunity for LDCs

Except for a number of countries in Asia, the decade of the 1980s was a disaster for the LDCs, especially in Africa and Latin America. One indicator of the basic problem of this decade was the trade imbalances that characterized many of the LDCs, although Asia was an exception. For example, in the earlier period (1970-1980) the amount of exports Asia had, increased faster than the amount being imported by a significant amount, thus simultaneously reducing debt accumulation and strengthening repayment capacity. In contrast, in sub-Saharan Africa and Latin America export volumes increased much slower than import volumes, with the opposite effect. For example, in sub-Saharan Africa, export volume increased by less than two percent per annum, less than the rate of population increase. In Latin America also, import volumes grew over three times more than export volumes (roughly six percent against two percent). The roots of a debt crisis were thus clearly planted in Latin America and Africa, rather than Asia.[23]

The debt crisis actually began with the enormous rise in oil prices of 1973-74. Oil exporter placed the larger part of the proceeds on deposit with the international banks; the banks needed borrowers. Under these circumstance, willing lenders found willing borrowers, and the external debts of the LDCs increased from less than $100 billion in 1972 to more than $600 billion by 1981

Understanding the Concept of Development 79

and on to $1200 billion in 1988. At the same time the international economy was particularly bad for the LDCs. As the World Bank has aptly noted, the "World economy in the 1980s was dominated first by sharp recession, then by steady and prolonged growth in the industrial countries, high real interest rates, declining real commodity prices, massive movements in exchange rates, and the collapse of voluntary private lending to many developing countries."[24]

In the 1980s, the international system shifted its emphasis to debt settlement, stabilization, adjustment, structural change, and trade liberalization. This contrasted strongly with the earlier emphasis in the field of development in the 1970s when development was conceptualized as increased employment, income redistribution, basic needs or reduction of poverty. This shift was associated with the ascent of neo-liberal ideologies, a shift in decision-making on development strategy to creditors, donors and international financial institutions. Perhaps the most symbolic development was the World Bank's shift out of exclusive project lending -- previously put forward as the soundest form of development assistance -- to balance of payments support in the form of structural adjustment lending and the establishment of a largely IMF-dominated "cross-conditionality" for World Bank action. The issue was clear, how do we help LDCs pay back their loans.

For all these countries, the 1980s proved a rude awakening from the illusionary growth of the 1970s. Over the five years 1982-87, the cumulative percentage falls in per capita GNP totaled nearly 17 percent for sub-Saharan Africa, approximately 10 percent for the highly indebted countries and roughly 12 percent for oil exporters. Thus, in many LDCs, which had seen great increases in the period of 1965-80, now saw their per capita growth drop to what it had been two and three decades earlier.

The 1980s can be best characterized as a lost decade for the LDCs for a number of reasons: (1) reduced import volumes by the developing countries with recession and protectionism interacting in the same direction; (2) highly unfavorable terms of trade, as a result both of high oil prices and a deterioration of other commodity prices in relation to their manufactured imports from industrial countries (the latter increased by high energy costs); (3) a reduction and, later, virtual cessation of commercial bank lending and a rise in real interest rates so that debt burdens were increased both through lower export earnings and higher service payments simultaneously; and (4) greater unwillingness among the MDCs to give aid due both to the recession and the spread of monetarist policy arguments.

Yet just at the time when the international climate became so disastrously hostile to development, the bastions of financial power in the industrial countries and in the leading financial institutions were captured by a new ideology which preached an all-out "outward export orientation" and "market orientation" as the secret of successful development. Such demands for greater privatization and economic liberalization were often justified as a necessary step for sustainable growth. However, many scholars in the LDCs were beginning to argue that the real purpose was to ensure LDCs' ability to pay their bank loans. Most economists of the MDCs still insisted that the spending spree of the 1980s required some reduction in investments, especially from sources that increased the debt that was already a serious constraint on future development. Yet a cutback in needed services, education, health, subsidized food prices, etc., clearly hurt the disadvantaged poor far more than minority rich of these countries and such demands for deficit reduction at a time when domestic needs were so high proved to be unrealistic, both economically and politically.

Yet while the structural adjustment programs of the international community seemed inequitable and insensitive to the real needs of the poor, the criticisms of earlier economic policies in the less developed world did deserve some consideration. It had become apparent to most LDCs, even those most committed to some socialist form of development, that a regime of overvalued exchange rates carried dangers of inefficient allocation, rent seeking, capital flight and so on; that prices and markets have a role to play in the efficient allocation of resources and are often better instruments than administrative regulations or controls. Others argued that the over expansion of the government sector might conceivably suppress the latent entrepreneurial spirit in the private sector which could be released by less regulations and that planning machinery can easily become over centralized at the expense of local initiative and popular participation. For many writers of the 1980s, trade liberalization was seen to be the way to go for the LDCs themselves. Equally persuasive were the arguments that proper price incentives to farmers would be a useful tool for stimulating domestic food production, that industrialization which is at the expense of agriculture can be self-defeating, and thus should be replaced by a type of development in which agricultural development and industrialization would mutually support each other. Especially important for the rest of this book will be the argument that policies should not be excessively "urban biased", that subsidies and other measures targeted at lower-income groups often have a way of failing to reach the poorest and sometimes benefit the better-off instead, and that public services no less than the private sector should be governed by principles of efficiency and low-cost services, etc.

Of course, the insistence on structural adjustment and greater liberalization as a precondition for new development is justified according to western economists on the grounds that it is not a policy imposed by the international financial institutions and big industrial governments, but rather an inescapable necessity. This is an argument which is obviously true as far as it goes. Given an international climate so unfavorable to development, the LDCs probably have no choice but to adjust themselves to it

The Decade of the 1990s: What Prospects for Development in the LDCs

Yet now in the mid-1990s, a new optimism is beginning to emerge. The severe depression of the early 1980s was sufficient to produce fundamental changes, if not in the actual international order then at least in the thinking about development. There is an increasingly visible wish now, to return to the business of development both in the MDCs and the LDCs. There is now more doubt about the social, political and environmental consequences of adjustment policies; less self-confidence in the structural adjustments being imposed on the LDCs; and less assertion of the doctrine that development is necessarily constrained by domestic mismanagement to the exclusion of external factors.

Both physical investment and human capital formation have received serious setbacks during this phase, when concern with development and growth has been largely displaced by adjustment and stabilization. The decline in investment in low-income economies other than China and India, and among major debtor countries and oil exporters, has been described earlier. Similarly, human capital has been deteriorating in an alarming way. As documented by the UNICEF studies on "Adjustment With a Human Face" and "The Impact of the World Recession on Children",[25] the cuts in government expenditures have affected the welfare of poorer people and particularly women and children disproportionately; the measures taken under the World Bank and IMF prescription for adjustment, such as abolition of food subsidies, devaluation, trade liberalization, privatization and so on, have contributed to greater inequalities of income distribution, with the well-to-do in a better position to protect their interests. The resulting deteriorating indicators of child nutrition, child health and schooling, as well as the rise of child mortality -- the ultimate indicator -- are particularly ominous since their impact on development is bound to be felt for at least another generation.

The reality today, unfortunately, appears that we have not learned much from our past mistakes, that all the previous approaches and recipes for development have been submerged by the new orthodoxy of primacy for coming to terms with the debt crisis, and of conforming to the deterioration of the international climate obvious since the early 1970s. New economic thinking for the 1990s will probably include portions of the following: (1) adjustment has not been sufficiently "growth-oriented"; (2) adjustment must be given a more "human face" in which some of type of "safety net is established to help the poor; (3) more external resources from the MDCs are needed to smooth the process of adjustment and make it politically possible; (4) adjustment must be made less harsh and stretched out over a longer period; (5) some element of debt relief is inevitable as part of the adjustment process; and (6) the optimistic view of open market economists is of doubtful validity in an unfavorable economic climate and especially when applied to low-income countries with difficult structural problems.

The adjustment problems which many of the LDCs have faced in the 1980s and now into the 1990s are unique in their abruptness and obvious negative but cumulative impact. The problem is at least three-fold: first is the rather static growth patterns in the MDCs which make projections for increased export growth in LDCs somewhat problematic. Second is the sharp decline in primary commodity prices and the subsequent steep deterioration in terms of trade between the LDCs and the MDCs. Trends in the late 1980s and early 1990s have brought commodity prices to their lowest real level since the 1930s. Third is the significant reduction in foreign aid and commercial bank loans presently available to the LDCs. This is even more difficult given the increased demand that past loans be paid as quickly as possible.

The failing of this process are now all too apparent. For some, the major cause is in the international market place where the MDCs clearly have the advantage and where LDCs will continually find it difficult to compete. Others will argue that the more domestic factors of governmental authoritarianism, bureaucratic inefficiency and over-centralization are the real culprits. Those who proclaim the dominant importance of domestic factors point to the very divergent records of different countries (some growing very nicely, others actually declining), even though they are faced with the same or similar international environment. They also argue that the LDCs must take the international environment given as a "fact of life", and that hence it is fruitless for them to keep on moaning about the international environment.

While some might argue that all the structural adjustment policies of the 1980s will prove to be useful in helping LDCs to initiate a new process of development, I am more inclined to question such optimism. During the past decade, according to World Bank figures, the proportion of central government expenditure spent on education has fallen from roughly 21 percent to less than 10 percent in low-income countries; from 18 to 13 percent in lower-middle income countries; from 15 percent to 11 percent in Latin America and from 15 percent to 10 percent in the severely indebted countries. There are similar declines in health expenditures as a proportion of government expenditures from five percent to three percent in low-income countries; six percent to four percent in the lower middle-income countries and from roughly 6 percent to just over four percent in the severely indebted countries.

As was described in an earlier section, Third World poverty has increased in absolute numbers although not as a proportion of world population. The current best estimate is that over 1.5 billion, or roughly 35 percent of the world's population, live in poverty; and more than half of them live in "extreme poverty". Thus, more people than ever are exposed to the vicious cycles of poverty or the "poverty trap". The amount of human capital destroyed in the process is incalculable. Part of this may be amenable by market processes and economic "empowerment" of the poor but not even the most ardent free market advocate would deny the need for complementary state action to provide opportunities and safety nets for the poor. The World Bank itself, in its 1990 *World Development*

Report, with poverty as its main theme, has opened the new decade with an impressive argument for such a "balanced' or "double-track" approach, combining labor-intensive growth with social safety nets -- back to the Redistribution with Growth strategy of the 1970s. Growth policies are more sustainable if they are simultaneously accompanied by poverty alleviation. Poverty alleviation in turn is more sustainable, or only sustainable, if additional resources are available from domestic growth or external sources. Thus we are back where we started at the beginning of the 1950s.

All governments of LDCs favor both growth and equity and declare their wish and intention to combine them. But in practice this turns out to be extremely difficult. Growth tends to go hand in hand with increased efficiency and increased efficiency often means less employment and less employment means more poverty. Similarly, emphasis on equity and poverty reduction all too often means increased taxation or more inflation or otherwise reduced incentives for the productive sector of the economy and thus may reduce growth. Again it is easy theoretically and on paper to point out ways in which growth and equity could be made to work together: growth could and should be labor-intensive and thus increase employment, and poverty programs could be of a kind to increase production by providing productive assets and employment for the poor; but once again all this is more easily said than done.

The equity element in the growth/equity combination encounters the further difficulty of targeting poverty reduction programs effectively on the intended beneficiaries. History does show us that almost by definition, the neediest and most vulnerable groups are also the ones most difficult to reach by public action, especially by public action emanating from a central government. It is here that the question of decentralization to regional and local levels and the involvement of non-governmental organizations (NGOs and PVOs) and the community itself emerges as a reasonable alternative for the next two decades. David Korten in his splendid book *Looking to the Twenty-First Century* presents a most persuasive argument for returning to history for the strategies and approaches that might be most useful in the future.

David Korten suggests that those seeking a model for economic development into the 21st Century should consider the growth strategies used by the Asian "tiger" economies -- Singapore, Hong Kong, Taiwan, South Korea and Japan. Korten argues that all five countries made major investments in achieving high levels of adult literacy and education. A strong commitment to education at all levels in society was an important part of their growth strategies. Three of these countries with consequential rural sectors (Japan, South Korea, and Taiwan) each instituted comprehensive and radical land reform, resulting in agricultural sectors that consisted predominantly or exclusively of small farms. Special efforts were made to strengthen local government systems, including a willingness to allow local organizations, associations, cooperatives and other forms of grassroots participation. Such rural areas were characterized by a growing number of farmer associations and women's and youth organizations. Such local institutions appear to have stimulated the much needed social energy that eventually was channeled into other productive activities.

Equally significant for these countries were the various government programs and policies structured to increase the productivity of the two most important rural assets, land and people. This consisted of increasing crop diversification and improving agricultural technologies. This emphasis on agriculture did not seek to benefit the rich farmers at the expense of the smaller farmer. In fact, government policy specifically targeted the smaller farmer, ensuring that all levels of the rural community were benefited with appropriate levels of credit and an emphasis on labor-using and capital-saving technologies.

One significant aspect of this approach was the realization that domestic industrialization is not possible without a strong domestic market with people having enough income to buy manufactured goods being produced. In contrast to other countries that have allocated scarce resources to the larger more commercially oriented farms which tended to benefit only the richer farmers, the "Asian Tigers" tended to pay agricultural prices that would reward the small farmer for increased production. With this increased income, the masses of the rural areas were in a better position to purchase the goods and services being developed in the manufacturing sectors. These new markets became the initial base for the "demand-driven" development of small rural industries to serve the needs of the rural population. This emphasis on rural industries was strongest in Taiwan where in 1961, only 16 percent of factory jobs were located in Taipei, the capital city.

Professor Korten has suggested that an equity-led sustainable growth strategy which is best suited for many of the LDCs into the 21st Century probably should involve six sequential stages:[26]

(1) Preparation for Change: a preparation for change stage which emphasizes basic education for all, with an emphasis on livelihood skills, along with the development of greater social consciousness and skills of active participation and citizenship and environmental sensitivities. This first stage must include the establishment of strong guarantees of freedom of speech and association in which private associations and individual initiatives and local participation are not only allowed but are strongly encouraged.

(2) Asset Reform and Rural Infrastructure Building: this stage seeks to implement a radical redistribution of productive assets, particularly land, making use of NGOs, people's organizations and local governments to assume a leading role in implementation. During this stage strong efforts will be made to promote farmer-controlled cooperatives and other local marketing associations, basic investments in rural roads, electricity, housing, marketing distribution centers, and other forms of agricultural extension to increase farmer productivity.

(3) Agricultural Intensification and Diversification: this stage will emphasis the need to increase the value-added of small farm units through intensification and diversification, adding high value crops to generate cash income alongside those grown for family consumption. Credit services, improved local agricultural processing and market facilities are emphasized in this stage. The government should review and adjust pricing policies to eliminate biases against small rural farmers, with special care to protect local farmers from imported food products favored by foreign subsidies.

(4) Rural Industrialization: this stage seeks to provide incentives and assistance for the establishment of small and medium-scale rural industries to serve the needs of the rural people for services, capital goods, agricultural inputs and agricultural processing. During this stage, the government should encourage productive efficiency by insuring that domestic markets remain competitive, while providing protection to local small- and medium-scale producers from competition from better established, subsidized and highly capitalized foreign competitors.

(5) Urban Industrialization: this stage gradually shifts priorities to expansion of urban industries that have strong backward and forward linkages to the rural agricultural and industrial sectors. At this stage, the growth of these industries should be governed primarily by the growing needs of local markets and consumers.

(6) Export Promotion: this stage encourages the use of residual production capacity to serve foreign markets with products that have a high value-added relative to their content of physical and environmental resources. The goal of this stage is to earn necessary foreign exchange based one's comparative advantage and to participate in international markets while exporting as little of the country's physical resources as possible.

From this section which has suggested that development can best understood as a consequence of historical forces, there is much in this approach that is useful. Development specialist, however, tend to reject this approach arguing that progress in our understanding of development requires a more theoretical perspective, a willingness to develop a more systematic analysis of the factors which influence development. The complexities of this phenomenon will never be mastered until generalizations derived from theory are developed.

Section Two
Development as a Paradigm

Many might argue that development, when tied to the problems and challenges of the LDCs, has no precise meaning, no generally accepted definition. Most scholars agree that development as a separate sub-discipline emerged after World War II, and they usually point out two paradigmatic approaches that are used to conceptualize development and underdevelopment: modernization and growth versus dependency and underdevelopment. A third model based upon notions of pluralism and interdependency appears to becoming more and more accepted. What follows is a brief outline of these three paradigms with an attempt to outline both their strengths and weaknesses.

The Paradigm of Modernization Theory

During the 1940s, the 1950s, and the early 1960s, most development thinkers stated that the problem of "underdevelopment" or "backwardness" could be solved by a more or less mechanical application of the economic and political systems of the West to countries in the Third World. Therefore, the central element of this paradigm was the metaphor of growth, and the identification of economic growth with the idea of progress. This implied that development was organic, imminent, directional, cumulative, purposive, and irreversible. This belief in modernization as a function of Western industrialization was reflective of both the capitalist and communist models of those decades.[27]

Modernization came to mean a process of societal rationalization involving the intermingling of a particular Western world view and a set of external factors leading to the industrialization of Europe and of the United States and to market-regulated economic systems in which the state played a complimentary role. The process of secularization, in which the Christian church lost its role in international relations, was one of the major outcomes of modernity which delegated a global moral responsibility to political institutions and to the legal order of modernized societies. The institutionalization of purposive-rational action based on Western models of science and bureaucracy thus became the mainstream framework for developmental schemes everywhere. In short, modernity in its broad sense, meant some form of Occidental rationalism which required the creation of new social organizations to replace the traditional ones, an industrialization of the economy, secularization, and the development of the nation-state in small and large-scale communities.

The modernization paradigm saw development as unilinear and evolutionary, and defined the state of underdevelopment in terms of observable, quantitative differences between "poor" and "rich" countries on the one hand, and traditional and modern sectors in the poor nations on the other hand. Development implied the bridging of these gaps by means of an imitative process, which occurs in stages, in such a way that the traditional sectors and/or countries gradually assumed the qualities of the modern ones. Thus modernization was defined as the social, political, and economic prerequisites for, and consequences of, industrialization and technological development. Proponents of this perspective pointed to the growth of scientific technology that allowed for greater control over nature, the dramatic improvements in transportation and communication , the rise of mass consumption made possible by the industrial revolution, the growth of global ties as a positive legacy of colonialism, and the extension of European American diplomatic and political ideologies. throughout the world.[28]

This process was initially seen as an economic process of capital formation determined by the level of investment and measured in GNP terms. As thinking about modernization continued, and as it was seen that a one-sided economic strategy of unbalanced growth did not lead to modernization, various so-called non economic factors were introduced. There arose the idea that the transition from a traditional to a modern society presupposed not only economic growth indices but also changes in socio-psychological attitudes, education, and social and political institutions almost always defined in Western terms. In fact, modernization was inevitably defined as a process of westernization. Development thus was a process by which the LDCs of the world gradually adopted the social, political and economic institutions of the Western World. One early attempt to conceptualize this process was Rogers in his analysis of the processes of diffusion and adaptation of innovations on a systematic, planned, and long-term basis.[29] Given the impact of modern mass media throughout the world, modernization, qua westernization, was perceived to be not only inevitable but right and proper. The sooner the countries of Africa, Latin America and Asia became like us the better for them.

Criticism of the Modernization Paradigm

As a result of the lack of any real development in most LDCs in the 1950s and 1960s, the modernization paradigm became subject to strong criticism. Two lines of criticism can be identified in the literature (Marxist theory and Dependency theory) both reflecting an opposition to the liberal capitalist model that provided the foundation upon which modernization theory was based. All dependency theorists have been influenced either directly or indirectly by the works of Karl Marx (1818-1883). This is certainly not to suggest that all anti-modernists are Marxists any more than all Marxists accept without qualification the sum total of Marx's effort. It is simply to acknowledge that they owe an intellectual debt to him in terms of their methods of analysis and certain critical insights into the functioning, development, and expansion of the capitalist mode of production. To appreciate Marx as a scholar, one does not have to ascribe to the views of Marx as a revolutionary.[30]

Karl Marx's work concerned mankind's historical growth process and movement toward final self-realization and fulfillment in a society he called communist. For Marx, history was not so much the story of the rise and fall of particular city-states, empires, and nation-states as it was the story of class conflict generated by economic modernization. Having evolved out of a feudal system, capitalism reigned supreme in nineteenth century Europe. Marx argued that capitalism -- which involves market exchanges, labor as a commodity, and the means of production held in private hands -- produced particular political, social, and cultural effects. Marx's discussion and analysis of capitalism have influenced dependency theorist in at least three ways:

First, Marx was concerned with exploitation of the many by the few. He may have recognized the historically progressive role played by capitalists, but his sympathies were with the downtrodden. Second, according to Marx, capitalism exhibited certain law-like qualities in terms of its development and expansion. He viewed capitalism as part of a world historical process unfolding dialectically, an economic system riddled with clashing contradictions or internal tensions that could be resolved only by transformation into a socialist mode of production. Finally, Marx insisted that a society must be studied in its totality, not piecemeal. An analyst must be aware of how various parts of society were interrelated, including those aspects not so apparent to the casual observer. Robert Heilbroner argued: "The entire contribution of Marxism rests ultimately on its effort to penetrate the veil of appearances, to discover the hidden essence of things, the web of relations that is the real ground of reality and not the surface manifestations that are its facade."[31] In sum, Marx has influenced contemporary scholars working within a broader international perspective by virtue of his emphasis on exploitation, discernible historical patterns of capitalist development and expansion, and the importance of understanding the "big picture" and then asking how individual parts fits into the whole.

Hobson and Imperialism

Marx's observations on capitalism in the nineteenth century have since been modified and generalized to cover the entire globe under various theories of imperialism. Imperialism assumes an international, hierarchical division of labor between rich and poor regions of the world, but the relation is not one of mutually beneficial comparative advantage implied in modernization theory. Rather, it is one of exploitation, greed and plunder.

Ironically, perhaps one of the most significant theories of imperialism was devised by a non-Marxist, the English economist John A. Hobson (1858-1940). Near the turn of the century Hobson noted that capitalist societies were faced with three basic interrelated problems: overproduction, under consumption by workers and other classes, and over savings on the part of the capitalists. As the capitalist owners of industry continued to exploit workers and pay the lowest possible wages, profits mounted and goods began to pile up. But who was to purchase the excess goods? Given the low wages, it would not be the mass of the working class, because members of this class did not have sufficient purchasing power. Hobson argued that the efficiency of the capitalist mode of production resulted, however, in the relentless production of more and more goods that society was unable to consume.

What could capitalists have done with excess goods and profits, and how could they have resolved the problem of under consumption? Redistribute wealth?

Highly unlikely. The solution reached by capitalists was to invest in what are now known as the LDCs. The result was imperialism: "the endeavor of the great controllers of industry to broaden the channel for the flow of their surplus wealth by seeking foreign markets and foreign investments to take off the goods and capital they cannot sell or use at home." Hobson argued against "the supposed inevitability of imperial expansion." He stated that it is "not inherent in the nature of things that we should spend our natural resources on militarism, war, and risky, unscrupulous diplomacy, in order to find markets for our goods and surplus capital."[32] Hobson hence rejected the determinism so often found in Marxist scholars who write on imperialism.

Lenin and His Theory of Imperialism

V. I. Lenin's (1870-1924) *Imperialism: The Highest Stage of Capitalism* is his most important theoretical work of interest to dependency theorists. Writing in the midst of WW I (1916), Lenin was interested in developing a theory that explained the necessity for capitalist exploitation of lesser developed countries and the causes of war among advanced capitalist states. He drew heavily upon the works of Hobson and the German Social Democrat, Rudolph Helferding (1877-1941).

From Hobson, Lenin accepted the key argument that under consumption and overproduction caused capitalists to scramble for foreign markets beyond Europe and to engage in colonialism. From Hilferding, Lenin took the notion that imperialist policies reflected the existence of monopoly and finance capital, or the highest stage of capitalism. In other words, capitalism had developed such that oligopolies and monopolies controlled the key sectors of the economy, squeezing out or taking over smaller firms and milking domestic markets dry. The result was a need to look elsewhere for investment opportunities. This logically entailed the creation of overseas markets. As markets expanded, they required more economic inputs such as raw materials which encouraged the further spread of imperialism to secure such resources.

Marx had seen that rates of profits would decline because of overproduction and under consumption and that greater misery for the working class would result because more and more people would be out of jobs or receive even less in wages. Proletarian, or working-class, consciousness would grow, leading ultimately to revolution in all capitalist countries. For Lenin, imperialism explained why Marx's prediction of proletarian revolution in Europe had failed to come about. Economic contradictions inherent in the capitalist mode of production still existed, but imperialism allowed capitalists a breathing space. Imperialism provided the European working class a taste of small portion of the spoils derived from the exploitation of overseas territories -- new markets, cheap labor, and natural resources. By buying off the European working class in the short term, imperialism delayed the inevitable revolution.

Dependency Theorists

By the end of the 1950s, some began to question the optimism that had prevailed among modernists in the early 1950s. Economic growth, at the least was uneven, and at most had failed to materialize in a number of the LDCs. Why was this? Most scholars, utilizing the widely used traditional-modernity dichotomy, had begun to argue that the cultural values of traditional society were both a cause and a reflection of their underdevelopment. Traditional society was thus defined as an obstacle to the entrepreneurial spirit which was perceived as a prerequisite to the processes of modernization and development. The causes for this lack of growth was seen as endemic to many of the LDCs.[33]

In the early 1960s a number of non-western scholars associated with the Economic Commission on Latin America (ECLA) and the United Nations Conference on Trade and Development (UNCTAD) began to question such explanations. Instead of seeing an explanation within the LDCs themselves, this group of non-western scholars observed that modernization literature usually neglected a society's or state's external environment, particularly international political and economic factors, and in the process had tended to ignore the state's or society's place in the world capitalist order. A new set of factors were seen as more crucial in explaining the inability of the LDCs to develop.[34] One significant factor was the unequal terms of trade that seemed to characterize the relationship between the MDCs and LDCs. The volatility of prices from minerals and agricultural products and the generally downward tendency of those prices contrasted sharply with the more stable and gradually increasing prices for manufactured items produced by industrial countries. Thus, the terms of trade were thought to be stacked against those less developed states that exported farm products or natural resources.

Others boldly emphasized political and social factors within the context of a capitalist economic system that bound Latin America to North America. Choices for the LDCs were restricted by the demands and the economic requirements of international capitalism. The result was an unchanging structure of domination and exploitation. This multifaceted web of dependency reinforced unequal exchange between the northern and southern parts of the globe. Opportunities for LDCs were few and far between because LDCs were consistently allocated a subordinate role in world capitalism The world was thus divided into two groups of nations: the core nations of Western Europe and the United States and the peripheral nations of Asia, Africa and Latin America. This international system of capitalist exploitation thus ensured the perpetual underdevelopment of the LDCs. Equally significant were the ways in which multi-national corporations and international banking interests established and maintained these dependency relationships.[35]

A number of other scholars emphasized the role of local elites within the peripheral nations themselves in perpetuating dependency. The inability of these nations to break out of this strangle hold was often reinforced through the great landowners, the political and economic elite who benefited from the instruments of foreign domination. This so-called *comprador* class, or national bourgeoisie, thus played an important role in the exploitation of its own society. Allied with foreign capitalists, its self-serving policies encouraged the expansion of social and economic inequality, which often had disastrous consequences for the poorer classes of society, especially in the rural areas. Although some limited development often did occur in the major urban centers, the countryside was generally allowed to stagnate, being perceived as a provider of cheap labor and raw materials. These local elites, therefore, had more in common with the elites of the core countries than they did with their fellow citizens of the periphery.[36]

Probably the most influential critic of the modernizationist perspective has undoubtedly been Andre Frank.[37] He claimed that the modernization perspective was empirically untenable and theoretically insufficient. He also claimed that as a practical matter, it was incapable of stimulating development in the Third World. As a result of the general intellectual "revolution" of the mid-1960s, the above-mentioned Western or ethnocentric view of development was challenged by a generation of LDC scholars, and a theory dealing with dependency and underdevelopment was born. Though the dependency paradigm can be said to be an indigenous Latin American creation, the "founding father" of this perspective is Baran, who is, together with Magdoff and Sweezy, spokesman for the North American Monthly Review group.[38] Baran was the first to argue that development and underdevelopment had to be seen as interrelated and continuous processes, two aspects of a single global process. He emphasized how all trade relations between the developed and the less developed countries not only created both financial and technological dependency, but also ensured that the pattern of income distribution within these countries favored the rich and disadvantaged the poor.

Dependency theorists were typically concerned with the processes by which some nations come to dominate other nations. Thus they were concerned with development and maintenance of dependency relations among northern industrialized states (in North America, Western Europe, and Japan) and the poor, underdeveloped, or industrially backward LDCs of Latin America, Africa and Asia. The basic argument was that these latter states and societies are underdeveloped not because they have failed to develop capitalist economic systems or because they are poorly integrated into the world capitalist system. On the contrary, it is not a matter of too little capitalism but too much. Far from being placed outside the mainstream of the world capitalist system, LDCs have become an integral part of it. The structure of global political economy has developed in such a manner -- intentionally and unintentionally -- as to keep the Third World countries underdeveloped and dependent on the rich northern states. The LDCs play a crucial role in the economic well-being of such countries as the France or Great Britain by providing cheap labor and raw materials necessary to fuel their economies, and markets for Western European manufactured goods. As part of the world capitalist system, LDCs were unable to choose their own path toward economic and political development. Autonomous development, thus for the dependency theorists, was not possible as long as the international capitalist system prevails in the world.

For the dependency theorists, it is necessary to trace the historical evolution of the present system if we are to understand this structure of domination and exploitation. The key historical factor and defining characteristic of the system as a whole is capitalism, colonialism and today modern imperialism. This particular economic system works to the benefit of some individuals, states, and societies but at the expense of others. Such dependency theorists assume that particular mechanisms of domination exist that keep LDCs from developing and that contribute to worldwide uneven development with some nations having incredible wealth and other nations being incredibly poor.

One may state that most advocates of the dependency paradigm believed that the most significant obstacles to development were not lack of capital or management skills (as argued by supporters of the modernization paradigm) but were to be found in the international division of labor. These obstacles were, in other words, not internal but external to the dependent society. This meant at the same time that development in the center implied and ensured underdevelopment in the periphery.

The dependency paradigm has influenced discussion on strategies on both a national and an international level. Chile under Allende, Jamaica under Manley, and Tanzania under Nyerere are examples of governments that have tried to set up a development policy within a dependency perspective. On the international level, *dependistas* argued that in order to remove the external obstacles each peripheral country (LDCs) should strive for self-reliance and search for new allies within the framework of a New International Economic Order (NIEO). It was assumed that a revolutionary political transformation would be necessary in order to achieve this goal.

While modernization scholars took the nation state as their main framework of reference, *dependistas* believed in a predominantly international level of analysis. They argued that the domination of the periphery (LDCs) by the center (MDCs) occurred through a combination of power components, that is, the military, economics, politics, culture, and so on. Nowadays the cultural component has come to be of greater importance in perpetuating the dependent relationships because of the rather paradoxical situation that, as the Third World begins to emancipate itself economically and politically, cultural dominance increases. Galtung distinguishes four mechanisms by which the Center nations of the North take advantage of the peripheral nations of the South: exploitation, penetration (using peripheral elite), fragmentation, and marginalization. While exploitation was seen as the cause of inequality in this world, the other three mechanisms can be seen as supporting factors, not all of them equally necessary.

Most studies on the cultural "bedazzlement" of the Third World countries do not go much beyond quantitative aspects. They mainly show how much information, entertainment, advertising, capital, and hardware material flows between center and periphery nations, as well as disparities within regions and countries (e.g., between urban and rural areas, between linguistic or ethnic majorities and minorities, and between rich and poor groups or classes). Most early *dependistas* took for granted that, together with the huge volume of Western media messages, a conservative and capitalist ideology and a consumer culture would be introduced and reinforced simultaneously. Thus for the dependency theorists, the processes of modernization brought through westernization lead to greater poverty and degradation in the LDCs.

Criticism of Dependency Theory

The dependency view, in its stress on external factors, appeared almost as the antithesis of the modernization paradigm. However, when one looks at the content of development -- for example, both approaches started from mainly economic and/or socioeconomic variables -- one sees that the difference is minimal. Dependency theory grew out of a dissatisfaction with the modernization paradigm, and now radical critics of dependency theory see it also being incapable of explaining the new realities of the post colonial world.[39] Critics of dependency theory argue that it sees the fundamental contradiction in the world between the center and the periphery and, therefore, fails to take into account the ways that local elites and indigenous systems of exploitation at the local levels inhibit economic development. Equally significant is its inability to explain and account for changes in underdeveloped economies over time that do not fit the dependency paradigm.[40] This is especially true for the Newly Industrialized Nations (NICs) of Asia (South Korea, Taiwan, Malaysia, Singapore, etc.) which do not appear to fit the dependency model.

The Need for Deeper Understanding

Recent critics have argued that the greatest weakness of dependency research is the lack of an analysis of the nature of the societal forces and the position of the nation-state in peripheral countries. *Dependistas* put too much emphasis on the contradictions at the international level, and thus overlook the existing contradictions at the local level between the interests of the state and the general population at large. The political results of the dependency view, say critics, is to turn attention away from these internal class relationships and focus it on the center. However, one has to accept the fact that "internal" and "external" factors which inhibit development do not exist independently of one another. Thus, in order to understand and develop a proper strategy, one must have an understanding of the class relationships of any particular peripheral social structure, and of the ways in which these structures articulate with the center on the one hand, and with the producing classes in the Third World on the other. To dismiss Third World ruling classes, for example, as mere puppets whose interests are always synonymous with those of the center is to ignore the realities of a highly complex relationship[41]. The very unevenness and contradictory nature of the capitalist development process necessarily produces a constantly changing relationship. At the same time, one must keep in mind that so-called peripheral countries differ vastly in terms of their natural resources, and so on. Peripheral countries thus have not remained static but have followed their own historical paths, often independent of international factors.

New Paradigm for Development Shift from the Theories of Development to the Politics of Transformation

The events of the past decade in Iran, in Russia, in Israel, and in China cannot be explained by the theories of modernization and development so confidently presented in the previous decades. Such theories which assumed a linear movement towards things Western were challenged by the events portrayed on evening television. No political scientist would have suggested the demise and fall of the Soviet Union, fewer would have projected that a group of traditional mullahs in Iran would not only call for, but actually organize and implement, a revolution based upon principles and concepts totally foreign and alien to the concepts of modernization, secularization, and capitalist-oriented democracy.

No longer would it be possible to suggest that all forms of change, of revolution, would necessarily follow the pattern of modernization as defined by the students of development, especially in the West. Any form of development was accepted by definition as a process leading to things Western, secular and rational. Obviously the earlier forms of Western thought dominated by the ideas of economic and political development, implying movement towards a one-world culture, and the gradually elimination of traditional forms of cultural diversity, needed to be challenged. A new framework of thought based upon concepts of transformation, an open-ended process acknowledging a diversity, a complexity, and an unpredictableness generally ignored in the old modernist and dependency paradigms.

A new perspective on development theory is now emerging based upon three new trends. It is the result of the criticism of both modernization and dependency theory which insists that long-term development must be based on industrialization and consumerism. The **first trend,** based on the notions of "Small is Beautiful" and a concern for the environment, seeks to challenge the obsession with growth at any cost approach which destroys our forests, pollutes our lakes and rivers, and uses up our scarce and often non-replaceable natural resources. In this perspective, one can discern the rejection of the dominant consumerist model by certain segments in both the MDCs and LDCs. A **second trend** is the rise of cultural diversity and the demands for greater ethnic autonomy, somewhat rising out of the earlier liberation movements in the Third World against their own national elites. **Finally** is the more recent trend toward what is called an "Alternative Development" approach which seeks to emphasize local institutions, grassroots participation and local community development. Let us review the broader aspects of this third paradigm.

Interdependence

On a global level, one starts from the assumption that there are, in fact, no countries that are completely autonomous and self-reliant, and at the same time, no countries that develop (or underdevelop) merely as a reflection of exogenous factors. This global perspective is often conceptualized in terms of ways in which all nations have now become more interdependent, both politically and economically. To some, interdependence merely reflects the basic assumptions of the modernists and the ways in which nations are becoming more interdependent merely confirms the modernization paradigm of the 1950s and 1960s. To others, it is no more than a more complicated explanation for the center-periphery dichotomy. In contrast to the more economic- and politics-oriented views of the modernization and dependency paradigms, the central idea in this third paradigm is that there is no universal path to development, that is, development must be conceived of as an integral, multidimensional, and dialectic process which can differ from one society to another. In other words, every country must find its own development strategy. This also implies that the problem of development is a relative one, and no part of the world can claim to be developed in all respects. Therefore, discussion on the degree and scope of interdependence should be connected with the content of development.

Because the previous paradigms were unable to combine economic growth with social justice, this new paradigm tries to rethink the problem of freedom and justice in the relationship between man and society, and the problem of the limits to growth as inherent in the relationship between society and nature. In what follows, I deal with two trends that, to my mind, constitute the core of this new paradigm: the analysis of power and ideology in (world) society, and the search for "another" form of development outside the demands of industrialization and consumerism.

Global Analysis

The globalization of development thinking did primarily emerge from the discussion on dependency. Wallerstein, for example, one of the best known representatives of the world system approach, describes the world system as capitalist because the basic economic processes characteristic of capitalism operated on a world system level, not on the level of nation states. Thus he avoids one of the pitfalls of the dependency paradigm, its center-periphery polarization. At the same time, he retains some of the weakness of the dependency paradigm; for example, its static historical view. However, Wallerstein's main contribution whereby he, in my opinion, goes beyond the dependency paradigm, is his proposition that the world system is a social system characterized by the fact that life within it is largely self-contained, that the dynamics of its development are largely internal, and that this internal nature implies an internalization of the external factors emphasized in dependency theory. He expresses the hope for a revolutionary transformation of the world system as a whole into a socialist world system. But Wallerstein immediately adds that this is a long term project because of the "limited possibilities of transformation within the capitalist world-economy".[42]

Many have challenged the Wallerstein model, arguing that his analysis seems to stress the dynamic of the capitalist system one-sidedly as a universally explanatory principle.[43] From this newer perspective, capitalism, while rather pervasive in the world's economy, is but only one form of economic life possible. In the margin of the capitalist system, all kinds of pre- or non capitalist organizational patterns maintain their own coherency and significance. This viewpoint stresses the special autonomy of superstructural institutions in the precapitalist forms of production, and also notes how de-colonization has gained the upper hand. From this, it appears that all kinds of non economic factors, such as principles like kinship and religion that gave the old forms of production their unique form, still have a direct influence in this coupling. Therefore these scholars are more interested in what is happening within the boundaries of a country or nation in which they examine social class and ethnic struggles, the varying contiguous forms of production, populist and nationalist trends, and the functioning of ideologies as social processes.

An Alternative Development Paradigm

This new paradigm is more normative in its approach. It deals with development not in terms of how it is, but rather in terms of how it should be. The focus of this paradigm is on the content rather than on the form of development. Even if one accepts the basic assumption that development must be conceived of as an integral, multidimensional, and dialectic process which can differ from one society to another, one must define the general principles and priorities on which such a strategy should be based. Numerous researchers have been trying to establish the core components of "Another Development".[44] This new concept of development is perhaps best summarized by and spread through the Dag Hammerskjold Foundation and its *Development Dialogue* journal. Their conception of "Another Development" reflects the following:
1. **Oriented to Basic Needs**; that is, development must be geared to meeting human needs, both material and non material. It begins with the satisfaction of the

basic needs of the dominated and exploited, who constitute the majority of the world's inhabitants. At the same time, it ensures the humanization of all human beings by the satisfaction of their needs for expression, creativity, equality, and conviviality, and for understanding and mastering their own destiny.

2. **Focus on the Endogenous**; that is, processes of development stemming from the heart and soul (culture) of each society, which defines its sovereignty, its values, and its vision of the future. Since development is not a linear process, there can be no universal model.

3. **Emphasis on Self-Reliance;** that is, a form of development whereby each society must rely primarily on its own strengths and resources in terms of its members' energies and its natural and cultural environment. Self-reliance clearly needs to be exercised at the national and international levels, but it acquires its full meaning only if rooted at the local level, in the praxis of each community.

4. **Insistence on a Global Perspective on the Ecology**; that is, development defined as the rational utilization of the resources of the biosphere with full awareness of the potential of local eco-systems as well as of the global limits imposed on present and future generations. It implies the equitable access to resources by all, and careful, socially relevant technologies which seek to protect nonrenewable resources.

5. **Belief on the Need for Structural Transformation** -- in social relations, in economic activities, in the spatial distribution of these activities, and in the power structure. The result of such structural transformations will be self-management and participation in decision making by all, both at the community level and at the world level. Without this, the above-mentioned goals cannot be achieved.

6. **A Hope for Pluralistic Democracy**, that is, a form of government that not only represents the people, but is accountable to the people, guarantees a system of law that protects human rights not only of the majority within a society, but also minorities, their languages, cultures and ways of life. The proliferation of minority demands for autonomy and the protection and enhancement of local cultures is a very important part of this Alternative Development paradigm.

These six characteristics are organically linked, "for development is seen as a whole, as an integral, cultural process, as the development of every man and woman in a given community. The concept of "Another Development" thus means liberation, alternatives and choices.45 This newly emerging paradigm is yet to be clearly spelled out, but there is enough evidence in the literature that a new form of development thinking is upon us.

---

[1]World Bank, *World Development Report 1994*, (New York: Oxford University Press, 1994), p. 196.
[2]John Maynard Keynes, *The General Theory of Employment, Interest, and Money*, The General Theory of Employment (New York: Harcourt, Brace, and Co., 1935).

[3] Raymond F. Mikesell, *The Economics of Foreign Aid,* (Chicago: Aldine, 1968; and Edward Mason and Robert Asher, *The World Bank since Bretton Woods,* (Washington, DC: Brookings Institution, 1973).

[4] Charles Kindelberger and Bruce Herrick, *Economic Development,* (New York: McGraw-Hill, 1977)

[5] Ragnar Nurkse, *Problems of Capital Formation in Underdeveloped Countries* (New York: Oxford University Press, 1976), first published in 1953.

[6] Albert O. Hirschman, *The Strategy of Economic Development* (New Haven: Yale University Press, 1959), p.72.

[7] A general review of the literature of early economic development theory is represented in D. E. Novack and R. Lekachman (eds.) *Development and Society,* (New York: St Martin's Press, 1964) and A. N. Agarwala and S.P. Singh (eds.) *The Economics of Underdevelopment* (New York: Oxford University Press, 1970).

[8] P.W. Rosenstein-Rodan, "Problems of Industrialization of Eastern and South-Eastern Europe, reprinted in A. N. Agarwala and S.P. Singh (eds.) *The Economics of Underdevelopment* (New York: Oxford University Press, 1970).

[9] W.W. Rostow, *The Process of Economic Growth,* (New York: Norton, 1952).

[10] Simon Kuznets, *Modern Economic Growth,* (New Haven: Yale University Press, 1966).

[11] K. B. Griffin and J.L. Enos, "Foreign Assistance: Objectives and Consequences," *Economic Development and Cultural Change* 18 (1970), pp. 313-327.

[12] W. Arthur Lewis, *Development Planning: The Essentials of Economic Policy* (London: George Allen & Unwin, 1966).

[13] Michael Lipton, *Why Poor People Stay Poor: A Study of Urban Bias in World Development* (London: Maurice Temple Smith, 1977).

[14] World Bank, *World Development Report, 1978* (New York: Oxford University Press, 1978).

[15] World Bank, *World Development Report, 1994* (New York: Oxford University Press, 1994).

[16] Ronald Muller, "The Multinational Corporation and the Underdevelopment of the Third World," in Charles K. Wilber, ed., *The Political Economy of Development and Underdevelopment* (New York: Random House, 1979, pp. 151-78; Paul Streeten, "The Multinational Enterprise and the Theory of Development Policy," *World Development* 1 (October 1973); and Sanjaya Lall, "Less-Developed Countries and Private Foreign Investment: A Review Article," *World Development* 2 (April, 1974), pp. 41-48.

[17] Dudley Seers, "The Meaning of Development," *International Development Review* 11 (December, 1969), pp. 3-4.

[18] John R. Harris and Michael P. Todaro, "Migration, Unemployment and Development: a Two-sector analysis," *American Economic Review* 60 (March, 1970) pp. 126-42.

[19] Lyn Squire, *Employment Policy in Developing Countries: A Survey of Issues and Evidence* (New York: Oxford University Press, 1981) and Edgar O. Edwards, ed., *Employment in Developing Nations* (New York: Columbia University Press, 1974).

[20] Theodore W. Schultz, *Transforming Traditional Agriculture* (New Haven: Yale University Press, 1964).

[21] Hollis Chenery, *et al., Redistribution with Growth* (London: Oxford University Press, 1974).

[22] Colin I. Bradford, Jr., "East Asian 'Models': Myths and Lessons," in John P. Lewis and V. Kallab, eds., *Development Strategies Reconsidered,* (Oxford: Transaction Books, 1986), pp. 115-28.

[23] World Development Report 1994, *op.cit.*, pp. 190-97.

[24] World Bank, *World Development Report* 1989 (New York: Oxford University Press, 1989), p. 6.
[25] A. Cornia, R. Jolly, and F. Stewart, (eds.) *Adjustment with a Human Face, A Study by UNICEF*, (Oxford: Clarendon, 1987.
[26] David C. Korten, Getting to the 21st Century: Voluntary Action and the Global Agenda (West Hartford, Conn.: Kumarian Press, 1990), pp. 74-85.
[27] Marion Levy, Modernization Latecomers and Survivors (New York: Basic Books, 1972).
[28] C. E. Black, *The Dynamics of Modernization* (New York; Harper & Row, 1966) and John H. Kautsky, *The Political Consequences of Modernization* (New York: Wiley, 1972).
[29] E. M. Rogers, *Diffusion of Innovations* (New York: Free Press, 1962).
[30] Benjamin Cohen, The Question of Imperialism, (New York: Basic Books, 1973.
[31] Robert L. Heilbroner, *Marxism: For and Against* (New York: Norton, 1980), p. 49.
[32] John A. Hobson, *Imperialism: A Study* (Ann Arbor: University of Michigan Press, 1965), pp. 85-86.
[33] For a review of the diverse branches of dependency theory, see: Ronald H. Chilcote, *Theories of Comparative Politics* (Boulder, Colo.: Westview Press, 1961).
[34] J. S. Caporaso, "Dependence, Dependency, and Power in the Global System: A Structural and Behavioral Analysis," *International Organizations* 32 (1) (Winter 1978): 14-43.
[35] Howard J. Sherman, *Foundations of Radical Political Economy*, (Armonk, New York: M.E. Sharpe, 1987).
[36] Ronald H. Chilcote, *Theories of Development and Underdevelopment*, (Boulder, Colo.: Westview Press, 1984).
[37] Gunder Frank, *Capitalism and Underdevelopment in Latin America*, (New York: Monthly Review Press, 1967).
[38] Paul Baran, *The Political Economy of Growth*, (New York: Monthly Review Press, 1957).
[39] M. Bernstein, "Sociology of Underdevelop vs. Sociology of Development" in D. Lehman (Ed.) *Development Theory* (London: Frank Cass, 1979) and C. Leys, "Underdevelopment and Dependency: Critical Notes," *Journal of Contemporary Asia*, 7 (1) (1982.
[40] A useful critique and bibliography of dependence theory are in Sanjaya Lall, "Is 'Dependence' a Useful Concept in Analyzing Underdevelopment," *World Development* 3 (1975), pp. 799-810.
[41] Note how Amin argues that the NIEO strategy favors the interests and views of the dominant elites in the Third World. S. Amin, *Classe et Nation dans l'Histoire et la Crise Contemporaine*, (Paris, Minuit, 1979).
[42] I. Wallerstein, *The Capitalist World Economy* (Cambridge: Cambridge University Press, 1979).
[43] E. Laclau, *Politics and Ideology in Marxist Theory* (London: New Left Books, 1977); J. Petras, *Critical Perspectives on Imperialism and Social Class in the Third World*, (New York: New York Monthly Review Press, 1978); N. Poulantzas, *L'Etat, le Pouvoir, Le Socialism*, (Paris: PUF, 1983); and G. Therborn, *The Ideology of Power and the Power of Ideology* (London: Verso, 1980).
[44] R. Chapel, *Towards a New Strategy of Development* (Oxford: Pergamon, 1980); J. Galtung, *The True Worlds: A Transnational Perspective* (New York: Free Press, 1980); F. Perroux, *A New Concept of Development* (Paris: UNESCO); and M.P. Todaro, *Economic Development in the Third World: An Introduction to Problems and Policies in a Global Perspective* (New York: Longman, 1977).

[45] M. Nerfin, (Ed.) *Another Development: Approaches and Strategies* (Uppsala: Dag Hammerskjold Foundation, 1977);K. W. Deutsch, *Eco-social Systems and Eco-politics* (Paris: UNESCO, 1977); K. Lederer, (Ed.) *Human Needs: A Contribution to the Current Debate* (Konigstein: Oelgeschlager, 1980); D. Lehman,(Ed.) *Development Theory: Four Critical Studies* (London: Frank Cass, 1979); and I. Sachs (ed.) *Strategies de l' Ecodeveloppement* (Paris: Presses Ouvrieres, 1980); Keith Griffin, *Alternative Strategies for Economic Development* (New York: St. Martin's, 1989); D. Simon (ed.) *Third World Regional Development: A Reappraisal,* (London: Chapman, 1990); J. Friedmann, *Empowerment: The Politics of an Alternative Development* (Oxford: Blackwell, 1992); and John Brohman, *Popular Development: Rethinking the Theory & Practice of Development* (Oxford: Blackwell, 1996).

Unit Two
The Concept and Processes of Rural Development

Case Studies in Rural Development

Chapter 5

The Concept of Rural Development
Case Studies and Lessons Learned

In the previous chapter, the concept of development was considered in both its historical and theoretical contexts. Much of what has been written suggests that the crucial issues of development are best considered at the national and international levels of analysis. As will become much clearer in the chapters that follow, this bias for the national and international must be confronted. Within this broader notion of development is the sub discipline of rural development which focuses on the rural areas of the LDCs and seeks to identify strategies and approaches appropriate for improving the standard of living in these rural areas. Much of the development literature takes a macro-level approach to development, suggesting that the problems of the rural areas would best be dealt with through national and international processes. It will be the conclusion of this book that no strategy or program of development that ignores or fails to consider the people of the rural areas will have any long-term hope for success.

Section One
Historical Assessment of
Rural Development Processes

Rural Development (1950s): Resource Transfers

In the 1950s, development was conceptualized as **a process of resource transfer,** in which domestic savings and/or international capital investments would finance the industrialization of the LDCs. Industrialization was perceived to be the key to economic development and was measured in terms of increased GNP. Rural development, even when it was considered, was seen as a passive process, merely providing cheap labor and the food stuffs needed for urban workers. As wealth in a society was generated through the process of industrialization, the benefits of such growth in the urban centers would eventual "trickle down" to the rural areas. Because capital investment was seen as a value-free concept, quite independent of any cultural value system, local cultural systems were generally not considered relevant in the process of rural development. Local involvement and community participation was conceived as a process by which villagers would be mobilized and organized to accept government sponsored programs and policies.

One of the unintended consequences of this passive approach to rural development was the lack of any significant improvement in the standard of living in the rural areas. In this period, part of the hope was that industrialization would become sustainable as demand for the goods from the urban sector would be purchased by the masses in the rural areas. With no sustained effort to increase the income of rural people, no serious demand for these market goods emerged. Many early efforts to stimulate manufacturing and new industries in many LDCs proved nonviable as the masses of these societies simply lacked the income needed for a sustainable process of industrialization and national development.

Rural Development (1960s): Technology Transfers

In the late 1950s and early 1960s, a number of serious famines caught the world unprepared. And while the US was able to export large amounts of grain to the LDCs, such imports were clearly only a short-term solution. Many observers questioned the wisdom in defining development in terms of a countries commitment to industrialization. When people are starving, there is little need for manufactured consumer goods. People cannot eat radios, shoes, or refrigerators. In the 1960s, which was designated by the United Nations to be a "Decade of Development," the new emphasize of this decade was to be in the sector of agriculture. Rural Development was seen as a **process of technology transfer**. Western technology in modern agriculture would be transferred to the LDCs and the problems of famine and food storage would be solved. This new technology was known as the Green Revolution in which genetically engineered high yield varieties (HYVs) of wheat, rice and corn, coupled with modern fertilizers and insecticides would ensure a surplus of food throughout the world. It was during this period that many experts charged with implementing the Green Revolution in LDCs came to see the local culture as an obstacle, that the cultural values and traditional methods of agriculture in these societies simply had to be eliminated. Participation and community involvement again were mainly used for administrative control and to facilitate surveys and other data collection activities to help bureaucrats determine the needs and concerns of the rural areas.

The unintended consequence of this decade was the fact that only the richest and biggest farmers in these countries were able to take advantage of the Green Revolution technology. With their increased yields and thus increased profits, the richer farmers began buying up the land of the smaller farmers forcing many of them to find work in the urban areas. Also many of these larger farmers turned more and more of their lands to commercial crops for export, thus reducing the land available for domestic food production. A number of scholars observed that during the decade of the 1960s, the rich did get richer, but the poor were much poorer. Rural development as a process of technology transfer clearly had mostly negative consequences for the vast majority of the small farmers and landless agriculture workers. Obviously, a process of rural development that increased the gap between the rich and poor and increased unemployment and poverty needed to be reconsidered.

Rural Development (1970s): Providing Basic Needs

In the 1970s, the World Bank announced a commitment to helping the "poorest of the poor" in the LDCs improve their quality of life. A Basic Needs strategy was proposed in which all members of society should have access to the basic requirements of life including: basic health, education, adequate food and needed social services. The process for providing these basic needs was to be through a central administrative systems, controlled and operated by the central government. The process of rural development was thus conceptualized as a top-down process in which government bureaucrats provided needed services. It was during this period that a number of development practitioners began to argue for more appropriate technology, a technology that was sustainable and affordable and more relevant to the actual needs of rural people. Anthropologists became members of several development agencies and began calling for greater sensitivity to the local culture and the need to understand and work with such cultures. Participation was re conceptualized to include opportunities for rural people to begin a process of consciousness raising, that through group discussions and various mobilization techniques peasants could be energized and stimulated to seek change and improvement in their lives.

The unintended consequences of the 1970s were related to the inability of the central government to provide adequate services to the villages and rural communities of their countries. Plagued with budget deficits and unskilled administrators many of the promises for better health and education services were never met. The reality was that most government services were limited mostly to urban areas. Rural areas were consistently plagued by this "urban bias" that characterized so many of the LDCs government bureaucracies.

Rural Development (1980s): Local Institution Building

In the late 1970s and early 1980s, a number of scholars began to argue that rural development required the active involvement of the rural people themselves, that without the active participation of local people working through local institutions, little long-term development was possible. Given the many problems identified in the earlier centralized systems of governmental control, it is not difficult to understand this new call for decentralized systems of local administration, demanding greater accountability and local initiative. A new recognition for the importance of both public and private sector involvement appears, stimulating a greater call for privatization and the use of markets and free enterprise characterized this decade. A number of evaluations of central government approaches to rural development suggested that many such efforts were not sustainable, seldom had positive long-lasting consequences for the poorer segments of society and failed to stimulate local initiative or any sense of local self reliance and responsibility. Much evidence was presented to suggest that most successful projects tended to have small budgets, were usually implemented by local people working through local institutions, utilized some formalized process of local resource mobilization to help supplement external sources of funding, and defined these projects within the values and traditions of the local culture. Many in fact argued that successful rural development programs must not only understand the local culture but must strengthen and revitalize these local cultural systems as a significant source of social energy and community motivation.

Some of the unintended consequences of the 1980s was the inability of central governments to generate the funds needed to support these local initiatives. Forced to meet the repayment demands of international creditors, many LDCs, in their efforts to make needed interest payments, greatly curtailed domestic spending in the basic needs areas of health, education and social welfare. The structural adjustment programs of the World Bank and International Monetary Fund proved disastrous in many LDCs already trapped in a cycle of inflation and government deficit spending. Thus at a time when poverty was still increasing in many LDCs, their governments were being forced to curtail needed services to the very poorest of the poor. Many of the local initiatives and self-help programs of the early 1980s were simply not allowed to continue.

Rural Development (1990s): Networking, Linkage Building and Social Mobilization

In the 1990s, rural development specialists are beginning to focus on the political dimensions of local community development. Until local political forces are mobilized and structured to influence government policy making, most of the reforms being suggested for rural development will never be implemented. Rural Development is now being conceived as an important part of the process of democratization and increased pluralism emerging in Eastern Europe, the former Soviet Union and in many areas of Latin America and Asia. The process of rural development requires among others: central government support and local government initiatives, networks of cooperation and effective links between all levels of government. This appears to be a decade of local empowerment, mass movements of disadvantaged people and other strategies of political influence. Equally significant is the emergence of a stronger demand for ethnic autonomy and cultural diversity.

The unintended consequences of this decade are still to be played out. Some are predicting that the demands for cultural diversity may result in greater social fragmentation and increased levels of community violence. What is not clear is whether such efforts at mass mobilization will be reflective of democratic processes of government with increased commitment to human rights and meaningful political participation or whether such efforts will stimulate a return to greater authoritarianism and dictatorship. Such is the challenge for the LDCs of this planet.

The Concept of Rural Development

General Summary of Rural Development Theory Over the Past Four Decades

The chart below defines the subtle shifts that have taken place in rural development goals, strategies, and approaches over the past forty years. It must be recognized that the shifts in emphasis are categorized by decade more to distinguish different thrusts than to suggest mutually exclusive periods of time. Economists for example have obviously played an important role in rural development programs as much in the 1970s as in the 1950s but their relative significance was clearly greater in the earlier period than it is today.

A Chronology of RD Theory and Practice (1950s-1990s)

	1950s (to)	1960s (for)	1970s (with)
Purpose	Increase GNP	Increase Production	Increase Equity
Focus	Industrialization	Green Revolution	Basic Needs
Approach	Total System	Sectoral	Integrated
Strategy	Transfer Resources	Transfer Technology	Use Appropriate Technology
Local Cultural Values	Ignore as Unimportant	Neutralize as an Obstacle	Accept and Learn to Work With
Participation Focus	Use to Build Unity/Cohesion	Collect Information Generate Support for Govt Programs	Stimulate Consciousness Raising
Profession	Economist	Planner/Sectoral Expert	Public Administration

	1980s (Through)	1990s (By)
Purpose	Increase Quality Of Life	Ensure Ecosystem Sustainability
Focus	Local Institution Building	Democratization/Pluralism in Political Systems
Approach	Decentralization of Bureaucracy	Networking/Coalition Building
Strategy	Greater Privatization of Govt Services	Greater Public/Private Sector Collaboration
Local Cultural Values	Encourage culture as a Key Source of Social Energy	Protect and Enhance Local Cultural Diversity
Participation Focus	Local Capacity Building Project Sustainability	Empowerment/ Emerging Mass Movements
Profession	Management and Political Science	Interdisciplinary Global Approach

It should be noted that each period is tagged with a particular proposition (**for, to, with, through, by**) as a means of focusing the reader on how central governments and international donors have tended to relate to rural communities. In the 1950s and 1960s rural development required the transfer of technology and resources **"to"** the local population. Service Delivery Systems were established **"for"** the benefit of the local peasant farmers. Later in the 1970s and 1980s there is a greater awareness that development requires local involvement in which government officials and donor representatives work more closely **"with"** local communities in designing and implementing rural development projects. During the 1980s, there was a gradual acknowledgment that locally established private organizations, somewhat independent of the central government, were appropriate vehicles **"through"** which local political and entrepreneurial talent could be developed and channeled for rural development. Into the 1990s a new trend is emerging suggesting a greater commitment to democracy and local autonomy in which local communities in a much more decentralized local government system would implement rural projects **"by"** their own efforts and initiatives quite independent of the central government. A review of the history of rural development (RD) theorizing suggests not that earlier models were wrong but merely that they were often irrelevant to the needs of the peasant farmers of this world.

Section Two
The Three Stages of Rural Development:
An Integration of the Five Dimensions of Rural Development

The process of rural development is complex and often unpredictable. People who visit a rural village for the first time are often frustrated by the slowness with which change seems to take place. Often we want to see the problems of poverty, disease, and illiteracy eliminated quickly and effortlessly. Many assume that such problems will be overcome if we just spend enough money, or if we simply build a school or if we help them establish a health clinic. This chapter will seek to demonstrate how rural development is to be conceptualized as a three stage process working within the five basic dimensions of rural development and often requiring at least five to ten years for it to be effective and sustainable.

After thirty years of experience in the field of rural development, we are beginning to understand that the problems of poverty, illiteracy and underdevelopment are not easily solved, that the processes of development require slow, often painful changes that must come from within the village community itself. While outsiders may help stimulate this process of change, the long-term solution of these problems will require a gradual integration of a number of activities related to the village systems of culture, education, health, employment and ecology that must be developed over an extended (often at least five to ten years) period.

In the final analysis rural development must be thought of as "rural people development." This concept must acknowledge that motivation and proper incentives are the key ingredients of change and growth in people, and that the release of such energy is usually sparked by a learning process that widens one's mental constructs, activates a consciousness of what is and what is not possible, and introduces mental and behavioral skills needed to solve the problems of rural communities. Those seeking to initiate rural development must be aware of the incentives and disincentives for change that exist within the communities of their concern. They must become familiar with the structures, cultural norms, and value orientations of these rural communities.

One of the most common mistakes among outsiders coming into a village community, is to assume that they, who are western trained, should be able to introduce change with logic and reasonable persuasion. This is especially a problem among outsiders who are in the village for a limited period of time. For example, interns who are placed in a village for six months, often feel a strong urgency to accomplish something while they are in the village. Often with only six months to prove themselves as effective development facilitators, they seek to demonstrate their expertise, their competency, their ability, both to themselves, to the villagers and to those who have sent them into the field. In seeking to justify their existence in the village, they often feel compelled to introduce changes, any changes, to build a health clinic, complete a water system, establish a marketing activity, etc., so that when they leave they can say "Look what I have accomplished!!" What is not understood by the outsider is that the project completed was the intern's project, not the villagers. No matter how much the villagers may say that they accept the ideas, the suggestions, the projects defined by the intern, when the intern leaves, their project will die, and his or her ideas will often be forgotten. This is the challenge of sustainability. I hope that each intern and professional RDF that might read this book, will remember this simple but most profound truth.

Key Weaknesses in Past Development Strategies

Before we outline the various steps related to an effective and sustainability process of rural development, let us outline the common problems associated with past rural development projects. Organizations and governments seeking to deal with rural poverty in the world have generally approached this problem from one of three different ways. **First**, when there is a famine, a drought, or some natural calamity, the rich nations of the world are generally willing to provide short-term relief, ensuring that food and clothing are distributed to those in need. **Second**, while government programs do allocate budgetary funds to provide schools, health centers, and other government programs, they are too often based upon a political process that tends to benefit the urban and near urban areas first. If there is any resources available, and unfortunately there seldom is, they will then consider the needs of the more difficult to reach. These are the poorest of the poor, those in isolated rural areas, often disadvantaged minority groups, with ethnic and religious backgrounds different from the urban majority, and thus are more often apt to be forgotten or ignored. **Third**, are the non-government organizations (NGOs) that do seek to reach the rural poor, but again tend to help those who are easiest to reach, where the paved roads go, where people already have many of their basic needs met.

I am increasingly appalled and frustrated at how resources are allocated and distributed in the world of poverty alleviation. I have four major concerns related to how resources have been allocated and distributed in the past. These concerns are related to: (1) how funds are allocated through a highly centralized, top-down process, (2) how such funds tend to be used for quick, one time solutions to the problems of the poor (3) how such programs to help the poor are seldom sustainable and often cause more problems than they solve, and finally (4) how such programs too often reinforce dependency relationships common to most welfare systems rather than to strengthen self-help systems that build self-esteem, dignity and the skills and local resources needed for people to be able to solve their own problems.[1]

Challenge of a Centralized, Top Down Distribution System

Since the early 1950s, it is estimated that probably $100 billion have been given to Less Developed Countries (LDCs) and yet less than 1 percent of that money would have ever reached this bottom twenty percent of humanity. This is because the money is too often allocated for the middle and upper poor of these societies, because of the administrative costs that are retained in urban centers, and sadly because of the corruption of many local politicians and officials. Secondly, another $20 billion have been given through private voluntary organizations (PVOs) and non-government organizations (NGOs), and yet only about 30 percent of these funds have reached the poorest of the poor, again because of relatively high administrative costs and also because there is still a tendency to distribute such resources to the middle and upper poor who are more readily available in and around urban centers.

The Problem of the Quick, One Time Solution

Too often, development programs are designed and implemented with the idea of providing a quick, one time solution. The solution is generally defined in terms of the amount of money spent. The implicit assumption is that the more the better. Such approaches will pour millions of dollars into a given area, regardless of the capacity of that area effectively to absorb such resources in the time allocated for the implementation of the project. When it comes to a process of long-term development, the issue is not how much is available, but how it is distributed and used. If I had one million dollars to spend on rural poverty in a given area, I would rather spend only $100,000 per year over ten years or even $50,000 over twenty years than to spend the entire million is just one year. Development is a long-term process that requires the gradual stimulation of local initiative, the strengthening of local institutions based upon local leadership, self-help, and local resource mobilization. The worse thing you can do is to pour huge amounts of resources into an area in a short period of time. Generally such resources are squandered on inappropriate technology and complex administrative systems with the outsiders responsible for implementing the project taking the lion's share of the resources available.

The Issues of How to Make Programs Sustainable

One of the crucial issues in Development Administration is the problem of sustainability, that is, how to ensure that after a project is completed that the programs and services established will be sustained after the outsiders leave. Most large development projects require a number of outsiders: experts, administrators, consultants and various professionals. Studies commissioned by the World Bank have documented that less that one of these large projects in five are truly sustainable after they have been implemented because the administrative and operational costs of the project simply cannot be sustained by the community where it is established. I have seen millions and millions of dollars wasted on projects that were designed and implemented by outsiders that did not consider whether the program being established could be sustained over time. Generally, the local people simply do not have the money, the resources, and the skills to support large, programs being established by outsiders.

The True Purpose of Development is Often Forgotten

The key to long-term development in these local areas requires that the people themselves learn to identify their own problems, design their own programs, and then implement and manage those programs through their own resources. The development strategies of the past simply ignored the fact that most outside development projects merely reinforced the feelings of dependency and apathy that too often characterizes the poorest of the poor in a given area. What is needed is a strategy that will stimulate local initiative, encourage local capacity building, provide incentives and motivation to solve their own problems and to mobilize their own local resources needed to solve their own problems. Often a few thousand dollars a year from an outside source will stimulate more local initiative and sense of self-help than many millions of dollars dumped into an area with no regard for the long term consequences of such funding.

The Need for a Community-Based Approach

There are many organizations that are attempting to help the less developed areas of the world, and I would suggest that such organizations tend to fall into one of four kinds of groups:

A. **Short-term Disaster Relief Organizations.** Such organizations seek to provide food, clothing, shelter and medical care for people faced with serious drought, famine, and natural catastrophes. The purpose of these kinds of organizations are for immediate and short-term relief activities, and are very important in times of need. Roughly 13 percent of all development organizations fall into this category, and collectively spend approximately 9 percent of the resources available for the less developed countries dealing with problems of world poverty.

B. **Large-scale Technical Assistance Organizations:** Outside experts funded by national and international organizations implement programs in economic and social development. Such organizations as the World Bank, USAID, UNDP and other large donor agencies introduce new techniques in agriculture, literacy, health services and other types of outside interventions. Too often, the work is done by outside experts and little time is spent on developing local leadership or local institutions that will sustain the technical assistance after it has been implemented. Such organizations make up only about 10 percent of the development organizations, but account for nearly 60 percent of all world-wide development expenditures.

C. **Small-Scale Technical Assistance Approach.** Private Voluntary Organizations (PVOs) and Non-Government Organizations (NGOs) make up over 75 percent of development organizations in the world, but probably provide less than 30 percent of world-wide spending. Such programs are often based on private sector initiatives which seek to encourage small-scale enterprises and to provide local health, welfare and literacy programs. While the efforts of this third type of development organization are certainly based upon good intentions, too often such interventions simply strengthen feelings of dependency and welfarism that characterize many poverty programs both in this country and abroad. We have learned that when you give food, money and technology to people with no effort or sacrifice required of the people receiving the assistance, the results are almost never sustainable and often create more problems than they solve.

D. **Local Institution Building/District Networking and Empowerment Approach.** There are a few organizations today that are approaching development from a different perspective. This fourth approach to development recognizes that only when people organize and manage their own efforts, utilize their own resources, and utilize local institutions and local leadership, will long-term development be sustainable. Experience of the past decade, in particular, has reinforced the notion that community development and local institution building (cooperative, village development committees, mother's clubs, small credit groups, etc.) is a much more effective way to ensure that projects will be relevant, sustainable and appropriate for a given community. Long-term sustainability requires a coordinated linkage system between clusters of villages and district level government and non government groups, agencies, and institutions willing to emphasize local institution building and popular empowerment strategies and interventions. In Chapter 16 below, this approach is outlined in detail, suggesting a new form of implementation through Non government Networking Organizations. Such organizations make up less than two percent of all development organizations and probably have access to less than one percent of the resources available for development work. One major conclusion of this book is that foreign aid strategies of the future must seriously consider this approach in allocating resources for future sustainable processes of rural development.

A New Coordinated Strategy Ready to be Implemented

A careful reflection on these types of organizations and the four characteristics of traditional development strategizing mentioned above should provide the basis upon which a new more effective strategy might be implemented. In a study of the kinds of approaches that have proven to be successful in the implementation of effective, sustainable rural development projects, the following five pre-requisites have been identified: (1) successful projects were generally much smaller than unsuccessful projects, and thus structured to reflect the absorptive capacity of the community, (2) the people responsible for the design and implementation of the project tended to be local people, rather than outside experts and officials, (3) the project tended to use appropriate technology which could be implemented using local resources, skills and materials, (4) the project was carefully planned to ensure that local leadership and local institutions, were strengthened and used. Local institutions were encouraged to develop their own system of local resource mobilization through strategies of networking and linkage building to outside sources of funding and support, and (5) the system of development used was based upon the local cultural, the local social structure and local traditions that provided a sense of pride, continuity and self-esteem in the community.[2]

As a way of helping the reader understand how an effective community-based village development program might be implemented, let me outline a program that I have been intimately involved with for over ten years. Using the success of this program as a case study may make the process we are advocating become more real. In 1986, an organization called CHOICE (The Center for Humanitarian Outreach and Inter cultural Exchange)[3] was established to field-test this five-prong approach in a number of areas in Latin America, Asia, and Africa. Through a gradual process of learning, a strategy has been field-tested in a number of areas and is now being implemented, on a much broader scale, in a number of areas.

This strategy used by the CHOICE organization has three components that are being integrated and synchronized in order to maximize the utilization of the scarce resources that might be available. The **first component** requires the organization and implementation of short-term expeditions into various isolated rural areas both to determine needs and to develop a working relationship with the local people. The **second component** requires the training and placement of a group of student interns willing to live and work in these areas for at least 6-12 months at a time. The **third component** requires the recruitment and support of local villagers, trained to be rural development facilitators (RDFs), who are willing to work in their communities for a five to seven year period.

1. Expeditions:

Very few development organizations have seen the value of organizing expeditions into the areas where the poorest of the poor live. It is much more common for such organizations to merely give their resources to some agency which is then responsible to use the money as they see fit. The value and importance of expeditions became apparent only after several years of working with such expeditions. The idea of allowing a group of non-professional people from America to visit and work in an isolated rural village in Africa, Asia or Latin America actually happened by chance. In response to an ad in a local newspaper asking if there were any carpenters that might be willing to bring their own tools and pay their own expenses to go and help build a small school in Bolivia, we were amazed at the number of people who indicated an interest in going and working in a rural setting in South America. This spirit of humanitarian voluntarism is one of the truly unique qualities of American life. These expeditions which generally last two to three weeks in length have some very interesting characteristics that have come to be an important and integral part of this strategy for rural development in the less developed countries of the world.

Great Learning Experience. These expeditions have been a great learning experience for the participants. People who have never traveled into isolated rural areas are amazed at the beauty of the countryside, the uniqueness of cultural diversity, and the hospitality and warm hearts of the villagers toward them. These CHOICE expeditions provide a consciousness-raising experience that cannot be duplicated in any other way. People, with little experience outside the US, have had their mind sets expanded and they have come to realize how blessed they are and how just a few resources used in appropriate ways can have an incredible impact on the lives of these village people. Equally significant are the number of participants from all over the United States, after seeing what a few dollars can really accomplish in a disadvantaged village, have become active fund raisers and advocates for overseas development programs.

The Concept of Rural Development

An Alternative Vacation Experience. Some people might wonder if the funds used to bring these people to Africa or Asia or Latin America might better be donated directly to these poor people. While most of the American volunteers tend to go on some type of vacation each year anyway, to give them an opportunity to spend this money on some humanitarian project instead of going to Disneyland or Hawaii is a wonderful way to expand their horizons. Many participants have said that an expedition into a poor village with no electricity, no potable water, and certainly no tourist facilities, was one of the most meaningful and significant events in their lives; and that their family, through interacting together in these villages, was closer and more appreciative than ever before.

Help Meet a Local Need. These expeditions are organized to help complete a village school, a health facility, a water project or other need activities. Choice expeditions only go into villages where they are asked to assist with a project the community has determined it needs and is already seeking to implement. It is important that whatever we give, will be only a small part of the overall cost of the project; that our resources are used to leverage local resources. We want the villagers to see the project as theirs and not ours. Over the past ten years CHOICE has seen several hundred projects completed: village schools, primary health care units, greenhouses, various income generating projects, and small community water systems, including wells and pumps, etc.

Building a Trusting Relationship. Finally these expeditions help develop a relationship between the CHOICE organization and these villagers. They help build trust and better understanding, and most significantly, stimulate community cooperation, social energy and excitement. For many of these villagers this is the first time that any outsider has come into their village, has worked side by side with them. I am convinced that these expeditions, while not absolutely necessary for a village to develop, are nevertheless an important component in the process of sustainable development for it simulates greater community cohesiveness and cooperation and gives the villagers a sense of hope and excitement that is not always easy to stimulate in many of these poor villages. It is important that these expeditions be seen as a crucial part of the process by which a community comes to take responsibility for its own development. Such expeditions build upon and help reinforce the next two components of sustainable village development. Also it is important to see that the process of expeditions is completely self-funding since each expedition participant pays his or her own expenses.

2. Internships:

The second component of this sustainable process of village development allows a number of students to participate in a mini-Peace Corps experience of 6 months to a year. Such interns need to be mature, competent young people, willing to live and work in village community and completely versed in the process of rural development. We have come to see these interns as an important part of this strategy for the following reasons:

Opportunity of Field Experience. Such internships offer students interested in pursuing a career in development an opportunity to gain field experience in a foreign country. Many of these students already have language skills and a strong desire to work in overseas situations. Many companies have trade relationships with other countries or are seeking to develop such relationships in the future and are happy to support this internship program as it gives potential employees the opportunity to work overseas, to gain greater awareness and understanding of other cultures and peoples. The CHOICE organization has raised money to support roughly 20 interns a year. Those supporting this intern program have been very impressed with the quality of student interns, with their dedication and commitment to work in less than comfortable surroundings. There is no question that such an experience has positive consequences for these young people.

Importance of Follow-up. One of the motives for organizing internships was the realization that after the excitement of an expedition, the villagers often felt abandoned. Frequently, there is no one in the community that can and will reinforce this social energy into a longer-term process of community development. Interns have been extremely useful in structuring a series of follow-up activities.

Identification of Local Leadership and Future RDFs. One of the major aspects of long-term development is the identification and recruitment of local people to eventually become full-time rural development facilitators (RDFs). An important advantage of having these student interns living and working in the village for an extended period of time, is that it allows us to become better acquainted with the community, its culture, its way of life, its long-term needs, what resources are already available, and who are the real leaders in the village, both present and potential. One of the significant purposes of the internship program is to allow these students to help us identify local people from the village areas who can be trained and supported as long-term RDFs.

On-Going Assessment of Projects. The final advantage of having an intern living and working in the village is his or her ability to monitor how resources are being used, and who can be trusted to use such resources effectively. These interns are encouraged to build relationships with local government officials, and other agencies and organizations that might have resources to help meet the needs of the villagers. Some organizations tend to use only outsiders as their representative in the village, feeling that local people often cannot be trusted to use their resources in a responsible way. Of course, as long as outsiders are the only one's able to utilize and allocate such resources, local leadership and responsible self-help activities will probably never develop. On the other hand, a number of organizations have gone the other way, tending to rely mostly on local people to represent their organization in the village. While village people are generally much more effective than outsiders, local representatives are often tempted to use an outside organization's resources for their own personal use. Many development organizations have been burned by their inability to monitor all that was going on in a given community. All too often, such resources are used for the benefit of family members and other close friends of the local representative. CHOICE has found that a successful long-term process requires the placement of interns to provide a "check and balance" system which includes regular communication back to the supporting organization.[4] While one highly qualified local RDF can be ten times more effective in organizing and stimulating sustainable programs than most outsiders, the interns, however, will still play a significant role in helping us identify and assess who should be recruited, trained and supported. Having such interns in the village has proven to be invaluable to this process.

3. Rural Development Facilitators (RDFs)

Importance of a Long-Term Local RDF. As has been stated before, a local person trained and supported by an outside organization can be far more effective than an outsider if there are mechanisms for monitoring and assessing his or her performance over time. Such RDFs generally can be hired for something less than $6000 a year. One common mistake made by development organizations is to keep such RDFs on their payroll for long-periods of time. When RDFs are in their twenties and thirties, they are much more willing to live and work in the village, but when they are in their forties or fifties, they start wanting to live in urban areas, they insist on much higher salaries to help pay for their children's education and other expenses related to living in a town or city. From the experience of CHOICE, it appears better to hire RDFs and to explain right up front that the commitment to them is not intended to be more than five to seven years. In fact as they approach five years, they should be looking for a new job and should be training a younger person to take their place. When RDFs have had five years experience in village work, it is relatively easy for them to find work with various government agencies or other organizations that are willing to pay a high percentage of their budgets for administrative and personnel costs. It is important that these RDFs are committed to living and working in the village and not in a nearby town. When their salaries get above the average salary of the local professionals (village teachers, health workers, extension workers) they gradually want to live in a more comfortable situation, where the amenities of urban life are found. When salaries for RDFs are greatly increased, their willingness to live and work in the village on a full time basis is dramatically reduced.

Expanding to Clusters of Villages. Such RDFs can be effective in creating a network of village projects, perhaps covering as many as 50 to 100 villages over a 4-5 year period of time. From my experience, a well trained and culturally sensitive RDF can visit a number of villages, help the villagers prepare to have an expedition visit these villages, identify potential health care workers, literacy workers and small scale enterprise entrepreneurs. The RDF recruits and trains these para-professionals, who generally will be supported by their own community with some supplemental funds from outside sources. Such non-professionals can start the process of health, education and employment generation activities until government resources become available. I have seen RDFs in a number of countries organize whole clusters of villages, identifying and encouraging local leaders, helping to encourage community decision-making, stimulating local resource mobilization and thus starting the process of community development in a number of villages.

Implementing Projects in the Five Dimensions of Rural Development. Such RDFs can be a conduit for the efficient introduction of outside resources from governmental and non-governmental agencies in the **five basic dimensions** of rural development: 1) educational programs, including school construction and the encouragement of adult literacy, 2) primary health programs, sanitation and fresh water systems, 3) small scale enterprise encouragement and the use of appropriate technology to increase agricultural productivity. 4) increasing the community's awareness of their environment (lakes, forests, soils and wildlife) and how it can be protected and preserved over time. 5) the strengthening of local cultural systems in the arts, dance, music, poetry and local handicrafts,

The strength of this **three-component strategy** is dependent on the integration of the expeditions, the internship program and the RDFs in a targeted area. Successful long-term development requires the gradual improvement of local leadership, the opportunity to develop local capacities in problem identification, program design and implementation. The long-term goal is to establish local institutions that can function without outside support and help: such as cooperatives, village health committees, women's organizations, small scale enterprises that enhance employment opportunities, and social and cultural organizations that stimulate villager pride and individual dignity. Such a process probably requires ten perhaps twenty years, as old ways are changed and new ways are learned.

The Time Has Come
to Create a Long-term-Sustainable Program

My experience in working with rural development programs over the past thirty years suggests lessons that need to be emphasized.

First, many organizations will start a project with an adequate budget to continue their work in the village for usually one year, two years at most. Such short-term commitments merely reinforce the notion that nothing can be done unless there are outsiders working in our village. This tends to reinforce dependency, frustration and apathy. What is needed is an strategy that can guarantee a long-term commitment in an area, at least five to ten years minimum.

The Concept of Rural Development

Second, most rural development organizations structure their programs around single year commitments for they are totally dependent on their annual fund-raising efforts. If the fund raising is successful, projects can be funded. If the fund raising is unsuccessful, projects cannot be funded. I have seen many organizations start and then discontinue their projects because of a lack of funds, and thus the cumulative impact needed over a number of years is never realized.

Third, when an organization is totally dependent upon its annual fund-raising capacity to maintain its presence in a given rural area, much organizational energy and expertise is taken away from the process of village development to the more mundane task of raising money. It is for this reason that the final characteristic of this strategy for village development must be the establishment of an Endowment Fund, large enough to provide a steady stream of income from the interest earned each year. For example, with an Endowment Fund of $5-10 million, a community-based approach would probably be in a position to guarantee $500,000 or more each year on an almost perpetual basis. RDFs would then know that their salary did not depend on any fund raising campaign that might or might not succeed and thus would be much more apt to make a long-term commitment. By keeping overhead down (a common problem among most NGOs and PVOs) and ensuring that no RDF would be allowed to work beyond the seven year mark, the funds from such an Endowment Fund would be available indefinitely.

Over the past twenty years I have watched millions of dollars allocated for short-term projects, generally with no planning as to how such programs would be sustained over time. In one project, I saw $15 million spent to implement a water pump project in several hundred villages in the Indonesia. When I was invited to review the impact of that $15 million, I was appalled to see that nearly 85 percent of the pumps were not working. No one had thought to teach the villagers to repair or maintain these pumps and the resources used had no long-term impact at all. Imagine what that fifteen million dollars might have done, if it had been put into an Endowment Fund, where the interest earned could have been used to provide water pumps conditioned on the local community's demonstrated ability to repair and maintain these pumps. Such an Endowment Fund would still be providing support to the villagers in Indonesia long after those earlier pumps had worn out and were discarded. It is absolutely amazing what a RDF can do in a village community with even a few hundred dollars along with the mobilization of the villagers' own local resources, materials and labor.

Section Three
The Three Step Process of Rural Development

People who visit a Third World village on some type of humanitarian expedition, often wonder if their efforts really will make a difference. There is much evidence to suggest that these expeditions play a very important role in stimulating local social energy and a sense of hope and excitement that cannot be developed in any other way. While such expeditions may build a school or a clinic, dig a well or help repair a road, what is far more important, is the impact of these expeditions on the people themselves. For the first time, they begin to realize that they are not alone, that some of their problems can be solved through their own efforts, and there is a new pride and an enhanced sense of enthusiasm that cannot be measured and will not always be apparent to a group of outsiders staying in the village for only a few days or weeks. Let us now review how the sequencing of certain activities are to be structured and how such sequencing will have a more cumulative impact over time.

I. Sequencing of the Three Stages of Rural Development

```
            Year 1 Year 2 Year 3 Year 5 Year 7 Year 10
Stage One   ---------------->
Stage Two           ------------------------------------>
Stage Three                 ------------------------------------------------------------->
```

Stage One: Trust Building
Time Frame   (One to Two Years)

Stage One is a period of time when helping and trust building are the dominate activities.[5] During the first year or so when individuals and groups are initially coming into a village community, the various activities being implemented are far more humanitarian than development in their impact. After all, during this stage of the process, much of the initiative, the resources, and the responsibility rest with the outsiders. During this stage it will generally be an intern and/or outside expedition participants who have initiated the process and helped to build the relationships needed for a community to move to stage two. In the first stage the following things are happening:

(1) **Awareness** of the villagers reality: their problems, concerns and needs are being identified and documented,
(2) **Sensitivity** and appreciation for the local culture are encouraged,
(3) **Trust Building** between the outsiders and the villagers is being strengthened by identifying and working with formal and informal leaders.

Activities in the Five Dimensions of Development During the First Stage

During this first stage of village development certain types of activities will be encouraged in the five dimensions of development.

1. **Culture:** Information on the history and culture of the community (dances, music, rituals, important concepts, ideals, values and traditions) will be collected.

The Concept of Rural Development

2. Health: The level of infant mortality and the need for potable water will be determined and the community will be encouraged to discuss ways to deal with these health problems. Some preliminary health projects will be implemented.

3. Education: The level of illiteracy and the level of interest in building a primary school will be determined. Some preliminary efforts to build a primary school will be implemented.

4. Income: Determine the level of income in the community, the role of agriculture in generating present levels of income, the opportunities to create credit groups and small scale enterprises will be assessed.

5. Ecology: The opportunities for protecting and enhancing the productive capacity of the land and the environment in the community will be assessed and discussed in the community.

Stage Two: Capacity Building
   Time Frame   Three to Five Years

During Stage Two, the relationship between the outside agency and the village is more of an equal partnership with the villagers beginning to take far more responsibility than was noticed in Stage One.[6] In Stage Two, there will be a full-time professionally trained Rural Development Facilitator (RDF) living and working in the village for extended periods of time to help in the Capacity Building phase of village development. During Stage Two the following kinds of activities will dominate the process:

(1) **Develop ownership** among the villagers for the problems that need to be solved using group discussion techniques and local participation activities. Develop ownership for possible solutions that the villagers can implement to solve these problems.

(2) **Encourage and Support Local Problem Solving Groups** Using training and group development activities to stimulate capacity building in the planning, implementing and evaluating of projects, problem solving groups will be developed over time.

(3) Encouraging the use of **Appropriate Technology** that utilizes local resources and material, utilizes or helps develop local skills and competencies, and does not increase dependency on outside groups.

Activities in the Five Dimensions of Development During the Second Stage
1. Culture: History and culture of the community will be collected and published in a simple form and such material will be distributed to the community as a whole

2. Health: A small clinic will be built and a number of village health care workers will be trained and supported by a combination of local and outside resources.

3. Education: Both a children and an adult literacy program will be implemented in the community and the curriculum will be structured to reflect the real needs of the villagers.
4. Income: A number of villager credit groups will be trained and organized and/or a program to help increase agricultural productivity and develop a number of small scale enterprises in the community will be developed related to greater food production and increased income.
5. Ecology: Implement some type of environment protection and enhancement program, including improved housing, sanitation facilities and beautification of the community.

Stage Three Local Institution Building
     Time Frame   Five to Ten Years
The ultimate goal of village development is the establishment of local institutions managed and supported by the community itself. The process of **Institution Building** is a cumulative process that builds on the first two stages and thus may take anywhere from six to ten years.[7] During the third stage local village leadership begins to take over the process of village development. The full-time RDF gradually withdraws from the community as the villagers demonstrate their own ability to mobilize their own resources and manage their own institutions. This is the what village development is all about. The following activities dominate this stage:
(1) **Institution Building** ensures the sustainability of village projects through the strengthening of local leadership and systems of local participation.
(2) Successful **empowerment** of the community to solve their own problems with less dependency on outside help with a focus on building of networks and linkage mechanism between the villagers and various outside agencies and organizations, and through the establishment of coalitions and local resource mobilization efforts.
(3) **Commitment** to the creation of autonomous local institutions and action steps that allow the local community to pursue activities that meet their long term needs for a better quality of life defined and determined as they see fit.

Activities in the Five Dimensions of Development During the Third Stage[8]
1. Culture: Establishment of local institutions that enhance the cultural life of the community in the fields of literature, music, art, dance and community values.
2. Health: Establishment of a self-sustaining health committee that guides and directs the work of local health workers in the community and ensures local resource mobilization to help pay for all or at least part of the salaries, supplies and equipment needed in the community health facility.
3. Education: Establishment of a local PTA organization accountable to the community and organized to provide feedback and support to the local school teachers in the community

The Concept of Rural Development

4. Income: Establishment of locally managed credit systems and productive cooperatives and other small scale enterprises linked to various regional or national systems of credit, marketing and production systems.

5. Ecology: Establishment of a Village Environmental Protection Committee committed to planning and organizing activities and projects that will enhance and protect the local environment, improve the quality of housing for all and the institutionalization of a community beautification program.

An understanding of the processes of village development requires that we understand both the **sequencing** of the three steps outlined above and the **integration** of the five dimensions of rural development: both interns and RDFs must come to see the interrelationship that exists among the five dimensions of rural development and the process of leadership building in the community. The process of identifying local leaders, establishing local problem solving committees, and other activities related to rural development must understand both the impact and interrelationship of all five dimensions and the process of moving from an unorganized rather simplistic process of village problem solving to a much more institutionalized sustainable process of problem solving. A detailed description of this process will be outlined below in Chapters Eight and Nine.

Analysis of the Five Dimensions' Impact on Each Other
1. Awareness of the Impact of the Local Culture on:
Health: The traditional ways of dealing with health and maternal needs.

Education: The traditional socializing mechanisms for teaching children about the traditions and customs of the community

Income: The traditional ways of making a living, the technologies and methods used and why such methods have proven so appropriate in the past for the community.

Ecology: The relationship between the people and the land, the forests, the rivers, the animals and plant life in the area, an appreciation of traditional housing and traditional systems of community beautification.

2. Awareness of the Impact of Health on:
Culture: How traditional health workers might be introduced to modern medicine and how the two systems (traditional and modern) might learn to work together

Education: How the local health system might be used to teach concepts of sanitation, nutrition, and better health care systems in the local schools.

Income: How many hours are lost each year when villagers are ill and how productivity might be improved if the level of health in the community could be improved.

Ecology: How better health is related to the quality of the environment through better systems of sanitation and cleanliness.

3. Awareness of the Impact of Education on:

Culture: How the school system might enhance and help strengthen local traditions and cultural values that are revered by the community.

Health: How the school system might teach students about sanitation, good health and nutrition and the importance of good health in the community.

Income: How the school system might teach skills and competencies that would increase the income generating activities of the community.

Ecology: How the school system might teach about the environment and how its needs to be protected, through community cleanliness and beautification.

4. Awareness of the Impact of Income Generating Activities on:

Culture: How local resource mobilizing activities could be used to finance cultural awareness and the strengthening of local traditions in the community.

Health: How local resource mobilizing activities could be used to finance better health services, pay the salaries of village health workers, and purchase needed supplies.

Education: How local resource mobilizing activities could be used to finance better educational opportunities in the community for children and adults.

Ecology: How local resource mobilizing activities could be used to finance the protection and enhancement of the local environment, help finance better housing, and by implementing a community beautification program.

5. Awareness of the Impact of Ecology on:

Culture: How the local environment impacts on the local culture, on people's pride and their sense of community.

Health: How the local environment impacts on the local health system through improved health and sanitation.

Education: How the local environment impacts on the local school system.

Income: How the local environment impacts on the local economy.

Both interns and RDFs must carefully assess how these five dimensions impact on each other, must help the villagers to understand these interrelationships, and must assess the impact that a project or activity in one of these dimensions would have on the other dimensions. An awareness and sensitivity of these interrelationships do not come easily and outsiders, in particular, must be patient and open-minded to the ways in which these five dimensions are defined and understood by the villagers. In Units Three and Four, the reader will find a very detailed outline of programs, strategies and interventions that interns and RDFs can use in helping villagers to move through these three stages of rural development.

We are now ready to consider a series of case studies which should provide a better understanding as to how rural development programs have been implemented in the past, how individuals seeking to introduce change in a given rural situation have accomplished their tasks, and to what extent we might be able to generate a set of specific principles that seem to be related to successful rural development activities. Having been exposed to the three stages of rural development outlined in this chapter and having considered how the five dimensions of rural development are interrelated, the reader is invited to review these case studies and to assess to what extent they confirm or disconfirm the ideas outlined above.

Case One
The Y. C. James Yen Story[9]

Dr. Y. C. James Yen is an extraordinary man. Now in his nineties he can look back on nearly sixty years of a life of total dedication to mass education and rural reconstruction, first in China and now throughout the world. Rural development and widespread concern for the peasants and farmers of the underdeveloped world is generally conceded to be a post World War II phenomenon, yet in the 1920s James Yen had already mapped out his life's work. He would commit himself to the rural peasants of China. With fierce determination and engaging enthusiasm, he recruited a group of devoted coworkers who, with great patience and perseverance, lit a new beacon of hope for the rural communities of China.

In 1943 at the age of 50, Dr. Yen along with such greats as Albert Einstein, Henry Ford, John Dewy, Orville Wright and others, was awarded the "Copernican Citation" as one of ten "modern revolutionaries." Dr. Yen had indeed sparked an educational revolution in China. In less than twenty years -- using a strategy of rural development that is as "modern" today as it was unique and innovative in the 1920s -- a transformation of gigantic proportions commenced in which some 50 million rural Chinese were introduced to the wonders of education.

Concern for the poor and illiterate peasants of the countryside had challenged men in many countries: Mahatma Gandhi in India, Pere Aryout in Egypt, Paulo Freire ii, Brazil, Akhter Hameed Khan in Bangladesh, Magsaysay in the Philippines, Dr. Puey in Thailand and many others. Dr. Yen is unique, both because his work in rural areas predates that of most of these men by many decades, but most importantly because he moved beyond the limited region where his effort began to the important task of sensitizing the world's intellectual community to the poverty, exploitation, and tragic waste of human resources to be found among the majority of this planet's population. His ultimate contribution is the work he initiated in the Ting Hsien district of rural China where a pioneering "social laboratory" was established to develop, test, and put into operation a comprehensive strategy for development through rural reconstruction.

Y. C. James Yen was born in China in 1893 in the province of Szechuan, the son of a venerated scholarly family -- a family that traces its genealogy back to the time of Confucius through a long line of teachers and scholars. As a young boy James was given a classical education in ancient Chinese learning including the Four Books and the Five Classics, poetry, and the religious tradition of Confucianism and Christianity. A love of learning was a part of his family tradition, and his father recognized the importance of exposing his son to the science and technology of the West. At the age of eleven, James Yen entered the Chinese Mission School in Paoning. His formal education eventually culminated in a degree from Yale University in 1918.'

World War I came to be an important turning point in his life when young Yen was recruited by the YMCA to help supervise some 5000 Chinese laborers performing construction work in the trenches and battlefields of France. Here for the first time, James Yen, the scholar, found himself face-to-face with a level of Chinese society that he would never have experienced in his homeland. Here were the "coolies," which in Chinese means "bitter strength," far from their families and homes, assigned the backbreaking tasks that no one else would do. Mostly of the peasant class, they could neither read nor write. Education in China has always been the prerogative (If a small group of intellectuals. Yet Yen came to know these men -- their problems, their concerns, their fears. Often in the evening this young Chinese intellectual was asked to transcribe simple letters of love and communication to friends and family in far-off China.

Pearl S. Buck describes this first encounter between James Yen and the coolies in these words: "He found them ignorant and helpless when it came to expressing themselves on paper but he knew by watching them that they were strong and resourceful and able with their hands. That they could not read and write was no fault of their own. He came to see that though these men wee illiterate they were not really ignorant. They thought shrewdly and profoundly, they understood, with a sort of practical common sense, the things they saw around them in France, they had lively humor and warm hearts.

It was here in France, working with these illiterate Chinese coolies that James Yen discovered his destiny -- his life's mission. For a man of less conviction, his task of bringing education to the masses of China would have appeared an impossibility. Yet as he himself loves to say, "The journey of one thousand miles must start with the first step." How does one explain the life, the commitment, the sense of purpose that has motivated this man for over sixty years? It is clear he saw a *challenge* -- how to make complex and extremely difficult written Chinese intelligible to illiterate and presumably ignorant peasants. He also had a *dream*, a premonition of what could be. He envisioned that, while written Chinese has in excess of 40,000 unique characters, and that a minimum of 5000 are needed to perform the basics of reading and writing, a simplified version of say 1000 characters could be devised that would allow a simple peasant to learn the magic and joy of education. When he challenged his coolies to this monumental undertaking only forty volunteered, they themselves being rather skeptical. Yet a miracle did happen. Within four months thirty-five of his original group of students demonstrated, to the amazement of their fellow workers, that a Chinese peasant could learn to read and to write. Motivated by the clamor for more classes, and recognizing the need to provide additional reading material, James Yen established his one thousand character newspaper -- The Chinese Laborer's Weekly. In seeking an explanation for the way in which the spiritual/emotional dimension becomes operational it is significant that James Yen was piqued by the tragedy of his people's illiteracy and compelled by the possibility of changing them, but a simple event in Yen's life cemented his conviction. From a peasant he received the following letter: "Mr. Yen, big teacher: Ever since the publishing of your paper I began to know everything under the heavens. But your paper is so cheap and costs only one centime a copy, you may have to close down your Paper soon. Here please find enclosed 365 francs which I have saved during my three years labor in France."

Yen comments: "That is the kind of thing that touched me. I determined to use my life to enlarge his life. The word 'coolie' became for me a new word. I said, I will free him from his bitterness and help him to develop his strength." No one can help but be moved by the simplicity yet profundity that characterized this interaction. Out of this type of experience dedication was early engendered and commitment was to be sustained. In a lecture given in 1979 Yen talked of the letter described above and of his feelings at that time: "This letter started a revolution in me. For centuries we had taken for granted that these peasants -- these coolies -- were far beyond educating; that they were stupid, lazy and all that. But I made a personal discovery -- these coolies were men of tremendous potential. After twelve hours hard work in the trenches, they would come to my camp, without supper sometimes, because they were afraid to miss my course. They were able to master the basics of the Chinese spoken language. I began to realize that what these humble, common people of my country lacked was not brains, for God has given that to them, but opportunity. Right there and then I resolved that upon my return to China, I would not go into politics nor business. I was going to devote the rest of my life to finding opportunities for education, for development of these wonderful, educable millions of my country. . . . They had potential powers waiting for development, waiting for release. Our basic philosophy is not relief, but release. These self-respecting hard working peasants do not want relief from anybody."

James Yen returned to China in 1921, his soul burning with a desire to bring literacy to the masses in China. Working through the Chinese YMCA, the young student recruited a corps of teachers who gradually spread throughout China. In 1922, utilizing his "People's Thousand Character Reader," a program of speeches, parades, and public discussions, James Yen and his associates organized classes in temples, shops, in private homes. The success of his first reader made a second and third inevitable. Soon this project was so successful in Changsha that the YMCA established similar programs in other cities.

James Yen, the scholar, became James Yen the "master organizer. Supported and encouraged by Madame Hsi-ling Hsiung, wife of China's then prime Minister, Yen spearheaded the establishment of the National Association of the Mass Education Movement in Peking in 1923. His salary, as executive director was $50 per month and his staff was limited to on part-time clerk. During the following six years, he vigorously pursued his literacy campaign -- reaching many tens of thousands during this period. It was not difficult to interest the people of China in this literacy movement. It made an appeal to the patriotism of the people in their realization of China's appallingly high percentage of illiteracy compared with most other countries.

The Ting Hsien Experiment

It was not long before Yen came to realize that the idea of giving the farmers and laborers of China an opportunity to join the ranks of the literate through devoting no more than an hour a day for four months to a study of a thousand specially selected characters would only lead to grievous disappointment if those who possess this hastily acquired knowledge found that it left them no better off economically or socially than had they not spent the time in acquiring this new skill. Yen describes an incident that dramatized this need to move beyond the mere eradication of illiteracy:

There was this farmer who had just learned how to read. One day, he approached me and said: "Teacher, I can read. My neighbor cannot read. But my stomach is just as empty as his stomach." What that simple man said, it seemed to me, was not just a simple remark but a challenge. It made us feel so inadequate. For the first time in Chinese history, we had created a new literature for them. We did something very simple and modest about feeding their empty heads, but did nothing to feed their empty stomachs.

The challenge of that simple question "What good does it do to increase literacy if we fail to deal with the tragic problems of poverty, hunger, disease, and misgovernment?" set the stage for a fourfold program developed and institutionalized in Ting Hsien. Thus while literacy might be a first step, obviously a more extensive and more far-reaching program was needed. Yet the challenge of developing a broad approach that might have an impact on some 300 million rural peasants was not only formidable, to say the least, but it was presumptuous to even consider it.

The basic unit of government in China of the 1920s and 1930s was the *hsien* or county. Since there were some 1900 such units of government, Yen realized that if a workable pattern for rural development could he established -- empirically validated, perhaps tested in a "social laboratory" of one hsien -- then that pattern or model could be duplicated in the other 1899 *hsien*. Ting Hsien was a county area of nearly 500 square miles, with a population of roughly 400,000 people divided among some 472 separate village communities. The vast majority of the people (at least 90 percent) were illiterate peasants who sweated out their merger livings in separate family plots of land.

Responding to a friendly invitation by one of the leading gentry in the area, Yen and his few companions decided to go to the peasants in Ting Hsien. They would seek to understand their customs, master their techniques for farming, and win their confidence through friendship and service. The leader of the movement, actually living among the farmers for nearly a decade, would gradually come to appreciate the farmers' problems and concerns. Eventually through an interactive process of mutual study and learning, the peasants would he stimulated to consider practical ways in which they themselves might tackle their own problems. The atmosphere of the "social laboratory," which included in the early stages just a few village communities, would emphasize data collection, experimentation and carefully considered action steps. The constant focus of this effort was to see their experiments as part of a pilot project that once developed and tested, with some preliminary support and outside help, could be implemented by the farmers themselves in other *hsien*. Dr. Yen describes this early experience in Ting Hsien as follows: "There were no books on the peasants 50 year ago -- in Europe, in North America, in all other countries of Africa, Latin America and Asia -- nothing! Chemists have a chemical laboratory, physicists have a physical laboratory, so those of us who study human problems must have a social laboratory. If you are just sending questionnaires out, it is one thing to ask a beautiful question and quite another thing to get a beautiful answer. If we really want to help the uneducated people who comprise two thirds of the human race, we will not send out questionnaires; we are going to the people ourselves. If we want to help them, we must know them. If we want to know them, we must go to them where they happen to live? They are scattered in those thousands of dirty, poverty-stricken villages of the world."

So, a group of us, composed of college presidents, pharmacists, agriculturists, medical men, government bureau heads, and even senators, for the first time in Chinese history, left our ivory towers and went humbly to live and work with the dirty, poverty-stricken peasants. . . . For almost nine long years we stayed and learned from the people. Many in the group left, for they could not stand the strain. Several of them had the starting power but not the staying power. Some of those who went had wonderful hearts and intentions; but when they came face-to-face with the actual problems of the peasants, they were at a total loss. Others left because, with all their intentions, with all their book knowledge, they did not know what to do. Finally, there were thirty in the group who stayed, struggled on, and did not give up. Of course one must recognize that the difficulties were not only with these urban scholars. The peasants themselves were extremely suspicious that the newcomers were in quest of information about their villages upon which the government might tax them more heavily. Some others were suspicious that they might be a group of preachers seeking to introduce Christianity.

Although the inauguration of this "experiment" in Ting Hsien was greatly assisted through the introduction afforded by Mi Chien-shan, an influential member of the gentry in one village of the hsien, it was some time before the village elders throughout the hsien could be persuaded to extend to Yen and his coworkers a formal invitation. How completely they were able to generate support for their program among leading members of this hsien is evidenced by the fact that within two years after their arrival, Ting Hsien was voluntarily assigning a significant portion of its local budget in support of Yen's experiment. Yet obviously additional funds would be needed if this project were to have an extended impact.

Through a gradual process of experimentation, trying new things, succeeding and failing, it became apparent that the problems of the peasants could not be approached in a non-systematic way. The economic problems were too closely related to the social and political systems. Education programs could not be divorced from health programs, and cultural values early influenced organization efforts. Once the most crucial problems of the farmers were identified, Yen and his collaborators sought to develop a strategy, a program by which the problems of the farmers could be tackled in an integrated way. It dawned on this group of rural reconstruction people, almost as a new discovery, that certainly the most fundamental and universal problems could be classified under four key areas: poverty, disease, illiteracy and civic disintegration, and that no successful program of rural reconstruction could ignore any of these four fundamental issues.

As this staff of urban educated scholars began to move from the theories and concepts of their books to the realities of peasant problems, another discovery emerged -- the life of the village had the characteristics of a unified whole in which change introduced into one segment had deep repercussions in other segments. Thus emerged the fourfold program of integrated activities in education, health, livelihood, and local self-government.

Education

Dr. Yen acknowledges that his first village schools were very experimental. Through a trial-and-error process a set of techniques, a curriculum, and gradually a refined village level primer were produced. Initially three or four demonstration schools were established in several centrally located villages.

Once they saw how practical the teaching material was and how simple the teaching methods, they would start classes of their own and teach the illiterates in their respective communities without pay. These schools, taught and supported by the people themselves, are the people's schools. The responsibility of staffing and financing the people's schools falls upon the people. The people of Ting Hsien ran 472 people's schools, that is, one for every village, all supported by themselves.

The schedules of these schools were structured to meet the needs of the individual farmers and their families. The "elementary people's schools" allowed a busy farmer or laborer to complete the four basic 1300 vocabulary primers in 96 hours of classroom work, studying one hour each day. Four months constituted the full term of the elementary course and the price of the four books for the farmer was roughly 12 cents in Chinese currency. Each village was organized with an education subcommittee to facilitate and encourage the work. Ting Hsien itself was divided into six sub-districts and these into further subdivisions to facilitate the work of the three general supervisors who went about on their bicycles coordinating and encouraging the teachers and students in the various sections.

Of great significance in supporting and reinforcing this program of literacy was the establishment of a rural newspaper call "The Farmer." It was devoted to providing written material within the limits of the program's vocabulary. It provided carefully structured articles on local, national, and international news items in addition to a variety of short discussions on animal husbandry, horticulture, use of fertilizers, the need for cooperatives, and other items related to community responsibility and citizenship.

By the mid-1930s over 30,000 young men and women had passed through the people's schools. These young graduates were then encouraged to organize themselves into "Fellow-Scholar Associations," first for the purpose of encouraging their members to pursue advanced courses in agriculture, health, rural cooperatives, and civic responsibility, and second to provide their members with leadership opportunities in various community service projects. Many of these Fellow Scholar Associations became crucial sources of organized effort and leadership in the whole reconstruction effort. They organized drama and debating clubs, operated radio sets for the benefit of their village, chalked up news items on the village newswall, mediated in conflicts arising among neighbors, and sponsored a whole series of projects in tree planting, road repairing, agricultural exhibits, and anti-narcotic and anti-gambling movements. Clearly the Ting Hsien experiment had sparked an educational revolution among the peasants of this isolated district.

Livelihood

It was widely recognized that the typical Chinese agricultural specialist was usually from the upper class, had studied Western technology abroad and was essentially illiterate concerning the needs and problems of the Chinese peasant. As was pointed out earlier, Yen in his most persuasive way was able to convince a few agricultural experts from several urban-based universities to join his crusade for rural improvement. If foreign-trained Chinese experts were really to have an impact, if they were to help the vast majority of the Chinese people (the farmers) in any practical way, these experts themselves would have to become students again, must literally move to the village and learn from the peasants the social, cultural, economic, agricultural, and political conditions of these rural areas. Out of this experience came part of the Rural Reconstruction credo: "Go to the people, live among the people and learn from the people."

With the establishment of an effective system of rural education, a cadre of Fellow~Scholar Association members was recruited to help in educating the farmers to see the utility of modern agricultural practices. With the creation of the Farmer's Institute, farmer leaders were introduced to new strains of wheat, vegetables, and cotton which could greatly increase local yields. Also different varieties of hogs and chickens were introduced and cross-bred with local stock with amazing results.

A unique characteristic of this livelihood program was the way the graduates of the people's school system were recruited, trained, and encouraged to establish demonstration projects on their own farms from which agricultural innovations could be disseminated. Those who had passed the literacy test and had adopted some of the improved ideas in connection with better animals or better crops were given certificates as demonstrators. Such certificates were proudly displayed at the entrance of their homes for all to see. Thus with neither government administrative systems nor the use of especially trained extension workers, the farmers of Ting Hsien were exposed to a systematic process of agricultural extension.

Another lesson learned was the fact that while Ting Hsien is clearly an agricultural district, a significant variety of village industries existed. Most of these small enterprises, which manufactured simple implements and utensils, some clothing and food stuffs, were limited to an extended family or sometimes to neighbors in the village. Through careful observation, it became apparent that the methods of fabrication and qualities of the goods could be improved with no additional cost to the family -- thus increasing the marketability of its goods and a cash income to supplement a meager living. Eventually several families were encouraged to combine their efforts, thus increasing the output and providing much needed work opportunities during slow winter months.

In many ways the crowning glory of the livelihood section of this "experiment" has to be in the cooperative movement that was established. Multipurpose rather than sector-specific cooperative were encouraged to utilize most effectively limited capital and trained personnel in the village, to compensate for the diversification of Chinese farming and the relatively small volume of business in any one type of agricultural production. In some villages where the economic and leadership levels were too low to accommodate an "integrated cooperative" approach, small "Self-Help Societies" were encouraged to generate "pre-cooperative" social organizations structured to provide limited credit and some warehousing facilities.

Thus through the efforts of this strange breed of PhDs and university professors, the life and ideas of the peasants went through a remarkable transformation. Superstitions and traditions were subtly modified through acceptance of scientific methods. Instead of struggling alone in the darkness of isolation and exploitation, these farmers of Ting Hsien saw the utility of organization and cooperation

Health

Dr. Yen was able to recruit a physician, Dr. C. C. Chen, a graduate of the Rockefeller Medical School in Peking, who with the support of that institution, was able to train a cadre of staff and to organize a central training clinic in Ting Hsien. The great challenge in public health for Yen and his colleagues was to create a system "practical under existing conditions, to make elementary medical relief and health protection available to the masses." Village elders were encouraged to recruit and nominate local members of their village who could be given a ten-day health training course to begin with and then periodic follow- up courses over one to two years. Each village health worker was furnished with a small box of ten simple remedies among which were copper sulfate for treating trachoma common throughout North China, aspirin, iodine, Vaseline, etc. The whole kit cost but one dollar local currency. In the 1920s, in a society said to have had less than one physician per 75,000 inhabitants, the notion of using village health workers was indeed a revolutionary concept.

Vaccination was widely popularized through the work of the people's schools. Midwifes were complimented for their services in the village, acknowledged as important sources of medical care, and encouraged to attend the health training courses. As an incentive they were given a box of medicines and awarded a special certificate of graduation. In order to ensure better nutrition for the children, milk goats were introduced into Ting Hsien. In addition, special care was taken to help farmers improve their diets through the use of dairy products and vegetables.

Health centers were eventually established in strategic locations throughout the county and one of the main objectives was the eradication of superstitious beliefs concerning illness and disease and then wide distribution and availability of common medicines and other remedies in each of the sub-districts, health stations were set up to provide more specialized medical care when necessary. Local universities were contacted and advanced medical students were recruited to organize various health education programs, to implement immunization campaigns, to provide birth control materials, and to design general prevention strategies in public health. Here the village health workers received special training in: (1) keeping records in births and deaths in the village; (2) introducing vaccinations against small pox; (3) reconstructing a sanitary well according to an approved design; (4) giving simple treatment with the contents of their "medicine box"; (5) "introducing" patients whose ailments did not come within their scope of competency to the sub-district health station; and (6) serving as "health extension agents" encouraging good health practice in the home, providing free medical care to their neighbors, and introducing the science of medicine to their villages.

While it does seem impossible that these simple "peasant doctors" performed these services for no fee, it must be again recognized that the incentives were built within the culture, and the special relationship of Dr. Yen and his team with the local people was unique to the Chinese countryside at that time. As one observer noted, "The village health worker was paid nothing, but he gained big face in the village, and on Chinese New Year was presented with small gifts, to the accompaniment of speeches and fireworks.

Self Government

At some point during Dr. Yen's interactions with the central government it was suggested that he might accept the position of Ting Hsien magistrate. He refused for the reason that he wished to operate free from political affiliation. However, the high authorities appointed a new magistrate who proved to be thoroughly sympathetic with the mass education movement. When Dr. Yen became president of the Institute of Political Reconstruction he was able, with the support of the new magistrate, to institute a number of reforms, including a simplified administrative system, standardized salaries, the elimination of incompetent and corrupt officials, and a major shift in local government from a limited tax-collection and police security system to one with a much broader emphasis on public service more reflective of the "Fourfold Program."

In spite of some strong local opposition, significant reforms were finally initiated throughout the county of Ting. Eventually the villagers were given the opportunity to elect their own councilmen in the local government system while democratic ideals were preached and implemented in the cooperatives and other local agencies. Pearl S. Buck nicely quotes Dr. Yen's sentiments about this process:

"What is most gratifying is this, that after people had learned to run their own People's Schools, their modern farms, their cooperatives, their health clinics, they demanded that they should run their own government. Is there anything more natural and more inevitable? After all, what is government for? Is it not an agency for the welfare of the people? . . .To me self-government is the inevitable result of a people who are educated and capable of carrying on their own social and economic welfare.

A review of the Ting Hsien experiment is impressive in its simplicity, its impact, and its obvious workable strategy for rural development. Many of the techniques developed in Ting Hsien were clearly creative innovations. There is no question that the "mystery ingredient" in this whole process was the magic of Dr. Yen's personality, the contagious excitement and enthusiasm that he and his staff felt in designing, testing, and modifying their "own" creative approach to rural development, and the sensitivity and empathy with which the peasants were approached and helped.

Case Two
The Village Bank System of Egypt[10]

During the 1950's a young Egyptian graduate student, Ahmad al-Naggar, was given a fellowship to complete his Ph.D. in Germany. He began to study local savings banks and their development during the late nineteenth century. He noted their role as a financial institution but was more impressed with the role these banks played in the social and political development of Germany's rural areas. It was then that he first realized what this kind of an approach could mean for rural Egypt. He returned to Egypt and attempted to present his idea to various government officials and ministries. Many officials scoffed at the idea, arguing that an independent local savings bank among the *fellahin* [Egyptian peasants] was an impossibility. Others, especially the senior officials, were not so harsh but indicated that at least twenty years would be needed before such a system could be introduced.

After several months of seeking support, one influential man, Dr. Adel Mon'im al-Qaysuni, deputy prime minister for economy and finance, did listen with a sympathetic ear and indicated his willingness to consider the possibility of such a program. In an attempt to gain some international support, Dr. al-Naggar wrote to an old friend, the president of the largest savings bank in Germany and a leading figure in the field of international finance. He invited the German banker to consider his bank's supporting a joint project to study the possibility of introducing this kind of banking program into rural Egypt. Later he convinced Dr. al-Qaysuni to invite the bank president to Egypt. This he did, and the result was the signing of a German-Egyptian agreement to finance and support a rural banking system in Egypt.

During the initial stages of the rural banking system, Dr. al-Naggar and his staff postulated four conditions that would have to exist if the local bank system was to be effective in Egyptian villages:

1. Employees of the bank must be carefully selected and trained to ensure that they have not only the knowledge and skills required by a bank official but also the dedication, sympathy, and desire to effectively work with the *fellahin*.

2. No bank is to be established until a strong bond of trust and mutual acceptance has been created between the bank workers and villagers to ensure a continuous and open line of communication between the community and the bank.

3. Every effort must be made to discover and utilize the formal and informal leaders of the community in order to ensure that all significant groups are allowed to participate and share in the functioning of the banking system.

4. National and local administrative support is vital if the banking program is to start, but equally important is the fact that this government support must be indirect and subtle. Every effort must be made to create the feeling that this is the villagers' bank and not the government's.

The four assumptions became the foundation upon which Dr. al-Naggar developed a program to train future bank officials. The author spent several months interviewing and observing these young bank officials both in the bank's training institute and in the villages where banks had been established. My interest in these young men stems largely from the tremendous difference noted in their attitudes and behavior toward the fellahin when compared with the vast majority of bureaucrats working with the rural peasants. Much of their devotion, dedication, and enthusiasm appears to have been generated through their training program.

Selection

In early July 1962, Dr. al-Naggar placed advertisements in two Cairo newspapers (al-Ahram and al-Akhbar) twice a week for a two-week period. The advertisement stressed that candidates were needed to pioneer a project that would stimulate the rural people to help themselves, that there would be a certain amount of risk involved, but that, potentially, the program could be highly beneficial to the development of the country.

There were some 622 applicants, who were screened through a series of tests and interviews. Dr. al-Naggar, working closely with Dr. al-Said Muhammad Khairy, assistant professor of industrial psychology at 'Ain Shams University, presented a series of industrial psychology tests to measure intelligence, personality traits, leadership capabilities, integrity, and patriotism of the applicants. Second, each person was individually interviewed by Dr. al-Naggar or Dr. Khairy in an attempt to determine (1) their reasons for seeking employment with the local savings bank program, (2) how willing they were to work in the rural areas, (3) if they would accept work for three or four months without a salary and if they would be willing to take a possible salary cut from their present employment, and (4) the extent of their motivation, and understanding of the problems facing rural Egypt.

Of the original 622 applicants, 209 were disqualified through this first stage of screening, which was conducted during a five-day period. The remaining 413 were divided into groups of six to eight individuals. They were instructed that they would be given a series of topics and that they would have one hour to discuss these topics. Some of the topics for discussion included (1) the Arab League -- should this organization be encouraged or discouraged? (2) Housing -- should new housing projects be built in the centers of the cities or on the outer areas of cities? (3) Sex and women -- should mixed education be encouraged or discouraged? (4) Youth problems -- what are the basic problems of youth today in the Egypt and what solutions are possible? (5) Transportation and traffic problems -- what solutions can be recommended for the present crowded bus situation? (6) What projects are best conducive to alleviating the problems of the *fellahin*?

These discussion groups were not guided or directed, but were allowed to develop spontaneously. Each group was observed carefully in an attempt to measure each candidate's ability to work in a group situation. Upon the completion of these group discussions, Dr. al-Naggar, Dr. Khairy, and their assistants made the final selection of twenty- one candidates. These candidates ranged in age from twenty-four to thirty-two, although the majority were under thirty. All had graduated with a B.A. from an Egyptian university -- two in sociology, two in business administration, twelve in accounting, two in economics, and two in psychology. Four of the twenty had only recently completed their university work, four had been employed in various ministries, one was in journalism, and the other eleven had been working for private companies. Six of the candidates were from a village background, while the other fourteen came from Cairo, Alexandria, or Ismailia.

Training Program

The training program started in September 1962 and ended in April 1963. The training program included the following techniques: reading assignments in Egyptian history; the culture of the Egyptian fellahin; economic history of the underdeveloped countries; economic situation in the United Arab Republic; principles of community development; leadership techniques; group dynamics; history of savings banks; banking systems in Germany, Great Britain, the United States, and the Soviet Union; economics, with an emphasis on banking and finance; the new local government system in the U.A.R.; techniques of social research; interview techniques; survey techniques and objective reporting; and, finally, public relations and publicity.

One of the most important and effective means of training the candidates was the informal discussion sessions. Each student would prepare a lecture or two on some phase of the training. This technique not only provided an opportunity for independent reading and research, but it also developed confidence among the trainees as they presented and explained the material they were studying. Following each lecture there would be a question and answer period. Dr. al-Naggar indicates that many of the unique aspects of the present local savings bank program were developed during these discussion periods. During the discussion of how a new savings system could best be introduced into the villages of Egypt, the idea of a "non-interest-paying account" came into existence. Subsequent discussions broadened and conceptualized this non-interest-paying approach into a bank system with three types of savings account.

Dr. al-Naggar felt that the real problems of the *fellahin* were questions of behavior and attitude rather than poverty or lack of intelligence. During these discussions, Dr. al-Naggar and the trainees sought to conceptualize more clearly the ways and means by which the peasant's behavior patterns could be changed. The value of this kind of approach to training cannot be overemphasized. Group participation stimulated individual creativity and initiative. Each member of the group felt that the techniques and solutions being developed through these informal exchanges of ideas belonged to them. The ability of Dr. al-Naggar to present key questions that would stimulate a broad range of responses, ideas, and solutions not only provided an intellectual growth for the trainees, but also suggested a whole new range of creative solutions to the problems of community development in Egypt.

Research Papers

Each trainee was required to write a series of research papers on some of the following topics: What is community development? How can one introduce new ideas and techniques among rural people? What problems and aspects must be considered in preparing talks or discussions with groups of peasants, women, students, etc.? How do you discover the real leaders in the village? What are the latest up-to-date bookkeeping systems for banks? What are the major problems involved in administering a local bank? The major value of this kind of research in depth was not fully appreciated by the trainees until they actually began their work in the project itself. Within a matter of months, however, the value of these research papers became apparent. Not only was the information found in these training research papers applicable and valuable for a solution of the kinds of problems faced by the trainees in their new employment, but the expertise and confidence generated by an actual application of knowledge recently gained greatly reinforced their confidence and commitment to the whole banking program.

Practical Exercises

During the latter part of the training program, the trainees with Dr. al-Naggar spent a week camped outside a village in the governorate of Menufia, just north of Cairo. During the week, the trainees were encouraged to mix with the villagers. Following the age-old tradition of Arab hospitality, village shaykhs and heads of different families invited small groups of trainees into their homes. The primary purposes of this week's training were to:

1. Provide an opportunity for the trainees to live in a village under somewhat controlled conditions, thus allowing them to observe and participate first-hand in the lives of the rural *fellahin*.

2. Provide an opportunity for the trainees to apply some of the techniques of community development, such as developing a sense of who the "real leaders" are,

means of cultivating their friendship, and methods of influencing and motivating these real leaders.

3. Provide an opportunity to gain through informal discussions with the villagers a clearer picture of the attitudes, behavioral patterns, group norms, common expressions of the *fellahin*, concepts of themselves, their families, outsiders, the government, and the outside world in general.

Once a reasonable amount of trust and friendship had developed between the villagers and the trainees, special meetings were called in which the savings bank project was explained to them. Perhaps more important than explaining the project itself was the opportunity afforded by these meetings to probe deeply into the *fellahin's* attitudes toward savings, development, and investment. Special meetings were held for women, students, the shaykhs, and the *fellahin*. Each group was encouraged to speak frankly, to discuss and debate their personal feelings about a village savings bank. Many assumptions, fears, and prejudices voiced by the *fellahin* themselves provided insights for the trainees in how the program would have to be modified when introduced into Mit Ghamr.

During the training session itself each trainee was required to submit a tentative plan for introducing the bank system into a village. These plans were to be formulated in terms of planning, coordination, organization, control, reporting, and evaluation. Trainees were also introduced to the techniques of public relations, interpersonal communications, group dynamics, interviewing, and social research, which included methods for observing, conducting surveys, and presenting questionnaires. In addition, the trainees were given a refresher course in accounting skills, use of business machines, and even a driver-training course in the use of automobiles, trucks, and motorbikes. What proved to be a most important part of their training was a "refresher" course in the Islamic religion. Villagers are keenly aware of the "proper and improper" ways of praying and performing the rituals of a true Muslim. The trainees were encouraged to be aware of and practice the finer points of the Islamic faith. Also there was instruction on the use of the Koran and the various Hadiths that were applicable to the banking program. One of the most effective ways of introducing the banking program into the village was through the local religious leader. His support was often crucial in determining how readily the villagers would accept the banking project. Thus, it was extremely important that the trainees be aware of the practices, rituals, and religious teaching prevalent among the rural fellahin.

3. High morale and motivation: By far the most important factor in analyzing the effectiveness of this banking project is the individual attitudes, motives, and sense of mission of these original twenty trainees. In evaluating the training program, as well as the bank project itself, this crucial element must be taken into consideration. It is my impression that this program, devoid of personnel imbued with the motivation and desire to succeed that existed among these original twenty, would never have achieved the early success that it has. It is readily

admitted by all the original twenty that their commitment to the project is primarily due to Dr. al-Naggar -- his personality, his devotion to his work, and the sense of mission that he feels. This charisma, this personal relationship between Dr. al-Naggar and his trainees, must be institutionalized, impersonalized, and made a part of the program itself if the program is to succeed outside the sphere of one man's influence and personality. The crucial nature of this bond between teacher and student, however, is not easily impersonalized or made a function of an institution.

Importance and Practicality of the Project

Dr. al-Naggar explained and analyzed the problems and obstacles that the Egyptian peasants must overcome if they are to enjoy a higher standard of living and the comforts and blessings of modernization. He explained the relationship between savings and development and the need to change many common attitudes and beliefs of the *fellahin*. He created a feeling among the trainees that the savings bank project would be one of the most effective ways of improving the condition of the *fellahin*. The validity of this belief (that the bank could change attitudes and conditions of the rural villagers) was not fully appreciated until the trainees actually began to introduce the project among the peasants. As the trainees saw the attitudes of villagers toward savings actually change through their own efforts and powers of persuasion, as new cottage industries were established, and as personal needs and financial problems were actually solved, the trainees gradually, probably imperceptibly, internalized a commitment to the bank that no training program could have ever developed.

Personal Relationship to the Bank Program

The trainees were constantly reminded that this was their own program, that each of them had a unique opportunity to participate in a pioneer project that would eventually have a tremendous impact on the lives and future of a majority of the Egyptian people. One aspect of this early training program that may well be extremely difficult to duplicate in future groups of trainees was the very fact that the development of the project was still mainly a loose set of generalizations in the mind of Dr. al-Naggar. Thus, in the course of this first training period, the trainees were active participants in clarifying, conceptualizing, and making operational many of the techniques, procedures, methods, and modes of operation that are now regular procedures for the entire banking staff. The very fact that these "original twenty" played such an active role in developing and implementing the new project provided an added bond to the program that will indeed be difficult for future trainees to experience.

The Sense of Risk

As was noted in the pre-training interview sessions, Dr. al-Naggar probed deeply into the feelings of the candidates concerning salary and risk taking. He emphasized that members of the banking program would be paid according to their work output, that their salaries might be less than they were presently making, and that in the initial years of the project there might be months when salaries would have to be reduced. At the same time he appealed to their willingness to take a risk in a program that would fail or succeed according to their own efforts. This approach, known in Arabic as *mukafa'a shamilah* emphasized that employment would be based on a free contract with no guarantees of salary, promotion, or permanency. All salaries and promotions were to be based on work performed. The common system of employment known as *daragat*, which assumed that once a person is hired he can never be fired and whose salary and promotion depend primarily on the degree and year of graduation, was completely rejected in the banking system. Again, because of the unknown quality and future of the banking project as a basis for a meaningful career, the risk taken by the original trainees certainly strengthened their commitment to the bank program. This kind of psychological reinforcement will also be difficult to duplicate among future trainees who are already aware of the bank's success and its ability to provide a comfortable salary.

Meaningful Title and Position in the Banking Project

Upon completion of the first three months of training, the trainees were given the title *bahith* (researcher), and upon completion of the six month program they were given the title of *khabi*r (expert). The purpose of these titles was twofold: first, to encourage the trainees to believe that this training course had given them the necessary knowledge and skills in a new field of endeavor which justified and validated their new title; and second, the title provided them with a measure of prestige, which not only gave them confidence and self-esteem but also provided the villagers and townspeople with a symbol of rank so very necessary in the inter- relationships of a rural community.

Personal Relationship between Dr. al-Naggar and the Trainees

Each trainee was given special individual attention, and they were encouraged to come to Dr. al-Naggar whenever they had a problem. Dr. al-Naggar went out of his way to arrange special dispensations to meet the personal needs of his group: he arranged to have the wife of one trainee move to Mit Ghamr after the project started; he was ever ready to provide personal loans for short-term needs; and he even loaned his personal automobile for non-bank matters. These many examples of genuine personal concern for the trainees created a bond of loyalty and devotion that will be very difficult to duplicate in future training programs. One might add also that Dr. al-Naggar made it a special point to "over stimulate" their motivation and dedication to the program. During the early days of the project, they were all subject to a certain amount of pessimism and cynicism from government officials and academicians, many of whom deliberately tried to discourage the idea of a local savings bank among the *fellahin*. As Dr. al-Naggar admits, it was the challenge of these negative attitudes coupled with an intense loyalty for the banking project that has created these "super-motivated" individuals.

Dr. al-Naggar himself argues: "Most of the success or failure of the educational aspects of this experiment depends to a great extent on the skill, zeal, enthusiasm, and attitudes of those working in the field -- this is in addition to their capacity for influencing the attitudes of the people. Actually the selection of these employees can be considered as the corner-stone for the success of the project."

Implementing the Bank System

When the training program was completed, the group of trainees with Dr. al-Naggar moved to Mit Ghamr. During the first few weeks they made an effort to meet the formal leaders in the community: members of the town council, the government administrators such as the clinic doctors, headmasters of the schools, and the chief social worker; also the shaykhs of the various mosques and the local Coptic priest, the chief of police, the members of the ASU *lajnat al-'ishrin*, and influential members of the five leading families.

At the same time the town was divided into three sections and the twenty bank "experts" were also divided into three groups and encouraged to get acquainted with as many people as possible within these areas. The initial reaction on the part of most of the peasants was one of great suspicion and doubt. Some argued that they were tax collectors, others were convinced that they were seeking information for the ASU, others suggested that they must be Communist agents, while some thought they were members of the Muslim Brotherhood. The bank workers seldom discussed savings or banking but merely encouraged the peasants to talk about their problems and ways in which these problems might be solved.

Once the curiosity of the villagers had been aroused sufficiently, Dr. al-Naggar asked the town council chairman to call a series of formal meetings with various leadership groups in the community. In these formal meetings with the members of the leading families, the ASU, the schoolteachers, the labor union, the youth clubs, and women's organizations, Dr. al-Naggar explained the purpose of the banking program and the procedures that would be used. In order to appeal to a broad class of people, the bank provided three kinds of accounts:

1. Savings Account: This account would pay no interest. The minimum deposit was live piasters (twelve cents), and withdrawal was possible at any time. An interest-free savings account was a unique innovation developed during the training session, and proved to be a key factor in gaining supporters from among the conservative Muslim population. The Koran prohibits usury and this new approach to banking galvanized a large number of Muslim religious leaders to openly support the banking project.

2. Social Services Fund: Each pious Muslim is supposed to give a portion of his income as a donation to the poor. Working with the local religious leaders, Dr. al-Naggar suggested that this religious tax (*zakat*) be collected and allowed to accumulate in the bank. A committee of local leaders would meet periodically to determine how this money could be distributed as charitable gifts. Surprisingly enough, many people contributed to this fund who had never before given *zakat*. All bank depositors were eligible for this "disaster insurance." While I was staying in Mit Ghamr, a local horse drawn taxi was in an accident in which the driver's horse, his sole means of livelihood, was killed. Within two days the bank, through the social services fund, replaced his horse. It is obvious how this kind of activity would greatly add to the reputation and acceptance of the bank.

3. Investment Accounts: This account requires a minimum of one Egyptian pound and can be withdrawn only after one year. Once a year each depositor is given a share in the bank's profits earned from the projects financed and supported through investment funds.

After these formal meetings with specific leadership groups, the bank experts moved out among the people. They spent many hours in the coffee houses talking with the elder members of the town, they visited homes, and they followed the *fellahin* out to their fields. Special attempts were made to suggest goals that the *fellahin* might achieve if they saved a little each week. Farmers were shown they might have a new plough or a gamoosa. Students were encouraged to save for a bicycle or a new soccer ball. Women were urged to consider the value of a kerosene lamp or a sewing machine. Many group discussions were held in the local factories, the schools, and in local clubhouses.

Gradually a few peasants would give ten or fifteen piasters to one of the bank experts and then a few hours later they would demand their money back. As their confidence in the bank officials grew, more and more people began to bring their money in. A temporary bank office was set up in one of the central buildings of the town. Within the first year, over a thousand individuals became depositors, and after three years, there were fifty thousand in the area of Mit Ghamr alone. Finally, in August 1964, the bank moved into its own building constructed on land donated by the governorate.

The major purpose of the bank is to finance local projects that will stimulate economic growth. The bank will not extend loans to any individual until he has been a depositor for at least six months. The bank extends two kinds of loans: non-investment loans are extended to individuals who need a quick short-term loan to cover some emergency or to replace some item required for their livelihood. The borrower is required to repay only the amount borrowed (no interest charged) and may repay the loan at his convenience; investment loans are offered to depositors who wish to invest in some local industry or commercial endeavor. During the first year loans were made to start a brick factory, a shoe factory, a bamboo basket factory, a bakery, and several other cottage-type industries. In each instance, the bank gives technical assistance on how to buy raw materials, internal procedures of production, record keeping, and efficient marketing of their products. The bank has one employee whose major function is to locate customers in Cairo for the products of these bank investors. The loans are repayable over a reasonable period of time, based upon costs, rate of growth expected, and profits to be earned. Each borrower agrees to share a portion of the profits earned during the term of the loan. Again it should be noted that the borrower is not paying interest -- he is only sharing his profits with the bank.

One bank official proudly indicated that during the bank's first year about 80 percent of the depositors put their money in the savings account. At the end of the year, when those who had their money in the investment account were given a 6 percent dividend for their invested money, about half the savings account depositors shifted their money to the investment account. The Peasant quickly learned the advantage of long-term savings and investments.

One aspect of the program that needs to be noted is the "evening session." Each evening all the bank experts met with Dr. al-Naggar for two or three hours to discuss their day's experience and to plan for the next day's work. All of the twenty officials were asked to describe their daily experience with people they met, what new approaches they had discovered for gaining "new converts," what were people saying, who are the "real leaders," and what were their recommendations for improving the program. Thus, each evening these bank workers came together as a board of directors, each was treated as an equal, and many new ideas were generated through these "brainstorming sessions."

Dr. al-Naggar concludes a report on the results of the new bank program after its first two years of operation: "The question now is, what does it mean when 33,000 persons become savers. . . . This is an important social operation which includes three aspects: a) the people have moved out of their seclusion, b) they have expanded and widened the circle of their social contacts, and c) confidence and trust have been created, thus making the people move away from the fatal effects of passivism. Response and activity were thus stimulated because the piaster means much to these people."

One point that Dr. al-Naggar has consistently emphasized is the fact that the bank has more than just an economic function in so created to encourage savings, to limit consumption, and to provide capital investment for local development projects, but there are other functions just as important. The bank has a social and political role, and, in the long run, these may well be more significant, at least in terms of the various organizations and institutions that the government is trying to create in the rural areas.

In one government program established to increase egg production, an administrative agency wanted to give away some prize chickens to various villagers scattered throughout the Delta. But the *fellahin* refused to accept a free chicken from the government because they feared they would have to pay a fine if anything happened to the "government's chicken." Dr. al-Naggar made arrangements to distribute the chickens for the government free of charge. He then announced through a meeting of the depositors that the bank had some chickens it would sell for a nominal fee. The depositors purchased 27,000 of these prize chickens.

The doctor of a village health unit went to the director of the local bank branch and complained that he had tried for six months to bring the women of the village together for a lecture on the methods and values of family planning. The bank director merely called a meeting of all the women depositors in the village, giving the doctor an audience of over three hundred women.

The education committee of the Mit Ghamr Town Council invited several members of the bank's board of directors to their monthly meeting to discuss the question of building a secondary school. The bank officials suggested that the bank finance the project with the stipulation that all students be required to pay a certain fee until the school is paid for.

In one village outside Mit Ghamr, the branch bank director had developed, in conjunction with the local social worker, a rather successful family planning project. Two new ideas were incorporated in their program. First, prior to announcing the family planning program, the bank director and the social worker visited all the midwives in the village. From past experience it was known that these women had vigorously opposed the government's family planning program in other areas. From casual conversation, it was learned that the midwives earn about three and a half Egyptian pounds a month for their services. The bank director asked them if they would support the family planning program if the bank paid them four pounds a month, to which they readily agreed. In addition, these midwives were given an official title and sent to a nearby combined unit for a few days training. This made a tremendous impression. The salaries for the midwives were allocated from the Ministry of Social Affairs, but disbursed by the bank director whom all the midwives greatly trusted.

Second, instead of giving the doctor or the social worker one pound for each woman converted to family planning, it was agreed that the person bringing the woman to the clinic would take fifty piasters and the other fifty piasters would be placed in a community fund. When I visited this village, they were saving money for a youth clubhouse, and the director mentioned that many of the teenagers were taking their mothers to the clinic so that fifty piasters could be put in the community fund.

Reasons for Success

The obvious source of this new institution's success lies first in its leadership -- men with knowledge, skill, but even more, men with initiative and a deep sense of mission. Equally important was the fact that the villagers trusted this new structure in their midst. The bank was legitimate in their eyes because it sought to satisfy their needs and was clearly fulfilling their emerging aspirations.

The bank, as a new institution, was not incompatible with the needs and behavioral patterns of the villagers. The *fellahin* had traditionally saved, yet their savings were usually hidden in jars under the earthen floors of their homes or invested in golden ornaments worn by their wives. Often these savings were unwisely spent on a wedding or a funeral or other uneconomic consumption. Most fellahin borrowed from a local money changer at exorbitant interest rates. Given these obvious needs (a place to save their money and an institution through which fair and convenient loans could be obtained), the bank was certainly not inconsistent with their needs. However, government banks had existed in Egypt for many years. The local post office, after seventy years of encouraging a savings program, had only seven thousand depositors in all of Mit Ghamr prior to the establishment of the savings bank. In the late 1950's, the government instituted an agricultural credit bank, yet after ten years experience more than 60 percent of the loans were never paid back. In contrast, 100 percent of all loans made to the people in Mit Ghamr by the savings bank had been repaid. One fellah explained to me that money from a government bank did not have to be repaid because "they have lots of money." When asked why he would repay his loan to the local savings bank, he pointed out that "the money in the savings bank belongs to my neighbors, my relatives, my friend -- if I didn't repay that loan I would be stealing from them."

Dr. al-Naggar notes also: "The people are still clinging to the intellectual and spiritual aspects that are closely related to the values in which they believe. Interest, for the people is prohibited and unlawful, and the people believe that God will bless this project because it fulfills the teachings of religion. This simple but deep belief has been the motive driving thousands of people to deposit their few piasters in full trust and confidence, without having any material benefits drawing or attracting them to it."

In reflecting on what this bank program might mean for the long-term benefits of the *fellahin*, Dr. al-Naggar had these words to say: "How are we to evaluate the spiritual achievements and the noble motives that have once again been brought to life? How are we going to evaluate the changes in our society -- its values, its morals, and behavior? If we seek to evaluate them now, we shall fail. For despite all of these achievements we must admit that all we see are buds, but in the future these buds will yield their fruits to us."[11]

Case Three
Sarvodaya: The Other Development[12]

Mohandas Karamchand Gandhi, born in 1869, was thirty-four years old when a young friend, seeing him off at Johannesburg, gave him a book to read during the journey. It was John Ruskin's "Unto This Last." This collection of "Four Essays on the First Principles of Political Economy," first published in the monthly "Cornhill Magazine" in 1860, had a determining influence on Gandhi. Under the title "The Magic Spell of a Book" he tells us in his autobiography that "the book was impossible to lay aside, once I had begun it. It gripped me. I determined to change my life in accordance with the ideals of the book. I translated it later into Gujarati, entitling it "Sarvodaya" (the welfare of all).'"

In his book, Ruskin argues vehemently against the theoretical construct of an "economic man," because this model isolates the individual from social affection and from society. Political economy, he says, teaches us only the art of a "mercantile economy," namely the establishment of the maximum inequality in favor of a particular group of privileged persons. Their mercantile wealth can realize its value only as a claim upon many others' labors and, through the ruthless application of the "law of supply and demand," creates injustice and hatred among people. A guaranteed equality of payment should be wholly independent of any reference to the number of people willing to do the work. . . . The real science of political economy "is that which teaches nations to desire and labor for the things that lead to life and which teaches them to scorn and destroy the things that lead to destruction." The final object of a mature political economy should be to provide, through "good methods," a "good quantity" of products for "wise consumption," which Ruskin considered to be the aim of any productive undertaking. Thus the vital question for the individual and for the nation should never be "how much do we make" but rather "to what purpose do we spend our time."

"People in the West," Gandhi wrote in the introduction to his paraphrase of Ruskin's essays in 1908, "generally hold that the whole duty of man is to promote the happiness of the majority of mankind, and happiness is supposed to mean only physical happiness and economic prosperity. If the laws of morality are broken in the conquest of this happiness, it does not matter very much. Again, as the object sought to be attained is the happiness of the majority, Westerners do not think there is any harm if this is secured by sacrificing a minority. The consequences of this line of thinking are writ large on the face of Europe."

Independence (*Swaraj*)

This opening criticism of western materialism is further developed in the three pages of conclusions. Here Gandhi tries to convince his countrymen in South Africa, but especially those in India, that "Swaraj" cannot mean independence in the narrow political sense of the word: "New ideas are in the air in India. Our young men who, have received Western education are full of spirit. This spirit should be directed into the right channels, as otherwise it can only do us harm." "Let us have Swaraj is one slogan; let us industrialize the country is another. But we hardly understand what Swaraj is. Swaraj really means self-control. Only he is capable of self control who observes the rules of morality, does not cheat or give up truth, and does his duty to his parents, wife and children, servants and neighbors. Such a man is in enjoyment of Swaraj, no matter where he lives. A State enjoys Swaraj if it can boast of a number of such good citizens."

Thus Gandhi condemns violence as a means of achieving independence and deplores the "foolish Indians" who rejoice in bomb throwing. If these killers became the rulers of the country, India, would only have a change of masters." Swaraj was not to be attained by the sin of killing Englishmen and it could not "be attained either by the erection of huge factories."

If real Swaraj meant freedom of the personality through self-control, then an economic system that had to create ever new wants so as to maximize the productive potential of its industrial agglomerations was unnecessary and harmful. In it "gold and silver may be accumulated but they will not lead to the establishment of Swaraj. Ruskin has proved this to the hilt. Western civilization is a mere baby, a hundred or so years old. And yet it has reduced Europe to a sorry plight. Let us pray that India is saved from the fate that has overtaken Europe, where the nations are poised for an attack on one another, and are silent only because of the stockpiling of armaments."

Against this analysis of violence and aggression Gandhi visualized a new India that would attain Swaraj through "righteous methods." "Our Swaraj must be real Swaraj, which cannot be attained by either violence or industrialization." Truth (*Satya*) is for Gandhi the philosopher's stone, which alone could effect this kind of transformation. Thus he ends his conclusion with the words: "If every Indian sticks to truth, Swaraj will come to us of its own accord."

In his autobiography written twenty years later Gandhi reasserts that he discovered some of his deepest convictions reflected "in this great book of Ruskin." The teachings of "Unto This Last" he understood to be:

1. "That the good of the individual is contained in the good of all."
2. "That a lawyer's work has the same value as the barber's, in as much as all have the same right of earning their livelihood from their work."
3. "That a life of labor, i.e. the life of the tiller of the soil and the handicraftsman, is the life worth living."

Civil Disobedience

He became more and more involved in public issues, volunteered for medical work in the so-called Zulu War in 1906 and then became the devoted leader of a movement in which the Indians in South Africa protested against the discriminatory legislation planned by the government. In the course of this campaign Gandhi, inspired by Henry D. Thoreau's then hardly known essay on "Civil Disobedience," that was first published in Boston in 1849, developed his concept of Passive Resistance; it crystallized into the final form of Satyagraha, the holding fast to Truth.

In a letter addressed to a member of the Servants of India Society, Gandhi explained in 1935: "The statement that I derived my idea of Civil Disobedience from the writings of Thoreau is wrong. The resistance to authority in South Africa was well advanced before I got the essay of Thoreau on Civil Disobedience. But the movement was then known as passive resistance. As it was incomplete I had coined the word *Satyagraha* for the Gujarati readers. When I saw the title of Thoreau's great essay, I began to use his phrase to explain our struggle to the English readers."

In 1909, sailing back to South Africa from unsuccessful negotiations with the British government in London, Gandhi wrote his famous dialogues on "*Hind Swaraj* or Indian Home Rule," strongly advocating the right of a minority to fight against unjust laws. "It is a superstition and ungodly thing," he explains to an imaginary reader, "to believe that an act of a majority binds a minority. Many examples can be given in which acts of majorities will be found to have been wrong and those of minorities to have been right. All reforms owe their origin to the initiation of minorities in opposition to majorities. If among a band of robbers a knowledge of robbing is obligatory, is a pious man to accept the obligation? So long as the superstition that men should obey unjust laws exists, so long will their slavery exist. And a passive resister alone can remove such superstition."

Tolstoy Farm

To put the Indian minority's struggle against the unjust rule of the South African government on a firm economic basis, Gandhi decided to set a new farm complex, aimed at making the *Satyagrahis* and their families self sufficient, no matter how long the struggle would go on. With the financial and technical assistance of Herman Kallenbach, a wealthy Johannesburg architect of German origin, Gandhi started a settlement of about 1,100 acres in the vicinity of Johannesburg in 1910. He named it "Tolstoy Farm," showing humble respect for the grand old man in Yasnay, Polyana who lived a life of voluntary simplicity among his former serfs. "Next to the late Rajachandra," (a Jain reformer), Gandhi wrote in his "Young India" in 1921, "Tolstoy is one of the three moderns who have exerted the greatest spiritual influence on my life, the third being Ruskin." He[Tolstoy] wrote to Gandhi: "The longer I live, and especially now when I vividly feel the nearness of death, I want to tell others what I feel so particularly clearly and what to my mind is of great importance namely, that which is called passive resistance, but which in reality is nothing else than the teaching of love, uncorrupted by false interpretations. That love is the highest and only law of human life and in the depth of his soul every human being (as we see most clearly in children) feels and knows this; he knows this until he is entangled by the false teachings of the world."

It was precisely this firm belief in the natural goodness of man that led Gandhi further and further on. The Tolstoy Farm was now his laboratory and the Movement against the Smuts Government provided a unique testing ground for his experiments with truth. Having won the battle, Gandhi wrote in "Indian Opinion" that Civil Disobedience had proved to be an instrument with which a world-wide revolution could be achieved. "It is a force," he wrote, "which if it became universal, would revolutionize social ideals and do away with despotism and the ever-growing militarism under which the nations of the West are groaning and are almost being crushed to death, and which fairly promises to overwhelm even the nations of the East."

Constructive Program

Gandhi returned to India in 1915 and settled in a small *ashram*[farm] on the outskirts of Ahmedahad in Gujarat; his home province. Now he knew his tools: truth and self discipline. Through them he molded himself into the world-famous charismatic leader of the Congress Movement for independence. For Gandhi, however, unlike most of the Congress workers, independence meant much more than just a political issue. Constructive work, i.e. home-spun cloth, village industries and local self-reliance, was not simply a timely tactical instrument in a non-violent struggle against the colonial regime and its industries; for him it was the heart of the matter. In 1931 he wrote: "My work of social reform was in no way less than or subordinate to political work. The fact is that when I saw that to a certain extent my social work would be impossible without the help of political work, I took to the latter and only to the extent that it helped the former. I must therefore confess that the work of social reform or self-purification of this nature is a hundred times dearer to me than what is called purely political work."

The "Constructive Program" is central to the understanding of Gandhi's concept of *Swaraj*, which was for him a step towards the ultimate goal of "*Ram Raj*," the Kingdom of God, where an equal share was given "even unto this last." As an outcome of conversations with coworkers in his *ashram* at Sevagram, Gandhi issued a "thoroughly revised" edition in November 1945 so as to show the connection between the Constructive Program and Civil Disobedience more clearly. In the concluding remarks he repeats "that Civil Disobedience is not absolutely necessary to win freedom through purely nonviolent effort, if the cooperation of the whole nation is secured in the Constructive Program. Gandhi thus expects it to be clear to the reader that "Civil Disobedience in terms of Independence without the cooperation of the millions by way of constructive effort is mere bravado and worse than useless."

The Concept of Rural Development

The Constructive Program itself lists eighteen items of Social Work, namely: the building of communal unity; the removal of untouchability; the introduction of prohibition; the development of *khadi* [home spun cloth]; the promotion of other village industries; the improvement of village sanitation; the adoption of a new (craft centered) basic education; the introduction of universal adult education; the improvement of the condition of women and equality of status and opportunity for them: education in health (and hygiene; the preservation and development of provincial languages; the adoption of Hindustani as the national language; working towards economic equality; organizing the peasants and protecting their rights; organizing industrial labor on the basis of truth and non-violence; the welfare of the tribal peoples; and, finally, working with students to improve their mental, moral and physical equipment.

Khadi and Self-Reliance

For Gandhi, *khadi* [the making of home-made cotton cloth] is synonymous with self-reliance. It means a wholesale *Swadeshi* mentality, a determination to find all the necessities of life in India and through the labor and intellect of the villagers. That means a reversal of the existing process. To liberate the farmer from the uncertainties and fluctuating demands of distant markets, Indian farmers are advised to grow only what they need themselves: The farmer needs to know that his first business is to grow for his own needs. When he does that, he will reduce the chance of a low market ruining him. The same holds true for the essential village industries such as "hand-grinding, hand-pounding, soap making, paper-making, match-making, tanning, oil-pressing, etc. All should make it a point of honor to use only village articles whenever and wherever available. "Given the demand," Gandhi concludes, "there is no doubt that most of our wants can be supplied from our villages. When we have become village-minded, we will not want imitations of the West or machine-made products."

Gandhi did not consider his list of eighteen items of constructive work exhaustive nor did he attach any importance to their order. Yet "economic equality" remained for him the "Master key to non-violent Independence." He believed that a non-violent system of government was an impossibility " so long as the wide gulf between the rich and the hungry millions persists. The contrast between the palaces of New Delhi and the miserable hovels of the poor laboring class nearby cannot last one day in a free India in which the poor will enjoy the same powers as the richest in the land. A violent and bloody revolution is a certainty one day unless there is a voluntary abdication of riches and the power that riches give and sharing them for the common good."

Self Realization Through Service

Gandhi's *Sarvodaya* concept, a social ethic for the welfare of all, is a unique reaction against the barriers of a Hindu social system, in which functional cooperation and ritual separation coincide. The ritual purity of the upper castes depends upon specific relations with lower castes, who thereby become impure. Gandhi tried to break this circle of depending origination of purity and untouchability and was proud to be his own sweeper. Cleaning a latrine, removing one's own "night soil" was for him not a symbolic gesture to praise the image of "Harijans," but an essential part of his own struggle for self-realization. "Service unto this last" and true self-realization were interdependent.

Gandhi never made a secret of the fact that this quest for self realization was the driving force behind all his activities. He declared openly in "Young India" in April 1924: "I am a humble seeker after Truth. I am impatient to realize myself, to attain Moksha in this very existence. My national service is part of my training for freeing my soul from the bondage of flesh. Thus considered, my service may be regarded as purely selfish. For me, the road to salvation lies through incessant toil in the service of my country and there through of humanity. I want to identify myself with everything that lives. So, my patriotism is for me a stage in my journey to the Land of Eternal Freedom and Peace."

Even more revealing is the answer that Gandhi gave to a Polish engineer who came to see him on a rainy day in August 1936. He asked why Gandhi had retreated to a humble hut in a Gujarati village and whether his aim was simply humanitarian, just to serve the villagers as best he could. Gandhi's answer put in a nutshell his "this-worldly asceticism" as the true driving force of his life. "I am here to serve no one else but myself," Gandhi replied, "to find my own self realization through the service of these village folk. Man's ultimate aim is the realization of God, and all his activities, political, social and religious, have to be guided by the ultimate aim of the vision of God. The immediate service of all human beings becomes a necessary part of the endeavor simply because the only way to find God is to see Him in His creation and be one with it. This can only be done by service of all. And this cannot be done except through one's country. I am a part and parcel of the whole, and I cannot find Him apart from the rest of humanity. My countrymen are my nearest neighbors. They have become so helpless, resourceless and inert that I must concentrate on serving them. If I could persuade myself that I should find Him in a Himalayan cave, I would proceed there immediately. But I know that I cannot find Him apart from humanity."

Sarvodaya Shramadana in Sri Lanka

The Sarvodaya Shrmadana Movement of Sri Lanka traces its history back to the year 1958, when 27-year-old Ahangamane Tudor Ariyaratne, a science teacher at Nalanda Vidyalaya, a leading Buddhist High School in Colombo, took his students and some other teachers and volunteers to Kanatoluwa, a backward village 67 miles from the capital to hold a Shramadana Camp there. Ariyatne later admitted that this first experiment was meant mainly as an attempt to give the urban elite an insight into the real living conditions of some of their low-caste fellow-country men in the rural areas. "It is fair to say," he wrote, "that the pioneers of the Movement belonged to a higher class both economically and socially than most other youth in the country. The community they selected for their experiment, on the other hand, was one of the worst communities in Ceylon at that time." The crucial question was whether the young people from the towns would be able to "build a psychological bridge to close the gap between these two classes as a first step towards total integration of these two groups?"

The students had received three months' training to prepare them to face all the obstacles and hardships of a village camp, including the caste barrier they were determined to break. For eleven days they worked, "they sank wells, dug latrine pits, cleared home gardens and planted various crops, inaugurated a formal educational program, organized literacy classes for adults, conducted health lessons and demonstrations, child and maternity care work, singing and dancing classes and they even established a place for religious worship for the people," something which had never been accepted by the Buddhist clergy before. "Kanatoluwa was a hive of activity," A.T. Ariyaratne recalls in a report given later: "Hundreds of visitors from far and near visited the camp. Surrounding villagers in particular had the shocking experience of seeing men, women and children, led by this group of teachers and students who were supposed to be from a higher stratum of society, living and sweating with the so-called outcasts, whose very sight had made them tremble only a couple of days before. The lectures, discussions and meetings held every evening made Kanatoluwa a real school of life for all, young and old. How these suspicious observers gradually appreciated our mission and changed their attitudes towards the innocent people was apparent as the days passed by. A revolution in the minds and hearts of every one of us was complete and the first experiment in selfless labor to realize the lofty ideals of a Sarvodaya Society was successful."

What were these ideals? What were the new implications of "*Sarvodaya*" in the context of a Buddhist culture? "We in Ceylon were inspired by this Sarvodaya thought of Mahatma Gandhi and the Bhoodan-Gramdan action of Acharya Vinoba Bhave," A.T. Ariyaratne explains. "We do not allow our national pride to stand in our way when we choose to accept the best of any culture. While the word "Sarvodaya" with its literal meaning was adopted from India, the interpretation of its deep meaning as relevant to our own Sinhala Buddhist Culture and national population is completely our own. We have our own indigenous character both in thought and action as far as the Ceylon Movement is concerned."

At the same time it is, however, admitted that "the Sarvodaya philosophy of the movement is a synthetic ideology and a universal concepts. All forms of creative altruism and evolutionary humanism, be it from Marx's aim of material integration, Rousseau's option of social integration or Asoka's endeavor of moral integration, just to give a few examples, are inherent in title. Sarvodaya philosophy practiced by us for ours is an attempt to bring about total human integration. The philosophy that influenced us most in evolving our Sarvodaya concept in Sri Lanka (Ceylon) is Lord Buddha's teachings."

Buddha taught that "craving" (*tanha*) is the root cause of all suffering. He realized that the solution to man's suffering can only be found within the individual himself since all his actions are conditioned by the mind. In the *Dhammapada* it is further explained that "all states have mind as the forerunner, mind is their chief and they are mind-made. If one speaks or acts, with a defiled mind, then suffering follows one even as the wheel follows the hoof of the draught-ox." But if one speaks or acts with a pure mind, then "happiness follows one as one's shadow that does not leave one." According to this basic tenet of Buddhist philosophy Sarvodaya's development theory in Sri Lanka starts from the individual as its main element and tries to change his perceptions and attitudes. Though lack of documentary evidence makes it rather difficult to reconstruct the gradual evolution of the concept in the early years, I think it is correct to say that a Buddhist revivalism was the strong motive force at the beginning of the Movement. Here was a group of western-educated citizens with a middle-class back- ground formulating a Buddhist Ethic of Social Work so as to overcome the colonial spirit of capitalism in their country. The hard core of these part-time volunteers structured themselves in a loose association with Mr. A.T. Ariyaratne as their Convenor. They continued to organize and participate in Shramadana Camps in backward regions over the weekends or during their holidays. At a camp held in the ancient ruins of the former Buddhist capital of Anuradhapura in 1961, a resolution was passed: under the sacred Bo-Tree and all the participants firmly pledged their further energies to the cause of the Movement in the service of the spiritual and economic regeneration of Sri Lanka according to Buddhist principles.

Hundred Villages Development Scheme

The plan for a Hundred Villages Development Scheme first came up at the annual conference of the Movement held in 1966 where the participants discussed how best to celebrate the Mahatma Gandhi Birth Centenary in 1969. The idea was accepted and steps were taken during the last quarter of 1966 to select the hundred villages in such a way as to have them evenly distributed throughout the 22 Revenue Districts of the island. In each of these hundred villages a *Gramodaya* (Village Reawakening) Program was to be started so as to spread the basic development principles of the Movement in a more systematic way than had been done before.

As we have already seen, the sarvodaya development concept starts with the individual. The individual should have a clear and integrated idea as to why, from what and how he has to liberate himself, his own village community, his nation and his world. The Movement assumes that "one cannot go very far as an agent bringing about effective social change, unless one's ideological conditioning is non-fragmentary and embraces harmoniously one's own welfare with the welfare of others." Sarvodaya's philosophy tries, therefore, to achieve a two-fold liberation in every individual: "First, within one's own mind or thinking process there are certain defilements one has to recognize and strive to cleanse. Second, one has to recognize that there are unjust and immoral socio-economic chains which keep the vast majority of people enslaved. Thus, a dual revolution pertaining to an individual's mental make-up, and to the social environment in which he lives is kept foremost in the Sarvodaya Shramadana worker's mind and behavior." In this way Sarvodaya hopes to overcome the inner passions of greed, anger and ignorance that hinder a person's own, and thereby also others' realization and emancipation as a human being according to the Eight Noble Steps of Buddhist philosophy.

How was such a theoretical concept made to work at the practical level of a Hundred Villages Development Scheme? Ariyaratne explains that the unified approach of Sarvodaya Shramadana in Sri Lanka operates on three levels: education, development and participation are the foundations on which a new social order in rural Sri Lanka is to be built. (l) Through Shramadana, i.e. through working and sharing together, an educational reawakening process is initiated; (2) this new atmosphere and self-esteem is made use of and followed up by the Sarvodaya Village Reawakening and Development Program; (3) through peoples participation in the decision making process at all the various stages of the planning and implementing of Gramodaya (Village Re-awakening and Development) a non-violent process of emancipation is generated.

Education through Shramadana

During the Shramadana Camp, at the daily family gatherings and group discussions about performance and results achieved, Sarvodaya tries to reawaken in each participant "four principles of personality development" which the Movement understands as the very foundation of Lanka's Buddhist rural culture. They are *Metia* (Loving Kindness), *Karuna* (Compassion), *Mudita* (Sympathetic Joy) and *Upekkha* (Equanimity). These Four Sublime States of mind *(Brahmin Vihara)* are already mentioned in the old Buddhist scripts; they provide an answer to all the social situations and problems that arise from worldly contacts. Nyanaponika Thera explains them as "excellent or sublime, because they are the right or ideal way of conduct towards living beings. They are the great removers of tension, the great peacemakers in social conflict, the great healers of wounds suffered in the struggle of existence. They are called Abodes (*vihara*), because they should become mind's constant dwelling places where our minds feel at home; they should not remain merely places of rare and short visits, soon forgotten."

A Shramadana camp is understood by the Movement as "a place where both the physical and psychological requirements are fulfilled for every individual to imbibe these qualities in him." '*Metta*' is interpreted as the thought that motivates one to work with loving kindness and friendliness towards all and with respect for all life. '*Karuna*' is the action that leads one to help people overcome their suffering, fear and grief. '*Mudita*' is the immediate result experienced when fellow humans are made happy during the shramadana campaign. '*Upekkha*', however, is seen as the long-term result of a balanced personality that has learned to maintain equanimity at times of sorrow as well as joy

    A Shramadana Campaign aims at reshaping not only these four individual qualities but also group behavior. (1) In a camp each shares his labor and skills with others according to his capacity; sharing (*Dana*) is the first of the four principles of the Buddhist group-ethic and the first of the ten perfections for Buddhahood. (2) During their shared work people address one another in a pleasant language generally used in Sinhala only among members of the same family; "Pleasant Language" (*Priyavacana*) is the second Buddhist principle of social behavior. (3) By working together to reclaim a water tank or to cut an access road, by putting up a community building or a village school, the Shramadana family realizes "Constructive Activity (*Artha Chariya*), the third principle of Buddhist social behavior. (4) Sharing the same food, the same camp facilities for lodging and bathing without consideration of caste, class, race or political commitments is an example of "Equality" and Non-Partisanship" (*Samanathmatha*), the fourth principle of Buddhist Social behavior. It should be clear from the chart that a Shramadana Camp "with its song and dance, work and study" is seen as a microcosm of the "ideal human family where self-fulfillment and joy of living become a reality." For the Movement a camp is "an educative experience for young and old alike" from which three major benefits are expected: (1) Provision of a first-hand opportunity for rural and urban groups to meet in a beneficial manner, thus bringing about mutual-understanding and confidence in the achievement of common goals. (2) After generations of inaction and dependence the rural communities are stimulated into a new life of self-reliance and self-help to improve their conditions. (3) The emergence of a new rural leadership which is not split by caste, religion or political commitments but which has been trained for a new development.

Development through *Gramodaya*

    "The meaning intended to be conveyed by the term '*Gramodaya*' is the awakening of rural people, though its literal meaning is awakening of the village. If there is to be awakening of the nation there has to be awakening of the village. Our country consists of nearly 23,000 villages. Almost 90 percent of our people live in the villages. We in Sarvodaya are of the firm belief that it would be possible to develop a prosperous society in Sri Lanka by a process whereby villages are developed and village autonomy is established. So, Gramodaya is one of the most important aspects of the Sarvodaya program." By means of national Sinhala and Tamil newspapers, radio broadcasting and the Movement's official monthly journal ("Sarvodaya"), very wide and repeated publicity was given to the "Hundred

Villages Development Scheme." The Movement's headquarters asked for applications from or nominations of villages. On the basis of various reports and the data collected the Executive Council of the Movement decided which villages to include in the scheme. In each of the villages selected development work began with a "series of Shramadana Camps which aimed at meeting the need which the community felt most urgently and which could be completed with voluntary labor and a minimum of capital expenditure. This initial phase of the development work was handled with special care by a- team of experienced camp organizers assisted by groups of urban volunteers. The Movement found that the least difficult task was that of getting community cooperation. "The Sarvodaya philosophy provides a basis for everybody to meet at a common level and rise above all divisive forces in the village," Ariyaratne explains. "A workable and realistic program which can be carried out without dependence on governmental funds and bureaucratic procedures sets a tangible goal. Given the necessary sincere leadership and a scientific plan of action, a dynamic community action program is set in motion. Such is the manner in which initiation of the development program in each of the hundred villages is done. During the first year the Movement tried to realize the following targets in each of the hundred village:

-- To complete those projects that had been started by the first Shramadana camp and which aimed at the improvement of local irrigation, communication, farming and housing facilities.

-- To cultivate nobler individual and social values; to acquire elementary scientific and technical skills and know-how; and to learn to participate actively and intelligently in group ,and community programs.

-- To pick out a group of young and intelligent village leaders from among the members of the village community and provide then with the necessary training in the Sarvodaya methods and techniques of community development with a view to training them ultimately to be village level Sarvodaya extension workers.

-- To combine existing village-level leadership with new blood to form a common village planning body.

-- To link up with the village development scheme an educational or similar institution close to the village in order to train a group of young people selected from such a body and obtain their active and voluntary participation in village projects.

-- To conduct a thorough house-to-house survey of all the families in the community with a view to collecting all possible data pertaining to their present economic, social, educational and cultural life, to the health and medical services and the families' expectations in regard to the latter.

-- To provide opportunities for three national-level Sarvodaya workers (preferably university graduates) to gain a thorough understanding of the conditions prevailing in the village and trends of future changes with a view to becoming part of a body

of 3,000 rural reconstruction resource personnel drawn from all the 100 villages in the scheme.
-- To form for each village project a link with one foreign community group or welfare agency for mutual help and fraternal understanding.
-- To form for each village project a link with one private local voluntary body and/or supporting agency with some financial resources to assist the program.

In a report given four years after the program began Ariyaratne had to admit that "not all targets can be achieved by the movement in every village." He attributed the shortcomings to two main factors: (l) the Movement's inadequate financial resources and (2) the lack of sufficiently trained full-time workers. However, we must not forget that the main aims of the Movement are not material development targets as such but "the fulfillment of man. The Sarvodaya appeal is directed towards the transformation of the individual and through the individual the family, the village, the nation and the world." The practical application of this Sarvodaya thought is the participation of every villager in the solution of the numerous day-to-day problems in his immediate local environment.

Expansion

In 1969 A.T. Ariyaratne, "the little Gandhi of Sri Lanka, "received the Ramon Magasaysay Award for Community Leadership in Manila. In the same year Jayaprakas Narayan accepted an invitation to spend two weeks with the Movement in Sri Lanka to study and encourage its work and to celebrate the Gandhi Centenary. In 1970 a substantial donation from the World Assembly of Youth allowed for the first time a systematic expansion of the educational program for young community leaders. In 1972 the Movement, was incorporated in Sri Lanka by an Act of Parliament; thus the main condition for a Dutch organization's considerable financial commitment was met. A.T. Ariyaratne was now able to resign from his post as science teacher at Nalanda Vidyalaya and concentrate exclusively on the Movement's work.

Ten Basic Needs

In an attempt to identify the development targets in the villages more clearly and to make Sarvodaya work more specific, a ten Basic Needs Program was developed with the participation of some 660 village people. These needs are:
1. A clean and beautiful environment.
2. A clean and adequate supply of water.
3. Minimum clothing requirements.
4. A balanced diet.
5. A simple house to live in.
6. Basic health care.
7. Simple communication facilities.
8. Minimum energy requirements.
9. Total education.
10. Cultural and spiritual needs.

Each of these needs has been subdivided and detailed, making 167 items altogether. In his foreword to the brochure that lists these items, A.T. Ariyaratne explains that the "analysis of the Basic Human Needs has been based on the status of the weakest population group in the society and with the objective of improving their level of living." To achieve this improvement every village is advised to take the following steps: -

(1) Understanding the problem: The village or group of villages should be demarcated into self-sufficient and self-help units with between 100 and 150 families each. For each unit a detailed bench-mark survey should be conducted to obtain accurate figures on shortages and resources.

(2) Building up the organizational infrastructure: The village is advised to organize itself into various functional groups on the basis of the social infrastructure in a Sarvodaya village. The suggestion is also made that the Gramodaya Committee should not be composed only of the delegates of the various 'Haulas' but that steps should be taken to include delegates from the governmental and non-governmental units operating in the area.

(3) Developing service units: The brochure mentions twelve items of which the Sarvodaya PreSchool Service Center and the Sarvodaya Community Center are of special importance. Other service units that should be brought to the village either through the government or self-help are a junior school, a secondary school (in a large village), a place of worship, cooperative stores and a public market place, a playing field and an open air theater, a cemetery, a nursery and a seedbank, rural banking and insurance services, and a village library.

(4) Collective activities: Here sixteen forms of collective action programs are listed. They refer to the improvement of the local infrastructure, sanitation, irrigation, soil conservation and soil improvement. The last item, however, puts special emphasis on "economic units capable of producing furniture, earthen-ware and other utensils for the household, building materials such as bricks, sand, doors and windows, and implements like axes, crow-bars, katties, etc.

One should not, however, take the list of Ten Basic Human Needs as a doctrine; this would be totally contrary to the "Middle Path" approach the Movement has always tried to follow. The list is distributed to the villagers only as a guideline for educative self analysis, social and physical resource mobilization and joint action. Ariyaratne describes the present phase of the Movement as a "Struggle to integrate without Acquiescence"; this is the title of a chapter in his recent published booklet "A Struggle to Awaken." He sees the two decades' of Sarvodaya work in Sri Lanka as a struggle for survival, during which the Movement developed an infrastructural model of rural reconstruction that has gained public importance and thereby brought the movement "into the sphere of national and international development. Recognition of Sarvodaya philosophy and programs recently by political leaders, policy makers and administrators of development and welfare programs of our country is a pointer to the bigger and bigger national role we have to play."

Case Four
The Grameen Bank of Bangladesh[13]

In rural society no persons are more economically powerless than those who own no land, especially unmarried or widowed women. Traditionally the landless have survived by doing odd jobs, or by working for people who do own land. Policy makers have seldom given the landless a central place in their plans for rural investment. The lion's share of national bank loans has gone to landholders; people with no land or collateral were assumed too great a risk. In Bangladesh, such policies and assumptions held little promise for the landless poor -- more than half the population. A new bank, the Grameen (rural) Bank, set out to prove the common assumptions wrong.

The Grameen Bank had come a long way since 1975 when Mohammed Yunus, an economic professor, laid the foundation by lending his own pocket money to the landless poor near Chittagong University in southeast Bangladesh. Anyone with an income-earning venture could qualify-- rickshaw pullers, bicycle repairmen, traders hawking all kinds of goods and services. In the beginning Yunus simply wanted to know if borrowers would repay their loans. They did, he found, when conditions were right. He expanded in the Chittagong district under the wing of the national banks. By 1983 he had fully tested his model in the south-central district of Dhaka and got permission from the government to operate as an independent bank. Funding for expansion came from the International Fund for Agricultural Development, based in Rome. By 1987 Grameen Bank was reaching 6,000 villages in 6 of the country's 64 districts, with 335 branches and 300,000 borrowers; by the end of 1988 it had about 500 branches serving 10,000 villages. The target was 17,000 branches by 1995. Loan repayment was exceeding 95 percent, according to bank records. Most striking, three quarters of the loans went to the most economically vulnerable of villagers -- women.

"Of course, if you want to open banking to the landless poor -- people who are utterly powerless and have little or no collateral -- you need a different approach from what you'd do for the owners of land," explained Muzammel Huq. "We at Grameen Bank do not lend to individuals but to groups of borrowers -- five-person groups. This is our way of protecting the bank, as well as strengthening the individual borrowers." He pointed to a bank brochure elaborating the point. Group borrowing was a means of protecting bank interests, since borrowers came under pressure from their groups to pay back loans. Borrowers themselves also benefited from group borrowing. If one borrower became ill, the group could keep up his or her loan repayments. In other cases group support could be essential for encouraging a timid member to learn the loan procedure and accept its discipline. "So this group borrowing mechanism has been key to reaching the landless," said Huq. "To reach the more severely disadvantaged, we think you've got to have an alternative approach like this. The fact that it's more difficult to reach the poorest doesn't mean that they're unworthy of loans, or unreachable. It simply means you need an approach that's capable of reaching then, while protecting the bank at the same time. We have no doubt this can be done."

We got off the bus just outside Tangail at a village called Basail. A meeting of women borrowers had just begun. thirty women were seated cross-legged on mats spread across the ground in a shaded clearing. Barefoot, bare-chested children looked on from the doors and windows of bamboo huts. "This is a borrowers' organization we call a center, a Center," said Muzammel Huq. "Its comprised of six five person groups, and meets every week. The weekly meeting allows our bank agents to keep in touch with borrowers and collect regular loan repayments. For many women borrowers these meetings are their first encounter with participatory democracy. They elect a new chairperson for their Centers each year.

Seated at the front of the Center, facing the women borrowers, was a young woman banker. Rules of the bank allowed only female bankers to serve women borrowers, male bankers men. Beside the banker knelt a young mother in a bright green sari, clutching a naked baby with her left hand, a bankbook in her right. The baby's eyes, outlined with eye pencil, looked twice their real size. Muzammel Huq asked the woman a question in Bengali, then turned to translate. "Her name is Sharashawti Raj Bengshi," he said. "She's the wife of a village fisherman, mother of four. She inherited a family trade of fishnet making, and has taken out a loan to market her nets more widely around the area. It's brought a nice income for her." The young woman held up a net for Muzammel Huq's inspection. "As you can see," he said, "it's a fine mesh, made with an intricate hand-woven technique. Some of these family trades were endangered by the floods of 1974. Fine cloth weaving is another. Our loans help to rejuvenate these trades."

Sharashawti returned to her business with the bank agent, and signed her name on a loan form. Though illiterate, she had learned to write her name as a precondition for taking out loans. The sight of illiterate women transacting business in organized groups was one I had rarely seen in village society. My memory flashed back to a meeting some time before with a young Bangladeshi economist who had come home after finishing doctoral studies in the United States. It was the first time he had witnessed the women of his country taking out loans. "I'm not emotional by nature," he said, "but when I talked with these women I choked up. To believe that, in my own lifetime, I would see illiterate village women, their saris drawn up around their faces, explaining to me, an outsider -- a male outsider -- how the bank works, when their only way to count is on their ten fingers, and all they can write is their name -- I mean, I was taken aback. It's a kind of joy that's hard to explain."

As the fishnet maker returned to her seat among the borrowers, Muzammel Huq conversed in Bengali with another borrower. He turned to translate. "This is Ag Elashin," he said. "Her husband was disabled several years ago. She was left supporting him and three children. She already had some skills making pottery, and now decided to go commercial. With a bank loan she found new ways to market her work in neighboring villages. It's a scenario you'll hear time and again from women in these villages. For one reason or another they've had to become breadwinners, or starve." Muzammel Huq stood up before all the borrowers and asked how many were widows. The majority raised their hands. "You get the point," he said. "But the nice thing about the bank's approach is that there's absolutely no charity involved in helping people like this. European and American agencies have run relief programs here since the floods of 1974; they've given out charitable aid but asked nothing in return. People got dependent on handouts. Grameen Bank, on the other hand, gives out loans to landless people on the condition that they get more productive and repay -- including 16 percent interest. It sounds incredible, but their repayment rate is running well over 95 percent.

If Grameen Bank was doing much to improve the economic image of the landless poor, it still had not silenced ill doubt about their "viability." Some national planners downplayed its promise as a tool for economic growth. If the bank had shown that people at the margin can be reached with credit, that did not mean a country like Bangladesh should invest scarce resources in quite this way. Bank loans for micro enterprise, critics argued, could not make a significant dent in the problem of poverty among the swelling ranks of landless people. Of the nation's 55 million landless poor in 1990, Grameen Bank was reaching fewer than 500,000. Sufficient employment and improved incomes, critics argued, could be generated only by medium- and large-scale industry in the countryside, not the kind of small-scale enterprise supported by Grameen Bank. The Grameen concept had its merits, they admitted. But it should be considered more in the category of welfare, not a serious tool in the kit of national economic planners."

By the late 1985 some analysts were contending that Grameen Bank was surviving as an institution not because it was truly profitable, but because its operations were still subsidized by international agencies and other donors. Whatever the truth about the bank's financial sustainability, Yunus's justification of his bank as "good business" was puzzling. In one sense I could understand his argument perfectly well. The late 80s had brought growing international recognition that private enterprise and free markets must play a major role in boosting economic growth in poor nations. Since Ronald Reagan had come to the American presidency in 1981, political support had been growing in the United States for aid programs that encouraged entrepreneurship, including Grameen-style credit. Policies in developing nations also were coming to be more supportive of entrepreneurial activity, and of programs that promote it. In such a business-friendly international climate, Yunus's "good business" rationale would clearly be persuasive. Yet why did Yunus justify his bank so exclusively in business terms? Had he abandoned his original goal of elevating the landless poor on the list of national priorities, demonstrating their human and economic "viability"?

On returning to the capital city of Dhaka, I determined to press the Director in person for the answer. I found him one hot afternoon at the bank's head office. The building -- a modest office block on the outskirts of the city -- was the antithesis of the high-rise headquarters of the Agricultural Development Bank of Pakistan. Yunus was seated behind a large desk in a dimly lit, scantily furnished office. Slight of build but forceful in speech, he cut a handsome boyish image, accentuated by a shock of wavy black hair. Why, I asked, have you become so adamant about this good-business argument? Surely you do not believe the value of Grameen Bank will be judged by its performance as a business? "We are bankers," he replied. "If you're looking for a movement for social justice, or an institution to ease unemployment and poverty, you need to look elsewhere. Here we give loans, not plans for social reform. I'm not against reform, of course. I'm just saying that our purpose is to be bankers. There's a public demand for our services. We seek to make a profit on our lending. Though we take out loans from the national banks, we are not drawing down government resources -- in fact, the government makes money from us. So Grameen Bank is justified because it is a business venture that benefits its employees, the people, the government."

For all Yunus's seriousness, his voice carried a hint of tease, as if to admit there was more to his motivation than entrepreneurship. I made a last attempt to draw him out: "Surely you would not deny the humanitarian goals -- alleviating poverty, unemployment, showing the economic worth of the poor, and so on?" He yielded no ground. "We try to wear just one hat here -- the hat of a banker, not social or humanitarian reformer. That would confuse people, especially our borrowers. They might think we have special goals in mind, and then concoct artificial ideas for loans they think we'd approve. Instead, we say, `Look, we are bankers. You are people who need to earn a living. You know what you do best. If you need money, talk to us. If we think you'll earn money and repay, we'll give you the loan. You make a profit, we earn interest, we're both better off. With this approach, the initiative is theirs. It's their project, their planning. They must be the ones to initiate and carry through."

Here, then, was at least some explanation for the good-business rationale. Beyond claiming for the bank a legitimate place in the economy, it was a way to keep goal setting in the hands of bank borrowers, not the bankers themselves. Still, this did not explain everything. Grameen Bank was unquestionably one of Bangladesh's more visible symbols that the landless poor were worthy of inclusion in national development. Why downplay the social and humanitarian aspects? Could not Yunus permit himself a few moments to celebrate the act of reaching poor people, changing their prospects -- however modestly -- for the better? Perhaps he felt the benefits spoke well enough for themselves. Perhaps he was tired of debates over which strategies do the most to ease poverty. I left his office with only partial explanations, a collection of hunches. That seemed the most I could expect to find -- until, that is, I visited a town called Chilmari.

Chilmari was, in some ways, the extreme in a land of extremities. Simply getting there was in itself an extremity. From Dhaka in the south-central part of the country, the journey took five hours by bus to the northwest, three hours by ferry up the Brahmaputra River to the city of Rangpur, then two more hours of hot, dusty driving to the east. Life in rural Chilmari seemed to go on in utter remove from the more frenetic urban pace of neighboring Rangpur. Along its narrow winding streets, the shops of Bengali merchants were interspersed with Chinese restaurants, stores selling British bicycles and Japanese motorcycles, and retail outlets for Bridgestone tires and Philips TV. By contrast to cosmopolitan Rangpur, the tiny village of Chilmari seemed a settlement just off the edge of history, little touched by the winds of commerce or by the "universal language." It was a spread of small one-story stucco structures, surrounded on its outskirts by huts of elaborately woven bamboo and roads leading to villages beyond.

For sheer survival, Chilmari and other outlying villages were built on high ground. Everyone knew that the wet season each year would bring new flooding from rain rushing down from the Himalayas. To ensure the passage of vehicles, roads also were elevated on embankments, some six to ten feet high. In addition to facilitating traffic, the banks trapped water in vast pools ideal for cultivating rice and fish. Occasionally, the floods' angrier moods proved too much for the banks. In 1974, rising waters repeatedly breached the barriers, washing away huts and destroying crops. Many thousands died in village streets or on roads leading to urban centers. In Dhaka the government was slow to respond with relief for the northwest. Only when starving country folk began to stream into the capital and die in its streets was the extent of rural crisis taken seriously.

By the time I arrived in Chilmari, where Grameen Bank had established a branch, the village had enjoyed more than a decade of flood-free years, though few could forget the disaster of 1974. The bank's representative was S. M. Musa, a young college graduate from Tangail who had come to the area with his wife after serving the bank in Tangail. "That was child's play compared to here," explained Musa, as we walked through the dusty streets. "We've had enormous difficulty getting people just to accept the idea of a bank. The existence of charitable relief agencies in the area made it nearly impossible even to launch the bank at all." Like many of the college graduates attracted by the bank, Musa spoke excellent English. His slacks and trim open-neck shirt distinguished him in appearance from less-advantaged village men who wore the skirt like lungi and tattered shirts. "When we first came here several years ago," he said, "European relief agencies had, for years, been giving free services in nutrition and health. People got so used to handouts they couldn't comprehend the idea of taking out a loan and paying it back with interest. We finally got the idea across, but it wasn't a foregone conclusion."

Making our way to huts on the outskirts of town, we were met by two women bank workers and Momena Bewa, leader of a local women borrowers' association. Mrs. Bewa had lost her husband during the 1974 floods. After the first flood hit in June he had tried to rebuild the family hut. His efforts were decimated by a second flood in July. When the third flood hit in September he was sick and exhausted, and died leaving Mrs. Bewa to fend for herself and two small children. For eight years she roamed from village to village, trying to eke out a living doing odd jobs. When Grameen Bank came to the area, she took out a loan and started a business selling household wares. Profits made it possible to put a down payment on a hut. For the first time in ten years she had an address. Her daughter soon married the son of a respected family, and things began to look up.

Why, I asked Mrs. Bewa, had villagers finally embraced the idea of Grameen Bank, when they could have continued to take handouts from charities? "I remember when Dr. Yunus first came and told us about the bank," she said. "We were skeptical. He asked if we remembered the floods of 1974. Yes of course, we said, that was a terrible time, people dying everywhere. Then he asked if any of us had lost relatives. We were quiet. All of us had losses. He asked if we thought the suffering of 1974 would come again. We were still quiet. He said, "I tell you, the suffering will come again, because you are doing nothing to prevent it." Now that got us thinking. We knew he was right. We had to do more to help ourselves. But what? He told us we could take out loans. "Expand your businesses", he said, "but you must understand the bank's rules and pay back what you borrow. Then you'll be more secure." We did. Now most all the women in my group are better off. I don't know if we could survive another 1974, but we will have a far better chance.

If Yunus's early work in Chilmari had served to awaken in villagers a desire to reduce dependency and do more for themselves, by now the bank was itself a symbol of reduced dependency in the countryside. I was beginning to think I had my answer about why bank workers, and Yunus himself, shied away from the language of poverty alleviation and welfare. Justifying the bank in those terms would risk having it linked to ideas of charity, which the bank was trying to overcome. To the extent that Grameen Bank proved itself "good business," it would show that the "unviable poor" were not so economically unviable after all. Otherwise the bank would not be able to retrieve its loans, and would cease to exist. Far from an abandonment of his early humanitarian goals, Yunus's good-business rationale was a confirmation of them, and in the most convincing of bottom-line terms. He still had a long way to go to prove that the bank was sustainable; but he had also come a very long way.

Although Yunus and his colleagues were determined to wear just one "hat" -- that of the banker -- they had certainly not abandoned the idea of using the bank to promote social change. Studies were constantly undertaken to chart the impact of bank efforts. Bank activities appeared to be loosening age-old social restrictions that inhibited economic growth in the countryside. Restrictions on female enterprise were easing and male labor was experiencing improved working conditions. Men, traditionally employed on farms at substandard wages, increasingly received better pay offers from employers. These were trends bank workers encouraged. Employers realized that, without improved wage offers, landless laborers might be able to earn a living by taking out Grameen Bank loans and expanding their off-farm business activities. In some cases the influence of village headmen as judges in village courts declined as Grameen Bank members began to settle disputes among themselves. In short, the bank encouraged the poor to strengthen their position *vis-a-vis* more powerful groups by organizing self-help Bank workers also reported that rising self-respect among borrowers led to reductions in the social frictions of village life. "A husband who beats his wife," explained M. S. Musa, "will find his wife's borrowing group knocking at the door demanding explanation. Often the embarrassed husband stops the abuse, and in a very short time." What significance would a venture like Grameen Bank ultimately have for villagers like these -- twenty, thirty, forty years hence? In some ways, critics of the bank were probably right: Fuller reductions of rural poverty would require national policy changes that encouraged employment opportunities on a much vaster scale, largely through industries more sophisticated than the tiny micro enterprises supported by Grameen Bank. Still, activities like the bank's might be helping to create conditions for such economic expansions to take hold.

Muzammel Huq had argued as much some weeks before. "You have to realize," he had insisted, "that the people we're talking about -- the landless poor -- have had excruciatingly little opportunity for generation after generation. If you want to help them progress, you cannot bypass the channels of education they need, or push them ahead too fast. There have to be ways for them to develop confidence in themselves and what they can do. But once this confidence grows. they get involved in all kinds of activities they might have avoided before. This is the confidence Grameen Bank inspires."

The "up side" of Grameen Bank's system of loan repayment is that borrowers are allowed to repay a small amount each week, rather than all of it at the end of the loan period. This mechanism is clearly one reason the bank has been so popular. While landless laborers might find it inconceivable to repay a $ 50 loan all at once, they are comfortable with paying back $1 per week over a one year period. The "down side" is that the bank must maintain a labor-intensive system of loan collection and meticulous bookkeeping by hand. Week by week, bank officers must meet face to face with borrowers. It might be argued that more efficient methods can, and should, be found. Bank officials attribute the high repayment rate to various factors: 1)Interest rates are extremely attractive 16 percent per year, compared to the rates of local moneylenders, which can run as high as ten percent per week). 2) Since each person's prospect for getting loans depends on the loan repayment record of others in the group, peer pressure urges repayment. 3) Since national banks will not lend at all to people with no collateral, borrowers come to see Grameen Bank as "their own bank" and want to keep it alive. 4) Weekly payments look good compared to the moneylenders' requirement that loans be repaid at once, often at the penalty of seizing land or a homestead. 5) The possible penalties of failure to repay, litigation or loss of homestead, are costly and discourage cheating the system. 6) Since poor people generally receive small loans and make very modest profits, in contrast to large landowners who ask for large loans, they do not become oriented to "milking" the system.

In short, poor people's stakes in repaying their loans tend to be very high, while their ambitions and power to cheat the system are low. On the administrative side, the banks success might be partly explained by what economist Judith Tendler terms its "minimalist" approach to credit -- the financing of lower-risk activities, mainly in trade and commerce, rather than the potentially high-risk activities of manufacturing and services. This approach also avoids the longer time required to evaluate larger, more risky investments, and demands less extensive technical or business training for bank agents.

Case Five
ACCORD:
Action for Community Organization, Rehabilitation and Development for the Tribal Peoples of Southern India[14]

March 1984. Our first day in the Nilgiris. Stan and I were in a crowded bus. Two seats were unoccupied. The lone occupant of the three person seat was an old Panlya women. No one sat near her. They preferred to stand. A few stops later a Panlya girl in a sparkling white "mund," hair oiled and shiny, face scrubbed clean, sat in a vacated seat. The non-tribal woman next to her muttered angrily and inched away from the girl. "Cheek of these people" she grumbled, "Now they dare sit next to you, next they'll be on our laps." The Panichi sat uncomfortably at the edge of the seat. She had a blank expression on her face. As though the comments went over her head.

Months passed and our experiences confirmed the fact. The non-tribal community had belittled and denigrated the tribals' customs, culture and way of life. To the extent that people walked tall, happy and carefree in the confines of their own isolated hamlets, crept through the towns silent and scared. Ashamed of their origins, they were beaten and subdued.

To understand this, one has to go back in time. The tribals of the lower Nilgiris -- the Moolukurumbas, Paniyas, Bettakurumbas, Kattunaickens and Irulas were a proud people who lived isolated lives in the mountains and densely forested slopes of the Gudalur valley. When the region was opened to tea estates many of the Paniyas and Kattunaickens were trapped like animals and sold into slavery. After the abolition of Slavery Act in the 19th century, slavery gave way to the bonded labor system.

After independence, settlers from Kerala began migrating to the region. They tempted the tribals away from the Chettys with offers of cash. This broke the back of the bonded labor system. Throughout this process there was a steady undermining of their culture and ethos. The favored epithets were "savage, uncivilized, jungli, wild." People denigrated their language, dress, religion, land customs. Economically they were consigned to the lowest rung of society -- an unskilled labor force. The forests, once their domain, became forbidden territory. They were barred from collecting forest produce. Their environment was taken away from them. They had begun to believe what society told them -- that they were its dregs.

The Birth of ACCORD

ACCORD began functioning out of Gudalur town, the taluk[district] headquarters, as a response to this situation. Stan and I, and K.T. Subramanian, a

Moolakurumba tribal, started ACCORD in 1986. We planned to spend the first year moving around the taluk, getting to know the people. We discovered that there were a number of young people who had some education -- not enough to get them jobs -- but a little too much to allow them to earn their living as labors. We thought that this would be the starting point -- to create awareness among these youngsters, so that they could become agents of change. They wanted to do something for their people. These formed the core team -- the animators [RDFs].

Stan began training them in social analysis. For the first time the questions were asked. Why are we poor? Where has our land gone? Why? How? As we tried to answer these questions, directions emerged and slowly ACCORD began to take shape. First the **Analysis:** (1) the loss of control over the forests and the alienation of their land had rendered them impoverished and dependent on non-tribals. (2) with the disappearance of forests, land was their last resource. Change would necessarily involve recovering their lands. (3) they were totally powerless -- politically and otherwise. Their only strength was their numbers [-- roughly 30,000 scattered over several disunited tribal areas]. This meant that they had to unite. (4) they must organize themselves to fight for their rights, to recover their lost lands, to change the social and economic structures that had kept them underfoot.

Realty: (1) All very well, but the tribals were totally dependent on the very people who controlled these structures. (2) How would people get the courage to unite and stand up for their rights unless this dependence could be broken? (3) The situation of their health was so bad, could we just sit back and say wait till the structures have been changed.

Strategy: (1) Start organizing small groups at the hamlet level through local tribal animators [RDFs]. (2) While the focus would be on the formation of these groups, development programs would also be initiated to sustain them. (3) In about 10 years, ACCORD should pull out. The people had to take control of their own lives, or we would have failed in our job.

Forming the Sangam (Village Community)

Now began the arduous task of community organization. The concept of unity being strength was a new concept to these tribals. The idea of the sangam or village based action group took time for the people to understand. There were no role models in their experience. And then one day: "A local landowner who had moved up in the world, wanted to get a tractor down to his paddy field. But Chorian, a Paniya tribesman, and his tiny patch of coffee trees stood in the way. No problem, he thought, he would simply cut a trail through Chorian's property, including cutting down a number of the tribesman's coffee trees. Hundreds had done it before on other tribesmen's land. But this time there was a difference. Chorian had been to some of the sangam meetings. So he appealed to them for help. Within hours 200 Adivasis (tribal people) had arrived. They rebuilt the fence and demanded justice. Their clamor was heard, the police came, filed a case and

Chorian's land rights were restored. That was not all. A young lawyer, A. C. Chacko, sympathetic to the tribals, filed a civil suit for damages, and for the first time an all powerful landlord was brought to heel. Suddenly the concept of strength through unity meant sense to the tribals. All over, people started coming together in small groups. Sometimes just ten families. But they all added up and soon everywhere tribals were talking of their rights, of their lost lands and of the need to fight for change. A.C. Chacko, eventually became part of the ACCORD team, giving para-legal training to the tribals, taking on their cases against landlord atrocities, arbitrary arrests and false cases. The tribals have drawn courage from the fact that they have their own lawyer.

Cultural Activism

Community organization was not just the land problem and political awareness. Each tribe lived its isolated life. Rarely interacting with each other, it was necessary that they came together as a group and developed a pride in their tribal identity. Interaction with the non-tribal people around had resulted in a tremendous erosion of tribal culture. People were becoming increasingly ashamed of their own traditions. To combat this we hit on the brain wave of a Tribal Cultural Festival. The first festival was held on January 10, 11, 1988. All the five tribes participated together. Old leaders lit a common lamp and performed a common *puja* to symbolize tribal unity. This was the first time anything like this had happened. Then the music and dancing started and went on right through the night. In the day time there were games and sports. Tribal events -- archery, catapult shooting, and other games -- were held. The festival has been held every year since 1988. It has become a tradition. Many old forgotten dances, songs and games have been revived, and most significantly more and more young people have begun to participate.

National Attention is Finally Received

During this time an organization of tribal groups was established: the Adivasi Munnetra Sangam (AMS). It is now recognized as the legitimate representative organization of the tribals -- by the government, by the local non-tribals and most important of all, by the tribals themselves. The AMS was to spearhead the campaign for tribal land rights. Groups of youngsters formed a drama troupe to spread awareness about the need for land. The campaign culminated in a massive demonstration in Gudalur town on December 5, 1988. Ten thousand people arrived in a mammoth show of solidarity. They submitted their demands in a Memorandum to the Governor of Tamilnadu. It was a turning point for the tribals -- for the first time they realized their strength, their potential power. The news of the demonstration became a major front-line story that reached Madras and even Delhi. Several others happened simultaneously. Stan Thekaekara received the National Youth Award and most significantly the Prime

The Concept of Rural Development   171

Minister, Rajiv Ghandi, when presenting the award, agreed to meet the tribal team. Later that year the tribal leaders did meet with the Prime Minister and he agreed to follow up the land question. When the team reached Madras on their return, they were met by the Minister for Tribal Welfare. He promised to come and see for himself. A whirlwind tour followed. The tribals finally made inroads into the corridors of power. During 190-91 many land disputes were settled in favor of the tribals. Possession certificates were issued to those who had land. Many tribals who had been prevented from cultivating their traditional lands for want of proof of ownership now reclaimed their land.

Activism vs Development?
    We viewed our role primarily as one of creating awareness and getting the people to fight for their rights. This was fine as long as an issue emerged to fight around. But to sustain the movement something concrete was needed. Land in the hands of a penniless Paniya meant nothing unless he had the resources to develop it. Could one talk about rights to a grief stricken who had lost six children because of acute anemia?
    Tea Planting: From the very start, as part of the land campaign we were looking for ways to prevent land alienation. To make land productive so that tribals would value it, tea planting was introduced. Half an acre was easy to plant and take care of and would generate profit of nearly 600 rupees per month. Becoming a planter was a good political move -- it increased the people's pride in themselves. From 1986 when we had to beg tribals to plant tea, by 1992 we had a waiting list of 400 people. Based upon lobbying activities of ACCORD, both the Horticulture Department and the Tea Board are now providing resources and training
    The Adivasi Credit Fund: One of the basic problems was indebtedness. During the lean season when no work was available, tribals were forced to borrow at exorbitant rates of interest. Often the tribals were forced to sell their crops of pepper, tea or coffee at one tenth its price to meet the costs of an illness or a death in the family. The end result was mortgaged land and unending debt. To combat this, the people worked out the dynamics of the Adivasi Credit Fund. It started spontaneously when people contributed one rupee a week towards a credit fund for anyone in need. ACCORD matched the collection. Peer pressure ensures that the money is repaid on schedule. Otherwise there is nothing in the kitty when the next borrower comes along. An old abandoned traditional rice scheme was revived by the Kappala women's sangam. Each woman saved a handful of raw rice for the sangam before starting her cooking each day. Every week this came to the sangam. Women who needed a loan came and borrowed rice when needed.
    Livestock Development: We have always felt that it was necessary to explore other sources of income for the people. The IRDP program concentrated on the distribution of milk animals. However, the veterinary infrastructure was

very poor and most of the tribals were not at all familiar with dairying. We therefore decided to recruit a veterinary doctor. Dr Marimuthu Swaminathan, fresh out of college was full of enthusiasms and energy. With his expertise, we have launched numerous experiments in poultry farming, dairying, rabbitry and piggeries. He has also trained a small team of barefoot veterinary assistants.

Health: Every monsoon and every winter death visited the tribal hamlets. They succumbed with respiratory infections or common colds that worsened progressively. In the summer the killer was diarrhea and dehydration. All throughout the year, in all kinds of weather, women died in childbirth. In March 1987 we met Roopa Nath and Narayanan Devadasan. They had just graduated from medical training, were about to get married, and wanted to work with the rural poor. They agreed to a stint in Gudalur until post graduation time. Deva and Roopa started working with their first batch Health Workers and in a few months they were hooked. They decided post graduation could wait and plunged headlong into a community health program that centered around a core group of tribal women health workers.

Training Health Workers: The women were trained in an intensive three week session. This was followed by weekly teaching sessions. The Health Workers were taught to deal with basic illnesses -- diarrhea, colds, coughs and virals. They were trained to conduct deliveries and to recognize when mother and child were in danger and needed emergency treatment. Once a week, the mobile clinic also visited the base villages. Health Workers who had been visiting the houses in their care rounded up the sick people and brought them to the mobile clinic. In health also we witnessed the astounding phenomenon of fear. People quietly lay down to die in their homes, preferring a quiet dignified death to the unknown specter of the government hospital. The health team had a formidable task before them. They had to convince people about the necessity for immunization, about the importance of boiling drinking water, of nutritious food, and how ORS would save children plagued with diarrhea.

It was still very disheartening when deaths occurred inspite of the Health Workers presence in the hamlet. Old habits die hard. In some cases there was active opposition. In Bettakurumba hamlets, where the old ones decreed the anger of the Gods would descend on all those who abandoned traditional practices. Going to the hospital was taboo. The health team was often cursed in the villages. It was bad enough for the doctors, but the Health Workers who lived with the community bore the brunt of it. Slowly the tide turned. There are a few landmark events. In Bettakurumba, the Health Worker managed to convince one mother to allow her children to be immunized against measles. The others scoffed at them. Then the epidemic struck and the immunized children were the only ones who escaped the attack. The Health Workers were jubilant and slowly the number of mothers who brought their children for immunization increased.

Starting a Community Hospital

Ironically, the very success of the community health program created a new problem. Increasing numbers of serious patients began to arrive. We tried the government hospital but the treatment was so bad that patients' belief that hospitals were where you went to die was being reinforced. Private hospitals were the next resort. Even with the concessions from friendly doctors the bills were exorbitant and we had to really strain our resources to pay them. We put this problem to our team of animators (RDFs) and everyone came back to the same solution -- start a hospital of our own. There were pros and cons: We were opposed to the idea because it seemed to violate our philosophy of small scale activities that could be sustained after we left and Deva and Roopa feared the community health program would be swallowed up. Most important was the question of how we would finance such a major project. Yes, we have tried our best with government hospitals and Roopa had even offered to work there voluntarily and had been refused. We had ended up with two beds in the office. Without the infrastructure of a hospital or nursing services, Roopa and Deva were now often on duty 24 hours. How long could this go on? Our own hospital seemed the only way out. The clinching argument was that the hospital could be instrumental in empowering the people.

We had all agreed that we need a hospital, so when Shyla and Nandakumar dropped in to check us out, we could not believe our luck. A gynecologist-surgeon combination was too good to be true. We managed to convince them that we were not too bad. So they stayed to start the Gudalur Adivasi Hospital (GAH). In keeping with ACCORD pullout plan, the GAH was a separate entity. ASHWINI, a society to run GAH was registered. Intense and often heated discussions took place about what kind of hospital we wanted. We had to create an atmosphere where people would feel at home. To do this we recruited as many tribal staff as possible. All the nurses are tribal, so is Maran the lab assistant. The fact that people could be greeted in their own language by women of their tribe made them perceptibly relax. Another big fear was falling off beds, so we did away with all but two beds for emergencies. The others have mattresses on the floor. The nurses and doctors go out on the mobile clinic so when a patient arrives there is generally instant recognition from both sides. This reassures patients and makes for a warmer relationship immediately. A hospital committee was formed of tribal leaders, animators (RDFs) and Health Workers for a feedback system on how the patients perceives us. With limited support from international donors and other local supporters, the hospital was completed. It is simple but very functional, the staff are paid reasonable salaries but no one is getting rich. The biggest problem for the tribals is the unemployment that accompanies sickness. Hospital meant two unemployed people -- the patient and the family members watching over them. Both would borrow to tide them through the illness. Often ten days in the hospital meant a debt of up to 100 rupees, which often took a year to pay off. We have planned a vegetable garden that could provide part time employment for patients' relatives to cover living costs at least. To encourage tribal knowledge and revive healthy old practices, we intend calling on the reserves of herbal knowledge that tribal people are rapidly losing. A herbal garden will be an essential part of the hospital. Also we envisage creating a cluster of birthing huts close enough for comfort and companionship but with space for families to rally around with being in the way. Finally we hope in the future to hand over the management of GAH completely to a tribal body which will determine its policy.

The Insurance Scheme: Financing a hospital is always a nightmare for any voluntary organization. The obvious solution , of course, has been the Robin Hood one -- charge the rich to pay for the poor. But then who really owns the hospital? How could we say that this was truly a tribal hospital if they were to be the recipients of charity? It was then that the much advertised Mediclaim Insurance Scheme gave us an idea. Could the insurance company think of a much simpler insurance scheme suited to the needs and the pockets of the tribals? Such a scheme would not cover expensive treatments like kidney transplants, but diarrhea and pneumonia. The idea was put to a couple of insurance companies. The New India Assurance Company promptly responded. There was a lot of parleying that went on for several months, but with the support of the Divisional Manger and his staff, the scheme finally came through. For an annual premium of approximately 60 rupees per annum, a family of five would be covered for the following risks: (1) damage to hut and belongings up to 1500 rupees, (2) death or permanent disability to head of family up to 2500 rupees, and (3) all illnesses requiring hospitalization up to 1500 rupees. At present nearly 5000 individuals have been insured for five years. While this insurance scheme will not meet the costs of hospital care, we felt that this was one way of providing health care with dignity, not charity.

Education in the Tribal Communities

When a tribal child goes to a government school his name is changed. He is forbidden from speaking his own language and must switch to Tamil. His cloths, customs, speech and dress are denigrated and derided. The child who survives this cultural onslaught is a tough individual. He or she emerges completely Tamilized having accepted the verdict of the majority that theirs is the superior culture. Ram who coordinates the ACCORD school program estimates that there is only about 25 percent literacy among the tribals of taluk. Education was not seen as a priority by either the tribal team of animators(RDFs) or the people, so our initial attempts floundered. Jacintha Vincent who began the Kadachankolly school for us was an excellent teacher and worked wonders with Bettakurumba children there. The Kadachankolly school progresses inspite of its ups and downs. The children come even though the facilities are minimal. The Bettakurumba culture has been kept alive in the school with sons, stories and dances. The government infrastructure had 14 Government Tribal Residential Schools (GRT) which had been reduced to a farce! We had frequently discussed the possibility of placing tribal teachers in these schools to improve them. This has finally been achieved. Also some adult literacy projects have been established using local volunteers fired with a zeal to teach. Another education effort has been the starting of tutorials to help high school students pass their exams. Since their standards were so poor, tutorials were held for the 9th and 10th class kids. Now it has turned into a parallel high school running quietly with no fuss by three young tribals. This is a unique achievement.

The ACCORD Family
It is above all, people who make things work. In ACCORD we count ourselves blessed because of the people who make up the team. We work as a cohesive group, without a hierarchical structure and with a fair amount of democracy. Our greatest strength has been the fact that we have gotten together a strong team of tribal men and women who believe in the future and working towards it. Like all NGOs, the emphasis in ACCORD is on field work. Yet the administrative and support team here has been an integral part of all the action -- with everybody making their own unique contribution.

Section Four
Lessons Learned

We are now ready to consider a preliminary list of pre-requisites for success, a set of principles that successful RDFs have used to implement rural development programs. A careful review of the five case studies suggests a set of common themes, approaches, strategies that appear relevant to any rural development project. These principles are by no means exhaustive or all encompassing. Although certain ideals do appear to be relevant for most types of village development, RDFs must realize that while these principles must always be coupled with what David Korten calls a "learning process approach" which allows for risk taking, mistakes and the learning from such mistakes. The sole determinant of success cannot be found in one magical factor. Future projects may find these examples useful and appropriate but only if they are adapted to the needs and situations of the particular community where RDFs find themselves working.

Principle One: Long-Term Commitment
It Takes Time to Develop a Relationship of Trust and to Establish Mutual Understanding.
The life of James Yen is an embodiment of this first principle. While in the trenches of W. W. I, Dr. Yen discovered the importance of listening and seeking to

understand the people he was working with. He could help these people only after he had become acquainted with them in an intimate way. Ironically, he had to travel to France before he really came to see the peasants of China as they really were. It was later in China that this principle became truly operational. After living and working with the peasants for ten years, and after many failures and misfortunes, was he able to be truly helpful. In his own words: "If we want to help them intelligently, we must know them. If we want to know them, we must go and live with them."

Dr Ahmad al-Naggar recognized the importance of this principle as well. He insisted that no village bank be established until a "strong bond of trust and mutual acceptance" was first established. Dr. al-Naggar and his twenty facilitators spent many days and weeks interacting with the *fellahin*, trying to see reality as it was experienced by these peasants, understanding their idioms, their way of life, their customs and traditions. The power and significance of trust and mutual acceptance were very evident in way new ideas were introduced and accepted by the peasants. Government officials, who had been working in these villages for decades, without this trust and understanding, were simply incapable of having a positive impact on these people.

In his quest for "Sarvodaya," professor Ariyaratne understood the value of inter-cultural and inter-caste understanding. By taking a group of upper caste students into a number of low caste villages, he sought to build a "psychological bridge" between the educated and the impoverished. Ariyaratne further sought to comprehend the villagers' problems by conducting a thorough house-to-house survey seeking to collect economic, social, educational, health, and nutritional data. This effort to obtain in-depth information on the lives and concerns of the villagers proved to be an invaluable source of learning.

One of the special examples of this first principle is in the lives of Stan and Mari Thekaekara. Well educated, coming from an upper class background, there was little to suggest why these two would leave the comforts of urban life to live and work with the poorest of the poor tribals in southern India. They spent many days and nights seeking to understand the culture and way of life of these tribal peoples. Few Indians were concerned with these people, and even fewer were willing to give their lives to establishing a relationship of trust and understanding with such tribal people. They viewed their role as one of "creating awareness and getting the people to fight for their rights."

All of the five case studies document how successful intervention is not a short-term process. Only when one is willing to devote one's life to living and working with the less fortunate of this world, will long-term, sustainable kinds of programs be implemented.

Principle Two: Teaching Self-Reliance
Successful Programs must be Built upon the Concept of Self-Reliance and Local Resource Mobilization.

There is evidence from all the case studies that successful projects consistently encouraged the local people to use their own resources as much as possible. When local people mobilize labor, materials, and income for a project, they are much more willing to accept ownership, to take greater pride and responsibility to maintain the project, to see that it is sustainable. The successful RDFs in these case studies were all sensitive to the importance of only using outside resources as a leverage for local resources. Dr Yen could have hired doctors to come into the villages where he was working, but he choose to train and organize a group of local "barefoot doctors" who received their pay through small donations from the villagers themselves, including the satisfaction they received in helping their neighbors. Dr. al-Naggar's local bank system and Dr Yunus's Grameen Bank system both demonstrate conclusively that local people can be motivated to mobilize their own resources when systems consistent with the local culture are implemented. Stan Thekaekara, in south India, has been able to establish a modern hospital with a most limited budget. Relying on local people's volunteer labor, recruiting professionals willing to work at minimum salaries, creating a kind of HMO system in which local people pay something into the cost of operating the hospital, all combined to created a very cost-effective system for these poor tribal people. Ariyaratne followed in Gandhi's footsteps, insisting that villagers should be self-reliant, arguing that anything they cannot make or provide for themselves, they don't really need. Any activity or planning process that requires that the community becomes dependent on outsiders should be rejected. Long term sustainability requires that people develop their own systems of education, health, income generating projects, etc.

Principle Three: Using Appropriate Technology
Successful projects utilized simple technology, simple systems of implementation, and project activities that can be maintained by local resources, local knowledge and know-how.

Dr. Yen sought to present technologies that were simple and easy to understand. In his "formula for success," Dr Yen presented the essence of the third principle for success: "What you teach must be simple. It must be simple enough so that the peasant farmer can understand and adopt it." Dr. Yunus formula for success was simplicity at its best. "Look, we are bankers. You are people who need to earn a living. You know what you do best. If you need money, talk to us. If we think you'll earn money and repay, we'll give you a loan. You make a profit, we earn interest, we're both better off." Many rural development projects are quick to introduce complicated water systems, expensive agriculture equipment, and special technologies that require outsiders to provide maintenance and spare parts. All these case studies were implemented utilizing local technologies whenever possible, to only use outside technology after it had been adapted to the needs and capacities of the local people.

Principle Four: Develop Program Ownership
Successful projects emphasized the importance of involving local people in the implementation and development of the local projects utilizing traditional values and the local culture.

Dr al-Naggar insisted that the local bank system being developed belonged to the villagers and not to him or some other group. He emphasized how the bank was based upon the local culture and was consistent with traditional religious values. Stan Thekaekara involved the local tribal people in the planning and design of the project from the very beginning. There was no question that the program belonged to the tribals for they were intimately involved in all aspects of the program's activities. Without the involvement and participation of the people themselves, the program will remain something alien to the villagers. Professor Ariyaratne sought to conceptualize the whole system of village development on the basis of Buddhist concepts and values. The common people felt a strong identity and close affiliation with the program as it reflected values and goals that they already shared. When people feel an ownership, when they feel the project is theirs and not something foreign, they will take responsibility. They feel motivated and there is a social energy that stimulates development. No project that violates or ignores the basic principles of the local culture will be sustainable. We, in the field of development, are just beginning to understand this. Projects can be introduced by outsiders, but only when the project is seen as theirs and not the outsiders, when they truly develop ownership for the success and long-term sustainability of the project can be called a successful rural development program.

Principle Five: Confront Opposition Openly
Successful projects required leadership willing to confront those who would oppose the efforts of the villagers to help themselves.

All of the RDFs of these case studies faced significant opposition at one time or another. Dr. al-Naggar faced opposition from several government officials who saw his program fostering capitalism and an open market approach, when the government's policy of socialism rejects such activities. Stan Thekeakara, in his efforts to help the tribals gain control over their traditional land rights, he faced severe opposition from government and private interests who refused to accept the rights of the tribals. Very courageously, he helped the tribals confront the government and through the use of the courts was able to help the tribals gain control over their lands. Dr. Yen faced much opposition from the rich landowners and other elites who rejected his efforts to provide services in health, literacy and income enhancement to the peasants. Later, he faced the Japanese invasion into

The Concept of Rural Development 179

his area with great courage and resolve. After the Japanese were defeated, he faced the moral dilemma of siding with the communists who promised a better life for the peasants or working with the Nationalist government who tended to be dominated by the landed elite. In the final analysis, he rejected them both, seeking to carry on his work in the Philippines where his personal convictions would have to be compromised.

Principle Six: Strengthen Local Leadership and Local Institutions Through Indigenous Management Systems
Successful projects sought to strengthen local leaders, to build local institutions, and local indigenous management systems among both men and women.

Most of the successful programs outlined in the case studies emphasized the identification and training of local leaders, the strengthening of local institutions as much as possible, making certain that the systems of implementation where reflective of the local culture. With great foresight, both Gandhi and later Ariyaratne, trained young village leaders in the Sarvodaya methods. In the hundred village program, Ariyaratne argued that we must: "pick out a group of young and intelligent village leaders from the among the members of the village and provide them with the necessary training." He also emphasized the concept of :"Gramodaya" (awakening of rural people) suggesting that we must first "liberate" the leaders within the village, then the villagers themselves, and only then, can the nation be developed. Muhammad Yunus early recognized the need to identify leadership among the poorest members of the micro-credit groups being established, both because they would be able to represent their fellow peasants in the processes of expansion, but also because they would ensure that the benefits of the banking system would be fairly distributed to all the members participating. The management system which was developed was based upon indigenous processes of decision-making, conflict resolution and evaluation. Such management practices were considered legitimate because they reflected local customs and practices. Perhaps the most impressive example of this principle of strengthening local leadership was in the ACCORD project among the tribals of south India. Stan Thekaekara insisted that all the RDFs working among the tribals would be from among the tribals themselves. Stan noted that "Our greatest strength has been the fact that we have got together a strong team of tribal men and women who believe in the future and are working towards it."

Principle Seven: Program Expansion Through Networking and Linkage-Building Activities: Successful projects tended to expand their activities into the broader environment. RDFs encouraged various networks of government agencies, national and international NGOs and other organizations, public and private, that supported long-term change and reform. Jimmy Yen created a multi-district system of village development that eventually was replicated in many other parts of China. Ahmad al-Naggar's village bank system gradually set up bank branches all over the Delta area of Egypt. ACCORD set of clusters of tribal groupings that were able to confront the government for a number of reforms and the Grameen Bank quickly expanded into a multi-level system of banking. The Hundred Village program in Sri Lanka is an excellent example of this principle of expansion. While it is appropriate to begin the process of rural development in individual villages and single community problem solving groups, eventually, the process of expansion must be considered. Successful projects invariably found ways to build up from the grassroots level, linking their efforts to broader district and provincial levels. This principle suggests that RDFs may play an important role in working with villagers to help them acquire the motivation, confidence, status and skills necessary to identify their problems and needs, press for their own interests with governmental authorities and other donor supported non-government organizations, and thus eventually to assume responsibility for decision-making in the implementation of self-help projects.

---

[1] For a summary of these past development strategies and their major weaknesses, see: David C. Korten, *Getting to the Twentieth First Century* (West Hartford, Connecticut: Kumarian Press, 1990); Bill Rau, *From Feast to Famine: Official Cures and Grassroots Remedies to Food Crises*, (London: Zed Books, 1991); Sheldon Annis and Peter Hakim, (eds.) *Direct to the Poor: Grassroots Development in Latin America*, (Boulder, Colorado: Lynne Rienner Publishers, 1989)

[2] James B. Mayfield, *Go to the People: Releasing the Rural Poor Through the People's School System*, (West Hartford, Connecticut: Kumarian Press, 1986).

[3] CHOICE's national headquarters is located at 643 East 400 South, Salt Lake City, Utah, 84102, Telephone (801) 363-7970.

[4] A detailed process for the training of interns and RDFs will outlined in Unit Three of this book.

[5] For a detailed discussion of stage one, see Chapter 8.

[6] For a detailed discussion of stage two, see Chapter 9.

[7] For a detailed discussion of stage three, see Chapter 10.

[8] For a more detailed discussion of how programs in each of the five dimensions of rural development have been successfully implemented, in a number of rural settings, see chapter 11 (promoting literacy and non-formal education); chapter 12 (creating primary health care); chapter 13 (stimulating income generating activities); chapter 14 (protecting the local environment); and chapter 15 (strengthening and preserving the local culture).

[99] This case study is quoted from: James B. Mayfield, *Go to the People: Releasing the Rural Poor Through the People's School System*, (West Hartford, CON.: Kumarian Press, 1985).

[10] This case study is taken from: James B. Mayfield, *Rural Politics of Nasser's Egypt: A Quest for Legitimacy* (Austin: University of Texas Press, 1971).

[11] Ahmad al-Naggar, *Bunuk al-'Iddikhar al-Mahalliyah*, (Cairo, 1966) p. 27.

[12] This case study is taken from Detlef Kantowsky, *Sarvodaya: The Other Development* (New York: Advent Books, 1974).

[13] This case study is taken from: Richard M. Harley, *Breakthroughs on Hunger: A Journalist's Encounter with Global Change*, (Washington, DC: Smithsonian Institution Press, 1988).

[14] This case study was taken from: Mari Marcei Thekaekara, *Action for Community Organization, Rehabilitation and Development (ACCORD)* (New Delhi: Voluntary Health Association of India, 1994).

Unit Three
Becoming a Rural Development Facilitator (RDF)

Challenges of Training and Implementation in the Three Stages of Rural Development

Chapter 6

Is a Career in Rural Development For You?

Many books deal with the theories and techniques associated with the general field of Development Administration. Few books deal specifically with the problems involved in pursuing a career in this field or what it takes to become a professional in rural development. There are many sub fields in development related to agriculture, public health, non formal education, project management and policy implementation. This section focuses on the work of those who specialize in village development, who tend to work at the grassroots level and who seek to become facilitators in the process of village development. This unit seeks to outline what it takes to become an effective development professional by focusing on what it takes to become a rural development facilitator (RDF). This is a challenging profession that requires people willing to work in isolated rural communities in Africa, Latin America or Asia over an extended period of time.

This chapter will focus on the struggles, anxieties, and uncertainties of overseas development work. In addition, you will spend some time exploring the demands and strains of the rural development profession and its effect on an aspiring RDF. I encourage readers to examine their personal motives and needs to work in isolated rural communities, and challenge you to be honest in assessing what you might get from development work. Because many people are often conditioned to be passive learners, I should like to urge you to take an active stance in this educational and training experience. Being active implies taking responsibility for your own learning, but also applies to seeking opportunities to participate in overseas expeditions and applying for internships for extended experiences in a less developed country.

One of the first things we must do is to explore the belief systems of effective and ineffective RDFs and to discuss the positive and negative effects of a variety of assumptions they can have on one's effectiveness. Values are an integral part of the RDF/villager relationship, and I want you to devote considerable attention to an analysis of how they influence the rural development process. I define the process of rural development in terms of how an RDF can help villagers define their own values rather than training RDFs to impose their values on others. RDFs must appreciate cultural and lifestyle differences if their interventions are to be relevant and appropriate.

Much of this unit will provide an overview of the skills and knowledge required to be a successful RDF at each of the three stages of rural development. The focus of this part of the book is not on skill development but, rather, on the personal characteristics that enable RDFs to be effective. Effective RDFs must continually ask village community people to examine their perceptions, behaviors, their values and the way they do things and why they do such things as a way of helping them gain greater self-awareness and understanding. For that same reason, I will be asking you to be equally committed to an awareness of your perceptions, behaviors, your values and the way you do things and why. Much of the initial interaction between an outsider (RDF) and the villagers will be very stressful for both. The RDF is seeking to understand the customs, the behaviors, expectations and roles that characterize a particular group of villagers. Inexperienced RDF's are often unaware that their lack of experience in the village is the major source of their ineffectiveness, that until they understand how the villagers perceive them and are reacting to them, their relationship with the villagers will be strained and open communication will be almost impossible.

Beginning and even seasoned RDFs face common problems in their work, ways of dealing with resistance, with loneliness and discouragement, with the stresses of introducing change into communities that have few resources, less willingness to support change, and often downright opposition to the things you are trying to do. In this chapter we will also review ways of working with difficult communities and individuals, on how to deal with such stresses that are common in this type of work and the long-term consequences of burnout and frustration, and on ways to stay committed and energized both as people and as professional RDFs.

Section One
What Motivates One to Become an RDF

As you consider a career in the field of rural development, you are probably wondering: "Is the field of development administration really for me? Do I know enough and/or will I learn enough to be really helpful to the rural villagers of the world? Will I be able to apply what I will learn in this training program to my work in the field? Will this career be satisfying and meaningful to me in the long run? This book is intended to help you answer these and other questions about this field called Development Administration. The focus of this book is on you and on what you need to know personally and professionally to be the best RDF possible. I also want to emphasize the realities you are certain to face when you enter the professional world of development administration. You will be best able to cope with the demands of rural development if you get an idea now of what lies ahead.

Examining Your Motives for Becoming an RDF?

In choosing a career in rural development, you would do well to begin by examining your motivations for pursuing this path. It is critical that you be honest with yourself about the needs you will satisfy by entering this field. Your motives and needs can work either for or against both you and the villagers you will work with. As you reflect on the needs described in this section, ask yourself: "Do I deny having certain needs? How might I be able to satisfy both my own needs and those of the people I might work with? What needs of mine, if any, might I be inclined to meet at the expense of the people I might work with? Are some of my needs so intense that in meeting them I might hurt those that I am working with?

Typical Needs of Rural Development Facilitators

The Need to Make a Difference. It is natural after having reviewed the terrible levels of poverty, disease and illiteracy throughout the world, to want to help these people solve their problems. Many RDFs profess altruistic desires to make the world a better place. However, few RDFs admit that they are entering the field of development to satisfy a diverse range of their own needs. They may want to know that they are important and that they have the power to help people help themselves. Although they recognize that they won't be able to change the world in dramatic ways, they still want to make a dent in some corner of that world. When villagers are not interested in changing or don't want their help, however, a new RDF sometimes become frustrated. It is quite possible that a person may work in a community or country for several years and feel that they have not really made a difference. Your entire worth as a person should not be a reflection of this need to make a difference in the lives of others.

The Need to Follow a Role Model. The desire to emulate a role model often plays a part in the decision to become an RDF. Envisioning the work of James Yen, or having an older brother who was a Peace Corps volunteer, or perhaps a teacher or professor may have kindled your interest in the field of development. While such role models may prove to be instrumental in your decision, it is important that you reflect on whether this is what you personally really want to do. Such introspection is important in this process.

The **Need for Self Improvement and Development.** Many people pursue graduate training because they feel it will develop skills and attitudes that they presently don't have. Many people are naturally timid and have a great deal of difficulty in asking directly for what they want from others. They often say yes when they really mean no. Such people seek out training in assertiveness and public speaking. Others are too aggressive in their relationships with people and feel they need training in interpersonal skills. Others unable to adjust to the competition of their own society, seek less stressful experiences in other countries. Such people often see the opportunity to work overseas as a way of finding ways to develop the skills and competencies in a less threatening environment. While it is true that advanced training in these kinds of self-improvement activities can be helpful, it may be misleading to assume that the problems one is having in their own culture and society will somehow go away once they go into another culture or society.

The **Need to be Needed.** Very few RDFs are immune to the need to be needed. The problem arises when they deny that they want to feel needed. It may be psychologically rewarding to you to have the community people where you are working say that things are getting better because of your influence. These villagers are likely to express their appreciation for the hope that you have given them. You may value being able to take care of other people's wants, and you may get a great deal of satisfaction from doing so. For many RDFs, satisfying this need is perhaps one the greatest rewards of working in development. I would hope that you will not be apologetic about having this need and will not deny that you like being needed and appreciated.

Wanting to feel appreciated for what you are doing for others can be perfectly all right. The danger exists when you must receive appreciation and recognition in order to feel worthwhile. If you depend exclusively on others to feel like a useful human being, your self-worth is on shaky ground. The reality is that many people especially in communities where there is some conflict or competing elites will not readily express their appreciation and more often you may feel your efforts are resented. Furthermore, many private voluntary organizations (PVOs) often do not have the resources to give adequate rewards and incentives for good work. In fact, in some organizations, no matter what you may accomplish, they will want you to do more. Eventually, you may feel that whatever you do will not be enough. Some professional RDFs love their work because they have so many opportunities to feel needed. In many ways their work becomes their life. The possible danger with relying completely on your work to satisfy your need to feel needed is that your purpose and meaning in life might vanish if you could no longer work in your chosen career.

The **Need for Financial Security.** While everyone generally pursues a career expecting that it will provide economic security, significant financial rewards should not be your major goal. If a student or trainee needs to make a great deal of money, they might look elsewhere than the field of development. In most cases, beginning RDFs are expected to accept a modest salary adequate to meet daily needs but seldom equal to what other professions might be earning . At the administrative level, development professionals are often given free housing and other cost of living allowances including education costs for their children while they are living abroad. While some top administrators and consultants in the field of development do make very good money, such financial rewards generally come only after ten to fifteen years of experience. There are, of course, some RDFs who may wish to devote perhaps three to five years in development work, expecting later to return to the United States to pursue other kinds of professional work.

The **Need for Prestige and Status**. You may have hopes of acquiring a certain level of prestige, if not a certain income level. Yet if you work in a development agency or organization, the people you will be working with will tend to be the poorest of the poor, the illiterate and the disadvantaged of a given society. Because you are working with those of little status or influence, you will frequently not be given the prestige and the status you deserve. In fact, society in general may not even respect you, even resenting the fact that you are helping the people that they themselves should be helping.

On the other hand, you may work in a setting where you can enjoy the status that goes along with being respected by communities that you work with. If you have worked hard and become good at what you do, allow yourself to accept the prestige that you have earned. If you become arrogant as a result of your status, however, you may be perceived as unapproachable, and thus those you work with will be put off by your attitude. Again, if you want your self-esteem to rest on a solid foundation, it is essential that you look within yourself to meet your status needs, rather than looking to others to provide you with affirmations that you are indeed worthwhile as a person.

The **Need to Provide Answers**. There is a common tendency for some RDFs to have a strong need to give others advice and to provide "solutions" to their problems. People often have trouble dealing with ambiguity and insist on seeking for certainty and fixed answers to life's challenges. Such people feel good when they can influence others in the direction they want them to move. They may find satisfaction in influencing others, but it is important to realize that such answers may not be best for others. The true purpose of an RDF is to provide encouragement and to assist community people in discovering their own course of action. People with this need often find that their efforts to provide advice and answers sometimes gets in the way of effectively relating to others. A thoughtful RDF may find it more appropriate to back off and let people struggle with their own problems and to develop solutions through their own efforts.

How Your Needs and Motivations Operate

In the ideal situation, your own needs will be met at the same time that you are meeting the needs of those you are working with. Most of the needs and motives described above can work either for or against RDFs and the individuals they work with. There is nothing wrong with most of these needs, nor do they have to get in the way of effective development work. When you are unaware of them, there is a greater likelihood that they will determine the nature of your intervention. If an RDF is attempting to work through unconscious personal agendas by focusing on the problems of others, for example, there is more chance that he/she will use other people to meet their own needs. For instance, if your need for control is so high that you consistently attempt to determine the path that others take, this influence could easily interfere with their development of independence and personal initiative. When an RDF feels a strong need to provide answers to every problem that community villagers might identify, this may meet the RDF's needs at the expense of those being helped. Learning to reflect on those needs in our lives and consider both the negative and positive implications of such needs is the first step in becoming an effective field worker in development.

Section Two
Attributes of the Ideal Rural Development Facilitator

Although it is useful to describe some of the characteristics of the ideal RDF, even the most effective rural facilitators do not meet all of these criteria. If you try to match the ideal picture being presented here, you will be needlessly setting yourself up for failure and frustration. It is surely possible to become a more effective RDF if you are aware of those areas that need strengthening. You can hone your existing skills and acquire new ones. You can integrate knowledge that will enhance your abilities. You can make personal changes that will allow you to be more effective as you intervene in the lives of those you work with. People who have these characteristics have generally had many years of experience. Such skills do not come easily and most people develop them gradually. What follows are some of the characteristics that I consider an integral part of being an effective RDF working with rural people (the peasant/farmers of this world).

Ideally, you are committed to an honest assessment of your own strengths and weaknesses. You recognize that who you are as a person is the most important instrument you possess as an RDF. You realize that you are unable to inspire others to do in their lives what you are unable or unwilling to do in your own life. You are open to learning and have a basic curiosity. You realize what you don't know, and you are willing to take steps to fill the gaps in your knowledge. You recognize that your education is never finished but is something that you are continually acquiring. You have the interpersonal skills needed to establish good contact with other people, and you can apply these skills in the process of implementing rural development projects.

You genuinely care for the people you work with, and this caring is expressed by doing what is in their best interests. You are able to appreciate and deal with a wide range of behaviors, thoughts and feelings as expressed by people with different backgrounds, cultures and experiences. You share your persistent reactions to such people in appropriate and timely ways. You realize that it takes hard work to bring about change in a rural community, and you are willing to stick with these people as they go through this difficult process. You seek to enter the world of these peasant/farmers and to see the world through their eyes, rather than imposing your own vision of reality on them. You are able to offer support when it is needed and to confront these people on their unused potential when this is required. You realize that peasant/farmers often limit themselves through a restricted imagination of possibilities for their future. You seek to inspire such people to dream and to take the steps necessary to fulfill their dreams in reality. It is often your faith that enables such disadvantaged people who have little hope to begin with to believe that they have the potential for a better future. You are willing to draw on a number of resources to enable village people to move toward their goals. You are flexible in applying strategies for change, you are willing to adapt your techniques and interventions to the unique situation of each community you work with. In working with people whose ethnic or cultural background is different from yours, you are able to challenge them to examine how well their cultural values are working for them. You show your respect for these people by not fitting them into a neat mold.

You take care of yourself physically, mentally, psychologically, socially, and spiritually. You do in your own life what you ask of the people you are working with. You are capable of establishing meaningful relationships with at least a few significant people. You periodically question life and engage in critical self-examination of your beliefs and values. You are aware of your needs and motivations, and you make choices that are congruent with your life goals. Your philosophy of life is your own creation. Drawing on a multiplicity of sources, religious leaders, great books and ideals you seek to integrate that which is good from all cultures thereby blending the notions of justice, moral values, ethics and service into a meaningful vision of the good life.

This is not a complete list, and while no one fits the portrait of this ideal RDF completely, hopefully it will stimulate moments of self reflection and provide a set of ideals worthy of emulation throughout your career. James Yen, once in talking to some of his colleagues, announced that the effective RDF must have "*the Four C's.*" He describes these Four C's in his own words as follows: *"The **first C is competence.** A person must be competent in a particular competency -- agriculture, education, medicine or whatever. The **second C is creativity.** A person must know how to simplify highbrow knowledge and skill to be understood by the peasant. Such a person must be creative enough to humanize this scientific knowledge and translate it into terms that the peasant, who is wallowing in the mud with his carabao, can understand and apply. The **third C is commitment.** This is terribly difficult C. I have often said that when you are dealing with human development and human betterment, it is a thousand-year job. Many often have the starting power because they find the experience noble and very exciting. But when troubles and problems come, they run away. They do not have the staying power. One admirable trait of the communists is their commitment. Their work is their religion to them, no sacrifice is too big and no price is to high. I admire them for that commitment. My friends, unless you have that commitment, you will not get very far, no matter how clever you are. Your country cannot be saved without it. **The last C is unpopular. It is character.** Character is something very few people care about. Nobody knows the meaning anymore. People ask me, 'What is your greatest problem in your whole 58 years of work?'*

Many think it is money. Money is difficult to raise but that is not the foremost problem. My greatest problem is to find men and women with the four Cs.".[1]

Another set of qualities often deemed important for a person working with people of other cultures includes: (1) **Sensitivity** - How interested are you in others and the personal welfare of others? (2) **Personal Consistency** - How respectful and genuinely involved are you in your interpersonal interactions? (3) **Compassion and Empathy** - How able are you to respond to the needs of others with concern and understanding? (4) **Flexibility** and a willingness to receive feedback -- Can you openly consider feedback offered by others and make changes in your attitudes and behavior? (5) **Integrity** - How well do you demonstrate self-respect and respect for others in your interactions? (6) **Modeling** - Can you model functional human behavior and coping processes? (7) **Insight** - What is your capacity for perceiving, understanding, abstracting, and generalizing from professional sources and personal experiences?

Section Three
The Personal Challenges of self-awareness, Self-Assessment and the Need for Interpersonal Skills

In the past several years I have been interviewing a number of development practitioners asking them to list the specialized knowledge and skills they saw as most important in their present development work. Their comments were informal. I did not conduct a comprehensive sample of practitioners. These reactions give some idea of what is useful in development education and training.

Most of these professionals commented on the value of internships and fieldwork placements. These supervised-practical experiences had helped them learn about "the system of development" and how best to survive in it. The skills most people needed included rudimentary skills in agriculture, public health, literacy training and small scale enterprise development, counseling and supervisory skills, communication and conflict resolution skills, the ability to interact with different levels in the system from peasants to government officials to donor agency professionals. Other skills included the ability to write a proposal, various organizational and project management skills, fund raising and other local resource mobilization skills and especially important the ability to network and establish coalitions of support people. A number of professionals pointed out the value of self-exploratory experiences, especially working with groups aimed at personal and interpersonal growth. These group experiences gave them opportunities to look at themselves and to deal with their own feelings and problems, activities that were seen as especially helpful in preparing them to relate to people with different backgrounds and in different cultures. Even those professionals who were primarily engaged in the administration of development projects commented on the value of self-awareness and the understanding of interpersonal dynamics as some of the most valuable tools they utilized in their managerial functions. Even people at the country director level acknowledged that they would not be able to develop and coordinate their programs if they did not know how to work effectively with people.

In my view there needs to be an integration of what you know, what you can do, and the person who you are. Mere knowledge alone is not sufficient, yet without it you cannot become an effective RDF. If you focus mainly on acquiring interpersonal skills but neglect theory and knowledge, these skills will be of little importance. Furthermore, your ability to use the skills and knowledge you have is very much a function of your being sensitive to the interpersonal dimensions of the rural development process. The RDF who has a low degree of self-awareness is at best a skilled technician, and I doubt that he or she will make a positive difference in a community development effort. Rural development is more than set of techniques; it is an art that is an expression of who the RDF is personally.

As an RDF you will encounter a range of special concerns throughout your career, but some problems will be particularly pressing when you begin working in a village community for the first time. One challenge you will face is learning how to deal effectively with the feelings that some of the villagers will have toward you and the corresponding feelings that they evoke in you. Even experienced RDFs must show an interest in learning creative ways to deal with difficult people, especially those who exhibit great resistance to new ideas and suggestions. In this section we address the important issues of gaining greater self-awareness, developing interpersonal skills and managing your own feelings as you work in a difficult community environment.

This section will probably raise more questions than it answers. We are not interested in providing simple solutions to the many complex and challenging situations that you will encounter in village development work. Our purpose is to introduce you to a range of common concerns that beginning RDFs typically face. We will be stressing the value of learning to pay attention to yourself at least as much as you do to the villagers. Too often RDFs become riveted on getting resistant villagers to change and they underplay the importance of being aware of their own dynamics and reactions as they interact with difficult situations. Don't overwhelm yourself with the belief that you should know exactly what to do in every situation. More important at this point is your capacity for being open to what is emerging inside of you as you confront resistant behavior in the people you are working with. As this chapter will show, your willingness to work on yourself is an index of your ability to work with others.

One of the key challenges of a new RDF is the tendency to take personally the reactions both positive and negative that come from the people they meet: both with officials in a local agency or administrative office they must work with and with the men and women in a village community. Such emotional reactions are generally reflective of the RDFs thoughts and feelings in reaction to a strange environment, whether prompted by the villagers themselves or by events in the RDFs own life. The RDF needs to attend to the feelings he or she is experiencing in relationship with the villagers and then to identify the sources of these emotional reactions. Simply having feelings toward an official or a villager(s) does not automatically mean that you will be less effective in your interaction with these people. You may feel deep empathy and compassion for some of these village people as a function of your own life experiences. You may also be "turned off" by the pompous authoritarian attitudes of some officials. Such feelings do become a problem only if your own personal needs or unresolved personal conflicts become entangled in your professional relationships and blur your sense of objectivity.

Dealing with the challenges of this life, whether your own or the people you are working with, entails making an assessment of personal assets (strengths) and liabilities (weaknesses). If RDFs expect villagers to make an honest assessment of their situation, RDFs themselves must be committed to this same quest for self awareness and the development of key interpersonal skills.[2]

The Need for a Interdisciplinary Approach

While development is often defined in economic or political terms, it must also be defined in psycho-social terms and the purpose of this chapter is to encourage new RDFs to come to see the importance of an interdisciplinary approach to the processes related to village development. Some experts see development strictly in economic terms, others see it as an administrative or management process. It is my hope that you will begin to see other aspects of this process that often have more to do with culture and the individual psychology of people than the dynamics of economic and institutional development so often emphasized in the literature. .

To apply the concepts of psychology to the processes of village development, one could focus on a number of different aspects of the human psychic. This section deals with developmental themes found in the literature on individual growth and development. The idea in this chapter is not to teach you about the stages of human development but, rather, to use key concepts of these stages as illustrations of problems that you are likely to encounter with villagers and local officials seeking to find problems to their own situation. One of the more useful models of the stages of human growth and development is Erik Erikson's psycho social perspective.[3] Erikson describes human development over the entire life span in terms of eight stages, each marked by a particular crisis to be resolved. For Erikson, crisis means a turning point in life, a moment of transition characterized by the potential to go either forward or backward in development. These moments point to both dangers and opportunities. From a positive perspective, crises can be viewed as challenges to be met rather than as catastrophic events that simply happen to you. It is also possible to fail to resolve the conflicts and thus regress. To a very large extent an individual's current life is the result of earlier choices. Life is a continuity.

From Erikson's perspective each transition stage represents a psycho-social crisis, or a turning point when individuals are faced with fulfilling their destinies. Each of these developmental stages builds on the psychological outcomes of earlier stages. In Stage 1 infants develop a sense of trust if traumatic events do no halt this process of growth. The basic trust paves the way for children to expand their range of experiences, leading to autonomy in Stage 2. With a trust in self and environment, children are able to take the initiative in Stage 3 that results in widening their social circle and achieving a sense of competence. If these earlier tasks have been successfully accomplished, children are ready to begin meeting the challenges associated with formal schooling in Stage 4. The search for an identity that is characteristic of Stage 5 is made possible by the foundation of trust, autonomy, initiative, and industry that has been formed during childhood. Many of the tasks of Stage 6 involve the young adult's establishing and nurturing intimate relationships, which can be done to the extent that the individual knows how he or she is and feels a sense of self-worth. Stage 7 represents the crisis of middle adulthood, which relates to living a productive life and to showing care and concern for others. How one ends life has a lot to do with how he or she has dealt with the life challenges presented at earlier phases. Stage 8 brings with it the possibility of achieving a sense of integrity if one can look back without getting stuck in regrets. The purpose of this brief overview is to suggest that each of these developmental stages is influenced but not necessarily determined by earlier psycho social tasks and that such tasks have implications for individuals but also for communities and even societies.

Infancy

Trust versus mistrust. In infancy (the first year of life) the basic task is to develop a sense of trust in self, others, and the environment. The core struggle at this time is between trust and mistrust. If the significant persons in an infant's life provide the needed warmth and attention, the child develops a sense of trust. This sense of being loved is the best safeguard against fear, insecurity, and feelings of inadequacy. Children who receive love from parents or parental substitutes generally have little difficulty in accepting themselves. Some characteristic behaviors of people who have a high sense of basic trust include asking others for emotional help when it is needed, a tendency to focus on the positive of other's behaviors, having a generally optimistic world view without being Pollyannaish or unrealistic about it, and preferring a balance between giving and receiving. Insecure children come to view the world as a potentially hostile place. They have a fear of reaching out to others, a fear of loving and trusting, and an inability to form or maintain intimate relationships. The implications of such an orientation for village or community development should be obvious For generations, villagers have been exploited, have been taken advantage of, have been cheated, lied to, and abused over time. High levels of mistrust are natural consequences of these experiences with outsiders.

Early Childhood

Autonomy versus shame and doubt. The most critical task of early childhood (ages 1-3) is to begin the journey toward autonomy by progressing from being taken care of by others to being able to care for one's own needs. Some characteristic behaviors of people who have developed a sense of autonomy include making their own decisions about matters that are important to them, resisting being dominated by people who want to control them, working well by themselves and with others, listening to their own inner voice when deciding on a right and appropriate course of action, and feeling at ease in group situation.

Children who fail to master the task of establishing some control over themselves and coping with the world around them develop a sense of shame and feelings of doubt about their capabilities. Parents who do too much for children hamper their proper development. If parents insist on keeping them dependent, these children will begin to doubt the value of their own abilities. During this period it is essential that feelings of hostility, anger, and hatred be accepted rather than judged. If these feelings are not accepted, children may not be able to accept their own feelings later on. They will become adults who feel they must deny all of their negative feelings. People who have not learned to express feelings of anger and frustration in socially acceptable ways often direct such feelings inwardly in ways that is psychologically very damaging or outwardly towards others that are socially very damaging. The processes of village development are fraught with the problems of frustration, hostility and anger. Change is always a difficult thing in any society. Learning how to deal with the negative consequences of change and to be able to confront such consequences does take considerable skill and patience.

PreSchool Age

Initiative versus guilt. During the preschool years (ages 3-6) children seek to find out what they are able to do. They imitate others, they begin to develop a sense of morality, they increase the circle of people who are significant to them, they learn to give and receive love and affection, they learn basic attitudes regarding sexuality, they begin to learn more complex social skills , they take more initiative, and they increase their capacity to use and understand language. According to Erikson, the basic task of the preschool years is to establish a sense of competence and initiative. If children are allowed realistic freedom to choose their own activities and make some of their own decisions, they tend to develop a positive orientation characterized by confidence in their ability to initiate and follow through. Some characteristic behaviors of people who have a sense of initiative include having a high energy level, being a self-starter, being able to complete tasks at hand, having a strong sense of personal adequacy, being able to set goals and to accomplish them, accepting new challenges, and having a sense of ethics with being overly moralistic.

If children are unduly restricted or not allowed to make decisions for themselves, they develop a sense of guilt and ultimately withdraw from taking an active stance toward life. Parental attitudes toward children are communicated both verbally and nonverbally. Thus, children often develop feelings of guilt based on negative messages from their parents. Strict parental indoctrination tends to lead to rigidity, severe conflicts, remorse, and self condemnation. Each society and culture have their child-rearing practices. It will be important to understand these practices, the implications such practices have on the adults that make up a given community. Such awareness enhances the ability of an RDF to understand and appreciate the differences that one sees in a various culture systems. Hopefully, such understanding and appreciation increase tolerance and empathy for such differences and stimulate in RDFs a greater patience for the different kinds of people they must work with.

Middle Childhood

Industry versus inferiority. For Erikson, the major struggle of middle childhood, or the school years (ages 6-12), is between industry and inferiority. The central task is to achieve a sense of industry; failure to do so results in a sense of inadequacy. Children need to expand their understanding of the world and continue to develop an appropriate sex-role identity. The development of a sense of industry includes focusing on creating goals, such as meeting challenges and finding success in school. Some characteristic behaviors of people who have a sense of industry include enjoyment in learning about new things and ideas, being excited by the ideas of being a producer, having a sense of pride in doing at least one thing well, taking criticism well and using it to improve one's performance, and tending to have a strong sense of persistence.

Children who encounter failure in their early schooling often experience major handicaps later in life. Those children with early learning problems may begin to feel worthless. Such feelings often dramatically affect their relationships with their peers, which are also vital at this time. Problems that can originate during middle childhood include a negative self-concept, feelings of inferiority in establishing and maintaining social relationships, conflicts over values, a confused sex-role identity, dependency, a fear of new challenges, and a lack of initiative. Many school systems are structured to prepare students for higher education. As a consequence, many millions of children are conditioned to see themselves as failures very early in life. One of the great challenges of village development work is to focus on the educational systems being established in these villages to ensure that children who do not go on to higher levels of education are given a form of education that develops competencies and skills that make them successful and productive members of their society. In a later chapter when we deal with the dimension of education in development, the importance of developing a curriculum appropriate for the many instead of the few will be emphasized as well as how adult education programs in the villages can strengthen feelings of competency and progress for those who did not go on to higher education.

Adolescence
Identity versus identity confusion. Adolescence (ages 12-18) is the time of testing limits, and there is a strong urge to break away from dependent ties that appear to be restricting freedom. Although many adolescents feel frightened and lonely, they often mask their fears with rebellion and cover up their need to be dependent by exaggerating their degree of independency. Much of adolescents' rebellion grows out of the context of wanting to determine the course of their own life. Adolescence is a critical time for integrating the various dimensions of one's identity. For Erikson, the major development conflicts of adolescents center on the clarification of who they are, where they are going, and how they are getting there. The struggle involves integrating physical and social change. Adolescents may feel pressured to make career choices early, to compete in the job market or in college, to become financially independent, and to commit themselves to physically and emotionally intimate relationships. Peer-group pressure is a major force, and it is easy to lose oneself by conforming to the expectations of friends.

During the adolescent period a major part of the identity-formation process consists of separation from the family system and establishment of an identity based on one's own experiences. The process of separating from parents can be an agonizing part of the struggle toward individuating. Although adolescents may adopt many of their parent's values, to genuinely individuate they must choose these values freely as opposed to blindly accepting them.

Some characteristic behaviors of people who have a sense of identity include having a stable self-concept that does not easily change, being able to combine short-term goals with long-range plans, resisting peer pressure, having a reasonably high level of self-acceptance, believing that they are responsible for what happens to them, feeling physically and emotionally close to another person without fearing the loss of self, and being able to make decisions without undue vacillation. Many societies are faced with this identity crisis. What makes it so especially difficult in much of Latin America, Africa and Asia are the challenge of dealing both with the **generational aspects** of the identity crisis that characterizes all societies but also **the cultural aspects** of the identity crisis that many societies face in the onslaught of Westernization and modernization imposed through the mass media of television, movies and radio. Many young people in less developed countries feel caught between the demands and perceived constraints of their own culture and traditions and the enticing opportunities of "modern life" and thus struggle between the need to be who they are (Bambara, Kekchi, Maasai, Dinka) and the desire to accept the perceived opportunities of modern life. Very few societies are free of this crisis and many are struggling with the negative consequences of a society confronting this identity crisis. RDFs must be sensitive to both the positive and negative consequences for people rejecting their own cultural orientation and to consider ways in which the best of their own culture can be preserved. Many people see only two options in this crisis: (1) that development specialist who assumes that modernization is inevitable, that the quaint traditions of many societies must be forgotten if these societies are to become "developed and modern" and (2) those anthropological purists who assume that the traditional ways of life must be preserved at any cost, that the negative consequences of modernization must not be allowed into these societies. Somewhere in between these two extremes is a position that argues for a process of community development that empowers a given community with enough information and awareness of the options, that they begin to determine for themselves ways of preserving those aspects of their culture that are most important and consider ways to restricting the negative aspects of the Westernization processes that bring both blessings and problems.

Early Adulthood

Intimacy versus isolation. According to Erikson, we enter young adulthood (ages 18-35) after we master the adolescent conflicts over identity. Our sense of identity is tested a new in adulthood, however, by the challenge of intimacy versus isolation. The ability to form intimate relationships depends largely on having a clear sense of self. One cannot give to another if one has a weak ego or an unclear sense of identity. Intimacy involves a sharing, a giving of ourselves, a relating to another based upon on our strengthens, and a desire to grow with that person. If we think very little of ourselves, the chances are not good that we will be able to give meaningfully to others. The failure to achieve intimacy often results in feelings of isolation from others and a sense of alienation. Erikson's concept of intimacy can be applied in any kind of close relationship between two adults. Relationships involving emotional commitments may be between close friends of the same or the opposite sex, and they may or may not have a sexual dimension.

Some characteristic behaviors of people who have a sense of intimacy include the ability to establish a firm sense of their own identity, tolerance and acceptance of differences in other people, trusting others and themselves in the relationships they form, establishing close emotional bonds without fearing the loss of their own identity, and being able to commit themselves to relationships that demand cooperation, sacrifice, and compromise. In the field of village development, one of the crucial pre-requisites for a community to function effectively, is the ability to form bonds of cooperation and self-help. In Kenya, the word that epitomizes this process is **Harambe**. Forming groups and associations is absolutely essential in any village development process and the degree to which such bonds of affection, trust and cooperation are available in a given community will largely determine the degree of success such a process will have.

Middle Adulthood

Generativity versus stagnation. Middle adulthood (ages 35-60) is a period when people reach the top of the mountain and become aware that they must begin the downhill journey. They might painfully experience the discrepancy between the dreams of their younger years and the harsh reality of what they have actually accomplished with their life so far. According to Erikson, the stimulation for continued growth during middle age is the core struggle between generativity and stagnation. Generativity includes more than fostering children. It includes being creative in one's career, finding meaningful leisure activities, and establishing significant relationships in which there is giving and receiving. During this time people become more aware of the reality of death, and they may reflect more on whether they are living well. It is a time for reevaluation and a time when people are at the crossroads of life. They may begin to question what else is left, and they may establish new priorities or renew their commitments

During middle age there is sometimes a period of depression. When people begin to see that some of their visions have not materialized, they may give up hope for a better future. Some women who married and made a family their main priority may begin to wonder if this is all there is to life. At this time many women may choose to return to school or to work full time or to combine the triple roles of homemaker, student, and worker. Some men wonder if they want to stay in their career. They may have to cope with depression when they realize that they have not reached some of their important dreams.

As is true with any stage, there are both dangers and opportunities during this time. Some of the dangers include slipping into secure but deadening ruts and failing to take advantage of opportunities for enriching life. Many individuals experience a mid-life crisis, when their whole world seems to be unstable. A few of the events that lead to such a crisis include the realizations that youthful dreams will not come about; an illness or the onset of the aging process; the death of one's parents; the realization of one's ultimate aloneness in this life; the realization that life is not always fair and just; a marital crisis or the break-up of a long-established relationship; children's leaving the nest; the losing of one's job; and other major changes. A problem of this period is the failure to achieve a sense of productivity, which then leads to feelings of stagnation. What is important is that individuals realize the choices they have in their life and see the changes they can make, rather than giving in to the feeling that they are a victim of life's circumstances.

From a village development perspective, villagers in this period of their life are most apt to have had the experiences and to have achieved a level of status to provide both the leadership and wisdom needed to stimulate and foster community development kinds of activities. RDFs must understand that age is often greatly respected in traditional societies and that most leadership positions of such societies are dominated by the older members of the community. While it is important to get the youth involved in community development activities, one must not forget the fact that the real leaders of a community are more apt to come from older people and that they must be involved in determining what the problems are and what solutions are most appropriate.

Late Adulthood

Integrity versus despair. During this period of life (about 60 years in most developed societies but can be much younger in less developed societies where life expectancy may be considerably shorter) some of core developmental tasks include adjusting to retirement, finding a meaning in life, being able to relate to the past without regrets, adjusting to the death of a spouse or friends, accepting inevitable losses, maintaining outside interests, and enjoying grandchildren. Erikson sees the central struggle of this age period as one of integrity versus despair. People who succeed in achieving ego integrity are able to accept that they have been productive and that they have coped with whatever failures they faced. Such people are able to accept the course of their life, and they do not endlessly ruminate on all that they could have done, might have done, and should have done. Instead, they are able to look back without resentment or regret and see their life in perspective. Although they may not welcome the notion of death, they can view it as natural.

Some characteristic behaviors of people who have a sense of integrity include believing that who they are and what they have become are largely the consequences of their own choices; accepting death as an inevitable part of the life cycle; looking back on their lives without regret but with a sense of pleasure and feeling of accomplishment and appreciation; being reasonably happy and satisfied with their lives; approaching the final stage of their lives with a sense of personal wholeness; and integrating their past experiences with current realities. Again such people can be a great asset to a community seeking to solve problems and improve the quality of their lives. An RDF must see the elderly as a source of wisdom and experience that can be used to link the younger generation with their cultural traditions, histories, and identities. Too often development experts ignore the potential of the elderly to participate in decisions affecting the future of a given community. If the model of development espoused in this book confronts both the mindless rejection of anything modern and the equally perilous adoption of everything modern, it may well be the elderly, who can play an important role in defining and helping others to reflect on the really important aspects of a given culture. It will often be the elderly in a given society, who can help to capture the essence of a given cultural system, and who can help to legitimize certain traditional values for the younger generations.

Section Four
Is Rural Development Work for You?

As should be apparent by now, rural development as a career is not for everyone. In assessing whether rural development work is really for you, it is suggested that you reflect carefully on the following questions and consider their implications for your future:

1. What has attracted you to the rural development profession? Who in your life has been instrumental in your decision to consider this role for yourself?
2. What is the main motivation for wanting to be a Rural Development Facilitator?
3. What needs of yours are likely to be met through your work as an RDF? To what degree do you think that these needs might either enhance your ability to work in rural areas or diminish it?
4. Think about the attributes of an effective RDF. What are a few traits or characteristics that you would identify as being the most important?
5. What do you consider to be some counter productive attitudes, beliefs and behaviors of RDFs? Can you identify three personal characteristics that are likely to strain the ability of RDFs to form effective relationships with those who are seeking their assistance?
6. At this time in your life, how prepared (from a personal standpoint) do you feel to enter the field of development? As you reflect on this profession, ask yourself this question: "what qualities, traits, attitudes, values, and convictions are central to the person who you are?" "How might these personal characteristics either be assets or liabilities for you as you pursue a career in rural development?"
7. What kinds of education and training program do you think best fits your interests and talents? How do you see this program of training as a means to attaining your career objectives? If you could pursue a career in rural development at this time, what would your ideal vision be: Where would you be working and what would you be doing? What work particularly appeals to you? With what kind of people would you most like to work? What kind of work do you think will bring you the greatest meaning and satisfaction?

General Summary:

A career in development is not for everyone. I hope you will keep open the question of whether it is right for you. In deciding whether to pursue the field of development, do not decide too quickly. Be prepared for doubts and setbacks. Although the "Ideal RDF" does not exist in reality, a number of behaviors and attitudes characterize effective RDFs. Even though you might not reach the ideal, you can progress, especially with the willingness to question what you are doing and why? It is essential that RDFs examine their motivations for going into this field. RDFs do meet their own needs through this kind of work, and they must recognize these needs. It is possible both for village people and RDFs to benefit from the processes of rural development. Some of the needs for going into the field of development include the need to be needed, the need for prestige and status, and the need to make a difference. These needs can work both for you and against you in becoming an effective RDF. In selecting an educational program, follow your interests. Be willing to experiment by taking a variety of classes and by getting experience as a volunteer worker and by going on short expeditions. In choosing a career path, consider factors such as self-concept, interests, abilities, values, occupational attitudes, socioeconomic level, parental influence, spouse preferences, ethnic identity, gender, and physical, mental, emotional, and social strengthens and weaknesses. Be willing to seek information about careers in development from others, such as professionals in the field and faculty members, but realize that ultimately you will decide which career path is best for you. Do not consider the selection of a career as a one-time event. Instead, allow yourself to entertain many job possibilities over your lifetime. Realize that you must have a beginning to your career. Be patient, and allow yourself time to feel comfortable in the role of an RDF. You don't have to be the fully functioning RDF during your first and even second assignment overseas. **Generally there are four career levels in the field of development administration**:

The Four Career Levels of Development Administration

First is the rural development facilitator (RDF) who lives and works in the village community. Often the RDF is responsible for a cluster of villages in a given area and helps to train and encourage paraprofessionals (rural development workers) in community development, health, literacy and other development projects. Such paraprofessionals are usually volunteers from their own communities working under the guidance of the RDF.

Second is the supervisor and trainer of RDFs who may live right in a village community or a nearby town and is responsible for the training of full-time RDFs in a given project area. The Supervisor RDF usually has some skills in various sectors or service delivery activities, including: health, literacy and income generating programs and often helps other RDFs in recruiting and developing paraprofessionals in the many village communities of their region. Much of the material in Unit Four is useful in training new RDFs.

Third is the country director who coordinates and manages a number of rural development supervisors. The country director is responsible for the overall management of the various project areas in a given country, develops linkages and support relationships with governmental and non-governmental agencies, and ensures that the projects and programs being implemented are sustainable and meeting the real needs of the people. Also the country director works closely with outside consultants and experts in conducting research and evaluation of the projects being implemented in the various areas of the country. At this level there are other sub fields including budgeting and finance, personnel, planning and management information systems, research and evaluation, fund raising, public relations and policy implementation. At this level you also find sector experts in agriculture, public health, literacy, small scale enterprise development, local institution building, women in development programs, etc.

Fourth is the consultant who often teaches development administration at the university level and/or works with various donor agencies in a number of countries helping in the design and strengthening of the management system used to implement rural development projects, establishes training programs for local trainers, country directors and supervisors of RDFs and conducts research and evaluation of projects to determine and document lessons learned and ways to make the process of development more cost effective, sustainable and culturally sensitive.

---

[1] Quoted in James B. Mayfield, *Go To The People*, p.16.
[2] A workbook has been prepared to assist students in developing greater self-awareness and these kinds of interpersonal skills. The workbook is best used in a formal classroom or training workshop format. See: James B. Mayfield, *Rural Development Facilitator Workbook*, (1997).
[3] Eric H. Erickson, *Childhood and Society*, (New York: Norton, 1950) and Eric H. Erickson, *Identity: Youth and Crisis,* (New York: North, 1968).

Chapter 7

Getting the Most from RDF Education and Training

Once an individual decides that a career in rural development is a possibility, then comes the challenge of preparing oneself. The theme of this chapter is that future professionals in the field of development will only get out of their training what they are willing to put into such experiences. It is strongly encouraged that students and trainees see the process of becoming a development worker as long-term, not something to be completed through formal course work, training workshops or through a few months of being an intern in the field. It is important to understand that no one class, not even a university degree will totally prepare an individual to become an effective development specialist. The purpose of this chapter is to raise people's consciousness about pursuing a career in development. As was suggested in the last chapter, there are various career levels in the field of development. It is strongly encouraged that a future development specialist seek hands-on, in the field experiences as a grassroots rural development facilitator (RDF) over several years before they consider moving up the career ladder to various administrative and management positions. It is for this reason that a peace corps experience or an internship experience can be so valuable. Organizations generally prefer to hire management and administrative people who have had a wide-range of village-level experiences and have demonstrated their willingness to work face-to-face with villagers over an extended period of time.

In this chapter we will focus on several issues that relate to the process of becoming a professional development worker, by emphasizing the importance of first becoming an experienced RDF. My experience with beginning students suggests two kinds of extremes: those who feel that the skills needed to become a development worker will come fairly easily and those who sell themselves short assuming that they could never be effective in working with villagers and other disadvantaged people of the LDCs. Many might suppose that after they have completed several courses in rural development, have attended some workshops in various aspects of development, have even spent six months in the field as an intern, are now ready to make a significant difference in the lives of people they will be working with. Others might assume that even with coursework, workshops and internships they still would never be able to make a difference. The challenges, the obstacles, the constraints are perceived to be just too great. This chapter will seek to challenge both of these extremes: It has been said that there are two kinds of people in this world: those who blame others for their failures and those who take responsibility for their own successes. Becoming an effective RDF will take hard work, perseverance, and commitment. The challenges and obstacles are great, but the rewards and opportunities are incalculable. Let us review two specific activities that can influence your decision as to whether development work in the LDCs is for you: (1) a service learning experience while you are in school, and (2) an overseas internship experience where you actually life and work in a rural village setting.

Section One
Learning Styles
Their Impact on the Work of RDFs

Before we outline the process by which one prepares for a career in development, let us consider a conceptual framework developed to explain the process by which people learn.. A concept often used in institutions of education is experiential learning that is often described in terms of some type of internship, group interaction, and field-work opportunity. The acceptance of these learning strategies owes much to the work of John Dewey,[1] who argued that learning must be grounded in experience not just in traditional classrooms. Similar to Dewey, Kurt Lewin[2] expressed support for the individual learner as an active agent in the learning process through his or her interaction with the surrounding environment. A third theoretician to whom supporters of experiential learning are indebted is Jean Piaget.[3] He sought to conceptualize leaning as a process where intelligence is shaped by experience over time. His work confronted many of the traditional approaches opposed to experiential learning and provided a developmental framework through which we can better understand the process of intellectual growth.

The work of Dewey, Lewin, and Piaget provided the foundation for the more recent contribution of David A. Kolb.[4] Looking for ways to foster an individual's ability to best adapt to and master the changing demands of one's job or career, Kolb set out to develop the Experiential Learning Model. Experience is the cornerstone of this model, and like Piaget, learning is viewed as a process. Kolb's model outlines the learning experience as a constantly revisited four-step cycle. This model is perceived to be value-free in that none of the resulting styles formed from the interaction of the four steps is considered inherently better than another.

When viewed in its theoretical sequence, the model's four steps, begin with (1) concrete experience, followed by (2) reflective observation, (3) abstract conceptualization, and (4) active experimentation. Initiated by an individual's concrete experience, the process moves through a period of reflection on the experience. That reflection stimulates the learner to organize observations about the experience and create concepts (we might say mental constructs) around that organization to better understand his or her world. Through that new understanding, individuals find the confidence to experiment actively and thereby enhance their learning. That experimentation and specific action lead the individual to revisit the four steps of the cycle beginning with a new set of concrete experiences.

Styles of Learning

Kolb's four steps or sets of learning abilities (concrete experience, reflective observation, abstract conceptualization and active experimentation) interact to form four learning styles. These four learning styles are arranged graphically in a quadrant to form a "learning wheel," for easier understanding. Initially, all learning begins with a concrete experience, therefore it is best to begin exploring those styles where a preliminary concrete experience interacts with the subsequent reflective observation on that experience.

Diverger. In the first quadrant lies the diverger style. The learning strengths of divergers lie in their imaginative abilities; they exhibit ease in **brainstorming and generating ideas** and alternatives. As a result, they are able to view issues and problems from a variety of perspectives. With a strong interest in people, divergers are sensitive to individuals' feelings. They generally value others and have a keen ability to **appreciate the needs and concerns of others.** Divergers can often be found in the arts or service fields. Their potential for empathy makes divergers excellent candidates for **counseling**, advising, and facilitative work.

Assimilator. Next on the learning wheel lies the assimilator learning style. In this quadrant, reflective observation and abstract conceptualization interplay. Prone to **inductive reasoning**, assimilators are more interested in the logic of ideas and theory rather than practical applications to specific problems. This style is associated with **intellectual competencies**. Assimilators' interests are more attuned to ideas than to people, and assimilators are drawn to information and scientific positions. Within the various careers, assimilators serve well as **researchers** and theoreticians.

Converger. Like assimilators, convergers have the ability to conceptualize in abstract ways but at the same time combine that with an ease to active experimentation. Convergers apply their ideas in a practical manner, are highly organized, and tend toward **deductive reasoning**. Their strengths lie in the ability to **evaluate, make decisions, and apply ideas**. Being good at making decisions, convergers are often in technological or specialist occupations. Within the various careers, convergers serve as excellent directors and **managers** of services and program operations.

Accomodator. Sharing strengths in learning from concrete experience and through active experimentation, accommodators are **risk takers (entrepreneurs)**. They best learn from "hands-on" experience and gravitate to situations where they must adapt to changing and immediate circumstances. Accomodators focus on people and action. Though they are found to excel in the **marketing and sales** fields, accommodators also serve well in crisis-intervention and front-line service positions.[5]

Kolb, through his own research, has determined that each individual tends to favor one of these four styles over the others. However, individuals who limit themselves to just one style generally are less effective in their individual careers than people who have learned to use more than one style.

Individualizing Service Learning Through an Understanding of Learning Styles

In organizing the curriculum and the experiences of students seeking to develop their abilities in the field of development and in becoming an effective RDF, understanding the Kolb Learning Model can be very helpful. As an example, accommodators and divergers, due to a focus on people and field experiences are, in theory, more prone to engage in more hands-on kinds of activities (internships and field activities working directly with people). In contrast, assimilators and convergers would be more at ease in a more traditional classroom and library research setting. Every effort should be made to help all students move out of their "comfort zones" and seek experiences in areas where they are less comfortable. Many students may need face-to-face contact with disadvantaged people and people with different cultural backgrounds, while others need more time to reflect on their experiences (keeping a daily journal and participating in a discussion group) and/or seek to connect their experiences with various theoretical perspectives (writing a more abstract research paper or seeking a higher level of understanding of some issue or group situation). Some type of service learning process can be invaluable in preparing people for the rigors of rural development work.

Section Two
Promoting Learning Through Community Service:
A Design and a Strategy

One of the most effective ways of determining if rural development work is for you is to engage yourself in some type of humanitarian service in your own community.[6] While in school, there is some value in actively involving yourself in your own community in order to develop a better understanding of the needs and realities of the world around you. In his ground breaking book *When Dreams and Heroes Die*,[7] Art Levin supports this view, recommending that in order to combat apathy and emphasize civic responsibility, community service has to receive a higher priority in colleges and universities. In many universities, service learning programs have been established to help students integrate their own university experiences into the realities of the broader world in which they live. In many universities, students are now allowed to participate in some type of service learning experience where they can combine the classroom experience with an opportunity to participate in some type of service project in the community. The Service Learning Model developed here includes five phases of a student's development that result from the student's engaging in certain kinds of service-learning interventions.

Exploration. This phase reflects a student's initial concrete experiences in the realm of service learning. As an example, consider a new student who during freshman orientation opts to participate in a group service-learning activity composed of a day-long project at a local Hispanic community center. This student is exposed to other students and to a unique environment. Before that experience can be reflected on, it needs to be felt and sensed. Exploration is the service-learning phase in which these types of experiences occur.

Clarification. Students come to the clarification phase after having explored a variety of community-service opportunities. As a student begins to participate in service in a more systematic manner, the student not only feels and senses these experiences, but also begins to intuit meaning. Through placing an increased value on other volunteers as well as on service clients, the student begins to appreciate different points of view, a major characteristic of the reflective-observation stage of learning.

Realization. Considered the "Aha!" phase, realization is the moment when the student becomes the active agent in his or her service learning. Reflection no longer remains in the realm of intuition but involves the use of logic. The student spends time and energy on systematically collecting information and forming a conceptual framework. As an example, a student who volunteers once a week at a soup kitchen also has a paper to write for a nutrition class. Through the research conducted for the paper, the student becomes aware of some of the interrelationships between government policy, societal trends, and the existing conditions of the hungry. Research and the ability to draw interconnections are the kinds of behaviors endemic to those at the learning stage of abstract conceptualization.

Activation. No longer comfortable in a service role confined by peer and academic structures and norms, a student in the activation phase takes a more self-directed service role. Thus, the student because of his or her experiences and reflections, seeks to establish, for example, a hunger-action program on campus. Through negotiations with the student government, the dean of students, and the academic vice president, the student succeeds in getting the campus to dedicate a quarter to the theme of hunger. Food drives are conducted, speakers and symposia are presented, faculty are encouraged to weave the theme of hunger into their classes. The example student thus exemplifies learning through active experimentation, by influencing people and changing situations through a practical application of what he or she has learned and experienced.

Internalization. The final service-level, internalization, finds the student at a different, more mature level of learning. He or she is open to new intuitions and feelings, ways of thinking, and taking action. Sometimes defined as the "Mother Teresa" or "Gandhi" phase, now students are no longer content with seeing their work in the community only as a function of their school experience. Long-term goals and possible career options are now being considered and the lessons learned are being translated into a mature desire to complete advanced training in some type of service-related career. Such students begin to take specific courses related to some type of service work; they seek opportunities for internships and field experiences that will develop their skills and help them better determine if some type of service work (either domestic or international) is for them.

Section Three
The Concept of Moral Development

In exploring service learning as an intervention in student development, I should like to argue that the concepts of moral development are equally useful in seeking to conceptualize the process by which students develop the skills need to be effective rural development facilitators. Before we discuss in detail how this process works, let us review the work of three authors who have sought to outline contrasting approaches to study of values.

Perry's Cognitive-Developmental Model. On the basis of interview research with Harvard and Radcliff students in the 1950s and the 1960s, Perry[8] developed a cognitive-developmental model outlining an individual's intellectual and ethical development through nine stages. These stages, or positions, imply growth from simple dualism (positions 1 and 2), through multiplicity (positions 3 and 4) and relativism (positions 5 and 6), to commitment within a relativistic framework (positions 7 through 9).

More specifically, individuals at positions 1 and 2 support the notion that knowledge is absolute, that things are either black or white. There is a right answer to every question. Individuals at the next two positions have a multiplistic approach to knowledge. Questions that once had only one right answer now may have many answers. All viewpoints seem valid. Individuals at positions 5 and 6, the relativist stages, assume that knowledge is contextual and that each component of knowledge is a piece that fits into a larger whole. The move from multiplicity to relativism is critical, for it is a move from the cognitive to the ethical realm of development. In the final three stages, individuals have established their identity in a pluralistic world. Their actions and beliefs are integrated, yet the students have an appreciation for the diversity of their surrounding world.

Kohlberg's Moral Development Model. Lawrence Kohlberg[9] provides a model that outlines three levels of moral development: the pre conventional, the conventional, and the post convention. In the pre-conventional level there are two stages. The first stage identifies a person's motivation for obeying rules as the avoidance of punishment, a belief in the power of authority, and the search for gratification. The second developmental stage, the instrumental-relativist stage, describes morally correct behavior as that which satisfies one's own needs; consequently, much effort is spent in manipulating others to achieve one's goals.

Stage three, the interpersonal-concordance stage, begins the conventional level of moral judgment. An individual's peer group assumes increasing importance. The individual begins to move from a self-centered viewpoint to adopting opinions that please others and result in the approval of the larger group. Stage four, the "law and order" stage, takes the conventional level of moral judgment a step further: individuals begin to believe that social order should be maintained at any price.

Stages five and six outline the post conventional level of moral judgment. While individuals in stage four perceive law and order as paramount in importance, those in stage five understand that laws may be unfair and may need to be changed through appropriate channels. People in stage six assume universal moral judgment. Their respect for the dignity of the individual becomes critical and must be defended above any existing law. Civil disobedience may result from adopting this higher level of moral judgment.

Gilligan's Model of the Development of Women's Moral Judgment
Carol Gilligan[10] looks at moral development as gender specific. While previous theoretical models were developed from a male perspective, they were considered not to be specific to gender. Gilligan studies the difference between male moral development, which is generally seen as rationalistic and individualistic, and female moral development, which is viewed as embedded in relationships. Her theory is a three-level model including two significant transitions between levels. It contributes significantly to the practical application of student-development theory.

Level 1 represents an orientation toward individual survival. At this stage the focus is pragmatic and on the self. A feeling of powerlessness is sensed by the individual and relationships are seen as painful but necessary. The transition from level 1 to level 2 is characterized by moving from selfishness to a sense of responsibility to others. During this time, one redefines the meaning of self-interest. Attachment and connection to others become important, and there is an increasing ability to see one's limitations and self realistically.

Level 2 represents a morality of goodness as self-sacrifice. At this stage, society's values are adopted, acceptance by others becomes of the utmost importance, and there is a tendency to hold others responsible for the choices they make. Protecting dependent and disenfranchised individuals, avoidance of self-assertion, and fear of abandonment are issues facing the person at this level. The transition from level 2 to level 3 is characterized as moving from goodness to truth. At this point, there is a questioning of the logic of self-sacrifice. Moral actions are no longer based on what other people think but on the realities of intention and consequences.

Finally, level 3 also represents the morality of nonviolence. Here, there is a reconciliation of the diverse concepts of selfishness and responsibility through an understanding of one's self and a redefinition of morality. Nonviolence (not hurting others) is fundamental; caring becomes a universal obligation.

Enhancing Values Through Service Learning

Influenced by members of the school of radical educators, particularly Paulo Freire,[11] Kolb asserts that the Experiential Learning Model promotes not only the development of individual learners cognitively and intellectually, but also in the reinforcement of their value system. With this assertion, the Service Learning and Experiential Learning models work together in their contribution toward the development of values. By engaging in deliberate and planned service-learning interventions, particularly those designed through a learning-styles filter, students are challenged to clarify and act on their values. It is at this point that Kolb introduces the concept of virtue in the process of learning. He highlights four virtues: love, justice, wisdom, and courage. Each builds on the other and relates to a particular learning style or set of learning abilities. All four are governed by the master virtue of integrity.

Love/Empathy. Divergers tend to see reality through their own self-oriented powers of analysis. The virtue of love helps move divergers beyond their self-centered, more analytical observations. Personal experience in the world of real people can stimulate the feeling-side of human interaction and a greater sympathy, understanding and respect for others. When such experience is filtered through the concept of love, the learner's ability to empathize with others' feelings and conditions can be greatly enhanced. The resulting empathy challenges the learner to reflect on his or her own experience and to create new meanings that can stimulate a love and appreciation for people who are different. This broadening process is absolutely crucial for an RDF working in isolated villages.

Justice/Fairness. The next virtue, that of justice, assists us when we are using the assimilator learning style. Often when we approach an accumulation of facts, we make expedient assumptions, failing to see the fairness or moral implications of the facts observed. A sense of justice filters the learner's observations and thoughts about these accumulated facts, forcing the learner to consider the moral implications of the facts identified and thus to make decisions based upon fair and inclusive judgments.

Wisdom/Good Choices. Convergers are caught between the tensions of fact and meaning. The virtue of wisdom assists us when using the converger learning style. Wisdom holds random thinking or accumulation of facts in check by encouraging meaningful choices about one's behavior and by helping people to consider the moral implications of such behavior.

Courage/Application. For those found challenged when using the accommodator style of learning, the virtue of courage comes into play. Courage provides an individual with the motivation to find meaning in his or her actions and thus to continue in the practical application of new knowledge. Courage helps the learner prevail over situations that challenge him or her to abandon planned and intended strategies.

Integrity/Commitment. The overriding virtue, integrity, monitors the four virtues mentioned by calling us to respond to life's conditions in an active and empathic manner. This process forces us to be true to ourselves, our potentialities, and the opportunities that are given to us. Where it may be easier to choose a less complicated and difficult road, integrity encourages us to opt for the more challenging paths, seeking the road that promises greater self-actualization and self-fulfillment. This course results in more creative and productive outcomes than those paths that are easy and that offer little challenge in this life.

As the Service Learning Model previously described indicates, the process of moral development in students takes place gradually, moving from a stance characterized by a focus on the self, limited commitment, and inaction to a life-long concern for the larger world and its needs. The pages that follow will address the unique contribution that the community (locally in the poorer areas of the United States and/or internationally in the disadvantaged urban and rural areas of the world) can make to the process of values development described by the Service Learning Model.

Section Four
Four Aspects of the Community Role

There are three important areas where a community experience can make a contribution to the values education of students. They are stated here in terms of student experiences and include the following: combining rigor with relevance, encountering new cultures and needs, learning the realities of power, and becoming a member of a group and of the larger society. While each aspect is significant, the first is discussed at greater length, because of its pivotal importance to community service as a values-education methodology.

1. **Combining Rigor with Relevance.** In his book *The Reflective Practitioner and Educating the Reflective Practitioner,* Donald A. Schon[12]

speaks of the dichotomy that has long existed in our educational process between theory and practice, rigor and relevance. Schon notes our common desire to avoid the uncertainties that characterize the world of practice by remaining at a level of abstraction. He calls for an education process that is more context sensitive and explores some stimulating examples of what he calls "reflection-in-action." Schon's comments provide important insights for those involved in the process of teaching and learning new values.

There is perhaps no area where the connection between theory and practice is more important than the area of values education. Expressed values take on meaning only when they are realized in a tangible form in the life of a person. And yet, this problem of joining thought to action is the very one that Richard Morrill finds the least adequately addressed in his survey of recent practices of teaching values in a university setting. "Our earlier question concerning the relationship of knowledge to action, or of moral theory to practice, seems to fall decidedly short of receiving an adequate answer. Given that values, morality, and ethics have to do precisely with deciding and choosing -- with action -- this particular relationship between knowing and doing, by nature, presses for full connection. Yet, we find partial answers, avoidance of the issue, or acceptance of the separation."[13]

In response to this surprising omission, service learning provides a model in which the effort to establish and maintain the connection between knowledge and action is central. Involvement in reflective community service offers students the opportunity to focus their concerns and set a more selfless, more "other-directed" agenda for the rest of their education.

What means are available to make certain that the link between rigor and relevance is maintained? It may be helpful here to think of the linking of rigor and relevance as depending on a two-way movement, from campus to community and from community to campus. Opportunities for students to become involved in service activities both locally and internationally through internships, field work, and assignments to various Private Voluntary Organizations (PVOs) would appear to be especially helpful. Reflection must be carefully built into every project to assure that students have sufficient background to understand an issue as well as why some actions may be more effective than others. Also attention must be paid to the process of personal development that each student is undergoing. If we are serious about seeing service learning as a means of values education, then we need to attend to the development of each student who participates. This can be done more directly through helping students examine their own relationship to the different phases described by the Service Learning Model, or more indirectly through the use of tools such as writing journals and performing group exercises in a class setting.

2. **Encountering New Cultures and Needs.** One of the most significant benefits of many community-service experiences for students is the exposure such experiences give them to people different from themselves in race, class, culture,

age, and life experiences. What benefit does such exposure provide to values education? Charles Kammer writes that "our experiences also shape our moral feelings and intuitions. Growing up in a white, middle-class neighborhood may make it very difficult for us to empathize with the pain, desolation, and difficulties of minorities or the poor in our culture. . . . Being immersed in a minority culture, becoming a minority in another culture, may help us to better understand and empathize with the situation of persons whom our society regularly degrades and dehumanizes. Such experiences may awaken new moral feelings in us and so offer us new moral possibilities."[14]

As part of their service-learning experience, students can be exposed to community events that speak to questions of racial and cultural differences. Intense discussions with people of different backgrounds can help to deepen student understanding of the issue of race and the ways in which minority cultures are misunderstood and devalued by the majority culture. Students can gain insights into the experience of others that they could not have gotten any other way.

Service learning can be the means for students to move from a sense of personal isolation to a sense of their place within the community. It can be away to help students know more and care more about the places in which they live. By bringing them together with people who are different from themselves in culture, race, and economic status, it can help them see the common aspirations that all people share. From such learning , a new vision of community, one that is more inclusive and respectful of diversity, can begin to develop in students.

To be involved with people and situations first-hand is to take on people's life dilemmas as one's own. We must not become so identified with the group we are trying to service that we loose our sense of perspective. We must acknowledge that any human social phenomenon cannot be understood entirely from the view of the outsider, but that we must acknowledge that we share to some extent the humanity of the person we study. We must also learn something of ourselves. Service learning provides the most vital opportunity to put this kind of attribute into practice.

3. **Learning the Realities of Power.** As the Service Learning Model indicates, the higher levels of moral development are characterized by an increasing concern for justice and for social transformation. Issues of socio-economic power and control that may be invisible in the classroom become particularly important when it comes to planning a strategy for community action. Ignorance in this area leads to ineffective action and disillusionment, and to a perpetuation of dependency among those who are in need.

Placing students in the service role without giving them the opportunity for reflection on the structural causes of injustice and inequity creates the danger that their participation will help to preserve an unjust system. If part of the meaning of justice includes participation in determining one's own destiny, then service learning that serves the ends of justice also requires the active involvement of the community in defining its own needs and how these will be met. Such sharing of power may present difficulties both administratively and academically, but without such sharing, university faculty and staff may give their students the message that the interests of those to be served do not really count or worse that there really is nothing that can be done. As will be described in greater detail in Chapter 10 below, the final stage of successful rural development seeks to encourage local communities to determine their own destiny as much as possible.

Service Learning: Some Preliminary Conclusions

Many university environments have placed undue emphasis on the individual and on a process of moral reflection abstracted and thus often distanced from the real world context. As a result, students have difficulty connecting what they have learned in their course work with the real needs of people they encounter beyond the confines of the campus.

Our communities and our world can no longer afford a moral education that encourages the isolation of reflection on values from lived reality. As a growing population competes for the planet's finite resources, unprecedented cooperation and involvement in community-concerns both locally, nationally and internationally will become even more important than they are now. Service in the community, combined with carefully designed study and reflection can begin to prepare students for the complex and often pain-filled world they will enter on graduation.

This section has sought to introduce students to the importance of awareness and values in the broader field of Development Administration. In considering this field and the processes of Development Administration, one must consciously consider one's own cultural orientation, one's own mental constructs, one's own value commitments. Before one can begin to understand the role of an RDF in a village community, the relationship between one's own culture and the culture where one is working must be clearly and carefully defined. The role and impact of culture will be described in much greater deal in later chapters of this book. Let us now move beyond the training and experiences in a university or college setting and reflect for a moment on the importance of living and working in a less developed country, perhaps even in an isolated community in some rural area.

Section Five
The Fieldwork Experience

One of the most important ways that RDFs and interns as well, are to become sensitive and experienced in the importance and significance of a local culture is to live and work with such people. The field of Anthropology has elaborate techniques and methodologies for helping students, scholars and RDFs to work effectively in a given society. The study of ethnography is a valuable field of study in helping to prepare people who must live and work in a local culture. Below is a series of guidelines for future RDFs that should be carefully reviewed and integrated into their thinking and into their behaviors.

Future RDFs must learn to think and perceive in the categories of the people they are studying, this ability to work in two or more cultures is extremely important for RDFs. They must admit that these villagers are able to subsist in ways that would be impossible for the outsider. In many ways these villagers are far less dependent than the RDFs are for day-to-day survival. RDFs would be quite presumptuous in assuming they have something to teach these villagers about survival and self-reliance. Future RDFs must consider how they will explain why they are there and how their presence in the village will often be confusing and disconcerting to many of the villagers.

Future RDFs must acknowledge that the period of adjustment is often very difficult. One student described her experience thusly: "after two months I began to see myself as a total failure. The anxiety I suffered was so agonizing that I still find it hard to describe. Every time I returned to my stifling room after a series of futile 'interviews,' I sat down and cried. . . .Meanwhile, I fought a losing battle with an obsessive desire to eat. For several weeks I alternatively stuffed and starved myself. Finally I surrendered and ate almost all the time. In three months I gained thirty pounds."[15]

Berreman argues: "successful research [in a village] is most often the result of being viewed and accepted as a trustworthy, interested and sympathetic outsider. This has advantages in that an outsider can be naive. He can ask blunt, embarrassing, trivial or simple-minded questions, he can do or say the wrong thing, he can repeat his queries and pursue his interests *ad nauseam*, he can consort with people of every status and reputation. Such behavior would not be tolerated in an insider, yet is crucial to the research. The outsider derives the benefit of an immunity borne of difference and ignorance."[16]

Adjusting to a village community will require some time and will include a number of activities: learning their language, eating their food, listening to their stories, and joining in everyday work and recreation. Most important, participation also entails learning to function properly within the context of the community. Learning how to behave appropriately takes time. Outsiders, even trained RDFs, often make embarrassing blunders and violate rules of etiquette, which can cause people to become angry and upset. An anthropologist working among the Yanomamo Indians in Venequela once uttered the name of a woman who had recently been killed in a raid. In this society it is a flagrant breach of decency to ever mention the name of a deceased individual. The man he was talking to jumped from his chair, raised his fist and said: "You (#&&*), if you ever say that name again I'll kill you!" Obviously, RDFs must learn to address people correctly, to avoid tabooed subjects with certain individuals, to reciprocate in precisely the right amount for favors received, and if unduly imposed on, to fly into an appropriate rage just as the locals do in similar circumstances. Such skill does not come easily and certainly does not come from a few months experience in the village.

Early anthropologists often concluded that people from the same community or culture generally thought alike and their behavior was uniform and consistent.[17] Others strongly disagreed and suggested that even in the smallest of villages, individuals do not think or act alike. Nor is there much evidence now that uniform socialization tends to produce a common personality type. C. W. M. Hart working among the Tiwi tribe in Australia, noted among five brothers significant personality differences as varied as anything in modern society. The first brother was a follower, not a leader, very unsure of himself, and preferred to be by himself, the second brother was assertive, domineering and convinced of his own importance, the third son was a rebel obsessed with seducing other men's wives, the fourth son was known for his gaiety and humor, happy-go-luck, had many friends but had no political ambitions, the fifth son seem obsessed with a need to conform to others' expectations, generally was unnoticed and wholly uninfluential. It can be very misleading to assume all people in a village are the same. The longer you live in a community the more you will become aware of these differences.

Informants can be helpful and a hindrance. If they are trustworthy they can be helpful, but they may present their own biases as reality. The Yanomamo Indians once perpetuated an elaborate hoax that had an ethnographer recording false information for five months before he discovered the deception.[18] RDFs must be willing to see the diversity in every village. It is a common mistake to assume that everybody in the village thinks alike and has the same values and assumptions about what is right and wrong, what is good and bad. For example, using a school teacher who happens to speak a little English to explain some customs or traditions in the village, may well introduce bias and distortion because they will be using ideas and perceptions not necessarily reflective of how the people see things. Thus it is important to remember that no one informant will present a complete picture of the village. In one village, the religious leader, the anarchist blacksmith, and the village midwife will all have very different views on the values, the norms and none should be seen as having the "correct" interpretation of the village.

Factionalism is a common problem in many village communities which RDFs must be aware of. The web of intrigue and hostility bred of village factionalism, jealousy, or class antagonism frequently binds the RDF more closely to one group than another, despite all efforts to remain neutral. The sampling of community sentiments is therefore biased by forces beyond the fieldworker's control. Anyone who reads Gerald Berreman's marvelous account of his fieldwork in a Hindu village will be made aware of these possibilities.[19] Berreman shows how the two interpreters he used at different phases of his research affected the kind and quality of information obtained. Low caste villagers were unwilling to voice resentment they felt at their treatment by members of the upper castes as long as Berreman used a high-caste interpreter. When he used a Muslim interpreter, a whole new set of emotions, feelings, and perceptions emerged in the course of interviewing.

How Can RDFs and Interns Become Prepared for the Reality of Village Life?

One important aspect of one's training to become an RDF requires some exploration of the challenges that Interns and RDFs may face when they first enter a village community. No matter how much one has read or seen in movies or television, there is no way in words to describe the reality of village life. Yet I would be remiss in my duty if I did not try to prepare the unsuspecting intern or RDF to what he or she will most likely experience. Just remember no matter how bad it sounds, it will still probably be worse than you have imagined. Having said that, I must also acknowledge that getting through the initial shock is possible, and some of the most profound and meaningful experiences of my life took place in the kind of villages that I will describe below. Living and working in villages is both a challenge and a great reward. I hope you see both.

In my first experience in the villages of Egypt, the issues that I was forced to confront are, unfortunately, still quite common in villages as diverse and different as those found in Bolivia, Guatemala, Mexico, Kenya, Indonesia, Philippines and India. When I first arrived in Egypt, I sought to obtain permission from the Ministry of Local Administration to live in a village for a year in order to learn as much as I could about life in Egyptian villages. After several months of establishing my credentials as a graduate student who was hoping to document the process of development being implemented by the Nasser Government in Egypt, I was finally given the necessary papers and approval. Even though I had permission to live in an Egyptian village, I was told that the local leaders of the villages I might live in would have to give their permission also. I was given the names of ten villages some in Upper Egypt and some in Lower Egypt that I was told I could visit and seek local leader permission. I selected a village in Upper Egypt in Assyut and the first time I sought to meet with the village leaders, a few days previously, something had happened which had thrown the whole region into a state of consternation. In a nearby village, a Mosque had been burnt to the ground. Neither a motive nor any indication of who might be responsible for this outrage had been determined, although within the Muslim community, anyone who was Christian was suspect. Consequently, newly arrived strangers, especially an American, were not to be trusted. I approached the village chief, to whom I had previously talked with in Cairo about the nature of my stay in his village; but was told I would not be able to come to his village at this time.

I let some time elapse to allow the incident of the Mosque to become past history and once more set out to make contact, this time with a highly respected family in the same area. Now I learned that there was a rumor that I was a CIA agent, who was supposedly trying to infiltrate communities to impose alien ideas and sow divisions in the villages of Egypt. I retreated once more to Cairo. To cut a long story short, it was only after two more abortive attempts that I eventually won an introduction to the town chief of Mit Ghamr in the Delta of Lower Egypt and was able to convince him that my research would be useful in documenting the "great progress" that was being made in his area.

During the first few weeks my presence was greeted with much suspicion. Even the government officials who knew that I had central government permission to live in this area were reluctant to meet me in their home or in their offices. I was told later that anyone who was observed talking to me was later interrogated by the local secret police to determine exactly what we had talked about. Over the next several months I developed a friendship with the two local doctors, a husband and wife team, that were working in a nearby village outside Mit Ghamr. Through their contact I was able to meet with groups of men and women in their village.

One evening a small group of influential villagers came to me to solicit my help in starting a project for milk production. They had hoped that I might help them in arranging a loan with a bank in Cairo. Their assumption, that I, a rich American, would easily be able to arrange such financing, was unfortunately unfounded. Fortunately, I was unable to help in this project, because when the cows were eventually purchased through the connections of a local rich landowner, within just a few months, three of the cows had died of some mysterious disease. Yet, despite the disillusionment of the group, at least I had achieved some sort of acceptance and was beginning to get to know some of the villagers. I therefore decided to rent a small house to establish a better relationship with the whole community. I observed a local social service worker in the village and was impressed with her ability to work with the people. She had started a series of weaving classes for children, and this gave her the opportunity to visit the women in their homes. Through these visits she had hoped to convey to them the possibility of undertaking a group activity to improve their economic situation.

Between the female doctor and the social service worker, they had managed to get together some eleven women to stock and breed quality laying hens to improve the communal diet. Another fifteen women joined this group and a productive activity had begun. I had not realized that the lack of self-esteem of these peasant women was more of a problem than their poverty. I had arranged to obtain some information from a local extension agent on the proper feeding and care of these chickens. In spite of having been instructed in the rearing of the birds, most of the women appeared from my vantage point, to be quite irresponsible. They did not accept the obligations of active participation in the work of the group. On six occasions hens were returned in a state of such neglect that they were dying. There were cases of women forced to give up their chicken project because their husbands, not content with simply beating their wives into submission, threatened to sell the birds. On man, indeed, did kill two hens, just to make his wife suffer and frighten her into leaving the project. These early experiences were very discouraging to me and I often felt that I would never be able to make a difference in this environment.

It was during this period that I first met Dr. Ahmad al-Naggar and was introduced to his simple but very profound village bank system. It might be useful to reread his case study in Unit Two of this book, for his experiences, his methods and approaches were an inspiration to me. Through my work with Dr al-Naggar, I was able to feel much satisfaction in the work that we were doing.

Section Six
Realities of Village Life: What Hope Is There?

Lest, you doubt my sense of the challenge that all interns and RDFs must face, let us describe village life as it will be found in many rural areas throughout Africa, Asia, and Latin America. My description of such villages is based upon nearly 30 years of personal experience. Some of my observations are somewhat exaggerated to make a point, but unfortunately, too many peasants of this world still live under the conditions that I am describing.

My initial findings when I first began living and working in villages was that men and women worked as individuals or at best with members of their family, without the opportunity of wider support. Most of these peasants tended to be apathetic, devalued, frustrated, weak and occasionally rebellious. It is important to understand how this conditioning has become a major determinant of their lives; and one that will be difficult to overcome. When the Spanish arrived in South America, or the French and British arrived in Africa and Asia, they subdued the local population by force of arms, making them understand through repression that total submission was necessary for their survival. Following a process that is not too unlike what behavioralist today call operant conditioning, a system of conditioning rewards were also established: the more intelligent were given menial tasks in the colonial administration, and the western clergy promised them a good life after death if they were obedient and submissive to authority in this life.

For centuries many of these people were conditioned in this manner. Unfortunately, many of these same societies, even after the colonial masters have gone, are still under strong, centralized, and highly authoritarian regimes, with the message of control carried over in the modern systems of television and radio. The message now transmitted in many of these societies is of conformity and unquestioned obedience with opportunities for a few of them to receive education and health services from the government as their reward. Yet for most of these people, especially the rural poor, there is little opportunity to consider what their society is and who controls and manipulates it for whose benefit and advantage.

In contrast to the material possessions of the landed and governmental elite, is the squalor in which most rural people must live: half-naked children, people going barefoot in muddy streets beside which run filthy gutters, drunken men, wooden or mud (adobe) shanty dwellings, and an inadequate diet of corn, rice, beans or sorghum. The living conditions are demoralizing. There are government projects without number for the improvement of their living standards, but they almost always come to naught either because the finances dry up or because the officials in charge of the project are less than effective or even worse, cruel and corrupt. Little wonder, then, that the community is apathetic and has no incentive to embark on yet another project seemingly doomed to failure as all the others have.

Psychologists have long been able to explain how frustration engenders aggression. The blows and insults from the men to their women and children, and the sexual abuses of women are not chance happenings. I have witnessed a father burning his own son on the face with a lighted cigarette, another forcing his little son's hands into a fire, a drunkard slashing the hands and arms of his wife because she was not attending to his needs. The women in their turn strike and scream at their children when they fall over or break something, with no thought of reassuring them.

Frustration also engenders guilt. Particularly among the women it is commonplace that, after an outburst of anger with their husbands or children, they feel guilty and become totally submissive. These sudden changes of mood create confusion in the minds of children, with serious consequences for their mental health and growth to maturity.

Finally, aggression reflects back to the subject himself. Hence the chronic alcoholism, drug abuse and other forms of stimulant intake, especially among the men, are nearly always reinforcing. In the Latin American culture, drunkenness is a sign that the man is *macho*. Anyone who refuses to drink up loses his masculine image in the eyes of his peers. Drinking becomes competitive and those who can hold their liquor best are accepted and respected even though -- and this they would vehemently deny -- drink makes them sexually impotent, irresponsible, criminal and sick, even to the extent of putting their lives at risk. The women in many of these societies, in contrast, tend to neglect themselves, have no personal aspirations and sometimes fall victim to psychosomatic illnesses.

Most village people live in a constant state of fear, anxiety and uncertainty. They worry about the lack of resources to meet basic needs, unexpected illness, the devastation that a bad storm may bring. This leads to a kind of mental paralysis, a reluctance to try anything new, an inability to think through approaches to a solution to their problems. Sometimes this state of mind activates all their defense mechanisms, so that they block out reality. They become vulnerable, incapable of confronting any situation that is different from their normal lives. RDFs must be sensitive to these perceived realities.

From my work in many village communities in Africa, Asia and Latin America, village women are often very afraid of physical violence from their husbands or being deserted for another woman and so are very obedient to their husbands, asking permission for their every move. While I have observed hundreds of exceptions to this next observation, village women generally lack self-esteem, reflecting the fact that they are generally if not universally undervalued in their societies. They survive only in the hope of seeing their children grow up, showing neither the interest nor the courage to become involved in measures to improve their condition. It is difficult to picture them outside the familial framework where they are all but slaves of a masculine society of father, brothers, and husband. People in rural village communities tend to regard household tasks as exclusive to females, and this ensures that women see themselves as workers at home or in the fields, always obeying and following the demands of male members of society.

Women often appear to accept this uncomplainingly in the belief that the survival of the family unit depends on the preservation of the distinction between their role and that of their husbands, the providers. Not that the latter fulfill this function well: too many men seek comfort in alcohol, social drugs, gambling and various sports events. This is not too surprising, since there are few paying job opportunities for them. Male chauvinism is prevalent in nearly every rural society that I have worked and lived in, for this is the way rural societies are generally structured. Given this reality, female interns assigned to various rural villages may feel some trepidation and concern, wondering how they might have any positive impact in such a reality. The best that an outsider can hope to accomplish (especially an intern with only a few months) is to come to understand the power of tradition and custom. It is probably wise not to interfere in such customs in any open or confrontative way. Most westerners, coming into such societies for the first time, must be prepared for the shock of seeing these forms of male-female interactions.

In the Egyptian villages where I first worked, some of the women, whose men folk thought the activities suggested by the outsiders was a waste of time, would fail to attend work meetings when their husbands were at home. However, I observed that most of the men accepted some outside work for their wives, even if it meant neglecting house, husband and children, provided their work guaranteed a regular monthly income. Some women actually left the village group to engage in the production of plastic shoes in a workshop set up in another village, working a twelve-hour shift, often without a lunch break. They worked to earn less than the minimum wage, yet such minimal income enabled them to solve the problem of meeting their household expenses. Unfortunately, this extra income also added to the irresponsibility of their husbands since it allowed them to spend more of their own earnings at the local tea house.

In most villages of the less developed world, there is a general apathy and even a great fear towards introducing any changes, even when such changes might allow the peasants a better quality of life. This stems from a lack of work opportunities, the absence of creative activities and social involvement, and most assuredly a neglect of most rural areas through centuries of exploitation, violence, and pain. This reality will not be readily apparent to a newcomer, but let me assure you that it is does exist in many villages.

The attitude of village peasants obviously is derived from past centuries of submissiveness and degradation. From my perspective, their passivity tends to destroy them as human beings. Unfortunately, they have been conditioned by the local system of life into thinking that their situation is normal. Some even believe that it is their preordained lot to live in misery and ignorance. The poverty of these people has obliterated their capacity to experience themselves as self-reflective beings. All their other capacities -- of love, of creativity, of empowerment -- have been nullified or at least devalued, since these have no place in the reality of their lives.

It is important to understand that both men and women generally lack self-esteem. They attach no value to what they do or are or know. They do not realize that the empirical knowledge acquired from their everyday experiences is a kind of wealth. They do, however, often prize academic learning: a peasant may even make great sacrifices so that his son may go and study in the belief that a graduation certificate will help him to escape the poverty trap. Those who have such certificates, he believes, are respected and revered. Any certificate will serve; he does not ask himself whether it actually equips his son to attain a higher standard of living. The father may go into debt, even be forced to sell off part of his land. Girls do not generally have the same opportunities; there is the assumption that their daughters will eventually abandon their studies anyway to get married, and thus the time girls spend in school is perceived to be a waste of time.

Once they have completed their studies most youth seldom return to their villages. This is one of the reasons for rural depopulation in many areas. However, there are few employment opportunities in the cities either, and the sacrifice of the parents is often in vain. Life is not necessarily better and often is worse in the cities.

The psychological attitude of most rural peasants wherever they might live, struggling to achieve a precarious survival, is evident in their isolated and individualist approach to life, an attitude which at times I have found most discouraging, but which is a consequence of this long history of oppression and exploitation which these people have suffered. Those who live in rural areas demonstrate considerable insecurity over material possessions and seldom allow others, even in their own village, to know what they have. Clearly this is an instinct of self-preservation, since at times their lives may actually depend on it. Yet, while in this pattern of behavior is generally evident in most situations given their limited resources, they can often be very generous towards visitors and even to members of their own community on special community occasions (fiestas, holidays, and special events in the village). Thus is the contradiction of their lives.

Some Conclusions

You may find my description of village life perhaps harsh, even exaggerated, and perhaps insensitive to the problems and challenges that such people have had to endure in their struggle for survival. My purpose, however, is not to belittle or unfairly criticize what I have seen, but to sensitize you to a number of problems that will not easily go away, and certainly will not go away because an intern or RDF is willing to live and work among these people for a year or two. The process will take much longer. Again, may I share a personal story. Because of my work in rural Egypt in the mid-1960s, I have had a wonderful opportunity to compare and contrast rural Egypt in the 1960s with Egypt in the 1990s. When I visit the villages of Egypt today, I am very conscious of the changes that have occurred in the past thirty years. Yet in early 1991 I took a group of Americans with me to visit some of the villages that I had worked in before. I was proud of the changes that I could see: For example, the infant mortality rate is now nearly half what it was thirty years ago, illiteracy even among young girls is significantly less than what it was in the early 1960s. I now see schools and health clinics that were not there before. Yet for the Americans, this was their first experience with rural Egypt and they were aghast at the poverty and the dirt and squalor that they saw. One woman, tormented by the reality of her constructs, painfully said to me: "I see no hope for these people, I see no progress. Look, how the flies cake on the eyes of the children." For her, there was no hope, no change, only the relentless and impossible tragedy of poverty. Yet for me with the hindsight of thirty years, I was excited with the changes I could see, I was excited with the progress that these villages had made.

Now that we have reviewed the reality of these villages, I hope you will be able to see beyond the "flies on the eyes of the children." This section has sought to sensitize you to the many challenges related to introducing change into village communities, of the importance of taking a long-term view of development, and of seeing the challenges that a different culture presents to future RDFs and especially student interns, facing the realities of village life for the first time. While this chapter should make you aware (if not discouraged and even somewhat cynical), concerning the challenges and problems RDFs must face as they seek to introduce change, the next several chapters should provide you with a set of strategies, interventions and approaches that should give you some feeling of hope and optimism for the future. Our job is how to balance out these two seemingly contradictory feelings of pessimism and optimism. There is room for both in the field of rural development. Most programs organized to introduce students into the field of development, structure some kind of internship experience as part of the program. Let us now review some specific ways in which students can best take advantage of these internship experiences.

Section Seven
Overseas Internship Field Experience

Most training programs in development education require some type of fieldwork or internship experience. Fieldwork is perhaps the best way for you as a prospective RDF to gain enough experience to determine whether rural development work is really for you. Fieldwork is generally structured to allow a student to live and work in a LDC for several months. This experience helps to provide students with concrete knowledge of the varied approaches and methods used in rural development work. It clearly helps students both extend self-awareness and achieve a sense of professional identity. Obviously this is an important way to broaden student's sociocultural understanding of an alien or different culture from his or her own. Fieldwork in an isolated village gives the student a taste of what it must be like to live and work in the field of development over an extended period of time. Many students have acknowledged how such an experience was invaluable in assisting them to understand and appreciate cultural diversity and to offer ways of utilizing this understanding in the work of development. Finally, many student internships take place within the organizational structure of a development agency and fieldwork can help students expand their awareness of the professional role relationships within such development organizations as well as the organization's role in the community.

Making the Most of Your Internship Experience

For a variety of reasons, students often do not derive the maximum benefit from fieldwork and supervision. It is important to understand that development work often requires that you work in communities that you did not personally choose and are often required to work with a supervisor who is very busy and may consider your presence an imposition on his or her time. We offer some practical strategies for making the most of these applied experiences.

First let yourself fit into the situation you find yourself, instead of trying to make it fit you. Be open to learning from the staff and the people in the community. Attempt to suspend your preconceived judgments about what you should be learning and focus instead on what lessons are available to you. Learn as much as you can about the politics of the organization and the community by talking with people who work and live there, by attending staff meetings and community meetings, and by asking questions. All of your learning will not result merely from interacting with community people. You can learn a good deal about an organization by being attentive and by talking with co-workers.

It is important to be aware of the toll that this new experience might have on you both emotionally and physically including the confusion often associated with culture shock. The symptoms of culture shock were first documented in follow-up research on Peace Corps Volunteers. The most common symptoms are the feelings of disorientation, uneasiness, excessive concern over cleanliness, excessive irritation from delays and minor frustrations, resistance to learning the language or eating the local food, longing to be home with family and friends, feelings that the people are strange, different, possibly stupid, and somehow less than human. Certain aspects of your life that you have not been willing to look at may be opened up as you get involved with the community where you are working. It is important to realize that your increased awareness will lead to more anxiety in your life, especially when you are faced with the trauma of a totally new situation.

Experience from many other students suggests the importance of recognizing the limits of your training. It is for this reason that you must put yourself in situations where you will be able to obtain supervised experience. Regardless of your educational level, there is always more to learn. It is essential to learn the delicate balance between being too confident and doubting yourself.

Students often find it helpful to be flexible in applying various development approaches. Avoid falling into the trap of fitting the people of the community where you are working to one particular approach or theory. Use theory as a means of helping you understand the behavior of these people but recognize that such theories are mental constructs that may facilitate your understanding but may also distort your understanding of a given reality. Realize that people with different cultural backgrounds see things very differently and that care must be used in communicating with them.

If you find yourself in a place that you do not particularly like, don't write it off as a waste of time. At least you are learning that working in a given type of community or culture, for example is not what you want for a career. It helps to realize that none of your decisions need be cast in concrete. Determine what you don't find productive about the placement and why. You can also think of ways to make your assignment more meaningful, rather than just telling yourself that you'll put in your time and get your credit. There are probably at least a few avenues for creating learning opportunities. Welcome all experiences as resources that can teach you what you will need to know in future situations.

As early as possible in your internship experience, it will be helpful to make connections in the community. Learn how to use community resources and how to draw on support systems beyond the organization you are working with by developing a network of contacts. This kind of networking may well lead to a range of job opportunities.

Many students find it very helpful to keep a journal, recording your observations, experiences, concerns, and personal reactions to your work. Your journal is an excellent way to stay focused on yourself as well as to keep track of what you are doing and feeling, in this experience.

It is important to be open to trying new things. If you have not worked in an agricultural setting before, for example, observe how the farmers engage in agriculture, if possible, work with an agricultural extensive worker working in the area. Avoid setting yourself up by thinking that if you do not succeed perfectly in a new endeavor, you are a dismal failure. Give yourself room to learn by doing, at the same time gaining supervised experience. Look for ways to apply what you are learning in your academic courses to your experiences in the field. For example, one professional recalls having taken a medical anthropology course as part of her graduate program. Through her internship she was able to see some of the concepts she had studied come to life in the field. One important lesson she learned was that one had to look carefully to find the traditional health workers in a given community and that some of the things she had learned in class did not fit the community where she was working.

Be prepared to adjust your expectations. Don't expect an organization to give you responsibility for implementing some aspect of a project before it has a chance to know you. You'll probably start your fieldwork by being in an observing role. Later you may sit in on a community planning group, for example, and function as a discussion facilitator. Remember it takes time before you will gain the trust of a community. Find ways to work cooperatively with other staff and community people and to combine your talents with theirs. Look for means of tapping into your own creativity. If you are talented musically, for example, look for a way in which you might incorporate music into your field-placement activities. Other types of talents like sports, story telling, art and dance are all activities that will stimulate interest and involvement.

Experience suggests that students adjust better when they treat their field placement like a job. Approach fieldwork in much the same way as you would if you were employed by the organization. Demonstrate responsibility, be on time for your appointments and meetings, and strive to do your best. Although you may be in an unpaid placement, this does not mean you can be irresponsible on the job. Often an unpaid internship can turn into a paid position. Learn as much as you can about the structure of the organization where you are placed. Ask about its history, its policies and organizational structure, about the way the programs are administered, and about management of the staff. Most likely, as you pursue a career in development, you will often be involved in the administrative aspects of a development program.

Finally, it is important to remember that one of the major challenges will be the loneliness, the isolation and strangeness of this experience. Interns must learn to think and act in a self-directed way by involving themselves in a variety of activities. If you merely wait for a supervisor or other workers to take the initiative and give you meaningful assignments, you may be less than satisfied with your placement. Focus as much time as possible in learning the local language, write detailed field observations along with your impressions and feelings about what you are observing, seek to learn as much about the local culture, how they are able to survive in a situation with so many disadvantages. Review the questions in the section on Cultural Dialoguing and seek answers to these questions. Keep yourself busy and the time will go much faster.

Learn to challenge your self-doubts

Interns are often unsure, apologetic, and unwilling to credit themselves with what they are able to do. Ask yourself how you deal with your own feelings about what you know and don't know. Consider how you might deal with a disgruntled staff worker or even a community leader who challenges you. At the initial session, the staff member might admit he has no time to baby-sit a student intern, or the community leader might be surprised at your age. "Who are you to be offering me advice?" He asks. "You look so young, and I wonder if you have the experience to deal with our problems." Assume that these kinds of challenges open up some of your own fears and doubts.

Can you imagine saying any of the following things silently to yourself?

1. "He's right. There are many years separating us. I wonder if I can understand his situation?"

2. "This guy's attitude really makes me mad. He's not giving me a chance, and I feel attacked before I've even had a chance to know him."

3. "Well, I don't feel comfortable with this confrontation, but I don't want to back down. I feel like letting him know that even though we differ in age, we might have many similarities in our struggles. I'd like an opportunity to at least explore whether we can form a relationship."

4. "He's right. What makes me think I have anything to offer him? Maybe I should have chosen another line of work. Maybe I should not be here."

Most professionals have feelings of self-doubt and question their competence at certain times and in certain situations. The purpose of an internship is to provide you with an opportunity to begin the process of gaining the confidence and skills needed to be an effective RDF. I would hope that you would have the courage to face your feelings of incompetence rather than running from them or pretending that they do not exist.

Understand the Value of Good Supervision

Be clear in your own mind what you expect from the supervisors to whom you are assigned, and discuss your desires with them from the outset. This section suggests how to approach your supervisors and how actively to participate in this process. Remember you will limit your opportunities for learning if you assume a know-it-all stance. Be open to input and suggestions from supervisors but also from teachers, peers, other staff and even community people. Have the courage to admit your imperfections, and don't become frozen out of fear of making errors. Be willing to make mistakes, and talk openly with your supervisor about them. If you don't have the courage to fail at times, you won't be willing to try anything new. Take advantage of your student role, for as a student, you are certainly not expected to know everything. Give yourself permission to be a learner.

Being willing to admit your ignorance and feeling of inadequacy is all important in interactions with both your supervisor and the people you work with. I observed a young intern struggling with the newness of his assignment in the Philippines. He appeared arrogant and withdrawn, found it hard to smile and seemed hostile at times. His supervisor asked him what was going on. At first the young man merely stated that everything was OK and that he merely needed time to adjust. Later the young man admitted to me that he was greatly intimidated by the supervisor and was afraid that he would not measure up to the supervisor's expectations. Knowing the supervisor quite well, I suggested to the young intern that he should share his fears with the supervisor directly next time they were alone. Several days later the young man approached me with a big smile and acknowledged that the supervisor had proven to be not only understanding but quite helpful in reducing his uneasiness.

It helps to realize that supervisors are people, too. They get bogged down with their own burdens. As their own work load grows and pressures increase, they may not initiate the regular supervision sessions that they have promised. Furthermore, some practitioners do not volunteer to become supervisors but are told that they should add interns to their already heavy work load. At times their training for being a supervisor is minimal, and they too are expected to "learn by doing." If you are able to understand the predicament of supervisors you are more likely to establish a basis of communication with them. Within a climate of open communication, you can sensitively and assertively let them know that you need help.

I would suggest that you give your supervisors credit for wanting to do their best. If you approach them with a genuine attitude of letting them know what you would like from them, they are more likely to respond positively than if you keep your distance from them and expect them to make the first move. My experience suggests that many students have negative experiences with fieldwork and with supervisors. The relationship between the field supervisor and the student seems to be a key variable in determining whether the student's experiences are positive or negative. Supervisors certainly play a key role in the student's learning and it is part of the student's responsibility to communicate with them even if they are less than ideal.

Recognize and Appreciate the Effective Supervisor

One of the key responsibilities of a supervisor and trainer (**see the four career levels mentioned in the previous chapter**) is to supervise and monitor interns, to foster their personal and professional development, and to assist them in learning the basic skills needed in rural development work. What follows are examples of some of the characteristics of effective RDF supervisors observed over the years.

1. Professional supervisors demonstrate personal characteristics that enable them to carry out their roles and functions. For instance, supervisors are encouraging and optimistic, sensitive to individual differences, able to demonstrate a sense of humor, comfortable with the authority of their role, and committed to updating their own skills as a RDF and as a supervisor of RDFs.

2. Professional supervisors are knowledgeable about ethical, legal and administrative aspects of the profession.

3. Supervisors demonstrate knowledge of individual differences with respect to gender, race, ethnicity, culture, and age and understand the importance of these characteristics in the supervisory process.

4. Professional supervisors possess appropriate levels of empathy and respect, genuineness, concreteness, and self-disclosure.

5. Professional supervisors are knowledgeable and experienced both in methods of intervention with community people and in supervising interns and trainees as they intervene with the people of rural communities.

6. Professional supervisors set clear goals and use these goals to guide them in using various teaching techniques; they state the purposes of the supervisory relationship and explain the procedures to be used.

7. Professional supervisors provide direct and immediate feedback that is closely tied to the intern's behavior. This feedback is systematic, objective, accurate, timely, and clearly understood.

You may meet and work with some supervisors who do demonstrate effectiveness in some of the areas listed above. Some supervisors feel ill-equipped to do what is expected of them, and some may be as insecure in their supervisory role as you are in your role as an intern. However, it is up to you to get the most from your supervisors, inspite of any limitations that may exist.

It can benefit you to learn how to function under a range of supervisory styles, both now as a student and later as a professional RDF. One supervisor may believe that harsh confrontation is a way to cut through a peasant's stubborn defenses. Another treats peasants as victims who are not responsible for their problems. Another provides unlimited advice for peasant/farmers and promotes a problem-solving orientation for every community problem. There are supervisors who foster a supportive and positive orientation and who give out "warm fuzzies" exclusively. Other supervisors seem to thrive on crises and problems and therefore tend to escalate such situations rather than defuse them. Some work very hard at becoming friends with their interns, whereas others create a professionally aloof relationship. Be open to supervisors with various orientations, and learn to incorporate their viewpoints into your style of facilitation. Don't be too quick to criticize a style different from yours, but consider it an opportunity for learning.

If you do have trouble with a supervisor, the answer is not always merely finding a new one. You can learn a great deal by working with supervisors who have perspectives different from yours and from supervisors who initially appear to be difficult for you to make contact with. When you experience conflicts with a supervisor, it is a good idea to discuss them and do all that you can to work them out. Rather than convincing yourself that your supervisor will not be cooperative, assume that he or she will be open to your suggestions. Later, when you accept a position in an agency, you typically do not have the option of changing supervisors. What is more you often don't have choices in who your co-workers will be. Thus, it is important to learn the interpersonal skills necessary in working out differences while the stakes are not so high.

Section Eight
Some Common Myths About Working in Development

Let us review some of the common myths that many people may have about how things will be different once they have finished their professional training. My experience with people new in the field suggests that many of following comments are typical. It would be appropriate to consider you reactions to these ideas:

1. **As soon as I have a job, my problems will be over.** Starting in a new career is never easy. Most students underestimate how much time and energy it takes to reorganize your personal and professional life in order to start a new career.

2. **My new associates will welcome me enthusiastically and accept me as one of them.** New colleagues may be perceived as a threat to some of the old-timers. Recently graduated students often have to prove themselves before they can be fully accepted.

3. **I have been trained immediately to master the varied demands of my new job.** Success in school based upon memorization and doing well on exams do not guarantee success on the job. Coordinating the multiple tasks and job expectations can be draining and difficult. One crucial step toward mastery of the many demands of a new job is to admit that they cannot be mastered immediately.

4. **I must perform perfectly, lest someone discovers that I am incompetent.** You do not need to perform all aspects of your job instantly and flawlessly. Setting reasonable goals and being open to feedback can lessen the

pressure on you. By consulting with former peers in graduate school, you can form a support group and laugh together about some of your unreasonably high standards.

   5. **Because I have worked so hard to get here, I will automatically love my job.** You may feel somewhat disillusioned because all aspects of your job in the field of development do not meet your expectations.

One Last Piece of Advice

Many interns fail to distinguish between the role of an RDF and that of a student intern. Many interns have the mistaken view that they will be able to make a significant contribution to some poor village in a 6-12 month period. Students who have a strong need to see some progress, to have made things better because of their being in the village, may find their internship very unsatisfying. It is crucial to lower your expectations, to see the internship as an opportunity to observe how people live, to learn their customs, their way of life. This should be a time of deep reflection and assessment: Is development work really for me? Do I have the temperament and patience to work in this field for 5-10 years or more, and realize that the really important work of this process must be done by the villagers themselves.

In the chart below, the work and activities of RDFs and interns are contrasted. Review these differences very carefully. There must be no illusions about what a student intern will be able to accomplish. From my perspective, student interns are there to learn, not to change people or situations. In order of importance and probability of being accomplished, the following five activities might be considered:

   1. Observe and learn something about how development organizations work in the field. Be careful not to make judgments too quickly. Many development organizations have many challenges, often have few resources, must follow government regulations that constrain and slow things down, have local personnel who appear authoritarian and rigid. However, be not too quick to judge.

   2. Gain an appreciation for the difficulty of development work, assess your own motivations for wanting to work in the field of development, evaluate your own personality, your needs, your personal goals and determine if this is something you really want to do. In many ways, this is the most important purpose for the internship.

   3. Keep a detailed diary, using the questions in the section on Cultural Dialoguing, to stimulate your thinking and sensitize your observations. You will have a lot of free time, especially in the evenings, and your personal writing will keep your mind from loneliness and homesickness.

   4. One important task for student interns, is to keep their eyes open for local villagers who might eventually be recruited and trained as future RDFs.

Effective RDFs are often the informal leaders, those who are quietly working without fanfare or notoriety.

    5. The last task will be to consider working with the community on some small project. Again the challenge is to develop a project that is theirs and not yours, a project that will still be there a year after you are gone. Many interns make the mistake of imposing some activity, out of the mistaken belief, that their internship will be a failure if they don't build something in the village or implement some project. If there have been earlier interns in the area where you are working, you may be asked to follow-up on earlier activities.

Chart 7-1
The Contrast Between an Intern and an RDF

	Intern	RDF
Period of time in the village (no salary)	6-12 months (paid salary)	3-5 years
National Background	Generally American	Generally Local Indigenous
Level of Academic Training	Some University or above	Some Grade School or above
Focus of Activities	Phase one mostly and some phase two in RD	Functions in all three phases of RD

Major Purpose for being in the village

Intern	RDF
1. Builds trust and good relationships through conversations and discussions	1. The RDF does all the six things listed as purposes of the interns.
2. Engage in Cultural Dialoguing and Awareness Building	2. Builds on the problem solving groups established in the community, strengthening these groups to deal with one or more of the five dimensions of RD.
3. Learn the local dialect and as much of the local culture and way of life as possible. Keeps a detailed diary of what is observed and learned.	3. Seeks to build links and relationships with outside agencies and organizations that might provide needed resources.
4. Starts the process of problem solving group development and initiates some small project in one of the five dimensions of RD.	4. Begins the process of local institution building. Focuses on local resource mobilization to ensure greater sustainability.
5. Help the community prepare for the arrival of possible expeditions coming into the village	5. Recruits and provides training for villagers in basic health and literacy programs
6. Builds on the projects and programs started by previous interns in one	6. Seeks to identify other villagers that might become RDFs in the future. Seeks to

of the five dimensions of rural development (RD). work in a network of villages where the process of rural development is replicated.
7. May begin the process of administrative reform, networking, empowerment, and political awareness. (See Chapter 10).

It will be extremely important to reflect on these differences between being an intern and being an RDF, especially if the internship is to be a positive experience. When expectations are too high, many interns become very frustrated and disillusioned. Becoming a professional development worker requires time, patience and perseverance. Graduation from a university or even the completion of an internship is not the end, it is only the beginning. It is essential that you discover ways to maximize the benefits of your university training and internship experiences, to extend your education beyond graduation, for your knowledge and skills will soon be outdated unless you take steps to keep abreast of new developments in the field. Keeping professionally alert implies that you avail yourself of in-service and continuing-education programs. Below are a set of suggestions for a person seeking to enter the field of international development:

1. Join the Section of Comparative and International Administration (SICA) and attend the annual workshop scheduled in conjunction with the American Society of Public Administration annual meeting. Write to ASPA for an application form: ASPA, 1120 G Street, NW, Suite 700, Washington, DC 20005-3885. Equally useful is to become familiar with internet and the many Web Pages that specialized in development studies.

2. Perhaps one of the best ways of keeping yourself up to date is to be involved in a professional network with colleagues who are willing to learn from one another as well as assume a teaching role. One example is Larry Cooley, Management Systems International, 600 Water Street, SW, NBU 7-7. Washington DC 20024, Telephone (202) 484-7170.

3. Begin to subscribe to the 4-5 key journals in the field.

Public Administration Review
Journal of Development
Public Administration and Development
World Development
Journal of Economic Development and Cultural Change
Development and Change
International Journal of Public Administration
Journal of Peasant Studies
Journal of Applied Behavioral Science
Canadian Journal of Development Studies

Development Studies
The Journal of Cultural Survival
    4. While the literature on Rural Development is vast, it is important to become familiar with some of the best in the literature. The following are a small suggested list to begin with:

David Apter, *Rethinking Development: Modernization, Dependency and Postmodern Politics* (1987).
Robert Bates, *Towards a Political Economy of Development* (1984).
Peter L. Berger, *Pyramids of Sacrifice* (1976).
J. Black, Development Theory and Practice (1991).
John Brohman, *Popular Development: Rethinking the Theory and Practice of Development* (1996).
Coralie Bryant and L. White, *Managing Induced Development with Small Farmer Participation* (1985).
Stan Burkey, *People First* (1993).
Thomas F. Carroll, *Intermediary NGOs: The Supporting Link in Grassroots Development* (1992).
Michael M. Cernea, *Putting People First*, (1985).
R. Chamber, *Rural Development: Putting The Last First*, (1983).
Ronald Chilcote, *Theories of Development Underdevelopment* (1984).
Ken Darrow & M. Saxenian, *Appropriate Technology Sourcebook* (1986).
Eric Dudley, *The Critical Villager* (1993).
Frank Ellis, *Peasant Economics* (1993).
Charles J. Erasmus, *Man Takes Control* (1961).
Milton J. Esman and N.T. Uphoff, *Local Organizations* (1984).
Frantz Fanon, *The Wretched of the World* (1966).
R. E. Galli, et al., *Rethinking the Third World*, 1992).
Guy Gran, *Development by the People* (1983).
D. Harrison, *The Sociology of Modernization and Development* (1988).
B. Hettne, *Development Theory and the Three Worlds* (1990).
Albert Hirschman, *Getting Ahead Collectively,* (1984).
D. Hulme and M. Turner, *Sociology and Development: Theories, Policies and Practices* (1990).
Bruce F. Johnston and W.C. Clark, *On Designing Strategies for Rural Development* (1982).
David C. Korten, *Getting to the 21st Century* (1990).
Uma Lele, *The Design of Rural Development* (1975).
James B. Mayfield, *Go to the People* (1986).
James Midgley, *Community Participation, Social Development and the State*, (1986).
John Montgomery, *Bureaucrats and People* (1988).
Jon Morris, *Managing Induced Development* (1981).

K. P. Padmanabhan, *Rural Credit* (1988).
Samuel Popkin, *The Rational Peasant* (1979).
Brian Pratt and Jo Boyden, *Field Directors Handbook* (1985).
M. G. Quibria, *Critical Issues in Asian Development* (1995).
M. A. Rahman, *Grass Roots Participation and Self Reliance* (1984).
M. Redclift, *Sustainable Development: Exploring Contradictions* (1987).
Lawrence Salmer, *Listen to the People* (1987).
Teodor Shanin, *Peasants and Peasant Society* (1987).
James C. Scott, *The Moral Economy of the Peasants* (1976).
A. Somjee, *Development Theory: Critiques and Explorations* (1991).
Norman Uphoff & M.J. Esman, *Local Institutional Development* (1986).
James H. Weaver and K. Kusterer, *Achieving Broad-Based Sustainable Development* (1996).

---

[1] John Dewey, *Experience and Education*, (New York: Macmillan, 1938)

[2] Kurt Lewin, *Field Theory in Social Science* (New York: Harper & Row, 1951).

[3] Jean Piaget, *Origins of Intelligence in Children*, (New York: International University Press, 1952).

[4] David A. Kolb, *Experiential Learning: Experience as the Source of Learn and Development* (Englewood Cliffs, N.J.: Prentice-Hall, 1984)

[5] A copy of the instrument used to help individuals determine which learning style is most natural for them is found in James B. Mayfield, *Rural Development Facilitator Workbook* (1997)

[6] Much of this section, which describes a Service Learning Program being introduced on many university campuses, is taken from Cecila I. Delve, Suzanne D. Mintz, and Greig M. Steward (eds.) *Community Service as Values Education* (Oxford: Jossey-Bass, 1990)

[7] Art Levin, *When Dreams and Heroes Died* (San Francisco: Jossey-Bass, 1980),

[8] W. Perry, *Forms of Intellectual and Ethical Development in the College Years: A Scheme* (New York: Holt, Rinehart & Winston, 1970).

[9] L. Lawrence Kohlberg, "The Cognitive-Developmental Approach to Moral Education," *Phi Delta Kappan*, 56 (1975), pp. 670-677.

[10] Carol Gilligan, *In a Different Voice* (Cambridge, Mass: Harvard University Press, 1982).

[11] Paulo Freire, *Pedagogy of the Oppressed*, (New York: Continuum, 1974).

[12] Donald A. Schon, *The Reflective Practitioner* (New York: Basic Books, 1983) and *Educating the Reflective Practitioner* (San Francisco: Jossey-Bass, 1987)

[13] Richard Morrill, *Teaching Values in College: Facilitating Development of Ethical Moral, and Learning in the Professions*, (San Francisco: Jossey-Bass, 1980). p. 54.

[14] Charles Kammer, *Ethics and Liberation*, (Maryknoll, N.Y.: Orbis Books, 1988), p. 29.

[15] Rosalie Wax, *Doing Fieldwork: Warnings and Advice* (Chicago: University of Chicago Press, 1971), pp.71-72.

[16] Gerald Berreman, *Behind Many Masks: Ethnography and Impression Management in a Himalayan Village*, (Ithaca, NY: Society for Applied Anthropology, Monograph No 4, 1962)

[17] See Ruth Benedict *Patterns of Culture* 1934)

[18] Napoleon A. Chagnon, *Yanomamo: The Fierce People* (New York: Holt, Rinehart and Winston, 1968)

[19] Berreman, *op.cit.*

Chapter 8

Stage One of Rural Development
Trust Building and Cultural Awareness

As was mentioned earlier, the first stage of rural development must focus on trust-building and inter-cultural understanding. Many rural development programs and projects fail because they are structured with no understanding of the local community, its traditions, culture, and way of life. The process of developing understanding and awareness is complex and often unpredictable. An understanding as to why some programs of development are successful and appropriate and why others are not, requires that such programs be understood within the context of the local culture and value system of the society. Before one can appreciate the importance of culture and the value orientations of a given society, one must understand the epistemological assumptions underlying that society. Epistemology is the study of how we come to believe that what we know is true. For an RDF approaching a new village setting, the real challenge will come when what he or she thinks is reality is suddenly confronted by what the villagers think is reality. Which system of "truth" is right and how do we reconcile the concepts of science and secularism with the concepts of cultural traditions and spiritual values? Are these two systems of "truth" mutually exclusive, or is it possible that both could have some measure of value and utility?

Section One
Understanding How We Think We Know Something

In any review of the material used to understand the reality of a given cultural system, there are interesting methodological and epistemological assumptions one can make in deciding what we think we know. Following in the traditions of positivism, the scientific method that dominates Western thinking, has consistently been proposed as potentially best able to provide a methodological guarantee that what we think we know would be valid and thus based on truth[1] More recently, hermeneutics has been proposed as a similar candidate for determining the validity of knowledge.[2] The Western world is based upon a culture obsessed with the desire for Truth, Objectivity and Certainty, one where these notions are often deployed interchangeably. In recent years, there has been some skepticism about the utility and even the desirability of such scientific certainty.[3]

For most of the period since Newton, the influence of a scientific account of knowing has exerted an immense influence not only within the natural sciences but beyond, and indeed has influenced our very notions of knowledge. Yet in the last fifty years the very rationality of science itself has come under scrutiny by a number of scholars.[4] Still others have criticized those who would reject the validity and utility of scientifically derived knowledge.[5] Today the status of even the most sacrosanct scientific "truths" may now be questioned. One of these "truths" is that the scientific method places the products of science (scientific knowledge) in some way beyond its knowers. In other words, that scientific knowledge somehow transcends its knowers by virtue of its "objectivity." This approach to epistemology is often called "Monism," the belief that there is a direct relationship between the knower and reality spelled with a big R.

The Knower --------------------------> Reality

Thus, what one experiences through one's five senses is reality, is the truth if you will. If it can't be seen or experienced through the senses then it cannot be true. Much of Western science is based on this Monistic principle that clearly would reject the traditional systems of religion and cultural values found in most village communities, simply because they are non-verifiable in the scientific sense of that word.

An alternative approach to epistemology is call "Dualism" that argues that the relationship between the knower (he or she who thinks they know something) and reality is indirect and is conditioned by what are called the mental constructs that all people have.

The Knower ---------->(Mental Constructs)----------> Reality

Mental constructs are the categories of thought that we gain through the experiences of our childhood, our schools, families, and work relationships. They emerge out of each individual's culture and way of life. Each culture has its own set of constructs that have proven to be very useful. Thus the Eskimo culture has a set of constructs found useful in surviving sub zero temperatures over long periods of time with very limited resources. The Taouregs of southern Algeria and northern Mali have almost a sixth sense when it comes to finding their way in the vast spaces of the Sahara desert. Many Indian tribes in the Amazon basin have incredible knowledge of the plant and animal life in their environment. Such subtle awareness of these secrets of the forest is a function of their culture, traditions and tribal wisdom (what we are calling the mental constructs of a given society). Such constructs are filters that allow us to see and comprehend things in one culture in ways that other cultures would never understand or appreciate. Such constructs are also significant in determining what we perceive to be right, appropriate, beautiful and good. For this reason, an appreciation for cultural diversity is a prerequisite for those who would work as an RDF.

Let me give you an example of how "mental constructs" can condition an entire society. In the time of Gallileo, the society of his day believed firmly that the earth was the center of the universe and that the sun and stars circled around the earth. This belief that the world was at the center of the universe was accepted for several reasons. First, the dominant religions of that day held that scripture had confirmed that God had created the earth as the center of the Universe and anyone who would deny such religious truth would be excommunicated. Second, the scholarly community of that day held this view (a set of mental constructs) that the Sun circled the earth to be both reasonable and scientifically correct. Yet what was most persuasive was the evidence of the senses. For one merely had to observe the sun raising in the morning, crossing the sky during the day, and setting in the evening to "know" the validity of this mental construct (the earth is at the center of the universe). Thus when a given society is confronted with such overwhelming evidence (religious, scientific and common sense) it is not difficult to understand why such mental constructs would be assessed as truth.

Gallileo was faced with a serious dilemma. For through his own observations, he recognized that there was one phenomenon that could not be explained if one accepted the mental construct (the beliefs) that the earth was at the center of the universe, and that was an eclipse of the moon. In seeking to find a reasonable explanation for this anomaly, he suggested a different set of constructs, contrary to those of his society -- the "heretical" idea that the earth was not the center of the universe, but that, in fact, it was the earth that is going around the Sun. Once we begin to see how our constructs may blind us and force us to see reality in a given way, then we can begin to appreciate that how other people see reality may not necessarily be wrong. Epistemological dualism argues that our mental constructs (the assumptions and methods we use to ascertain truth) are neither true nor false in any logical or philosophical sense, but must be assessed in terms of their ability to achieve specific human purposes. Human purposes are not determined scientifically, but culturally. What is of value for a given society is based upon such concepts as goodness, justice, fairness, beauty and aesthetics -- concepts not determined scientifically. Thus even the scientific truths of today may be shown to be wrong (the dualist would say less useful) in the future. When Einstein challenged the notion of Newtonian physics and suggested a new set of constructs (relativity) to help explain the workings of the universe, the dualist would argue that Einstein's mental constructs were neither true nor false, but simply more useful, able to answer more questions and that some future great thinker will find a new set of constructs even more encompassing and useful than Einstein's Theory of Reality.

Dualism keeps one humble in the realization that what we think we know is always open to new experiences, new theories, new ways of looking at reality and that the arrogance of the Western scientific model, which is useful for many human purposes in transportation, communication, medicine, and comfortable living, cannot answer all the great questions of this life -- questions related to the nature and purpose of man, the role of religion and spiritual values in shaping the long-term survival of mankind. It is possible that we may have much to learn from the cultural values, traditions, and knowledge systems of the tribal and ethnic groups, the disadvantaged and isolated village people of the less developed world.

While dualist are often accused of extreme skepticism, the real Father of Skepticism was David Hume who argued most persuasively that there are no truths that can be ascertained logically, that truth will always be elusive and thus relative. Emmanuel Kant, while acknowledging the brilliance of David Hume's arguments, sidestepped the issue by announcing that Hume was right, one could not prove anything, not even that David Hume was right. Kant simply argued that it was more reasonable to assume that some things might be true and that "pure reason" was not the only source of truth. Thus the emergence of dualism that saw various forms of truth possible and that both science and religion might have some value in helping mankind achieve their individual and collective purposes. Such an idea should cause an RDF to consider how the diversity of cultures and values of the many tribes, communities and societies of this world may have value that once might have been denied.

In my approach to epistemology, I should like to suggest that "to know" is not to possess true representations of reality, but rather to possess ways and means of acting and thinking that allows one to attain the goals one happens to have chosen. To know, thus, is not to have the right set of constructs (mental concepts reflecting what is believed to be true) but rather to have a set of action strategies that prove to be useful in achieving desired human goals. Instead of insisting that true knowledge must reflect reality independent of our own perceptions of that reality, it is more appropriate to seek knowledge that is verified by its functional utility. Thus the reality of a given set of ideas, whether cultural, social, physical, or spiritual must be tied closely to their viability/utility, their adequate functioning in one's physical and social environment, their usefulness in establishing significant purpose, identity and meaning for this life, and their ability to furnish the key to a reasonable comprehension of the individual's experiential reality.[6]

In seeking to understand the cultural realities of a given community or culture, it is better now to see human life as an enterprise committed to the production and consumption of systems of meaning. The generation of "mental constructs" of individuals, or perhaps as Geertz would say "to spin out webs" of meaning, emerge in a society as people are socialized and educated in a given society.[7] Any particular person is simultaneously creating for themselves and consuming the products of his or her traditions. Such traditions are the accumulated creations of the past. As we interact with the reality of a given situation, we seek to understand, to interpret what we see. Yet as we seek understanding, we are interpreting (constructing) what is there in terms of our own cultural or mental constructs that both give meaning to the situation as well as extract meaning from them. This sort of meaning resides neither in the situation nor in the observer but rather in the interplay between them and thus reality emerges as a process of social construction. [8]

Towards the end of the last century Wilhelm Dilthey proposed a distinction between two sorts of knowledge. The **natural sciences** sought explanation whereas the **human sciences** sought meaning; thus the hard sciences could no longer be the model for social sciences.[9] From his point of view, the natural sciences might have a rational, empirical foundation, and generate criteria for their own objective progress, whereas the human sciences would recognize that there can be no beginning of meaning and no single, "correct" interpretation of any social situation, any written text, or personal perception of reality. This was a critical set of ideas for it denied Marx's wildly positivistic and influential notion that: "There is one science, not a division between natural and social sciences"[10]

Over the past half century this question about two forms of knowledge has stimulated much debate. Philosophers of science are today much more tentative and reluctant about claims of the ahistorical objectivity and progress of the natural sciences. More especially, the attempt to provide demarcation criteria to distinguish scientific knowledge from other sorts of knowledge has proven impossible to defend; Popper's majestic attempt to do so has dissolved under the criticisms of Lakatos and Feyerabend[11] Nothing, even on the natural science side of Dilthey's conceptual framework, seems so certain now; the objectivity, method and progress of such knowledge have all been demonstrated to be questionable, at best. In the field of anthropology that is clearly relevant to our study of village communities and the work of an RFD, a similar group of thinkers is clearly questioning past paradigmatic approaches to knowledge.[12]

The self-understanding of the human sciences has undergone its own transformation. Hermeneutics had traditionally sought a "correct" interpretation and usually found this in the intentions of authors or social actors. Recognition of the fact that there is neither a single truth to be found in acts of interpretation, nor a single method by which to proceed in such work, has been the central contribution of contemporary hermeneutics.[13] Thus, today we find ourselves in the position where works on both sides of Dilthey's subtle distinctions now lack the foundational certainties they once had. In fact, several have now sought to dismantle the distinction between natural and social sciences. Feyerabend has argued that there is nothing at all special about scientific knowledge for they are but a set of constructs that have been found to be useful, but certainly not necessarily a reflection of reality. In fact, Michael Foucault, has claimed that all knowledge is simply the reflection of strategies used by those who hold power in a given society. These "power holders" thus have the ability to determine which constructs are to be consider as "true" and the power to impose such views on others.[14]

While I am arguing that each individual has the capacity and the tendency to perceive that which one is accustomed to see, given ones constructs, there is a much more persuasive implication for this position. Each individual is the person he or she is because of their membership within human communities and cultures. These are the agents of our socialization and even our forms of education.[15] These experiences are the sources of our language, our sentiments and, indeed, to a large extent, our thoughts. While it is true that any particular socialization process with its accompanying set of constructs does limit the individual to one particular set of perceptual options, still I want to emphasize the positive side of this process. Each set of cultural orientations provides a unique way of looking at reality with each set of constructs having its own special set of potentials and opportunities for relating to reality. Cultural diversity in this way can be described in very positive terms for it offers a myriad of opportunities to contrast, compare and reflect on the values and traditions of the many cultural systems presently existing on the planet each with their own contrasting and potentially useful mental constructs. This need to protect and encourage cultural diversity helps explain why we have suggested that cultural enhancement is one of the **five key dimensions** of rural development

Key Conclusions

First, as I have suggested, notions of science and of truth that we in the West have taken for granted, have undergone radical transformation in our time. Second, any accounting of cultural learning will have social and political implications. Thus people can influence the sort of world they live in. It should be clear that there are innumerable different ways by which the world can be intellectually understood and as well as morally justified. One of the most important aspects of this process is its commitment to understanding learners as active rather than merely passive, acting in and on their worlds rather than merely receiving knowledge or forever controlled by their social reality. Both cultural and methodological pluralism is a very reasonable order of the day. Epistemological Dualism challenges the would-be RDFs of this world to consider the reality not only of the scientific truths of our own society, but also the cultural truths of the communities where we might be working.

Let us now focus on the ways in which students interested in becoming RDFs might develop a set of values appropriate and useful for development work. The first requires a self-assessment of one's own cultural value system and how your own value system may be an obstacle to your effectiveness as an RDF. The second looks at the importance of understanding the impact of culture on the lives and societies that make up the rural areas of the LDCs. The purpose of this chapter is to sensitize future RDFs to the importance of understanding the reality of rural poverty, of the challenges that must be confronted, and of the importance of taking a long-term view of the changes that will be needed to deal with this reality. It clearly will not be an easy process.

Section Two
Role of Values in the Development of an RDF

Once one understands the way in which our constructs determine how we think and how we relate to our own society and to other societies in which we might work, it is time to consider both our own value preferences that have largely been defined within the confines of our own cultures and then we must consider how we as RDFs must operate in a world of great cultural diversity.

This section is designed to help you clarify your values and to identify how they are likely to influence your work as an RDF. Toward this end we will explore how values operate in the processes of village development. To assist you in clarifying your values and identifying ways in which they might interfere with effective village development work, especially during the first stage of rural development, let us describe practical issues about which you may find yourself perplexed. One great challenge that all RDFs must face is the possibility that they will work in communities who have values, practices and beliefs that the RDF is opposed to. What should you do when you and the villagers you are working with have sharp value differences? Often we are torn between showing tolerance and understanding and wanting to confront and change such values and cultural practices.

At this point in your professional development, it is essential that you be open to considering how to establish contact with people who differ from you in age, gender, ethnicity, race, culture, socioeconomic status, sexual orientation, lifestyle, life circumstances, or basic values. Consider a personal value that could get in the way of you being objective in working in a community with very different value orientations. Examples might include: tendencies to reject family planning, the acceptance of abortion, the use of native narcotics, the practice of sexual relations before marriage, the use of traditional witchcraft, the encouragement of polygamy, the acceptance of female circumcision, support of authoritarian patron-client relationships, etc.[16] Preparing oneself to work with people with such different value orientations is not an easy process. What is essential is that you respect different cultural group's right to hold a set of values different from yours. Even if you do not endorse their values, you may still be able to work effectively with them if you are able to refrain from pushing your values onto them. See Chapter 15 for a detailed set of strategies for dealing with these dilemmas. It should be apparent that trust between people of very diverse lifestyles and practices will not be easy to establish. What are your options?

First, you do not need to be the same as those you work with or to have experienced the same life circumstances in order to form a facilitative relationship.

It is useful, perhaps necessary, that you have a range of experiences on which you can call as a basis for understanding different people in different situation. Experience suggests that universal themes do link people in spite of their differences. However, what is crucial is your openness to learn from the lessons that life has presented to you, that you show respect for contrasting perspectives, develop an understanding of the diverse world views of the people you work with, and strengthen your capacity to break out of the narrow mental constructs that filter your reality. If you have grown up in a monocultural world, it may be quite difficult for you quickly to understand people with a different world view, and it definitely will demand a good deal of reflection and soul searching on your part concerning your own attitudes, beliefs and views.[17]

In the previous section, we focused on the influences that your mental constructs will have on your own perceptions, values and approaches. This theme continues as we examine the basic role that cultural values play in every village development situation. Both you and community people bring attitudes, behaviors, and life perspectives into the relationship. If these values are continually clashing, there is little chance for a village development relationship to form. In order to function effectively as an RDF, you need to remain aware of people's cultural attributes and to realize how cultural values operate in the development process. For example, in nearly all village communities, religion plays a very significant role in their daily lives. Now assume that you do not share any of the villagers' religious values, that you are intolerant of such religious beliefs, and that you see such beliefs doing far more harm that good for people. Given these values, would you accept to work in such an environment? Would you be able to work with them objectively, or would you try to find ways to sway them to give up their view of the world? How you respond to these kinds of questions will greatly determine your effectiveness as an RDF, especially in the first stage of rural development.

The field of development is becoming more aware of the relationship between religion and development. Many RDFs may wonder whether the goals of religion and those of development are compatible. Some RDFs are attracted to the field of development because they see it as a vehicle for teaching people about the value of religion as a way to find meaning in life. Some students are concerned that their own religion will not be respected by others in the development field. Thus, they feel they must hide their values. Others wonder about their ability to work objectively with people who have different religious values.

A number of scholars are beginning to understand that religion is a pervasive force in most societies and is often over looked in the field of development. The training literature in development is beginning to support an integration of religious values with rural development and to suggest that the RDFs need rigorous training in the religions of the areas where they might be working to be better prepared to deal with the religious issues that impact on the processes of development in a given community. Some scholars, especially development specialists from Less Developed Countries (LDCs) are beginning to argue that there is a spiritual dimension of human experience that can contribute to improving both psychological and social conditions. Such scholars argue that religious values and traditions often provide a sense of identity and purpose in life that has been destroyed by the impact of alien cultural values thus intensifying the tendencies for apathy and anomie. These sets of issues will be described in detail in Chapter 15 below.

I would argue that development specialists tend to pay too little attention to the ways in which rural people view the world. I believe that it is crucial that RDFs become aware of the world view held by the people they are working with. From this perspective, this world view is always an essential part of a community's problems, and must be understood with sympathy and open-mindedness. In this broader frame of reference a religion is a basic part of how individuals view the world and, consequently, how and why they decide to act or not to act in a given situation.

One common error, is the assumption that someone born in a given society automatically has the cultural sensitivity to work effectively in a rural village setting. Often an RDF who has lived in the city for many years, has completed extensive schooling, will often be unaware of how his/her ideas, values and orientation to things have changed from those who live in villages. Much care must be made to ensure cultural sensitivity, even among the indigenous RDFs invited to work in the rural areas of their country.

This chapter is not designed to teach you all that you need to understand about diversity. If you have not given much thought to how your cultural frame of reference (your mental constructs) will affect your work as a professional RDF, this chapter hopefully will initiate a process of self-reflection about the intricate manifestations of culture in all human endeavors. You are encouraged to take a course in cultural diversity both in the United States and abroad which focus on gender concerns, ageism, racism, multicultural issues, physical disabilities, and issues pertaining to sexual orientation. We would hope that you would approach such courses not merely as a "requirement" to get through but as a challenging and awakening experience that can broaden your vision of the world. A good course in cultural diversity is a necessity in helping you formulate alternative perspectives and in giving you tools for working with people in many different kinds of cultural environments.

In the broad domain of social and behavioral science, more and more people are seeing the importance of training professionals in the processes of cultural diversity. A multicultural perspective must consider a variety of different variables: (1) ethnographic variables: nationality, ethnicity, language, and religion; (2) demographic variables: age, gender, and place of residence; (3) status variables: educational and socioeconomic background and formal and informal affiliations. A multicultural perspective encourages one to recognize the complex diversity that exists in this world of ours and suggests bridges of shared concern that link all people. This perspective looks both at the unique dimensions of a person and also at how this person shares common themes with those who are different.

Overcoming Cultural Tunnel Vision

My work with students in the field of development has shown that many of them have cultural "tunnel vision." They are limited in cross-cultural experiences, and thus, in some cases, they see it as their role to transmit their values to other people. I have found that many students are unaware of the difficulty of dealing with people who have a cultural background different from their own. Some students have made inappropriate generalizations about a particular group of people: Blacks, Asians, Chicano, American Indians, etc.

Regardless of your cultural heritage, it is essential that you honestly examine your own expectations, attitudes, assumptions about working with various cultural and ethnic groups. Effective RDFs need to understand and accept people who have a different set of assumptions about life, and they need to be alert to the likelihood of imposing their world view. One of the common mistakes made by inexperienced RDFs is to underestimate the controlling impact of one's own culture and how easy it is to operate on the unquestioned assumption that one's own value system and one's own set of mental constructs best reflect "reality" with a big R. If you accept the idea that certain ways of looking at reality are necessarily superior, you become limited by refusing to consider alternatives.

If you possess cultural tunnel vision, you are likely to misinterpret many patterns of behavior displayed by villagers who are culturally different from you. Unless you understand the values of other cultures you are likely to misunderstand much of the community life you are experiencing. Because of this lack of understanding, you may label certain villager behavior as resistant, you may make an inaccurate diagnosis of a particular behavior as maladaptive, and you may be seeking to impose your own value system on the villagers quite unconsciously. For example, many Indian women in Latin America might resist changing what you view as excessive dependency on their husbands. If you were working with an Indian community in Mexico, you need to appreciate that they are likely to live by the value of remaining with their husband, even if he beats her, is unfaithful and is gone for long periods of time. Indian tradition tells these women that no matter what, it is not appropriate to leave one's husband. If you are unaware of this traditional value, you could find yourself being ostracized by these women and not understand why.

Experienced RDFs understand that certain basic values that are part of a given culture should not be challenged, attacked, or degraded especially in the in the first stage of rural development work, what we are calling the trust building phase of rural development. If RDFs are not aware of these core characteristics that are deeply ingrained in a given culture, they may irrevocably alienate many of those they are seeking to work with. The process of acculturation (encouraging or forcing one group in a society to conform to the linguistic and cultural requirements of the dominate group) has historically been a fundamental tenant of American life and epitomized in the notion of the melding pot. Such ideas are now being challenged as a greater appreciation for cultural pluralism is growing. Yet a similar process for what is called acculturation exists in other parts of the world. People from the developed nations of the world often assume that the problems of the less developed nations would be solved if they would become like us -- thus communicating: "Leave your cultural heritage behind, and allow me to show you a better way." Many people of the LDCs want the advantages of Western technology and the quality of life implied in the modern world, without sacrificing those qualities that make them different. In many countries, the less advantaged and those most apt to be experiencing extreme forms of poverty are part of various ethnic minorities and other marginalized groups who make up a given society. For example, among the various Indian communities in Guatemala, adopting the values and behaviors of the Latinos (Spanish White community) means alienating themselves from their own culture. Equally frustrating is the paradox that even if the Indians of Guatemala do adopt values of the dominant culture, they rarely find acceptance, understanding, or success in the non-Indian culture. Such cultural issues have political and economic roots and will not be easily resolved. Nevertheless, RDFs must be sensitive to these issues and understand how such issues may have significant consequences for the process of rural development.

These examples illustrate how important it is that RDFs respect the cultural heritage of the villagers and that they avoid encouraging villagers to "give up" this culture so that they can "make it" in the dominant culture. Certainly, villagers need to consider the consequences of not accepting certain values of the society in which they live, but they should not be pressured to accept wholesale a set of values that may be alien to them. Although villagers who must exist in more than one culture are likely to struggle in finding ways to integrate what is best for them from both cultures, the synthesis is bound to be richer with possibilities.

RDFs from all cultural groups need honestly to examine their expectations and attitudes about the community development process. Realize that there is no sanctuary from cultural bias. We all tend to carry our biases around with us, yet we often do not recognize this fact. Most of us are culture-bound and encapsulated to some extent. It takes concerted effort and vigilance to monitor our biases and value systems so that they do not interfere with establishing and maintaining successful trusting relationships.

Western and Eastern Values

Most of the theories and practices of the development process that you have learned are grounded in Western assumptions. Most of the people with whom RDFs will work will have a cultural heritage associated with Eastern values. A comparison of Western and Eastern systems shows some striking differences in value orientations. For example, Western culture places prime value on choice, the uniqueness of the individual, self assertion, and the strengthening of the ego. By contrast, the Eastern view stresses interdependence, underplays individuality, and emphasizes the losing of oneself in the totality of the cosmos. From the Western perspective, the primary values are the primacy of the individual, youth, independence, nonconformity, competition, conflict, and freedom. The guiding principles of action are found in the fulfillment of individual needs and individual responsibility. From the Eastern perspective, the primary values are the primacy of relationships, maturity, compliance, conformity, cooperation, harmony, and security. The guiding principles for action are found in the achievement of collective goals and collective responsibility.

Behavioral orientations are also different. The Western view encourages expression of feelings and striving for self-actualization, whereas the Eastern view encourages control of feelings and striving of collective actualization. In talking with experienced RDFs, we have learned that their focus is on the individual in the context of the social system in which they work. In their working relationships with villagers, they are much more apt to pay attention to the family and clan than to the individual's interests. They have learned to balance a stress on personal growth with what is in the best interests of the family and community. They are able to respect the values of the villagers where they work, yet at the same time they are able to challenge the villagers to think of some ways to change. Most successful RDFs admit they must demonstrate patience and understanding in working with villagers. They saw it as essential to form a trusting relationship before engaging in confrontation. Although this necessity applies to development processes in general, it seems especially important in working with village communities.

Section Three
Challenging Your Cultural Assumptions

Culturally learned basic assumptions deeply influence the ways in which we perceive and think about reality and how we act. A willingness to examine such assumptions opens doors to seeing others from their vantage point, rather than from a preconceived perspective. RDFs often make cultural assumptions that they are unaware of. We give a few examples of assumptions that could interfere with effective village development in multicultural situations. By reflecting on them, you can begin to see ways to challenge your assumptions as you work in a village setting.

Assumptions about time. Many cultures emphasize the present and past far more than the future. Many people in these cultures are not ruled by the clock and simply will not be rushed. Thus being late for a meeting does not mean that they are uncooperative or resistant to authority. Rather it means that time will wait and if one is late to a meeting, they can always hold it "manana."

Assumptions about self-disclosure. Many professional RDFs in the field of community development, especially those with training in psychology, assume that no effective development will occur unless those being helped reveal themselves through a process of self-disclosure. For such RDFs, unless villagers are willing to verbalize and communicate their thoughts, feelings, attitudes, and perceptions, there is no basis for empathic understanding by the RDF. While I tend to agree that until villagers engage in some form of self-disclosure, it will be very difficult for an RDF to function effectively in a given community setting. However, you can recognize and appreciate that some villagers will struggle in letting you know the nature of their problems. This struggle in itself is a useful focus for exploration. Rather than expecting such villagers to "let it all hang out," you can demonstrate respect for their values and at the same time ask them how the RDF might be most useful in dealing with their problems. RDFs can also assume an advocacy role for the villagers vis-a-vis other outsiders, can help villagers build on their natural sources of support, or can teach them to use the resources with the community. As you will see in Chapter 15, a number of community-based interventions may be more appropriate for some cultural systems than interventions often used in Europe or the United States.

Assumptions about family values. In many western cultures, the concept of family refers to the immediate family (father, mother, brothers and sisters). In other societies a family may be broader, an extended family that could include relatives from a common great grand father. Questions related to whom one can trust, whom does one go to for help, who needs to be apart of any decision being made by an individual will all be different depending on how a family is defined, what roles the family plays and how much influence the individual expects and in fact wants from the family.

Assumptions about nonverbal behavior. Villagers can disclose themselves in many nonverbal ways, and thus it is a mistake to rely solely on what they talk about. Many westerns often feel uncomfortable with silence, and thus they tend to fill in quiet gaps with words. In some cultures, in contrast, silence indicates a sign of respect and politeness. You could misinterpret a quiet villager's behavior if you did not realize that she might be waiting for you to ask her questions. There are no universal meanings of nonverbal behaviors. Thus, it is essential that you acquire sensitivity to cultural differences in order to reduce the probability of miscommunication, misdiagnosis, and misinterpretation of behavior.

You may have been systematically trained in attending and responding as part of interpersonal skill building, which include keeping an open posture, maintaining good eye contact, and leaning toward the personal who are talking to. Villagers from some cultural backgrounds may have trouble responding positively to or understanding the intent of your body language. You have probably been taught that good eye contact is a sign of presence and that the lack of such contact is a sign of evasiveness. Many Asians and Indians in the Western hemisphere may view direct eye contact as a lack of respect. In some cultures lack of eye contact may even be a sign of respect and good manners. Many native Americans consider a direct gaze as indicative of aggressiveness; in cross-gender encounters it usually means sexual aggressiveness. Effective RDFs have learned not to make judgments about a particular behavior until it is understood and defined within the cultural context in which it is given.

Assumptions about trusting relationships. Many Americans tend to form quick relationships and to talk easily about their personal life. This characteristic is often reflected in their approach to other people regardless of their cultural background. Thus, the inexperienced RDF often expects that villagers will approach their relationship in an open and trusting manner. It is important to remember that among many cultures it takes a long time to develop meaningful relationships. What is more, you have to earn the trust of these people before they will confide in you.

Assumptions about self-actualization. It is understandable why many RDFs assume that people in general will want to become fully functioning and would naturally be committed to learning and improving themselves as individuals. You will recall that in the Eastern orientation one of the guiding principles is the achievement of collective goals not just individual goals. In many tribal societies, a person will judge their worth primarily in relation to how their behavior contributes to the harmonious functioning of their tribe and society. If an RDF pushes individuals to adopt certain behaviors that would be perceived as seeking some advantage or gain of one individual over another in a given community, such efforts, such behaviors, could quickly become very counter-productive. Such activities are especially disruptive in a cultural system where the community believes there is only a limited amount of material goods available in the world and if one person is seen obtaining more, then by definition someone else in the community must be receiving less. Anthropologists have described this concept of the "limited good" as characteristic of a number of societies. Again the key to these kinds of issues is to help describe the interventions being suggested by the RDF in terms that reflect the cultural values of the community, i.e., helping the villagers to see that such interventions are not just advantaging individuals, but the entire community.

Assumptions about directness. Although the Western orientation prizes directness, some cultures see it as a sign of rudeness and as something to be avoided. If you are not aware of this cultural difference, you could make the mistake of interpreting a lack of directness as a sign of being unassertive, rather than as a sign of respect. Some Latin American cultures value finding indirect ways of communicating.

Assumptions about being assertive. If you are operating from a Western orientation, you will assume that people are better off if they can behave in assertive ways, such as telling people what they think, feel, and want. Many training programs in the West teach participants to focus on assertiveness and coping skills that involve taking an active stance toward life.

As is true of directness, being assertive is not always viewed as appropriate behavior. Many from an Indian culture are likely to appear to some as shy, unassertive, passive, and highly sensitive to the opinions of their family and peers. RDFs are constantly faced with the dilemma of whether to accept a cultural trait or seek to change it. Assume that you are working with a group of women who seem very unassertive to you. They rarely ask for what they want, they allow others to decide their priorities, and they almost never deny a request or demand from members of their families. If you worked hard at helping them become more assertive women, it could well create conflicts within their family system. If they began to change their roles, they might no longer fit in their culture. It is important that both the RDF and the people being worked with consider the consequences of making too many such changes, too quickly.

Given all these faulty assumptions, we hope you see the importance of challenging some of the views about villagers that you take for granted. One way to respect such villagers is to ask them to tell you about themselves and listen to their underlying values. We are not suggesting that you merely listen in an accepting way, for you can still challenge villagers who are culturally different from you. For example, it is not inappropriate to discuss with a villager if she sees any problem with not being assertive or direct. Perhaps she may change certain aspects of her cultural conditioning yet retain other aspects that she deems important. Asking the villagers what they want from you is a way of decreasing the chances that you will impose your cultural values on them.

Section Four
How to Become a Culturally Skilled RDF

Training programs need to recognize that no one style or theory of development will be appropriate for all societies and situations. Instead RDFs must be able to adapt interventions to meet not just the development needs of villagers but also their cultural needs. Training programs that are grounded primarily on a single theoretical school may be doing a disservice to their trainees. To become culturally skilled RDFs, it is necessary to: (1) to be aware of one's own cultural heritage and of biases, values, and preconceived notions that can intrude in trust building and helping relationships; (2) acquire knowledge of culturally diverse groups that will pave the way for grasping the world views of a variety of cultural groups; and (3) develop a range of intervention strategies and skills that are appropriate, relevant, and sensitive for different cultural groups.

What follows are a series of ideas, competencies and standards that should be continually reviewed during your career in village development work. No one aspect of this work will ensure success, but a careful review and reconsideration of these kinds of ideas will help reduce cultural bias and insensitivity.

Beliefs and Attitudes of culturally skilled RDFs. First, effective RDFs recognize and understand their own values, ethnocentric attitudes, and assumptions about human behavior. They do not allow their personal biases or problems to interfere with their ability to work with people who are culturally different from them. They do no allow their fear of discovering and owning up to their prejudices block them from a multicultural perspective. They seek to examine and understand the world from the vantage point of the people they are working with. They respect villager's religious or spiritual beliefs and values. Because these RDFs welcome diverse value orientations and diverse assumptions about human behavior, they have a basis for sharing the world view of the villagers, as opposed to being culturally encapsulated (believing that their culture is necessarily superior in all respects to other cultures). Rather than being ethnocentric and maintaining that their cultural heritage is superior, they are able to value and accept cultural diversity.

They value bilingualism and do not view another language as an impediment to the development process. This is a tough issue in a number of countries where various tribal and ethnic divisions are exacerbated by efforts to impose a single common language. In India, English has become a common language for the over 300 different language groups in that country. In Kenya, Kiswahili and English are often imposed upon various tribal groups in order to provide a common language base. In Guatemala, the many Indian dialects are under constant pressure to adopt Spanish as the language of social, political and economic interaction. The philosophy of development being espoused in this book suggests that one's mother tongue is an important part of one's self identity and perhaps key to one's self-esteem, and that when one is forced to reject one's language, one is being forced to reject one's culture and perhaps even one's ability to become a self-reliant and productive member of society. This does not mean that villagers should not be encouraged to learn Spanish, French, English, Kiswahili, or Chinese as a way of functioning more effectively in a given nation-state system. It is equally important and appropriate and perhaps, as will be argued later, even crucial for a given cultural group to maintain and enhance their own language and cultural identity if they are to participate in a self-defined process of development.

Knowledge of culturally skilled RDFs. Second, culturally effective RDFs possess certain knowledge. They know specifically about their own racial and cultural heritage and how it affects them personally and professionally. Because they understand the dynamics of oppression, racism, discrimination, and stereotyping, they are in a position to detect their own racist attitudes, beliefs, and feelings. They seek to understand the world view of those they are working with. Because they understand the basic values underlying the processes of change and development that are too often derived from their own cultural background, they appreciate and seek to be sensitive to how these values may clash with the cultural values and traditions of the various tribal and ethnic groups that make up any given society. They understand that external sociopolitical forces may have influenced culturally different groups, and they know how these forces operate with respect to the treatment of minority groups in a given country. Such RDFs are aware of the institutional barriers that prevent illiterate peasants, especially if they also happen to come from a disadvantage tribal or ethnic groups, from utilizing governmental services in health, education, credit systems and agricultural extension available in a given area. They possess knowledge about the historical background, traditions, and values of the groups with which they are working. They have knowledge about the family structures, social hierarchies, patron-client systems, and other political and economic factors that determine how a particular group functions in a given society. Culturally skilled RDFs view diversity in a positive light, which allows them to meet and resolve the challenges that arise in their work with a wide range of community populations. They know how to help a village community make use of indigenous support systems. The greater their depth and breadth of knowledge about culturally diverse groups, the more likely they are to be effective RDFs.

Skills and Intervention Strategies of Culturally Skilled RDFs Third, effective RDFs have acquired certain skills in working with culturally diverse populations. Effective RDFs seek to use methods and strategies and define goals consistent with the life experiences and cultural values of the people they are working with. Such RDFs modify and adapt conventional approaches to village development in order to accommodate cultural differences and political dimensions. They are able to send and receive both verbal and nonverbal messages accurately and appropriately. One last thing that one must understand in preparing for work in rural development is a better understanding of the reality of village life and the ways that a culture influences this village situation. Being culturally sensitive is obviously important, but being prepared to live and work in a different culture and a different way of life is even more difficult. In the next several sections we will seek to address these kinds of issues.

Section Five
Cultural Awareness:
A Key to Effective Rural Development

Now that we have reviewed the ways in which RDFs must understand their own culture and how that awareness can be invaluable in becoming an effective RDF, it is now time to reflect on the impact of culture within the context of village life. Perhaps the greatest challenge facing an RDF will be the difficulty of adjusting to the culture of the people you are working with. Even RDFs who is from the culture of the people they are working with, must understand that by the very nature of becoming an RDF, their mental constructs have been changed, and they will never be able to see the reality of the humble peasant in exactly the same way as peasants experience their world. Becoming aware of the power and influence of one's culture requires much study and experience. Let us review some of the ways in which cultural and social realities have positive and negative consequences for the work of an RDF.

The Meaning of Culture

Culture is defined as systems of meanings. The capacity to bestow meaning on the things and the behaviors around us, and then to live according to these meanings is unique to human species. The principal mechanism through which these webs of significance are created and imposed is human language.

The process through which individuals become cultural beings is known as enculturation or alternatively as socialization. It starts in childhood and continues throughout life. This code consists of prescriptions, rules, and norms that individuals can bring to bear in appropriate situations. A social/cultural system consists of people who tend to acknowledge and accept most of the same rules. Most people follow a consistency of behavior formed out of the expectations imposed upon them as they grow up. Some people shake hands, others bow at the waist, some are quiet at a funeral, others wail in loud shrieks.

In his book, *The Structure of Scientific Revolutions*, Thomas Kuhn has shown how scientists, once they operate under a common paradigm, come to share the same set of assumptions about the world. They begin to think in similar ways and to investigate a similar range of problems. Thus scientists see what they are trained to see, and, what is more, they systematically ignore aspects of nature that fail to conform to prior expectations. Said in another way, all people, even carefully trained scientists, tend to be controlled by, what we have called, their mental constructs. This process is even more pronounced among various cultural groups who have all been socialized into a common group of mind sets, assumptions, or mental constructs.[18]

Cultural behaviors and values have the same addictive quality as do tobacco or drugs. Cultural usages influence our perceptions and shift of muscular patterns so that each individual becomes not only a user of the culture, but also a product of it. The consequence, of course, is that one's own customs appear "natural," since both body and mind have been molded to accommodate those forms, whereas different usages appear "unnatural" and even perverse. The Japanese carpenter naturally pulls the plane toward himself, centripetally. The western workman pushes it away from his body, centrifugally. American gardeners poison snails, French people eat them with great relish. To a black native a blond European is grotesquely ugly, the scars and tattoos of the black women are beautiful to the native man. Americans on the Atlantic coast are avid clam-eaters but make no use of the mussel, whereas Europeans prefer the mussel and pay far less attention to the clam.[19]

Individuals are bound by quite specific rules of conduct even though they do not normally feel the constraint. Goffman's work makes us aware of the large number of rules that people obey even in the most casual circumstances of their everyday lives. We keep a certain distance when in conversation, Latins prefer to speak very close to each other. We tend to engage in "civil inattention, staring is impolite, but in many African societies staring has no social stigma attached.[20] While a common culture does generate similarities in behavior and thoughts, there is still much diversity in every society. There are many reasons for diversity: (1) Not all people are socialized in the same way. (2) All people can be unpredictable because of the power of different emotional responses, for example, a refusal to shake hands can communicate anger, wanting to be insulting etc. (3) In every society, compliance to societal values is often relative, obeying traffic laws, income tax payment, premarital sex, degrees of honesty, etc. RDFs must never assume that a common culture guarantees conformity or even a consistent response in a given situation. Diversity between and within cultures is a common trait in all societies.

Why People Do What They Do and Is Change Possible?

The struggle to make compatible the processes that introduce change and that maintain the traditional reflect two processes: those that stem from the external reality of climate, physical landscape that stimulate adaptive behaviors and the internal factors that give meaning, purpose and a sense of identity. Both sets of factors are not necessarily functional but still have an important place within a sociocultural system. Thus behavior may be more than simply adaptive to external factors, internally derived customs can be understood by viewing them as part of the logical, meaningful order of the actors in any particular society. Thus, there is the world of the physical to which he must adapt and the world of the subjective that he creates and through which he is created.

Eskimos have both the capacity to survive in the snow-covered tundra by their knowledge of snow, animals and the needs for survival, but they also have a most complex system of ghosts, demons and evil spirits that greatly determine their behaviors. There are elaborate supernatural measures taken to protect themselves from harm. Eskimos also surround themselves with numerous amulets and charms designed to ward off a particular calamity or to enhance a certain skill. By far the most important means of warding off danger, however, is through the observance of taboos. A taboo is a prohibition against certain acts or types of behavior. For example, before they drag a seal carcass into a dwelling, the hunter must lift a cup and gently pour drinking water over the dead animal's snout, then before butchering the animal, there are numerous thing that should not be done. Rasmussen notes: "In winter, while the sun is low in the sky, no women may sew or do any other work as long as the seal brought into the house has not been cut up. Nor may men work in ordinary stone or soapstone, or in wood or iron. No footwear may be dried over the rack and no woman may comb her hair or wash her face. . . . If there is old blubber from last season's [hunt] lying in the house, this must be taken out through the window -- never through the doorway -- before the seal is even brought in."[21]

How are we to interpret all of this. Functionalist try to find meaning by tying all behavior to survival, but the custom of giving dead seals a drink, or the laborious procedure of removing blubber through an airtight window instead of simply taking it out the door -- how are these acts to be understood? The best resort of the anthropologist in such instances is to attempt to penetrate the mental world of natives -- to ask them what they think they are accomplishing when they do these apparently impractical things. If you ask an Eskimo why he gives a drink to a dead seal, he would reply that he does this to "please the seal's soul." Probing further, we would discover that the Eskimo believes not only that animals have souls but also that the soul is thought to return to the sea to be reincarnated as another seal. If the dead animal therefore considers that the hunter has treated his body with thoughtfulness and respect, the reincarnated seal will then be willing to become prey for that hunter again. If he shows disrespect, refusing to give him drink, or to engage in other activities before attending to the carcass, the animals will avoid the hunter in the future and he will be plagued by lack of success in the hunt.

This knowledge, then, helps to "explain" the Eskimos' behavior. Once we understand their beliefs regarding souls and animal reincarnation, the practice of giving dead animals a drink and the various ritual expressions of respect embodied in the system of taboos all follow logically: they are means, we would say magical ones, that the hunters employ to ensure their future success. I remember as a young graduate student in rural Egypt, being initially very unhappy with peasant mothers. I observed their lack of care and sanitation in the treating of their children. Children were often allowed to play in the most filthy of conditions, mothers almost never washed their children, or removed the flies that often rested on the eyelids of their children. My mental constructs saw the behavior of these mothers as uncaring. It was only many months later that I was introduced into the reality of that behavior. Visiting with a grieving mother who had just lost her youngest child, I sought to understand how she could be so saddened by the lost of the child and yet so uncaring of her children in regards to health and cleanliness. It was then that the impact of her constructs finally made sense to me. For in her world, the greatest cause of death for the children were the evil spirits (*ginn*) that sought to destroy the children, especially those children that were beautiful and attractive. The only way that a mother with that set of constructs could possible act rationally, would be to keep her children as dirty and unattractive as possible. Behavior, which from my constructs was evidence of an uncaring and insensitive mother, was from her constructs, evidence of great love and concern for the safety and welfare of her children.

No matter how exotic or bizarre a behavior may be, close scrutiny of such beliefs has invariably shown that there is an impressive logical consistency to them once we grant the premises on which they are based. The most famous demonstration of this point was carried out years ago in 1937 by Evans-Pritchard in his study of the Azande, a tribal people in central Africa. The Azande are a people who are intensely preoccupied with witchcraft and magic. The major premise of this system of beliefs is that certain unidentified men and women, living among them, posses inherent power to do others harm. By a mere act of will these witches are thought to be capable of sending a spirit entity called *mbisimo mangu* ("the soul of witchcraft") through the night to feed on the organs and flesh of their intended victims, causing illness and death. The Azande attribute virtually all serious sicknesses and all deaths to the evil machinations of witches.

Even the activities of daily living are caused by witches, if a potter's ware is cracked in the kilm, if a farmer's ground-nut crop is ruined, if a child's toe is stubbed on a root, he suspects witchcraft. Once a group of people in the heat of the day were in the granary to get away from the heat, it suddenly collapsed from termites in the wood. Evans-Pritchard tried to argue that the accident was easy to explain by the fact of termites and people's desire to get out of the heat of the day. The villagers asked him but why did these two things happen together. He replied it was coincidence, the villager saw it as witchcraft. Once the mystical premise -- that witches exist and they do people harm -- is granted, there is no difficulty in following the logic of their arguments. It is only the underlying premise that we might disagree with. All people create elaborate systems of shared meanings that guide and constrain behavior. If RDFs are to gain more than a superficial knowledge of the society they are working in, they must understand these meanings.

Section Six
Cultural Dialoguing:
Creating Social Energy for Village Development

There are many available strategies for entering and stimulating village community development. Some argue you must start with some type of health project such as a vaccination program or a potable water system, others insist that such a village development strategy must be based upon literacy and the establishment of non formal education. Still others would argue that because of the widespread nature of poverty, the first step must emphasize income generating projects which will enhance the family's resource base for better housing, more food and increased standards of living. While all of these strategies have been used and while there are many examples of success using these strategies, I should like to suggest that a slightly different sequence of events, a slightly different approach, will have greater chances for success

It will be argued that these sector-specific strategies, while often successful, sometimes are not and in fact, there is evidence that such approaches without a solid base of cultural dialoguing, will have less chances for short-run success and even less long-term sustainability.

How to Start

In assessing the way to enter a community and to develop greater trust and awareness, we should appropriately contrast two different perspectives by which one might define the process of getting started in a village community. First, there is the "Problem Identification" approach and the second, let us call the "Cultural Dialoguing" approach. Both have been used to help outsiders like interns, peace corps volunteers and rural development facilitators (RDFs) begin their work in a village community. Yet, as will be argued, one approach tends to emphasis what is wrong in the community as the basis for explaining why the outsider is in the village and the other tends to emphasis what is right in the community as a basis for explaining why the outsider is in the village.

What is Wrong in this Village? Many village development specialists have sought to justify their presence in a village community by helping villagers assess their needs, determine the problems that exist, and the major concerns that people have. Such a strategy has several unreflected assumptions that need to be considered. Assumption One: All villages have problems that require new information, skills, knowledge, and technologies from outsiders to solve their problems. Assumption Two: The community's present information, skills, knowledge, and technologies are not appropriate to solve these problems. Assumption Three: The outsider is the only one available to help them solve their problems. Assumption Four: The outsiders have many useful ideas for which they are very proud and very happy to share with the villagers as they assume that their ideas and technologies will solve the problems of the villagers. Assumption Five: The villagers have many inappropriate ideas and many old-fashion customs for which they should be very ashamed and which should be discarded if they are to improve the quality of their lives.

What is Right in this village? A process of cultural dialoguing suggests a different set of assumptions and begins the interactions between the outsider and community from a very different perspective. Assumption One: This community has been in existence for a long time and has generally been reasonably successful in surviving the many challenges and problems in their history. Assumption Two: The village community knows what has worked and what has not worked in their community over time far better than any outsider. Assumption Three: Following the traditions, the customs and the old ways of doing things gives the members of this village community much satisfaction and a sense of pride in the value and utility of their present way of life. Assumption Four: While the villagers acknowledge that outsiders have many wondrous things to share with them, there is some hesitation to accept the ideas of the outsiders if it will change their old ways of doing things. Assumption Five: Outsiders must be very careful before suggesting new ideas, technologies and approaches until they have carefully considered not only the advantages but also the disadvantages of such ideas, technologies and approaches. Many ideas and technologies introduced by outsiders often have unintended consequences that must be understood and considered carefully.

In contrasting these two perspectives, I should like to consider the types of discussion that will characterize the interactions between the outsider and the villagers.. In the Problem Identification approach, the beginning discussions would emphasize the many problems, the issues, the concerns, and negative aspects of the villagers' present situation. The outsider, while seeking to be sympathetic and understanding, reinforces feelings of inadequacy and failure. While no one would disagree with the notion that such communities do have problems, the tendency of these early discussions is to reinforce in the community the ideas that they are incompetent, unskilled, illiterate, sick, and incapable of solving their own problems. The implication of such discussions includes the thoughts: "thank goodness, there is now an outsider who has made us more aware of our problems and our failures and will now help us to solve these problems." Obviously, these outsiders are offering something that we could not have done by ourselves." The major goal of such discussions is to determine what is wrong, what needs to be changed or modified, what new ideas, activities, behaviors, technologies and values are now needed to fix what is wrong or broken. The unintended consequence of this approach is often the reinforcement of feelings of inferiority, apathy, and dependency.

In the Cultural Dialoguing approach, the beginning discussions would emphasize a different set of ideas, beginning with a clarification of what is important, valuable, and good in their present way of life. The outsiders, while aware of the many ways that they might help these villagers, seek to reinforce feelings of pride and gratitude for the things that are good and useful in their culture and their present way of life. The focus of this type of discussion is to help the outsider understand and appreciate the way of life that has characterized this community over the past many years and to help the community to articulate what makes the people of this community special, unique, worthy of praise, and appreciation. The outsiders must communicate their sincere desire to know what makes this cultural system function as it does, how this way of life works for these people. Such a discussion does not begin with what is wrong with their village, but with what is right with their village.

At this point it is important to emphasize why the Cultural Dialoguing approach is being suggested. Rural Development Theory over the past fifteen years has tended to argue that a grassroots approach that emphasizes local participation and local institution building will have the greatest probability of being effective and sustainable. In the process of introducing such rural development projects, most management documents have espoused a commitment to involving the local community in the processes of implementation. Yet a number of evaluations of such projects suggest that local participation does not always ensure project success. In assessing the reasons why participation may in some situations lead to success and in other situations to failure, I have observed in my own research, that one pre-requisite often over looked is the way that the community perceives the process of participation being used.

The connecting causal link between participation and project success is not the existence of discussions and the verbal agreement between outsiders and villagers, but the perceptions of the villagers, how they felt about those discussions and those verbal agreements, whether they felt serious commitment, whether genuine feelings of social energy were stimulated, whether the villagers felt good about what was happening, whether they saw the project as theirs and whether the project was consistent with and appropriate for their way of life.

Thus, while outsiders may assume that because villagers have been brought together, were involved in a discussion, helped identify their problems, and agreed to cooperate with the outsiders in solving these problems, success has now been assured. In reality, such discussions may have reinforced feelings of inadequacy, feelings that nothing can happen without outside help, that it will be the outsider who will solve our problems. Thus the whole process may have merely confirmed feelings that they are incapable of solving any of their own problems by themselves.

Please note that the problem identification approach has been successful in some situations, has stimulated projects that have brought schools and health clinics and other problems solving processes into village communities, but the issue before us requires that we struggle with a much more important question. Does the completion of a school or health clinic reinforce feelings of inadequacy and dependency or does it stimulate social energy and feelings of confidence and self-reliance? From my review of the literature on Rural Development, too many of the rural development projects being implemented over the past two decades have failed to remain sustainable after the outsiders leave. It makes little sense to mobilize resources for village projects that will fall into disrepair and disuse within a year or two after the outsiders leave. The argument should be clear. Unless the community owns the project as their own, perceives the project as appropriate and worthy of maintaining, then outsiders have merely engaged in a process of subterfuge, building up hopes with unrealistic expectations, and in the long-run merely reinforced social apathy and a kind of community fatalism that can be devastating.

What is the alternative? From my perspective, the process of Cultural Dialoguing implies the following steps or categories of action:

An outsider seeking to live and work in a community for several weeks, months or even years must begin to build personal relationships and establish trust with the people in that community. At first, the villagers will have an assortment of feelings from suspicion to curiosity toward the outsider and some may even express hostility and rudeness. Villagers will want to know why you are there, what is your purpose or agenda in coming into their community? While there are many ways to begin this process of trust building, I would like to suggest that trust building is a process that takes time, that there are various levels of trust, and that without some modicum of trust the outsider will have no success at all. Even the beginning levels of trust may require several weeks or months to establish. The fact that you are living in the village will stimulate interest. Your interest in their culture, their way of life, how they farm, raise their children, the kinds of games they play, the songs they sing, and the activities they perform each day is a place to start. Paulos Freire describes this process very nicely by suggesting that outsiders should: "begin their own visits to the area, never forcing themselves on others but acting as sympathetic observers with an attitude of understanding toward what they see . . . .they register everything in their notebook, including apparently unimportant items: the way the people talk, their style of life, their behavior in various situations. They record the ideas of the people: their expressions, their vocabulary, and their syntax (not their incorrect pronunciation, but rather the way they construct their thoughts) . . . .It is essential that the investigators [outsiders] observe the area under varying circumstances: labor in the fields, meetings of a local association (noting the behavior of the participants, the language used, and the relations between the officers and members), the role played by women and young people, leisure hours, games and sports, conversations with people in their homes (noting examples of husband-wife and parent-child relationships). No activity must escape the attention of the investigators during the initial survey of the area."22

Basic Questions in the Process of Cultural Dialoguing

Below is a set of questions that have been found to be very useful in any process of cultural dialoguing:23

First, some effort must be made to determine the past history of the community, past notable leaders, past events that the older members of society pass on to the younger generation, to list and understand the function and purpose of the various organizations, institutions, groups or associations that are presently, or that have in the past, existed in this community. There is some value in asking people to describe how the village is different today from what it was like ten, twenty, fifty years ago. How are people, their customs, their behavior, their beliefs, their work, their way of doing things different today from earlier times?

Second, what resources are available in the area? Who controls the use of these resources? How is this control distributed? What are the sources of wealth in this community, (land, water, forest, education, commerce, etc.)? What systems of reciprocal exchange and mutual aid are available between people in the community?

Third, How do people make their living in the area? What are the various types of productive activities? What are the various forms of agricultural production for self-consumption and for commercial sale? What are the constraints on production? What other types of work are available in this area? How does one market one's surplus in this area and who are the intermediaries (middle men) who facilitate these marketing systems? Where does one obtain credit, what interest is charged, and what is the system by which these loans are paid back?

Fourth, Who are the poor and disadvantaged in the area? What do the poor themselves see as the causes of their poverty? What are other causes of their poverty that others might suggest? What restraints are hindering their development? What is the land ownership system in the community: types of tenure, renting, selling, concentration, etc.?

Fifth, What is the degree of economic and social homogeneity in the area? What internal divisions are there in the communities? What are these divisions based upon (income, religion, ethnicity, caste, tribe)? Who are the political leaders, how are they chosen, what aspects of social life are controlled by the local political leaders, and how do they make decisions?

Sixth, What dependency relationships exist between the poor and others? Is there exploitation of the poor? What forms does exploitation take? What is the degree of exploitation? What types of patron-client systems exist and how are they organized? Are their factions, disputes or divisions in the community that have caused conflict and what are the sources or causes of these conflicts? How are conflicts and disputes handled in this community? Who are the people most likely to act as intermediaries in these conflicts and how effective are they and why?

Seventh, In what ways are the interests of the various socio-economic groups similar? In what ways are they opposed to each other? Which of these contradictions are mutually antagonistic and which are non-antagonistic?

Eighth, What natural or physical factors, such as water, soil conditions and erosion, are causes of poverty and hindrances to development? Have these conditions worsened during the past 20 years? If so, why? What is the potential for improvement?

Ninth, What is the pattern of social conditions among the poor, e.g., disease, nutritional status, literacy, hygiene and sanitation? What are the causes of the unsatisfactory conditions? Which factors are primary causes of continued poverty?

Tenth, What are the cultural and religious beliefs and practices of the people? Are these shared by everyone? Which of these benefit the poor? Which are detrimental? Why? Do they distinguish between natural and supernatural phenomenon and people (spirits, demons, angels, gods)? It would be very useful to understand the important ceremonies in a given community: ceremonies related to birth, circumcision, rites of passage, marriage, death, etc. What systems of prayer, sacrifice, witchcraft, magic, sorcery exist in the village? Who are the people in the community who perform these activities?

Eleventh, Which governmental services and programs are operative in the area? Who are they available to and who is taking advantage of them? What other local and external organizations are active in the area? Who is benefiting, and how, from their programs?

Twelfth, A special effort must be made to develop awareness and understanding of the categories of thought that define the local culture. What words are used to describe relationships between family members, extended family members, clans, tribes and communities? There would be some value in drawing a map of the village indicating where people live and how they are related to each other (family, friendships, special groups, commercial interests, etc.). What are the characteristics admired in people -- what are the standards of behavior by which people are judged, compared, and looked up to? What are appropriate and inappropriate behaviors for men and women, child and young adults and the elderly?

Thirteenth, What systems of cooperation presently exist (cooperatives or associations)? There are many types of associations including voluntary associations, para-military associations, secret societies, age sets, and men's and women's associations. What are the criteria by which one becomes a member of such groups: residence, kinship ties, sex, order of birth, wealth, influence, etc.

What are the functions and purposes of these associations and how important are they in this community?

All of the above questions should be investigated through discussions with individuals, families, and small groups. Such discussions should be held with all socio-economic groups, but especially the poor. Discussion should also be held with officials, teachers and medical personnel as well as with other external agents such as bank officials and cooperative officials. Through internal discussions, comparisons of findings, writing and revising notes, the outsider will gradually build up a comprehensive picture of the local situation. This broad picture will form the basis of their developing understanding of the condition of the poor in the village community.

Advantages of this Process of Cultural Dialoguing
If an outsider follows these activities, there will be several significant advantages both for the outsider and for the community:

First, in engaging in cultural dialoguing, the outsider will gain a variety of insights about the culture and way of life, coming to appreciate and understand the complexity and interrelationships that exist among the various components of the culture.

Second, the outsider would be in a much better position to understand what types of interventions, technologies, and approaches would be appropriate and inappropriate, would be more aware of the various contingencies and constraints that must be considered in introducing innovations or changes into a given community.

Third, the villagers have the opportunity to reflect on and share with the outsider those aspects of the local culture that make the community special, unique, and to identify those aspects of the culture that bring meaning and purpose to individuals within the community.,

Fourth, such cultural dialoguing develops a greater sense of identity and pride for the members of the community as they are asked to articulate and clarify the positive dimensions of the local culture. Sharing and observing those stages of life that bring both joy (a new child, rites of passage for a teenager, a marriage, etc.) and those that bring sadness (an illness, a death, a poor crop, etc.) helps the outsider to appreciate the role of traditions and values in helping the community to deal with these events of life.

Fifth, the process of cultural dialoguing stimulates greater confidence and trust between the outsider and the community and reduces the tendency for the outsider to reinforce feeling of cultural inferiority, attitudes of apathetic dependency, and a mind set associated with welfarism and fatalism.

Sixth, the process of cultural dialoguing helps initiate the processes of social energy within a given community as local people are able to interact with the outsider in ways that stimulate self-reliance, reinforce community cohesiveness, and ensure a set of activities that are sustainable and culturally relevant and appropriate.

Seventh, if careful notes are prepared, written down and reviewed, a detailed document will result that can be very helpful for future interns, RDFs and others who may wish to work in this community. If such documentation is not prepared, future outsiders will waste much time in seeking to help these villagers help themselves. One of the most important tasks of an intern or RDF working in a village will be to ensure that there is a continuity of learning between past and future interns and RDFs and others working in this village. **Please take this responsibility very seriously.**

Conclusion

The process of cultural dialoguing must be seen as an important part of the first stage of rural development. Trust building is a two-way process in which understanding and appreciation emerges gradually as both the outsiders and the community people come to know each other. There is no alternative set of activities more important than cultural dialoguing for ensuring that appropriate and meaningful changes are considered. Change in these communities is always a two-edged sword with specific trade-offs. The advantages and disadvantages of such changes must be carefully considered. If the outsider is to play an appropriate role in this process, he or she must be willing to live and work in the community for an extended period of time, to engage in a serious process of cultural dialoguing, and then to reflect carefully with the community before introducing something new. Let us now move to an analysis of the second stage of rural development: the process of capacity building.

---

[1] M. Berman *The Re enchantment of the World* (Ithaca: Cornell University Press, 1981).
[2] G. Warnke Gadamer: *Hermeneutics, Tradition and Reason* (Stanford: Stanford University Press, 1987).
[3] F. Feyerabend, *Farewell to Reason* (London: Verso, 1987).
[4] Examples include: Karl Popper *The Logic of Scientific Discovery* (London: Hutchinson, 1959) and Paul Feyerabend *Against Method: Outline of an Anarchistic Theory of Knowledge* (London: New Left Books, 1975), Thomas Kuhn *The Structure of Scientific Revolutions* (Chicago: University of Chicago Press, 1970), Imre Lakatos *Philosophical Papers,* Volume I: *The Methodology of Scientific Research Programmes,* edited by J. Worrall and G. Currie (Cambridge University Press, 1978) and Norwood Russell Hanson, *Patterns of Discovery: An Inquiry into the Conceptual Foundations of Science* (Cambridge University Press, 1972).
[5] D Stove, *Popper and After: Four Modern Irrationalists* (Oxford: Pergamon Press, 1982); R. Trigg, *Reality at Risk: A Defense of Realism in Philosophy and the Sciences*, (Brighton: The Harvester Press, 1980; W. Newton-Smith, *The Rationality of Science* (London: Routledge and Kegan Paul, 1981); and I. Scheffler, *Science and Subjectivity* (Indianapolis: Bobbs-Merrill, 1967).

[6] C. D. Smock and E. von Glasersfeld (eds.) *Epistemology and Education* (Athens, GA: Follow Through Publications, 1974).
[7] C. Geertz, *The Interpretation of Cultures* (New York: Basic Books, 1973).
[8] P. Watzlawick *The Invented Reality* (New York: Norton, 1984).
[9] R. Palmer, *Hermeneutics: Interpretation Theory in Schleiermacher, Dilthey, Heidegger and Gadamer* (Evanston, IL: Northwestern University Press, 1969).
[10] Karl Marx *The Economic and Philosophic Manuscripts of 1844* edited by Dirk Strvik (New York: International Publishers, 1964), p.148.
[11] Karl Popper, *The Logic of Scientific Discovery* (London: Hutchinson, 1959); I. Latakos, *Philosophical Papers, Volume I: The Methodology of Scientific Research Programmes* edited by J Worrall and G. Currie, (Cambridge: Cambridge University Press, 1978); and P. Feyerabend, *Farewell to Reason* (London: Verso, 1987).
[12] (See George Marcus and M. Fischer, *Anthropology as Social Critique: An Experimental Moment in the Human Sciences* (Chicago: University of Chicago Press, 1986).
[13] (See: Hans G. Gadamer, *Truth and Method* (trans by G. Barden and J. Cummings) (New York: Crossroads, 1975).
[14] P. Feyerabend, *Against Method: Outline of an Anarchistic Theory of Knowledge* (London: New Left Books, 1975); Michael Foucault, *The Order of Things: an Archaeology of the Human Sciences* (trans by Alan Sheridan) (New York: Vintage Books, 1970).
[15] M Oakeshott " Education: The Engagement and its Frustration", in R. F. Dearden, P. H. Hirst and R. S. Peters (eds.) *Education and the Development of Reason* (London: Routledge & Kegan Paul, 1972).
[16] For a detailed set of workshop interventions to prepare future RDFs to work more effectively with cultures that have moral values, traditions and customs somewhat repugnant to the intern or the RDF, see: James B. Mayfield, *Workbook for Rural Development Facilitators,* (1997).
[17] In Chapter 15 below, there is a very detailed discussion of the ways in which RDFs in the past have dealt with the dilemmas being identified in this chapter.
[18] Clifford Geertz, *The Interpretation of Cultures* (NY Basic Books, 1973); Bronislaw, Malinowski, *Argonauts of the Western Pacific* (NY Dutton, 1922) talks of three kinds of data to collect and the ultimate aim of fieldwork "to realize {the natives} vision of his world; and W. Hortense *Powdermaker, Stranger and Friend: The Way of an Anthropologist* (NY: W.W. Norton, 1966) an excellent book on fieldwork in three different societies.
[19] For an analysis of the impact of culture on various societies see: Mary Douglas, *Purity and Danger: An Analysis of the Concepts of Pollution and Taboo* (London: Routledge and Kegan Paul, 1966); also her book, *Natural Symbols: Explorations in Cosmology* (NY: Pantheon Books, 1977) and E.E. Evans-Pritchard, *Witchcraft, Oracles and Magic Among the Azande* (Oxford: Clarendon, 1937).
[20] Erving Goffman, *The Presentation of Self in Everyday Life,* (New York: Doubleday, 1959).
[21] Knud Rasmussen, *The Netsilik Eskimos: Social Life and Spiritual Culture.* Report of the Fifth Thule Expedition, 1921-24 Copenhagen: Blydendalske Boghnadel., 1931, p. 167.
[22] Quoted in James B. Mayfield, *Go to the People,* pp. 100-101.
[23] I gratefully acknowledge that many of these questions were derived from a list developed by Stan Burkey, *People First: A Guide to Self-Reliant, Participatory Rural Development* (London: Zed Books Ltd, 1993), pp. 115-119.

Chapter 9

Stage Two of Rural Development
Capacity Building and Problem Solving

Much of village development programming of the past four decades reflects a frustrating dilemma: the realizations that too many projects implemented in LDCs tend to fail and yet the obvious need to increase resources available if the problems of the LDCs are to be dealt with. Is the only alternative to increase rural development funding in order to implement more programs that appear to have high probabilities of failure? Of course the high rate of failure is often attributed to an insensitive awareness of the local culture and the rather simplistic approaches often used to confront the complex problems of Third world poverty. We are beginning to understand that tossing money at problems, especially social and cultural problems, is not the solution. The issue is not so much "do we spend more," but how do we use the resources we have in the most appropriate and useful way possible.

What is often not understood, is the contradiction that often reflects our efforts to help those who live in poverty. It is easy to assume that poor people simply need more money and their problems will be solved. We are beginning to understand that money by itself is a two edged sword: rural development resources allocated for rural poverty alleviation too often benefit the urban elites. Government officials, technical consultants, even the RDFs themselves, generally receive the lion's share in the form of salaries, per diem, and travel allotments. Alternatively, money that is distributed at the local level often stimulates feelings of dependency, demanded entitlements, and a kind of fatalistic assumption that nothing can be done without outside help. Effective utilization of scarce resources requires a gradual process, through which four kinds of pre-requisites must be understood. first, the utilization of resources requires a certain level of capacity and understanding on the part of the community receiving the help. Second, such capacities only become an integrated part of society when the community as a whole understands the logic and contextual demands of the new knowledge and resources being made available. Third, local leadership must be developed and supported in ways that ensure the acceptance and understanding of the new resources and knowledge being introduced into the community, and fourth, community involvement and wide-spread participation are absolutely crucial if the capacities, understandings, resources and knowledge are to be sustainable.

Section One
An Understanding of Capacity Building

The Role of the RDF

The work and challenges of a village rural development facilitator is often ignored in the literature. It is too often assumed that if there are adequate resources, if you have a professional staff of managers and administrators, that the work of rural development will be relatively easy to implement. Little information is available about the everyday challenges of working in a village community. Few in-depth studies are available that identify and clarify the activities, strategies, interventions and interactions that have been successful and those that have been unsuccessful and most important -- why? This dearth of useful information and concern has been the major stimulus for the writing of this book. Experience does suggest that effective RDFs must be generalist, able to integrate the problems of illiteracy, sickness, poverty, environmental pollution, cultural disintegration and civic or political apathy into a coherent program of rural development. This multi-disciplinary approach requires individuals with experience and knowledge in many fields. Such people are seldom available and even when they are available, there is a real danger that such RDFs may be so overburdened with the challenges of such a complex program that the RDF is unable to accomplish a meaningful task in even one of the dimensions of rural development, let alone in all of the areas being suggested.

Effective Planning

Many development experts in past years have assumed that projects that have been planned well (blue print approach) would automatically be implemented as the plan requires. In practice, most development plans require specific activities, roles and functions that are often ignored and even at best are modified or changed in ways not acceptable nor anticipated by the original planners. Such planners often fail to distinguish between what is possible and what is probable and generally forget to consider what can possibly or even probably will go wrong in a given environment. Design plans for hand pumps assume that local people using such plans will have the material needed, will cut and manufacture the parts to exacting measurements, and that construction skills are available to manufacture the hand pump as described in the plan. All such assumptions almost never exist in a village environment. Early efforts to implement "Green Revolution" technologies in the village were disappointing as the assumed levels of training, resources and facilities needed to implement such modern agriculture were again generally not available or inappropriately assumed to be unimportant. Many experts view such failures as merely the results of illiteracy, conservatism, carelessness and village superstition. The technology obviously works in the

United States, so failure is not in the technology, the failure must be in the people, the culture, the situation over which the expert has no control and therefore cannot be held accountable for the failure. RDFs involved in capacity building activities must be concerned not only with what might work, because it works in the developed world, but also, and even more important, why it might not work, what cultural obstacles, environmental constraints, social limitations, and community oppositions might exist to prevent implementation.

David Korten over a decade ago argued that rural development was best conceptualized as a learning process, that learning from failure was as important as success, that learning requires that we consider what has worked and what has not and why. Korten even argues that the sharing of failures should be rewarded as a valuable part of the process of learning. Yet the very nature of an RDF working in a village seems to prevent such learning from taking place. Unfortunately, most donor organizations are driven by the demands of their donors far more than by the needs of the villagers. Money is given on the assumption that specific schools, health clinics, wells and latrines will be built. Success is defined in terms of such money being spent, failure to implement such projects within the budget year are simply unacceptable. Any conscientious RDF will not be free from the pressures of the home office to meet the schedule of project completions required. The fact that the trees planted eventually died because of a drought, or that the shiny new latrines sit unused because of cultural obstacles, or that the carefully constructed health clinic remains unoccupied because of some conflict between two major families in the village, would almost never be mentioned in an RDF report. Such failures are neither accepted nor appreciated by the people who so generously provided the resources in the first place. It is much easier to suggest that everything is rosy in the village, that progress is eternal and that all problems have been dealt with. It will be argued that a new set of criteria is needed if RDFs are to be effective. Long-term success will require that RDFs not be judged simply on the completion of projects funded by the outside organization. The clarification and careful analysis of problems, obstacles, failures must not only be encouraged, but actually rewarded by the organization supporting the RDF. A totally new conceptualization of this process of capacity building is needed.

The Capacity Building Process

Successful capacity building requires approaches that are consistent with and comparable to the processes that villagers are already using in developing and adopting new knowledge, skills, technologies, and social interactions. My experience with villagers in general, suggests that villagers are far more adaptive, shrewd and calculating than is generally understood. They are neither naive, unaware, nor impractical when it comes to questions of survival and change. They are inherently skeptical, untrusting, and hesitant to accept advice from outsiders. They are continually assessing their own resources, their needs and their options.

Outsiders seldom have a clear understanding of the calculations and assumptions such villagers use in their daily struggle to survive and improve their own conditions.

The role of the RDF has been conceptualized in a number of different ways:[1] from (1) **a provider**, one of change agent, solver of villager problems, mobilizer of resources, and an expert in dealing with the needs of villagers, giving free resources, information, and technology; to (2) **motivator** one of animator, stimulator, external source of change and development, in which the villagers had to be motivated to change, which assumed that they were inherently passive and unmotivated; to (3) **facilitator**, one of being an enabler, a helper in which the major focus was on the villagers, the source of change was in the villagers not in the RDF, the motivation was internal and a reflection of the inner dynamics of the community itself.

The facilitator model tends to define development as a process by which local people have an opportunity to broaden their choices, their options, allows them to determine their own activities and strategies to achieve these choices. The role of the facilitator is not to determine the choices or the solutions, but to encourage a process of reflection and decision-making that is consistent with and appropriate for the community. Such a process hopefully facilitates a set of discussion activities that will ensure that the right questions are being raised and answered if they are to be successful in achieving their goals and satisfying their needs. Before any RDF can be successful in this second stage of development (capacity building), it is obviously true that the processes of stage one (trust building) will require that the RDF understand and appreciate the situation of the villager from the villager's perspective.

Basic Questions to Ask in the Process of Capacity Building

Before villagers will be willing to develop and accept the skills, technologies, ideas, suggestions needed to broaden both their choices/options and the abilities to implement such choices, several sets of questions must be answered:

(1) Do the words, ideas, and concepts being presented and discussed clearly reflect the mental "constructs," the thought patterns and traditional ways of looking at things as was identified in the previous chapter. A consistent effort to engage in cultural dialoguing will be crucial if the RDF is to know what ideas are acceptable and what ideas are not acceptable and why this is from the perspective of the community of villagers.

(2) What activities are most appropriate to ensure that the projects, suggestions being presented are meaningful to the people involved? What types of discussion formats, participation strategies and group interactions are most appropriate to ensure that RDFs and villagers have a common sense of understanding and appreciation?

Capacity Building and Problem Solving 271

(3) What specific things must be done to ensure that the projects, suggestions being discussed will be implemented effectively and sustained over time? What incentives and traditions of the community are available to ensure the legitimacy and favorability of the ideas and projects being discussed will be established?

The Need to Understand Sources of Support and Opposition

The basic idea of the intervention being proposed must be clarified by identifying the necessary background knowledge needed for it to succeed and specific behaviors or practices considered essential, if the project is to provide the benefits anticipated. The key question is: What are we trying to accomplish and what can cause it to fail? Using some form of Force Field analysis, RDFs and villagers can better understand both the conditions needed for the project to be successful and the realities that exist to cause failure.[2] How might the basic idea be misunderstood, misapplied, and misperceived? RDFs must emphasize what conditions are needed for it to work rather than how the benefits of the idea may be maximized. What has to happen, what types of opposition must be confronted, what types of incentives exist or need to be created, to encourage the change anticipated?

The Need to Work Through Established Institutions

Many rural development experts have advocated the use of local institutions in any process of project implementation. While as a concept this seems reasonable, reality in the village may suggest something different. There are many local institutions that can be significant obstacles to any meaningful change and development: the caste system, land tenure systems, apartheid, middle-men systems of exploitation, etc. Too often, efforts to strengthen local institutions may be strengthening institutions of inequality and exploitation. Much care must be made to ensure that the local institutions used will not be an obstacle to the change. Generally, however, if appropriate care is taken, local institutions can be more effective in introducing needed changes, technologies, and projects, than the importation of outside systems of management and organization.

Importance of Integrating the New with the Old

In the field of health care in Nepal, there were two sources of legitimacy: the *dhami* (traditional health worker) and Durga, a Goddess associated with medical cures. Most dhamis, when presented with a child with diarrhea, would prescribe withholding liquids in order to dry the child out. This is often fatal since the major cause of death among small children is not diarrhea but dehydration. In seeking to introduce Oral Rehydration Technology (ORT), it was assumed that a new set of local village health workers would need to be recruited and trained. Not only was such an effort extremely expensive, but often did not work as villagers simply did not trust the new health workers. Rather than trying to set up a competition with the dhamis, UNICEF later chose to recognize the legitimacy of these traditional health workers and to support their activities while at the same time trying to persuade them to promote ORT. To reinforce and complement this approach they produced a promotional card, the size of a playing card. On one side of the card were graphic instructions on how to prepare the oral rehydration mixture, while on the other side was a color reproduction of a familiar image of the Goddess Durga. This obviously associated in the villagers' minds, the practice of ORT with the blessings and wisdom of Durga, it also demonstrated to the *dhamis* that UNICEF valued the traditional methods and values of Nepalese culture. Since the dhamis were given stocks of the cards to distribute, their status was enhanced since the cards were modern, colorful and shiny. [3]

Section Two
An Understanding of Participation

The obvious answer to the problem of implementation and sustainability is the need to ensure local community participation and involvement. Nearly every program document today has a section on local participation. We all know it is needed, yet very few of us really know what it is, how it is to be implemented, or why it often fails even when it is implemented. These kinds of questions will be the major focus of this section.

As a first step, participation must be seen as inherently political. True participation among the more disadvantaged of a given community will nearly always be perceived as a threat to the elites and those who have the power. RDFs are naive if they believe that meaningful participation can be benign, neutral or non-controversial. Paulos Freire, the great champion of the poor, acknowledged that liberation from the chains of illiteracy, poverty and exploitation, would require not only participation and unity, but also may lead to conflict and even bloodshed. Many political systems will often use the concept of participation to justify their own neglect of local areas. Participation in this context is simply a guise used by central governments to justify their own inability to provide educational, health and other community services by "allowing" the local people to solve their own problems through their own community institutions, knowing full well that such efforts are doomed to failure. Even those of us committed to the use of participation to ensure that projects reflect the needs and sensitivities of the local people, must acknowledge that participation stimulated by an RDF does not guarantee that the process will necessarily benefit the participants. Many such efforts have had little if any positive impact and some such efforts have caused more harm than good. This has to be the major challenge of the second stage of rural development.

In any serious discussion of participation and empowerment, some effort is needed to conceptualize these two terms in ways that are helpful to an RDF. In the next section we shall distinguish between participation activities that would be appropriate during the first two stages of rural development (trust building and capacity building) and those types of participation (including empowerment and coalition building) that are far more appropriate in the third stage of rural development: the local institution building stage. Participation during the first two stages is thus best conceptualized as a process of problem identification and solution implementation focusing on individual and group capacity building. The RDF must ensure that problems identified and solutions suggested can be resolved and implemented within the organizational and resource constraints of the community. Participation at this level is concerned with developing capacity in the planning and implementation of needed projects. The emphasis will be on group and local leadership development related to planning, designing, implementing and evaluating small scale village development projects. These types of activities are less political and more administrative in style and consequence and thus less apt to generate conflict or repression. The processes of participation and training related to these early stages in rural development are to be explained in the next section of this chapter.

There are a number of reasons for structuring the processes of capacity building and local leadership development in a given rural community. First, RDFs must understand that the needs of rural villages are changing rapidly and are clearly different even between villages in the same area. What a village near a major urban center and an isolated village might need are often very different. With the advent of mass media, television, and movies, increased travel and work opportunities, and the expansion of government and international donor development activities at the local level has introduced a whole new set of expectations, perceptions, needs and wants. In many areas, significant ecological degradation has changed village life from what it once was, new social and cultural institutions and norms are evolving. In today's world, very few things are static, change appears to be almost ubiquitous, and RDFs must be sensitive to these developments. While some will want to preserve the traditions and customs of the local people, it must be understood that some outside information will still be needed if the problems of villagers are to be solved.

Section Three
The Value and Structure of Participation

Early involvement by the community offers opportunities for greater understanding of the projects to be implemented, and for direct participation in different elements of the program process. In many societies, much of the planning and organizing of village level programs are completed by outsiders with little input from the villagers themselves. Individuals who have not participated in the definition of problems and needs, or have not provided information to the effort are less likely to be satisfied with or have the same degree or "ownership" of what was produced as those who were involved. If anything is characteristic of participatory program effort in the early stages of rural development, it is an abundance of meetings. Yet, all too many of them are exercises in frustration. Discussions are often unfocused, tangential, and rambling. A small number may dominate the interchange while a sizable group does not participate. In some cases, the formality of some meeting (tape recorders, microphones, large crowds, government officials, and foreigners) intimidate all but the most aggressive individuals. Often, meetings wear participants out by their length, overload them with too much information, dazzle them with brilliant, ingenious graphics, or confuse them with excessively technical presentations.

Meetings involve a gathering together of people. Each person is a source of resources that include information, energy, time and material goods. Every meeting is an opportunity for mobilizing these resources. How well the resources are drawn upon depends, among other things, on the leadership, the process and the structure of the meeting. Access to an individual's time and energy depends largely upon the degree of "ownership" of the group's decisions, process, or proposed action achieved by that individual. "Ownership" is a consequence of the perceived exercise of influence by individuals in the group's problem-solving effort. How a meeting is organized, whether equal opportunities to participate are provided, and the extent to which individual ideas are visibly accepted, will determine the access to the resources of participating individuals and thus determine their ownership and commitment to the process.

Section Four
A Typology for Distinguishing Various Types of Participation

In an attempt to cut across both the euphemisms and the rhetoric of people participation, let us consider a typology which seeks to clarify various levels of participation -- from pseudo to real participation.[4]

Pseudo Participation

In the name of people participation, members of a community are allowed to assemble for the express purpose of "educating" them or engineering their support. In such meetings, it will be the local government officials who educate, persuade, and advise the citizens, not the reverse. The purpose is to manipulate the people into accepting some outsider government program, some policy condition, or some new requirement of a central ministry. Such meetings are

Information Sharing

Informing community members of their rights, responsibilities, and options can be the most important first step toward legitimate people's participation. However, too frequently the emphasis is placed on a one-way flow of information rather than on two-way and shared awareness communication -- from outsiders, both private and public officials, to community members -- with no channel provided for feedback and no power for negotiation.[5] Meetings can also be turned into vehicles for one-way communication by the simple device of providing superficial information, discouraging questions or giving irrelevant answers.

Consultation

Inviting community member's opinions, like sharing information, can be a legitimate step toward their full participation. If consulting them is not combined with other modes of participation, this rung of the ladder is still a sham since it offers no assurance that common people's concerns and ideas will be taken into account. The most frequent methods used for consulting people are attitude surveys and community meetings.

When outsiders or government officials restrict the input of people's ideas solely to this level, participation remains just a window-dressing ritual. People are primarily perceived as statistical abstractions, and participation is measured by how many come to meetings, take brochures home, or answer a questionnaire. What community members achieve in all this type of activity is that they have "participated in participation" and what outsiders and government officials achieve is the evidence that they have gone through the required motions of involving community residents.

Placation

It is at this level that villagers begin to have some degree of influence though tokenism is still apparent. Examples of this type of participation include program planning committees where a few carefully picked village members are allowed onto the committee. If they are not accountable to the village itself and if the traditional power elite or government officials hold the majority of seats, the disadvantaged of the village can be easily outvoted. Another form of placation is to allow a village based council to advise and plan *ad infinitum* but retain for the outside government officials the right to judge the legitimacy or feasibility of the advice. The degree to which villagers are actually placated, of course, depends largely on two factors: the quality of technical assistance they have in articulating their priorities; and the extent to which the village community has been organized to press for those priorities.

Partnership

At this rung of the ladder, power is in fact redistributed through negotiation between villagers and officials. They agree to share planning and decision-making responsibilities through such structures as planning committees and mechanisms for resolving impasses. After the ground rules have been established through some form of give-and-take, they are not subject to unilateral change.

Partnership can work most effectively when there is an organized power-base in the village to which their leaders are accountable; when such village-level committees have the financial resources to pay its leaders reasonable honoraria for their time-consuming efforts; and when such committees have the resources to hire (and fire) its own technical experts and community organizers. With these ingredients, community members have some genuine bargaining influence over the outcome of the plan.

In most community development efforts where power has come to be shared generally it was taken by the members, not given by the officials. Thus a true partnership is often stimulated by angry community leaders demanding an equal share of the process of decision. There is nothing new about this process, which is often characterized by hostility and rancor. Since those who have power normally want to hang onto it, historically it has had to be wrested by the powerless rather than proffered by the powerful. In one village situation, a village spokesperson threatened to mobilize a protest against a suggested project unless the officials agreed to give the village members a couple of weeks to review the project plans and recommend changes. The officials agreed reluctantly. At the next meeting, the village leaders handed the officials a substitute member participation section that changed the ground rules from a weak members' role to a strong shared power agreement. Again the officials reluctantly agreed especially when they came to see how shared power did tend to motivate the local community leaders to take much more responsibility for the implementation of the project being offered.

Delegated Power

Negotiations between village leaders and government officials can also result in communities achieving dominant decision-making authority over a particular plan or program. It is in this type of participation system that RDFs are generally allowed to function. Often before an RDF will be allowed to work in a given village community, there must be government approval. In a sense the government is delegating a certain level of power and authority to the RDF to work with the village community. At this level of participation, village leaders and their members are still somewhat dependent on outsiders for the resources and materials needed to implement a given project. Nevertheless, the villagers will have a significant amount of discretion in how these resources and material are to be used. Outsider officials tend to play the role of auditor and monitor to ensure the project is implemented according to certain standards of operation.

Community Autonomy

In many societies, demands for community controlled schools, health clinics, and development programs are on the increase. Village members are simply demanding greater autonomy and authority that guarantees that community institutions can govern a program or project, be in full charge of policy and managerial aspects, and be able to negotiate the conditions under which "outsiders" may change them. A village council or development center at this level will seek to mobilize their own resources through user fees, local taxes and with links to other resources.

Village Local Government

The ultimate level of village participation would be the creation of a local government system in which a village council and village leaders would be elected and held accountable to the local community. Community Autonomy and Village Local Government are still not widely available options for most village communities. In order to identify the strategies currently being employed to stimulate these kinds of village participation systems and to evaluate their effectiveness, let us review some of the more common ones.

From a local provincial, municipality or district point of view, there clearly are advantages to encouraging a process that will ensure that village and other community groups have the opportunity to communicate with and become an autonomous part of the local administrative system of a given area. There is evidence that active local institutions become effective and thus sustainable to the extent that they have real political power and are able to actively pursue their own interests.

Section Five
The Challenges of Introducing Change
Through Participation

When one emphasizes the importance of participation, one is emphasizing the importance of listening, of making certain that what is being communicated is what is being intended and understood. Effective communication requires concrete and systematic efforts to reduce the biases found in RDFs identified above, but also the many factors that make communication with villagers very difficult:

Local Language and Dialects: Few RDFs are sensitive to the horrendous challenge they face when the native language of the villagers they are working with is different from their own. When an RDF or villager speaks Spanish, French,

English, even Swahili, Arabic, Hindi or Chinese, such outsiders must understand that these dominant languages are often second languages for many villagers, that while they may appear to understand and speak these languages, they will often miss the subtleties and nuances that a native speaker will catch. In many such communities, the men will have learned these dominant languages, while the wives and children often have not. Communication is difficult enough even among people with the same language, the challenges of rural development workers is doubly difficult because of the cultural and language differences that often exist between RDFs and villagers. In coastal Kenya there are a half dozen tribal languages as well as many dialects and the national *lingua franca* of Swahili. Even for Kenyan RDFs there is frequently a need for a translator. In some instances, for a non-Swahili speaker, comments may have to pass through two translators. In such circumstances, any notion of the visitor casually listening in on a free exchange of views must be illusory.

History of Exploitation and Feelings of Inferiority: RDFs must understand that past interactions with outsiders have generally been exploitative, with promises that were not kept, being taken advantage of, and unreasonable taxes collected, conscription of their sons into the army, destruction of crops, lands and property. It is not surprising that villagers will remain suspicious, guarded, disbelieving, and frankly unconvinced of what is being said or promised. Such an environment makes candid, open conversations and discussions almost impossible.

The Constructs of Villagers: Indigenous cultures reflect a set of categories of thought, understanding, values and expectations concerning roles, norms, assumptions that are generally quite incompatible with the thought processes of the outsiders, even RDFs from the same culture. RDFs have generally been exposed to western learning, western science and thinking. They are not aware of how these kinds of experiences make them quite different from the illiterate peasant they must work with. Words have very different meanings when analyzed in terms of the "mental constructs" identified in the last chapter. Such differences make meaningful communication nearly impossible. In Northern Pakistan, UNICEF has built a large number of drinking-water installations, in which clean spring water is piped to village stand pipes. This is considered by the aid establishment to be a major contribution to tackling the health problem associated with using water that has been taken from open and polluted irrigation ditches. In one village, a stand-pipe stood next to an irrigation ditch and a group of villagers was asked the question, "From where do you get your drinking water?" The question appeared stupid to both parties since the answer seemed obvious. The peasant responded, "Of course drinking water would come from the irrigation ditch!" It emerged that running water is considered clean, and cold water is considered particularly clean. Since the irrigation channel is fed from glacial melt-water it is cold, while the spring water is relatively warm and thus dirty. To the villager, the answer was obvious and rational given the constructs they used to explain clean and dirty water.

Past Experiences of Villagers With Development Projects: RDFs must understand that nearly all villages have had some experience with development projects of some kind. With the thousands of development agencies, donor organizations, government programs and institutions, few villagers have been totally ignored. Such experiences will color their perceptions of the "new" outsider coming into their village. For most villagers, outsiders are seen as the bearer of gifts, and RDFs must consistently confront the "Santa Claus" syndrome, the assumption that outsiders are expected to bring free food, clothing, housing, seeds, fertilizers, etc.

Who Happens to be Present: Conversations with villagers will provide different kind of information depending on who happens to be present. A very poor villager may be very unwilling to admit problems of poverty when some of the richer villagers are present. Observations about village problems are seldom raised by villagers if the village chief is present, since raising such problems in his presence would be rude and inconsiderate. In one study, it was found that when a housing improvement worker was present the villagers generally reported satisfaction with these new technologies, but that when a housing worker was absent the bulk of the reports was more negative. When the health worker in the community was present in a general meeting, most people commented on the positive impact of having a village health worker in their village. In more private meetings, individuals were much more negative about the health worker, suggesting that the health worker was not properly trained, did not have medicine when it was needed, etc.

Matching technology with Village Competencies: Too many projects require a level of technological understanding that simply does not exist at the village household level. In Hunza, Baltistan, and Ladakh the composting latrine was introduced by outsiders as an agricultural tool. It was assumed that individual families would quickly see how it should be used, what methods and materials would be needed for its construction, when it should be emptied and what crops could benefit most from the fertilizer. Outsiders must understand that such understanding requires cultural, institutional, family and social knowledge and experience not found in many areas where such latrines have never been accepted. In Hunza, where such latrines were integrated into the agriculture system, it is reported that the emptying of the latrines was made an integral part of the springtime religious festivals that coincide with the sowing. Thus, the religious leaders being involved, were able to give the timing of the emptying of the latrines some cultural legitimacy. An RDF seeking to introduce latrines and new composting techniques would need to be able to integrate these new concepts into the established structure of skills, responsibilities, incentives and seasonal cycles of the area. Knowledge has to be matched with the appropriate competence in two senses; not only does a new idea have to be targeted at the correct person but it also has to be introduced by an appropriate person or organization.

Ensuring the proper scale: The methane or bio gas digester has been widely advocated as a way of providing sources of fuel for cooking and heating and for generating electricity in the village. Yet in reality, only a small number of this kind of project has been successful as the technology required appears efficacious only at a certain scale of operation. The small scale experimental household digesters have tended to clog up, produce little gas and in a few instances they have exploded. Other problems included the cost of the materials which villagers could not afford and practical considerations such as the lack of sufficient cow-dung to sustain the digestion process..

The Principle of Recognized Authorities

The use of village health workers has been widely advocated for several decades. Few village health worker programs have succeeded in becoming an integral part of most village communities. Most villagers still feel appropriate medicine can only come from a real doctor, who is seen as having the competence and medicines needed to help sick people. This core idea makes all village health workers as suspect, second best, and thus by definition, less than helpful. Even a doctor, though he or she recognizes the value of latrines and the importance of nutrition and hygiene, will generally be listened to, but the advice will be ignored. The doctor will be listened to politely and respectfully but his advice will be ignored since it is perceived as being significantly outside his area of recognized wisdom. Often the best strategy for introducing modern medicine is to work with the traditional healers and medicine men, and midwifes, rather than simply training new people who are not perceived as having any competency in medicine.

In seeking to use an agronomist, the problem is even more difficult. The concept of an agronomist is very confusing: He is young, trained in urban centers, has no land of his own and you the local farmers are supposed to have confidence in this kind of young person. A person who is being paid to do something but who has no recognizable function does not make sense. Some care is needed to help villagers to develop some reasonable understanding as to what an agronomist does, what an RDF does? Many progressive doctors who may wish to take off the white gown and work directly with the people in their homes and among their traditional health workers will often be frustrated by the villager's unwillingness to accept this new role, these new functions.

Adult education makes no sense to villagers. Schools are for children. By being placed in a childlike situation their competence as adult is under threat. Some schools in Yemen were designed and fitted out to conform with the Arabic *mufraj;* the sitting room where men spend long afternoons chatting, smoking and chewing local, mildly narcotic leaf. Carpets and mattresses on the floor created an instantly recognizable pattern in which an adult male felt comfortable in his role. Such a context was the natural one in which novel ideas were considered at leisure and problems could be shared and dissected with one's peers.

Section Six
The Inter-Personal Dimensions of the RDF in the Process of Implementing Capacity Building.

The main purpose of this section is to highlight the central role of interpersonal skills and how the basic assumptions and beliefs of RDFs have concerning people will greatly determine their effectiveness in the process of introducing change and capacity building. Studies suggest that what makes an effective RDF is directly related to their level of interpersonal competency and the assumptions they have about people. Studies have shown that RDFs often operate without a clear awareness of their beliefs and attitudes. It is essential to recognize how you came to acquire your beliefs and how they affect what you do with community people, especially those with a different cultural background.

The Orientation of RDFs to Helping Others

In one interesting study that examined some 13 studies in five helping professions to identify the characteristics of the effective helper/facilitator, Combs (1986) suggested there were at least four areas of beliefs that seem to discriminate clearly between good (or effective) facilitators and poor (or ineffective) ones.
1. Beliefs about the value of focusing on the client's personal world. Effective facilitators are people-oriented; that is, they focus on internal personal meanings rather than external behavioral data. They are primarily concerned with how the world appears from the vintage point of those with whom they work.
2. Beliefs about people. Effective facilitators hold positive beliefs about people, seeing them as trustworthy, capable, and dependable.
3. Beliefs about self. The facilitator's self-concept is vitally related to effective practice. The studies suggest the importance of a positive view of self, confidence in one's abilities, and a feeling of oneness with others. Effective facilitators identify with others rather than feeling isolated, and they feel wanted rather than unwanted.
4. Beliefs that influence methods. Research on specific facilitator/helper methods has not established that methods alone serve to discriminate between effective and ineffective professionals. The most promising research on effective facilitator/helpers seems to lie in studies of specific traits. Characteristics of effective facilitators tend to include empathy, congruence, warmth, compassion, genuineness, or authenticity, and unconditional positive regard.

The views and beliefs that RDFs hold about human nature are very much related to the facilitative strategies they will employ while working in a village community. If one believes in being active and directive in the facilitative process, they will do much of the talking, will give much advice, will provide a high degree of structure, and will make sure that the community meetings and group discussions keep moving. Some RDFs focus on the feelings of the villagers and thus seek the more slow process of group discussions ensuring that all the feelings and concerns are fully discussed. Others will focus on what people are thinking and how they rationalize their present situation. Such a facilitator will see change as a result of helping the villagers to eliminate faulty thinking and replace it with constructive thoughts and more logical levels of analysis. Some RDFs employ a good deal of confrontation, thinking that villagers will surrender their defenses and agree to change only under pressure of being challenged. Other RDFs think that support is far more useful than confrontation. Depending on your beliefs, your interventions will have the effect of either supporting or challenging.

Establishing a relationship of Trust. If villagers are to feel free to talk about their problems, RDFs need to provide attention, active listening, and empathy. Community members must sense your respect for them, which you can demonstrate by your attitudes and behaviors. You reveal an attitude of respect for villagers when you are concerned about their best interests, view them as able to exercise control of their own destiny, and treat them as individuals rather than stereotyping them. You actually show villagers that you respect them through your behavior, such as actively listening to and understanding them, suspending critical judgment, expressing appropriate warmth and acceptance, communicating to them that you understand their world as they experience it, and helping them take the specific steps needed to solve their problems.

I am convinced that the early phase of rural development requires highly developed listening skills. In this first stage, the first step is to define and understand the community, its values, cultural traditions, its history, its way of life economically, socially, and politically. Too often RDFs are eager to begin the process of change and problem-solving without understanding the mental constructs and the realities of the villagers themselves. To be able to do this, RDFs must possess listening and attending skills. Your capacity to understand and respond with empathy, genuineness, respect, acceptance, and caring greatly influences your ability to help the villagers to share in greater detail and with less distortion what they are really feeling and thinking.

Although it may seem deceptively simple merely to listen to others, the attempt to understand the world as others see it is demanding. Respect, genuineness, and empathy are best considered as a "way of being" not as mechanical techniques to be used on villagers to influence their behavior to induce change. In fact, there is much evidence to suggest that people who fake empathy or respect will communicate unintentionally messages that increase defensiveness and actually increase feelings of distrust.

The Significance of Confrontation for the Effective RDF

In every village community you will find some villagers with some levels of hostility and rejection. Such people will often not voice their feelings of hostility to you in public. You may hear that some opposition exists to a given idea that you have been discussing with the community. Some may suggest that the ideas will never work and should be rejected. In a non defensive way you can explore with such people their unwillingness to consider the ideas being suggested. If you are patient, you may discover that these people have some good reasons for rejecting the ideas being discussed. It may be helpful to be somewhat skeptical of any project or idea where there is absolutely no opposition or concerns about its utility or appropriateness. Opposition and conflict, which we will discuss in greater detail later, must not be seen as necessarily a bad thing.

One of the qualities of an RDF that is misunderstood, is the importance of confronting and challenging villagers with new ideas and perspectives. First, it must be understood that confrontation is not generally appropriate in the first stage of rural development, especially when the RDF is trying to establish a relationship of trust and understanding. However, at some point some forms of confrontation will be needed. There are many misconceptions about the purpose and value of confrontation and conflict. Some RDFs see it as producing defensiveness and withdrawal in villagers. Or they view it as an adversarial stance between them and the villagers, which can lead to premature termination of the community development process. Many RDFs sometimes see confrontation as a negative act with destructive potential. Because of this connotation, they sometimes avoid it at all costs, when it is the very thing that they need to provide as the impetus for growth. Without confrontation, villagers often remain stuck in self-defeating behavior and do not develop the new perspectives and skills needed to make needed changes. Some RDFs provide plenty of positive support but are reluctant to confront villagers. RDFs cease to being effective catalysts to other's growth if all they offer is support and empathy. Constructive and caring confrontation invites individuals to look at discrepancies, distortions, games, excuses, resistance, and evasions that are keeping them unable to solve their problems. Done with sensitivity, confrontation ultimately helps villagers develop the capacity for self-confrontation that they will need in working through the problems of their community.

Confronting villagers effectively entails focusing on their awareness of what they are thinking, feeling, and doing. If the confrontation is successful villagers are able to overcome blind spots and develop new perspectives on their life situation, and thus will be influenced to make changes based on this self-understanding. Thus, confronting aims at enabling villagers to participate actively and fully in the process of helping themselves. Ideally, they will learn the art of self-confrontation.

Here are a few suggestions for making your confronting effective. First of all, earn the right to confront. Know your motivations for confronting. Is it because you want more deeply to understand another, or is it because you want to control the other person? Do you care about your relationship with the villagers? Are you really interested in getting closer to them, and are you aware of what gets in the way of a closer relationship? Challenge villagers only if you feel an investment in them and if you have the time and make an effort to continue building the relationship with them. If you have not established a working relationship with a villager, your confrontation is likely to be received defensively. The degree to which you can confront the villagers you are working with depends on how much they trust and like you and how much you trust and like them. Learn the skill of giving non-evaluative feedback.

Using self-disclosure appropriately. Sharing yourself can be a powerful intervention in making contact with rural villagers. We are not encouraging an indiscriminate revealing of your personal problems to the people you are working with. It can be very helpful to talk about yourself in ways that allow the villagers to know you in a more intimate way. Often such disclosures help villagers to talk more honestly about themselves. Self-disclosure does not mean to share detailed stories about your past or present problems. Perhaps the most important type of self-disclosure is that which focuses on the relationship between you and the villagers. Self-disclosure for me implies sharing information about yourself that another person should know if your relationship with that person is to grow.

Section Seven
Village Problem Solving Group Development[6]

In seeking to conceptualize the process of helping groups of villagers become effective problem solving groups, it may be helpful to think of this process as an on-going cycle of activities in which the RDF plays a significant role at times and at other times must back off to let the villagers begin to take responsibility themselves.

Introducing a problem-solving approach into a rural setting is always very difficult. Too often RDFs focus only on the structure and procedures (how to organize, how to make decisions, what will be the responsibilities of the members of the group, etc.) rather than on what the villagers are feeling. There is a need to train RDFs to be sensitive to the feelings, the behaviors, and the perceptions of the village people before they begin to emphasize the problems of organization. Often the RDF is so eager to introduce new approaches that s/he forgets first to check the perceptions, concerns and attitudes of the village people. It is crucial that the rural problem-solving process go through a continual cycle of first checking feelings and perceptions using the process consultation skills associated with *maintenance* (M); next the RDF might suggest techniques, approaches, procedures, and systems that might be used using the process consultation skills associated with *task* (T); then checking again on feelings, perceptions, concern(M); then suggesting new approaches, possible solutions, procedures (T); and then again checking feelings, perceptions (M), etc.

In the chart that follows the process of institutionalizing a problem-solving approach in a given village is outlined. It is assumed that a village may seek to introduce a project or activity at: (1) the **small group level** of interested villagers (a group of villagers wanting to build a bridge across a small stream or a group of mothers wants to understand how to deal with diarrhea); (2) the **sectoral level,** which would include a significant portion of some sector (the farmers, the mothers, the youth or the village development committee, etc.); and (3) the **total village level**, where the project, the program or activity would affect the entire village. It is assumed that RDFs would play a significant role at the small group level helping villagers to gain some confidence in solving problems that are important to them. Yet such small group level activities, in the short run, often have little impact and often are not sustainable. At the total village level, the RDF should be backing off from the process, as village level institutions begin to have the capacity to provide solutions to problems that will be sustained and have some significant long-last impact. If the introduction and successful completion of projects are to be reinforcing and sustaining over time, it is assumed that it is better to implement a small project with a high probability of success than a large project with a low probability of success.

Chart 9-1
Process of Building Village Problem Solving Capacity

Low Impact	Medium Impact	High Impact
A. Small Group Level	B. Sectoral Level	C. Village Level
1. Desiring (M)	5. Hoping (M)	9. Envisioning (M)
2. Searching (T)	6. Planning (T)	10. Organizing (T)
3. Trying (M)	7. Implementing (M)	11. Integrating (M)
4. Accomplishing (T)	8. Testing (T)	12, Evaluating (T)

This chart suggests a series of steps that may be appropriately considered as an RDF seeks to introduce projects first at the small group level, then the sectoral level, and finally at the village level. Each step implies a series of skills and training experiences that must be developed prior to moving to a higher step. For example, the first step suggested is **desiring.** It is assumed that the RDF with a small group of village people must first help the villagers to develop a desire on their part to change some situation in their village. This step is designated as a process maintenance (M) step since the RDF must focus on perceptions and feelings of the group members. The skills needed in this step include the ability to share perceptions (mental constructs), ideas, goals, concerns; the ability to communicate more effectively, employing the skill of active listening and dialoguing; the ability to brainstorm without the ideas generated being criticized or evaluated in ways that increase defensiveness in people; and the ability to use the ways of increasing group effectiveness -- more openness, more trust, more awareness of each other and the processes of communication, decision-making, and conflict resolution. As the sense of group awareness begins to emerge, it has been found that a desire to initiate some activity that is perceived by villagers to be important begins to emerge.

The second step involves **searching**. This is designated as a task (T) step since the RDFs will begin to introduce a set of procedures that will facilitate the process of searching for a project and the means to accomplish it. At this step the group will seek to consider alternative projects and goals and to search out the availability of resources and funding (both within and outside the village).

The third step is **trying** -- again designated as a (M) maintenance step because it is important that the RDF work closely with the village group to ensure that this early attempt to try some new project is successful encouraged and supported. Such support requires very close communication between the RDFs and the village group to ensure that feelings and perceptions of the village people are continually considered as they try to introduce a new project. This is the point where a village group actually embarks upon some project and tests the RDF's belief that effort and activity can lead to its successful

The fourth step is **accomplishing,** designated as a task (T) step since it implies a commitment to some type of system or procedure. This is the difficult step of assessing whether the goals of the group projects have or have not been accomplished. The RDF will try to help the members of the group evaluate what they have done, why they were or were not successful, the lessons they have learned, and what procedures and relationships need to be developed or changed if the project is to be more successful in the future, and if it is to be expanded to the sector or village level.

In analyzing the first level of the small group approach, it is important to recognize the following four characteristics. First, although each step is designated as a M (maintenance) or a T (task) step, it should be emphasized that these are not mutually exclusive concepts. Thus, the RDF's awareness of feelings must be checked and considered in all four steps, just as in each one some task procedures, and techniques must be utilized. The point is that both feelings data and systems/task data must continually be considered. However, it appears that different steps require a different emphasis and mixture of the two types of data.

Second, there is no inevitability about any of these steps. It is just as possible that a specific step may be a success as it is that it may be a failure. This whole approach invites the RDF to go back again and again to earlier steps if it appears that the latter steps are not successful.

Third, at the group level the role of the RDF is very crucial. Here RDFs play a key role in teaching, encouraging, monitoring, and evaluating the skills and new procedures needed to help the group achieve the envisioned goals. Training at the group level is still mainly at the awareness stage. It is during the first four steps (desiring, searching, trying, and accomplishing) that the RDF helps to make village people aware of the skills and procedures needed. At the sector level, the next four steps, 5 through 8 (hoping, planning, implementing, and testing), tend to provide village leaders with the opportunity to practice the skills and to receive feedback on how well they are doing. The village level, which includes the steps 9 through 12 (envisioning, organizing, integrating, and evaluating), provides village leaders with an opportunity to begin to internalize the skills and approaches needed to make the village programs self-sustaining.

Fourth, at the group level, the RDF is generally responsible for training. At the sector level the RDF begins to help the leaders trained earlier to become trainers themselves. Thus, as the earlier trained leaders are moving through the practicing phase of steps 5 through 8, they are also being encouraged to train new groups to go through steps 1 through 4. Only at a later phase will some leaders begin to emerge who have internalized or are in the process of internalizing the skills in step 1 through 12 with the hope of eventually developing a village wide project that can have a major impact. In this final stage the RDF gradually withdraws from the village as the people themselves become capable of running their own projects. This eventually allows the RDF to move into a new village where he/she can then start the whole process over again at the group level.

At this point it may be helpful to reemphasize the ways in which the twelve steps are distinguished. For the purpose of analysis it has been found useful to discriminate between the processes of training (awareness, practicing, feedback, and internalization) and the processes of group/leadership development (climate building, date flow, goal formation, and control).

Let us review the four dimensions of group/leadership development. For example, steps 1, 5, and 9 are all manifestations of the first dimension (A - Climate Building); 2, 6, and 10 are associated with the second (B - Data Flow); 3, 7, and 11 are part of the third (C - Goal Formation); and steps 4, 8, and 12 are characteristic of the fourth dimension (D - Control/Evaluation). Gibb has suggested that these four dimensions can best be remembered as a reflection of his TORI theory (T= Trust, O = Openness, R = Realization, and I = Interdependence). On the basis of experience with the People's School System, the utility of this TORI model is found in its ability to sensitize in RDF to the issues that must be considered if leadership and group development are to take place in a rural setting.

Trust Building

From the words listed below, the reader may clearly see why the emotional climate is the dominating factor. All other processes of problem solving, goal setting, action research and program implementation are colored by the climate of trust or distrust. It should not be difficult to distinguish between those situations in which a RDF is functioning in a village with a low-trust and those in which high trust prevails

Chart 9-2
T = Trust -- Climate Building

(1. Desiring   5. Hoping   9. Envisioning)

Low Trust	High Trust
Fear	Trust
Hostility	Confidence
Criticism	Acceptance
Coldness	Warmth
Envy	Respect
Inadequacy	Esteem
Cynicism	Sympathy
Defensiveness	Love
Alienation	Affection
Anxiety	Less Defensiveness
Distorted	Appreciation of Diversity
Conflicting Values	Non criticism
Antagonistic Perceptions	Caring

In step 1 the goal of training and leadership development must be to heighten some awareness for the need for greater trust. Out of a milieu of greater trust will emerge a desire for some action, a desire for more cooperation, a desire for greater interaction. Often during this phase, with its emphasis on developing awareness, the process of trust building is based upon an intellectual or cognitive commitment to the notion that trust is better than distrust. However, such early awareness will often be characterized as less than sincere. Nevertheless, it is this early desire -- even if the skills and behaviors to build trust are not yet developed -- that is the first step in developing effective leadership and group building.

In step 5, at the sectoral level, there is some opportunity to practice the skills and the behaviors needed to develop an environment of trust building. A crucial variable in this first dimension, as has been said, is climate. Is the emotional climate conducive to trust building? How would you characterize the climate of the sector in terms of trust and acceptance? It is usually in this phase of practicing that leaders and members move from a desiring mode to a hoping mode. On the basis of their experience in steps 1 through 4, a certain degree of optimism emerges, and as the skills needed to reinforce greater trust levels are practiced and developed, a larger number of the village people begin to accept the genuineness and the sincerity of the individuals making up the sector with which the RDF is interacting. Hoping implies a certain confidence and trust not only in the RDFs and the groups to which they belong, but also in the environment. It is this improved climate of trust that can motivate various groups in the village to move to the practicing level of training and leadership development. A climate of desire requires help from the RDF. It is a dependency relationship, and the villagers' desire to try something is a reflection of their awareness that trust is necessary if they are to solve some of their problems in a cooperative manner. A climate of hope implies less dependence on the RDF since steps 1 through 4 have given them some sense of accomplishment and an awareness that specific skills are still needed if they are to move from the group level to the sector level. Hope generates greater motivation to practice the skills needed to succeed at the sectoral level.

In step 9, at the total village level, the process of internalizing the skills and behaviors associated with high trust generates a new vision of what is possible. This ninth step of envisioning suggests a degree of competency, awareness, and high trust that allows the village leadership to see beyond the present to the future, gradually to replace the RDF as the source of sympathy and respect for different opinions comes to characterized the village leadership structure. Only as village leadership begins to internalize the skills and behaviors associated with higher levels of trust will the climate be conducive to a self-sustaining and self-reinforcing process of growth and development in the rural community.

Openness

The key component of the second dimension is Data Flow -- the tendency for communication to be valid and distortion-free or, on the contrary, restricted and characterized by hidden agendas and games people play to deceive and/or to manipulate.

Chart 9-3
O = Openness -- Data Flow
(2. Searching   6. Planning   10. Organizing)

Low Openness	High Openness
Deception	Empathy
Masking	Spontaneity
Formality	Active Listening
Strategizing	Intimacy
Politeness	Rapport
Hidden Agenda	Receptivity
Role Playing	Open Brainstorming
Distortion/Deceit	Candor/Frankness
Ambiguity	Conflict Confrontation
Caution	Clarity/Directness

In step 2, the goal of training and leadership development must be to stimulate some awareness that communication patterns need to be open and distortion-free. Effective development of good ideas and appropriate alternative goals require a process of searching that stimulates the generation of valid information. At the group level individuals must be exposed to the necessity of giving non-evaluative feedback, a greater awareness of what "shared meaning " communication implies, what the negative consequences of role playing, distortion of intention, and deception can be on the whole process of data flow.

In step 6 comes the opportunity to practice the communication skills needed to increase the quality of planning at the sectoral level. It is in this phase that feedback skills are practice, planning skills are developed, skills in interactive listening and brainstorming are stimulated and reinforced. Effective planning implies open access to a variety of information sources both in and outside the village. Developing linkage skills with the village, district, and provincial government officials should be emphasized and practices with the support of the RDF. Practicing the skills needed to reduce defensiveness and game playing in the whole decision-making and planning process should be encouraged during this step.

In step 10 effective interpersonal and inter group communication skills must be internalized if the organizing structures of the village's formal institutions are to be strengthened. Organization implies a set of procedures and decision-making approaches that aim at maximizing the flow of data within the rural community. The internalization of certain behaviors associated with empathy, active listening, two-way communication, and valid and distortion-free data are a slow process, yet absolutely essential if the quality of decision making and planning is to be up to the long-term needs of rural villages.

Realization

The third dimension of the group/leadership development process is primarily concerned with the action steps required to complete some task, to achieve some goal, or to institute some change strategy. The goal-formation aspect of this whole process emphasizes the obstacles of apathy and resistance.

At the group level the crucial awareness needed for step 3 is the importance of trying. Here some awareness of the relationship that appears to exist between coercion and passivity, manipulation and resentment, persuasion and indifference, and between forcing and apathy should be developed. Although the RDF plays a crucial role in stimulating and supporting local leadership, the group seeking to complete the task or achieve some limited goal will gain an awareness of the satisfaction that comes from simply trying something new, setting a goal and the sense of expectation in seeing a plan unfold.

Chart 9-4
R = Realization -- Goal Formation
(3. Trying   7. Implementing   11. Integrating)

Low Realization	High Realization
Coercion	Achievement
Passivity	Commitment
Guidance	Fulfillment
Apathy/Withdrawal	Takes Responsibility
Manipulation	Eagerness
Resentment	Self-determination
Resistance	Enthusiasm
Disinterest	Goal Integration
Irresponsibility	Excitement
Indifference	Well-being
Rivalry	Involvement
Diffused Goals	Creativity

At the sectoral level, step 7 endeavors to generate an opportunity for village leaders to practice the skills needed to implement, monitor, and follow through. Specialized training in problem solving, goal setting, and action research strategies should provide such incipient leadership with the opportunity to experience the sense of achievement and urgency that comes from seeing a project actually implemented from beginning to end in a larger group (sector) setting.

The ultimate goal of "integrating," during step 11, is the internalization of these skills and behaviors associated with actually taking personal responsibility for a project and seeing it through to completion, that sense of deep commitment that comes to a person who totally identifies with the project being implemented. This step implies not only a sense of enthusiasm for some goal, but the actual integration of the individual's goals with his/her village's goals; also, the excitement and high productivity that comes from the feeling that one is free, not coerced; genuinely responsible without unfair persuasion; and self-determining, not forced.

Interdependency

The key component of the fourth dimension of the leadership/group development process is control and evaluation aimed at understanding the process by which groups of people build the mechanisms needed to increase effectiveness and progress. This dimension focuses on the issue of how best to structure evaluation, quality controls, and improvement over time; how to instill internal commitment to change and increase effectiveness; and how to release human potential through useful feedback and evaluation. It is at this step that significant individual, group, and institutional growth begin to take place. The opposite of interdependency is dependency (submission and discouragement) or counter-dependency (tension and hostility). Groups that have tried to implement a project and have failed feel impotent. Groups that have succeeded feel the exhilaration of accomplishment and competence.

Chart 9-5
I = Interdependency -- Control and Evaluation
(4. Accomplishment   8. Testing   12. Evaluating)

Low Realization	High Realization
Dependency	Freedom
Inadequacy	High self-esteem
Rebellion/war	Participation
Tension	Mutuality
Submission	Potency
Defeat	Synergism
Uselessness	Adequacy
Discouragement	Efficacy
Power Struggles	Informality
Restrictions	Leadership Sharing

In step 4 the goal of leadership training and development is to generate some awareness that the group can accomplish a task. The role of the RDF is crucial at this awareness stage since the feelings of inadequacy, dependency, and uncertainty still tend to dominate. In a society characterized by authoritarian leadership styles, legalistic rules and procedures, power struggles, and counter-dependency, there is little room for a spirit of interdependency to emerge among members of the group. In steps 1, 2, and 3 the RDF helps to increase an awareness that through a process of desiring, searching, and trying, specific projects with positive results will emerge. In this early phase, when the dominant norms of distrust, suspicion, and skepticism underlie most interpersonal relationships, there is little willingness to evaluate carefully or to test out openly the success or failure of a project. If the project fails, the old patterns of apathy and discouragement will be reinforced. If the project succeeds, some group members may become aware that they have, in fact, accomplished a task. Yet in this early phase this sense of accomplishment may be weakened by the realization that it was the RDF, or outsider, who is most responsible for the accomplishment. From a group development point of view, the reader should recognize how important project success is in developing these early feelings of success. Small projects with high probability of success constitute the formula for stimulating this positive awareness.

It is at the sectoral level of step 8 that the group may actually begin to practice the skills needed to create an environment of interdependency. The development of higher levels of trust and interpersonal competence required to plan and implement a project by themselves with only peripheral help from an RDF can set the stage for some open testing of where the members of the group are, why they are succeeding or failing, how they may begin to improve themselves and move to a higher level of competence. This step of testing is a delicate point in a group's development for it is here that a group begins the process of project evaluation.

If the process of testing is characterized by power struggles, formal rules and regulations, and an environment of defensiveness and tension, then the responses of hostility and counter dependency will be reinforced. If, on the other hand, the process of testing encourages a participative mode of interaction, with some freedom to confront in non evaluative ways, to interact spontaneously with no need for formal procedures and rules, then the new responses of high self-esteem, confidence, and cooperation will be strengthened.

In the final analysis, it is step 12 where the whole process of group leadership training and development reaches full circle. It is here that a group of individuals attempts to internalize the skills needed to evaluate themselves without outside interference or structure. There is much evidence in the literature of rural reconstruction documenting the utility and appropriateness of interacting, patterns that emphasize leadership sharing, freedom of choice in decision-making, openness, and self-awareness. The type of evaluation described here implies an openness to a review of all aspects of the process so far discussed. Once the process of self-evaluation, group-evaluation, and institution- evaluation is perceived to be not only useful and appropriate, but even absolutely necessary, then the locked-in potential for growth and improvement can be released. As feelings of impotence, fatalism, power struggles, and game playing are replaced by feelings of efficacy and confidence, a sense of being needed and the freedom to be yourself, then, and only then, will the individual's, group's, or institution's full potential begin to emerge. That is the exciting challenge facing rural development facilitators as they seek to introduce sustainable change.

The Process of Making Villagers Action Research Oriented:
The previous section has sought to conceptualize the process of helping villagers develop their competencies in problem solving and project implementation. There are two aspects to this process: (1) the need to help villagers become RDFs themselves, to become researchers and implementors in developing their own skills and competencies and (2) the challenge of recruiting and nurturing local leaders who can play a positive role in developing these problem solving competencies.

Helping Villagers to Become Their Own Researchers:

The above conceptualization of how to develop problem solving groups can lay the foundation upon which a process is institutionalized that helps villagers implement this process on their own. This process has three distinct aspects to it: search, discover and capacity building:

Search: The search occurs when villagers have identified problems that are significant and important to them personally. The reflection on such problems often stimulates tremendous energy and community involvement. I have found that people only really begin to search, to find answers when they have identified the questions clearly in their minds, have a problem, a concern, a need that motivates the search. RDFs can play an important role in stimulating people's awareness of the questions that need an answer, that provoke a search for answers. This is the first step in the capacity building process.

Discovery: Learning happens best when villagers are given a chance to discover the knowledge, the skill, the new competency by chance, through a process that does not hurt one's pride, is not embarrassing, nor contrary to the way things should be organized. Self-discovery is a process that few villagers have experienced. Too often RDFs are too quick to solve the problem, show them the solution, do the thinking and analyzing for them. Effective RDFs are those who create environments where such individual discovery on the part of villagers is a reoccurring experience.

Capacity Building: There is a great need to establish opportunities to develop one's capacity. Often it is not what the RDF or villager might do individually, but more important what they are trying to do together. When there is a relationship, there is trust and appreciation for each others point of view, and often a magical serendipity can emerge through this kind of interaction. Often the first ideas presented will be unacceptable, inappropriate, hair-brained schemes that simply ignore the realities of the situation. If the process of capacity building is appropriately structured, such early efforts may still be important, for they give both the RDF and the villagers some time to come to understand where each is coming from, and gradually as they come to learn more of each others knowledge base, and the reasons why they do things as they do, real learning will begin.

RDFs must understand that before a peasant will accept new ideas, such ideas need to be explained in terms that are understandable, that are part of their own vocabulary, and if possible using words from their native tongue. Too often, RDFs assume that because peasants appear to understand English, Spanish, French, even Kiswhahili, that what you say to them is intelligible.

I remember interviewing a group of women in a small village in Upper Egypt, who had just had a three hour discussion of the use of oral rehydration packets. It became all too clear that these peasant women had not understood what the Egyptian health worker from Cairo was trying to communicate. Highly educated and raised in Lower Egypt, the health worker simply was unaware of the linguistic and cultural differences that separated these villagers from this sophisticated urbanite from Cairo. She was a *Khawaga* (a foreigner) to them, for while she was speaking Arabic, her Arabic lacked any appreciation for the word forms, slang and the idioms, even the parables and thought processes that characterized the *Sa'idis* (the people of Upper Egypt).

Before peasants can evaluate and adopt an idea, this new idea must be connected to peasants' own mental constructs, there must be a word that reflects the idea. Until the idea is truly comprehended by the peasant, discussions using the RDF's language will lead to superficial acceptance at best, and actual misunderstanding and confusion and even rejection at worse. Generally when peasants reject the ideas presented to them, it is often difficult to determine if the rejection is due to a lack of intelligibility or if the rejection is based upon the peasants good sense of what is possible and what is not possible, given the world in which they must live. Either way, idea rejection must not be seen as stubbornness or stupidity but as a perfectly logical process that reflects the RDFs inability to make his or her ideas intelligible and appropriate for the community. Of course even more dangerous, are the peasants that appear to accept an idea, not wishing to offend or confront the guest in their village. This kind of adoption is very common, but again is part of the challenge of making the idea intelligible. Until a peasant truly understands the idea (described in their own native language), has reflected on the implications of such an idea on their culture, social structures and community interactions through a series of community discussions, and clearly sees the advantages and the disadvantages of the idea by allowing such an idea to be debated and challenged openly, then any acceptance by the community will be doomed to failure. Only when an RDF has been a part of these discussions, has heard the opposition's arguments in their own language, and has some appreciation for the disadvantages of such new ideas, will the community begin to share their feelings, their concerns, their ideas and their commitments with the RDF.

The Challenge of Effective Rural Leadership

The effectiveness of any rural development project is clearly dependent upon competent and committed leadership. The literature is full of examples of different styles of leadership in rural development efforts, some of which were proven to be effective and some detrimental. In this stage of rural development, we have been looking at the relationship that must exist between the RDF and community leaders. Also we have been seeking to analyze the process by which local leaders are identified, recruited, motivated, and trained if this second stage is to be effective in stimulating a self-sustaining process of development in a village community.

An understanding of rural leadership requires some understanding of the patterns of collaboration and conflict found in rural villages. Only through collaboration among individuals will there be enough unity of purpose to maintain a project. Competition and conflict, even acquiescence and apathy, all forms of counter dependency and dependency, characterize the interactive patterns within and among village groupings. In many societies there are specific cultural manifestations of conflict stemming from the concept of honor and "face." It is based upon the notion of a "limited good," which generally is obtained only at others' expense. As in a zero-sum game, the success of one person is a threat to all the other players, a characteristic that generates competition and jealousy. One's status in a village setting is often based upon the ability and willingness to use force. This does not necessarily mean force is resorted to frequently. It is enough to create the impression that one is willing and able to use force. Generosity is demonstrated not to the general public, but toward individuals who will then be obliged to render their support. Blood feuds, a form of one-upmanship, including revenge for a previous defeat or insult are common. Such feuds often become very long, involved, and explosive, but they continue even when people are aware that after so much trouble, even multiple killings, with their accompanying expenses, pain, and sorrow, they will still have nothing tangible to show. A person whose status and reputation are increasing attracts followers and allies who hope to benefit; but such a leader also attracts the jealousy and fear of others who are likely to band together behind the scenes to plot strategies to limit or reduce him. In such an environment, collaboration comes slowly, often requiring an outside arbitrator with great sensitivity and patience. Many skills are necessary for resolving problems and managing conflict situations in a rural community, but of all skills, the art of knowing how to work with people within the constructs of their cultural values and expectations is of foremost importance. Essential to this skill is knowing how to listen, being sensitive to conflicting perceptions of reality, being empathetic to other points of view, and knowing how to communicate with others in ways that do not produce defensiveness.

Rural development projects can change many things in a community, but if the people themselves do not change, self-sustaining development will be very difficult. In the final analysis, development of a community is functionally correlated to individual development -- their awareness, sensitivities, knowledge, and skills. This is the challenge of a RDF seeking to encourage and stimulate effective local leadership and small problem solving groups in a village setting.

A Case Study in Women Problem Solving Group Development in Bolivia

Between 1991 and 1995, a group of Aymara Indian women from the village of Ayamaya, Bolivia began a process of change, in cooperation with two RDFs (Wilma Johnson and Lidia Choque Hoyle). The Aymara women are faced with the challenge of adjusting to a painful transition from ancient systems of barter and exchange to a modern cash economy and wage labor system that sends their husbands off the cities and greatly increases their own work responsibilities on the family farm. The women of this village came to see the value of literacy, the importance of access to credit, and the need for greater autonomy as they participated in a group development process, organized and supported by the RDFs.

These RDFs sought to help these peasant women to reflect together on ways that they could solve their most pressing problems. They gradually came to see that any improvement in their health and well-being would require changes in the social and economic relationships between men and women in the village. The strategy developed focused on negotiation and collaboration, rather than on confrontation. Through a 3-4 year process, some 40-50 women established a weekly discussion group in which consciousness raising through reflective dialogue was first emphasized, then leadership and group solidarity skills became dominant. In time, various extension workers, representatives of different NGOs and community development workers provided appropriate training in agriculture, primary health care, micro-credit systems, literacy and family planning. Within a year of their first meetings, the RDFs provided access to limited credit sources that were used to finance small income generating projects.

A new social energy was seen among these women and their relationship with their husbands changed as the men perceived benefit to themselves and their families from the income generating projects. The model of this community clearly follows the stages identified in the Village Problem Solving Group Process outline in the previous section. Clearly the process of group formation instilled in the woman's self awareness, consciousness raising, group solidarity and increased commitment. As their confidence increased, they were more willing to engage in literacy training, taking a risk in obtaining a loan, and seeking additional information about health, sexual reproduction, and ways of negotiating and persuading their husbands that a pregnancy did not have to happen every year.

This broadened knowledge, increased income, added confidence and new status did not emerge overnight. It took many months, if not years. Both men and women interacting over time developed new attitudes, new roles, new relationships and new options. Thus was the women's quality of life improved over time. Note the following changes: (1) In 1991, only 56 percent of the women could sign their names, add or subtract figures, yet by 1995, 100 percent of the group could perform these basic tasks. In 1991 none of the women in the group rode or owned a bicycle, by 1995, over 70 percent were riding bicycles and 20 percent owned their own bicycle. In 1991 only 16 percent had traveled to La Paz, while by 1995, 52 percent had been to the big city. By 1995, 52 percent of the women had three loans or more, 36 percent had two loans and only 12 percent had only one loan. In 1991, only 16 percent of the married women had not lost at least one child to diarrhea and dehydration, 81 percent of the deaths occurred before the second birthday, 29 percent between 2-5, and 10 percent after the age of 6. When the women were asked what was the most important lessons learned from the Women's Group discussion, 40 percent mentioned family planning and reproductive health, 24 percent mentioned the loans for income projects, 20 percent saw reading and writing as most important, and 16 percent mentioned training in agriculture, veterinary classes, handicrafts, knitting and sewing.[7]

This case study demonstrates the power of group development processes that emphasizes group dynamics, consciousness raising, capacity building and community interaction.

Conclusion

With the implementation of the activities and strategies identified with the processes of participation, problem solving, and capacity building, we are now ready to review the third stage of rural development: The Stage of Community Empowerment and Local Institution Building.

---

[1] Robert Chambers, et al., *Farmer First: Farmer Innovation and Agricultural Research*, (London, Intermediate Technology, 1989); Stan Burkey, *People First: A Guide to Self-Reliant, Participatory Rural Development* (London: Zed Books, 1993); Eric Dudley, *The Critical Villager: Beyond Community Participation*, (London: Routledge, 1993); Salmon, *Listen to the People* (1988); and James B. Mayfield, *Go to the People*, (1986).

[2] For an explanation of the use of Force Field Analysis, see: James B. Mayfield, *Workbook for Rural Development Facilitators*, (1997).

[3] One book that has been very helpful in clarifying my own ideas about these issues is Eric Dudley, *The Critical Villager: Beyond Community Participation*, (London: Routledge, 1993. Some of the anecdotal material used in this chapter has come from this very insightful book.

[4] The typology of participation is adapted from Sherry Arnstein, "A Ladder of Citizen Participation," *Journal of the American Institute of Planners* 35 (July 1969), pp. 216-224.

[5] Mayfield, *Handbook, op.cit.*

[66] This section is an edited version first developed in James B. Mayfield, Go to the People (1986).

[7] Wilma Johnson, "Ayamaya Women's Program: Empowerment, Income Generation, and Reproductive Health Options", (research paper submitted for Political Science 537, University of Utah, June 1996).

Chapter 10

Stage Three of Rural Development
Local Institution Building, Empowerment, Networking and Coalition Building

Participation as described in Chapter Nine is often defined as an administrative process in which groups of villagers determine their needs and concerns and then seek to plan and implement various projects structured to solve their more immediate problems. Many of these activities are related to effective administration of scarce resources and the management of a process of project implementation. Rural Development, of course, is more than an administrative process in which central government officials or outside donors transfer technology and resources into rural areas or simply a process by which groups of villagers work together to meet their basic needs in health, sanitation, water or literacy. Development in the long-run implies change and the essence of change is conflict.

If RDFs are to be helpful in encouraging village members to be significantly involved in the implementation of a village development program, they must recognize that different levels and types of participation and community empowerment are appropriate depending on the stage of rural development that a given community finds itself. Let us now in this chapter seek to emphasize the political dimensions of participation in which empowerment and coalition building become the dominant forms of villager involvement.

Early development theorists tended to hold a "Harmony Model" that assumed a harmony of interests among the inhabitants of a rural area regardless of their socio-economic status in the village. By bringing the great landowners, the small farmers, and landless peasants together, community development was the process by which a spirit of unity and community cohesion could be inspired among all groups generating a feeling of cooperation for change. This is how community development was often conceptualized in the 1950s/60s.   In reality most peasants, through long and painful experience, have come to expect a "conflict model" of interaction that emphasizes a zero-sum approach to the village society. The elite have what the non-elite will never have. The realities of these inequities generally foster a sense of apathy and acceptance. On the basis of this set of assumptions change only comes through violence and conflict. Stability and peace require acceptance and conformity to the world as it is. It is somewhat strange that many scholars still cling to the image of peasants as apathetic, fatalistic, and resistant to change. This view flies in the face of strong peasant movements in Russia, China, Algeria and Indochina.

Luis Taruc, an important leader in the Huk peasant-based movement in the Philippines, described his strategy for involving peasants as follows: "I first sounded out the people about their problems and grievances, and then spoke to them in their own terms. Instead of carrying out frontal assaults on the ramparts of capital, I attacked a case of usury here, an eviction there, the low crop price elsewhere. These were things that we could fight and around which the people could win small, but enormously encouraging victories.

I had to prove to the people that our organization and its leaders were of them and close to them. I sat down with them in their homes, shared their simple food, helped with household chores. I walked in the mud with them, helped them catch fish, crabs and shellfish, worked with them in the fields. It was not hard for me, nor was it new to me. I was merely rejoining my people."

This quotation is presented not to challenge RDFs to become revolutionaries but to challenge them to do some soul-searching about what it takes to gain a peasant's trust? Just how do the peasants perceive their RDF? What is the level of commitment and dedication needed to succeed in the work? Can we learn from successful organizers what it takes to reach peasants, penetrate their minds and souls, and release their potential energy.

Local indigenous RDFs (not outsiders from another country) who have a direct and personal interest in such political reforms should also be sensitive to the dilemmas of social and political change. Preparing a given community or rural area for such politically sensitive issues takes time best left to the third stage in the process of rural development. It is during this third stage of rural development when the emergence of peasant consciousness generates a desire for change and the development of peasant awareness of how such changes are both possible and necessary. The approach defined in this book rejects the reactionary and passive consequences of the "Harmony Model" and the bloody and revolutionary consequences of the "Conflict Model." Somewhere in between these extremes is what I am calling the "Reflective/Confrontive Model" in which confrontation, organization, and reform dominate a process of gradual but meaningful local institution building, empowerment and coalition building. There are too many examples of this moderate course of action to deny its utility and appropriateness.

Problems related to needed land-reform against a local landowner or government policies that pay farmers an unfair price for their crops, or the unfair distribution of government services to an isolated village are all very significant issues that cry out for solution, yet the RDF must understand that participation and empowerment to deal with those kinds of problems require political skills in coalition building, resource mobilization and empowerment strategies that are difficult to implement and will take time to develop. Without such political skills, pre-mature efforts to force reform or needed change often deteriorates into a lose-

lose situation in which violence and repression becomes the norm. These words should not be interpreted to imply that communities should not confront nor seek to change unjust and exploitative situations, merely that such major changes require a level of organization and political skill that must be developed gradually over time.

If an RDF becomes involved in such political issues too early in the process of village development, he or she is certain to experience failure, certainly in the short-run. It should also be clear enough that an RDF who is not a citizen of the country where he or she is working should never get involved in such politically sensitive activities. In the long-run, it must be the villagers themselves who must seek to bring about meaningful change in the political and economic situation of their village. Many such efforts are doomed to failure from the start because the people are not prepared. Successful efforts in confronting those who would prevent the disadvantaged of an area or a society from achieving their long-term interests require careful planning and preparation. A gradual process of empowerment is necessary if the villagers are to have the skills, the confidence, the political will and economic resources needed to challenge the obstacles and barriers to meaningful and equitable change and reform. Let us consider what this process of empowerment entails.

Section One
The Process of Empowerment

Powerlessness of poor people in isolated rural villages arises through a process whereby valued identities and roles on the one hand and valuable resources on the other are denied -- all of which are prerequisite to the exercise of interpersonal influence and effective social functioning. Much of the challenge in dealing with the problems of the people in most rural areas is that such communities are haunted by the severe limitations of their self-determination and an inevitable sense of dependency. The disadvantaged, the peasant and the other rural poor, have for decades, if not centuries, been subjected to negative treatment from the larger society to such an extent that powerlessness in the group is pervasive and crippling. One of the more insidious of these consequences is an overriding sense of one's powerlessness to direct one's own life in a course reflective of one's values and standards of personal gratification.

In recent years there has been a strong call for a process of de bureaucratization, greater flexibility among local officials in order to adjust the rules and procedures and to maintain a maximum range of discretionary behavior among such officials for the benefit of the disadvantaged. In the early 1980s, several scholars advocated a program of reorientation for local administrators, thus helping to make local bureaucracies work for the disadvantaged and the poor instead of against. The process known as "bureaucratic reorientation" encompassed some combination of changes in the structure of the bureaucracy, the procedures of operation, and the attitudes of local officials towards the local citizenry.[1]

Others are now arguing that administrative reform and extensive training of local officials will simply not be enough. Unfortunately, local administrative systems do not modify their behaviors very readily. Recent studies in local administrative behavior suggest that significant changes are not likely unless the upper echelons of the organization demand such changes, then appropriately monitor and also reward such new orientations or unless the local communities are able to force such changes in administrative behavior by making such officials accountable to the community.[2]

Empowerment is best conceptualized in terms of individual and community power building, district and provincial networking, and processes of coalition building and mass movement integration. Bertrand Russell has observed that the concept of power is fundamental in the social sciences in the same way that energy is fundamental to physics. Yet the social sciences are not a single discipline but many, and there is disparate conceptualizations of power depending upon whether one deals with it from a psychological, economic, political, sociological, or even philosophical perspective. Power is most often studied as a macrosystem concept, useful in understanding détente, apartheid, or urban revolts but is generally limited in providing insights into the chronic unemployment of a landless peasant, his wife's chronic illness and his children's illiteracy. However, from my perspective, power may be the key concept linking microsystem and macrosystem processes. In fact, people generally described as socially disadvantaged, illiterate, incompetent, even mentally ill, may be better perceived as persons deprived of adequate social solutions to the problems they face not only in their daily lives, but also in their own personal growth development, with powerlessness at this level better conceptualized as a lack of self-esteem and personal efficacy. Furthermore, even community-level disruptive behavior often stems from a lack of power and influence to provide adequate social solutions to the problems of both community growth and personal development.

What is important in this analysis of empowerment are the many factors and levels of concern that must be considered in determining how best to implement a process of empowerment. I will be arguing that there are at least four levels in which empowerment can be defined, conceptualized and implemented in a given situation: (1) the level where the individual is allowed to develop his/her own sense of self-esteem and personal confidence through some type of local community building experiences, including village discussion groups, interpersonal and group process training, and opportunities to interact with others at the village level in experiencing the broadening impact of consciousness raising and increased awareness of one's community and its environment, (2) the level where groups of villagers are allowed to develop their abilities and capacities to solve their own problems through local institutions, using local management and administrative processes, local resource mobilization strategies, and competencies in project planning, implementation and evaluation, (3) the level where clusters of village communities, generally organized into groups of formal and informal local leaders who develop district-wide linkage systems which connect their own individual communities into the broader political and administrative environment. This level of empowerment requires the development of management and political skills among a significant cadre of local leaders willing to expand their network of contacts and sources of support beyond their own immediate village community areas, and finally (4) the level where networks of village leaders broaden their focus out to the provincial, national and even international environment. This is the level of coalition building, an empowerment process that gradually integrates such coalitions into broader mass movements. Here the emphasis is on policy and administrative change and reform. The dynamics of this level of empowerment reflect significant levels of risk, political confrontation, and active pressure on political systems that support and reinforce processes of inequity, exploitation, and the violation of human rights. Each of these levels of empowerment require some careful planning and conceptualization. Let us now review these levels in some greater detail.

Individual Level of Empowerment

Powerlessness is defined at the individual level as the inability to manage emotions, skills, knowledge, and/or material resources in a way that allows one to achieve one's goals and values in a self-satisfying way. The power deficiency so often seen among the landless and the disadvantaged peasantry stems from a complex and dynamic interrelationship between the disadvantaged person and his relatively hostile social environment.

Growing up in a disadvantaged community can have a profound impact on the social, economic and political attitudes of such people. Various socialization experiences reinforce notions of apathy, powerlessness, and frustration. Societal forces may block individual access to the resources and experiences needed for the development of interpersonal and technical skills. Given the centrality of these kinds of negative experience in the lives of the disadvantaged and the poor, empowerment may be seen as an important goal and process for development work in the disadvantage areas of the Third World. Empowerment is defined here as a process whereby the development facilitator engages in a set of activities with these disadvantaged community members that aim to reduce the powerlessness that has been created by generations of exploitation and discrimination.

There is an assumption that each individual in the society will proceed through a certain sequence of events that constitute a hostile or benevolent cycle of interactions. Generally, most individuals experience a complex series of events monitored by the family or surrogate family that involve the self, significant others, and the environment. These experiences result in the acquisition of personal resources such as a positive self-concept, cognitive skills, health, and physical intellectual competencies. These personal resources lead to the development of certain interpersonal and technical skills such as sensitivity to the feelings and needs of others, organization skills, and leadership ability. The personal resources as well as the interpersonal and technical skills can then be used to perform effectively in valued social roles such as parent, farmer, employee, or community leader.

The Community Level of Empowerment

From the individual perspective, powerlessness is often defined as the inability to obtain and use resources to achieve personal goals. However, from the level of community groups, powerlessness is better seen as the inability to use resources to achieve collective goals. Disadvantaged groups, especially in rural areas, are often prevented from completing some task or achieving some goal due to power deficiencies existent because of that community's lack of confidence and influence. In Chapter Nine above, it was pointed out how careful an RDF needs to be in introducing some project or solution, which may have little chance of being implemented successfully. Such experiences in project failure clearly reinforce these attitudes of apathy, acquiescence, and withdrawal from community involvement.

In the case of many minorities or disadvantaged groups of poor people, there is greater likelihood that the initial growth and development of such communities will be limited. Past experiences will have reinforced certain destructive elements inimical to maximum community development due to the stigma and inferiority of poverty and village life communicated from the larger society. Such messages constitute an indirect power blockage that stifles the development of community identity and cohesion. Many of the more disadvantaged and isolated villagers tend to see their present condition as "right" or at least inevitable and therefore make no effort to exert power at all. The powerlessness that they exhibit can be considered power absence rather than power failure.

It should be clear from the foregoing that the concept of empowerment may be an appropriate goal for social development intervention in any community or with any individual or group, especially when there is the pervasive condition of systematic, structural, or institutionalized discrimination and exploitation. It seeks to confront and challenge various forms of community apathy and inferiority that are imposed or reinforced, sometimes subtly and sometimes not so subtly, by the broader, external society. Let us now look at empowerment as a process of networking and coalition-building in which political influence and organization dominate.

Section Two
Rural Development Facilitators (RDFs) and the Process of Empowerment

In the early stage of problem solving already described in the last chapter, empowerment activities should be directed toward overcoming the feelings of apathy and frustration found in the disadvantaged villagers in order to engage the community members in the process of finding solutions to their most basic needs. Succeeding stages in that process also relate to the location and removal of obstacles and the identification and reinforcement of supports to effective problem-solving. Thus empowerment activities must be designed to insure that the problem solving process itself serves to counteract the perceptions of inadequacy and impotency.

The RDF must demonstrate an understanding of the dynamics of powerlessness and its consequences in order to develop some expertise and practical skills in the service of empowerment. These activities can generally have one or more of the following goals, especially at the individual and community levels of empowerment:

1. Helping the villagers perceive themselves as causal agents
in achieving a solution to their problem or problems
2. Helping the villagers to perceive the RDF facilitator as having
knowledge and skills which the villagers can use.
3. Helping the villagers to perceive the RDF as a peer collaborator or
partner in the problem-solving effort.
4. Helping the villagers to perceive the "power structure"
as multi-polar, characterized by varying degrees of support and opposition
to the status quo and therefore open to some
influence for change.

Thus, the overall goal is that of helping village communities that have been subjected to systematic and pervasive mistreatment and exploitation to perceive themselves as capable of exerting influence in the world of other people and capable of bringing about some desired effect. It should be made clear that this does not deny the power and the significance of external forces in the creation of their problems or problem situations; however, it does place an overarching emphasis on the inherent weakness of "giving up" and on the latent potential in isolated villages to deal more effectively and more creatively with their own problems including oppression and exploitation. This emphasis on individuals as causal agents does not necessarily imply that they are the cause of their problems or that their problems can be solved by merely effecting change in themselves. On the contrary, it focuses greater attention on the complexities of the multiple, contributory factors in any problem situation. Thus the conceptualization of the individual as a causal entity tends to emphasize the processes and interventions that can effect change or solve problems rather than the inimical forces that created the problem in the first place.

During the 1950s and 1960s the more traditional approaches to community development tended to teach the individual how to adjust to the "realities" of living in a given village community. There were some basic assumptions associated with this traditional approach, including the assumptions that government officials knew what was best for the villagers, that central government programs would easily solve the problems of the village, that villages were generally homogeneous with little social or economic differences within their communities, and thus that consensus and cooperation among villagers was natural and that conflict and disagreement within a village community was unnatural and to be avoided at all costs.

In contrast, village development of the 1980s and 1990s assesses the problems of a village in the context of the larger political and economic systems of society. Development is much more apt to be defined in political terms, with much greater emphasis being given to constraints and obstacles to development in a given community. Village development today requires that villagers be encouraged to empower themselves, to engage in political activities so that they can begin to change some of the inequities in society. While many private voluntary organizations have been hesitant to engage in politics, especially in the first two stages of rural development (trust building and capacity building). Nevertheless, during the third stage (local institution building) of rural development, if villagers are to become autonomous and self-reliant, they must be willing to challenge and confront the economic, social and political forces that are preventing them from achieving their goals for a better life.

Local indigenous RDFs who are active in their community need to recognize the importance of establishing and maintaining a personal network, especially involving people who may be in a position to help the disadvantaged members of their community. Equally important is the importance of achieving credibility and standing within the community, and developing leadership among the members of the community being served. From a longer-term perspective, effective RDFs must seek to develop relationships, more involvement and cooperation among those involved in policy reform, learning to apply and understand systems theory to problems, and understand planning and its relationship to action.

Many people would argue that RDFs can foster real and lasting changes only if they have an impact on the overall milieu of people's lives. While RDFs by definition will be working both with individuals and groups of individuals, in the final analysis, the context of development requires some awareness of the community and the broader environment in which the processes of development are being introduced. Some initial steps that an RDF might follow: (1) RDFs can demonstrate a spirit of activism by becoming involved with special-interest groups found in rural areas: peasants, farmers, women, and other rural workers, (2) RDFs can become activists on the local, district, regional and national levels. For example, RDFs could work with local PTAs in their efforts to communicate community concerns about the quality and relevancy of village-level education to the educational professionals at all levels within a Ministry of Education, (3) RDFs can play a crucial role in advocating fairness in the distribution of government and non-government services in a given area. Becoming an advocate for a particular ethnic group or a cluster of villages often ignored, are examples of this advocacy role. Agricultural, educational and health services should no longer be tailor-made just for the higher status people of a given community.

During the trust building and capacity building stages of rural development, empowerment tends to emphasize community awareness and local problem solving group development. Eventually, however, RDFs need to see empowerment in its broader context in which individuals, groups and communities become linked to the broader environment with the role of the RDF becoming more concerned with "combining forces" rather than giving aid and assistance. Again the distinction may be subtle but it is unquestionably important in the pursuit of empowerment. The approach being advocated requires that eventually development must be conceptualized more as a **linkage building or coalition building** process rather than merely the distribution of assistance more reflective of welfare and handouts.

Section Three
The Local Institution and Linkage Building
Level of Empowerment [3]

During the third stage of rural development, the key question for the RDF is how to help the local community build and sustain local institutions by harnessing and creatively using limited resources. RDFs at this stage, will generally be working in conjunction with various government agencies or non-government organizations often in various administrative capacities at the district, provincial and even national levels. Kessler[4] points out that the ability to choose agencies with which to ally from among the diversity of organizations in a "pluralistic" environment may be critical to success in helping communities create linkages with outside organizations. To do this, RDFs must be skilled in **networking and linkage building**; they must also be able to assess accurately the ideological orientation of potential allies. These are skills that are not typically covered in development administration courses, yet they may be essential in establishing self-sustaining local institutions.

A number of theories and research efforts can assist us in developing the social technology to address the challenges of supporting the development, maintenance, and growth of large numbers of local community institutions and the longer-term goal of establishing networks of support groups for sustainable development at a given district or provincial area. Relevant theories that can provide important insights for RDFs concerned with these issues include: general and open systems theory, network theory, social learning theory, adult education, and behavior theory. An understanding of these theories will aid the RDF and other community development workers in designing the support system for community based and community development initiatives. Let us quickly review some of basic components of these theories.

General systems theory[5] has been applied to human social organizations in a number of different settings.[6] Open systems theory assists us in understanding what it takes for new institutions to develop, maintain themselves and grow, by examining the flow of resources or energy needed. The basic open system concept, applied to local institution building (self help groups, for example), tends to suggest that local institutions must receive various inputs from its environment (e.g., information, potential members, financial resources, and political support) if it is to be sustainable over time. Such inputs are transformed through the internal workings of the institution and become throughputs. Within the institution are various structures and functions performed that constitute subsystems with the purpose of using energy or resources to either maintain the institution (i.e., making sure the institution remains viable) or to produce the intended goals of the institution.

Organizational activities result in intended and unintended outcomes, or outputs upon leaving the institution (services provided, goods produced, changes in behavior or community standards). Such outputs become part of the environment, which in turn send new information or feedback (an input) back to the community institution. Community organizations, like all systems, have forces that push toward disorganization and "death" (entropy). To survive, community institutions must counter these processes through some form of "negative entropy," importing more energy from the environment than they will use. A system will first spend its energy collecting inputs or resources, later transforming them for the maintenance of the organization and then for production of goods and services. Community organizations expend high levels of energy collecting inputs (recruiting members, mobilizing resources) and transforming them into throughput (activities and programs). These organizations must build a highly efficient capacity to gain access to and use resources in order to survive.

Community institutions must be capable of receiving information on their environments such as assessing community needs and strengths. Negative feedback -- criticism from the community, or a failed project -- hopefully allows the system to make adjustments to enhance its ability to maintain itself. Local community institutions require information concerning the resources in their environment (e.g., grants, technical assistance, other groups they could work with, innovations) and their immediate environment's conditions (e.g., community needs and information on competing systems).

New institutions, especially in a village setting need information about their own internal functioning in order to make appropriate adjustments. Key indicators need to be identified (e.g., needs and concerns of members, bookkeeping records to ensure appropriate expenditure of funds, quality and accountability of management, etc.), and regular monitoring is necessary. Effective RDFs must learn to use various interviewing schedules, perhaps even survey-guided feedback methods on key components of the organization's internal functioning. Such internal monitoring and consistent assessment work are crucial if such village institutions are to be sustainable.

Network theory and analysis provide a paradigm to examine networks. The structure of the network can be examined in terms of its density (frequency and completeness of interaction) and its components (e.g., nodes, linkages, brokers). Networks are interconnected and interactive social relations among various nodes or points. A node can be an individual or an organization. Fischer[7] has described networks as a "specified set of links among social actors." Network theory also examines the flow of resources. A network can be defined by the recipients involved in transactions, where common resources are exchanged.[8] Reciprocity is important to the network in order to maintain its balance and viability. The transactions within the network are often indirect and not always mutual.[9] The network, therefore, needs to encourage within itself as many combinations of exchanges as possible. There is also a norm or a mutually held expectation of reciprocity that overshadows all relations, among individuals and organizations within a network.[10] An important strategy for a facilitative process (perhaps initiated by the RDF) is to provide many sustained and unrestricted opportunities for exchange, sharing, or interaction among various key participants (e.g., community organizations, village leaders, technical assistance providers (NGOs), government agencies at all levels, etc.).

The distribution of resources within many networks is often controlled by what are called "brokers." RDFs seeking to expand networks of support groups (government agencies, NGOs, etc.) must learn to play the broker-role which can be crucial in mobilizing resources and systems of support and influence.[11] Network density is another important consideration for the design of a broader village development alliance or mass movement. Density is determined by the number of lines of exchange or communication within the network. Dense networks frequently exchange among themselves; there is greater overlap among exchanges, and they rarely exchange outside their networks. A cohesive ethnic community would be considered a dense network. Members of less dense networks or ones with "weak ties"[12] often exchange as much or more with individuals and groups outside the network. Cohesive and dense networks provide greater support for its members and rapid communication. According to

Granovetter[13], however, more open kinds of networks are more conducive to the transfer of appropriate technology and other innovations and they provide greater potential for collaboration in a broader context of political influence and support. An enabling system needs to balance the strengths of ties among its members. It appears to be essential to keep the network open to exchanges with other networks, to interact and incorporate other social policy areas, to involve interdisciplinary actors, and to strengthen the sense of community among its members.

Social learning theory[14] and theories of adult education[15] offer numerous insights into how local institution building can be furthered through the development of strategies that build the capacity of local communities through the education and development of citizens. The long-term development of various local institutions according to these theories, will require a training approach that is problem oriented; is based on experiential learning, simulations and actual real life-experiences; is directed by the learner and his/her needs; allows for different learning styles; is sustained and readily accessible as questions and barriers emerge; uses role modeling and peer learning (learning from people like oneself); is proactive; offers on-going support to participants; uses multiple, mutually reinforcing methods; provides incentives for participation; and promotes the adoption of new ideas. Social scientists have begun to document the effectiveness of methods based on these theories for supporting community development corporations,[16] voluntary community organizations and other neighborhood association,[17] health promotion programs[18] and self-help groups.[19]

A Rural District Approach to Networking and Linkage Building in Rural Development

Over the past fifty years a number of strategies have been developed to focus on an intermediate level between the upper stratum of central governments and the lower levels of grassroots efforts usually in individual villages. These mid-range efforts generally focused on regional decentralization, growth centers or some other mixture of district or provincial level programs of implementation. Most of these decentralization efforts emphasized "functional" approaches in which the rural areas of a country were to be integrated into the overall process of national development. A number of scholars quickly noted that such strategies were based on neoclassical assumptions of international development and while economic growth could be encouraged by such an approach, the unintended consequences were to increase socioeconomic inequities, often accentuating both inter- and intra-regional inequalities. The anticipated spread effect of these so-called "growth poles" never materialized as the machinations of urban bias expropriated surplus resources out of the countryside into the urban centers, exacerbating regional areas of poverty and inequalities.[20]

In the 1970s, an Integrated Regional Development Planning (IRDP) approach emerged as a new strategy structured specifically to stimulate growth in the peripheral, rural areas of the LDCs. This approach, very much a central government driven strategy, emphasized communication networks of roads, telephones and railroads, new market centers, financial and credit facilities and networks, service delivery linkages, and increased administrative decentralization. Following the work of Rondinelli and others[21], a number of specific advantages were identified with this new approach: first, by improving the quality of life in the regional capitals, this would hopefully discourage mass migration from the rural areas to the major urban centers. Second, it would allocate more resources out into the rural areas, alleviating pockets of poverty by providing more services in health, education and social welfare. Thirdly, the increased emphasis on marketing, storage and processing of agricultural products would greatly stimulate the local rural economy. Finally, the commitment to greater administrative decentralization was supposed to improve government responsiveness, accountability and efficiency.

Rather predictably, the IRDP approach did stimulate economic growth in many rural areas. Unfortunately, the benefits went mainly to the local elites, landlords and rural and urban business people. Unwin argued: "In a free-market system, it is difficult to see how those with economic and political power are going to be persuaded to relinquish some of the advantages currently accruing to them for the benefit of the urban and rural poor."[22] While the approach ostensibly sought to encourage local participation and grassroots efforts, the reality was quite different. Actually the systems of integration, resource allocation, and services delivered, tended to benefit the wealthy and the powerful. A key problem with this strategy was that it paid scant attention to the distribution of benefits, tended to ignore the power structures and the elite networks that easily dominated the economic activities being stimulated. According to many analysts of this approach, the major weakness of the IRDP approach was its inability to deal with the underlying social, economic, and political realities of the rural areas.

Nearly all systems of government in the LDCs have historically extracted surplus from the peasants through a variety of taxes, pricing systems and cooperative controls. Such integrated development programs, which have characterized most efforts at rural development, simply have failed to confront, to work out strategies, or to encourage systems of political influence, coalitions of the poorer members of the society that can and will confront the realities of exploitation and unfair restrictions. Such strategies are not asking for an equally sharing of the wealth, they are asking for a more equal sharing of opportunity.

During the 1980s, a new approach known as the Territorial Regional Planning Approach gained some prominence in the rural development literature. Spread headed by the research and writing of John Friedman, this approach argued for "territorial integration" in which the resources generated in a given region, province or district would remain within the area for the benefit of the local people. Contrary to the growth pole approach or the IRDP approach, which generally structured economic activities to benefit the core urban areas of society, the Territorial Regional Planning approach argues for a more endogenous form of development, in which local areas pursue territorial integration, defined as "the use of an area's resources by its residents to meet their own needs."[23]

This sub-national approach rejects the more conventional strategies of development that tend to focus on an integration of local systems into the broader systems of the world economy. Much greater emphasis is given to the strengthening of the local economic, political and social systems, in which local leadership, local resource mobilization, and local income generating activities are structured to meet local needs, to reflect grassroots concerns, and to build local capacities. In defining my sub-national approach to development, with its emphasis on broadly defined community empowerment and district level linkage and network building strategies, this book reflects a solid commitment to the role of RDFs who work in clusters of villages usually at the district level. One serious effort to define this sub-national approach suggests the following key elements: First, the processes of rural development must reflect the empowerment of peasants, landless villagers, and other disadvantaged people through grassroots interventions related to local problem solving, improved self-reliance, and community pride. Secondly, is the emphasis on alliance building activities that strengthen the capacities of broader networks and coalitions of such disadvantaged people to confront the structural, social, and economic constraints that reinforce systems of exploitation and extreme poverty.

This is not an easy process, nor will such constraints be eliminated without significant political pressures and reforms. But I am arguing that this is where such forces for change will first begin. Second, such sub national level activities must also reflect a much greater concern for the clearly disadvantaged, the class, gender and ethnic divisions of these rural societies, with specific strategies emphasizing basic needs in health, education, nutrition, and income. Programs that emphasize the role and contribution that women can make in rural development must be encouraged and strengthened. Third, a much greater emphasis should be given to the rural agricultural sector, especially ensuring more favorable pricing and terms of trade for the smaller scale farmers. Increased efforts are needed to structure extension programs, to provide appropriate technology, and to establish adequate credit systems to stimulate and benefit the small farmers who, with proper inputs and support, can greatly increase the productivity and financial well-being of these rural areas. Fourth, local government institutions need greater autonomy and freedom from central government controls. A key to this sub national approach rests on the assumption that local institutions, both public and private, are key in the long-term and sustainable growth of the rural areas of a country. Decentralized decision-making, greater accountability, and increased local resource mobilization and independence must characterize the political and administrative processes of these local areas if social energy and local initiative are to be stimulated.

Specific government policies are needed to protect the local resources of these areas from being confiscated by and exploited for outside interests whether at the provincial, national or international levels. The sub national approach being presented here rests on the assumption that sustainable growth requires that specific rural areas must become as independent and self-reliant as possible, that patterns of productive flows must benefit the local people first, and then if there is surplus, it might then be sent to higher levels in the system. Fifth, and in many ways most important, the sub national, district level approach, has as its major advantage, the ability to build systems of growth, equity and development that are reflective of the local cultures and traditional value systems that provide people with their sense of identity and community spirit, feelings of self-esteem and pride, self-reflected notions of where they are and where they may want to be in the future.

I have no doubt that this characteristic, the ability to preserve and enhance people's sense of who they are, their sense of identity, purpose, and meaning, are absolutely crucial in helping communities of people move through the four levels of empowerment: the individual's sense of self esteem, the community's capacity for self-initiated problem solving, the linkage/networking processes of the district and province, and the coalition and mass movement building efforts that can transcend and in the process, can transform the structural (political, economic and social) constraints that must be confronted and changed if meaningful and appropriate developments are to be implemented.

Professor Friedman has developed a model very similar to the sub national approach I am suggesting. He argues that the most appropriate level of emphasis for rural development is what he is calling the "agropolitan" district, which is generally a geographical unit of some 50,000 people, usually consisting of a number of villages and a single rural market town. He argues that such rural districts are "large enough to meet most of the basic needs of the population out of its own resources . . .[yet]small enough so that the entire population of the area might have reasonable physical access to the center for political decision making, planning and administration"[24] He argues
that the processes of rural development require a more decentralized approach, structured to encourage local economic and political autonomy.

Too many past approaches to rural development tended to stimulate economic growth that benefited the central, more urban areas of a country. Programs of investment, increases in productivity, and resource exploitation were so dominated by local and national elites that the general mass population of a given rural area never benefited from such economic growth. What is needed is an economic orientation that encourages local accumulation and investment of resources, that rewards a broad base of increased productivity, and ensures that surplus is integrated into the local economy in ways that benefit the local communities. Rural development is best founded upon small-scale and labor-intensive kinds of activities that spread the benefits of growth in ways that meet basic human needs and increase opportunities to improve a rural area's overall quality of life. Such decentralized systems of rural development are much more apt to stimulate a more balanced and endogenous form of development.[25] What the sub national approach herein envisioned does, is to reinforce greater inter-dependency (mutually beneficial systems of growth), stimulates greater local coalition-building that challenges exploitative systems of dependency, encourages a more horizontal perspective that better develops local human resources, and establishes political and economic networks that are reflective of local needs and interests.

Friedmann argues that a sub national perspective with its emphasis on local territoriality has a number of definite advantages over highly centralized, top down approaches that have characterized so much of what we call development strategizing: He argues: "Territoriality is one of the important sources of human bonding: it creates a commonweal, linking the present to the past as a fund of common memories (history) and to the future as common destiny. Territoriality nurtures an ethic of care and concern for our fellow citizens and for the environment we share with them."[26]

Both government and non government organizations must play a role in the implementation of these strategies. Again, this book is not arguing that such programs must be based simply on some normative ideal, nor is the argument based upon some naive hope that beneficent governments and local and national elites will see the morality of this approach. In reality, such changes in society will require organizational and political skills, networking capacities, and the establishment of coalition building abilities that may generate conflict, perhaps even violence. However, this sub national perspective has the ability to generate forces for change that do not necessarily lead to violence. In fact, in Unit Four of this book are many examples of sub national programs and interventions that have brought about significant change and reform, using a political approach that emphasizes pressure without violence, influence without corruption, and confrontation without human rights violations. There are thousands of examples of people who have made a difference, working without fanfare, prodding along day in and day out, addressing an injustice here, challenging an exploitative relationship there, and confronting the challenges of life at the village, the town, the district and provincial levels over time. This is where such efforts need our support, where a larger allocation of resources should be made and where the real important processes of rural development must begin. Many might assume that these calls for decentralization and grassroots efforts are nice in theory, but the realities of these areas suggests that local and national elites are much too powerful. Yet, I am arguing that such dominating systems of exploitation, greed, and violence, are not inevitable nor impervious to human will, agency and reflective thought. The sub national model of development implied in this study recognizes this capacity in the human spirit to reflect, to challenge, to organize, and thereby to change such structures over time. History is replete with such examples of individual effort. Let us now review how RDFs may contribute to this broader process of empowerment.

Section Five
The Coalition Building Level of Empowerment:
The Final Dimension of Rural Transformation

Building a coalition of like-minded people: peasants, local RDFs, local teachers, health workers, local officials, associations, donors and others at the local district, provincial and national levels who are interested in the process of rural transformation is a long-term process fraught with many challenges and many opportunities. There are a number of activities related to this process, including: local, district, and national membership recruitment building, political influence networking, and organization and management systems development. Let us now focus on effective strategies, skills, and leadership styles that will be useful in the processes of alliance- and coalition-building. Most analysts of community organizing agree that the major resource of social action groups as they exert pressure for social change is a large base of committed activists that both legitimize and empower a larger group of people to act.[27] The work of RDFs to involve people is what Fisher refers to as "building the base." Involving, engaging, and sustaining a large and strongly identified group of participants is important to achieving desired goals.[28]

Recruiting, engaging, and maintaining participants receives a great deal of attention in the literature.[29] Many RDFs bemoan, that even among those who are interested, few people are prepared to work actively for change, especially among illiterate and impoverish villagers. Organizers also complain that too often they are unable to attract the right kind of people to their organizing meetings, particularly those who would bring valuable talents or traits. Many complain that people are either unwilling to assume roles or could not perform them adequately because they lack skills or live far from the area where organizing meetings are being held. Others worry that some people accept institutional roles as a way of maintaining their power and control, then resist including others in decision making and planning. Consequently, newcomers are excluded from taking on responsibility. RDFs bemoan the time they spend negotiating internal conflicts, managing member relationships, or finding and training someone to take on organization responsibilities. Sometimes people get involved for a specific project directly related to their needs but fail to stay with the organization as it seeks to tackle new problems.

Organizing requires a large group of activists, but economic and social realities restrict the ability of many people to even begin to participate in social action organizations. When people do participate, they invariably and appropriately bring their own agendas, questions, and status needs which create additional demands on the RDFs. Too many RDFs resent the need to recruit people who have so many different agendas. They have not learned to accommodate to these demands as the source for future energy and commitment, therefore, question how much time and energy should be expended on recruiting and working with participants.

It is my observation that many RDFs hold biases that predispose them to be inattentive to members. First, many RDFs articulate goals for substantive change, not membership development, suggesting their priorities are for outcomes, not involvement. For such RDFs, working with members of a coalition or larger mass movement is viewed as a diversion from issue and strategy work, only indirectly related to the substantive gains on issues they seek. Second, some RDFs appear to believe that true commitment cannot be developed, and that people who have to be convinced, are by definition, less reliable members. Thus, these organizers only pay attention to those already converted, doing little recruitment or member development work. Third, RDFs have an acute sense of the importance of their own expertise to the organization. Their status is primarily a reflection of their expert knowledge. Consequently, these organizers may see recruiting and working with unskilled participants as a potentially presumptuous threat to their own power in the organization. Working with members takes time and effort, requires interactive skills rather than issue expertise, is never-ending and often frustrating, and requires RDFs to have continual contact with strangers who may disagree with them. RDFs often do not realize that they are signaling that the organization can function effectively without participants, that it is in the capable hands of the staff, confirming people's notions that non-involvement, passivity, and episodic engagement are acceptable. The economic realities of most rural communities with high levels of poverty and illiteracy and civil inertia make it inherently difficult for RDFs to find and maintain members. This difficulty is exacerbated when organizers, themselves are ambivalent or neglectful about giving attention to member participation. Some RDFs complain of lack of participation, but are bewildered about what might change this.

Training RDFs to function effectively at the local level

At the membership recruiting level, RDFs generally focus on building local problem solving groups at the village level, described in Chapter Nine, encouraging the key leaders in these groups to meet with leaders from other villages. These key activists have the potential to help establish a district- or provincial-wide source of social energy and commitment. Such groups of village leaders provide a broader base of discussion and involvement that is precursory to more formalized networks of decision-making, problem solving, resource mobilizing and political involvement. At some point, such groups of leaders may seek to organize themselves into a more formal organization, perhaps a local NGO which seeks to network with a variety of government and non government organizations. RDFs at this level may agree to play a more administrative or management role in institutionalizing this district level organization.

In the final analysis the advancement of rural development work requires the development of RDFs into a politically influential interest group at the local, provincial and national level. Viewing rural development decision-making as highly political, pluralistic and competitive, I want to emphasize the importance for RDFs to shape rural development decisions affecting local service delivery systems in local communities through development of political knowledge, skills and alliance building. Weinbach[30] discusses the importance of the task environment in which any kind of service or policy oriented organization must function. Unlike business organizations, human service agencies have multiple constituencies that can either support or oppose the organizational goals of the service agency. Whereas paying customers will determine whether they desire an organization's product in the for-profit world, nonprofit organizations serve many persons who cannot pay for the services they desire. RDFs do not have to "sell" their products to their consumers. It is external decision-makers, the gatekeepers for both public and private sources of funding, who must be convinced that vulnerable villager groups should be served. Therefore, RDFs working in private voluntary organizations (PVOs) or nongovrnment organizations (NGOs) must be skilled in negotiating through a politicized environment and in pursuing strategies to acquire power within that environment.

First, fundraising is developing into a daily activity for many NGO administrators, and few can expect to rely on boards of directors to perform these functions. Developing and honing skills in these areas will thus be increasingly important, as will skills in locating alternative and often competitive funding sources in a changing environment. Second, traditional management skills involving the ability to maximize productivity and utilize limited resources have been and always will be critical to obtaining successful results in such environments. Third, such rural development administrators still cannot focus exclusively on internal operations, no matter how skilled they are in matters of personnel, policies, and procedures. To the contrary, the importance of external factors means that rural development administrators must continue to hone their skills in dealing with multiple constituencies, networking with organizations, and understanding political forces in order to successfully obtain necessary resources from their environments. Avoidance of service cutbacks may well rest with the ability of RDF administrators to analyze the environment and in establishing viable relationships.

Building on the work of several political scientists interested in development policy implementation, I wish to present a systems framework for understanding local community decision making at the local level. In my opinion, RDFs do not always recognize the potential for decision-making influence as one of the multiple actors presenting demands or resources that must be responded to by such key decision-makers as the mayors of villages and towns, their key staff in health, education, and economic development. Thus they are rarely a consistent part of the political process generating specific policy decisions. Second, they often fail to recognize that program directors at the district and provincial level hold considerable formal and discretionary power over the direction that a rural development strategy might take.

Formalizing the Professional Status of RDFs

In the face of the many changes being introduced and dealt with at the national level, most RDFs are relatively isolated individually and collectively as a professional discipline. Most of these RDFs tend to assume that national level organizations and associations concerned with the issues of policy reform and change would represent their needs and concerns at higher levels. As a result, generally there is almost no concerted effort by RDFs at the local level to influence public policy or reform agendas.

Let us seek to identify four specific strategies that might strengthen the impact of RDFs at the local, regional and national levels:[31] All four strategies are interactive and the primary mode of influence integral to all four will be inducement rather than force or agreement. These strategies can be seen as part of an over-all planning process in which successive levels of influence-building will be geared to "getting an issue on the policy agenda"[32] and gaining increased recognition as a necessary and useful party in the development of solutions.

1. **A Strategy to Build Associations of RDFs.** Establishing some form of Association of RDFs in a given area can be an important first step to: (1) help isolated RDFs become aware that they are not alone, (2) bring such RDFs together on a regular basis to discuss common problems, identify useful interventions and new approaches, (3) help build consensus among RDFs to see the importance of working together, and (4) help RDFs to see ways in which they can be involved in influencing local and national government officials to consider needed policy and program changes. The first step would be to develop an association of RDFs into a local unit of political activity. A political assessment would be needed to identify potential supporters and natural allies. Such an assessment would also identify potential obstacles, vested urban interests, and others apt to oppose rural development reforms and change. Specific efforts must be made to train the leadership of such an association, to mobilize resources, and develop specific

strategies for working within the political environment where they live. This association then must anticipate and act on public policy trends and decisions that directly affect RDFs and local community development programs in a given area. As a corollary, such an association of RDFs may be crucial when other organizations can not be relied upon to take action in the group's behalf. Gradually a network of such local associations of RDFs must be developed within a broader province or region. An active leadership core eventually must take responsibility for expanding the network into other regions, communicating the need to take unified action, and seeking practical strategies for confronting the consequences of the present approach to rural development.

2. **A Policy Definition Strategy** seeks to redefine issues and to shape perceptions related to key power brokers, and potential allies at the local, provincial and national levels. One of the impediments to RDFs organizing on their behalf in the face of budgetary cutbacks at the national level is often the perceived lack of credibility of their cause. Little value is generally placed on the utility or usefulness of RDFs in the rural community development system. This is primarily due to a lack of understanding of the contribution RDFs make to community development, and to a perception that RDFs are simply generalists with little if any technical training. Often efforts by RDFs to prevent budget cuts are seen as self-serving and questionable for a professional association. As a result RDFs are not always unified on the question of fighting for budgets and other resources. Much work is needed in educating and building consensus among the RDFs themselves. Also the RDF leadership must systematically identify and present the development implications of social, cultural and familial factors absent from many governments' programs. The case must be made for the inseparability of rural development and the broader questions of national development.

Specially, such associations of RDFs must articulate the crucial role of the RDF in providing culturally relevant programs, using appropriate technology, and emphasizing local institution building as the key components of any national program of rural area transformation. Shaping perceptions of the issue in these ways will make it possible to unite the profession and mobilize its resources.

3. **Political Strategy**: The long-term goal of such associations must be to improve and expand the utilization of RDFs in the rural areas of the country. To achieve this goal, such associations might embark on three interrelated processes: (1) fact-finding and program design on state of the art rural development work and support service models in community development programs; (2) outreach to local influentials to build a constituency for community development in all areas of the country. and (3) fund-raising to expand the organizations' staff resources devoted to advocacy in rural development.

The key to the development of a National Association of RDFs in a given country or region requires an integration of these three interrelated processes. To enable such an association to be more effective in the future, the factors limiting support, resources and unity will need to be addressed. The political process responds to numbers, money and influence. Thus, the long-term goals of an effective rural transformation may be harder to achieve, given the profession's mission, lack of money, influence and numbers relative to others competing in the same field of interest. Furthermore, the enduring tension between a professional association as a "self-interest" association and an "advocate for sustainable rural development" type association will need to be sensitively handled for collaboration and coalition with others to occur. This will be the long-term challenge of such associations of Rural Development Facilitators.

Basic Conclusions

The processes related to empowerment described in this chapter suggest a number of activities, strategies, interventions and organizing skills that will be needed if RDFs are to play a significant role in the third stage of rural development. And while the first two stages of rural development are crucial in the early processes of individual and community empowerment building, and while RDFs have the potential to play a role in the processes of coalition building and mass movement stimulation, I wish to argue that from a practical point of view, the major focus of effort for RDFs working at the third stage of rural development should emphasis a district level Community Empowerment and Linkage and Coalition building Approach which will be described in much greater detail in Chapter 16.

---

[1]David C. Korten and Norman Uphoff, "Bureaucratic Reorientation for Participatory Rural Development (Washington DC, NASPAA Working Paper No. 1, 1982; Harry W. Blair, "Reorienting Development Administration" *Journal of Development Studies* 21 (3) (1985), pp. 449-457.
[2]Arturo Israel, *Institutional Development: Incentives to Performance* (Baltimore: Johns Hopkins University Press, 1987).
[3]Much of the material in this section comes from: Terry Mizrahi and John Morrison (eds.) *Community Organization and Social Administration: Advances, Trends and Emerging Principles* (New York: the Haworth Press, 1993).
[4]M. Kessler, Inter Organizational Environments, Attitudes, and the Policy Outputs of Public Agencies: A Comparative Case Study of Legal Service Agencies, *Administration and Society*, 19, (1987), pp. 48-73.
[5]L. von Bertalanffy, "An Outline of General Systems Theory," *British Journal of Social Science*, 1950, 1, 34-65; S. H. Berrien, *General and Social Systems* (New Brunswick, NJ: Rutgers University Press, 1968).
[6]D. Katz and R L. Kahn, *The Social Psychology of Organizations* (2nd ed.) New York: Wiley, 1978);S. Murrel, *Community Psychology and Social Systems* (New York: Behavioral Publications, 1973);J. P. M. Plas, *Systems Psychology in the Schools*, (NY: Pergamon Press, 1986).
[7]C. S Fischer, et al., *Networks and Places* (NY: Free Press, 1977).
[8]S. Cook, "Network Structures From an Exchange Perspective," In P. V. Marsden and N. Lin (eds.) *Social Structure and Network Analysis*, (Beverly Hills: Sage, 1982).
[9]C. Levi-Strauss, *Elementary Structures of Kinship*, (Boston: Beacon Press, 1969).

[10] A.W. Gouldner, "The Norm of Reciprocity: A Preliminary Statement," *American Sociological Review*, 1960, 25, pp. 161-179.

[11] P. V. Marsden, "Brokerage Behavior in Restricted Exchange Networks" In P.V. Marsden and N Lin (eds.) Social Structure and Network Analysis, (Beverly Hills: Sage, 1982).

[12] M. Granovetter, "The Strength of Weak Ties," *American Journal of Sociology*, 78 (1973), pp. 1360-1380.

[13] M. Granovetter, "The Strength of Weak Ties: A Network Theory Revisited. In P.V. Marsden & N. Lin (eds.), *Social Structure and Network Analysis*, (Beverly Hills: Sage, 1982).

[14] A. Bandura, *Social Foundations of Thought and Action: A Social Cognitive Theory* (Englewood Cliffs, NJ: Prentice Hall, 1986); G.S. Parcel, et al., "Translating Theory into Practice: Intervention Strategies for the Diffusion for the Health Promotion Innovation", *Family and Community Health*, 12 (1), pp. 1-13.

[15] P. Freire, *Pedagogy of the Oppressed* (New York: Herder and Herder, 1970 and P. Freire, *The Politics of Education,* S. Hadley, MA: Bergin and Garvey, 1985; M.S. Knowles, *The Adult Learner: A Neglected Species (*2nd ed., Houston: Gulf Publishing, 1978); and A. B. Knox, *Helping Adults Learn* (San Francisco: Jossey-Bass, 1986).

[16] A.P.C. Vidal, et al, *Stimulating Community Report: An Assessment of the Local Initiative Support Corporation* (Cambridge, MA: John f. Kennedy School of Government, 1986).

[17] D. M. Chavis and P. Florin, Sustaining Voluntary Community Organizations : Through Action Research, Unpublished manuscript (New Brunswick, New Jersey: Center for Community Education, 1990; and H. Spiegel, "Coproduction in the Contest of Neighborhood Development, *Journal of Voluntary Action Research*, 16 (1987).

[18] R. P. Merino, "Technical Assistance Offered to Community Health Programs Through a Resource Model. *Public Report,* 100 (1985), p. 30.

[19] A. Bernstein, "A Comparison of Systematic and Personal Characteristics that Support Self-help Groups", *American Journal of Community Psychology* (in press);T. M. Julien, The Relationship Between Self-Help Groups and the Community Organization that Provide their Resources. Unpublished doctoral dissertation, Columbia University, 1988. K. I. Maton, *et al.*, "Factors Affecting the Birth and Death of Mutual Help Groups: The Role of National Affiliation, Professional Involvement, and Member Focal Problem, *American Journal of Community Psychology*, 17 (1989) PP. 643-671.

[20] H. Brookfield, *Interdependent Development* (London: Methuen, 1975); M. Conroy, "Rejection of Growth Center Strategy in Latin American Regional Development Planning, *Land Economics*, 49, pp.371-80; M. Santos, "Underdevelopment, Growth Poles and Social Justice, *Civilization*, 25, pp. 18-30.

[21] D. Rondinelli and K. Ruddle, *Urbanization and Rural Development: A Spatial Policy for Equitable Growth* (New York: Praeger, 1978.

[22] T. Unwin, "Urban-rural Interaction in Developing Countries: A Theoretical Perspective." In R. Potter and T. Unwin, (eds.) The Geography of Urban-Rural Interaction in Developing Countries, (London: Routledge, 1989), pp. 11-32.

[23] C. Weaver, "Development Theory and the Regional Question: A Critique of Spatial Planning and Its Detractors," In W. Stohr and D. Taylor (eds.) *Development From Above and Below? The Dialectics of Regional Planning in Developing Countries,* (Chichester: Wiley, 1981), pp. 71-105.

[24] John Friedmann, "The Active Community: Towards a Political-Territorial Framework for Rural Development in Asia, *Economic and Cultural Change,* 29, (1981), p. 284.

[25] W. Stohr, "Development From Below: The Bottom-up and Periphery-inward Development Paradigm. In Stohr, W. and Taylor, D. (eds.), *Development From Above and Below? The Dialectics of Regional Planning in Developing Countries* (Chichester: Wiley, 1981), pp.39-72.

[26] J. Friedmann, *Empowerment: The Politics of an Alternative Development,* (Oxford: Blackwell, 1992), p. 133.

[27] Haggstrom in F. M. Fox, et al (eds.), *Strategies of Community Organization* (Ithasca, IL, F.E. Peacock, 1987).

[28] R. Fisher, *Let the People Decide* (Boston: Twayne, 1984).

[29] G. Brager and H. Specht, *Community Organizing* (New York: Columbia University Press, 1973); P. Henderson and D. Thomas, *Skills in Neighborhood Work* (London: George Allen & Unwin, 1980); A. Twelvetrees, *Community Work,* (London: The Macmillan, 1982); and L. Staples, *Roots to Power,* (NY: Praeger Press, 1984).

[30] R. Weinbach, T*he Social Worker as Manager: Theory and Practice* (NY: Longman, 1990).

[31] J.E.Tropman and J.H Erlich, "Strategies: Introduction. In F.M. Cox, J.L. Erlich, J. Rothman and J.E Tropman (Eds.) *Strategies of Community Organization: A Book of Reading* (Itasca, IL: FE Peacock Publishers, 1979.

[32] H. J. Rubin and I. Rubin, *Community Organizing and Development* (Columbus, OH: Merritt Publishing, 1986).

Unit Four
Five Dimensions of Rural Development

Strategies, Programs, Interventions and Approaches

The Fourth Unit will present field-tested programs, strategies, approaches and action step interventions for the five dimensions of rural development: health, literacy, agriculture/small scale enterprise, ecology and local culture enhancement. In writing this book *One Can Make A Difference*, I am very much aware of the fact that rural development facilitators that will make a difference must have the commitment, the cultural sensitivity, the social awareness, and field experience needed to help people help themselves, but also they will need specific information, knowledge, and competency in areas of interest and relevancy to villagers themselves. One of the interesting dilemmas of this work of village development facilitation is the seemingly contradiction that the more effective the RDF might be, for example, the more technically trained and the more competent the RDF might be in programs related to rural health, village literacy, small-scale enterprises, village credit systems, or in organic agriculture, the greater the danger that the villagers will remain dependent upon that RDF and thus will fail to generate their own sense of responsibility and as a consequence will be unwilling or unable to take initiative in their own development. Clearly, there are certain skills, competencies, and technical abilities that an RDF needs to be aware of in order to work in a village setting. However, experience also suggests that there needs to be a balance between what the RDF does for the villagers and the extent to which such an RDF is willing to let villagers make mistakes and learn for themselves, to let the villagers develop a sense of self-esteem and self-reliance, quite independent and often in spite of the RDF's efforts. Finding this balance and conceptualizing this process is the purpose of this book.

Let us now again review the Three Stages of Rural Development and the kinds of activities and interventions that might be appropriate in each of these three stages:

Stage One: Trust Building
Time Frame **(One to Two Years)**

(1) **Awareness** of the villagers reality: their problems, concerns and needs are being identified and documented through a process of cultural dialoguing,

(2) **Sensitivity** and appreciation for the local culture are developed and encouraged,

(3) **Trust Building** between the outsiders and the villagers is being encouraged by identifying and working with formal and informal leaders.

Stage Two: Capacity Building
Time Frame **Three to Five Years**

(1) **Develop ownership** among the villagers for the problems that need to be solved using group discussion techniques and local participation activities. Develop ownership for possible solutions that the villagers can implement to solve these problems.

(2) **Encourage and Support Local Problem Solving Groups** Using training and group development activities to stimulate capacity building in the planning, implementing and evaluating of projects.

(3) Encouraging the use of **Appropriate Technology** that utilizes local resources and material, utilizes or helps develop local skills and competencies, and does not increase dependency on outside groups.

Stage Three Local Institution Building
    Time Frame   **Five to Ten Years**
(1) **Institution Building** ensures the sustainability of village level projects and programs through a strengthening of local leadership, management and organizational skills and systems of local participation.

(2) Successful **empowerment** of the community to solve their own problems with little dependency on outside help. This includes the building of networks and linkage mechanism between the villagers and various outside agencies and organizations, and through the establishment of coalitions and local resource mobilization efforts.

(3) **Commitment** to the creation of autonomous local institutions and action steps that allow the local community to pursue activities that meet their long term needs for a better quality of life defined and determined as they see fit.

Both interns and RDFs must carefully assess how these stages relate to each other, how they build upon each other, and how each of the five dimensions of rural development described in detail below impact on each other. RDFs must help villagers to understand these interrelationships, and must assess the impact that a project or activity in one of these dimensions would have on the other dimensions, within each of the three stages. An awareness of these interrelationships do not come easily and outsiders, in particular, must be patient and open-minded to the ways in which these five dimensions are defined and understood by the villagers.

Each of the following five chapters will be organized to accomplish the following: (1) present a general introduction to the issues and concepts related to the dimension being discussed, (2) present a conceptual framework that will contrast the way that this dimension has been defined in the past and the way that it needs to be defined for long-term sustainable village development, (3) define various strategies, activities, interventions and approaches that would be appropriate for each of the three stages of rural development and finally (4) present a set of case study materials that provide insights into how an RDF might learn from the successes of others in other parts of the world, how an RDF might help the villagers help themselves, how an RDF might make a difference in a village setting.

This last unit is in many ways the most important section of the book. No one book can present all the lessons learned, or give examples of all the successes implemented throughout the world or even begin to outline the many ways in which an RDF might interact with a village community in ways that would facilitate long-term sustainable change and development. It is strongly recommended that an RDF be encouraged to read this Unit Four over and over on a fairly regular basis. This unit is to be seen as an idea stimulator. Each time one reads these five chapters, a new set of linkages or connections will be developed in the mind of the RDF. Some RDFs, while working in a village, may feel that some of the material presented in this unit appears to have little relevance for their present situation in that particular village. However, from my experience in rereading these ideas over an extended period of time, new possibilities come to mind, new connections that were not apparent before suddenly appear. Reading and rereading this kind of material over and over is crucial to the reflective process of problem solving and capacity building and empowerment and networking outlined in Unit Three of this book.

Chapter 11

First Dimension of Rural Development
Non Formal Education and Grassroots Literacy Programs

Basic Education and Literacy in the LDCs Today

Today there is a basic agreement that primary education has the potential and in many ways is vital to self-sustaining development in the LDCs. Primary education is the first organized phase in a life long process of learning. It is not just a matter of imparting the basic skills of reading, writing, and arithmetic (the 3Rs), but also strengthening the ability to express oneself and to think in problem-solving terms related to the challenges of village life. Primary education should enable people to live productively in their environment and to develop abilities that help them to better their living conditions and make rational decisions concerning their communal life. More and more we are understanding that such education must also integrate the local languages and cultures of the people seeking to improve their quality of life.

Section One
Primary Education in Village Development

The advantages of primary education have now been carefully documented, showing how even 4-6 years of education can have a direct and positive impact on family income, farming productivity, family planning, nutrition, health, and child-raising. As relevant studies have demonstrated, education tangibly improves the prospects for poor children to escape from their poverty. As labor power is all that the able poor have to rely on, raising their labor productivity obviously offers the best chance to fight poverty. Farmers with four-years of education or more are far more amenable to innovation and are far better able to digest information than farmers who have less education. The impact on productivity and income is even greater, when basic education conveys relevant skills that have a direct application in the lives of village people.

Primary education also has positive effects on health and nutrition. The mortality rate of children whose parents are literate is only half as high as those whose parents are illiterate. Studies have shown that for every year that a woman attends school, there will be roughly a reduction of 10 percent in child mortality. Women with a minimum of basic education in turn place greater emphasis on the education of their own children, they tend to give their children a healthier diet and encourage them to attend school regularly.

Of people living in absolute poverty, women suffer most. A quarter of poor households are headed by women whose incomes are substantially below the average income found among poor people in general; and within these households fertility, and maternal and infant mortality are significantly higher. The children tend to suffer from lack of protection, accidents, violence, abuse, and neglect. Low educational levels and poverty go hand in hand. In many societies, 80 percent of those defined as living in absolute poverty were classified as illiterate compared to 25 percent of the population as a whole; and 75 percent of children from these households did not attend elementary school compared with 20 percent of the general population.

Most international conferences on literacy emphasize the role of the central government in initiating school reform: more teachers, more classrooms, and curriculum reforms to make the classroom material more relevant to the needs of the local situation. Materials and aids for teachers and pupils must be developed in line with the cultural setting and made available in sufficient quantities to the schools. The schools in the LDCs must drastically increase the number of teaching hours actually given. It is not enough to simply furnish the schools with additional material; the teachers must also learn to effectively handle such material in teaching situations. Yet if such countries wait until the government has adequate budget to accomplish all these reforms, thousands and thousands of communities in the LDCs will be waiting far into the next century. Alternative methods of illiteracy alleviation are needed. In rural areas in particular, such methods must involve both children and adults, and they must include lessons dealing with survival and increases in productivity, health, and problem solving skills.

Unfortunately, a growing number of LDCs are spending less and less on education, especially primary education as structural adjustment programs demand cuts in government spending and the curtailment of budget deficits. Often rural school funding is the first to be cut in such government austerity programs. At the same time, the quality of education imparted in schools is worsening to a shocking degree. Schools in the LDCs are often open for 500 hours or less in the year, while figures for the MDCs are almost double. On average, African countries spend almost 60 times as much (a ratio of 60 to 1) on a university student as on a primary school student. In the MDCs this ratio is around 3 to 1. As a whole, public spending in the developing countries on education dropped by 25 percent between 1970 and 1980, whereas it rose considerably in Europe and North America during the same period of time. In several African countries, the amount of real resources available for education dropped significantly in the late 1980s and early 1990s, with government budgets often having 30-40 percent less budget monies than the average available during the whole period 1970-85. Despite a verbal commitment to education, these much lower budgets must now cater to twice as many students as in 1970. Thus resources for teachers' salaries, school facilities, and curriculum materials are simply not available in many rural areas of the LDCs.

Forty years have passed since the international community defined education as a universal human right and called on all nations to provide adequate education facilities for their populations. Almost one billion people worldwide are unable to read and write and of these, two-thirds are women. Instead of intensifying efforts to increase literacy rates, many developing countries have allowed school enrollment to fall in the past decade. Some countries have succeeded in giving their children an education of at least 4-6 years, yet more than 100 million children are deprived of the opportunity to attend any type of school. Worse, school attendance is by no means a guarantee that they will acquire basic skills in reading, writing, and arithmetic. Few children who have finished grade school have meaningful opportunities to strengthen and improve their meager educational skills as adults. Millions of children abandon school after a short period thus short-circuiting the potential of many educational opportunities that are available. Many children even after 6-8 years at school have not learned the essentials they need to survive the challenges they face as adults.

These figures also obscure further anomalies, especially with regard to girls and women. Of the over 100 million children who do not attend school, 60 million are girls, and of those that abandon schooling (some 40 percent), far more girls tend to leave than boys. Unfortunately the enrollment rate in at least 12 developing countries has dropped by up to a third in the last decade. Here, again, it is the girls, the children of rural and poorer families, that are hardest hit. Eradicating illiteracy among girls and women is essential in improving health and nutrition and curbing unwanted pregnancies.

The overall debt crisis, economic stagnation, rapid population growth, and widening economic inequities in the LDCs may provide an explanation for the situation but there is no reason to remain passive. The situation in basic education is deteriorating dramatically. Lack of basic education of broad sections of the population in LDCs increasingly impedes development policy efforts and contributes to ecological destruction, hampers efforts to reduce population growth, and makes people prone to blindly accept radical political and religious systems that promise relief from their misery.

Many countries have used literacy programs to integrate minority groups into the dominant culture of a given society. In many countries, literacy campaigns have been used to prepare illiterate peasants for jobs in the large plantations and urban sweat shops. Literacy was thus used by the political elites to encourage migration to the cities as low-wage workers. Literacy in this way has worked in the interests of those in power, providing a pool of wage workers of the agro-business and factories of the city. Literacy is not necessarily a bad or good thing.

When literacy is used to exploit and control the poor of a given society, we must raise questions as to the purpose and consequences of literacy.

Section Two
Contrasts between Central Government Education and Village Community Education

Too many government programs focus on educational objectives that are related to intellectual development through institutionalized curricular processes. Such learning often creates artificial learning environments, isolates students from the relevant socio-cultural contexts that villagers find themselves and emphasizes learning that is distant from people's real needs. It distorts, ignores or underestimates the natural learning processes whereby adults and children grow and develop. In addition, formal education systems, by starting the process when children reach the age of 6 or 7, ignores the earlier years that are equally crucial for development and learning.

At this point we need to distinguish between two forms of education at the village level: traditional central government sponsored education and village community education (VCE). It is important to see these two forms of education as ideal types that merely help an RDF to compare and contrast different village education systems.

Chart 11-1

Central Government Education	Village Community Education
1. Highly centralized with decisions concerning curriculum coming from outside the community.	1. Mostly decentralized with decisions concerning curriculum coming mostly from the community itself.
2. The focus of education is on teaching children usually between 6 and 16 to enter higher education system (high school/college).	2. The focus of education is on teaching all age groups to solve problems relevant and useful to the community Thus men, women, and children can be involved.
3. This system tends to be teacher-centered with the teacher deciding what is successful learning	3. A VCE system is learner-centered with teacher and community deciding together what is successful learning.
4. Families are often excluded if the parents are illiterate since clearly they have no role to play. In fact, students are often encouraged to see parents as backward and of no value.	4. Families are encouraged to play an important role in defining what is learned and when students are to be there and to see their parents as resources for learning.
5. This system too often emphasizes rote memorization of material defined by the teacher	5. A VCE system encourages open discussion and critical evaluation of material and ideas

and the education system.	that are relevant and important to the learners.
6. The goal of education is often structured to help students pass government structured exams.	6. The goal of VCE is to help learners develop problem solving skills relevant to their environment.
7. The teacher is usually from the dominant culture of society and encourages students to see the student's own culture as inferior.	7. The teacher helps the student to see the value of knowing both the learner's own language and culture and the culture and language of the dominant group in their society.
8. Illiteracy is generally defined as an inability to read and write and use math.	8. Illiteracy is defined as the lack of awareness concerning what the individual needs to know to deal successfully with the challenges of life.
9. Literacy is generally defined to complete a certain number of years of school and certain skills in the 3Rs.	9. Literacy is defined as the ability to solve problems that are relevant and important to the learners in dealing with their families, communities, and the outside world.
10. Much greater emphasis given to educating boys than girls with resource allocations generally reflecting this gender bias at all levels in the education system.	10. Much greater emphasis is given to encouraging girls and women to participate in all literacy and educational programs

The Basic Characteristics of Village Community Education (VCE)

Village Community Education (VCE), thus, is conceived as a process of human development and social transformation. It must transcend the traditional concept of education as the accumulation of knowledge and cultural transmission, and open up the possibility for each person, regardless of age or socio-cultural conditions, to satisfy basic learning needs and develop the potential to respond in a creative and critical way to the challenges of developing a more just and humane society.

Village Community Education, in contrast to what happens in conventional school settings where learning is most frequently an individual concern, turn learning into a social process. This concept implies profound transformations in the objectives, principles, and strategies of the system. The flexibility it generates leads to radical change in its structure, administration, curriculum, and agents and at the same time opens the learning contexts and environments to the home, the community, and other natural settings. The concept of time similarly shifts away from being institutionally defined and toward responding to the needs and characteristics of the learners. Thus it will broaden access to educational services to populations living in exceptional conditions: working children, migrants, rural people, etc. It places the community at the center of the process, sharing with it the role of educational planner, administrator, and curriculum specialist.

Conceived this way, Village Community Education for all becomes a powerful tool for qualitative improvements in educational processes and outcomes. Below are six characteristics of most Village Community Education programs:

1. In Village Community Education, every person -- child, youth, and adult -- should benefit from the process of education designed to meet basic needs.

2. The satisfaction of these needs should empower individuals both in solving their own internal problems and in interacting with the outside world in more effective ways.

3. Village Community Education is not an end in itself but the foundation for lifelong learning and human and community development.

4. The most urgent priority is to ensure access to and to improve the quality of education for girls and women, and to remove the obstacles that hampers their active participation.

5. The focus of Village Community Education (VCE) must be on whether people actually learn. Active and participatory approaches are particularly valuable in assuring that learners achieve their fullest potential. While village teachers/literacy workers and RDFs have an important role to play, a crucial role must be found for the community and the families, given that learning begins at birth.

6. The traditional learning systems that already exist in most village communities and the actual demand for education services should be identified, preferably through active and participatory research processes involving groups and the community.

Section Three
Appropriate Activities in Education
for the Three Stages of Rural Development

Let us now review some of the kinds of activities that are best implemented in each of the three stages of Rural Development. Each stage has a different focus and each requires different kinds of skills and interventions.

Stage One: A general assessment of the education system in the village should be implemented: including determining the level of illiteracy among children and adults, attitudes and feelings in the village toward schools, education, literacy, past experience with outsider teachers and literacy workers, the quality and effectiveness of the village school if one exists, and the level of interest in building a primary school if one does not exist. If there is interest in building a school or improving or adding on to the present school, interns and RDFs in this first stage might consider inviting some outside group, agency or organization to help provide some of the resources needed in the building or expansion of the village school. Some preliminary efforts to build a primary school might be implemented in this first stage. Some initial efforts might be made to contact central government officials to determine their willingness to provide a school teacher or to provide additional resources for the community.

Trust Building and Awareness Enhancement through Cultural Dialoguing -- One of the greatest needs in working with people is to establish from the beginning a relationship of mutual respect and understanding. To achieve this requires the adoption of certain attitudes from the moment the idea of a village education system emerges. The cultural arrogance that has been cultivated in so many of us for so long has to change to an attitude of cultural and professional humility: We must learn to listen to what people have to say until an understanding of their point of view has taken root; we must establish a process of cultural dialoguing (See chapter 5) wherein people are involved and learn from each other. Their ideas must be incorporated into the plans and they must be involved in the action steps developed. There must be mechanisms for negotiation and for the resolution of conflict. When this happens, a partnership is established and together professionals and community leaders, parents and children can start the long journey to learning, to growing, and to changing their present conditions.

When RDFs enter village communities, there are certain key points they must understand before introducing literacy in those communities. RDFs must first determine if there is a school in the community, who are the teachers, whether the villagers (men, women, youth, and children) see the school in positive or negative terms and why. RDFs must be sensitive to the fact that learning is going on in this village regardless of whether there is a formal school with a trained teacher. Even more important, just because there is a teacher who holds class does not necessarily mean that meaningful education is taking place. In assessing the present education system in the village, RDFs must have a clear understanding of the differences between traditional education and what we are calling Village Community Education.

RDFs after they have been in a community a while will begin to recognize certain words, phrases, and general themes that are continually being mentioned. Examples might be such words as sickness, hunger, mother, market, or such phrases as being cheated, being hungry, having bad luck, or such themes as the number of children that seem to die in our village, the struggle to have enough income, a conflict with a land owner, or the importance of some religious or culture event. RDFs should write these words, phrases, and general themes down in their diaries. At some appropriate point, the RDF might invite some of the villagers to a meeting to present these words, phrases or themes for discussion. In many ways, this process is similar to the cultural dialoguing process described earlier in Chapter Five, except that now the RDF is seeking to focus on ways to introduce some system of education into the community. The point here is to develop a clear understanding of the words and phrases people use, the problems they define and talk about, the themes that are important and significant in their lives, both positive and negative.

Cultural Enhancement and Self-Expression -- Providing services or education that are consistent with the local cultural of the group participating in the program is an important dimension for success. Understanding their cultural and historical perspectives and using approaches that develop new understandings about their own culture, the present conditions in their village, and the reasons for those conditions, are all vital to the first phase of any project. Understanding how the concept of time is managed in a given society in which one is working and the community's availability for certain activities and for certain members of the community is crucial to the success of any program. This requires observation and listening skills as well as the ability to ask questions before formulating specific plans. It also requires the involvement of the participants (students and parents) in the process of reflection and analysis prior to taking action. The anticipation and analysis of the potential consequences of the possible actions to be taken are important elements in the process of reflection. Often this first step is ignored or rushed, with disastrous consequences, because organizers want to get on with the task of meeting objectives. Moreover, these processes need to be maintained throughout the development of the VCE system because the complexities of a culture are not wholly learned or understood at one point in time. Cultural manifestations change with different social and political conditions. Several case studies in this chapter reflect this need to go slowly and to integrate the local culture into the processes of village education.

During **Stage Two** the RDF could consider introducing the concept of a Village Community Education Program. Both a children and an adult literacy program might be implemented in the community and the curriculum would be structured to reflect the real needs of the villagers. Much effort would be needed to bring teachers, parents and students together, to structure programs that facilitate a better relationship between what happens in the school and what is happening in the village. Some effort to organize a village education committee might be started in an attempt to encourage village problem solving in the area of literacy and education.

Underlying this process of VCE are certain principles and processes that are essential for successful outcomes. There is clear evidence that the best results come when the processes are achieving objectives set by the participants and when agreed principles underpin the processes. The process of a meaningful system of education must start with the community and its perception of what its needs and interests are. RDFs must be careful to let the people decide what the educational agenda will be. VCE implies helping a community to define its problems, to determine possible solutions, and to implement such solutions through a set of specific action steps defined by a collaborative decision-making process including both the community and the RDF. For some communities, the first priority might be to build a potable water system or to reduce the number of children who are dying from measles or malaria. For other communities it might be the need to increase agriculture output or to learn how to raise more productive chickens or fatter cattle. Still for other communities, it might be the need for adult women to learn how to use numbers and to read bus signs so they can go to the market to sell their goods. Of course, many communities will suggest that what they need is a school where their children can learn. The point is that a VCE approach must be flexible and based upon the needs of the community.

There are a number of issues and concerns related to introducing and developing a Village Community Education program.

First Issue: Does the community already have a traditional education system and if yes, will the RDF be allowed to initiate some type of Village Community Education approach? If there is a government sponsored school in the village most teachers in such a system will prefer the traditional education model. Some discussion and open dialogue will be necessary between the RDF and the local school teacher, if some combination of the traditional education and the village community education approaches is to be developed. RDFs must be careful not to offend or to suggest that what the teacher is doing is wrong or not valued. Experience suggests that if the teacher is not from the community, there is a much greater tendency for the teacher to follow the system established by the central government and to resist making any changes in the curriculum. Ideally, the best teachers for a Village Community Education system would come from the same area, or at least have a strong familiarity with and an appreciation for the community's language and culture.

Second Issue: Assuming the RDF is allowed to help develop a Village Community Education approach, there will be the issue of community commitment and ownership of the approach developed. A number of community meetings will be needed to ensure that the village community understands the options being presented and accepts the approach agreed upon: Should the VCE approach focus on basic literacy for the children with an emphasis on the educational needs of the children or should the VCE approach emphasize adult education and community problem solving or perhaps a combination of both? Eventually it would be helpful if the community selects a group of villagers to form some type of Village Education Committee (perhaps a Parent-Teacher Association) made up of villagers who have an interest in implementing an effective VCE program.

Third Issue: What is the best way to combine both the requirements of the traditional education system with its emphasis on basic reading, writing, and arithmetic in the language of the dominant culture and the efforts of the VCE approach to include some classes in the local language and culture? What is the best way to reconcile the needs of both approaches? An RDF must be willing to help develop curriculum material for both approaches. Using the words, phrases, and themes collected by the RDF, a basic primer or dictionary might be developed in which both the dominant language, the local language and perhaps English could be included. For example in the altiplano of Bolivia it would be Spanish and Aymara, in the central highlands of Guatemala, Spanish and Mom or Quechi, in south Mali, French and Bambara, in Mombasa, Kenya Swahili and perhaps Diga or Giriyama, in Timor, Indonesia, Bahasa Indonesian and Timorese, in northern Thailand, Thai and Karen. Some effort needs to be made to encourage the integration of dominant and local cultural systems in order to help develop a sense of pride and self-esteem in one's own traditions, values, language and culture.

Fourth Issue: What is the best way to integrate the needs of the community and the needs of the children in a given community? Often the scheduling of the school system is insensitive to the requirements of the adults who may need the children at key times in the agricultural processes of the community (planting, weeding, harvesting, etc.). A number of strategies have been developed to ensure that parents are involved in the scheduling of the school to ensure that family and community needs are considered. Traditional education system alienates the children from their parents. It has been found to be useful to involve the parents in the schooling process, giving parents a role to play in teaching traditional values, agricultural techniques, identification of local plants, animals, cultural skills in story telling, music and dance, etc. In one system to be described in more detail later, a strategy was developed whereby the children were in school for a month, then home for two weeks to share with their parents things they had learned about agriculture, health, and literacy, and the parents were encouraged to teach the children traditional stories, customs, music and dance. The Village Community Education approach is a two-way process in which adults and children are communicating and learning from each other.

Fifth Issues: What is the best way to ensure that the curriculum is relevant and meaningful to the people being educated? While it is important to emphasize the basic skills of the 3Rs, it is also helpful to structure such instruction to reflect material that is meaningful and relevant to the needs and problems of the community. Curriculum materials need to be developed on problems of health, sanitation, nutrition, on questions of better farming techniques and procedures, on small scale enterprises, supplemental income generation and marketing approaches, and finally on cultural values, traditions, and religious systems. There is no better way to motivate villagers to the value and excitement of education than to prepare reading materials that reflect problems, concerns, and values that are important to the people.

Mutual Respect and Meaningful Participation -- From the inception of a VCE program it is essential to involve participants in identifying problems, setting priorities, identifying roles and functions, analyzing strategies, and selecting and mobilizing resources. This approach to participation cannot be top-down, or outsider dominated. Meaningful participation requires the local involvement of the people in decision-making, problem identification, problem solving and conflict resolution in all aspects and phases of the implementation of the program. However, the management of a bottom-up approach often requires an external literacy worker (RDF) who serves mainly as guide and facilitator. Such an RDF is not expected to ignore her own feelings and ideas and accept blindly those of the community. Rather she needs to establish a relationship of mutual respect and understanding, in which dialogue and reflection lead to the identification of the best alternatives and ideas for implementation.

During **Stage Three** there should be consistent efforts to establish a local PTA organization accountable to the community and organized to provide feedback and support to the local school teachers in the community. It might be during this stage that RDFs would work with local villagers to develop associations of PTAs among a number of village communities that might seek to influence programs and policies of the central government level. It is in this stage that villagers take greater responsibility for the education system that is established in their community. If the villagers wanted to change their present central government approach to education to a Village Community Education Program, it would be in this stage that efforts would be started to enlist government support for such innovations through various political activities. (See chapter 10)

Empowerment of People -The main objectives of Village Community Education programs are to empower people to solve their own problems by using existing resources in appropriate ways and to take control over the main factors that affect their lives. This requires people to organize in ways that make sense to them in terms of what they want to achieve, and to expand their relationships with the broader environment at the district and even national level. The organizations of informal supportive networks, interaction, and self-help systems (PTAs, village education committees) are essential for sustaining community-based actions that lead to the identification and solution of participants' own problems with the minimum dependency on external sources and also to more complex organizational patterns. As people help one another they become stronger individually and collectively, with increased levels of self-confidence, self-trust, pride in their work, risk-taking abilities, and sense of direction. It also gives them renewed psychological energy to tackle more complex problems.

Self Initiative and Community Autonomy -- Every effort needs to be made to formulate a process of VCE that encourages autonomy and decreases unnecessary dependence. Important steps in that direction are to provide outside support to the community only in those areas where the community is unable to attend to its own needs; to use means that strengthen the community's ability to deal with the problems at hand; to identify the needs with the people themselves and together mobilize the resources from their own environment that can be used to address those needs. One of the great challenges that face many programs is to find ways of providing the educational services needed without destroying the desire for self-help. Governments and many donor institutions have in the past often worked in ways that encourage dependence and discourage self-help. Villagers must be encouraged to find ways to increase the allocation of their meager resources for education. Specific community income-generating projects can be developed to supplement those scarce resources available from government and other outside donors.

Networking with other villages is an important part of stage three, especially in seeking to improve the quality of education. Traditional systems of education, dominated by central government ministries of education are very difficult to change. In such cases, some system of community empowerment through the development of Parent-Teacher Associations will need to be developed, with networks of community PTAs being formed to present demands for needed reforms at the community level. Such reforms will require political dialoguing and policy reformulations -- activities that are time consuming, fraught with conflict and disagreement, and certainly not easy to implement. On the positive side of the traditional education approach, the RDF may play a helpful role in organizing community efforts to build or expand an existing school, help strengthen links to the district or provincial education departments to facilitate increases in educational resources: so that textbooks and teaching materials are available to the village, encourage the creation of a Parent-Teachers Association in the community to facilitate better communication between the teachers and the community, etc.

The Principle of Program Flexibility

Most central government programs seek generally to implement a single program in the same way in every region. What is needed is a willingness of the government to allow a set of diverse alternatives that can respond to the different socio-cultural characteristics of the groups/communities who have special needs and concerns. What is needed is a strategy of education that reaches more than just a few children. Such a strategy must focus on the most needy by creating an approach that is family and community based. This principle is best implemented in the course of various stage three activities related to empowerment, political influence on policy making, and other mass movement strategies.

Impact of Education on the other four Dimensions of Rural Development
Reflecting on how education can impact on the various dimensions of Rural Development and how each of the dimensions can impact on education in the village is an important part of the work that an RDF must do. His or her efforts in connecting the different dimensions of Rural Development will play a key role in initiating a process of sustainable village development. Note the following ways in which education programs and processes might impact on the dimensions of Rural Development:

Culture: Awareness of how the school system might enhance and help strengthen local traditions and cultural values that are revered by the community.

Health: Awareness of how the school system might teach students about sanitation, good health and nutrition and the importance of good health in the community.

Income: Awareness of how the school system might teach skills and competencies that would increase the income generating activities of the community.

Ecology: Awareness of how the school system might teach about the environment and how it needs to be protected.

Section Four
Lessons Learned from Past Literacy Efforts

For many development programs, the assumption is that education is the prime mover and thus must come first in a project design. Hugo Aceros, a former priest in Cartegena, Columbia had first organized a literacy program based upon Paulo Freire. He soon learned that the peasants were not interested in literacy and so he changed his strategy. He began to focus on helping the landless obtain new land for farming, giving them training on the problems of production, legal rights to land, cooperative formation, putting pressure on the authorities for needed public works. Once the farmers had access to land and services they began to show interest in having their children educated. Many of the farmers wanted to make certain that the curriculum had agriculture in it also. Thus education came after many other development activities and reflected their own needs.

On the other hand, a simple literacy program can stimulate interests in other areas. Dr. K. Yusus, of Malaysia, observed this tendency: "I started to go where the squatter people were living. After I talked to the people, especially the women, it was quite obvious that even though they had health problems, they didn't think it important, because they are living in a situation where other things determined what was important. They said they should have jobs and food and education for their children. So the first thing was a pre-school because that is what they wanted. It was only later that we were able to deal with immunization and malnutrition and hygiene."

Education and training that improves literacy, leadership, technical skills, and functional knowledge have been instrumental in increasing the economic strength of the family unit, the community and improving women's status in many rural communities. When women are considered as equals in the community development effort, rather than as separate, they gain confidence to voice their feelings and experience to participate in the implementation of community decisions. For example, in one village in Bangladesh, a women's cooperative that began with seven members, invited a Muslim teacher from the Mosque to be their formal teacher. They saved their money and gave some of it as a token to the teacher. The cooperative grew to 30 members within two years. All 30 members can now sign their names and manage their own finance. Before, such signing was done by an outside middle-man.

Learning can also take place outside the classroom. A number of RDFs have organized self awareness groups to facilitate discussion and interaction. By this method, rural people become aware of their problems and are mobilized for social action. Many villagers, because of past exploitation, have lost a sense of initiative and a sense of dignity. People must get to know their village, must understand the potential of the village. People learn a great deal by coming together and working as a team. RDFs can use several vehicles for this kind of education: small study groups spontaneously organized to deal with a particular crisis, meetings based on existing women's or youth organizations, simple literacy classes, and special camps for unemployed youth. Whatever the form, the intent is to enable participants to know and understand better the environment within which they operate and to decide their individual and collective response to it.

We must analyze what needs to be done to guarantee that parents and other family members participate in parent and village community education programs. There is ample evidence that programs that involve the parents in the education of their children yield the best results and have the best long-term effects. The strategies need to be designed to increase parental self-confidence so that, individually and collectively, they may have the skills to solve their problems and interact positively with their children. Many societies are at risk and will enter the next century in even more critical conditions unless people assume greater responsibility for creating a more just society for all. The processes and strategies of community education have a great potential to contribute towards the implementation of these strategies and to face educational and development challenges in the LDCs of the world.

During the 1920s and 1930s, James Yen was seeking to introduce literacy into rural China. He came to realize that his greatest challenge was finding ways to reinforce the ability to read and write after the formal training in literacy was over. Special writers were hired to prepare simplified written material on health, agriculture, entrepreneurship, accounting, etc. A rural newspaper based upon a very simple language system was started offering stories on local, national and world events, cultural traditions, bibliographies of past folk heroes, descriptions of upcoming festivals and theater.

In Latin America there is an alternative tradition in literacy training started by Paulo Freire in the 1960s. For Freire, literacy is not a technique that can be deposited in learners' minds as though the illiterate was an empty, ignorant container. Rather, literacy teaching must begin with the knowledge and the reality of the learners. Literacy is as much about reading the world as reading the word. Freire argues that the written word is associated with images that encode the contradictions of the way of life of those learning. In the process of discussing the image and the word ("codification" in Freire's language), the learner acquires what Freire calls a "critical consciousness," that is, the student becomes aware that the world is not static, that the student's world can be transformed. This consciousness raising process helps students to understand that through their efforts changes in their world are possible.

Some prosperous farmers organized short courses in gardening, beekeeping and the like for the poorer families in their community in Southern Chile. Then they heard about the **Maison Familiales Rurales Program** started in the thirties in rural France. After elementary school, in seventh and eighth grade and perhaps beyond, children whose parents are practicing farmers alternate throughout the school year, a period of one or two weeks in school, where they would be taught agriculture along with traditional subjects, then followed with two weeks at home. When at home, they were encouraged to apply some of the knowledge acquired at school. They were given a special kind of homework (cultivating plants, handling animals, etc.) which would latter be inspected by the teacher on a weekly basis. The purpose of this program was dual: to avoid the alienation from agricultural work that is frequently the result of prolonged schooling in purely academic matters; and to transfer the knowledge of modern agricultural practices from the children to the parents as the children apply the knowledge acquired at the school to projects at home.[1] Parents admitted to having learned something from the children: bee-keeping, the growing of asparagus and some other vegetables, and the importance of having cows vaccinated against certain diseases. The poorer farmers of the area, especially those who were of Indian background, were the major beneficiaries. Eventually the running of the school was turned over to a PTA in Alto Chelle.

In an attempt to deal with the problem of unemployable rural women in Jamaica, the Elders and Youth Skills Training Project was established. In various local schools, technical training in fields such as food processing, metal craft, needle craft, and soft drink production was linked with income generation in the form of small businesses and cooperatives. Since the program used the local resources of retired skilled elderly people both in the village and nearby towns, it broke down social, age, and financial barriers and helped preserve their cultural heritage. This type of vocational education was augmented with courses in personal development, family life, and management skills such as accounting and communications. Equally important was the ability of the elderly to share stories, traditions and past customs of their culture, demonstrating the importance and relevancy of past wisdom. Perhaps most significant was the way such education helped the retired people of a society to feel needed and appreciated.

In central Luzon, Philippines, a multi-institutional project was organized to help reshape a traditional pre-school program to facilitate greater involvement of the parents. There are several special features including a home program in isolated villages. In such villages, two teachers meet once a week in various homes teaching mothers on such subjects as nutrition, sanitation and basic literacy. Mothers were also given simple lesson outlines that they were taught to give to pre-schoolers on alternative days. The teaching team visited several different groups on different days each week. The cooperation of the mothers was voluntary. Following a training program, parents helped run the pre-schools on a daily basis. Each day began with a hour-long training session. This involvement of the parents in the development of the curriculum benefits both the school and the family. It gives positive reinforcement to the professional teacher and favorably aids the children's transition from a home environment to a school environment. Since most of the instructors in the schools are the parents themselves, both parents and children benefit. The professional teacher also changed their attitude from teaching a traditional curriculum to one that is oriented toward the parent's participation and the development of the community.

In northern Thailand, a group of community leaders in a Karen community lamented how the only way for their children to get any education required leaving home and being exposed to a foreign world that threatened the loss of their own culture and mother tongue. Even those who did go to the city schools often failed to graduate. In fact, no one from that village had graduated from high school in the previous ten years. The elders saw their people losing their pride, values and way of life. Those who were in school were about three grade levels behind children in other parts of Thailand. An education committee was formed that involved members of the community and an RDF from outside the community. After extensive discussion, they sought to design a program reflective of the spiritual base of their people. The clearest indicator of the change in the attitudes of the Karen was reflected in local school attendance rates that has increased to 95 percent in recent years. The school has become the community's culture center. Young girls that used to be sold into the brothels of Bangkok are now attending classes. A curriculum based upon the community's culture is a powerful way to strengthen a community's sense of pride and to stimulate various forms of social energy needed to introduce and implement change. In order to meet the cultural components of the new curriculum, local people had to be trained as teachers. Several local leaders have been the graduates of this new form of education and they have become advocates in other villages for this type of education.

Many traditional educators assume that sports channel social energy into wasted activities. Yet in a number of communities in Nigeria, school teachers began to encourage local boys to participate in a soccer league. The decision to play soccer meant not spending time at the local bar and the effort to build a soccer field often stimulated group consciousness that led to greater, more complex projects. For youngsters growing up in the countryside, playing soccer is a means of breaking out of the isolation of family and rural life, of becoming less timid and of becoming part of a wider community. Participation in sports can act as a great socializer and initiates these youth into the life of groups, organizations, and educational programs.

The south Indian state of Kerala has had one of the most successful literacy campaigns in the LDCs. Already literacy is up from less than 20 percent to 70 percent, and in some districts it is nearly 100 percent. It could be a model for other areas of the world. The state government has supplied needed budget money to set in motion a mass literacy program unique in the LDCs, but not unlike the Mass Literacy Program of James Yen in China in the 1920s and 1930s.[2] It is the thousands of grassroots literacy workers and volunteers who have made the goal of mass literacy a reality. In many districts it was a question of community pride and the desire to be fully literate before some of the other districts. Groups of volunteers visited every house in their villages and towns and drew up a list of people who were illiterate. In the rural town of Ernakulam, some groups of 4 and 5 educated young people visited 650,000 homes and listed more than 185,000 illiterates over a two year period. Later, when the teaching of the three Rs began, around 25,000 literacy workers or volunteers took regular classes at 18,000 centers. Woman's literacy workers have outnumbered men -- a significant factor in persuading many women to join classes. Most of the training centers were the homes and huts of the disadvantaged. Some central government funding was available for the salaries of the supervisors of the volunteers, and some NGOs and local notables also contributed some funding, but it was the excitement of the campaign, the thrill of helping their community be the first fully literate, that motivated most of the volunteers. One of the unanticipated consequences of this campaign has been the higher levels of awareness of health and hygiene among the newly literate and as a consequence, no cholera cases, once a common complaint, have been reported in recent years. Incidence of wife beating, alcoholism and drug addiction have fallen overall also as a consequence of greater levels of education.

In November 1990, a workshop was organized in Zimbabwe to allow representatives from 30 African countries to take a critical look at the problems of teaching about agriculture and the environment in village primary schools. They reviewed a number of recommendations of how to revise the curriculum. This new focus emerged as more and more policy makers came to realize that so-called academic subjects in primary schools were not enough to prepare children to cope with the problems that they will later have to face. It is not expected that we should make 12-14 year olds into perfect farmers, able when they leave to produce with complete self-reliance; rather, the intent is to familiarize their pupils with the economic realities of their country, and to teach them the importance and dignity of farming and rural life.

Familiarizing village school children with practical farm work has not always been the focus of many ministries of education in LDCs. Recently more and more countries are seeing the value, especially in times of economic crisis, to prepare pupils for adult life by means of practical activities at school. Unfortunately, most countries, even when village agriculture is part of the curriculum, only allow their teachers to spend one or two hours a week on such subjects, so it is hardly realistic to expect teachers to convey very much in the short time available to them. In many countries, agriculture lessons consist of the pupils themselves performing physical work on the school farm or in the local community. There is no theoretical component at all. Physical work is in the forefront, with little attempt made for the students to appreciate or come to appreciate the importance and value of agriculture knowledge. Concentrating on agricultural topics as a separate discipline is more an exception in most educational systems in the LDCs. A further problem is that most teachers are not trained to teach agriculture, and in only a minority of countries are there teaching aids or school textbooks on agriculture specially designed for children. The teachers usually have to rely on themselves when planning lessons and are obliged to manage with the sparse resources at their disposal; nor can they call on the advice of a specialist to improve their teaching. From the workshop in Zimbabwe, some specific recommendations for this kind of curriculum were developed:

1. Agriculture instruction must be linked to the science of agronomy, including organic farming and appropriate technology for small scale farming. For some specific examples, see Chapter 13.
2. Agriculture lessons must be conducted in the native language, so that the pupils grasp the main points and are not hampered by language difficulties.
3. Successful traditional farming methods must be presented in order to counter the development of a blind faith in so-called modern aids such as fertilizer and chemicals.
4. Local schools should use local stories, customs, history, folktales, songs, poetry, literature, etc., if the curriculum is to be interesting and relevant to the local children and adults.

One village women's association in Madhya Pradesh, India, that was organized to change the status of women through non-formal education and active participation in village development projects, were invited to form their own syllabus for a women's literacy program. They organized workshops for writers who could prepare literature for women. Such material sought to help women define their own goals in household work of the village and in society as a whole. They took up the theme of women's role as good housewife, mother and Annapurna (the goddess of giving good food to family members) as well as good citizens and agents for social change. A number of basic primers have been written and published and distributed through local communities. Motivation in literacy classes has been high as a result of the use of books like these.

Section Six
Zambia Case Study
Teacher Initiated Reform in Village Education

As was mentioned earlier in this chapter, a number of LDCs are faced with serious debt and government budgetary cuts which could have a very negative impact on local school systems. An example of these problems is found in Zambia. Ten years ago, the education system of Zambia was faced with serious problems. Most schools were grossly overcrowded in order to accommodate a growing student population. Books and educational materials were still scarce, and for many pupils there were no desks. Buildings had deteriorated as damage to floors, windows and roofs had not been repaired in several years. Classrooms were filled to capacity, and, especially in lower grades, many pupils crowded together on the floor with nothing to write on. Unfortunately, curriculum development was generally a highly centralized process, and emphasis was placed on the academic subjects in preparation for examinations, giving exclusive access to very limited salaried employment opportunities. Moreover, individual syllabuses revealed little attention to Zambia's environment, cultural heritage or traditional values.

Still, Zambia is an example of a society committed to strengthening its educational system, especially at the village level. Over the past decade significant efforts have been made to stimulate local resource mobilization and community education activities. Perhaps most interesting in this effort in Zambia are the initiatives developed by the teachers themselves. One area in which teachers were especially active was in school income generation activities. Most such activities were limited to agricultural production, including the growing of maize, a school vegetable garden, and occasionally the keeping of small livestock or the growing of fruit. Output generally remained low, due to insufficient training of teachers in agricultural activities, lack of tools, and poor access to credit. Still a number of teachers did press forward in their efforts to generate supplemental income for their local schools. Gradually such activities not only provided income for the school, but provided students with opportunities to develop greater skills in agricultural production. Such profits did have an impact as they were used to purchase stationery, some materials for repair and maintenance, and other needs including sports equipment and transportation. Because of the efforts of these teachers, money raised through such activities tended in many communities to exceed what was collected directly from parents.

Also parents have been told point blank about their new responsibilities for sharing the costs of education and that such local resource mobilization will not only be increased, but even institutionalized at the local level. One step in this direction is the proposed conversion of PTAs into formal cooperative societies. Thus, the current involvement of the grassroots is not going to be a passing phenomenon. Teachers will also be much more involved. Through resource work, a cadre of teachers is being developed who when organized in committees, are taking a greater responsibility for the actual teaching-learning activities in the schools. By so doing, they are effectively filling the gap left by the forced retreat of the central government with its education officers, inspectors and curriculum developers.

One major result of these developments was the range of practical skills that were brought into the schools; they included maintenance and repair of furniture and buildings, the production of simple tools and utensils, construction of toilets, and participation in community projects including the construction of teachers' houses and school classrooms. It was common for pupils to be involved in these projects. In many schools, pupils also produced sets of small articles for sale, ranging from coat hangers to brushes, baskets and belts, the proceeds of which were used to purchase new materials.

Several government officials from the Ministry of Education expressed concern about the young age of the pupils, their inability to produce items of marketable value, the danger of exploitation, the neglect of valuable core subjects in the curriculum, such as language, science and mathematics, as well as the unrealistic aims of such premature vocational education. The villagers challenged these observations, arguing that these types of economic activities are becoming accepted, by teachers and slowly also by parents, as an integral part of school life. In fact, it has contributed greatly to making the school -- especially at the primary level -- a much more important part of the environment, as pupils are involved in activities which are also commonly found in the wider community. Such efforts are unlikely to prepare boys and girls to be skilled workers -- indeed the quality of the items produced still leaves much to be desired -- but instead of separating them from the world of work, it brings them into a more systematic contact with it and offers an opportunity to explore different aspects of adult work in a protected environment. The major benefits, therefore, of school production have been in the pedagogical and social spheres, while from a micro-economic point of view its contribution to the physical environment of learning cannot be discounted.

Another important area of self-help activities in Zambia that is an important component of a village-directed approach involves the local teachers in developing teaching aids, new materials for the classroom, innovative curriculum suggestions, etc. Focal points for such activities have been "teachers' centers" established in central locations, which also host other self-initiated programs, such as in-service training and assessment and improvement of classroom practice. Perhaps the biggest gain, however, has been the restoration of many teachers' confidence in their own professionalism, and the overcoming of feelings of abandonment in the face of rapidly deteriorating financial, personal and professional conditions. Around the country scores of teachers have made a contribution to this development. They have been encouraged by the fact that they were identified by inspectors on the basis of merit and talent, and were given special recognition and responsibilities. There is ample evidence that this recognition and new responsibilities have led to personal sacrifice in terms of time, energy and money in the effort to mobilize fellow teachers, parents and the students themselves.

In order to stimulate the scope, quality and effectiveness of self-help activities, financial and material support from the central government are now being made contingent on the activity levels of the local teachers and parents in village education. Such support works as an incentive, and along with workshops and seminars for various cadre of personnel, this program has already initiated a trend of more schools and more teachers and head teachers participating in school income generating activities as well as in other resource mobilizing activities among parents. Thus the program has become part of a learning experience for teachers and officials up and down the system in moving towards greater coordination, more responsiveness to local initiatives, more school-community self-reliance in education development, and more joint efforts to grapple with the many problems in education. Clearly, a cluster of schools in a district, could work together, sharing information, materials and approaches, encouraging each other and seeking common solutions to new problems. In the long term, this type of teacher-initiated reform could be replicated in other countries. This type of reform in village education may be an appropriate approach for those LDCs facing stringent structural adjustment problems. One crucial unknown in many LDCs will be the willingness of central government Ministries of Education to allow such autonomy and grassroots initiative to be not only allowed but, in fact, rewarded.

General Conclusions

One of the most widely used literacy approaches in the world is Laubach Literacy International. One of the best descriptions of this approach is found in a book entitled *Literacy for Social Change* by Lynn R. Curtis. In this book he defines literacy as "the listening, speaking, reading, writing, and mathematics skills, adults and older youth need to solve the problems they encounter in daily life; to take full advantage of opportunities in their environment; and to participate fully in the transformation of their society."

In a very persuasive way, he suggests that successful literacy programs must have four components: (1) Fundamental Skills in basic language understanding: development of a basic sight vocabulary, and understanding of phonics and certain elements of grammar and punctuation. It also includes writing, listening, speaking and math. (2) Critical Thinking allows students not only to understand the meaning of what they hear and read, but to question its content, seek additional information, and synthesize information to identify and analyze the problems they encounter in daily life, the causes of these problems, and alternatives for action. (3) Cultural Expression suggests that what is real and important for literacy learners is experienced on an emotional or spiritual level. This form of social knowledge gives meaning, purpose, value and identity to people. Much of this type of learning is better expressed in music, drama, folklore, dance, literature, and art. Any literacy program that ignores this aspect of learning is doomed to failure. (4) Individual and Community Action suggest that literacy education is complete only when specific actions are taken to address issues arising through the learning process. Through action, learning is not only reinforced, it is fulfilled.[3]

The Village Community Education approach outlined in this chapter is based upon a set of principles that reflect these four components, as well as the importance of involving the entire community in the process. RDFs are encouraged to review all the various case materials in this chapter and in chapter 5 on a fairly regular basis as they seek to introduce education and literacy into a village community. This would be especially true when an RDF moves into a new community. For ideas and approaches that were perceived to be irrelevant and inappropriate in one community may prove to be quite relevant and appropriate in a different situation.

---

[1] For information write to Union Nationale des Maisons Familiales Rurales d'Education et d'Orientation, 59 rue Reaumur, 75002, Paris.
[2] For a description of this mass education program see: James B. Mayfield, *Go To The People* (1986).
[3] Any one seeking to become a professional RDF should seek to master the contents of: Lynn R. Curtis, *Literacy for Social Change* (New York: New Readers Press).

Chapter 12

Second Dimension of Rural Development
Primary Health Care in the Village

In 1978, a group of people aiming to change the state of health in the world gathered in Alma-Ata, a city in South Central Russia near the border with China.[1] The World Health Organization (WHO) and United Nations Children's Fund (UNICEF) sponsored the meeting, which involved delegates from 134 countries and 67 UN organizations. It culminated in the adoption of the Declaration of Alma-Ata, which enshrined health as a "fundamental human right." Its essential concern was with equity, the assurance that everyone have the minimal requisites for a healthy life.

Section One
History of Primary Health Care for the Village

The Director General of WHO, H. Mahler, at that conference outlined eight questions to stimulate a deeper concern for health policy in the world:

1. Are you ready to address yourself seriously to the existing gap between the health "haves" and the health "have nots" and to adopt concrete measures to reduce it?
2. Are you ready to ensure the proper planning and implementation of primary health care in coordinated efforts with other relevant sectors, in order to promote health as an indispensable contribution to the improvement of the quality of life of every individual, family and community as part of overall socioeconomic development?
3. Are you ready to make preferential allocations of health resources to the social periphery as an absolute priority?
4. Are you ready to mobilize and enlighten individuals, families and communities in order to ensure their full identification with primary health care, their participation in its planning and management, and their contribution to its application?
5. Are you ready to introduce the reforms required to ensure the availability of relevant manpower and technology, sufficient to cover the whole country with primary health care within the next two decades at a cost you can afford?
6. Are you ready to introduce, if necessary, radical changes in the existing health delivery system so that it properly supports primary health care as the overriding health priority?

7. Are you ready to fight the political and technical battles required to overcome any social and economic obstacles and professional resistance to the universal introduction of primary health care?
8. Are you ready to make unequivocal political commitments to adopt primary health care and to mobilize international solidarity to attain the objective of health for all by the year 2000?

Mahler's hope at that time was to stimulate a greater willingness and commitment among the leaders of the world to pursue a set of policies directed to alleviating the problems of health care in the world. Few nations among the less developed countries were willing or able to allocate the resources necessary to confront the problems of health within their respective countries.

In March 1988 in **Talloires, France,** a world health conference ensured continued commitment to the goal of universal childhood immunization by 1990. The principal foci of the meetings were sustainability of immunization, the addition of new and better vaccines, and the introduction of other major cost-effective health initiatives. When the Expanded Program of Immunization began in 1974, only 5 percent of the children in the less developed world were immunized; when the Task Force for Child Survival began in 1984, 20 percent were immunized. The truly great event of the conference at Talloires was the reconciliation between UNICEF and the WHO over strategy. Mahler went to the blackboard and drew a horizontal line along the bottom. He then drew five vertical lines representing immunization, diarrheal diseases, acute respiratory infections, family planning, and AIDS. He acknowledged that vertical programs could be inserted as low-cost, effective, and equitable measures into the overall plan for primary health care. Development, he said, consists of "knowledge and motivation; the immunization campaign was delivering both; and the result was not a weakening, as had once been feared, but an improvement of it."

Later, the Rockefeller Foundation convened a conference entitled **"Good Health at Low Cost"** to review four successful case studies: China, Sri Lanka, Kerala state of India, and Costa Rica. Four factors were identified as being common to all four countries: (1) political and social will; (2) education for all with emphasis on primary and secondary schooling; (3) equitable distribution throughout the urban and rural populations of public health measures and primary health care; and (4) assurance of adequate caloric intake for all.

In the summary of this Rockefeller Conference Report was the following: "For the last decade at least there has been a model for health in the developing world that can be called 'the **northern paradigm**.'" This approach to health care assumes the growth of a literate population living in comfortable housing, provided with piped water and sanitary facilities, and supplied with the fruits of industry and agriculture via good roads and communication The LDCs, in seeking to emulate this model have gradually over time generated huge foreign debts, forced unnatural systems of development onto their populations, and pursued processes of growth that have been ecologically unsound.

During the past several decades an alternative strategy has emerged quite successfully in the four countries mentioned above which is now being called the **"southern paradigm"** and which has been able to greatly reduce infant mortality rates and increase life expectancies at a substantial cost saving. Crucial in this approach is the stimulation of political will at the national, provincial, and community levels of a nation, the commitment to the development of an educated and literate population, a much more equitable distribution of primary health care services in both urban and rural areas, and a much greater emphasis on adequate nutrition for all through enhanced agricultural productivity.

The southern paradigm accepts primary health care services through paraprofessionals willing to integrate traditional forms of medicine into modern forms of medicine. This approach also emphasizes preventive medicine as much as curative medicine and acknowledges that central governments cannot do it alone but must be willing to decentralize authority and resources down to the community level for maximum impact.

In his inaugural speech, Hiroshi; Nakajima, the new director general of WHO, said the time had come to concentrate on the practical implementation of the concept of health for all and on the primary health care approach, which is now widely accepted. In terms of the challenges faced by many LDCs, John Evans, Director of the Population, Health, and Nutrition Department of the World Bank in the early 1980s, described three stages in the evolution of health systems. The first was dominated by infectious diseases linked to poverty, malnutrition, and poor personal hygiene; the second by chronic diseases, particularly cardiac and cerebrovascular diseases, cancer, diabetes, arthritis, and mental disorders; and the third by environmental hazards of air, water and food pollution. The industrialized countries evolved through the three stages over the course of more than a century, but the less developed countries (LDCs) face the challenge of coping with all three simultaneously.

The *New England Journal of Medicine* article on selective primary health care called attention to a World Bank estimate that the cost of furnishing basic health services to all the poor in less developed countries by the year 2000 would be between $5.4 billion and $9.3 billion or roughly 5 percent of GNP per annum. Very few LDCs have been willing to allocate this kind of money for primary health care that would provide one community health worker or auxiliary nurse-midwife for every 1,500 to 2,000 people and one health facility for every 8,000 to 12,000 people or every 10 square kilometers (roughly 4 square miles) whichever is greater.

In 1985, Rotary International launched an extraordinary initiative called the **"Polio Plus"** program, pledging to provide all the polio vaccine necessary for up to five consecutive years for any participating city, state or country. By 1986, Rotary had made 42 "Polio Plus" grants, representing a commitment of $37.3 million.

World Health Organization established the concerted immunization program in 1974. By 1990 steady progress had been made, reaching a global coverage of about 20 percent against the six diseases that earlier took the lives of more than 4.5 million children and crippled millions more: **tuberculosis, measles, poliomyelitis, diphtheria, pertussis and tetanus** still take the lives of three to four million children annually.

Section Two
Contrasting Perspectives on Health Care

The principal controversy for the last two decades has been between the so-called **vertical approaches** that seek direct, targeted programs using specific technologies such as drugs, vaccines, and insecticides, and the **horizontal approaches** that argue for a broad-based strategy including medical, ecological, sociological, and political factors that would improve health. The controversy centered around three basic issues: a negative versus a positive attitude toward science and technology; a belief in technique-oriented as opposed to community-based approaches; and whether the people or the "experts" should make the decisions.

Shortly after the WHO was established in 1948, a number of mass campaigns were initiated against tuberculosis, yaws, and malaria. The massive anti malaria effort begun in 1955 was prompted by the development during World War II of the insecticide DDT and of powerful new anti-malarial drugs. Fifteen years later, because the malaria parasite and the mosquito carrier had developed resistance, respectively to drugs and insecticides, efforts to eradicate malaria in many areas of the LDCs were postponed. Still one must acknowledge the great success of one vertical approach -- the eradication of smallpox by 1978.

Horizontal Approaches

Alternative strategies were suggested in the aftermath of this failure to eradicate malaria. Many scholars argued that the key to good health was not the development of advanced medical systems. In fact, one study by Thomas McKeown[2] suggested that water supplies and sanitation, decent housing, and, particularly, the availability of food were responsible for the dramatic improvement in health in the developed world. Thus it is largely due to socio-economic progress and not to specific medical interventions that improved the quality of health in these developed countries. Equally significant is the inequitable distribution of health resources that also has become a major concern. Large modern hospitals located in the major cities of the LDCs often provide health care for less than 5 to 10 percent of a country's population but require 50 to 75 percent of the health budget of that country.

The failure of major vertical, global campaigns to eradicate or control disease, the emphasis on socioeconomic development in the less developed world to the exclusion of more immediate measures, constituted the ground in which the seeds of a new strategy based upon a more community-based approach began to emerge. In 1973, a working group of the WHO completed a report on basic health services and concluded that there was "failure to meet the expectations of the populations; an inability of the health services to deliver a level of national coverage adequate to meet the stated demands and the changing needs of different societies; a wide gap (which is not closing) in health status between countries, and between different groups within countries; rapidly rising costs without a visible and meaningful improvement in service; and a feeling of helplessness on the part of the consumer." Two years later a joint WHO/UNICEF report described a range of successful or promising health systems in nine countries: Bangladesh, China, Cuba, India, Niger, Nigeria, Tanzania, Venezuela, and Yugoslavia. The report concluded that "a virtual revolution" was needed to bring about "changes in the distribution of power, in the pattern of political decision-making, in the attitude and commitment of the health professionals and administrators in ministries of health and universities, and in people's awareness of what they are entitled to." The report emphasized the importance of primary health workers modeled after the so-called barefoot doctors of China. The concept of these village workers -- who were chosen from and by their communities to be trained in a short, intensive course -- was originally field-tested by Dr. James C. Yen in the 1920s and 1930s.[3] For many people, these more horizontal approaches using local community health care workers were seen as a more appropriate approach to the health care needs of the millions of rural people then being denied basic health care services.

Vertical Approach
Yet one study published in 1979 approached the health care needs of the LDCs with a most creative perspective.[4] Instead of arguing for the long-term requirements of the horizontal approach, these authors argued for a straightforward approach that would seek to eliminate the major causes of death. The major infectious diseases of the less developed world were placed in the order of their importance based on the number of people afflicted, the number of deaths produced, and the disabilities caused, ranging from weakness and inability to work and learn, to crippling and disfigurement. Their analysis revealed that the two most important health problems in the less developed world were the diarrheal diseases and respiratory infections of infants and young children, each of which was responsible for billions of episodes and for 5 to 10 million deaths each year. Other major diseases mentioned in this study included malaria, measles, schistosomiasis, whooping cough, tuberculosis, tetanus, and diphtheria.

On the basis of these figures and the crucial element of feasibility of control (i.e. the availability of adequate, low-cost means of preventing or treating these problems), the article concluded that an application of four very low-cost (vertical) measures could save the lives of millions of children each year: (1) immunization against tuberculosis, polio, measles, diphtheria, whooping cough, and tetanus; (2) use in diarrhea of highly effective salt-sugar-water (oral rehydration therapy); (3) treatment of life-threatening malaria; and (4) breast feeding of infants, which provides the child with protective antibodies present in mother's milk. The paper did not discourage application of the (horizontal) so-called comprehensive primary health care package of Alma-Ata but stated that until it could be made available to all, "services aimed at the few most important diseases may be the most effective means of improving the health of the greatest number of people."

A Combination Strategy

Most LDCs are now seeking an integration of both the vertical and horizontal approaches. One dimension of this strategy must reflect the level of development found within the communities where the health strategy is to be implemented. If we conceptualize the interaction between local community and the intervention strategies to be encouraged by outside entities, the matrix deduced from such interactions would have two sets of factors:

(A) The first dimension includes the quality, experience, and commitment to development and change by the community's local leadership, their experience in local institution building, quality of life indicators reflective of degree of poverty, infant mortality, life expectancy, and past experience in development activities in health, education, and productive enterprise development. The scale emerging from these characteristics would help to categorize communities from very low capacity, to some initial capacity, to some high degree of capacity. Capacity was defined in terms of the quality of leadership available in the community, the degree to which local institutions were presently functioning in the community and the extent to which problems of poverty, illiteracy, and health and sanitation had been addressed in the community in the past.

B) The second dimension reflects various types of interventions that might be considered in seeking to implement a child-care program in a given community including:

(1) A **technique-oriented program** in which outside experts enter a village for some type of one-shot program: mass immunization, child growth monitoring, the establishment of a potable water system, the creation of a health care center staffed by urban trained health workers. The emphasis of this first level of intervention is reflective of the Specialized Primary Health Care programs that enter a local community, provide services that the local community cannot provide for itself, and maintain these services through external resource allocations from the central government or some international donor agency. Such a strategy is assumed to be relevant for communities with very low levels of leadership and community capacity.

(2) A **decentralized form of intervention** in which local administrative systems at the sub national level of government organize and support some type of community health care worker program. The focus of this intervention is best exemplified by the local community willing and able to select individuals from the community to receive some type of extensive health care training at a district or provincial training center. Often such local health workers are assumed to be the appropriate link between the community and the local administrative system with appropriate supervision being provided by local health officials. Such a strategy is assumed to be relevant for local communities where there is some initial or average level of capacity and thus while there is some community participation in the selection of the health worker, the emphasis is still on a top-down type of system with most of the resources and initiative coming from outside the community.

(3) A **local institution building form of intervention** in which the emphasis is on the community empowering itself to take responsibility for its own health services. The institutional framework through which this intervention is implemented requires autonomous institutions (perhaps a community health committee as part of a community council, or functioning women's clubs or health clubs) made up of local citizens willing to plan and organize the health care programs deemed relevant and desirable by the local community. This third form of intervention assumes a community with some high level of quality leadership, a willingness to engage in local resource mobilization to supplement or replace the scarce resources coming from the central government or some outside donor, and a sense of community development and consciousness raising that is reflective of a process of community empowerment and which assumes local communities can begin to take responsibility for their own children health care programs.

The principal focus of this matrix is a greater clarification concerning the relationship between the characteristics of a given community and the type of intervention that would be most appropriate. There is no implication that these categories of intervention are mutually exclusive. It is possible that in a given community all three types of intervention might be used at the same time or in some appropriate sequencing of activities. However, there is some sense that a strategy A would probably be more appropriate when there is low levels of capacity in a given community, that E would perhaps be more appropriate in a moderate capacity community and that a strategy I would be most apt to succeed in a high capacity community. There would need to be some empirical research to ascertain the sequencing of these interventions, the prerequisites needed to go from a strategy A to D to G in a low capacity community or from strategy C to F to I in a high capacity community.

Table 12-1
Intervention Strategy Matrix

	Low Capacity	Moderate Capacity	High Capacity
(1) Professional Health Facilitators	A	B	C
(2) Community Health Workers	D	E	F
(3) Local Health Institutions	G	H	I

In assessing the utility of each of the above mentioned forms of intervention, the following issues will need to be confronted: (1) the uncertainty of funding sources limits the size and scope of a given intervention, (2) community poverty naturally sets limits to the capacity of a community to mobilize its own resources, (3) excessive outside influence and funding generally increases dependency and apathy and leads to project activities which simply cannot be sustained over time, (4) expensive and erratically supplied drugs weaken local health care worker effectiveness and credibility, and (5) "most foreign or expert-based projects tend to have built-in implementation weaknesses. When the time comes for experts to depart, there is often inadequate social mobilization, training and competence among national and local cadres to ensure continuation of the project."[5]

There are a number of local community interventions that have resulted in substantial reductions in infant and child mortality.[6] One summary of such interventions suggests that "The elements of projects which have aided in success include: easily accessible and well-covered population, prior well-established relationship between the providers of care and the community, concentration on a small number of key interventions, easily accessible referral hospital, sustained funding, comprehensive surveillance system, good leadership, and an established supply system."[7] Thus the literature does provide evidence that community-based systems of intervention can work but only **if there is a fit** between the capacity of the community and the intervention being implemented. When a strategy focuses on outside interventions without serious community involvement there is a danger that such "high profile donor aided projects deflect attention from the real factors that empower people, and allow them to control their health: the political processes that allow and disallow the channels of dissent, of demand, of participation."[8] Much of what we discussed in Unit Two and Three of this book presents the basic components of this process of community involvement and local participation.

Village Community Health Program

It is generally acknowledged in the field of Primary Health Care that the key element in rural health care is the focus on preventive health care. Many of the illnesses seen in rural areas in both developed and less developed countries can be eliminated with basic preventive rather than curative health care. This emphasis on preventive rather than curative health care is causing a major shift in the field. Essential health care in most LDC village health care programs involves preventive measures such as immunizations, health education, nutrition training, sanitation and family planning along with some direct curative treatments. Let us briefly outline the differences between Traditional Modern Health Care and a Village Community Health program:

Table 12-2

Traditional Modern Medicine	Village Health Medicine
1. Focus is on curative medicine in which doctors do the work.	1. Focus in on preventive medicine in which villagers do the work
2. Considers Western Medicine the only reliable source of medical care	2. Combines an appropriate mix of Western medicine and Traditional medicine
3. Considers only professionally trained people qualified to provide health care	3. Considers local paraprofessionals also qualified to provide health care
4. Is a technique based approach that requires specially equipped hospitals.	4. Is a community-based approach that only requires a small clinic or even a village health worker with limited supplies
5. This system requires a highly centralized administrative system to function.	5. This system works best in a highly decentralized system.
6. Most decisions are made by medical professionals who issue top down decisions and policies.	6. Most decisions are made in conjunction with significant villager participation and involvement.
7. Emphasizes external funding and government budgets.	7. Emphasizes local resource mobilization to supplement outside resources
8. Is a short-term strategy providing a vertical implementation of programs	8. Is a long-term strategy providing a horizontal coordination of local resources and concerns.
9. Is urban based, capital intensive, with much greater concern for quality service to the few.	9. Is rural based, people intensive with much greater concern for equitible distribution of resources, servicesss, and personnel.

Section Three
Appropriate Activities in Health for the Three Stages of Rural Development

There are a **number of issues** that have to be dealt with for a RDF seeking to introduce a Village Community Health program. Also some care must be made to distinguish between health related activities appropriate for Stage One, Stage Two and Stage Three: Let us now review some of the kinds of activities that are best implemented in each of the three stages of Rural Development. Each stage has a different focus and each requires different kinds of skills and interventions.

Health Activities Appropriate for Stage One

First there needs to be a general assessment of the condition of health in the village. Efforts must be made to identify the sources of poor health in the community. The level of infant mortality and the need for potable water should be determined and the community should be encouraged to discuss ways to deal with these types of health problems. Some preliminary health projects might possibly be implemented with the help of some outside donor or local government agency. Some ideas that can be introduced in Stage One include:

Develop Awareness of Potential Danger: Human and animal feces contamination of water, fingers and hands, and the environment, sets the stage for the transmission of disease to a new host. Contaminated water may be ingested directly, it may be used in the preparation of food leading to contamination, or it may be used for washing utensils and vessels for drinking and storage. Fingers and hands are commonly contaminated during defecation or by touching contaminated articles and surfaces. Flies become contaminated with fecal pathogens by alighting on feces or fecally contaminated surfaces. They are one of most common carriers of pathogens to humans, especially to children. Trachoma, a common eye disease in many tropical areas is transmitted from the eye of an infected person to the eye of a susceptible person. Transmission may be by a variety of routes including fingers, flies, and shared towels or other articles used to wipe the eyes and face. Villagers need to be aware of these dangers and the specific behaviors that lead to the transmission of these diseases. Such awareness does not come easily, in fact, studies show that the education of sanitation often takes considerable effort and reinforcement over a long period of time. The most common dangers include:

1. Water borne or water related diseases: Amebic dysentery, Cholera, Giardiasis, Typhoid, Poliomyelitis, Hepatitis, etc.
2. Water washed (skin and eye infections): Infectious skin diseases, Infectious eye diseases (Trachoma), louse-borne typhus, louse-borne relapsing fever
3. Water-based: Schistosomiasis, Guinea worm, Chlonorchiasis, Dracunculiasis

4. Water-related insect vector: Sleeping sickness, Filariasis, Malaria, River blindness, Yellow fever, Dengue.
5. Other Sanitation related diseases: Hookworm, Strongyloidiasis.

Common solutions include draining stagnant pools of water in the village area, creating a village garbage collection system, building latrines and teaching people to use them, creating appropriate technology systems to turn human and animal waste into biodegradable fertilizers and to generate bio-gas systems to reduce the need to burn fire wood.

How to Provide Clean Drinking Water: Some of the basic questions to consider in Stage One relates to: What is the present source of drinking water in the village? How available and easy is it to get this water to the individual families? Is this water potable or does it need to be boiled? Does the village need new sources of water: wells, tapping into nearby springs, lakes or rivers. Can rain water be collected in the rainy season and stored for the dry season? What is the best way to teach local people to drink uncontaminated water, to understand the relationship between contaminated water and the sickness of their children? Do the mothers in the village know how to prepare oral rehydration packets that include one liter of boiled or potable water, plus a half teaspoon of salt and 6-8 level teaspoons of sugar.

Education of Mothers: RDFs in India have found it helpful to interview mothers, seeking to ascertain their understanding of immunization, breast-feeding, weaning, diarrhea, acute respiratory infections and family planning. On the basis of their response to a simple set of questions, a basic course of lesson material is presented, both to increase mothers' awareness and to encourage new behaviors. Initiating discussions with the women of the village to determine their attitudes and perceptions is an important First Stage intervention.

Health Activities Appropriate for Stage Two

This is the stage to seek to introduce a Village Community Health Program. A small clinic might be built and a number of village primary health care workers could be trained and supported by a combination of local and outside resources. Below are the kinds of ideas that need to be emphasized in Stage Two:

Village Commitment: First, is the issue of whether health is a concern of the leaders and the general community in the village? Without strong interest from the entire community, it is difficult to create a sustainable VHC program. A number of meetings will be needed to determine interest, to identify a key group of people (it needs both men and women) who will work on a village health committee, and to ensure there is consensus in the community for some type village health program. The RDF will have to take some initiative in the early stages, but gradually the village health committee (which should include people to represent a broad section of the community, key clans, families, and influentials) must see health as their responsibility, not the responsibility of the RDF.

Selection of the Village Health Worker (VHW). Second will be the issue of determining who in the village will be trained to be the village health worker. Again this decision must be the result of a broadly based discussion and decisions, including all elements in the village. Too often the village chief or one of the influentials will decide who should receive training and they pick a relative or a friend who may not be the best person. Experience suggests that it should be someone who is committed to staying in the village. When young men are trained they often use the medical skills received to find a job in the town or city. Generally women or men who already have demonstrated some interest in health care make the best candidates. Health workers should not be selected solely on the basis of education. Indeed, many of the most effective VHWs I have seen were illiterate or semi-literate, but were able to understand and communicate with the villagers in ways that an outsider cannot. While it is sometimes difficult to recruit traditional healers or tradition midwives, if you can develop some trust with them and show them how some training might improve their medical skills, they can make wonderful village health workers. There is also some value to identifying several villagers who can be trained in health care work in case the main health worker gets sick, looses interest or moves away.

Village Sanitation: What are the major sources of disease in the village: flies, mosquitoes, human and animal feces? What is the best way to eliminate these sources of disease: keeping animal penned and separated from the homes, building latrines and teaching the people to use them, teaching parents to wash their hands and their children before handling food, etc. Can the RDF obtain media material: charts, posters, films, or organize community discussion groups that will motivate people, parents in particular, to the importance of good sanitation. From experience it has been observed that village latrine programs seldom have any long-term positive impact. In the few places where success has been observed, the following **pre-requisites** have been identified: first when villagers are given options in how outside resources might be used. For example, if villagers are asked: "Do you want us to help build latrines in your village?" They will say "yes." If, however, you were to say, "we have a limited amount of money for a village project. How would you like us to use this money: a school, health facilities, potable water, latrines, etc.", they are much less likely to suggest latrines. Latrines seem to work best when they are family based, not community based, are simple to build and maintain, and when there is a simple way of emptying them on a regular basis. When the village leaders, a village health committee or women's clubs make latrine-use a major campaign and such leaders have been able to build a high level of commitment and consensus in the village, a latrine program can work. I have seen successful latrine programs sustained when funding for future projects were made contingent on the willingness of the village to actually use latrines on a regular basis, also latrine programs can work when there is enough conscious awareness of the relationship between flies, disease and human waste among adults and children and when there are latrines in the local schools and the teachers both use and encourage the children to use them. Finally, I have seen some successful latrine projects mostly in Asia, where animal and human waste are collected and used for the production of bio-gas and organic fertilizers. Without these kinds of pre-conditions, most latrine projects fail to introduce significant changes in behavior.

Village Malnutrition: An RDF can use a very simple formula for getting a grasp on some village nutritional needs. The following formula will indicate the total production of grain required to meet the nutritional needs for a given village. You calculate the number of people in the village, multiplied by 365 days in the year, multiplied by 3,000 calories, divided by 3,200 calories per kilo. This will give the number of kilos of grain (no matter which type) needed to feed the village for the year. The allocation of 3,000 calories per person a day is a bit high, but this is to allow for some wastage of grain in storage. Legumes have a slightly higher concentration of calories per kilo, but the difference is not so great that they cannot be included in the calculation as well. Once you have this figure, go around to the farmers and find out how much grain they produce in an average year. Is there enough to feed the village. Often you may be surprised to find that enough is produced, yet people are going hungry. Where this is the case, you need to start asking questions about the distribution system. If enough is not produced, you need to investigate what is needed to increase agriculture production (see Chapter Twelve). A clear picture of what amount is needed to feed the whole village, and a clear proposal as to how it can be produced and distributed may be just what people need to see.

Malnutrition is not a disease but rather the condition caused by not getting enough food or enough of the right kinds of food at the right time. People can be encouraged to find sources of supplemental fruits and vegetables. Fruit trees, greenhouses and various kinds of family gardens can be encouraged. Demonstration is one of the most powerful teaching tools. RDFs are encouraged to grow experimental plots of needed fruits and vegetables. Husbands and wives need to be mobilized to understand appreciate the importance of good health in the lives of their children. Much of UNICEF's work has emphasized the need to focus on four activities that involve women and children in a community: (1) child's growth monitoring, (2) encouraging breast feeding, (3) teaching mothers to prepare oral rehydration packets, and (4) immunization. There are many doctors, nurses and village health workers who have yet to adopt the simple procedures of checking the arm measurement of children or of recording on a regular basis the weight of infants as a means of detecting the otherwise often-hidden fact of malnutrition.

Village Immunization: It would be appropriate for the RDF to conduct a survey in the village to determine who has and has not be immunized, how long it has been and what types of diseases are most common. With such information, the RDF is encouraged to meet with the villagers or village health committee to raise consciousness, to explain the need for a vaccination program and to develop commitment to some type of total village immunization program. Also with such information it is possible to link up with local hospitals, government health agencies, and national non government health programs that may provide the vaccine and the health personnel to vaccinate the children. It is also important to realize that the challenge of building a permanent system capable of delivering to every infant every year and of educating every generation of parents about the need for immunization is to integrate this process into the very fiber of the community ensuring that a local village health committee is functioning, that village health workers are keeping track of who needs vaccinations, and that the immunization program is a part of the broader health and sanitation program being implemented in the village.

Health Activities Appropriate for Stage Three

This is the stage to establish a self-sustaining health committee that guides and directs the work of local health workers in the community and ensures local resource mobilization to help pay for the supplies and equipment needed in the community health facility. Perhaps some type of community based income-generating project could be implemented to help pay for some of the costs of a local health program. RDFs can help communities organize with other communities to pressure the central government to establish some type of on-going training for para-professional village health workers at the district or provincial levels of government

Below is a series of issues that RDF must consider in developing ways of introducing some type of Village Community Health program that would be sustainable over an extended period of time.

Health Care Sustainability: First is the issue of payment for health care services provided by the village health worker. Some village discussion will be needed on this topic. Many villagers have come to expect free treatment from government or outsider medical care. The sustainability of the VHC program will require that the village health workers be compensated for their services. It does not have to be a fixed salary, but it should be some amount that is motivating to the health worker, perhaps some money, produce or food supplies, or inkind services. Also the cost of medicine must be considered. While the government or an outside agency may be willing to provide some free medicine, it is better if the villagers come to understand that such free medicine may not always be available and that the village needs to start mobilizing their own resources to create a village pharmacy or a village clinic storehouse. Most village health programs that are not sustainable have not dealt with the issue of payment to the health worker and the cost of replacing the medicine. The RDF will need to spend a significant amount of time helping villagers to understand this process. Realistically, the issue is one of degree. What is the level at which local people can participate financially? What scheme will provide the needed care and at the same time enable people to have a sense of dignity and self-respect? At best, any financial scheme will be one of appropriate shared responsibility. The most successful village health projects have usually been funded by some village income generating activity that was created specifically to pay for the health care worker and the medicine needed in the village. In some villages, a kind of health insurance program is established in which each family donates some small but fixed amount each month, structured to reflect family size and income. This money is used to help defer the expenses of paying the village health worker and to buy needed medicine. The money is collected through the village health committee and deposited in a nearby bank. Those families that do not participate with a monthly donation are allowed to receive care but must pay a high service fee.

Long Term Training and Support: A key issue relates to long-term training. A common problem with many village health programs is the tendency for an outside group to train an individual and then assume that a one-time training activity will be adequate to keep the village health worker motivated and committed. In reality, an effective village health worker needs continuous in-service training. Experience suggests that an initial 2-3 weeks of training is a minimum to get the process started, but that at least once every 3-4 months there needs to be follow-up training of 2-3 days to build their competency, to create bonds of friendship and support with other village health workers, and to assist these health workers with the on-going problems of village health work. When outside medical experts visit the village they must be careful not to ignore or discredit the village health workers. Outsiders should communicate to the village how valuable and competent their own village health worker is, that he or she has been trained and has the skill to deal with most of the health problems of the village. Outsiders make a terrible mistake if they do not reinforce and praise the work of the local para-professional.

The Jamkhed program in India has a well-established VHW training system. Initially, those chosen are brought to the main health center for a one-week training program. Thereafter, they come to the main center twice a month. Most of the training is based upon actual cases encountered at the center or in the village during the week. Their training, in general, is geared to deal with the project's health priorities. Though the emphasis is on the promotion of health care and prevention of diseases, they also receive some training in the curative treatment of simple illnesses and the use of a few basic drugs. Along with this training, they have brief studies in the social sciences sufficient for their needs. At various stages in the training, project staff will stay with VHWs in the village and observe them in practice. Good VHW training must be a two-way process of communication. As the instructors gain knowledge on local beliefs and taboos, they and the VHW discuss ways and means of overcoming those that are of a negative nature. As the VHWs gain knowledge, they are encouraged to make and develop their own health education material. The curriculum for the VHWs is tailored to the needs of the local situation. It includes, courses on cures for minor ailments, personal hygiene, preventive measures against diseases and disabilities, nutrition, maternal and child care, sanitation, and accident prevention. One village health worker had this to say about his experiences in the village: "This work which I am doing is helpful to my village, it is helpful to all my friends, it is helpful to my family, and also I get the satisfaction that through my hands I am able to do something which is really useful. And it gives me a little sense of happiness that it works, and it is successful, it is not a failure. It is like giving blood to another person. Much more significant is my work with children. I have seen so many children dying in my village. Now not even one child is dying. How grateful I am for this opportunity."

Analysis of How Health Might Impact on the Other Dimensions
Both interns and RDFs must come to see the interrelationship that exists among the five dimensions of rural development and the process of leadership building in the community. The process of identifying local leaders, establishing local problem solving committees, and other activities related to rural development must understand both the impact and interrelationship of all five dimensions and the process of moving from an unorganized rather simplistic process of village problem solving to a much more institutionalized sustainable process of problem solving. A detailed description of these processes was outlined above in Chapters Nine and Ten. Note how health can impact on each of the other dimensions of Rural Development.

Culture: Awareness of how traditional health workers might be introduced to modern medicine and how the two systems (traditional and modern) might learn to work together

Education: Awareness of how the local health system might be used to teach   concepts of sanitation, nutrition, and better health care systems in the local schools.

Income: Awareness of the how many hours are lost each year when villagers are ill and how productivity might be improved if the level of health in the community could be improved.

Ecology: Awareness of how better health is related to the quality of the environment.

Both interns and RDFs must carefully assess how these five dimension's impact on each other, must help the villagers to understand these interrelationships, and must assess the impact that a project or activity in one of these dimensions would have on the other dimensions. An awareness and sensitivity of these interrelationships do not come easily and outsiders, in particular, must be patient and open-minded to the ways in which these five dimensions are defined and understood by the villagers. Let us now approach the dimension of health in some detail, to reflect on the major issues and concepts of this dimension, to consider alternative ways to conceptualize appropriate interventions in the field of village health, and to consider a number of programs, activities and strategies that have worked in various parts of the world.

Section Four
General Strategies and Approaches Used in Health Programs

There are four important concepts related to the implementation of village health programs. (1) Collective Awareness, Involvement and Ownership, (2) Integration of Modern and Traditional Methods of Healing, (3) Local Resource Mobilization for Service Sustainability Through Meaningful Systems of Participation, and (4) Cultural Enhancement and Self-Identity Through the Use of Para-Professionals Whenever Possible.

Villager Awareness, Involvement, and Ownership

An increasing emphasis is being placed on the training of local people themselves so that they understand and implement preventive health care practices. For example, in Nigeria in the early 1970s, there was a gradual shift from curative to preventive medicine. Working directly with village leaders, specific men and women were selected by the community to be trained in basic health care services. Full-time medical personnel traveled to the villages to supervise the village health workers and to provide pre-natal clinics and immunization. It became quite clear that the effectiveness of preventive measures depended upon the active participation of the villagers. Even in remote areas where usual medical services are not available, it was possible to produce remarkable results if the villagers were involved and engaged in practicing appropriate health care.

Any health program can contribute to or weaken the objectives of community development. For example, consider a basic village health care program which chooses as its main implementer someone well-qualified from outside a village. Such a person may be effective in dealing with disease, malnutrition and poor sanitation. If the project organization has the financial resources to sustain such a system, it may well be viable economically. Such a project will be implemented more quickly than one based on a village committee or a locally selected health worker. However, a health project using a village health worker from within the village as the base of a health system, or a village health committee, enables the development of a leadership dynamic within the community that can broaden its concern to all aspects of the community's well-being. RDFs who focus on the development of a team within the village to run a health program are making strides toward enabling the village to have self-confident, and investing in the future capacity of the village to do its own development

This concept of village involvement has been developed even more widely in India around the Jamkhed area. The key aspect of this approach was the delegation of the practice of health services out of the hands of the doctor and into the hands of the nurses, the para-professional and, most important, the village health workers (VHWs). They are the link to the rural community. They are trained to use simple, effective and low cost methods that meet the village needs. The project developed a three-tier system of health care delivery to meet the health needs of the most neglected segment of society, the rural poor of India. The first tier consisted of at least one village health worker (VHW) resident in each village. The second tier consisted of a mobile health team of trainers that visited each village once or twice a month for follow-up training, evaluation, assessment of progress being made. The third tier consisted of the main center in Jamkhed with facilities for diagnosis, emergencies and in-patient care.

It is estimated that 85 percent of the health problems found in a rural area can be solved with basic health training of 2-3 weeks with follow-up training of 2-3 days every 3-4 months.[9] The book *Where There is NO Doctor* is a marvelous source for training such village health care workers.

Integrating Modern and Traditional Medicine

People's attention world-wide is turning to alternative forms of medicine from Chinese acupuncture to homeopathic cures, from herbal remedies to traditional Indian pulse-readings. The basic principle behind traditional healing is the link between man and the cosmos, between the individual and his/her psychological well-being. In Africa, in particular several efforts are being implemented to strengthen the relationships between traditional and modern medicine. For example, Zimbabwe has set up a national professional organization of native medicine men; Ghana now allows aspirant "native doctors" to pursue their studies at the national university and so obtain a doctorate in their branch of medicine. The government of Mali has formalized studies for traditional medicine men and has granted to graduates the professional title of doctor.

For many areas of the world, most rural people have much confidence in their traditional healers. Modern medicine, along with other aspects of Western culture are often seen as part of the heritage of the colonial powers. Most traditional healers are herbalists, the heir of ancient practices with a deep knowledge of the efficacy of plants and roots for curing diseases. Native scientists are getting involved in research on the properties of natural substances. In Cameroon, a pharmacologist claims to have extracted from the roots of a local plant -- he keeps its identity a secret -- a substance with anti-inflammatory effects, and capable of curing the growth of cancerous tumors. The same mixture has been used to cure the tropical disease bilharziasis.

It is now argued that the whole future of traditional medical science depends on the commitment that doctors and scientists will have to discover and adopt the empirical secrets that the traditional healers have so closely guarded amongst themselves until now. In the highland plateau scattered with mysterious medicine men in central Mali on the borders of Burkina Faso, is the Banidagara Research Centre for Traditional Medicine. Here, a group of Italian doctors and technicians, under the coordination of Dr. Piero Coppo, is researching with a group of Mali colleagues the bases of traditional medicine and the medical plants used in the region. Their results have identified a number of new medicines with high effectiveness and low level of toxicity. Hapatisane is an infusion that stimulates the bile production of the liver, dysenteral is a great antidote for amebic dysentery, cassia is a laxative infusion, and balemo, a natural cough syrup.

Primary health care should not be built on a preconceived standard model of modern medicine, but needs to develop organically in each environment. It is now also clear that people's perceived needs in health care are molded by the culture and its understanding of what sickness is, how it is caused and what are its appropriate cures. Traditional health systems are holistic -- involving an understanding of the total culture, its religions, its folklore, its healers, and its herbal remedies. Professional RDFs, and especially professional health care workers, need to become acquainted with the concepts and healing methods that can be derived from them. Research in the Philippines has demonstrated that nearly all traditional systems of health care can be analyzed in one of three ways: (1) a significant 40 percent of all traditional health care remedies have some therapeutic value, are based upon methods, herbs and other practices that have been found to be useful in the lessening of pain, the healing of wounds and broken limbs, and the cure of certain kinds of diseases. Another thirty-five percent of all traditional methods appear to have neither a positive nor negative impact, from a scientific assessment point of view. Many simply have a placebo effect. Nevertheless, because people believe such remedies are efficacious, they can be helpful. Village doctors would do well to allow such practices to take place if only as a way of creating trust and a better relationship with the community they are working with. It is true, of course, that another twenty-five percent of the traditional methods used in village communities do have some potential danger, applying cow dung on wounds, excessive bleeding, denying liquids to children who have diarrhea, using herbs that are highly toxic, etc. Care is needed to separate these three different types of traditional medicine. From the RDF's perspective, it is important to note that roughly three-fourths of all traditional healing practices are either helpful or at least not harmful. Medical professionals need to have a more open mind concerning these traditional health care systems. Being sensitive to and aware of the valuable contribution that a traditional healer can make to the community's health will both increase trust and reduce opposition from the community and the traditional healers working in a given area.

The Role of the Paraprofessional in Rural Development

There are not enough RDF professionals to meet the demand for rural development assistance. Faced with this reality, many people in the field of rural development have concluded that non professionals should be given the training and supervision they need to provide some rural development services. There has been over the past decade a trend toward the use of paraprofessionals in rural development and related fields. Many PVOs have discovered that paraprofessionals can indeed provide many direct services as effectively as full professionals, for much lower salaries. More and more it has been demonstrated that training local community workers in the basic five dimensions of rural development is an effective strategy for reaching certain communities that would otherwise go unserved. The paraprofessional movement emerged partially in response to the exclusive practices of the medical profession, which made health services available only to the communities that could afford a practicing physician.

It has been found that a large part of the success of community health worker programs has depended on these non traditional workers receiving training, support, and supervision from professionals. Medical practitioners often do not have sufficient experience or training in working effectively with various racial, ethnic, and socioeconomic groups. This is also true in the field of education and literacy, agricultural extension, small scale enterprise development and other professional fields related to rural development.

It is essential for both professionals and paraprofessionals to acquire understanding of culturally diverse populations and to learn cross-cultural competencies, as we discussed earlier. The trend toward the increased use of paraprofessionals means that professionals, especially during the Third Stage of Rural Development, will have to assume new and expanding roles. They can be expected to spend less time providing direct services to villagers, so that they will have time for indirect services such as teaching and consulting with community workers, volunteers, and paraprofessionals. Utilizing paraprofessionals can benefit the community. It can also benefit paraprofessionals, for they will receive training and supervision. It can also benefit professional practitioners, for it gives them opportunities to develop new roles in carrying out community programs. Once professionals in health, education, agriculture and other fields related to rural development see the paraprofessional as a partner in extending their own influence into a larger number of communities than a single professional could ever accomplish alone, then the time and effort required to train and work with such paraprofessionals will be seen as legitimate and appropriate. RDFs must play an important role in helping other professionals see the value of such paraprofessional programs.

My experiences with paraprofessional village workers have been quite positive. Of course, there are both advantages and disadvantages to using such non-professional workers. One of the advantages is that village workers are often perceived more as friends and role models than are RDFs, which tends to make them less threatening than a professional RDF. One of the limitations is that the skills of such village workers are not as well developed as those of professional RDFs. Thus, these paraprofessionals need to be aware when problems are beyond their level of competence and to know when and how to refer such problems to a professional. This limitation underscores the need for professional supervision as the cornerstone of an effective paraprofessional program. There are many creative possibilities for professionals and paraprofessionals in working collaboratively to meet the health needs of the community.

Many planners and health professionals, who formerly disdained any perpetuation of traditional medicine, are now realizing the importance of linking traditional healthcare providers into the modern system. One thing that is clear is that modern medicine and all its trappings simply will not be available to the vast majority of people on this planet for many decades if not centuries. The millions of isolated rural poor in particular will remain neglected if they are to wait until sufficient numbers of doctors and nurses are trained and health centers are built to serve their hard-to-reach and sometimes less-than-inviting communities and villages. In the final analysis, common sense indicates that much could be accomplished and relatively quickly, by somehow tapping the resources that are already available locally.

Several government programs are being established which do seek to link the traditional to the modern. Examples include: set up a government licensing program and license indigenous practitioners willing to completed some basic training; supply them free of charge or at low cost with basic supplies and medications; provide ongoing supervision, continuing education and a re supply of materials as necessary; recruit local, traditional practitioners to become part of the teams assigned to rural health clinics; organize workshops for government health personnel in which they are given appropriate cross-cultural training, with specific emphasis on the beliefs and practices of traditional medicine, and finally modify modern medical school curriculum to include elements of traditional medicine with a view of personalizing the practice of village medicine and promoting an appreciation of traditional beliefs and practices.

The Role of the Local Culture in Introducing a Village Community Health Program

Let us now review in some detail a case study that demonstrates how a health care system was restructured to prepare a group of village health workers to be more effective in their efforts to introduce modern medicine into their communities. The conclusions of this case study are surprising for they suggest how important it is for rural development workers to be fully aware and knowledgeable of the local culture before they seek to implement some of type development program.

The Sikuani, one of some 70 indigenous groups in Columbia, number nearly 20,000 people living in small villages scattered among the savannas of the Orinoco River Basin, mainly in the department of Meta and territory of Vichada.[10]

"The women ignore us. They don't want to sweep their houses or boil drinking water. The grandmother say they never boiled the water and it hasn't kill them yet. When someone is seriously ill, the people in the community say the promoter should pay the cost of transporting the person to town and feeding him, that that's why we earn good money so we can pay for these things. They don't believe us when we talk about parasites and microbes; they think diseases are caused by witchcraft."

During a conference of discouraged village health workers, the above comments were common among the women hired to work as health workers. When they were asked what their major problems were as health workers in the village, they were very hesitant to talk about problems. They had become accustomed to coming to a training session to learn from the experts, no one had ever asked them about their problems. When they were pressed, they simply suggested that everything was OK in the village, that all they needed was more advanced training in nursing, more drugs and equipment, better transportation, and panels for the tin roofs of local health posts. This did not fit well with the fact that 60 percent of the health workers were dropping out (quitting their health care work) after less than one year. We began to realize that the problem was not in the lack of resources, but the way that their roles as health workers were being defined, both by the government and by the villagers themselves. The problem was to remove the barriers that kept the health workers from unleashing their creativity to work as Sikuanis as well as representatives of a government agency.

Only when they began to discuss their problems among themselves in their own language, did the RDFs assigned to this area understand their problems. After three hours of intense discussion, a number of issues began to emerge. The broad outlines of the participatory research program that the RDFs would undertake with them during the next two years emerged from RDFs increased awareness of their problems. The RDFs developed a totally new concept of training for these indigenous people that sought to integrate these health workers into the community by forging links with the village leaders on an on-going basis, that would not only emphasize curing the sick, but would also emphasize promoting health. The RDFs' preliminary research convinced them that the declining health among the Sikuani was related more to recent ecological and sociocultural changes than to strictly medical factors.

Until the 1950s, the Sikuani, like many tribal groups in the world, were generally able to maintain their traditional life. The Sikuani sustained themselves by hunting, fishing, gathering edible roots and insects, and by slash and burn farming, primarily of yuca amarga, or cassava. Gradually, settlers began moving into the area, forcing the Sikuani into far less favorable lands. One immediate consequence of reduced area was an impaired diet. The Sikuanis were cut off from many of their traditional sources of protein -- the game, insects, roots, nuts, turtle eggs, and wild fruits that were vanishing along with their habitat. The effects of malnutrition have been compounded by exposure to new diseases through contact with whites, while concentrated settlement in villages has facilitated the spread of contagions once they are introduced. The formation of permanent villages has also led to other problems. The accumulation of human waste and garbage, and the feces of increasing numbers of domesticated cattle, chickens, pigs, and dogs have polluted the streams that provide water for household use, making them primary sources of disease. The final result of all these factors has been high rates of intestinal parasites, tuberculosis and other respiratory illnesses, malaria, and skin infections.

At the same time, the Sikuani have been replacing traditional practices that promoted health -- such as breast-feeding, the use of medicinal plants, and a diversified diet based on local foods, -- with products -- such as infant formulas, pharmaceuticals, and canned goods -- that make cash-poor villagers even more dependent on a market economy.

How to Bridge the Gap Through Participatory Research

As a first step it was necessary to integrate the Sikuani health workers into the lives and minds of the people. Many of the newly trained health workers had lost interest in supporting themselves through agriculture, hunting and fishing, and preferred to wait at health posts or in their homes -- day in, day out -- for a patient to come in and ask for a drug. As salaried employees of a government agency they were in danger of being transformed into an indigenous elite with little connection to the communities that had selected them.

The RDFs decided to keep the former health workers, along with a few new ones. They did not want to waste the training that the health workers had already received, and in fact, those who had already been trained proved to be a necessary bridge between the Western and the traditional Sikuani medical systems. The RDFs adopted a participatory research approach, a methodology that involved the community in every phase of the process -- from formulating the problems and identifying resources and strategies, to interpreting results and taking corrective action. Participants not only benefited from the concrete results of such research, they also learned how to analyze and solve their own problems.

The first step was to hold a series of meetings with village leaders and traditional healers in the village. Research would focus on aspects of Sikuani culture and traditional medicine, but the village leaders and healers could stipulate which topics not to investigate, because they might expose tribal mysteries. Three specific areas were selected for analysis: the history and current situation of the community, Sikuani medicine, and the traditional diet.

What was crucial in this early phase that took several months to complete was the interaction between the health workers and the villagers, and the information that was collected and reviewed with a local doctor and nurse. The health workers became pivotal in the process, for they were learning far more from the villagers than the other way around. Often after several days of discussing a topic, the health workers would decide that they had to return to their communities to interview other people -- women, elders, shamans -- who were in a better position to know. Even after the information was collected, the health workers would visit with groups of people, explain what they had learned from individuals and seek group consensus on what they thought they knew.

Curiously enough, the topic that proved to be pivotal in defining the direction of the program was Sikuani history, and several meetings were devoted to it. The health workers began asking people in their communities several basic questions: Was the community healthier today than 20 years ago? Did people eat better before? What changes had occurred in the way people lived? How had these changes affected health and diet? Piece by piece a historical and social overview of disease began to emerge. At the end of the process, each health worker prepared a profile of his community that not only summarized its history, but also contained an appraisal of the general state of health, perceived morbidity rates, and local peoples' opinions about their problems. The reports were read at community meetings and discussed, sparking lively debates about which problems were most urgent, how they were caused, and what could be done to solve them.

From the outset of the discussions, the RDFs stressed that the Sikuani had a great wealth of cultural resources that was being lost and that must be recovered if efforts at autonomous development were to succeed. One interesting question did arise: "Were we suggesting that the Sikuani should once again use the casas mosquitero, or mosquito-proof communal houses built of thatched palm fronds." Such housing had disappeared several years earlier, when most of the palm trees had been cut down. This lead to a heated debate about progress, change, the value of the old ways, the impossibility of going back to old ways, etc.

A project to provide clean drinking water helped clarify how the old and the new could be linked effectively. The history the health workers were reconstructing clearly showed that the pattern of concentrated settlement in permanent villages, which had become prevalent in the past 20 years, had led to the pollution of the primary sources of water for domestic use. The traditionalists argued that the river caused illness because the proper rituals of purification had often been ignored. The health workers, of course, suggested a modern health explanation. What was important was that both explanations were given respect and people were encouraged to discuss their own points of view. As the possibility of perhaps digging wells closer to the village (as opposed to a long walk to the river), it became apparent that outside help would be needed. The health workers had to learn to prepare a project proposal -- complete with justifications, objectives, and activities -- in order to obtain outside financing. Hours were spent drafting the proposal, which was modified and expanded in response to community suggestions that were collected between the discussion meetings.

When women began to realize that wells would cut down on the time needed to obtain water, they became quit excited, until a few mentioned that now there would be no reason to go to the river, a time for visiting, meetings, chatting, and matchmaking. In the end it was decided that the wells would provide enough clean water for drinking and cooking, while bathing and laundering would continue at the stream.

In discussing the introduction of pumps and other modern gadgets, it was finally agreed that since they were instrumental in providing water, they too should be a part of the purification rituals used in the traditional ways. After such questions were raised and resolved, it was finally decided that the communities would not only contribute their labor to the project but would raise their own funds to buy tools and spare parts to maintain the system. With their written proposal finalized, the RDFs then began to encourage the local health workers to visit various PVOs and government agencies in the area that might provide some funding for the wells and pumps. Within a few months they had obtained funding which helped put wells and pumps in about half the villages during the first year

While well construction was under way, the health workers began implementing an educational campaign on the water problem, using posters in Sikuani that they prepared during the discussion meetings. As the communities learned how to use, repair, and maintain their new water systems, they made the project their own. It was now clear to the health workers and the RDFs that the important thing was not whether health resources were traditional or modern but whether or not they are controlled by the communities. Technological innovations can be assimilated when they are sufficiently discussed beforehand.

Please note that the lack of discussion and local ownership helps explain why government medical services in the area have been so under utilized, even though professional medicine has resources that could significantly benefit indigenous communities. That is, health posts, pharmaceuticals, diagnostic equipment, doctors and nurses, and paramedicals are often wasted precisely because the local population, despite its obvious need, lacks the framework for understanding how they work, and the opportunity to reflect how such resources can be appropriately incorporated into local development. Most people only came to the health center after a delivery of pharmaceuticals. Too many recommendations from the health workers were being ignored. Treatments for tuberculosis were not followed because the patient thought the symptoms of the disease were caused by witchcraft. Dietary regimens to counteract illnesses caused by nutritional deficiencies were ignored because they contradicted the suggestions of the *shaman*. The oral rehydration and breast-feeding campaigns conducted by the health workers for years appeared to have made no impression on mothers. The conflict between traditional medicine and the provision of modern health services that seemed to lie at the heart of such problems was the next issue that the program would explore.

Classifying Diseases in terms of Traditional Medicine.

Most studies of traditional medicine appear to assume that such traditional systems of medicine divide diseases into two classes -- those with natural and those with supernatural causes. Natural diseases are regarded as those that require treatment based on cause-and-effect relations, understood in terms of the scientific logic of Western medicine. Supernatural diseases are those attributed to spiritual causes that require treatment by magic or witchcraft.

In their participatory research project, the 15 Sikuani health workers challenged this view, spending several months of working out the rationale and internal logic of the medical practices and beliefs that they had learned as children, from their parents and grandparents. The work became truly exciting when the health workers began to realize that the knowledge in traditional lore could be organized into many categories. Traditional medicine ceases being a disjointed collection of names for diseases or a series of seemingly arbitrary treatments based on antiquated customs, and became, instead, a complex organic system whose structure and dynamics arose from the present and past history of the Sikuani people.

Before that could happen, however, it was first necessary to understand the very notion of "classification," which emerged gradually as a product of their work. First they compiled a long list of all the Sikuani names for diseases. Then they played what they called "the game of the little boxes," in which they identified those diseases that could be subsumed by other diseases. Little by little, broader categories were identified, until an approximation of the Sikuani system of classifying diseases emerged. The health workers then took their charts back to their communities for discussion before returning to the next meeting to make corrections. The health workers spent long hours collating the information they had gathered and discussing the concepts behind each category before finally assigning a disease to its given box. The local doctor who participated in this process was visibly impressed: "My image of traditional medicine was transformed. I always thought that indigenous peoples were superstitious, that their medicine was no more than herbal remedies and spells. Now we should understand each other better because I'll be able to appreciate the diagnoses patients offer when they come in for exams." He also acknowledged the value of clarifying the system of traditional medicine in a given culture: "This work has helped me see why patients are sometimes so reluctant to come to the health post, or why they take off in midtreatment to see the *shaman*. Before, I would scold the village health workers because I though it was their fault when things went badly. Now I don't think it's a simple problem. Instead, I should support them so they can work better with traditional medicine."

A new system of communicating between villagers, health workers and doctors was worked out. The health workers now give doctors, with each referral, a bicultural case-history form detailing the Sikuani diagnosis of the disease and the way the patient has been treated in the community, both by the health worker and the *shaman*. Charts now hang on the wall at the health center and at health posts in outlying villages so that medical personnel can better understand patients and prescribe treatments that respect the practices of traditional medicine.

This joint effort by health workers and medical personnel consolidated the participation of village health workers in the program. Health workers, aware of the essential knowledge they had as Sikuanis, gained the confidence to be more open with supervising doctors and nurses. Many of the problems that were cited before the program began were not problems of "laziness" or "vagrancy" at all, but misunderstandings that cleared up when the health workers were able to speak up and be understood. The health workers now realized that representing a medical institution did not require losing faith in their own traditions. Nor was it a question of becoming traditional healers. Rather, they were the indispensable mediators between Western and traditional medicine.

Decision-making Sparks Creativity

Promotion of breast-feeding is a priority of the national ministry of health, and rural health workers have been chosen as the best qualified group to spread the word in local communities. As we would later learn, Sikuani women did not share that assumption. In the early efforts to encourage the women to breast feed their young children, such advice seemed natural and logical. Children were weaned on average, at six months, and bottle feeding often commenced just a few days after birth. Surveys by the health workers of mothers in 30 communities revealed troubling data on the nutritional intake of small children. Why were these women rejecting the traditional method of breast-feeding. Gradually the dilemma to the problem began to emerge. Previous campaigns had failed because they ignored the changes that had occurred in women's work, the shifting relationship between Sikuani men and women, and the traditional explanation for the origin of many childhood illnesses interacted. The first explanation presented was simply that the women found a bottle much more convenient. When the Sikuani maintained a semi-nomadic lifestyle, women walked to their fields in 15-20 minutes. Today, settled in permanent villages and raising livestock, the Sikuani often have fields two or three hours away, making it difficult for women to bring young children along, especially when it is necessary to make the return trip home loaded down with produce. The bottle, then, has been a great convenience, enabling mothers to leave young children at home in the care of a grandmother, aunt, or other relatives.

Infant formula, however, is costly so it is often diluted with stream water, which as was later found to be contaminated with pathogens. Even with the advent of wells, a poor understanding of hygiene and the importance of sterilizing bottles poses grave risks of transmitting gastro-intestinal infections.

A shift in the traditional rules governing the relationship between men and women has occurred alongside the change in work patterns. Schooling and the learning of Spanish have given women a greater freedom in their relationships with both Sikuani and nonindigenous men, provoking increased jealousy and sparking lovers' quarrels. This, in turn, was linked to the way the Sikuani explain the rise in infant mortality from diarrhea and vomiting as an increase of the disease called *amibeje*, which can be roughly translated as "bewitched breast" and which affects children though a poisoning of the mother's milk, It occurs when a man who has been wounded by love touches a woman's breast and casts a spell. Any future child who suckles at her breast will grow ill and die. *Amibeje*, then, not only defines the nature of many childhood illnesses and explains the new practice of early weaning despite the high rate of gastro-intestinal infections associated with bottle-feeding, it also acts as a social control, reinforcing traditional mores. The danger of transmitting sickness becomes a mechanism for culturally limiting the disorder in sexual relations caused by social changes that outstrip the ability of people to absorb or assimilate them.

Such an analysis of the problem vividly demonstrated how formidable the obstacles are to linking traditional and modern practices. The health workers understood this and sided with the community saying, "For now we need to learn to properly handle the bottle so we can teach mothers how to protect their babies when breast-feeding is not now possible." That decision transformed the breast-feeding campaign into a study of nutrition that would provide mothers with the information they needed about the relationships between infant mortality, food hygiene, and family economy.

The message from this case study should be clear. Only when the local doctors and nurses understood the culture of the area where they were working could they be effective in training and working with village health workers. When you separate a health worker from his or her culture, you separate that person from the community. The integration of traditional and modern medicine generated greater cooperation and trust between villagers and the medical system, it gave the health workers a sense of pride and dignity -- knowing that they had found value in their own cultural way of doing things and in using modern medicine when appropriate. No RDF will be effective in a given community until this knowledge of the local culture is both understood and appreciated.

Section Five
CHOICE Rural Hospital Outreach Program

One interesting example of an approach appropriate for the third stage of rural development and found to be useful in establishing a long-term village health program in various LDCs is the Rural Hospital Outreach Program being established by CHOICE, a non-profit NGO, operating in a number of countries.

In an attempt to organize a self-sustaining program of village workers, CHOICE first identifies a rural district hospital which is willing to participate in a village health worker outreach program. Such rural hospitals are usually isolated from central urban areas, often lack adequate supplies and equipment, and are generally in great need of support and encouragement. Over the past several years, CHOICE has developed a network with various American hospitals, clinics, pharmaceutical houses and private doctors willing to donate and help distribute the kind of basic medical supplies and equipment that isolated rural hospitals can readily use. CHOICE contracts with the local rural hospital to designate at least one or two hospital staff to act as trainers and supervisors for a cadre of local village health workers in the participating district. In return for this service, CHOICE provides on a regular basis, significant amounts of supplies and equipment to the rural district hospital. Below is a general description of the CHOICE Village Health Corps program.

The next step after a rural district hospital has been identified is to recruit and assign a full-time rural development facilitator (RDF) to the district. Her job would be to visit all the villages in the district, seek to help organize village health committees who in turn would select individuals to be trained as village health workers.

In the United States, various physicians, dentists, nurses, public health workers and others with basic health care skills are recruited who are willing to spend at least 1-2 weeks working in the rural district hospital. Such medical personnel must be willing to pay their own living and travel expenses while in the rural district, bring some of their own basic medical supplies and equipment, and participate with the local staff in providing basic medical care and training for both local hospital staff and local village people, (including the village health workers and members of the village health committees).

The medical personnel selected to participate are **expected to spend at least five days** in the rural district, with the mornings devoted to training village health workers on the concepts and procedures outlined in the book by David Werner *Where There Is No Doctor* or the book by Murray Dickson, *Where There Is No Dentist*. In the afternoons of these five days in the district, the participating medical personnel are expected to conduct a public open clinic, to provide basic health care for the local villagers as well as supervise and support local village health workers to develop skills on concepts and procedures presented during the morning training sessions.

The CHOICE program has **several advantages** over other humanitarian medical programs in developing countries.

1. Many doctors have participated in humanitarian medical programs but have felt some frustration in knowing that what they did, while it was helpful to the individuals receiving medical treatment, probably had very little long-term impact on the community as a whole. By combining short-term professional health care and training of local health care workers, the **long-term impact** on these communities can be much greater.

2. Field research conducted by a number of donor agencies has determined that nearly **75 percent of all health-related deaths in rural villages can be prevented** by individuals with less than eight weeks of intensive training in: oral rehydration, basic awareness of communicable diseases, proper nutrition, the do's and don'ts of modern medicine in a village environment, care of simple respiratory problems, simple first aid practices, concepts of sanitation and basic public health, oral hygiene, etc.

3. The CHOICE Village Health Corps has designed an **eight stage training program** where village health workers receive intensive training for forty days: five days a week over eight separate weeks scattered over a two year period. **CHOICE has projects in Mexico, Guatemala, Bolivia, Kenya, India, Indonesia, Samoa, and Vietnam.** In most of these areas, there are both rural district hospitals which provide the follow-up supervision and training and also full time Rural Development Facilitators (RDFs) paid by CHOICE and assigned full time in the district area to provide on-site support and encouragement until the next level of training can be given. Each participant will be told what level of training the village health workers need in a given village. All training materials are adapted from the book *Where There Is No Doctor* (Dentist).[11]

4. In each village **there is a translator provided** to work directly with the medical personnel assigned to the various villages of the district. Generally, the rural district hospital doctors assigned to the CHOICE program participate directly with the American medical team, both to observe the work of the Americans, but also to provide cultural insights and suggestions on how best to work with the village health workers. CHOICE has learned from experience that the rural district hospital personnel are much more committed to this type of outreach program when they actually participate in the training program out in the field both with the American team and the village health workers. Personal relationships can thus be established which make it much easier for the district medical people to then later follow-up with their own visits and encouragement.

Basic Principles of an Effective Village Health Care Program

Over the past several years, CHOICE has developed the following eight basic principles for a Sustainable Village Health Program:

1. A Formal Network Linking Village Health Committees, Village Health Workers to a District Hospital Is Needed:
Problem: Many NGOs tend to provide training and support for health programs directly at the village level. While such programs can introduce health services, too often, as soon as the outsiders leave the project area, the local health workers often become discouraged, seldom receive follow-up training and supervision, and generally have no access to an on-going source of medical supplies. Such one-time programs of aid and support are almost never sustainable.
Solution: Sustainable Village Health programs require the formal linkage of village level programs to a district level hospital both for long-term supervision and encouragement, but also to ensure that the village level program becomes integrated into the formal health system of the country. Such a network requires the active support of the district hospital staff and the establishment of a network of village health committees, consisting of local villagers interested in improving the health situation in the village. They are also crucial in organizing health projects, mobilizing local resources and recruiting and supporting village health workers.

2. Long-Term Iterative Training is More Effective Than Short-term Concentrated Training Too many village health workers receive a one-time intensive crash course of several weeks and then are expected to function basically on their own. While such training in a concentrated period of time is quite common, without costly programs of follow-up, the impact will be limited.
Solution: Experience has shown that having shorter periods of training (five days) scheduled over a longer period of time (usually every four months over a two year period) will have much more long-term impact in ensuring that the training is understood, practiced and internalized. The training program established by the CHOICE Village Health Program seeks to provide eight weeks of training but scatters the training out over a two year period at an interval of every three or four months Because of the relationship established with a rural district hospital, a local physician participates directly with the CHOICE medical team assigned to the rural area. During this training, each village health worker is given specific assignments, is prepared in specific skills and interventions, and is provided with specific supplies that they are to practice using over the 3-4 months between each training session.

3. Focus on Very Basic Health Care with an Emphasis on Preventive Medicine: Most professional medical personnel are generally trained in curative medicine which works well in an environment where medical resources and facilities are readily available. Medical personnel who participate in the CHOICE Village Health Corps will often need to have their orientation to medicine modified. All trainers are expected to become completely familiar with the material found in David Werner's two books: *Where There Is No Doctor* and *Helping Health Workers Learn*.

Solution: Effective village health programs must combine both curative and preventive medicine, but emphasis should be placed on preventive strategies: sanitation, education, and nutrition. Effective trainers will seek to provide information, skills, knowledge and interventions that are readily understood by people with little education, easily introduced and incorporated into the local culture, and can be practiced by people with little training. CHOICE provides experienced interpreters and/or RDFs who are prepared to work with the medical professional in training village health workers.

4. **Training Must Include Hands-on Practical Emphasis Which also Encourages an Integration of Modern and Traditional Medicine:** Too many health care programs emphasis class room study, with a strong dose of reading and listening. Most para-professional health workers have had little schooling, are not able to take notes in a class room setting and will not retain much of what they hear in the training. Too often, the training staff is quite insensitive to the role and significance of traditional medical care.

Solution: The five day training program is scheduled as follows: In the mornings (8-12 a. m.), the trainer introduces the basic concepts of the program to the village health workers. Much of the training must emphasis a "learn by doing orientation." During each afternoon, (1-5 p.m.), an open public clinic will be set up. During the first two or three sessions of training the professional trainer will obviously take the lead, but is encouraged to involve the village health workers in the diagnosis, suggested interventions, and possible follow-up as much as possible. In the later sessions of the training, especially during the training of the second year, the medical professional is encouraged to take a back-seat to the village health workers: This is important as a crucial part of building the health workers competence, confidence and status in their communities. Equally, important is the way in which the professional demonstrates to the villagers that what the village health worker is doing is good, should be listened to, and that the professional has confidence in the village health worker. Villagers often believe that the only person who can help them is someone in a white coat who dispenses pills. The professional plays an important role in legitimizing the role and status of the village health worker among their fellow villagers.

The types of skills taught include the following: promotion of education in local health problems and methods of preventing and controlling them; promotion of improved food supplies and nutrition, with information on balanced diets, breast-feeding, weaning foods, and the growing of vegetables and fruit in home gardens; promotion of safe water supplies and basic sanitation, including the construction and use of latrines, personal hygiene, and the preparation and storage of food; promotion of immunization against major diseases, including referral of children under five to clinics for immunization; promotion of prevention and control of locally endemic diseases, including the recognition of symptoms of dangerous diseases such as diarrhea, tuberculosis, leprosy, malaria and malnutrition, and the referral of affected individuals for treatment; provision of treatment for common diseases and injuries, as well as first aid and accident prevention; promotion of maternal and child health care, the monitoring of pregnancy and recognition of abnormalities, antenatal care, basic delivery techniques, referral for abnormal delivery; and finally, provision of essential drugs, including aspirin and other first-aid medication; and the operation of basic dispensaries.

5. A Pay for Services Program Must Be Instituted: Many rural health care programs provide medical care and medicine at no charge. When such medical supplies are no longer available, and this is most of the time, the rural health program quickly dies.

Solution: CHOICE will provide each village health worker with a medical kit, made up of basic medicines, supplies and instruments needed. The village health workers are strongly encouraged to charge some fee for their services and to charge for the medicine dispensed. There will be times when some of the poorest of the poor may need to have these services and medicines somewhat subsidized. However, as a principle, it is hoped that the villagers are gradually prepared to see that medicine does cost money, that if the village health worker is to replenish his meager supply of medicine, he will need to receive some payment. CHOICE is committed to re supply the village health workers' medical kit every four months during the two years of the program, but the village health workers are encouraged to charge the villagers when they dispense supplies, to purchase local equivalents of the medicine given, and over the two year period of the program to establish their own slush fund large enough to purchase the supplies they need, independent of outside support. Implicit in this principle is the notion that antibiotics are to be used sparingly, that highly sophisticated drugs are inappropriate in a village setting, that when a villager has a serious medical problem, they should go to a professional medical person in the rural district hospital.

6. Full-Time RDFs are Needed to Supervise the VHWs: In many village health care programs, the village workers receive very little supervision, support or monitoring. Even though they have been give several weeks of training, within a few months without outside support, they soon become discouraged, apathetic and ineffective.

Solution: In each area where the CHOICE Village Health Corps is established, a full-time rural development facilitator (RDF) is assigned. This will generally be a local person, trained in community development and general rural development program implementation. He or she will generally be responsible to cover 10-20 villages and thus will be visiting on a fairly regular basis with the village health workers, assessing their effectiveness, determining what problems they are having, reinforcing the previous training that they had received, and perhaps even bringing them together periodically to share problems, successes, concerns and interventions that have worked or not worked. Equally important are the medical personnel assigned by the rural district hospital to work with and visit on some regular basis the village health workers trained in the rural district. CHOICE agrees to provide significant amounts of medical supplies but only on the condition that district hospital personnel are working with local village health workers in a supportive way and on a continual basis.

7. Specific Strategy to Integrate the VHWs into the Formal Health System: Many outside organizations have sent medical personnel into rural communities to provide modern medical care. Such humanitarian work is greatly appreciated, but unfortunately, such efforts seldom have any long-impact on the community. Even when the village health care workers receive adequate training and support, the program quickly dies when the outsiders are no longer funding the program in a given area.

Solution: As soon as CHOICE moves into a new area and sets up a CHOICE Rural Hospital Outreach Program, a system must be set up by which the village health workers are gradually integrated into the formal health system of their respective countries. Contact with local clinics, rural hospitals must be established, and specific personal in these facilities must be encouraged to see the value and competency of the village health workers. One way CHOICE seeks to build these kinds of relationships is to obtain donations from US hospitals, clinics, pharmaceutical houses, etc., to provide needed supplies to these formal health systems. Also, district health officials and hospital personnel can be invited to visit some of the training sessions, to see the quality of services being provided and the way that these village health workers can be an important component of the formal health service. CHOICE is committed to work in a rural area for two years and then seeks to move into another rural area and to start the whole process over again. This principle of integrating village health workers into the formal system is crucial to this process.

8. Localize the CHOICE Health Program: Many health care programs are implemented by Americans, based upon the belief that we have the training, the funds and the skill to help the less fortunate people of this world. While this kind of thinking is only partially appropriate in the short-run, the long-term consequences may not always be positive. In our attempt to help the disadvantaged of the world, we may be denying local people from developing the skills and commitments needed to learn how to care for their own people.

Solution: The long-term goal of the CHOICE Village Health Program in a given country would be to recruit local health professionals to initiate the principles of a sustainable village health care program themselves. From among the many VHWs trained under the CHOICE health program, 3-4 of the very best could be trained and supported by local sources of funding to duplicate this program independent of American professionals. This is the long-term goal of this program.

Lessons Learned from Successful Village Health Programs

One significant assessment of the district hospital outreach approach suggests the following pre-requisites for success [12]

(1) **Moral and Material Support of the District Medical Officer.** In successful programs, the district health officers manifest their commitment by supporting village health committees, by maintaining a functioning mobile health team, scheduling regular hospital staff visitations to the participating communities, regularly attending village health committees, responding immediately to health committee requests for assistance, and advocating the need for preventive and public health interventions to doctors and nurses and other hospital staff in the district.

(2) **An Operational Mobile Health Team.** Such teams generally consist of a variety of personnel: possibly a doctor, nurse, sanitary inspector and health educator, etc. By means of regular contact with the village communities (health surveys, seminars, village assemblies, medical visits, village health committee meetings, etc.), the health team creates a network of contacts that increases the skill, the confidence and the status of the village health workers.

(3) **Federation of Village Health Committees:** Some of the most successful district outreach programs not only established health committees in each village but also established an active federation of village health committees in the district. The federation serves as an essential mechanism by which individual health committees could approach and pressure the health system for more and better quality services. Other beneficial services provided by the federation included: lending money to health committees to finance activities and repair facilities, accompany health committee officers to the central ministry to request special services, linking experienced health committees with recently organized committees in order to lend technical assistance, financing transportation costs so that health officials can regularly visit distant communities, and training health committee officials in organizational, parliamentary and interpersonal skills.

(4) **Strong Village Health Committee Leadership.** Successful district programs invested considerable time and effort training both the village committee members and the village health workers both to mobilize their own resources in order to become more self-sufficient, but also to take more responsibility for the quality of health care in their individual villages.

Section Six
The Importance of Local Participation in Village Health Programs

The strategy being suggested in this chapter seeks to give some form to the principle of participation that might enable RDFs and villagers to consciously include this principle in their program plans and evaluations. It is still not clear what the basic ingredients of an effective process of participation might include, but the literature on participation does give us some clues.

One scholar argues that "Until those who have to make decisions about resources also have frameworks by which to understand and judge their efforts to extend public health care (PHC) beyond service delivery, it is likely they will continue to expect health to be related mainly to the provision of services and choose policies and actions that reflect this view. For this reason, it is important to attempt to develop a framework in which **professionals can see benefits of efforts to support participation**, alter their expectations accordingly and allocate resources and time to developing this approach. Until those who have control of resources are convinced that participation is a viable and desirable concept, it is likely to remain relegated to rhetoric."[13]

One extremely creative effort to measure participation in health care programs seeks to assess whether participation is fairly narrow and limited, or fairly broad and extensive or remaining generally unchanged within a given community or organizational setting.[14] The authors suggest that participation has three important components. The first is that participation must be active. The implication is that the mere receiving of services does not constitute participation. The second is that participation involves choice. Participation implies the right and responsibility of people to make choices and therefore, explicitly or implicitly, to have power over decisions that affect their lives. The third is that the choice must have the possibility of being effective. This suggests that mechanisms are in place or can be created to allow the choice to be implemented.

Many scholars seeking to define this process argue: "Community participation is a social process whereby specific groups with shared needs living in a defined geographic area actively pursue identification of their needs, take decisions and establish mechanisms to meet these needs. In the context of PHC, this process is one which focuses on the ability of these groups to improve their health and health care and by exercising effective decisions to force the shift in resources with a view to achieving greater equity.[15] Rifkin and her associates have suggested five factors which influence participation: (1) needs assessment, (2) leadership, (3) organization, (4) resources mobilization, and (5) management.

Needs Assessment

The first step in introducing a health care program requires an assessment of the health needs of a given community and their level of willingness to act upon those needs. Needs assessment can be made by professionals using their training and past experience either to define possible problems or carry out surveys in order to plan actions. When professional carry out the assessment alone participation is defined as narrow and more limited. It moves toward broader participation with actions that involve community members in the processes of research and analysis of needs. Questions to assess participation might include.:

1. How were health needs identified?
2. Did the identification include only health service needs or other health needs.
3. What role, if any, did the community people play in conducting needs assessment, in analyzing health needs?
4. Were surveys used? Who designed the surveys and who conducted them?
5. Were the surveys used merely to get information or also to initiate discussions among the villagers themselves?
6. Were potential beneficiaries (villagers) involved in analyzing the results?
7. Was the assessment used to further involve the beneficiaries in future plans and programs?
8. Was only one assessment made or is it an on-going exercise for change, review and further involvement of community people in program plans over time?
9. How were the results of the assessment used in the planning of the program?
10. If community people were involved in the assessment did they continue to be involved in the implementation"?
11. Was the assessment used to strengthen beneficiaries roles in decision-making about the program?
12. Did the process include various representatives from a wide range of possible beneficiaries (women, young and elderly, isolated members of the community) for which the health program was designed?

Leadership

In reviewing the capacity of a given community to implement health care programs, it is necessary to examine the present leadership structure of that community, who are the elites, how are leaders selected, who does the existing leadership represents, how does the leadership act on the interest of various community groups, especially the poor and how responsive are the leaders to change. Narrow participation is present if the leadership represents only the elites and the wealthy minority and continues to act only in their interest. The indicator moves toward the wider end if the leadership represents a variety of interests present in the community.

1. Which groups does the leadership represent and how does it represent these groups?
2. How was the leadership chosen and how has it changed over time?
3. Is the leadership paternalistic and/or dictatorial thus limiting the prospects for wider participation by various groups in the community?
4. Does a charismatic leader exist who is so influential that his support is absolutely essential if a health program is to be adopted in the community?

    5. How does the leadership respond to the poor and marginalized people, i.e., peasant, laborers, unemployed, women?
    6. What types of relationships and linkages does the leadership have with outside organizations in terms of gaining resources for the needs of the community?
    7. Have most of the decisions by the leadership resulted in improvement of the majority of the people, for only the elites, for the poor?
    8. What was the attitude of the leadership toward the introduction of a health program and what was the attitude of the leadership concerning health before the program was introduced?

Organization
    If the health program is to be community based, local organizations and institutions must exist among the community people to implement the program. If program planners and professionals do not use community organizations, experience suggests that programs will find it difficult to succeed. A rather narrow form of participation will exist to the extent that community organizations are imposed by outside planners. Where community organizations are locally established, include a broad constituency and incorporate or create their own mechanisms for introducing health programs, the process of participation will be seen as moving toward the broad end of the continuum. Questions that might be asked to determine this point include some of the following:
    1. Are there organizations in the community focusing on the development of health programs?
    2. What is the relationship of the health professionals to these organizations and do they have a decision-making role and if so, how important is that role?
    3. If new organizations were created, how do they relate to existing organizations
    4. How does the organization get resources?
    5. What kind of input do the resources holders have in the organizations, is it a large decision-making role?
    6. Has the representation and the focus of the organizations changed since they were created, if so, how and to whose benefit?
    7. Who staffs the organizations: professionals, para-professionals, beneficiaries and which beneficiaries -- the elite or the poor?
    8. Can the organizations meet needs other than providing health services if other needs have been identified?
    9. Is the organization flexible and able to respond to change or is it rigid resisting a change in control?

Resource Mobilization

In the strategy being suggested, local resource mobilization and self-reliance in terms of both resources and responsibility for programs is a major goal. While mobilizing indigenous resources is a symbol of commitment to a specific program, all too often it has been seen as a way in which governments can be relieved of allocating their scarce resources to these areas. If this situation exists, the commitment of resources limits the ability of participants to decide on allocations which have been defined by outsiders rather than enhance their control over programs. Thus the indicator for resource mobilization not only must take account of the commitment of community resources but also the flexibility that can be exercised in deciding how these resources can be used. A point at the narrow end of the spectrum therefore would be one that showed a program with a small commitment of indigenous resources (money, manpower, materials) and/or limited decisions about how local resources are allocated. Questions dealing with local resource mobilization might include:

1. What have beneficiaries contributed?
2. What percentage of requirements come from these groups?
3. What are the resources being used to support?
4.. Have these resources been allocated for support of parts of the program which in other circumstances would be covered by government allocations?
5. Who decides how indigenous resources should be used?
6. Do all groups that contribute have a decision-making role?
7. How do the poor benefit from allocations to which, because of their poverty, they can make little contribution?
8. Can resources raised to support a health program be used to support more than health services?
9. How are mechanisms developed to decide about allocations and are they flexible or rigid?
10. How are resources mobilized from the community?
11. Which groups influence mobilization how do they do it?
12. Whose interest are being served in both the mobilization and allocation of these resources?

The challenge of implementing a process of meaningful participation into any rural development program should be obvious. What we have tried to do here is simply provide a set of questions that RDFs should review and reflect on periodically to ensure that all the aspects of participation are being considered as they seek to implement a village Community Health Program. RDFs who short circuit the process of participation by ignoring any of the aspects of participation mentioned above, are reducing the chances that the projects being implemented will be sustainable. This will be one of your greatest challenges.

[1]Much of the material for this chapter was first prepared for a UNICEF Conference held in Tunisia in August 1992. For a full rendition of these materials see: James B. Mayfield, "A Preliminary Strategy Paper for the Implementation of a Sub national Primary Health Care System in North Africa and the Middle East." (New York: UNICEF Publications, 1992).

[2]Thomas McKeown, *The Modern Rise of Population* (NY, 1976).

[3]James B. Mayfield, *Go To The People* (Kumarian Press, 1986).

[4]Julia A. Walsh and Kenneth S. Warren, "Selective Primary Health Care: an Interim Strategy for Disease Control in Developing Countries,: *New England Journal of Medicine*, 301 (18), (1979).

[5]F. M. Mburu and J. Ties Boerma, "Introduction: Community-Based Health Care 10 Years Post Alma Ata, *Social Science Medicine*, 28, (10) (1989), pp. 1006.

[6]D. R. Gwatkin, et al., "Can Health and Nutrition Interventions Make a Difference?" Overseas Development Council, (Washington, DC., 1980; and W. L. Gerggren, et al., "Reduction of Mortality in Rural Haiti Through a Primary Health Care Program", *New England Journal of Medicine*, 304, p. 1324.

[7]Julia A. Walsh, "Selectivity Within Primary Health Care," *Social Science Medicine*, 26 (9), (1988), p. 901. See also: J. A. Walsh and K. S. Warren, (eds.) *Strategies of Primary Health Care: Technologies Appropriate for the Control of Disease in the Developing World.* (Chicago: University of Chicago Press, 1986).

[88]S. B. Rifkin and G. Walt , "Why Health Improves: Defining the Issues Concerning 'Comprehensive Primary Health Care' and 'Selective Primary Health Care.' " *Social Science Medicine* 23 (6), (1986), p.564..

[9]David Werner, *Where There Is No Doctor*, (Palo Alto, California: Hesperian Foundation, 1992)

[10]This case study is an edited version of an article: Xochitl Herrera and Miguel Lobo-Guerrero, "From Failure to Success: Tapping the Creative Energy of Sikuani Culture in Colombia," *Grassroots Development* . 12 (3), 1988.

[11]Potential participants who have an interest in working in a disadvantaged area and desire more information may write to the **CHOICE headquarters: 643 East 400 South, Salt Lake City, Utah, 84102 or call at (801) 363-7970.**

[12]Gerard M. La Forgia, "Fifteen Years of Community Organization for Health in Panama: An Assessment of Current Progress and Problems," *Social Science Medicine,* 21 (1), (1985), pp. 55-65.

[13]S. B. Rifkin , et al., "Primary Health Care: One Measuring Participation" *Social Science Medicine*, 26 (9), (1988), p. 931.

[14]P. Oakley and D. Marsden, "Approaches to Participation in Rural Development , (Geneva: International Labour Office, 1983).

[15]Rifkin, et al., (1988), *op. cit.*, p. 933.

Chapter 13

Third Dimension of Rural Development: The Role of Agriculture and Small Scale Enterprise in Village Development

Poverty is a reality for nearly two billion rural people. The major manifestation of this poverty among the poor is hunger and malnutrition, and the lack of productive resources and technology to increase productivity and the consequence inability to generate adequate income for their families. This chapter focuses on two aspects of poverty alleviation: (1) How to increase agriculture production among the small and landless farmers of the world? (2) How to stimulate small scale enterprise development and other income generating activities as a means of increasing the standard of living of the poorest of the poor?

Section One
The Role of Agriculture in Rural Development

Paramount to any discussion of the means by which the people of the world may experience more meaningful and productive lives is a more knowledgeable understanding of the role played, and the contributions made by agriculture. Today, less than a dozen nations produces enough food to feed their own people and still have surplus to export. In another 50 nations, mostly Second and Third World nations, local farmers produce enough to meet local needs but have little to export to other nations. All the rest, which includes nearly 120 nations, mostly poorer Third and Fourth World nations, are significantly dependent on outside sources for much of their basic grains and food stuffs. For example, in a country like Egypt, which was once the bread-basket of the Roman Empire, today their government is forced to import nearly 60 percent of its grain needs. What is equally tragic is the fact that nearly three-fourths of the people in these LDCs live in rural areas and thus logically should be able to produce their own food requirements. For many, maintaining even a subsistence-level life style is a daily concern. What has happened to make hunger and famine so common in many LDCs?

Recent Trends in World Agriculture

To understand more fully why rural populations in particular neither produce enough food nor have enough money to buy it, we must examine agriculture and its changing role in the world-economy in greater detail.

Essentially, people throughout the world can obtain food in two ways. They can either grow it or buy it. It is with the factors that control their ability to do one or the other that the real causes of a higher quality of life lie. To grow food, people must have access to the means to produce it, i.e., land, water, seed and tools, and be able to retain enough of what they produce to meet calorific requirements. Access to the means of production does not necessarily imply that they will satisfy their physical needs, since they may have to pay a proportion of what they produce as tribute, rent or sell some to pay taxes. In Southeast Asia high tax levels in the 1930s contributed greatly to famines by preventing peasant rice growers from storing surplus grain for times of scarcity For the vast majority of the landless and near landless, some type of income generating activity will be needed beyond the opportunities of agriculture. In a later section we shall describe some of the ways that many villagers have found to supplement their meager incomes.

In the MDCs most farmers no longer grow their own food; rather, they purchase it like everybody else. In many LDCs food production for subsistence is still an important aspect of farming. Few, if any agricultural societies have been totally self-sufficient. Moreover, for many centuries these pre-capitalist formations have engaged in some form of exchange, both internally and to a limited extent with trading partners. In general, farmers in Latin America are more oriented towards cash crop production than are African farmers. What is significant is that growing food for subsistence is everywhere becoming a less important component of production. Those who cannot or do not produce sufficient food for subsistence must purchase some or all of it. As subsistence economies give way to those founded on commerce, the pattern of income distribution becomes a critical factor in the provision of food. Because of this inequality, those who are poor cannot afford to buy what food there is on the market.

World-Wide Pressures on Traditional Agriculture

The internationalization of agribusiness, and particularly its spread into the LDCs is one of the main features of the world food economy. In Latin America intense agricultural investments have created conditions conducive to the rapid expansion of agribusiness. Tens of millions of peasants have been pushed out of agriculture as a result. For example, since the mid-1960s the number of people living solely off the land in Brazil has decreased by 50 percent, and the rural population now constitutes only 30 percent of a total of 155 million. One of the causes is the growth of commercial agriculture and the concentration of land in the hands of fewer landowners. Brazil is now the world's second largest producer of soya beans after the US. This high-protein crop contributes almost nothing to the diet of Brazil's malnourished population. Small land-holders who cleared the land in the 1950s have been ousted by large commercial farms run privately or by large international companies. US grain companies invested $50 million in soya bean processing in Brazil between 1973 and 1980.[1]

Industrial agriculture is currently expanding rapidly into many LDCs. Since their independence, however, there has been a renewed penetration of agriculture by agribusiness, encouraged by technical developments in tropical agriculture. Food production is no longer of much relevance; the trend started with the production of luxury beverages and fibers and vegetable oils for the industrial markets. If markets required flowers and exotic fruits, then that is what agribusiness produced. Much of the renewed penetration of peripheral agriculture takes the form of contract farming, whereby the farmer grows what the company requires. Effectively, the farmer leases both land and labor; the farmer bears the risks and the company takes the profits. A classic example of this type of venture is described by Feged in his analysis of the infamous "strawberry scheme" in Mexico.[2] These types of trends obviously have had disastrous consequences for the rural peasants of this world.

Modern agriculture technology has both a good and bad side. While we in the United States have come to understand the negative side-effects of chemical pesticides, many LDCs are still using such products. The pervasive problems of misleading advertising, inadequate labeling and unsafe use, found in a number of countries (for example: Brazil, Ecuador, Egypt, India, Indonesia, Mexico, the Philippine and Thailand) allow local farmers to use such products. Improper practices in the sale and use of pesticides can kill or disable humans, upset the ecological balance and inflict long-term damage on the environment. While many of these highly toxic products are banned in MDCs, they continue to poison many in the LDCs. A UN report estimates total world pesticides' poisonings at 2 million cases a year, including 40,000 deaths. The global impact on livestock, wildlife and flora is impossible to measure. Products banned or severely restricted in MDCs are freely available, and are manufactured in Mexico, Colombia, India, Indonesia and Thailand among others. Illiterate or semi-literate farmers are unaware of the hazards involved. RDFs must take the time to become familiar with these products.

Section Two
Contrasting Modern and Traditional Peasant Agriculture

As a starting point from which to consider the implications of agrarian transition of the mass of rural people, we shall first distinguish between the two poles, commercial and subsistence agriculture. The former represents production in the MDCs, the latter is more apt to be found in the LDCs. As has already been noted, the distinction is not entirely valid, since "modern" agriculture is present throughout the LDCs also.

Modern Agriculture: In most MDCs, agriculture is essentially another form of business no different in motivation from any other industrial enterprise. The agricultural products grown are for exchange, and the profit that goes with it, rather than for immediate use. In the context of the North American wheat belt, the product has value above all else because it can be sold or exchanged on the market, and not at all because it can be eaten. The fact that it will eventually be consumed as food plays almost no part in the commercial decisions governing its production.

Traditional (Peasant) Agriculture: Peasant agriculture, in contrast, has as its logic the survival of the family unit -- the provision of adequate subsistence, clothing, shelter and so on. Peasants have a great deal of experience with the crops they cultivate, inspite of great pressure for them to be integrated into the modern world economic system. Decisions for such farmers are taken not to reflect profit-maximizing goals, but rather long-term survival in the face of uncertainty.[3] Associated with a peasant style of agriculture, and essential to its continued viability, are institutions such as common lands and rights for the exploitation of resources, usually managed collectively. From the comments noted above, it is now possible to summarize the differences between modern (large scale) agriculture and traditional (small scale) agriculture

Chart 13-1

	Large Scale Commercial	**Small Scale Subsistence**
Purpose	Earn commercial profits	Family survival and improved quality of life
Source of Inputs	Expensive commercial inputs of fertilizers, HYV seeds and insecticides	Inexpensive traditional inputs, organic fertilizers, local seeds and natural insecticides
Major Work Source	Heavy equipment and mechanized technology	Human and animal energy with little or no outside energy
Source of Tools	Urban manufactured tools	Home or community made tools
Cultural Orientation	The purpose is to exploit the land	The purpose is to live in harmony with the land
Gender Orientation	Farming is seen as men's work, with men receiving the lion's share of the resources allocated.	Farming acknowledged as often women's work as much as men and in some countries women do most of the farming. They need greater access to resources.

A Need to Focus on the Marginalized Subsistence Farmers

Because of the trends mentioned above, it is important that RDFs focus on the subsistence farmers of the world. While large numbers of villagers are being integrated into the world economy, it must be understood that between 30 and 40 percent of the world's people and about two-thirds of the world's farmers are still living on intensively operated subsistence farms. Subsistence farming systems grow only enough food and fiber for their own needs, collect fuel and building materials from natural sources, and hardly enter into the cash economy at all. For many of these poorer farmers, it is a fact of life that the harder they work, the poorer they get. Their land is either too steep, too dry, or the soil too poor, to support more than a mean level of existence for a few people. Because of increasing populations and intractable patterns of land use and tenure, fragile environments are being subjected to more intensive use than they can sustain. Cropland is becoming scarce in relation to pressures from world population growth, and soil quality is decreasing at an alarming rate in many countries, primarily because of improper usage and management.

It is now well established that peasant agriculture is highly productive, and has provided a reasonable quantity of food for centuries without outsider help. Traditional agriculture has the potential to produce adequate supplies of food without being "modernized." In terms of the energy inputs required in subsistence farming, it is a far more efficient producer of calories than modern mechanized agriculture, the latter's being viable only through energy subsidies in the form of cheap oil supplies for the manufacturing of fertilizers and insecticides. Failing productivity in traditional agriculture, as a result of overuse of the soil and erosion, is not an inherent characteristic. It is merely a further symptom of the problem of extreme poverty, with its causes rooted firmly in the workings of the world-economy.[4] Let us now reflect for a moment on the activities that RDFs might pursue during the three stages of rural development as it relates to agriculture and income generation.

Activities During the First Stage

In the initial months, local RDFs should seek to determine the level of income in the community, the role of agriculture in generating present levels of income, and what opportunities are available to create credit groups and small scale enterprises. This is the time to learn from the villagers how they have been able to subsist in the past, what resources they have, what connections with markets are available, what specific strategies have they been using to survive in the past. The RDF is learning far more from the villagers than the other way around in this first stage. This is a time for intensive cultural dialoguing.

A crucial part of stage one for the RDF is to develop an awareness and appreciation for the traditional system of agriculture. One of the first tasks for an RDF entering a new village is to determine both the past and present types of crops and animals grown in this area. Answers to the following questions should give the RDF a first-hand knowledge of the farming schedule of the villagers:
1. When and how do they prepare the ground and plant their crops?
2. Where do they buy their seeds and how much do they pay

3. What tools do they use to prepare the ground, plant the seeds, spread fertilizer, weed the crops and harvest the crops?
4. How and when do the farmers weed their fields, apply fertilizers, and provide water for their fields?
5. How and when do the farmers harvest their crops
6. What role do family members or non-family members play in these agricultural activities?
7. If non family members help, when and how much are they paid?
8. When and how are their crops marketed? Do they use a middleman?
9. How much surplus is generated by the traditional system of farming?
10. What are the major advantages and disadvantages that the farmers perceive in farming the way they do?

Activities During the Second Stage

Increasing agricultural productivity is a priority task for professional RDFs in their work for rural transformation. At the same time, other forms of income-generation such as village-based industries, cooperatives and credit systems must be developed and expanded. A number of villager credit groups might be established and organized including a program to help increase agricultural productivity through some form of organic farming or regenerative agricultural. The RDF should also be involved in encouraging an entrepreneurial spirit in the village, seeking to find ways of developing a number of small scale enterprises in the community, especially enterprises related to greater food production and increased income.

Also in the second stage, RDFs must begin to help peasant farmers to improve agriculture production at the village level? The following specific questions related to this process would help in generating useful information for the villagers.

1. What specific things might a farmer do to increase his/her present crop yields?
2. What specific things might a farmer do to develop an organic vegetable garden?
3. Could local organic fertilizers be used to increase yields of crops in the area?
4. What new crops might be introduced (vegetables, fruit trees, grains, legumes)?
5. Could the source and use of water for crops be increased/used more efficiently?
6. Would any increase in yields actually benefit the farmer or would most of the surplus go to some elite?

Activities During the Third Stage

In traditional rural societies the power structure has not undergone significant change despite democratization and modernization in some areas. This structure operates to the disadvantage of the poorer villagers. The larger landowners have been able to develop better rapport with institutions and organizations working for the development of rural areas. Awakening the rural poor to their rights and to the opportunities available to them through national and state rural development programs is crucial to rural transformation and a significant part of stage three. It is during this stage, that farmers must learn to organize themselves to take advantage of developments in science and technology, in better marketing, storage, and distribution. During this stage RDFs should be working with local leaders in the establishment of locally managed credit systems and productive cooperatives and other small scale enterprises linked to regional and/or national systems of credit, marketing and production systems. Since the third stage is about networking and linkage building between the villagers and their wider environment, here are a set of questions that RDFs might consider:

1. Are there local colleges or universities that might have agricultural extension programs useful to local farmers?

2. Are there national and international NGOs and various government agencies willing to support networking activities structured to support meaningful land reform, a more equitable system of pricing and credit distribution, new forms of marketing, storage and processing that might benefit local farmers?

3. Are there demonstration plots in the area or innovative farmers willing to share their knowledge with smaller subsistence farmers?

4. Could an RDF seek to develop a network of small farmer groups in a single district that were willing to share information, identify effective local leaders and devise common strategies to confront local bureaucrats to be more accountable to the local community, to empower local leaders to challenge sources of ineffectiveness, inequality and corruption.

5. Are there other farmer associations scattered throughout the country that the farmers in a given district might join to facilitate various policy changes needed to improve the quality of life of the local farmers in the area.

One significant skill that an RDF must develop in all three stages of rural development is the ability to analyze how agricultural development and income generating activities will impact on the other four dimensions of rural development

Impact of Income Generating Activities on:

Culture: Awareness of how resource mobilizing activities could be used to finance cultural awareness in the community.

Health: Awareness of how resource mobilizing activities could be used to finance better health services in the community.

Education: Awareness of how local resource mobilizing activities could be used to finance better educational opportunities in the community for children and adults.

Ecology: Awareness of how local resource mobilizing activities could be used to finance the protection and enhancement of the local environment.

Both interns and RDFs must come to see the interrelationship that exists among the five dimensions of rural development and the process of leadership building in the community as these communities move through the three stages of rural development. The process of identifying local leaders, establishing local problem-solving committees, and other activities related to rural development must reflect both the impact and interrelationship of all five dimensions and the process of moving from an unorganized rather simplistic process of village problem-solving to a much more institutionalized sustainable process of capacity building and local institution building, and eventually to a broader form of networking and coalition building needed to challenge the political and economic constraints faced by local villagers.

Section Three
Breaking the Subsistence Cycle

Rural poverty is largely related to low agricultural productivity. Small marginal farmers who make up the largest number of operating units in many developing countries have not been able to take advantage of advances in agricultural science and technology. Many farms lack assured water supplies. Over the past thirty years a number of strategies and community interventions have been developed to break the subsistence cycle for small and marginal farmers. Subsistence farming traps people (because they do not have capital) into a pattern of farming in which they practice methods requiring the least investment and generally giving the least return. The tragedy of this approach is that it does not provide the surplus necessary for moving to a more productive style of farming. Even more tragic are the landless who are the poorest of the poor. Without productive assets their mainstay is seasonal employment that provides wages generally insufficient even for subsistence -- let alone for the productive investment required to increase assets. One particular strategy for increasing food production in subsistence villages is to introduce organic farming.

Organic Farming: A New but Old Technology.

The Green Revolution introduced high yield varieties of wheat, corn and rice, but also a high dependence on chemical fertilizers, insecticides and weed controlling substances. Over the years, this heavy dosage of chemicals has destroyed much of the natural quality of the soil and has often destroyed the delicate balance between harmful and helpful insect life. Healthy soil contains humus, available minerals, bacteria, fungi, acitinomycetes, earthworms, and many other organisms all working together to produce natural antibiotics that convey disease immunity to plants, animals and people. Earthworms alone will produce up to 20 tons of fertilizer per acre each year that is so perfectly balanced that humans cannot produce anything comparable to it.

Tested methods of farming can be adapted to the situation of small farmers and can increase productivity in even the most disadvantaged areas. RDFs should gain some familiarity with such concepts as diversification of land use, organic and natural farming approaches, soil development, conservation, wasteland reclamation, and small scale irrigation. Subsistence farmers resigned to their meager lot over the years can be awakened to these methods through demonstrations, literacy education, access to credit, and the use of new and simple technologies. A whole new science of natural agriculture is emerging which includes the use of simple methods of crop rotation, inter-cropping, manuring, and integrative use of trees and animals without the use of chemical fertilizers and pesticides. Such approaches help in replenishing the soil and in raising healthier crops and animals. It allows farmers to operate on a low budget and low energy input. The basic components of organic agriculture are as follows:

Basic Philosophy[5]

First, organic agriculture aims to be in harmony rather than in conflict with natural systems, and seeks to preserve the environment, while at the same time produce food which is of optimum nutritional value. Also, the organic approach does not use artificial fertilizers or chemical pesticides, and strives to be based on local markets, utilizing decentralized systems of distribution.

Soil is the one constant factor at the base of all organic farming operations. The soil relies on animals and plants for its food. It takes back what is left over from the manure and plant residues to be recycled and used again. The organic farmer gives the soil special care, ensuring that it is nurtured and fed with this soil food. Soil is a living entity -- it positively teems with life. The nutrients include carbohydrates (sugars, starch, and cellulose), proteins and lignin.

Soil Improvement Measures: Drainage and aeration are important factors in encouraging good biological activity: (a) Use of deep cultivation techniques like subsoiling will break plough pans and other compaction problems. (b) Aeration and loosening of the soil can be helped and stabilized by establishing a fast and deep-rooting green manure after appropriate cultivation. (c) Use various additives to reach the proper adjustment of ph: natural lime if magnesium is deficient, rock phosphate on acid soils and redlag on alkali soils, are all examples of ways to improve the quality of the soil in a given area.

Crop rotation is one of the corner stones of organic farming and very important in converting from a high cost input farming system to a low-cost organic system. It must be designed to minimize weed, pest and disease problems, to optimize nutrient use and cycling and minimize nutrient loss, to build organic matter and soil structure, and to provide feed for livestock and returns for the farmer. Crop plants fall into several distinct groups: legumes, bassicas, roots, cereals, etc. The organic farmer alternates these so that the gap between two similar crops will generally be augmented anywhere from three years upward. There must be a fertility building phase through rotation.

Earthworms are the great promoters of vegetation, by boring, perforating and loosening the soil and rendering it pervious to rains and the fibers of plants. Also worms by distributing their excrement throughout the soil as fine manure, are invaluable to farming.

Biological Cycle is another cornerstone of organic farming as it emphasizes the careful use of all waste products. This means returning back to the soil in good form all manure and plant residues produced on the farm. Health is considered natural. If plants are healthy, then pests and diseases should not be a problem.

High yields from modern farming is like force feeding with a narrow range of nutrients and excessive water and fertilizers. Organic farming uses natural fertilizers and tends to have higher nutritional quality with larger amounts of proteins, vitamins, and minerals than crops grown non-organically.

The problem with **pesticides** is that they destroy the predators of pests along with the pests. Indeed, these natural checks and balances are often more affected by pesticides than are the target organisms, because of their slower life cycles and dependence on the pest as their food source. This means that the pests are more likely to cause greater problems in the future than they did before. Pests quickly build up resistance to pesticides thus require more and more lethal formulas. Their impact on rodents and thus birds of prey are now being confirmed. DDT became so widely used and its impact on humans so pervasive that mother's milk in some areas was banned. There are many other types of insecticides and pesticides that are now being found to be very dangerous to human health.

Soluble fertilizers may be food for plants, but they are not food for soil life. They bypass the soil life and go straight to the plant. If the soil receives no other nutrients, then its biological activity will gradually die away. The fertilizers also inhibit and can even actually kill parts of the soil's flora and fauna. Some potash fertilizers are lethal to earthworms. Too much nitrogen causes a lush, watery growth. Too much potash causes thin cell walls. Both these make the plant susceptible to pests and diseases.

Only about half of the fertilizers reach the plants. The rest go down or sideways or out the farm gate. Nitrate fertilizers for example seep deep into the soil slowly, taking sometimes 20-30 years to reach the ground water. Some of the water being pumped now was, unfortunately, polluted by fertilizers of the 1950s and 1960s. Other fertilizers go into the rivers and streams stimulating water weeds and algae, which use up so much of the available oxygen that other forms of life, like insects and fish, are suffocated. Such water looks like pea soup and phosphate and nitrate fertilizers are the culprits.

In many ways, manure is the central hub of the organic farm. Well composted, the carbon to nitrogen ratio in the manure of animals will have dropped from 25:1 down to about 10:1. The nitrogen will probably have actually increased by the action of free living nitrogen-fixing organisms. However, potassium is likely to have been lost through leaching, and it is therefore important to be able to collect any run-off from stored or composing manure, or better still, to cover the heap to save this rather mobile and problematic nutrient. In this way, the manure will have been largely converted into a stable humus which will enrich the organic matter in the soil on a long-term basis. Composting properly is crucial in hot climates. The rule is 1 or 2 stock animals (such as cow, buffalo, horse, goat, sheep, camel, etc.) per hectare farmed in a given year in order to provide the needed manure for natural fertilizer.

Organic weed control starts with proper manuring techniques and ensuring that weeds are not brought on to a field. It continues with seed-bed cultivation, including the more normally recognized mechanical hoeing and various types of newer thermal techniques. It is complemented overall by careful rotations, choice of varieties and the use of green manure. Weed seeds can be stopped from coming on to the field in the manure by ensuring that your composting methods create sufficiently high temperatures to kill them. Prepare your seed beds about two weeks in advance of planting the crop. This allows one to remove weeds before the crop is planted.

General Conclusion

There is much evidence that this new form of "alternative agriculture"[6] described above can help subsistence farmers keep production levels high enough to provide for their families. RDFs must be knowledgeable concerning the ways that non-chemical technologies can be applied in a given area, how new mixes of crops can be tested and applied in the local area, how new cropping patterns can both strengthen the quality of local soils, but how soil erosion can be reduced. Even more intriguing are the ways in which alternative systems of tillage can reduce the need for weeding, increase soil productivity, increase earthworm activity and save much time and effort by the farmer.

The Art of Communicating Effectively

An effective RDF needs to develop an understanding of these appropriate methods and techniques of soil preparation, planting, irrigation and moisture control, appropriate technology, pest control, soil characteristics and conservation and testing on small plots. Small animal husbandry is an important skill for RDFs. Special emphasis should be given to feeding, breeding, and managing methods and techniques for raising small animals for food and resale. Equally important for an

RDF is the need to understand the principles of nutrition and preparation of nutritious and economical meals in a variety of cultural styles. This requires some awareness of what foods potentially grown in a given area can provide what forms of nutrition.

It should be clear that these kinds of skills will be of little use unless the RDF has the ability to communicate such information to the peasant. The following factors are crucial to agriculture extension according to Bunch[7]:
1. The program must work toward solving felt needs (i.e., the people must want the problem to be solved).
2. The people must believe it is possible for them to solve the problem (i.e., the solution must be simple and inexpensive enough to be within their means).
3. The people must believe that the RDFs know enough to be competent help, and are working for the people's benefit rather than to cheat or manipulate them.
4. The people should come to identify with the program's work and its successes by being involved in program planning.
5. The people must participate in the program's work so that when success is achieved, they will feel a sense of accomplishment. The challenges must be simple enough at first so that they can grow in their ability with problems and can feel an increasing sense of accomplishment.

Use problem-centered learning. Villagers will learn faster and better if you use actual problems and let them work out the solutions. The discovery of knowledge or the formulation of principles through the case-study method is an excellent approach. Most important, RDFs must understand the great wealth of knowledge and the experiences that villagers already have. Exploit this wealth of talent and expertise in a positive way. Make use of the experience and traditional knowledge through discussion and group participation.

The Role of Women in Agriculture[8]

It has been found that women in LDCs own less than one-fifth of the assets of men, but perform at least 70 percent of the work. Much of the work is "invisible": bearing the children, nurturing them, gathering fuel and drawing water, cooking the food, taking her husband's meals to his work place, milking the domestic animals and undertaking other household tasks. In Kenya it is estimated that at least 75 percent of the agriculture work is done by women. They produce most of the food grown for family consumption. Although the proportion of women in agriculture is already high, it is increasing, not only in subsistence agriculture, but in commercial production as well. The unskilled work in agriculture is not only done mostly by women, it is done for extremely low wages for a long working day. In one district in rural India, it was found that one-third of the households in most villages were wholly dependent upon the earnings of the women. In many countries in Latin America, well over 40-50 percent of the families in the rural areas are single-parent families, since many of the men have left for the cities to work and often do not send money to their families.

Although the evidence in the LDCs is that women are incredibly creative and effective in providing for their families, the general picture is that they are overworked and under-paid for reasons that are partly social/cultural and partly political/economic. Particularly urgent is the need to lighten the domestic work load that tradition has laid upon the women. Infrastructure improvements such as piped drinking water, better housing and drainage, the installation of electricity, biogas and solar energy could reduce the volume of their domestic work. Unless this is done, they will have neither time nor energy to take advantage of more varied employment opportunities, which would enable women to supplement their contribution to the family finances. In Tanzania, poultry production has been introduced to women and this has impacted on several areas of need. The women earn more (personally), the manure is used as a fertilizer for vegetables and maize and the community benefits from the protein the poultry adds to their diet.

The enormous disparities that exist between opportunities for men and women and the disproportionate burden that rural poverty and environmental degradation pose for women mean that expanded opportunities for women can result in significant returns for them, their families, and their communities. The disparities between men and women in the LDCs begin in childhood, when girls have less access then boys to education, and sometimes even less food and health care. In Nepal, to cite an extreme case, only 57 percent of girls are enrolled in primary school while the number for boys is over 90 percent; in Chad, enrollment is 29 percent for girls and 73 percent for boys. In Bangladesh, malnutrition is three times more common among young girls than boys. Maternal mortality rates -- as high as 1,000 per 100,000 live births in low-human-development countries compared with 10 or fewer in the MDCs -- are dramatic evidence of the neglect of women's health. The literacy rate of women in the developing world as a whole is three quarters that of men. [9]

In LDCs, development efforts in the informal sector have been particularly effective in increasing women's earnings. The elimination of laws and customs preventing women's participation in training and other development programs, their access to credit, education, and housing and property ownership could do much to increase women's opportunities. Increases in women's status, education, and earnings, along with the availability of maternal and child health care, also are significant factors in improving child nutrition and health, as well as reducing family size.[10]

Section Four
New Approaches to the Problems of Agriculture

RDFs need to be aware of the value of traditional crops and the importance of plant genetic diversity. The International Institute of Tropical Agriculture (IITA) in Ibadan, Nigeria, in 1975 established a Genetic Resource Unit, with the aim of collecting, documenting, and storing grain legumes, cereals, roots, and tubers whether wild or domesticated. Such research is needed to save Africa's genetic resources of food crop species, for use in plant breeding and related researches. Germplasm materials in the IITA have been drawn from over 100 countries around the world. Such germplasm from both wild and domesticated crops has served not only to increase resistance to disease and pests but also to provide materials that are tolerant of abiotic stresses such as drought, heat, cold, and soil toxicity.

By contacting local extension workers and national agricultural research centers, RDFs are in a better position to advise farmers on new varieties of crops better suited to the constraints of the local areas. It is through the use of naturally occurring variations in various germplasm collections that crop breeders have developed such things as cassava varieties resistant to the cassava mosaic virus disease, the cassava bacterial blight. Maize varieties have been developed with resistance to streak virus; long grained rice varieties that are tolerant to the blast disease and the yellow motle virus; and sweet potatoes resistant to weevil and other virus diseases.

Combining the Needs of Agriculture and Sanitation in the Same Village

Malnutrition is a chronic lack of sufficient energy-giving foods, proteins, vitamins, and minerals, or combination of these nutritive elements. One interesting approach to the challenge of malnutrition is to grow Spirulina in recycled village wastes. Villages could become self-sufficient by growing Spirulina themselves and by recycling waste in a digester to provide the raw materials for its production. Spirulina is a blue-green alga and a natural concentration of food. It is the richest source of vitamin B12 available in natural form. One gram contains 1.700 micrograms of beta carotene -- equivalent to more than half the daily requirement for vitamin A -- plus important amounts of vitamin B1, B2, and others. When dried, Spirulina contains about 65 percent high quality assimilable protein and compares very favorably with egg protein.

Spirulina is the most easily produced of all micro algae and has been eaten by humans in Africa and in Central America for hundreds and probably thousands of years. As much as 50 tons of protein per hectare per year can be produced by cultivating Spirulina.[11] As was pointed out in Chapter 12, lack of sanitation is a pressing problem in most rural villages. Leaving human waste uncovered in villages and at the edges of villages leads to microbial pollution of the soil, water, and the atmosphere. Parasites breed and eventually infect the villagers. Often as many as 80 percent of the members of a village may be suffering from intestinal parasites. A third of the food the farmers raise feeds the parasites that make them sick. The infection lowers the body's capacity to digest and assimilate food. In some villages, more than half of the food eaten goes to feed parasites.

The solution, of course, is latrines, where fecal matter is transformed rapidly by biological processes into a useful compost or effluent. Only the generalized use of latrines can control and eliminate intestinal parasitism and also increase the food supply by improving the soil. There is no scheme for improving agriculture output that can compare with the effective agricultural increase possible through proper sanitation practices. Since the early 1970s, the Laboratoire de La Roquette in France has been studying ways to end malnutrition. Projects have been implemented in India, Senegal and Togo. The goal is to assure a daily supplement of proteins and vitamins to pre-school children, pregnant and lactating women, older children, and other adults -- in that order of priority. This supplement is to be provided by Spirulina grown by the villagers themselves.

All photosynthesizing organisms require carbon dioxide, nitrogen, potassium, phosphorus, and many other minerals, and large amounts of these nutrients are needed for intensive mass culture such as growing Spirulina. These raw materials are present in village wastes and just need to be converted into forms usable by the algae.

From the central latrine, human waste passes through a 24-hour holding tank and then into a solar heated digester, or biogas plant, where cow dung and agrowastes are added. Disease-producing micro-organisms proliferate at human body temperature, but most die if kept for long periods at elevated temperatures. Fermentation of the wastes for 10 days at high temperature (55 degrees Centigrade) transforms them into harmless new materials. Any protozoans, bacteria, or viruses that survive the digester and filtration die under the ultraviolet light of the sun and the very high oxygen concentration in the algae basin as well as by heat during solar drying. A culture of Spirulina needs to be stirred. If the water is left stagnant too long, the algae may die and be decomposed by bacteria. These blue-green micro algae need only abundant sun, fertilizers and minerals obtained from biogas digester effluent, carbon dioxide (also coming from the digester), salt, a little bicarbonate to begin with, and gentle stirring. The cultures that take 90 days to mature in a laboratory in France in winter take only four days in India.

Value of the Neem Tree

One of consequences of the Green Revolution has been the spread of pest resistance to pesticides. Such new types of insects are indirectly threatening the livelihood of marginal farmers in the LDCs. The number of species resistant to insecticides rose from 25 to 432 between 1954 and 1980. FAO experts predict that some pests may soon be beyond "effective chemical control." Modern researchers are today becoming more aware of the possible use of traditional methods of insects control using poisonous plants.

The earliest mention of poisonous plants, or that with pest control properties, is found in the Indian Rig Veda, the classic book of Hinduism, compiled during the second millennium BC. Today, some 1,600 plant species are reported to possess such properties -- and the Neem tree is by far the most promising. Almost every part of the Neem tree, the roots, trunk, bark, leaves, flowers, fruit and seeds is utilized for some purpose in the countries where it is found. It is used as a medicine, pesticide, mosquito repellent, fertilizer, diabetic food and animal feed; to produce soap, lubricants, paper, hardboard, briquettes, fuelwood, gums and plastics; to build houses, boats and ploughs; and as a toothbrush and even as a contraceptive.

Farmers have for centuries been mixing neem leaves with grain, or soaking storage sacks in neem water to repel insect pests. Ground neem-leaf paste is also mixed with the mud used for making earthen containers. Neem effectively controls target pests with a minimum disruption of beneficial insects; it is inexpensive and easy to prepare using village-level technologies; it is absorbed by the plant tissues and so provides good crop protection even after heavy rainfall; it is environmentally safe, and non-toxic.

Neem's active substance, Axadirachtin, was isolated by British scientists towards the end of the 1970s and found to be effective in two ways: firstly as a repellent by inhibiting feeding (antifeedant); secondly by upsetting the insect's hormone balance so that it becomes permanently incapacitated. Neem is reported to control more than 100 species of insects, mites and nematodes, including such major pests as desert and migratory locusts, rice and maize borers, pulse beetle, rice weevil and citrus red mint as well as aphias and white flies. Since, unlike synthetic compounds, neem is a collection of some 20 active ingredients, it is difficult for any insect to develop a resistance to them all.

Building on Local Technologies

The process of sustainable development would be advanced by the development and use of labor-intensive, energy-efficient low-cost technologies that improve productivity or conserve natural resources in countries. However, one of the central lessons gained from small-scale development projects is that technologies already known and accepted by the people have a much higher rate of success than new and unfamiliar technologies. Thus, development of technologies for the poor countries needs to give a high priority to increasing the effectiveness and efficiency of locally known techniques.

We have learned of the unintended consequences of the Green Revolution that tended to benefit only the rich farmers or which introduced technology that was neither sustainable nor relevant to the needs of the subsistence farmers. RDFs must be sensitive to ways that appropriate technologies might be introduced into a village community. Examples of such technology include: pedal power devices for application to irrigation pumps and threshing machines, wind power devices for application to various farm and household tasks. Some examples include: (1) windmill so sensitive that it spins in breezes of under four miles an hour to pump nearly 4,000 gallons of water a day. (2) Water (hydrologic) power devices for generating direct or indirect (such as electric) power. For example, small hydroelectric generators that can obtain enough power from small streams to supply a farm or a school. (3) Solar power devices for water distillation and dehydration of foodstuffs. Another example includes a solar hot-water heater made out of burned-out fluorescent light tubes. (4) Small units for the generation of biogas and alcohol from waste products and plant growth. (5) Improved tillage and harvesting tools made from local materials with local labor. (6) New or improved varieties of plants and breeds of animals that are more efficient in food production. (7) Practices leading to improved nutrition for both humans and animals. (8) Effective communication and adult education programs, and improved practices in production management.[12]

Nonetheless, further research on improved technologies -- especially those applicable to agriculture or to rural life -- is important. In Africa, in particular, raising agricultural production among small farmers has the potential to combat poverty and promote economic growth. Building on the knowledge of rural people has already led to successes with inter-cropping, agro-forestry, small-scale irrigation systems, organic recycling, and improved tillage methods. To fully use the knowledge that local farmers have of their land and of ways to manage it, however, development agencies need to shift from a technical or bureaucratic approach to a participatory one.[13]

Section Five
Activities for Village Income Development

As an RDF approaches the third stage of rural development, and as he/she begins to feel the frustration of seeking to help villagers organize themselves, lessons learned from a number of different countries might be helpful to consider. While much of this stage three work will deal with organizing farmers to protect their interests, their lands and their access to inputs, other kinds of activities must also be considered. As more and more farmers are forced to leave their land, they will need help in developing alternative sources of income. Some of these activities will be related to agriculture, but many will not. In the literature on rural development there is much discussion of the importance of finding supplemental ways of increasing employment and generating additional income. It is important for the RDF to be able to distinguish two rather distinct forms of small scale enterprise development. Let us contrast the two approaches in the following chart.

The first, we shall call Income Enhancement, which tends to focus on the household, often involves some outside agency providing tools, resources and supplies to a poor family increase their income. While this strategy is based upon good intentions, such activities are almost never sustainable. The outside donor often gives the peasant a sewing machine, or a milk cow, or some seeds to plant --

hoping that the new tools or resources will help the villager. Such help can be useful but only if there are procedures for some type of pay-back, only if the villager has the marketing skills to sell the products produced by the project. A more sustainable kind of project tends to be much more business-oriented, is based upon careful training in management, financing, and quality control and is structured to reflect a solid marketing strategy to ensure the goods will be sold for a profit.

Chart 13-2

Income Enhancement	Small Scale Enterprise
1. Household/small group oriented	1. Business/Production group oriented
2. Marketing Issues de-emphasized	2. Marketing Issues strongly emphasized
3. Subsistence Income is the goal	3. Significant/Real profit is the goal
4. RDF needs Social Welfare/Extension skills	4. RDF needs Entrepreneurial, Marketing /Management skills
5. Activity decisions based on family needs	5. Activity decisions based on enterprise viability
6. Life of project related to donor schedule	6. Life of project is open-ended
7. Emphasis is horizontal to local markets	7. Emphasis is vertical to regional/national markets
8. Dependency relationship in which projects provide most of the resources	8. Interdependency relationship in which the business seeks to find its own long-term funding
9. Leadership based on group cohesiveness /individual trust	9. Leadership based upon management and financial effectiveness

Building Cooperatives: The Key to Successful Village Agriculture

Building on the advantages of economy of scale processes implied in the small scale enterprise approach outlined above, many small farmers have devised various forms of association to raise their income levels. Cooperative arrangements can help farmers to purchase inputs, share in the risk of innovation, and find new and more lucrative markets. Unfortunately, many village cooperatives do fail, and it is important that RDFs understand why. Most failures can be reduced to four simple rules: (1) the functions of the cooperative did not meet the perceived needs of its members (2) the rewards and incentives agreed upon were not equitably distributed or the dishonesty of one or two members destroyed the trust and commitment of the others, (3) the members did not all have the technical and financial skills needed to ensure the success of the cooperative, and finally (4) the cooperative was unable to purchase the inputs at a fair price or was unable to market the crops for a reasonable profit because of the opposition or restrictions of larger farmers, outside middlemen, or the government itself. The creation of effective cooperatives, tied to networks of participating farmers is a common strategy found in stage three and reflects a serious effort to keep as much of their surplus in the local community as possible

Let us look at a few case studies where organizational success can be reviewed: in Uruguay, an Inter-American Foundation program first established in 1974 has given over 90 grants to help support a network of rural cooperatives serving small-scale farmers. Today there are 80 agricultural co-ops and an equal number of *sociedades de fomento*, or small farmer development societies (35,000 small-scale farmers belong to these co-ops and societies); five cooperative marketing federations; two national associations representing farmer interests; and several membership organizations specializing in meeting minority group needs. Also part of the network are several research centers and two key intermediary organizations that provide services, not solely to the grassroots, but to cooperatives and federations as well. RDFs working in Latin America need to be aware of Inter American Foundation sources of money for rural development. Since 1982, the Inter-American Foundation has funded three projects for 10,000 Mapuche Indians in the Argentine province of Neuquen. With the money, the Mapuches have set up a network of small stores to sell basic necessities in their isolated communities, and a warehouse and communications system to enable them to market their goods -- principally goat skins and wool, thereby helping to keep the profits from such activities within their own communities.

Most of the small scale enterprises that can help villagers to improve their income are related to agriculture. In Kenya, the Kibwezi Women's Group was formed to help women start four projects: bee-keeping, honey and wax refining, improved goat breeding and stabilized earth brick-making. All are generating additional income for women who had no future beyond subsistence farming. No other livestock can survive in that area due to tsetse flies. Bee-keeping, traditionally a men's occupation, was taken up by the women. Following training organized by the Ministry of Livestock Development the women have formed a cooperative for this purpose. With the help of an NGO in the area some 100 acres have been fenced for honey producing trees and shrubs. Nineteen Women's Registered Goat Breeding Co-operatives are providing extra cash income and better nourishment. There are roughly 50 women in each co-operative, each with 30-50 goats.

Small and marginal farmers caught in the subsistence cycle are hesitant to take risks since they are uncertain of the results. When it comes to adopting new practices in farming or any other aspect of living, their intuitive reaction is to wait and see if anybody else nearby has taken it up, and if so, with what results. If the new methods are openly discussed with them they are likely to weigh the pros and cons of the new practices in the light of their own experience and most often react favorably . If practices are selected which meet their direct and immediate needs, the chances of their acceptance are even greater.

Simple Marketing Systems

One interesting marketing system was established in south Luzon, Philippines. For years, urban produce distributors had purchased vegetables from the local farmers at nearly subsistence level prices and then sold them in the towns at high prices. A group of small farmers organized themselves to set their prices high enough to provide for input costs and a reasonable profit, but still cheap enough to encourage town people to buy from the farmers directly rather than from the town stores. Several farmer's markets have been set up in a number of towns and provincial cities that benefit both the small farmers and the local consumers. In many areas of India, local village youth have been taught in cattle production and dairy farming. Training programs in the care of animal health, testing of the quality of milk and artificial insemination were provided by a local university research center when a local RDF introduced the farmers to some of the people in the research center.

In Santo Domingo, there were some 5,000 tricicleros (tricycle riders) that were too poor to purchase their bikes, and thus rented them often for 20 percent of their daily income. Accion Internacional, a Cambridge based group helped a group of tricicleros to buy their vehicles on the installment plan: but as each individual rider represented an unacceptably high risk this loan fund required that groups (grupos solidarios) of five to seven tricileros to be formed and be jointly responsible for everyone's payments. The IAF financed the operation with a grant. Today some 200 such groups called solidarios exist. Soon several groups organized a larger association that collected dues and sought other grants to start a rudimentary health insurance scheme and promoted contributions of members to funeral expenses for members, then they build a tricycle repair shop and bought parts at wholesale, Finally the association is able to put political pressure by having 500 vehicles come to a spot and paralyze traffic if some proposal is about to hurt the tricicleros.

In Coma, Peru a group of women got together to seek ways to increase family income. They joined forces with a PVO called *Centro de Estudios Sociales y Publicaciones* that was organized by a group of educators. With help from Dutch and German aid agencies they began to help the women to sew. Soon other courses were organized in literacy, history of Peru, and female health. After two years, the women trained asked if they could become instructors for other women. Soon they were involved in community issues and how the situation of women could be improved. Such experiences demonstrate the move from income generation to social conscientiousness.

Among the Aymara Indians in the Lake Titicaca region, not far from Puno, a number of villagers began to establish small coop grocery stores. As expected, the main benefits were in cheaper costs and not having to travel to the nearby town of Llave. Yet other benefits were noted. There was the great relief in not having to worry about being cheated by the city merchants. Also for the Aymara speaking Indians, the establishment of such small village stores is akin to a declaration of emancipation from the mestizo, Spanish-speaking merchants, who for them are very much a part of a system that has oppressed and exploited them for centuries. In a more positive view, the store is a symbol of the community's ability to undertake a joint effort and of its aspiration to better its condition, as a solidarity group.

To outsiders these stores seem insubstantial ventures whose principle purpose is to bring prices down for the articles farmers buy and of raising prices for the items they sell. Yet they may have long-term consequences like forcing merchants to reduce their own prices in the community in order to compete with the coops. Many would criticize such coops as not really making much money for the families participating in such ventures.

While it may not be the most useful or productive thing to do, still its great advantage is that it serves as a temporary outlet for the urge to cooperate. In the process, people are brought together and talk to each other about the problems of the community, with the results that they become aware of other more useful and productive, but also more ambitious and difficult, ventures that might be undertaken next. In this sense, the consumer store can have yet another intangible benefit: it leads to heightened interaction among the cooperating members who will now explore new forms of cooperative action. In the process, some of the more fundamental problems of the community may also be tackled.

Importance of Local Credit Systems

An area of emerging consensus is that to be sustainable, development projects must be participatory and community-based. Throughout the LDCs, successful development initiatives share a number of characteristics. They address needs identified by local people, involve people in the design as well as the implementation of projects, use techniques and principles suited to local conditions, and respond flexibly to changing circumstances, either correcting previous mistakes or incorporating new information.[14] Whether initiated by communities themselves or by outside donors, the most successful and sustainable development efforts have been those in which the intended beneficiaries had the opportunity to participate both in defining their problems and in choosing and implementing their solutions.

Some of the most successful projects are those initiated and run by local communities and indigenous NGOs. The Grameen (meaning "rural" in Bengali) Bank is perhaps the most well-known of the small-loan, self-help credit institutions. Founded in 1976 and formally established by government order in 1983, the bank now provides up to $10 million per month in loans averaging about $70; it has a 98 percent repayment record. Over 90 percent of its loans are to women.[15] Case Four found in Chapter 5 of this text outlines the steps leading to its success.

According to the International Fund for Agricultural Development (IFAD) -- which has similar activities throughout the developing world -- to be successful, credit programs must target women as well as men, foster the active and ongoing participation of the poor, not just as recipients of loans, but as integral partners in development, and draw on the experiences of grassroots NGOs. Remember the work of Ahmad al-Naggar in the case study of the Village Bank in rural Egypt and the special care he took in recruiting and training effective RDFs and then in developing trust and awareness among the villagers.

In the fall of 1995 a world-wide movement was established by the Micro Credit Summit[16] sponsored by representatives of some 400 organizations (including the World Bank, United Nations Development Program UNDP, USAID, and various Non Government Organizations (NGOs). The goal of this Summit group is to establish small income generating projects among the 100 million poorest families of the world by the year 2005. Most of these families earn less than 50 cents per day. By making credit and training available to such families, it is hoped they can establish productive enterprises for their own development. Note how the quality of life improves when families earn $1 or $2 a day in comparison with the subsistence type families who earn 50 cents or less a day.

Chart 13-3[17]

	Subsistence Poor (50 cents per day)	Middle Poor ($1.00 per day)	Sustainable Poor ($2.00 per day)
School attendance	5%	20%	60%
Access to Potable Water	15%	30%	65%
Use of Oral Rehydration	10%	45%	85%
Access to Nutritious Food	1%	33%	65%
Adequate Housing	1%	10%	40%
Infant mortality	120 per 1000	80 per 1000	40 per 1000

As part of the Micro-Credit Summit commitment, the CHOICE organization has sought to establish a micro-credit system in a number of countries in Africa, Asia, and Latin America. The system is structured to be implemented over an extended period of time and is generally conceptualized to include three stages:

(1) **Self-sustaining Savings Groups.** In this program, local RDFs will encourage the poorer individuals in rural villages to begin a program of savings, both to mobilize local resources for their own use and also to reinforce the commitment and discipline needed for such people to become self-reliant.

(2) **Flexible Small Credit Systems.** This program will establish small credit groups in these communities which allow men and women to obtain small loans for small scale enterprises, income generating projects of various kinds, and loans for emergencies and short term consumption needs.

(3) **Integrated Training Centers.** These training centers provide specific training through demonstrations, counseling, and instruction in marketing, agricultural production, small animal and livestock care, handicraft manufacturing, simple bookkeeping and other entrepreneurial skills needed to succeed in establishing various small income generating projects, and other activities that will improve the quality of life for these people.

The process by which this three-fold Rural Enterpreneurship program is established includes a number of specific activities to be implemented over a three to five year period.

Stage One. A Subsidized Savings and Small Loan-Giving Group Program

Step 1. Working in collaboration with CHOICE, local RDFs help villagers organize and strengthen small savings groups, each is organized to ensure a weekly deposit of some small amount into an account that provides the assets needed to establish a small group credit system.

Step 2. In step two, local RDFs help these small savings groups gradually evolve into small loan-giving groups. At this stage some financial resources are given at some ratio, generally for every dollar saved by the villagers, CHOICE contributes $2-3. The loans are small (generally less than $100), some minimal amount of interest is charged. During the period of this stage, the small loan giving groups gradually develop their capacity to pay such loans back, develop entrepreneurial skills in small scale enterprise, and establish a sense loyalty and commitment to the group of villagers working together. It generally costs $15,000 a year to start a stage one program in a given area.

Stage Two: A Transitional Micro Credit (Rural Bank) Program

Step 3. While CHOICE provides the resources needed to pay for the salaries of the RDFs and the other staff needed to build and monitor the activities of Stage One, in Stage Two, CHOICE helps establish a more formal micro-credit program (Rural Bank Program) among a cluster of saving and loan-giving groups. Generally this cluster of at least 20 groups of 5-10 women is located in a common geographical area, generally a rural district of at least 30-50,000 people, which allows for some interaction and instruction in a common Rural Entrepreneurial

Training Center. The goal of this transitional stage is to help the village microcredit groups to become a Village Banking Program, hopefully at this stage becoming somewhat self-sustaining.

Step 4. When a cluster of 20 groups or more is formalized into a district rural Bank Program, interest is charged that is higher than the commercial bank rate (1-2% per month), lower than the typical money lender rates (5-10% per month), but high enough to exceed the inflation rate and to cover most of the overhead costs of the Village Bank (3-4% per month). The major purpose of Stage Two is the create a cluster of village saving and loan groups who become committed to creating a self-sustaining banking system, structured to provide credit to the poorer individuals in the area.

Stage Three: An Integrated Commercial Bank System for the Rural Poor

Step 5. In stage three, when perhaps as many as 50-100 groups are functioning, the village bank system in a given district has generally created a large enough pool of savings that outside resources are less important, if the interest rates paid are at the rate of 3-4% per month, most of the costs of the bank program can be covered locally. If steps four and five have been successfully documented, demonstrating that the village participants have not only been repaying their loans, but have also been paying a commercially viable rate of interest, at this point the CHOICE RDF in the area will be encouraged to contact a commercial bank and to help convince the bank to consider opening a local branch in the area of the village bank. While the villagers participating in this CHOICE Rural Entrepreneurial Training Program were never able to obtain loans from commercial banks before because of their lack of collateral, it is hoped that a commercial bank might be encouraged to establish a line of credit for the participants of the Village Bank Program, perhaps with CHOICE guaranteeing these loans up to some fixed amount for some specified period of time (generally one year or less).

Step Six. In the final step of this program, the village bank system in a given district is fully integrated into a commercial bank system. While no individual participant before was able to obtain credit from banks before because of the lack of collateral, literacy and skill, the assumption of this program is that the demonstrated willingness of these villagers to repay their loans with interest in the CHOICE program becomes a form of collective collateral that should entice some commercial banking or credit union system to integrate these villagers into their formal financial system. It is anticipated that all three stages require roughly five years to complete, at which time CHOICE then moves to another rural district and starts the whole process over again. Below are some of the problems and constraints that many village banking systems face when NGOs first start.

Problems and Constraints:

1. **Little Awareness of the Informal Savings and Loan Systems Already Existing:** Many NGOs seek to introduce a system of financial services (primarily loans given to poor of a given area) with very little awareness or understanding of the informal and unofficial credit and savings systems that already exist in many rural areas of the LDCs. Often these NGOs are not aware of the negative unintended consequences that can happen when these NGOs bring such new sources of credit into a given community.

2. **Funds Disbursed on the Basis of Donor Agency Requirements:** Many NGOs seek to disburse their funds based upon a timetable established by the donor agencies supplying the funds in the first place. Having to demonstrate some success within the budget timetable established by the donor agencies (generally within the first year), many loans are given in a community with little attempt to ensure that the loans are being given for activities that have a reasonable potential of being repaid. Many NGOs have no commitment to assessing the absorptive capacity of a given community, little or no understanding about the marketing and small enterprise development potentials that exist in a given area.

3. **A Fairly Narrow Focus on Income Generating Projects**: Many NGOs are not sensitive to the wide variety of financial needs that the village poor often have. Too often, such NGOs are only willing to provide loans directly related to some productive activity that will earn immediate income. Most poor people have financial needs that reflect the physical reality and economic constraints that characterize most rural areas. While, credit for some income producing activity is important for many villagers, equally, if not more important, are their needs related to immediate and future crises: crop failure due to drought or flooding, the loss of an important asset (cow, buffalo, or oxen), sizable loans for traditional activities related to weddings, funerals, fiestas, etc., and even short-term consumption needs related to food, clothing, including school expenses for their children. Such non-income generating loans are almost never available through a typical NGO-organized credit program.

4. **A Philosophical Bias for Subsidized Credit to the Very Poor**: Most NGOs have a commitment to helping the poor through some form of low interest credit. While this type of motive is reflective of a sincere concern for the poor, it almost always has very negative and usually unintended consequences. Such unintended consequences include the disruption and even destruction of already functioning rotating savings groups and small informal lending groups that cannot compete with the cheap credit being offered by the outsiders. Unfortunately, wealthier peasants often seek this cheap credit to then reloan at a much higher rate, thus defeating the very purpose of the cheap credit program. Perhaps most troublesome is the inability of these cheap credit systems to generate enough revenue to cover the costs of the credit system, thus ensuring that such a credit program only lasts as long as the outsiders are willing to provide the subsidized

credit. Once the outsiders leave, the villagers often find themselves worse off than they were before the outsiders arrived.

5. **A Commitment to an All or Nothing Blue Print Form of Credit System**: Many NGOs providing credit to the poor, insist on a pure form of credit disbursement based upon a model or philosophy that has been perfected or field-tested in another country or another part of their own country. Convinced that they have found the correct system, they are unwilling to consider alternative systems, locally developed and often irrelevant to the local situation in terms of their cultural norms and social mores. As a consequence they tend to make two kinds of mistakes: first, they tend to refuse to consider different ways of organizing a saving and credit program, to seek ways of adapting their "blue print model" to the local situation. Secondly, they see no need to consider working with, perhaps even learning from, the local forms of savings and loans system already existing in the area.

6. **Failure to Establish Some Links With the Local Banking Systems in the Area**: Equally unfortunate is the tendency of many NGOs to remain independent and separate from the more formal and official financial institutions of the country. This tendency to reject the possibility of linking up with some formal credit or commercial banking entity is too often based upon the assumption that such organizations are either unwilling to work with the poor or are unable to do so. The long-term goal of any micro-credit program established by these NGOs should be sustainable programs of savings and loaning, structured to integrate the more traditional and unofficial systems into the formal or official organizations capable of providing a wide variety of financial services for all the people of the community, both rich and poor.

Ten Basic Principles of Successful Small Credit Systems

The difficulty of getting credit to villagers is often cited as a major bottleneck for development. Historically, most of the credit available in rural areas was monopolized by the larger, richer farmers. The small farmers and landless simply did not have the collateral to qualify for such loans. RDFs can play a very important role in helping poorer farmers and small-scale entrepreneurs to develop revolving credit systems. The whole process is based upon **the following ten principles:** (1) The basis for a successful small credit system is the creation of **small groups of men or women** who are committed to a common set of ideals, procedures and goals. Experience has found that women's groups are more apt to be successful than men's groups. Although some men's groups have been very successful, many are arguing that focusing on women has some long-term value both in terms of income generation, but also in terms of impact on the entire family. (2) Each group is generally around 5-10 people, most of who are **friends or close associates**. A cluster of 10-20 small groups makes up a village credit system. (3) Each person must participate in an **ongoing saving program** both to develop discipline and commitment but also to create a locally derived pool of money. Such money should be kept in a local bank or in some safe place that is acceptable to all the members of group. An outside organization such as CHOICE, will match in some agreed upon ratio, the money raised locally, and could provide an annual bonus when there is at least a 95% repayment schedule on the loans given. (4) The decision as to who will receive a loan must be a **group decision** with each member taking a turn at getting a loan. (5) A **Village Bank Worker plays a very important role** in training the group in income project assessment, marketing and bookkeeping skills. (6) All loans should go for some **income generating project** that has quick turn-around and good prospects for success, thus ensuring that the loan will be repaid. (7) **Some interest** should be charged usually more than the local bank rate, but significantly lower than the local money-lenders (generally 2-3 percent per month). (8) **Loans should be small** enough to be repaid in 3-6 months in the beginning. (9) **loan repayments** should be made on a **weekly basis,** with larger loans and longer repayment schedules allowed after the credit group has gained some experience and has developed more financial resources. (10) Each member of the **group guarantees the repayment** of the loans given to group members thus ensuring that adequate social pressure in placed on all the members to repay their loans.[18]

In areas of Egypt, Indonesia, India, Kenya, Philippines, Malaysia, Bangladesh, Vietnam South Korea and many other countries, women's credit systems of this type have been established where literally thousands of such groups have been able to collect significant resources over time, allowing these women to start a wide variety of different small-scale enterprises in their communities and thereby beginning the process of moving from subsistence poverty to a more sustainable kind of life. Obviously this third dimension of rural development will continue to be a crucial part of any development program.

---

[1]R. Burback and P. Flynn, *Agribusiness in the Americas,* (New York: Monthly Review Press, 1980), pp. 7-11.
[2]E. Feder, *Strawberry Imperialism: An Inquiry into the Mechanics of Dependency in Mexican Agriculture*, (The Hague: Institute of Social Studies, 1978).
[3]*Ibid.*, p. 18.
[4]P. M. Blaikie, *The Political Economy of Soil Erosion in Developing Countries,* (Harlow: Longman, 1985).
[5]Much of the information that follows is described in greater detail in Ken Darrow Mike Saxenian, *Appropriate Technology Sourcebook* (Stanford: Volunteers in Asia, 1986); Robert Rodale, *The Basic Book of Organic Gardening* (Emmaus, PA.: Rodale Press, 1971); John Seymour *The Self-Sufficient Gardener,* (New York: Doubleday & Co., 1979); Jules N. Pretty, *Regenerating Agriculture,* (London: Earthscan, 1989); Third World Network, *Return to the Good Earth: Damaging Effects of Modern Agriculture and the Case for Ecological Farming,* (Third World Network, 1990); and Coen Reijntjes, et al., *Farming for the Future: An Introduction to Low-External-Input and Sustainable Agriculture* (Leusden, The Netherlands, 1994). Especially useful is the book: Katie Smith, *The Human Farm: A*

Tale of Changing Lives and Changing Lands, (West Hartford, CT: Kumarian Press, 1994) and also the magazine *Organic Gardening,* Rodale Press, 33 East Minor Street, Emmaus Pennsylvania 18409.

[6] See: National Research Council, *Alternative Agriculture,* (Washington, DC: National Academy Press, 1989) and Richard Thompson, et. al., "Case Study: A Resource-Efficient Farm with Livestock," pp. 263-80 in C.B. Flora and L. D. King (eds.) *Sustainable Agriculture in Temperate Zones* (New York: Wiley, 1990).

[7] Roland Bunch, *Two Ears of Corn,* (1982)

[8] For a wonderful book for RDFs seeking to work with women in agriculture, see: Hilary Sims Feldstein and Janice Jiggens, (eds.) *Tools for the Field: Methodologies Handbook for Gender Analysis in Agriculture,* (West Hartfield, CT.: Kumarian Press, 1994)

[9] *UNDP Report* 1990, p. 31.

[10] Mayra Buveni and Margaret A. Lycette, "Women, Poverty, and Development in the Third World," in *Strengthening the Poor: What Have We Learned:* John P. Lewis, ed. (New Brunswick, NJ: Transaction books, 1989).

[11] Note that rice provides only 1/5 ton per hectare per year, wheat provides 4/5 ton per year, corn provides two ton per year, soybean provides 3 tons, and spirulina provides 50 tons per hectare per year.

[12] One of the best sources on appropriate technology is Ken Darrow & M. Saxenian, *Appropriate Technology Sourcebook* (1986).

[13] John Thompson, *Combining Local Knowledge and Expert Assistance in Natural Resource Management: Small-Scale Irrigation in Kenya,* (Washington DC: World Resources Institute, 1991`).

[14] Barbara Thomas-Slayter, C. Kabutha, and R. Ford, *Traditional Village Institutions in Environmental Management: Erosion Control in Katheka, Kenya,* (Washington DC: World Resource Institute, 1991); Walter V. Reid, J. N. Barnes, and Brent Blackwelder, *Bankrolling Successes: A Portfolio of Sustainable Development Projects,* (Washington DC: Environmental Policy Institute, National Wildlife Federation, 1988) and Kenneth Tull and Michael Sands, *Experiences in Success* (Emmaus, Penn.: Rodale International, 1987).

[15] Mahabub Hossain, *Credit for Alleviation of Rural Poverty: The Grameen Bank in Bangladesh* (Washington DC: International Food Policy Research Institute, 1988) and Muhammed Yunus, ed. *Grameen Dialogue,* No.8 (Dhaka, Bangladesh: Grameen Trust, 1991).

[16] Micro Credit Summit, 236 Massachusetts Avenue, NE, Suite 300, Washington, DC 2002, phone (202) 546-1900. Their email is micro creditsum@action.org.

[17] The information for this chart is based on observations of the author and a review of different United Nations and USAID reports.

[18] For a nice summary of micro-credit techniques, see: Susan Holcombe, *Managing to Empower: The Grameen Bank's Experience of Poverty Alleviation* (London: Zed Books, 1995); Maria Otero and Elisabeth Rhyne, (edsl) *The New World of Microenterprise Finance: Building Healthy Financial Institutions for the Poor* (New Hartfield, CT.: Kumarian Press, 1994); Alex Counts, *Give Us Credit: How Muhammad Yunus's Micro-Lending Revolution is Empowering Women from Bangladesh to Chicago* (New York: Random House, 1996). For a more critical assessment of these micro-credit systems, see Dale W. Adams and D.A. Fitchett, (eds.) *Informal Finance in Low Income Countries* (Boulder, Col.: Westview Press, 1992). For access to information on the internet, contact Hari Srinivas, his e-mail is hari@soc.titech.ac.jp.

Chapter 14

Fourth Dimension of Rural Development
A Concern and an Appreciation for the Local Environment: A New Ecological Perspective

Today the world faces a wide variety of critical environmental threats: degradation of soil, water, and marine resources essential to increased food production; widespread health-threatening pollution, stratospheric ozone depletion, global climate change; and loss of biodiversity. At the same time, it faces enormous human problems in the form of widespread, persistent poverty and human misery. Despite growing affluence for the few, a pattern of growth that is increasing rather than remedying such disparities, characterizes life for the many.

Such problems are troubling enough. If human societies in decades to come are to inhabit a world that is environmentally secure, economically prosperous, and characterized by growing peace, freedom, and human welfare, then current generations must also come to grips with underlying trends that threaten to make these problems far worse. One of the most basic trends is that world population has doubled since 1950 and is expected to roughly double again by the middle of the next century. Similarly, as people everywhere have struggled to improve their standards of living, world economic activity has grown at about 3 percent per year since 1950; if this rate continues in the decades ahead, then the world economy will be 5 times larger in the year 2050 than it is today.

Such growth in population and economic activity has the potential to increase dramatically the pressure on the natural resources and natural systems -- from farmland to fisheries to the global atmosphere -- which are already suffering serious levels of degradation. Consider just two examples:

1. Well over 1.5 billion people in the world are malnourished. To provide an adequate level of nutrition as the world's population doubles will require more than doubling current food production. Under the best of conditions, that would require making very productive use of the world's stock of arable land. Yet according to new estimates by the world's leading soil scientists, more than 1.2 billion hectares of vegetated land -- an area as large as farming lands of India and China put together -- has been significantly degraded since Word War II. If such degradation continues or accelerates, expansion of food production on the scale required will be extremely difficult, if not impossible, and a greatly worsened human misery will be increasingly likely. In the last decade, in fact, per capita food production has declined in 69 countries.

2. Fossil fuels provide about 95 percent of the commercial energy used in the world economy, and their use is growing worldwide at the rate of 20-25 percent per decade. Combustion of those fuels constitutes the largest source of emissions of climate-altering greenhouse gases to the atmosphere. Scientists convened under the auspices of the United Nations Environmental Program and the World Meteorological Organization concluded that a 60 percent reduction in carbon dioxide emissions would be necessary to stabilize carbon dioxide concentrations in the atmosphere at current levels. Protecting the Earth's climate therefore may require significant reductions in global fossil fuel use, even as the world economy expands; alternately, continued expansion of fossil fuel use at current rates will double atmospheric levels well before the middle of the next century and thus increase the risk of significant climate change.

Section One
Need for Sustainable Development

As these two examples illustrate, the world is not now headed toward a sustainable future, but rather toward a variety of potential human and environmental disasters. Let us now review some information on sustainable development that all RDFs need to understand as they work and live in rural areas of the LDCs. Over the past 25 years, since the Stockholm Conference on the Human Environment, the world has started to recognize that environmental problems are inseparable from those of human welfare and from the process of economic development in general and that many present forms of development erode those environmental resources on which human livelihoods and welfare ultimately depend. With this recognition, the United Nations established the World Commission on Environment and Development to examine these issues and to make recommendations.

In *Our Common Future*, World Commission on Environment and Development concluded that "a new developmental path was required, one that sustained human progress not just in a few places for a few years, but for the entire planet into the distant future." Sustainable development, as the commission defined it, is development that "meets the needs of the present without compromising the ability of future generations to meet their own needs."[1]

In an attempt to make the concept of sustainable development more specific, some authors have given a narrow definition focused on the physical aspects of sustainable development. They stress using renewable natural resources in a manner that does not eliminate or degrade them or otherwise diminish their "renewable" usefulness for future generations, while maintaining effectively constant or non declining stocks of natural resources such as soil, ground water, and biomass.[2] Implied in this kind of analysis is the notion that our economic systems must be managed so that we live off the dividends of our resources, maintaining and improving the asset base of this resource system.[3]

Economic development does not necessarily mean economic growth; the type of economic activity can change without increasing the quantity of goods and services. Many authors argue that not only is economic growth compatible with sustainable development -- as long as it is the right kind of growth -- it is in fact greatly needed to relieve poverty and generate the resources for development and hence to prevent further environmental degradation. The issue is both the quality of the growth and how its benefits are distributed, not mere expansion. Some argue, however, that "sustainable growth" is a contradiction in terms, and that a more equitable redistribution of wealth not growth is the way to combat poverty.[4] Sustainable development related to greater equity is thus defined as development that improves health care, education, and social well-being. Such human development is now recognized as critical to economic development and to early stabilization of population.[5]

As the *Human Development Report 1991* of the UNDP put it, "Men, women, and children must be the center of attention -- with development woven around people, not people around development." Increasingly, definitions of sustainable development stress that development must be participatory and must involve local people in decisions that affect their lives. Some authors have expanded the definition of sustainable development still further to include a rapid transformation of the technological base of industrial civilization. They point out that new technology is needed that is cleaner, more efficient, and more sparing of natural resources in order to reduce pollution, help stabilize climate, and accommodate growth in population and economic activity.[6]

Increasingly, definitions of sustainable development attempt to cut across or encompass several aspects or dimensions. The new strategy outlined by the World Conservation Union, *Caring for the Earth*, defines sustainable development as "improving the quality of human life while living within the carrying capacity of supporting ecosystems."[7] This report focuses on sustainable development as a process requiring simultaneous global progress in a variety of dimensions: economic, human, environmental, and technological.

Economic Dimensions

On a per capita basis, inhabitants of industrial countries use many times more of the world's natural resources than do inhabitants of developing countries. Consumption of energy from fossil fuels, for example, is 33 times higher in the United States than in India and ten times higher than in Western Europe. For rich countries, then, sustainable development means steady reductions in wasteful levels of consumption of nonrenewable energy and other natural resources through improvements in efficiency and through changes in life-style. In this process, care needs to be taken to ensure that environmental stresses are not simply exported to developing countries.

Industrial countries have a special responsibility for leadership in sustainable development, because their cumulative past consumption of natural resources such as fossil fuels -- and hence their contribution to global pollution problems -- is disproportionately large. In addition, rich countries have the financial, technical, and human resources to take the lead in developing cleaner, less resource-intensive technologies, in transforming their economies to protect and work with natural systems, and in providing more equitable access to economic opportunities and social services within their societies. Leadership also means providing an investment in the future of the planet, and technical and financial resources to support sustainable development in other countries.

In poor countries, sustainable development would mean the commitment of resources toward continued improvement in living standards. As an ethical matter, rapid improvement is especially critical for the more than 20 percent of the world's population now destitute. Alleviating absolute poverty also has important practical consequences for sustainable development, since there are close links between poverty, environmental degradation, and rapid population growth. People whose basic needs are unmet and whose survival may be in doubt perceive no stake in the future of the planet and have no reason to consider the sustainability of their actions. They also tend to have more children in an effort to increase the family labor force and to provide security for their old age.

Human Dimension

Sustainable development means significant progress toward stable populations. This is important not only because continued growth of the human population for long at anything like current global rates is clearly impossible, but also because rapid growth puts severe strains on natural resources and on the ability of governments to provide services. Within a given country or region, rapid population growth undercuts development and dilutes the natural resource base available to support each inhabitant. The final size attained by Earth's human population is also important, because the limits of the Earth's carrying capacity for human life are not known with any accuracy. Current projections suggest that, given present trends in fertility, world population will stabilize at about 12 billion, which would more than double the current population. Even at present levels, population pressure is a growing factor in deforestation, land degradation, and the over exploitation of wildlife and other natural resources; as expanding populations are driven to marginal land or must overuse current resources.

Distribution of population is important too: present trends toward increasing urbanization, especially the developments of megacities, have massive environmental implications. With currently employed technologies, cities concentrate wastes and pollutants and thus often generate conditions hazardous to people and damaging to surrounding natural systems. Thus, sustainable development would mean vigorous rural development to help slow migration to cities and adoption of policy measures and technologies to minimize the environmental consequences of urbanization.

Sustainable development also entails making full use of human resources by improving education and health services and by combating hunger. It is especially important that basic services reach those living in extreme poverty; thus, sustainable development would mean redirecting or reallocating resources to ensure that basic human needs, such as literacy, primary health care, and clean water, are met first. Beyond basic needs, sustainable development means improving social well-being, protecting cultural diversity, and investing in human capital -- training the educators, health-care workers, agricultural extension workers, appropriate technology technicians, community development workers, etc. Education can help farmers and other rural inhabitants to better protect forests, soil resources, and biodiversity.

The role of women is particularly critical. In many developing countries, women and children grow the subsistence crops, graze animals, gather wood and water, use most of the household's energy in cooking, and care for the household's immediate environment. In other words, women are the primary resource and environmental managers in the household -- as well as the primary care-givers for children -- yet their health and education are often neglected in comparison to those of men. More-educated women have greater access to contraception and, on average, lower fertility rates, as well as healthier babies. Investing in the health and education of women can have multiple benefits for sustainability.

Environmental Dimensions

Soil erosion and loss of soil productivity reduce yields and cause large areas of agricultural land to be taken from production every year. Overuse of fertilizers and pesticide pollutes surface and ground water. Human and livestock pressures damage or destroy vegetation and forests. Many freshwater and marine fisheries are already being harvested at levels that are now, or are close to becoming, unsustainable.

Sustainable development necessitates protecting the natural resources needed for food production and cooking fuels -- from soils to woodlots to fisheries -- while expanding production to meet the needs of growing populations. These are potentially conflicting goals, and yet failure to conserve the natural resources on which agriculture depends would ensure future shortages of food. Sustainable development means more efficient use of arable lands and water supplies, as well as the development and adoption of improved agricultural practices and technologies to increase yields. It requires avoiding overuse of chemical fertilizers and pesticides, so that they do not degrade rivers and lakes, threaten wildlife, and contaminate human food and water supplies. It means careful use of irrigation, to avoid salinization or water logging of cropland. It means avoiding the expansion of agriculture onto steep hillsides or marginal soils that would rapidly erode.

In some regions, water is in as short supply as land, with withdrawals from rivers threatening to exhaust the available supply and ground water being pumped at unsustainable rates. Industrial, agricultural, and human wastes are polluting surface and ground water and threatening lakes and estuaries in virtually every country.

Tropical forests, coral reef ecosystems, coastal mangrove forests and other wetlands, and many other unique habitats are being rapidly destroyed, and species extinction is accelerating. Sustainable development means that the richness of earth's biodiversity would be conserved for future generations by greatly slowing -- and, if possible, halting -- extinction and habitat and ecosystem destruction. Let us review some of the major problems that we face in the years to come:

1. **The ozone layer** that shields us from the full effects of the sun's ultraviolet radiation is in danger. An increase of ultraviolet radiation by even 2-3 percent could have severe consequences on human health, plant growth, and basic forms of aquatic life vital to the food chain and the balance of carbon dioxide in the atmosphere. Many concerned scientists believe the ozone layer is being depleted at any alarming rate caused by a range of chemicals being spewed into our atmosphere, principally chlorofluorocarbons (CFCs). According to some calculations, over the Antarctic some 97 percent of the ozone is missing and a similar hole in growing over the Arctic.

2. **Acid Rain**. Sulfur dioxides and nitrogen oxides from coal, oil and vehicle exhausts form acid rain which is causing severe damage to our forests and lakes. Canada has 14,000 strongly acidified lakes, and over 35 percent of Europe's forests are affected. Crop damage from acid rain in the US is estimated to be over $5 billion a year

3. The **Greenhouse Effect**. The warming of the atmosphere is caused by the accumulation of gases that retain heat from the sun. The speed of warming 1 degree every 30 years is unprecedented in human history, especially since 75 percent of the hottest years of past hundred years were in the 1970s and 1980s. Such heating of the atmosphere is likely to lead to massive changes in climate patterns, floods, droughts, storms, and crop failures.

4. **Deforestation:** Forests once covered 75 percent of the planet's land area. Today it is less than 30 percent. Tropical forests once covered 14 percent, today they cover less than 7 percent of the world's land. On the basis of recent estimates, at the present rate of 20-30 million acres of forest being destroyed annually, 99 percent of the world's rain forests will be gone by 2025.

6. **Species Extinction.** Estimates vary, but probably 50-100 animal and plant species are being extinguished every year and the rate in rapidly raising. Tropical forests contain 80 percent of all Earth's perhaps 30 million species. The impact of such loss of this animal and plan diversity will be horrendous.

7. **Toxic Chemicals.** Some 70,000 chemicals are in common use with 1000 new ones added annually. Such chemicals pollute our water and soil, cause cancer and other types of death. Nearly 50,000 people die each year in the Less Developed world of Africa, Asia and Latin America, as they are ever-increasingly becoming dumping grounds for chemicals banned in Europe and the United States. The breast milk of Nicaraguan women has been shown to contain DDT at 45 times the WHO tolerance limit. Their continual use increases various strains of insects resistant to such chemicals.

8. **Desertification.** The area of non-agriculture deserts increases 15 million acres each year and another 75 million acres in Africa and Asia are experiencing a significant decrease in yields each year. Estimates suggest that 35 percent of the earth's land mass are at risk as some 24 billion tons of top soil are blown or washed away each year. The principal causes of degradation are over grazing, over cultivation, water logging, salinization and deforestation. In 1950 there were 275 million Africans with 275 million livestock, today there are 600 million people in African with 550 million livestock. UN experts estimate that $4.5 billion a year (less than two day's worth of world military spending) for twenty years is needed to control the problem of desertification.

9. **Water Depletion.** Farming accounts for 70 percent of global water use. Falling water tables in all parts of the world promise serious water shortages within a decade or two. Twenty-four percent of the cultivable lands of the less developed world have been seriously damaged by the build-up of salts in the past two decades. A 1987 UN report predicts that pollution and population increases could cut per capita availability of water in Asia and Africa by up to 50 percent, while 2-3 billion people already suffer chronic water shortage. In the US, drinking water has been found to contain 129 dangerous chemicals and in terms of overuse, each American was flushing 34,000 liters of drinking water to remove 500 liters of body wastes.

Cause and Effect

The causes of these problems are complex and multifaceted, but all relate to too many people, with some people (in the developed world) consuming a disproportionate share of the world's wealth. Pollution and water depletion spring directly from industrial consumerism that systematically is destroying the unreplaceable resources of the world at an alarming rate. Some 15 million acres of tropical timber is shipped annually from the poor nations of the world to the rich nations, Over the past ten years, the amount of land in Africa and Latin America used for growing food exported to the Developed nations has increased 20 percent, land that before was used to feed local populations. The appropriation by the rich of the resources of developing countries leaves less and less for the indigenous poor, who are forced into the forests or on to marginal or fragile soils that simply cannot sustainably support them. Huge modern farms in South

America are forcing an army of landless people into the Amazon basin where ever increasing amounts of the rain forest are being destroyed daily.

Section Two
Now is the Time to Redefine Development

Signs of the planet's deteriorating health are all around us. Some, like global warming and the thinning ozone shield, seem remote and can be understood only with the help of scientists. Others, such as receding forests, contaminated water, and worsening air pollution are painfully real. Progress and development, as defined by modern economics, are destroying the very natural systems upon which we depend for health and prosperity. In the same way as an auto-immune disease, in which the body's own defense system attacks and destroys vital tissue, the world's consumer society is assaulting the very life-support systems that keep it functioning. That we persist in calling this progress is the grossest fiction -- and the greatest danger -- of our time.

Nothing less than a fundamental overhaul of the way we define, pursue, and measure well-being will enable us to halt the self-destruction. Use of Gross National Product, the total output of goods and services in an economy, as the prime indicator of whether people are becoming better off is increasingly deceptive. Such an indicator tends to ignore the destruction of forests, soils, water supplies, and other natural resources. A country can be on the brink of ecological bankruptcy and still register GNP growth, and thus appear to be making progress.

We all know that human well-being depends on much more than producing and consuming things valued in the marketplace. Good health, satisfying work, a sense of community, freedom of expression and religion, equal opportunity, and a healthy environment shape overall welfare as much as income does, often more so.

At the heart of the problem lies ecological shortsightedness and commercial greed. What we need, to overcome the energy crisis, is not more energy but less. Our ever increasing energy needs reflect the general expansion of our economic and technological systems; they are caused by the patterns of undifferentiated growth that deplete our natural resources and contribute significantly to our multiple symptoms of individual and social illness. The need to overcome our multifaceted crisis is not through the mindless expansion of more energy, but a profound change of values, attitudes, and life styles.

The Earth's resources are sufficient for all living creatures needs, if they are managed efficiently and sustainability. (1) There is enough food raised on this planet to feed every person, the problem is distribution. As Mahatma Ghandi says: "The Earth is sufficient to provide for every one's need, but not for everyone's greed." (2) Both poverty and affluence can cause environmental problems. In the industrialized world, at least 3,000 square kilometers of prime farmland disappear every year under new buildings and roads. In the LDCs the rural poor burn more than 350 million tons of dung and crop residue every year for fuel -- material that should go back to the soil to restore nutrients. (3) In the rich world, half the surface water and a significant amount of ground water has been polluted with industrial waste, and in the LDCs 60 percent of the water sources are polluted with human and animal waste. (4) The top 25 percent who live in the industrialized world consume 80 percent of the world's resources mobilized each year.

Economic development and care for the environment are compatible, interdependent, and necessary. If rich men own all the good land in the valleys, then the poor will farm the erosion prone hillsides. If the rich countries import beef for their hamburgers, the poor countries will burn their forests to provide range land for cattle. Natives of Tikopia in the South Pacific have strong rituals to control population, ensuring that there is never over crowding. Traditional homesteads on Bali incorporate complex systems of inter cropping, aqua culture, and animal care that recycle virtually all organic matter, never leave the soil bare to erosion, reduce pest infestations, and maintain high productivity. Small cities in Japan have clean, mechanized waste-recovery centers that return every form of urban waste to a useful purpose: organic matter is composted into fertilizer; bottles are washed and refilled; metals are reclaimed; paper is either recycled or burned to produce heat and electricity. Israel has pioneered water-conserving technologies so efficient that over the decade 1968 to 1978 it doubled agriculture production, while water use per hectare of irrigated land fell 21 percent.

Poverty is a major cause of environmental degradation. In 1980 more than 1.2 billion people were cutting wood for fuel faster than it was being replenished in Africa and Asia. Crop residue and dung when used for fuel can appreciably diminish soil fertility and crop yields. The women who use these fuels cannot be blamed for their poverty. In mountainous, rainy Costa Rica, the building of roads usually means landslides, a clogged or flooding stream, and severe disturbance of a whole watershed. Now the engineers are taught to build roads in ways that do not disturb the ecosystem of the area. In Hungary, the top soil in strip-mining areas is saved and put back after the mining. In Indonesia, the forest areas above new dams are carefully protected to regulated water runoff and prevent the dams from silting over.

Protecting the Environment

In poor countries, because of the close relationship between poverty, population growth, and environmental degradation, the most important actions to conserve natural resources are those that are aimed at stabilizing populations and alleviating poverty. However, specific efforts to maintain as much as possible of each country's natural and modified ecosystems, to halt deforestation, and to conserve biological diversity are also badly needed. Creating and maintaining protected areas and protecting threatened species are important components of the necessary strategy. Using both wild and managed biological resources in ways that allow stocks to renew themselves is also important.

The spiral of poverty, population growth, and environmental degradation that characterizes many poor countries is frequently aggravated by policies that actively encourage waste and resource degradation, particularly in agriculture, forestry, and energy. For example, holding agriculture prices artificially low to benefit the urban minority discourages investment in soil and tree conservation in rural areas. Subsidizing pesticides, fertilizers, and other agricultural inputs encourages their use and leads to residues and runoff that can be environmentally detrimental. Providing tax incentives that encourage forest clearing for timber and ranching creates short-term profits for a few while seriously degrading the environment.

Many developing countries subsidize the cost of fuel. Protecting the environment in poor countries would require economic incentives, including prices and tax policies, that favor resource conservation rather than resource degradation. However, the direction and impact of policy change are not always clear-cut and must be carefully suited to local conditions. Energy technologies are also of critical importance to poor countries. Poor rural populations throughout the developing world depend heavily on traditional biomass fuels -- fuelwood, charcoal, dung, and crop residues -- for energy. Such fuels provide approximately 60 percent of fuel needs in LDCs excluding China and India (22 percent including China and India).[8] In sub-Saharan Africa, such fuels account for two thirds of the energy consumption, with some four fifths of the population relying wholly or partly on them. In very poor countries, the proportion of traditional fuels is even higher, exceeding 90 percent of primary energy supplies in countries such as Ethiopia, Nepal, and Bangladesh. More than 50 million Africans already face acute fuelwood scarcities.[9]

This situation is getting worse as increased prices for other fuels, especially petroleum and electricity, result in greater reliance on biomass in urban areas as well. Fuelwood shortages require rural women to spend increasing amounts of time collecting wood, causing a host of negative social and economic consequences, such as decreases in child nutrition. Moreover, as farmers begin to burn dung and agricultural residues instead of using them as fertilizers, the cycle of poverty and environmental destruction is further aggravated. Development of more efficient domestic stoves or cooking methods would help to minimize fuelwood needs.

Governments and international organizations have sought to train local officials in the tools and methodologies of planning, finance, and materials acquisition; yet much more is needed, especially by providing small development funds to catalyze local initiatives; conduct more research to improve locally known and accepted techniques rather than promoting new and foreign practices; and they can train village-based and local specialists in terracing, reforestation, water development, and land management, instead of supplying outside experts.

Section Three
Contrasting Approaches to the Environment

The two great models of industrialism -- socialist centralized planning and liberal capitalism -- are both inadequate. The removal of the communist model from much of the world demonstrates the failure of centralized planning rather than the ultimate success of liberal capitalism. The latter system, especially in its laissez-faire conservative form, also cannot deal adequately with emerging regional, continental and global environmental problems through its favored mechanism, the decentralized free market. An RDF should be conversant with the two major paradigms that reflect people's relationship to the environment. These competing ways of looking at the environment should be carefully reviewed.

Chart 14-1

Economic View of Environment	Sustainable View of Environment
1. Dominance/exploitation of nature.	1. Harmony with nature in symbiosis.
2. The natural environment is a resource for humans to exploit and use.	2. All nature has intrinsic worth; biospecies are equally worthy of survival.
3. Material economic growth needed for growing human population is crucial.	3. Elegantly simple material needs (material/spiritual goals) are key to the goal of self-realization.
4. Belief in ample resource reserve.	4. Belief that earth's resources are finite.
5. High technological progress and solutions.	5. Appropriate technology/soft sciences.
6. Commitment to consumerism.	6. Doing with enough with a commitment to recycling
7. National/centralized communities.	7. Local communities/Ethnic diversity.

The Industrial Economy

The foundations of the modern world are rooted in the Industrial Revolution. Its father was the Scottish moral philosopher and economist Adam Smith, whose book, *An Inquiry into the Nature and Causes of the Wealth of Nations,* was published in 1776. Adam Smith saw the industrial revolution as the key to future wealth and argued that the industrialists of the world would be the wealth creators and that they should have the freedom to make profits through the exploitation of the world's resources. He believed that individual economic self-interest should be allowed to work through a free market, where, as by an "invisible hand," it would come to serve the common good.

Following this philosophy, the people of Western Europe and North America (including Japan and Australia) approximately 25 percent of the world's population have a standard of living like no other civilization in the history of the world. This system based upon industrial consumerism has created problems that Adam Smith could never have imagined. It is hard to imagine the 18th-century world of Adam Smith as he sat musing on the marvel of self interest: a population of less than a billion, all types of animal life (birds, beasts and fish in profusion; a vastly productive land mass rich in diverse plant life; and large expanses of rich green forests (nearly 75 percent of the landed areas of the planet)

In less than 200 years, more forests have been destroyed, more natural non replaceable resources have been used, more soil erosion and increased desertification as deserts continue to expand, than in the previous 6,000 years of human experience. It is time to consider a more sustainable approach to the environment using a community-based strategy that involves local people in the preservation of their scarce local resources.

Section Four
Activities in Environment Protection
for Each of the Three Stages of Rural Development

There are a number of issues that have to be dealt with for an RDF seeking to introduce a Village Community Environmental program. Also some care must be made to distinguish between ecological related activities appropriate for Stage One, Stage Two and Stage Three. Let us now review some of the kinds of activities that are best implemented in each of the three stages of Rural Development. Each stage has a different focus and each requires different kinds of skills and interventions.

Activities During the First Stage

First, the RDFs must take an inventory of the local environment: assessing and documenting changes in the environment over the past several decades. What are the trends in deforestation, lake and stream pollution, soil erosions and other degradation of the environment? The opportunities for protecting and enhancing the productive capacity of the land and the environment in the community need to be assessed and discussed in the community.

One approach to environmental protection used by RDFs in a number of countries is called the Participatory Rural Appraisal (PAR) approach. This approach recognizes that, although community residents have a good working knowledge of ecological and development needs, they do not necessarily have the means to systematize this information or mobilize the community to take action. The roots of the approach can be found in the philosophy of Paulos Freire and his use of village consciousness raising discussions and through Robert Chamber's notions of Rapid Rural Appraisal where local people are involved to help in collecting and analyzing needed information and data.[10] It brings multi-sector RDF teams who have skills in agriculture, water, forestry, and community development, together with village members to assess village needs and priorities and then create village resource management committees. Topics under discussion include perceptions of the community's most pressing problems, trends in resource access and use, and institutional effectiveness in fostering sustainable development.

These committees work out locally defined plans that become the basis for action in the rural community and enable local institutions, government units and NGOs to cooperate. The RDFs draw upon knowledge and skills already in the village; they create a setting in which local residents exchange information with one another and the RDFs assigned in the area who have some technical background. The RDFs use a range of visual instruments such as seasonal calendars and trend lines to organize data and present them to community members. They provide a structure for the expression and implementation of local aspirations and goals. They facilitate a ranked listing of village project activities that funding agencies can support through expeditions and longer-term consulting teams. In sum, this process of PRA sets in place a plan that village members and institutions can implement and sustain.

The Participatory Rural Appraisal model involves eight clearly defined steps, though the procedures may vary greatly, depending on local needs and preferences of the village committees. These steps, which all require extensive community participation, include: (1) site selection, and clearance of the proposed appraisal with the assistance of local administrative officials; (2) a preliminary site visit to meet the village leaders and members and formulate an initial identification of environmental problems; (3) collection of data relating to four aspects of the community's environmental problems: a)spatial, b)time-related, c)social, d)technical; (4) synthesis and analysis of data; (5) setting the problems in priority order and exploring opportunities for resolving them; (6) ranking the opportunities by priority order and feasibility and formulating them into a Village Resource Management Plan (VRMP); (7) community adoption of the proposed plan, and (8) implementation of the plan, including monitoring the results, by local institutions.

It places the burden of analysis, planning and implementation with local institutions rather than external or national agents. It identifies local leadership and rural organizations as the most effective units to undertake rehabilitation of LDCs degrading ecosystems and to launch truly sustainable development. This approach builds on the premise that individual rural communities reside in discrete ecosystems or micro-zones -- rainfall, soils, elevation, vegetation, etc. -- and require particular and unique combinations of farm, health, soil, water and woodland/grassland management. As a result, popular participation introduces a fundamental ingredient in project planning. In helping to devise locally maintained institutions and technologies, as well as sustainable economic, political and ecological inputs, it is more likely to achieve a reversal in environmental decline.

Originally conceived and implemented in Kenya, the Participatory Rural Appraisal methodology now functions effectively in a number of countries by engaging the rural community itself. It seeks to mobilize community institutions around issues of sustainable development by raising awareness of what can be accomplished as well as how local groups can do it. It systematizes rural participation by helping local communities to define their own problems and identify potential solutions to them. It enables villagers to rank solutions, based on local priorities related to feasibility, ecological sustainability, and cost effectiveness. It sets out priorities in a community-based plan for resource management. It offers prompt turn-around, requiring an average of only six day's field work and three days to organize priorities. It is cost effective because it uses technical officers who are already assigned to the field site. The RDFs should also help the community make contact with appropriate donor agencies to fund small scale projects.

Activities During the Second Stage

RDFs are encouraged to implement some type of environment protection and enhancement program, training the local villagers in the processes of measuring and assessing the consequences of development activities on the environment of their village.

An example of a Stage Two approach is found in Ghana. A major cause of the recurrent droughts and famines that devastate Africa is the loss of more than three million hectares of forests per year, accompanied by massive erosion of soil and water resources. The problem is particularly severe in West Africa where the rate of deforestation is seven times the world average. This dangerous trend results in part form unwise and short-sighted agricultural practices. Poor land management, over cropping, over harvesting of trees and overgrazing by domestic animals leads to soil erosion, removal of tree cover, flooding, loss of water resources and desertification.

This was the problem which the IIRR (Jimmy Yen's organization) and the Ghana Rural Reconstruction Movement (GhRRM) is addressing in an attempt to develop and share appropriate agroforestry strategies which can be widely adapted by African villages to meet their legitimate needs for food, fodder, firewood and shelter while conserving and restoring the natural resource base.

In GhRRM's area of operations in the Mampong Valley in the Adwapim District in Eastern Ghana, the following strategies are being introduced to encourage villagers to play an active role in conservation and reforestation.

(1) introduction of at least ten tree species to meet a variety of village needs: firewood, timber for housing, green manure to fertilize the soil. A nursery with 5,000 seedlings has been established at the GhRRM center on the Yensi river, to provide seedlings to villagers participating in the program; (2) RDFs are training villagers in a variety of agroforestry techniques like alley cropping (planting of different crops between rows of multi-purpose trees); (3) establishing demonstration woodlots and training village forestry workers to set up woodlots in their own communities, which will provide firewood without depleting the forest; (4) development of efficient, culturally accepted stoves to conserve fuel; (5) training in goat and sheep management to prevent overgrazing and to cultivate trees as sources of fodder.

The program also addresses the problems of declining food production, a severe problem throughout Africa, which is evidenced in Ghana by a rate of decline of 20 percent per year. IIRR is a world leader in regenerative agriculture, a system of technologies that maximizes food production, while sustaining and renewing the environment. Instead of costly and potentially harmful chemical fertilizers, pesticides and herbicides, regenerative agriculture relies on inexpensive and renewable resources like plant and animal wastes.

Suknomajri, India[11]

One of the most common sights in the foothills of the Himalayas is the obvious soil erosion, with canyon-like gullies and huge gorges cutting down through grazing lands and farming communities. Early 19th Century British accounts of these hills spoke of luxurious forests of oak, silver fir, deodar, and other species. In the 1830s, mining contractors began cutting trees to clear access to iron and copper deposits in the northern hills. More deforestation followed British efforts to secure military control of the region. Timber was also felled to build the railways that would carry tea and other raw materials to ships at port. Meanwhile nomadic herding people also began to settle in the valleys. They grazed their animals over the surrounding hills and allowed them to eat whatever vegetation remained. By the time India gained independence in 1947, the ground cover that once protected the rich topsoil of the Himalayan foothills had almost totally vanished.

While there are many examples of failure in trying to get farmers not to overgraze the hills, thus increasing the tendency for huge floods to wash down into the valleys, in one community, a solution was found. Sukhomajri, a small village in the state of Haryana, rests at the headwater of a major ravine, and is largely made up of impoverished herders. For years, the villagers had grazed their livestock across the hills, cutting down trees for fuel, denuding the hills of vegetation, and thus exposing soils to torrential monsoon rains. Inspite of threats and even arrests from government officials, farmers would stop for a while, but then after a time the old patterns of grazing would start up again. An RDF in the area began discussing with the farmers, asking questions, listening, interacting with both villagers, government officials, and environmentalists. In the process it was discovered that the real problem did not lie in the forest but in village poverty. Getting villagers to stop grazing animals and allow the hills to recover required giving the villagers some real economic alternatives, not just threats of jail. The alternative lay in the water trapped in the small dams in the area built to control the flooding. The RDF convinced the local agriculture office to help provide some irrigation piping to be built to get water to the farmers' fields. This would allow farmers to grow extra crops during the dry season. Villages, in exchange, would have to agree to voluntarily stop grazing their animals across the hills. This RDF began to understand that the old approach of the Forestry Department looked at conservation as a technical problem you could solve in isolation from poverty and human needs. From this standpoint you just tried to make the farmers stop cutting trees, plant new ones, and then wait twenty or thirty years before they could use the forest again. But this meant a lot of waiting, which poor people cannot afford to do. The RDF sought to treat ecological and economic needs together, not separately. You obviously needed reforestation, so you plant fast-growing trees and grasses. You also need a plan by which the local people could use the new vegetation immediately. The RDF taught the villagers to cut the top branches of the trees after two or three years, getting some of the fuel they needed while not destroying the trees. Also the RDF emphasized that by cutting the grasses above the root they would be able to get fodder for their cattle without destroying the soil-protecting grasses. Gradually over time the hills have regained a substantial new cover of grasses, shrubs, and trees. Not a single grazing animal could be seen feeding on the new plants. Cattle were now kept in enclosed areas and the grass was brought to them. Indeed, upon visiting this village in 1991, land around the village evidenced the greenness of the young wheat and vegetables made possible by irrigation. It must be understood by RDFs that poor people will participate in environmental preservation only if it also gives them a better livelihood. Finding this important link between poverty, the environment, and the villager's way of life takes time and careful learning both by the RDF and the villagers.

Activities During the Third Stage
   At this stage, RDFs are encouraged to help villagers to establish a Village Environmental Protection Committee committed to planning and organizing activities and projects that will protect farm land from erosion and enhance and protect the local environment, especially local forests, lakes and streams and wildlife. Also in this stage, RDFs help village committees to link with district and provincial level organizations and donors willing to develop area-wide ecology-protecting strategies.
   Environmental management for sustainability is an intensely political process, involving strategies and approaches best implemented during the third

phase of rural development, the stage of empowerment and mass movement organizations. Of all the dimensions of rural development, the protection and enhancement of the local environment is the most controversial and the one most fraught with conflict and even violence. Also there are many organizational constraints to an effective management of the processes related to environmental sustainability: the fragmented nature of policy making in key institutions, a failure to promote organizational learning; the lack of policy integration in economic management; the massive complexity of environmental problems; the difficulty in balancing "top-down" and "bottom-up" initiatives in environmental management and planning; and the great turbulence of the world as industrialism becomes a global condition.

Some RDFs will have to deal with externally caused pollution. One village in India had a nearby industry manufacturing rayon polyfibres and dumping their effluent in the river. The villagers began to suffer when most were unwilling to take their drinking water from the river. A few months later they discovered tons of dead fish in the water. They took the fish to a nearby research laboratory and discovered the cause of death to be oxygen insufficiency in the water. Although the local politicians were unwilling to take a stand since they received considerable contributions from the company's owner, the RDF mobilized the people of several villages along the river and forced the company to change its ways. This type of village mobilization is clearly a stage three type of RDF work, but still must be encouraged when the villagers are suffering from such types of pollution.

An RDF must see the processes of environmental protection as a key aspect of rural development, but one that requires longer time commitments and greater willingness to build linkage systems at district and provincial levels, along with policy makers and environmentalist groups at the national and even international levels.

Section Five
Case Studies in Environmental Protection at the Local Level

This book has sought to identify some ten tragedies related to the problems of world poverty and five policy areas that must be developed if there is to be sustainable and equitable development throughout the world in the next half century. Let us consider what an RDF might seek to do in a given village community in the area of environmental protection and long-term sustainability of our world's natural resources.

In recent years a program called Innovations in Development for Environmental Action (IDEA) has been implemented in a number of LDCs to enhance local management capability for addressing serious environmental problems. In each of these projects, there was an interesting set of formal and informal linkages established between national agencies concerned with environmental protection and local community organizations seeking to preserve their own community's environment. These case studies provide an illustration of the non-hierarchical, action-centered networking as a complement to traditional bureaucratic structures found in the common central administrative systems of the LDCs. These case studies also validate the usefulness of the action research methodology for local problem solving outlined in Chapter Nine. Equally important are the lessons to be learned for an RDF who is seeking to link local environmental problems with various agencies and organizations seeking to confront such problems from a national and international perspective.

The first step in most of these case studies involves the identification and linkage of various communities, organizations, agencies, NGOs and other donor groups working within the country where the RDF is located. One important aspect of the environment is the availability of water both for drinking and for agriculture. Many communities have learned to build small dams that allowed the formation of ponds, which in turn maintain the water table. Pump wells are usable as a consequence long into the dry season. Many specialists might object to encouraging villagers to create ponds that then spawn mosquitoes, bilharsis and other water-borne diseases. One RDF in Kenya has suggested that malaria can be prevented by adding a thin film of used motor oil to ponds, killing the anopheles larvae while leaving the water clear below the surface. Community problem-solving groups often encourage the construction of catchment ponds for irrigation and washing purposes. Such community groups must often be helped by an RDF to understand the ways in which rain water can be conserved. Using volunteers from the United States and an appropriate well digging technology, CHOICE, a non-profit organization, has helped a number of villages in South America and Asia to dig wells and to maintain them.

Ethnoecology is a field that all RDFs should have familiarity. Efforts should be made to gain extensive knowledge of local natural resources: agriculture, animal husbandry, ethobotany, and pharmacology. Such knowledge may be used to foster successful indigenous development projects in the place of externally-generated failures which were based on animal and plant programs not adapted to the local ecosystem. Examples of these kinds of local forest preservation activities include the Gavioes of Central Brazil who profitably collect and market Brazil nuts, and the Yanomamo of Venequela who have established beehives for the purpose of marketing honey. These examples of native systems of resource harvesting demonstrate that local groups can pursue sustainable development within environmentally sound frameworks.[12]

Reforestation

In many areas of the world tropical forests are often the single most important resource available to rural communities, providing them with food, shelter, and spiritual sustenance. Most RDFs working with local communities have found the following advantages to indigenous systems of forest management: (1) better policing and husbanding of forest resources; (2) more equitable distribution of benefits; (3) a greater commitment to sustainability because communities are closely knit and deeply rooted to the area; and (4) the display of remarkable resilience in the face of fluctuating markets and social changes. The community-based approach generally costs less and is more effective than government management of forest lands.

Community-based forestry programs require informed participation by local user groups to identify problems, propose workable solutions, and form alliances with outside interests to sustainably manage forest resources. Central to success has been the ability to merge local knowledge with outside (NGO) technical know-how and political influence. Let us now review several case studies that provide suggested action steps for RDFs.

In the Amazon forest of Brazil and Central America, the native peoples for many centuries lived in the forest and depended on the forest for survival. The forests provided them with building material, food, medicine and culture. As vast mineral deposits were found in the interior of the Amazon, roads were built to assist in the extraction of the raw materials . Cattle interest began to move into these areas, cutting down vast areas of forest for cattle grazing. Furthermore, the roads inland provided access for the poor in the cities to migrate in the hopes of finding a better life. People began to settle along the roads and clear forested areas for agriculture. Unfamiliar with the ecosystem of the areas, outsiders used inappropriate forms of slash and burn farming that robbed the soils of their nutrients. Within a few years huge areas of former forest were soon useless ground.

Beginning in the 1960s, the native population of the Amazon basin began to fight back against the policies of development that were invading their traditional lands. These Indian Tribals had no concept of ownership of resources and took only what they needed to provide them with subsistence. The large-scale agribusiness concerns which had invaded the Amazon basin now claimed to "own" the land and thus felt justified in pushing the local communities out of these areas. Out of this situation, with the help of some RDFs, several local people began to organize themselves against these outside intrusions. One such man was Chico Mendes, an uneducated rubber tapper, who had seen the work of the large rubber barons in exploiting the local Indian communities. Mendes organized a tappers' union to the protect the remaining virgin forest areas. His group of supporters began to argue that these forests should be protected from wanton cutting. They suggested that selectively cutting of trees and harvesting of forest products, rubber, nuts, flowers and medicines would provide both income for the local people and foreign exchange to the country of Brazil, while at the same time protecting the Amazon forest for future generations.

The Brazilian government resisted in the beginning and arrested those who attempted to stop economic development projects. Land owners and ranchers responded with their own way of hiring mercenary armies to "protect" their land and forcibly to remove anyone who stood in the way. By 1985 over 50 million acres were in dispute and more than 1.5 million people were involved in land disputes. By the mid 1980s people like Mendes found some allies in the international community, and the Brazilian government found itself forced to re-evaluate their policies regarding the Amazon forest. However, in December 1988, Chico Mendes was found dead. He was shot as he walked out of his house, in front of his wife and children. As of this point, no one has been prosecuted, even though two of the areas largest landowners had placed a "bounty" on his head. The international community was shocked by his death and in 1989, when the Brazilian government went to the World Bank to restructure its debts, they faced strong pressure to concede to environmental demands placed on renegotiation. The work of empowering local people is by its nature political and thus susceptible to conflict and violence. All RDFs, especially those from local areas who are seeking to protect their environments from mindless exploitation and destruction may take courage from people like Chico Mendes. While he is gone, the work that he started will have favorable consequences not only in Brazil, but throughout the world, and not only now, but far into the future.[13]

Shifting Cultivation of Palm Forests in Brazil

One particular forest area under great attack by outside commercial interest in Brazil are the great forests in the state of Maranhao in northeast Brazil. Here are found the babassu palms that constitute both a renewable agricultural input and an important household and economic supplement to local farmers. Palm stands are harvested by slash-and-burn techniques in four-year rotations that allow for nutrient recycling and weed control. Babassu palm forests provide local peoples with an array of household and market goods, including thatch, fiber for an array of basketry items, construction materials, fish traps, bird cages, planting medium, feed for cattle, horses and other stock, palm wine, oil or kernels for a nutritious beverage, and sale to local small-scale industries for the production of oil, soap and animal feed. The fruit husk is used to make charcoal, which is the principal cooking fuel, makes a substantial contribution to real income, and protects forests from excessive fuelwood harvesting. These native technologies have provided subsistence for centuries.

Babassu kernels are particularly important as a source of cash income in the period between crop harvests. More importantly, the peak of babassu harvesting does not compete with other critical subsistence events in the agriculture calendar such as weeding and harvesting, so natives are not tempted away from subsistence activities by those with an exclusive market orientation. In local belief systems, babassu palms represent an important "subsidy from nature", a gift from the gods which must be protected to be enjoyed and used by future generations.[14]

Recently scientists have documented the importance of the slash-and-burn process in horticulture in tropical ecosystems, disputing claims by Western agronomists that the archaic practice would never be capable of sustained development. Slash-and-burn techniques produce renewed garden soils with higher phosphorus levels used in plants as a nutrient. The gardens are also slightly less acidic allowing for greater plant viability. The deposition of ashes after burning may be responsible for this change. Newly "burned" soils have the highest ratings of organic matter, probably accelerating the nutrient cycling process. Nitrogen levels in the soils were rated high so a system of natural fertilization was occurring. Such case studies are adding to a growing body of literature reaffirming both economic and ecological soundness of native systems of horticulture. RDFs must see these indigenous modes of production as providing a subsistence living and often a surplus for local trade. Most of the time when such slash-and-burn systems have been found to be counter-productive, it was either because too many people were using the same piece of land or the time allowed for the land to remain fallow was too short a period of time or the people using the system were marginal farmers forced on to lands unfit for slash-and-burn agriculture.

The Resin Tappers of Honduras

Over half of the 6,000 farmer/resin tappers in Honduras have been organized with the help of several RDFs into 46 local cooperative since 1974. The pine trees provide a supplemental income source for farmers as tapping the trees for sap helps them through to their agriculture harvest. Modern resin-tapping methods can sustain the productive life of trees for up to forty years. Pine resin is sold for export as turpentine, or as resin for soaps, dyes, and adhesives. In addition, wood and other forest products are harvested.

By offering small farmers a long-term environmentally sound cash crop, resin tapping has led to increased farmer receptivity to more sustainable farming methods, and has protected the forest against the appeal of clear cutting which provides short term cash but precipitates rapid environmental degradation. Two indigenous goals have been supported by cooperative local resin tapping. First, preservation of the forests has insured continued species biodiversity, protected the watershed, and safeguarded this renewable resource. Second, tapping rather than cutting trees allows for sustained income generation.

Four lessons have been learned in the success of these cooperatives encouraged by local RDFs which are relevant to a variety of community-based environmental activities world-wide and can be applied to better understand the processes of environmental degradation and community response: (1) Members shared a common vision based upon local cultural traditions and their participation bound them together; (2) Building in multiple-use activities strengthens the conservation ethos and allows the cooperative to weather erratic price swings in one commodity; (3) Members organized a simple group credit scheme and learned its effective use early on to help buy modern tapping equipment; and (4) Strong participation within the cooperatives led to the diffusion of leadership skills [15]

Community Forestry in the Sierra Juarez Mountains of Oaxaca (South Mexico).

The forests of the Sierra Juarez are some of the richest in the world in terms of biodiversity. A local forestry enterprise has been cooperatively managing oak and pine harvests for the past ten years in response to a previous pattern of external exploitation wherein multinational timber companies depleted the forest to supply pulp and paper mills. Several groups of local harvesters were organized by a local RDF to boycott the paper factory and pulp mills with the objective of receiving more economic benefits as mill workers. Natural resource sustainability was not the main motive, initially.

With their success in organizing to obtain concessions from the multinational corporations, local leaders were confident they could do a better job of harvesting and milling the forest products as well. The local groups began to organize cooperative activities including an ecodevelopment strategy that halted indiscriminate cutting of precious tropical hardwoods, along with the setting-aside of permanent extractive reserves to be harvested in 25-year cycles, and the recruitment and establishment of technical teams which began intensive training in all aspects of forest management including forest inventories, logging operations, and small forestry enterprises.

With time and experience, the community cooperatives discovered that selling carefully selected timber provided capitalization opportunities that facilitated the purchase of new equipment, the establishment of furniture shops, and the channeling of profits toward socially beneficial goals such as schools, health clinics, roads, and waterworks. Most strikingly, the majority of these investments were made out of current income, with the few loans needed being quickly repaid.

An unanticipated consequence of these sustained development programs was the resurgence of a "forest culture," the concern with sustainability for both economic and ecological reasons. These productive enterprises have helped to stem the tide of migration to the United States in search of employment. As one leader described their future options, "We must decide whether we will be coffee farmers, timber producers, forest stewards . . . or maids and construction workers in Santa Monica."[16]

The Greenbelt Movement in Kenya

Thousands of Kenya women are actively involved in a significant environmental protection project started by Kenyan activist, Wangari Maathai. The Greenbelt Movement started slowly and only expanded when it was sure that the foundation was solid. The idea for the Greenbelt Movement was first conceived in 1974 but the early founders took another three years to field test this program before it was finally adopted by the National Council of Women in 1977. This movement is mainly the work of one woman who saw a need and decided to devote her life to the protection of Kenya's tremendous natural resources.

With the support of the National Council of Women, implementation was well-planned but still gradual, starting first with women's groups, then expanding out to schools and youth groups, then to the community at large. The movement's organizers knew that people needed to understand first why care for the environment was so important. Once people understood this, then they could become committed to caring for and nurturing the trees. Through this effort, along with community education and encouragement to conserve soil and water, a very successful strategy was developed. Maathai discusses the beginnings: "We approached the Department of Forestry in the Ministry of Environment and Natural Resources, which had a national network of tree nurseries. The head of the Department laughed when we told him that we intended to plant a million trees, and without hesitation promised us all the seedlings we needed. Less than a year later he had to go back on his decision when he found that we had distributed more seedlings than he could afford to give away."[17]

These women did not let a little thing like no seedlings stop them. They were then able to organize, build, and develop their own nurseries. Over the next 15 year period, over one thousand nurseries were established. About 80,000 women have been involved in these nurseries. Later, the movement began to work with whole communities to plant belts of trees (in lots of at least 1,000 trees), providing seedlings, tools, and a small salary for a caretaker to supervise community maintenance of the trees.

The Greenbelt Movement has spread across Kenya, involving thousands of people, mostly women. Well over a million trees have been planted, hundreds of community education programs on environmental protection have been organized, and several thousand women now earn a monthly income from seedling production and distribution. Village responsibility has been key in this movement that has emphasized the protection of forests and other local environments. A fundamental approach to reforestation has to do with locating the responsibility, benefits and work of tree planing all in one place: the village. Thus the Greenbelt approach in Kenya relies on local groups planting "greenbelts" of trees on school compounds and around community centers.

To begin a belt, a local Greenbelt committee is formed to direct the digging of holes and preparation of the land. The community then assumes responsibility for nurturing the trees. Many times the actual care is done by a group of children who are assisted by a Greenbelt ranger. These rangers are for the most part handicapped community residents who receive a small stipend for their work. They are key to the success of the green belts. It is easy for the RDF or a school headmaster to be enthusiastic for a week or two. It is another thing to maintain the interest of enough people sufficiently long to allow trees to reach the self-reliance stage. The presence of a Greenbelt ranger, whose work has to be reported on monthly and whose main role is to encourage children to participate, becomes a focus point for the whole movement. Over a ten year period, some 500 green belts were established in the rural areas of Kenya. It is interesting to note that today the Greenbelt Movement provides no seeds to the women for their seedlings. Instead, it teaches them how to find their own seeds in the surrounding area. This is done for two reasons: so that the women learn that the seeds are locally available, free, from nature, and so that the women learn not to become dependent upon the Greenbelt Movement.

    The Greenbelt Movement has become Africa's most significant environmental organization and has been a model for similar programs in about 12 other African states. Here is a perfect example of One Can Make A Difference, for it demonstrates the power and vision of one woman who engaged in what we are calling the third phase of rural development -- the empowerment of people to accomplish their own goals. This story would not be complete without some mention of the trials and difficulties that Maathai has had to suffer because of her efforts. The Kenya government was not always pleased with Maathai and her programs. Maathai, the first women in Kenya to receive her PhD (in anatomy) has often angered and frustrated the Kenyan government with her complaints, questions and challenges for reform. She was early on labeled as a subversive and was forced to give up her office in a government-owned office building. She is now forced to work out of her home. Maathai feels the government was threatened because "this was an organization of a group that officials tended to believe were powerless: poor, rural women -- ordinary people."

    The women involved in establishing this movement were very much aware that the long term success of any program would be dependent on some type of political support. For a project to be widespread, it must have both public and political levels of support to move rapidly at the local level. Thus a key event happened when Kenyan President Moi publicly agreed to plant trees in a public ceremony and encouraged his fellow Kenyans to do the same. This gave the Movement credibility and larger numbers of people became more readily involved. Also, the Movement's commitment to non-violence and its focus on helping the poorest of the poor gave it widespread legitimacy. The Ministry of the Environment and Natural Resources began to provide its expertise. Also the Department of Forestry also provided technical know-how and training. This was an important structural linkage because the Department of Forestry had field officers and staff throughout the country who were available for on-site advice and counseling. The reason for this successful co-operation was that the Greenbelt Movement consistently saw itself as working in collaboration, not in competition, with the existing government structures.

Chipko Movement in India[18]

The forest has always played an important role in Indian civilization and Aranyani, the goddess of the forest, has been worshipped as the giver of life and fertility. Trees are viewed as sacred entities and have spiritual meaning attached to them. When areas of forest were cleared for cultivation, it was done in an almost religious manner. Prayers would be said for the trees that were felled and certain trees were left standing. In the late 1960s, various communities began to complain to the government that areas that had never flooded before were being washed away with every monsoon rain and wells were drying up as the rate of recharge had been decreased. The peasants drew a correlation between the new environment problems and commercial logging. They appealed to the government to stop the widespread deforestation and to support the traditional ways of peasant forest production based on labor cooperatives and small scale industry. These pleas fell upon deaf ears in the Forest Department. In the early 1970s huge stands of ash trees were set aside for a foreign corporation to harvest and none were allocated to the local people who had depended on them for their livelihood in the past. A group of local villagers banded together to fight this move and out of their struggle, emerge a movement called "Chipko" or "Embrace the Tree."

The Chipko Movement is a Gandhian movement that uses *satyagraha* (nonviolent resistance) to preserve the Himalaya's critical mountain-forest ecosystem. It began in Garhwal in the 1970s when an Indian women activist, Vandana Shiva, began to organize women to protect with their own bodies the trees that contractors were trying to remove.[19] Shiva argued that women know instinctively that the environment needed to be protected. There was a spiritual dimension to this organization that saw the protection of the environment as a sacred calling. The holistic role women can play in their desire to protect the environment is reflected in the song of the Chipko movement: "The oak trees we must save and worship them, because their roots store water, their leaves have milk and fodder, the breeze blows cool over the beautiful rhododendron flower." Shiva's success was based on her ability to motivate women to see the role they could play in protecting the environment and in the way she encouraged local women to take responsibility for their own local areas.

In the mid-1980s, this movement helped support a group of villagers in Doon Valley in the Haryana and Uttar Pradesh provinces of northern India. The forests of the Nahi-Kala region of Doon Valley have been a rich pocket of genetic wealth, preserved and used skillfully by the local people for centuries. A group of 31 villages had traditionally managed these forests, conserving them for sustainable use. A large variety of wild fruit trees provide fodder for the farm animals, vital for sustainable agriculture. Other species provided timber, and fiber trees provided raw material for basket weaving.

Lime quarrying was first introduced into the area in 1962 when partition (in 1947, when India and Pakistan became two nations) brought refugee miners from the area that is now Pakistan. In the 1970s, the adverse ecological impacts of large-scale quarrying in the sensitive catchments of Doon Valley stimulated adverse public opinion about continued quarrying activities. The Department of Environment conducted an ecosystem study and concluded that the quarrying was destroying the rich forest cover and topsoil over large areas in the region. The areas in the hill slopes, not directly under the quarry lease, have also been covered by the rejects and overburdens from the quarries -- thus damaging a land area several times higher than the actual quarry lease areas. The combined result has been the destruction of the hydrological capacity of the hill slopes in reducing instant surface runoff and absorbing more water in the topsoil for recharging the parched aquifers in the Mussoorie Hills. More directly, the physical removal of the limestone deposit adds to the scarcity of water. The cracked and fissured limestone belt, as it is in the Doon Valley, has become a major aquifer or water-holding deposit over geological periods. Limestone in the fissures gets dissolved by moving rainwater, creating large cavities. Throughout the world, as a result, limestone belts play the role of underground aquifers, which hold and conserve water for slow release as springs and streams.

The vast quarrying processes had played a key role in destroying these natural aquifers, with the result that spring sources of all villages surveyed in the local catchments registered an average decrease of about 50 percent in their lean-period discharges over the last two decades. Agriculture is the oldest economic activity of the Doon Valley; the villagers have always tapped the area's abundant streams to irrigate their fields. This traditional agriculture provided the economic basis for a decent physical quality of life in the valley. The stability of the economic base was, in turn, linked with the stability of the water resources. The destabilization of the resource base has, in turn, destabilized food production. The irrigation channels in most of the villages that lie below the quarries have been destroyed by the flow of silt and other debris from mines or from mining roads. The village of Shitarli, in the Tons catchment, was completely self-sufficient in food grain and had surplus food and milk production before quarrying destroyed its food and fodder base.

Nearly the entire area below the limestone belt has been lost as a grazing resource, and large areas, covered by debris from the mines, have practically no vegetation. The few pockets of shrubs and forest that remain cannot be used for cattle grazing because of the perpetual danger of boulders rolling down the slopes from quarry blasting. An important economic activity based on animal husbandry was being destroy; the decline in the cattle population in areas affected by mining was as much as 40 percent. The decline in livestock population affected the production of milk for the villagers and the market, the production of energy for farm operations and the production of animal dung that provided soil fertility for sustainable agriculture -- the last function being the most important one in hill agriculture. As a result, the food production system in the area was on the verge of collapse.

The local government system seemed quite impervious to the calls for change by the villagers. Finally the people of Nahi-Kala working with several local RDFs in conjunction with some local activists of the Chipko Movement, organized a process of non-violent resistance. The villagers and the Chipko activists began their nonviolent resistance on 16 September 1986, bringing a complete halt to the functioning of the quarry and the movement of limestone. The struggle was not easy. For six cold months, the volunteers held day and night vigilance, making certain that their natural wealth was no longer turned into profits. Local courts had served the peaceful satyagrahis (nonviolent protesters) with notices of arrest. On numerous occasions, the main quarry operator and some of his men attempted to remove the protesters with little success, but within days they would return. The issue is still not resolved, but this case study demonstrates the way in which local villagers, working with outsider supporters, can be empowered to protect their own local interests. This is the very essence of local community empowerment, especially in the third stage of rural development.

The Appiko Movement in Southern India

Another example of this process of empowerment during the third stage of rural development is observed in the Appiko Movement in southern India. In 1950, Uttara Kannada district's forest covered more than 81 percent of its geographical area. The government, declaring this forest district a "backward" area, then initiated the process of "development." Three major industries -- a pulp and paper mill, a plywood factory and a chain of hydro-electric dams constructed to harness the rivers -- sprouted in the area. The industries have overexploited the forest resource, and the dams have submerged huge forest and agriculture areas. The forest had shrunk to nearly 25 percent of the district's area by 1980. The conversion of the natural mixed forests into teak and eucalyptus plantations dried up the water sources, directly affecting forest dwellers. As one RDF put it: " . . .in a nutshell, the three major p's -- paper, plywood and power -- which were intended for the development of the people, have resulted in a fourth p: poverty".

Such deforestation in the Western Ghats has caused severe problems in all southern India. The recurring drought in the provinces of Karnataka, Maharashtra, Kerala and Tamil Nadu clearly indicates watershed degradation. The Appiko Movement, a grassroots group of people seeking to challenge these developments has created community groups throughout southern India. The movement's objectives can be classified into three major areas: First, the Appiko Movement is struggling to save the remaining tropical forests in the Western Ghats. Second, it is making a modest attempt to restore the greenery to denuded areas. Third, it is striving to propagate the idea of rational utilization in order to reduce the pressure on forest resources. To save, to grow and to use rationally -- popularly know in Kannada as Ubsu ("save"), Belesu ("grow") and Balasu ("rational use") -- is the movement's popular slogan.

The Appiko Movement uses various techniques to raise awareness: foot marches in the interior forest, slide shows, folk dances, street plays and so on. These kinds of activities have stimulated the local governments in a number of areas to ban the felling of green trees in some forest areas. Appiko activists have successfully motivated villagers to grow saplings. Individual families as well as village youth clubs have taken an active interest in establishing decentralized nurseries. An all-time record of 1.2 million saplings were grown by people in the Sirsi area in 1984-85. No doubt this was possible due to the cooperation of the forest department. The villagers have initiated a process of regeneration in barren common land. The Youth Club has taken the responsibility for the project and the whole village has united to protect this land from grazing, lopping and fire. The experience shows that in those areas where soil is present, natural regeneration is the most efficient and least expensive method of bringing barren areas under tree cover. In the areas in which topsoil is washed off, tree planting -- especially of indigenous, fast-growing species -- is done. The thrust of the Appiko Movement in carrying out its work reveals the constructive use of local people. Through a process of local empowerment, depleted natural resources can be rebuilt. The movement's aim is to establish a harmonious relationship between local people and nature, to redefine the term development so that ecological movements today form a basis for a sustainable, permanent economy in the future.

Conclusions

An important component of virtually all definitions of sustainable development has to do with equity. Two types are embodied in the World Commission's definition -- equity for human generations yet to come, whose interests are not represented by standard economic analyses or by market forces that discount the future, and equity for people living now who do not have equal access to natural resources or to social and economic "goods." There is, in fact, some conflict between these two types of equity. Some authors point out that environmental issues in less developed countries cannot be resolved without alleviating poverty and calling for redistribution of wealth or incomes both within countries and between rich and poor countries. Others stress inter-generational equity -- the "sharing of well-being between present people and future people" -- and focusing on the need for reducing current consumption to provide for investments that build up resources such as knowledge or technology for the future. This conflict -- between increased consumption now for poor people and increased investment for future generations -- can also be stated in environmental terms. It is a conflict between increased burning of fossil fuel (or conversion of forests to agricultural uses as poor countries develop) and efforts on behalf of future generations to curb those actions to slow greenhouse warming, destruction of tropical forests, the devastation of our stock of biodiversity and the pollution of our present waterways.

The environment presently performs a number of invaluable functions both for our survival and our pleasure. The environment provides resources, absorbs and neutralizes our wastes, protects us from the burning sun, stabilizes our climate over time and provides us with the beauties of animal and plant life for our enjoyment. Sustainability means "development that meets the needs of the present without compromising the ability of future generations to meet their own needs." Rural Development Facilitators (RDFs) must learn to play a positive and aggressive role in helping communities to protect their own environment.

---

[1] World Commission on Environment and Development, *Our Common Future* (New York: Oxford University Press, 1987), pp. 4 and 8.

[2] David W. Pearce, Edward B. Barbier, and Anil Markandya, *Sustainable Development and Cost-Benefit Analysis* (London: London Environmental Economics Center, 1988), p. 6

[3] Jim Robert Repetto, *World Enough and Time* (New Haven, Connecticut: Yale University Press, 1986).

[4] James MacNeill, "Strategies for Sustainable Economic Development," *Scientific America*, 261 (3), (1989).

[5] United Nations Development Program, *Human Development Report 1991* (New York: Oxford University Press, 1991), pp. 1-2.

[6] George Heaton, Robert Repetto, and Rodney Sobin, *Transforming Technology: an Agenda for Environmentally Sustainable Growth in the 21st Century* (Washington DC: World Resources Institute, 1991).

[7] World Conservation Union, UN Environment Program, and World Wide Fund for Nature, *Caring for the Earth,* (Switzerland, 1991), p. 10.

[8] UN Statistical Office, *Energy Statistics Yearbook, 1989* (New York: UN Publications, 1989), pp. 90-111.

[9] The World Bank, *Sub-Saharan Africa: From Crisis to Sustainable Growth*, (Washington DC: The World Bank, 1989), p. 129.

[10] Paulos Freire, *Education for Critical Consciousness*, (New York: The Seabury Press, 1973) and Robert Chambers "Shortcut Methods of Gathering Social Information for Rural Development Projects. In *Putting People First*. Michael M. Cernea, ed. (Oxford: Oxford University Press, 1985), pp. 399-415.

[11] David Seckler and Deep Joshi, "Sukhomajri: A Rural Development Program in India," (New Delhi: Prepared for the Ford Foundation, 1981) and David Seckler, "Institutionalism and Agricultural Development in India," *Journal of Economic Issues*, 22, (4), (1986).

[12] Darrel A. Posey, *et al.*, :"Ethnoecology as Applied Anthropology in Amazonian Development", *Human Organization*, 43 (2), (1984), pp. 95-107.

[13] S. Hecht and A. Cockburn, *The Fate of the Forest: Developers, Destroyers and Defenders of the Amazon*, (London: Verso, 1989).

[14] S.B. Hecht, et al., "The Subsidy from Nature: Shifting Cultivation, Successional Palm Forests, and Rural Development", *Human Organization*, 47 (1), (1988), pp. 25-35.

[15] Denise L. Stanley, "Communal Forest Management: The Honduran Resin Tappers", *Development and Change*, 22 (1991), pp. 757-79.

[16] David B. Bray, "The Struggle for the Forest: Conservation and Development in the Sierra Juarez", *Grassroots Development*, 15 (3) (1991), pp. 13-25

[17] Wangari Maathai, "Kenya's Green Belt Movement" *UNESCO Courier* (March, 1992), p. 23.

[18] S.S. Kunwar (ed.) *Hugging the Himalaya: The Chipko Experience*, (Gopeshwar, 1982); R. Guha, *The Unquiet Woods: Ecological Change and Peasant Resistance in the Himalaya* (New Delhi: Oxford University Press, 1989; and United Nations, *Tree Growing By Rural People* (Food and Agriculture Organization, Forestry Paper # 64, 1985).

[19] Vandana Shiva, *Staying Alive*, (New York: Zed Books, 1989)

Chapter 15

Fifth Dimension of Rural Development
The Preservation and Enhancement
of Local Cultures
A Key to Long-Term Sustainable Development

During the post World War II era, there was an optimistic feeling among economists and in international agencies that the processes of development were essentially linear and nearly inevitable. Thus with appropriate allocation of investment capital and the use of Western technology all societies would eventually follow in the footsteps of the United States and Western Europe. Both Marxists and capitalist thinkers assumed that culture was immaterial in this process -- it could be ignored. However, by the early 1970s many scholars, at least admitting that the optimism of LDC development of the previous decades was clearly premature, sought some explanation for this slow growth. Thus Gunnar Myrdal blamed the slow process of development in India on the Hindu culture, suggesting that such societies would have to westernize their value system if meaningful change and development were to happen.[1] Frantz Fanon,[2] also lamented the ways in which traditional cultures were obstacles to the processes of modernization. Such scholars were quick to assume that modernization and economic progress would only happen when such societies gave up their "outdated" value systems and adopted western ways based upon secular value systems.

By the mid-1970s and early 1980s, many development agencies began to hire anthropologists, hoping to better understand the ways in which culture might impact on the processes of development. It became clear that development was in some profound way related to culture, that a more holistic view of society was needed if we were to understand the relationship between culture and development. A number of anthropologists began to argue that culture is a very complex concept, that changes in one area of society would have significant consequences in other areas, that every culture has some characteristics that could be an obstacle to modernization and development as defined in the West, but that other aspects of these traditional cultures were not necessarily incompatible with development and might even be facilitative. The incredible growth in Japan suggested that a local culture could play a very positive role in defining and even motivating people.

Section One
Local Culture Enhancement
The Very Essence of Village Development

The thrust of my own thinking goes even further. For me, a local culture has not only positive qualities for development, but may in fact be the very essence of development. A local culture, depending how it is defined, provides an individual with his/her sense of identity, it preserves and clarifies the notion of purpose, meaning and direction. From the first chapter in this book, I suggested that development is best defined as people development, as a process of consciousness raising, in which people reflect on what it is in their societies that needs to be preserved and what might need to be changed. When a family's child dies, when people are without potable water, when a woman cannot read the signs on buses going to market, people may seek changes. The issue is not should there be changes in these rural villages, but what kind and how much change. The mass media of television, movies and internet has brought and will continue to bring tremendous changes. My argument rests on the assumption, that unless villagers are given the opportunity to confront these kinds of changes in some reflective manner and are helped to develop strategies to preserve and enhance local cultures, such unique and diverse cultures will gradually disappear.

An RDF has a great opportunity to help local people to determine what in their culture is valuable, meaningful and worthy of being preserved and what might be changed or redefined to be more relevant and appropriate for their present situation. Unless there is a conscious effort to confront the onslaught of Western influences: rock music, drug use, violence, immorality and obsessive consumerism, to mention the most obvious messages being sent through western television and movies, much of what is beautiful and unique in these cultures will be lost.

Few development specialists of the 1970s would have predicted the rapid growth of Islamic fundamentalism in the Middle East of the 1980s and 1990s. For over thirty years, the US had supported the Shah of Iran in his efforts to modernize his people. Few Westerners were aware of the anti-Shah sentiment that existed because of his authoritarian and secularist orientation. His willingness to allow "modern" forms of entertainment, dress and culture to enter his society was praised in the West, but deeply offended the traditional value system of Iran. The Western world was shocked at the Khomeini revolution which in many ways reflected a mass rejection of Western cultural influences in their own society. Much of the violence and terrorism that characterizes LDCs can best be understood as a reaction against the negative value systems and anti-religion sentiments perceived to be emphasized in western culture.

In a very important book, written on the subject of cultural expression and its impact on development, in the forward we read how Western perceptions of tribal people are clearly ethnocentric and are often a disguise for their desire to control and exploit. The author notes that: "the invading Europeans have been arguing since the conquest that Indian cultures are backward and should be destroyed. The Indians were considered savages because of such customs such as cannibalism or human sacrifice put them beyond the pale. Those Indian societies that did not engage in such practices were considered savage because they were naked. If they went clothed, then they were held to be savage for being too egalitarian or un-Christian. These judgments were passed, with no sense of irony, by Europeans who practiced, for example slavery and judicial torture."[3] The film *Mission* graphically portrays the ways in which Europeans sought to christianize the natives in South America. It is clear to us now that the justifications used by the conquerors were rationalizations for their determination to seize the new lands and rule over their inhabitants. It is still common for many Americans to believe that the only way traditional peoples can survive in the modern world is to assimilate them into the dominant culture in which they find themselves. Traditional cultures are too often seen as obstacles to development

In many countries, especially in Latin America and South Asia, local tribal peoples are ignored, often pushed off their traditional lands in the name of progress and development. Many countries have bought into a model of development that favors a paradigm of progress based upon multinational corporations. ever expanding consumerism, and reckless exploitation of limited natural resources. As was pointed out in the last chapter, the building of huge dams, the establishment of international lumber projects, and the creation of vast agribusinesses consistently violates the rights of indigenous peoples.

This tragedy is even more pronounced in countries were Indians are in fact a majority as in much of Central and South America. Much of the economy of these countries is dominated by a "latino" elite often based specifically on the exploitation and misuse of the Indian populations. Among such elites, there is a reluctance to consider the possibilities of Indian cultural autonomy or even, on occasion, to admit the existence of their Indian populations at all. I wish to argue that there is scant possibility for genuine national development until there are both self and mutual respect among the groups that cohabit these countries. The important factor in any kind of development is the human factor. To be productive, men and women have to value themselves, which means being able to understand where they stand in society and in history. Cultural development goes hand in hand with economic development. From this perspective, a people must approach their culture as developmentalists. They will find resources for their development in their music, language, folktales, crafts, and dance. They will see these cultural forms as the basis for educational programs that teach self-worth, personal dignity and community pride. By inverting the symbols associated with shame, they create a kind of cultural capital that is as important and valuable as land, water, or seed.

In Africa and Asia, a similar pattern can be seen. Governments consistently seek to prevent tribal people from practicing swidden, or slash-and-burn, agriculture on the grounds that it impoverishes the soil. Again, study after study has shown that there is nothing inherently harmful to the soil in swidden agriculture. Indeed, it is often the most effective form of agriculture available to people who have few tools or other agricultural aids. Problems are created only when the elites force such tribals off their traditional lands into smaller more marginal areas and are thus forced to shorten the time the ground is allowed to remain fallow before replanting. Efforts along the coastal areas of Kenya to eliminate traditional farming practices have proven a failure as modern farming practices were found to be inappropriate for the climate and quality of soil available in the region. I am not arguing that traditional cultures always have the best answers for local problems, only that they often do. Outsiders tend to discount such systems without considering the fact that many such cultures have emerged over centuries of learning how to survive in a given situation and may be far more appropriate than ideas and programs developed in the West.

Modernization, war, and economic deterioration have hit traditional peoples harder than most and left them more vulnerable than ever. Massive geographical dislocations, national integration policies that emphasize cultural homogenization and assimilation into the dominant sector of society, and the penetration via mass media of the values and needs of an urban, Western-style consumer society, often overwhelm marginalized, politically weak, traditional peoples. All of society is made poorer by the demise of any one of its groups. Not only the moral stock of the society but also its cultural diversity is drastically reduced by such tragedies. Traditional ethnic groups offer vital practical knowledge in the areas of health, sustainable agriculture and forest management, and even social and political organization.

I have come to believe that development is best defined as a process of expanding one's mental constructs (levels of awareness of what is available and possible) and in expanding one's choices (ability to implement decisions based upon a process of reflective consideration of one choices). Different cultures provide a diversity of different systems of meanings/constructs, different ways of cooking, marrying, organizing, playing, relating to nature. Choice, for me, means that there are alternatives with which to compare and contrast one's own culture and one's own lifestyle with other cultures and lifestyles, and only with an awareness of the different cultural systems: their values, their music, their social systems, their traditional health care systems, and their philosophy of life, etc. -- will I be truly free to compare and choose. Such choice allows us to consider different ways of making our lives more meaningful, enriching and purposeful. Without such choices, people are not really free, for in the modern world of mass media, alien values and lifestyles are too often imposed upon them, with little or no options or alternatives considered.

Section Two
Contrasting Perspectives
on the Role of Culture in Development

In the world today, there are two very different ways of looking at culture. Some see Western culture as the epitome of progress, who would see the Cultural Values of Europe and the United States as superior, and thus will inevitably dominant the rest of the world. This perspective also questions the utility and appropriateness of religious value systems in the modern era. Secularism is the new religion and commitment to rationality, science and modern organizational forms are perceived to be right and thus morally right. Others are less certain of the Modernists approach to social values. Such people see great value in cultural diversity, in expanding the right of individual groups to protect and preserve their own cultural value systems.

In much of the literature, you tend to find two perspectives related to these issues: first, the western consumerists who argue that traditional cultures are an obstacle to progress and thus should be eliminated. This perspective argues that the sooner such people start wearing levis, buying western video tapes, and eating at MacDonalds -- the better for all concerned. Another perspective at the other end of the spectrum suggests that these traditional cultures need to be protected and preserved in their pristine state -- with no influence from the outside allowed. In my opinion, the first perspective is immoral, for it forces a mindless consumerism onto a defenseless community with no opportunity to preserve their own culture or to reject ideas and activities that often bring greater poverty, personal alienation, family disintegration and economic dependency. The second perspective is unrealistic, for it totally ignores the impracticality of keeping such societies in an incubator of forced isolation. For me development is about choices, about allowing people to determine their own futures, their life styles, their own economic and political systems -- all based upon time-tested cultural systems deemed meaningful and appropriate for their time and their situation.

What I am arguing for is the creation of a process of reflective dialogue, in which traditional people have raised their consciousness to the point where they can choose, they can see the advantages and disadvantages of adopting modern ways, they can see the strengths and weaknesses in their own culture and that through this process they become free to select what they want to preserve in their culture and what they want to change. The key in this process is the creation of systems of education and literacy, a consciousness raising process where people see their options, understand the consequences of these options and reflectively consider what they want to change and what they want to preserve. From my experience, the worst disasters and injustices committed in the name of development come about when people are excluded from the decisions that affect them or are excluded from consideration when such decisions are being made.

From the chart below you will see these two approaches in contrast:

Chart 15-1

Secularist/Western Perspective	Spiritual/Cultural Diversity Perspective
1. Traditional cultures are an obstacle to progress and ought therefore to be eliminated.	1. Traditional cultures are time tested systems of social cohesion and adaptability and need to be valued as such.
2. Western cultural values are superior to others and thus there is no need to study or understand or appreciate other cultures.	2. Both Western and Eastern forms of culture have a great contribution to make to humankind and both must be studied and understood.
3. The process of westernization is inevitable and therefore must be good, right, appropriate. Most forms of non-Western cultures will eventually disappear	3. While westernization may appear to be inevitable, one must not be surprised if non-Western forms continue and perhaps even surpass Western forms in some areas.
4. Secularism/Science offer humankind the best hope for a rational and predictable future.	4. While science and the secularist perspective will offer much to our societies, religious value systems will continue to offer important truths for our understanding of justice, equity and ethics.
5. Economic and political processes are most important in shaping the future of the world. All other factors will be less significant and thus can be ignored.	5. To the extent that we ignore or downplay the cultural, aesthetic and religious dimensions of life, our own lives will have less meaning and purpose, which is perhaps the greatest challenge of modern life.

The pluralism I am advocating thus entertains a wide variety of development strategies and deals openly with the population to be effected by those strategies. It also accepts their right to be different, if they so chose. This is particularly important when the populations are culturally or ethnically different from the majority of a given society. Yet I also wish to argue that while protecting cultural diversity and the rights of people to choose their own futures is largely a moral issue, I wish to emphasize that there is a practical reason for preserving and enhancing such cultural systems. Rooted in respect for the wisdom and ways of ethnic peoples and the poor in general, this approach seeks to retain their special cultural strengths and contributions while enabling them to achieve necessary changes in their social and economic condition. As I suggested earlier, a local culture is the very essence of community development, it is the source of the social energy, motivation and sense of purpose that is absolutely vital if a community is to confront the challenges of their existence. Only when there is a pride, a sense of self-esteem and dignity will village people began to take responsibility for their own futures.

A Concept of Social Energy

Albert O. Hirschman, based upon a detailed field study in the early 1980s, suggested that much development activity was being implemented at the grassroots level and that much of this activity was best understood in terms of a concept he called "social energy." I am defining "social energy" as a key source of motivation, commitment and enthusiasm in working together with the members of a given community to achieve common goals and to implement collective enterprises. Such examples of social energy and collective involvement are generally stimulated through common experiences of hardship, adversity and exploitation, through shared concepts of culture, history and religion, and through a gradual realization that their own community, their own people have special qualities, traits and characteristics that inspire pride, self-esteem and self-respect. Such common feelings and emotions mobilize and stimulate collective action, especially in times of disasters, external threats and danger. A sense of a common tradition, ethnic background and historical experience is generally defined within the parameters of a common culture, with reinforcing values, norms and sentiments. It is in only recent years that development specialists have come to appreciate the power of culture in helping to define a community, where it is and where it wants to go. While outside experts and outside resources may stimulate change and development in a given area, such changes when they are not integrated into the community's system of culture and traditions, will seldom if ever be sustained or incorporated into a long-term process of appropriate change and progress.

Without this social energy, most village communities will remain dependent, lethargic and passive, waiting for outsiders to come and solve their problems. This, in fact, may be the major reason that so many LDCs are plagued by massive poverty. Cultural stagnation is the consequence of centuries of outside manipulation and control, whether such control comes from the colonialists, the merchants, the priests, the landowners or the development specialists. Cultural stagnation leads to apathy, fatalism and inertia. Cultural enhancement leads to a sense of dignity and purpose; it motives and stimulates people to action, to taking responsibility, to finding solutions to their problems and most importantly, to seeing their lives as meaningful and important. We know that when people are forced to give up their culture, or when they give it up too rapidly, the consequences are normally social breakdown accompanied by personal disorientation and despair. The attachment of people to their culture corresponds, then, to a fundamental human need. My 30 years experience in rural development indicates that participatory broad-based development at the grassroots level is best built upon a foundation of strong cultural identity and pride and the resulting increases in group solidarity and energy.

Cultural expression (music, dance, popular theater, puppetry, artisan work, poster and mural art, and oral traditions) is a major means of generating and focusing on a process that I am calling enhanced social energy. This energy is a prime source of motivation that inspires people to confront problems, identify solutions, and participate in carrying them out. I am convinced that villagers need to know the history of their village, their people and culture, they must know the traditions and value orientations of their forefathers. When they have a keen sense of who they are, where they have come from, then they are ready to confront where they are now, to develop critical skills of assessment and analysis, and thus to understand the reality in which they presently live. With these skills and this kind of awareness and understanding, they are then much better able to change this reality, to transform it in ways that will be reflective of what is best in their culture, in ways that will reinforce, clarify, and direct the purposes and identities that are meaningful and satisfying to the community. The is the key role of social energy.

Section Three
Appropriate Activities of Cultural Enhancement in the Three Stages of Rural Development

Let us now review some of the kinds of activities related to cultural enhancement that are best implemented in each of the three stages of Rural Development. Each stage has a different focus and each requires different kinds of skills and interventions.

Activities During the First Stage

RDFs are encouraged to gather information on the history and culture of the community (dances, music, rituals, important concepts, ideals, values and traditions) in an attempt to truly understand and appreciate the local culture and the role it plays in the life of this community.

Activities During the Second Stage

The history and culture of the community should be written up and published in a simple form and such material should be distributed to the community as a whole. Such materials could then be used in the local schools, and as the basis for determining the best way to implement a given program or project in the village.

Activities During the Third Stage

RDFs should be encouraged to stimulate local efforts to establish local institutions that enhance the cultural life of the community in the fields of literature, music, art, dance and community values. In a broader context, district-wide associations committed to local culture enhancement can participate in provincial, even national activities supporting dance festivals, fiestas, handicraft exhibits, and other cultural affairs.

Section Four
Role of Cultural Enhancement in Village Development

Charles Kleymeyer[4] has done a marvelous job of identifying some six different ways in which the use of cultural enhancement can impact positively on the processes of development at the village level.

1. Strengthening Group Identity, Social Organization, and Community

He argues that "a strong sense of shared identity can energize people and inspire them to take collective action to improve their lives. . . Organizations built on the bedrock of cultural identity seem better able to single out common problems and collectively seek appropriate solutions. . . Such expressions of culture as feast days, work parties, celebrations, special songs, dances, and costumes establish and shore up a group's sense of identity and pride. Recognizing this, many groups actively promote such activities as an integral part of everyday life. When people's shared notion of uniqueness is lost or weakened, so is their sense of belonging to any community at all, and social organization is the first victim."

Example: Los Yumbos Chahuamangos, a music and dance group of lowland Quichua Indians from the Amazonian region of Ecuador, exemplifies this use of cultural enhancement. Los Ymbos's members are drawn from a large agricultural cooperative made up of eleven communities and 500 families. The group regularly performs at local festivals and important cooperative meetings, attracting broader attendance by injecting vitality into the proceedings and promoting organizational participation through song lyrics and by example. One of its songs explains in Quichua how a cooperative functions. Group members are also involved in mobilizing participation in a local Indian federation.

2. An Antidote to spoiled Identity and Alienation

"In contrast to the energizing capability of cultural expression, there is little that disheartens people more than a negative ethnic identity or sense of self, a shared perception of inferiority and low value within a larger social structure. People who feel inferior or despised participate less actively and perform poorly. . . A revitalized and revalued culture assists ethnic peoples in counteracting negative stereotypes that they may have internalized. Cultural expression can shore up people's self-perceptions and demonstrate the richness and complexity of their creative capacities to outsiders. . . Most important, a shared sense of self-worth provides the foundation for self-help -- a 'we can do' attitude --- encouraging a group to maximize the use of its own internal resources rather than turning too often, to much, or too soon to outsiders."

Example: In Israel, ethnic groups in conflict have formed theater groups to address social tensions before local audiences. Real-life incidents are dramatized. Israeli and Palestinian actors play the parts of members of the other group -- a rock throwing youth and a patrolling soldier, perhaps. Discussion among actors and audience follows.

3. Teaching and Consciousness Raising

"Forms of cultural expression can be very effective ways of teaching because they capture people's attention and imagination in ways that other forms of communication cannot do. In their very essence they are culturally appropriate, using understandable language and symbols to transmit messages in non formal training, in formal education, or in the course of everyday life. . . engaging people in the context of leisure and fun is a highly effective manner of reaching them with a message. . . a bilingual theater and music group presents educational dramas . . about the dangers of pesticides."

Examples: A puppet theater group in Kenya present plays using the local language and local cultural stories to emphasize the dangers of AIDs, drugs and alcohol in ways that keep children and adults entertained for hours. The Yumbos Chahuamangos present specific messages on the importance of boiling water to prevent children having diarrhea, in their performances in Amazonian Ecuador. Music and dance festivals among the tribal peoples of south India are used to build community esprit de corps and a sense of pride.

4. Creativity and Innovation

"Forms of cultural expression are primary sources of collective and individual creativity. They provide people with rare opportunities for looking at the world in a new way. They teach and inspire people of all ages, particularly the young to express and innovate."

Examples: Engaging a group of villagers to relate key aspects of their culture (music, dance, oral traditions) to the problems they are facing provides them with the opportunity to assess new possibilities and to ponder how things might be. This exercise of imaginative reflection can be the first step in creating an arena where problems and potential solutions can be identified, defined and redefined. Many RDFs have been able to use local theater groups to present images, questions and ideas that stimulate and involve the audience in discussions of adult illiteracy, low crop yields, the disappearance of the local forests, the need for potable water, the number of children who die of measles, etc. Many people make the mistake of assuming that a local culture is unchanging and thus irrelevant to the problems of the modern situation. In reality, local cultures are continually evolving over generations in a never-ending process of invention, elimination, and active borrowing from other cultures. Because cultural forms are creative and dynamic, they are especially compatible with what should be the most basic elements of the development process -- creativity and dynamism.

5. The Link to Production

"Traditional forms of culture are related to production, although the relationship is frequently more contextual than direct, particularly in rural settings. Here, music and dance are not set off from the rest of the human enterprise as mere entertainment but are integral to social structure and to forms of work."
For example, the Andean *minga* -- a pre-Columbian collective work system often used for harvests or for community projects -- is commonly mobilized and energized by songs and special foods, and the work is followed by a festive celebration. Cooperatives and worker-managed enterprises also use cultural expression to promote group solidarity and pride. Even though their resources may be extremely limited, these groups commission songs, organize festivals, design colorful banners (which are proudly presented to honored visitors), and so on -- a clear sign that cultural expression is an integral part of the group's productive process. A number of grassroots development projects draw upon this connection by promoting traditional handicrafts such as weaving, embroidery, leather work, and woodcarving." Many RDFs use traditional forms of agriculture to encourage various forms of low-input farming, better use of scarce water sources, and to see the value in traditional crops and animals in a given situation. Tradition systems of self-help, like *harambe* in Kenya or *minga* in the Andes, can be especially helpful in mobilizing members of a community in some type of productive activity.

6. Preserving Autonomy -- The Challenge of Pluralism

"Minority ethnic groups are frequently locked into the lower strata of society and commonly blamed for causing its problems, retarding its development or obstructing its integration as a nation. The blame often involves a labeling process -- the 'Indian problems,' the 'black problem,' and so on. The solution frequently offered for these 'problems' challenge the very essence of the group's ethnicity, usually by threatening to assimilate the group into the dominant culture. . . . Maintaining ethnic autonomy and cultural self-determination is a basic human right and is fundamental to broad-based development. . . In agriculture, nutrition, environmental protection and health care, native techniques have been adapted frequently by the Western world. Pharmacies and grocery stores are filled with products first developed by native peoples in Asia, Africa and Latin America.

Although these cultures should not be romanticized, neither should they be written off as quaint, primitive, or useless. Nor should they be asked to jettison their pragmatic technological heritage in favor of questionable 'modern' implants."

Section Five
Negative Consequences of the Local Culture

Some may raise the question as to whether, this chapter is advocating a completely relativistic approach to culture, suggesting that all forms of traditional culture must not only be tolerated but in fact encouraged. After all, there are many practices of traditional cultures that can and obviously, for many, must be confronted and even eradicated: cannibalism, headhunting, slavery, such practices as clitoridectomy and infibulation on young females, spouse and children abuse, witchcraft, human sacrifice and other forms of behavior that violate commonly held views on human decency and human rights. To answer this question, we must first review the three stage process of rural development as defined in Chapter Five above. As was pointed out, the first stage is one of trust building and establishing rapport with the community where the RDF or the student intern might be working. The appropriate behavior of the outsider in this stage should focus on developing an awareness and an understanding of the local culture. The major emphasis is one of understanding what people do and to seek to find some explanations (using the logic and beliefs of the local people themselves) for why they do what they do. This is a period where judgment, criticism, and rejection of local cultural values and norms have no place. An RDF too quick to judge or criticize may not only destroy his/her chances of truly understanding what is going in the community, but will undoubtedly destroy any chance of building close intimate relationships with the villagers.

The second stage of rural development would seek to apply the local culture as much as possible in designing and implementing capacity building activities: solving locally defined problems, assessing alternative ways to deal with certain needs or concerns, and in implementing projects in ways that do not violate sacred traditions, important values and strongly held beliefs. The focus of this second stage is **developing an appreciation** for the value and importance of the local culture and a willingness to use the local culture in as many ways as possible. Again both interns and RDFs would play an important role in this process.

In the third stage of rural development, the RDF is seeking to help build autonomous local institutions that will survive after the RDF leaves. In the third stage, the processes of empowerment generate community activities, changes and developments that are determined and implemented by the people themselves. In my opinion, it is in this third stage that individuals from within the culture itself would begin to reflect on how and why certain aspects of their culture should be preserved and what aspects might be changed. The focus of this third stage is developing a reflective and confrontative approach toward the local culture. The process of challenging or confronting certain aspects of a given culture requires great care and patience. An RDF must be very sensitive to the serious consequences of seeking to change or modify the rituals, rites, ceremonies and other norms deemed appropriate, important or eternally valid in a given community. The answer to the question of this section is best understood to suggest that cultural values that an intern or a new RDF might find repulsive, inhumane, crude or simply inappropriate can be confronted and in time perhaps even changed, but that is not the role of an intern or of a new RDF. Such confrontations and changes are best handled, not in terms of weeks or months, but in terms of many years and decades. Patience and a gradual process of education and training must be the key to this process of change.

Do all Customs Serve a Purpose?

Anthropologists seldom use the words weird, enigmatic, or strange to describe people and their cultures. Their job is to show how customs make sense, that they are reasonable or logical once we understand the set of cultural meanings in which they are embedded. Harris[5] argues that "particular sociocultural systems are an arrangement of patterned behavior, thought and feeling that contribute to the survival and reproduction of particular social groups. Traits contributing to the maintenance of a system may be said to have a positive function with respect to that system. Any careful analysis of the customs or norms that have been around for a long time generally have some adaptive and functional role to play for that society and should not, out of hand, be ignored or belittled.

For example, belief in witchcraft can serve the ends of social control in various ways. Because the individuals most commonly accused of practicing witchcraft are those who stand out as "different" and are also persons who tend to make numerous enemies, there is pressure on the individual to conform to accepted rules of conduct and to avoid giving offense to many people. It is not difficult to understand, therefore, how belief in witchcraft, by restraining deviance, can be interpreted as fulfilling definite social functions.

Others reject this functionalist perspective, arguing that many customs are not necessarily required for survival, but have emerged more out of habit and as a way of providing uniqueness and meaning or standards for behavior with no functional utility implied or required. There are two opposed tendencies: first, there is in every culture a dynamic element, one of practical adjustment to circumstances. Over time, the environment undergoes change, new technology arises, the population increases, or whole groups migrate to new areas. People see that the traditional way is not always appropriate for the changes that come and thus are forced to modify the acquired culture to cope with changing circumstances. Second, there is the tendency to conserve and defend established cultural practices. Resistance to change is just as ubiquitous a feature of human culture as is change itself. One important reason for this is that in every society norms and customs are imbued with emotional significance. The way we do things is seen as natural, hence any deviation appears unnatural. If we are forced to eat with individuals for whom it is customary to slurp, belch, or spit during the meal we experience discomfort, just as a Muslim might be revolted by our use of the left hand to convey food to the mouth.

Many years ago Ruth Benedict wrote a famous book, *Patterns of Culture*, in which she attempted to illustrate the enormous diversity and range that is to be found among human societies. Benedict contrasted the Pueblo Indians and the Indians of the Great Plains. She described the Pueblo./Hopi, Zuni Indians as "Appollonian", she meant that there was a marked distrust of individualism in the culture. Thus proper behavior in all spheres of life required that the Hopi Indian not be an innovator or a charismatic figure but rather should be one who conforms to tradition and keeps to the middle of the road. The individual avoids ecstatic religious experiences, the use of drugs or self-torture, or anything that would take him beyond the bounds of moderation.

In marked contrast to the Apollian Hopis, are the "Kionysian" Indians of the Plains. Benedict used the latter term to describe the various forms of immoderate behavior that were sanctioned in Plains culture and the relatively free hand given to individual initiative. Where the Hopis/Pueblos valued restraint and moderation, the Plains Indians craved all forms of violent experience. Benedict describes how Plains warriors sought visions as a means of attaining supernatural blessing: "On the western plains men sought these visions with hideous tortures. They cut strips from the skin of their arms, they struck off fingers, they swung themselves from tall poles by straps inserted under the muscles of their shoulders. They went without food and water for extreme periods. They sought in every way to achieve an order of experience set apart from daily living."[6] Ruth Benedict did not try to explain these differences but merely sought to describe them. Today most explanations of cultural differences are generally explained as a problem of cultural adaptation. Most would see the Pueblos as agriculturist tending to place a much higher premium on obedience, responsibility, and conformity to social rules. Any delay in attending a harvest could mean loss of the entire crop. Even individual initiative in attempts to improve techniques may be feared because no one can tell immediately whether the changes will lead to a greater harvest or to disastrous failure. Such reasoning is often used to explain the common conservatism of peasant society the world over.

In hunting and gathering societies, on the other hand, where food supply depends on daily foraging, there is a more immediate relationship between the effort and skill expended on any day and the resulting success. Individual hunters are therefore encouraged to develop personal abilities and initiative. Such a subsistence system put a premium on qualities of individual initiative, self-dependence, forbearance, and the capacity to size up a situation and act on one's estimate. Such contrasts in culture can be understood as the social consequences of fundamentally different ecological adaptations.

As was suggested earlier, RDFs and interns in the early stage of village development must not judge but must seek to understand, and thus are encouraged to subscribe to what is known as "cultural relativism" that is the belief that any particular set of customs, values, and moral precepts is relative to a specific cultural tradition, and that they can only be understood and evaluated within that particular milieu. Thus the Eskimo practice of infanticide, in our society would be considered a callous atrocity, but in north Canada is a rational practice of population control in a situation of harsh environment and narrowly limited resources. The Dani tribe in western New Guinea practices the custom of cutting a finger from the hand of the close female relatives of every man who dies. It is a standard part of their mourning rituals and by the time a woman is old she may have only one or two fingers left on each hand. Such practices give older women a sense of pride and status difficult for people outside their culture to understand or appreciate. Other kinds of practices and policies reflect religious and cultural practices quite unacceptable to the Western mind. The Dodoth tribe of Uganda painfully extracts the lower teeth of all the little girls, and this is seen as sign of female beauty. The Iraqi government announced in 1990 that "any Iraqi who kills . . .his own mother, daughter, sister, aunt, niece or cousin for adultery will not be brought to justice. In Pakistan, the Hudood Ordinance has been used to convict raped women of fornication and whip and imprison them. Most scholars acknowledge that such laws derive more from patriarchy and political power than from a "correct" interpretation of the Koran.

Muslim women in a traditional society are required to spend most of their lives sequestered in the home. Elizabeth Fernea, adopted the abayah (head covering) and limited her social life to the company of the women and children in their walled seclusion. She wrote: "I could tell my friends in America again and again that the veiling and seclusion of Eastern women did not mean necessarily that they were forced against their will to live lives of submission and near-serfdom. I could tell Haji (an Iraqi friend) again and again that the low-cut gowns and brandished freedom of Western women did not necessarily mean that these women were promiscuous and cared nothing for home and family. Neither would have understood, for each group, in its turn, was bound by custom and background to misinterpret appearances in its own way."[7]

Clitoridectomy and infibulation, commonly known as female circumcision, are practices found in many African cultures. They are deeply embedded in cultures where they occur because they affect the very definition of what it is to be female. Many Africans and Westerners feel that the practices are harmful but efforts to eradicate them cannot be divorced from the total cultural and political context. Studies in Sudan suggest that the major source of perpetuation of this practice was not merely from men, but from mothers and especially grandmothers.

In Asma El-Dareer's survey, the reasons given for continuing the practice of female circumcision were, in order of decreasing frequency: tradition, religion, cleanliness and beauty (uncircumcised genitalia were described as ugly and dirty), better marriage prospects, greater pleasure for the husband, preservation of virginity/prevention of infidelity; and increased fertility.[8]

Professional RDFs must come to understand that the way people believe and act is a function of their own reality that consists of their own mental constructs, values and traditions: Margaret Mead in 1935, *Sex and Temperament in Three Primitive Societies* argued that cultural conditioning can produce a situation in which our stereotypical sex roles can be nearly reversed. Among the Tchambuli people in New Guinea, women are the dominant and managing partners, whereas the males were emotionally dependent on the more aggressive females.

Cultural Persistence

Cultural behaviors and values have the same addictive quality as do tobacco or drugs. Cultural usages influence our perceptions and shift of muscular patterns so that each individual becomes not only a user of the culture, but also a product of it. The consequence, of course, is that one's own customs appear "natural," since both body and mind have been molded to accommodate those forms, whereas different usages appear "unnatural" and even perverse, The Japanese carpenter naturally pulls the plane toward himself, centripetally. The western workman pushes it away from his body, centrifugally. American gardeners poison snails, French people eat them with great relish. To a black native a blond European is grotesquely ugly, the scars and tattoos of the black women are beautiful to the native man. Americans on the Atlantic coast are avid clam-eaters but make no use of the mussel, whereas Europeans prefer the mussel and pay far less attention to the clam. There is the great story of an anthropologist Marriot visiting the Kiowa Indians, stating that he wanted to help the Indians protect their culture by writing down their traditions. The chief agreed that would be helpful to his children. But first he needed to get his record so the information would be correct. The anthropologist found out that the Indian chief was using a book that an Anthropologist, Mr. James Mooney, had written in the 1880s about the chief's people. Thus Marriot found herself recording a Kiowa version of Kiowa culture as interpreted at various points by a deceased anthropologist.

There is a strange paradox in comparing the life of the modern world and the life of the Amazon Indians. In Amazonia, for example, traditional Indians live in comfortable dwellings, warm at night and cool in the day. They eat well, a varied and healthy diet. They live in close community where loneliness is unknown, and they do it all on three or four hours work a day, leaving plenty of time for playing with their children, for contemplating philosophy, cosmology, and religion, and for externalizing whatever answers they find through profound rituals that make many of our own seem shallow and meaningless. For most city poor living in Brazil who have the benefits of the modern world, their children work 12-14 hours a day, they are often malnourished, serious disease is rife, infant mortality is high, life expectancy is low, alcohol and drug abuse common, and family life is characterized by anger, hostility and violence. Which society really is the happiest?

Section Six
Case Studies in the Process
of Cultural Enhancement

Let us now review a collection of case studies that demonstrate the power and utility of strengthening a local culture as a part of the process in rural development. Each case represents a specific way that culture facilitates one of the key areas in village development (education, health, etc.)

Cultural Enhancement in the South Sea Islands

This notion of cultural enhancement reflects a process by which the local language and history of a given culture are integrated into the local school system. One RDF working in a South Sea Island began tape recording stories from the villages' oldest residents in order to create reading material for her students. Tales from their tribal history, of traditional fishing activities, sailboat commerce, local game hunting, and practical herbal medicines were fascinating reading for the children of the small island, whereas stories about "Dick and Jane" were incomprehensible. The local stories in both English and the tribal language became so popular that several village schools obtained permission to use them in their own curriculum. One RDF noticed that many young people, especially if they were exposed to Western movies and television, were loosing their sense of the island culture. She began to argue that the young people of her island needed to experience some form of bonding with their own cultural traditions -- to know themselves and to carry on building their communities. Her comment was: "These young people have so much to be proud of, and they did not know it." She convinced a local high school principal to allow a group of juniors and seniors, to work on a book on the island's history and traditions. They began discussing among themselves what they knew about their own history, how they had learned it and from whom. Working groups were formed around topics of mutual interest: the old ways of the ancestors, the evolution of boat making, the history of specific islands and areas on the bigger islands, the use of herbal medicines, the impact of the Whites on their culture, and the sea lore of coastal fishermen. Each group practiced using tape recorders and cameras, and refined questions for interviews. When the students felt ready they chose informants among their family members and neighbors, people who had lived the history and could voice their own experiences. In visiting with the older members of their communities, they gained a new respect for the wisdom and experience these older people had. Picking the best pictures and interviews, they edited a small book on the history and culture of the island.

During the year of the project, other students wrote about the histories of their own villages, island handicrafts that were being lost or corrupted, detailed descriptions of marriage and burial ceremonies, the dangers of deforestation, insect bite cures, traditional recipes, and older folktales and songs that were being lost or forgotten. When students were asked to describe what they had learned through their participation, they pointed to improvements in their oral and written skills, their new familiarity with cameras and tape recorders, and the value of knowing and appreciating their own history. Until development specialists begin to understand the significance of this kind of cultural training, many traditional societies will continue to lag beyond in their efforts to find meaning and purpose and in the final analysis long-term success in their own development programs.

Cultural Enhancement in Colombia

In Colombia is an organization called the Asociacion Colombiana de Promocion Artesanal (ACPA), a unique institution that has developed a comprehensive strategy for reviving craft traditions during the past two decades.[9] The ACPA would seek to maximize it scarce resources by organizing communities of local artisans to help themselves. Because the business of crafts in Colombia had been dominated by urban intermediaries, RDFs working with ACPA decided to focus first on the artisans themselves rather than on what they produced. Beginning in 1977, with grant support from the Inter America Foundation, ACPA launched an intensive program to help artisan communities create their own development programs.

Most artisan communities were highly fragmented, sometimes because of family or political disputes, but often because artisans were competing on unfavorable terms for access to markets. In most cases that situation was exploited by intermediaries, who bought crafts on consignment or in return for a little cash and enough raw materials to keep production going. Organizing as a precooperative, which entailed fewer legal requirements than a cooperative, was one way to remove some of these bottlenecks and increase production. By pooling resources together in a credit fund, a precooperative were able to buy raw materials in bulk, providing members with a steady, economical supply of inputs to increase production. Sometimes ACPA agreed to buy a group's first inventory, either to encourage the formation of a precooperative or to help it capitalize its production fund. ACPA through its network of RDFs helped individual groups of artisans to develop their own strategy for direct marketing in order to provide higher rates of return for members and encourage the group's independence.

Since 1977, ACPA has assisted nine artisan groups, with varying degrees of success. Perhaps the most notable has been the *barnizadores* of Pasto. This relatively small group, primarily man, practices a unique craft whose roots extend back to pre-Colombian times. Using a complicated process, craftsmen convert the gum of the *mopa-mopa*, a tropical shrub like tree, into paper-thin sheets of dyed material, or *barniz*, which are applied with freehand artwork to wooden trays, boxes, animal figures, and other articles. The resulting products look something like Japanese lacquer ware, but are in fact unique.

Establishing this group of barnizadores of Pasto was no easy task. The people of this community were known for their lack of cooperation, their tendency to undercut each others efforts, and the failure of earlier attempts at establishing some type of cooperative. Several craftsmen had been able to sell their work through Artesanias de Colombia, but most were at the mercy of a few local middlemen who commissioned cheap curios for the tourist trade what were a pale reflection of past standards. The barnizadores also suffered from unsteady supplies of *mopa-mopa* gum, the crucial raw material for their craft. The only source was relatively small area of the Putumayo jungle, a 12-hour bus ride from Pasto. Prices fluctuated wildly, in part because intermediaries occasionally tried to corner the market. A better supply system was necessary to ensure the barnizadores' survival, but for that they needed to organize and build up a capital fund, neither of which seemed likely.

For three years ACPA's team of specialists worked patiently with the barnizadores, listening to their troubles and looking for ways to bring people together. A turning point came when several artisans were invited to produce some special pieces that could be presented at an arts fair. Freed from the restraints of producing for traditional intermediaries, many of the barnizadores made objects of striking beauty. Asked to comment on each other's work, men who looked past one another in the street began to express feelings of grudging admiration that soon gave way to questions of how a certain effect had been accomplished. A meeting became a workshop

In 1982, the workshop became a precooperative of 18 barnizadores. With a grant from the IAF, the new organization took its first step toward regularizing access to raw materials. A fund was established to ensure a steady supply of *mopa-mopa* gum from the Putumayo. The group also made arrangements with local woodcarvers, and opened its own wood-working shop, to obtain a dependable supply of objects for decoration. Each member received inputs free of charge, but finished work had to be submitted to a quality control committee for payment. When a piece was accepted, five percent of the payment would be deducted for the percooperative's capital fund. Another five percent would go to the group's solidarity fund, from which interest-free loans can be withdrawn for medical or family needs. The product was then marked up in price by 60 percent to cover the costs of raw materials and administrative overhead, and put up for sale.

With ACPA's help, the group attacked the marketing problem next. Several members traveled to craft fairs in Colombia and abroad, and a brochure was prepared detailing the group' history and promoting the artistry of its products. In 1986, the group used a loan from ACPA to buy an old colonial house in central pasto to provide office and meeting space, a gallery, and a store for retailing finished goods. This center has become the precooperative's primary source of income, and sales have been brisk. Artisan income has risen commensurably -- nearly quadrupling in the eight years the group has been together.

Feria Educativa in Ecuador

In rural Ecuador, a dozen campesinos had come from a neighboring village to watch a performance by the Feria Educativa, or "Educational Fair."[10] The Feria, a group of young indigenous musicians, had spent the entire Sunday afternoon in the village plaza, playing traditional Quichua songs, staging socio-dramas, putting on a puppet show, and encouraging members of the audience to comment on how the situations on stage reflected local problems, and how local people might find solutions. To appreciate the significance of the Feria's role, and the culture action methodology that underpins it, requires a look at the history of grassroots development in Chimborazo. The province has one of the highest concentrations of poverty-stricken native peoples in Ecuador, even in South America. Living in more than 1,000 villages, at altitudes that sometimes exceeds 13,000 feet, the quarters of a million indigenous inhabitants of the province have only recently emerged from an exploitative hacienda system that greatly limited their possibilities for self-sufficiency, social development, and economic development. Most development organizations that have worked in the area generally included white collar representatives who come from a social and cultural background far removed from that of the local campesinos. They would drive to villages accessible to the village by the Pan-American Highway and meet with a small group of leaders, invariably men, explaining to them in Spanish how their particular organization intended to set up a development program for the benefit of the local residents. Then the visitors would pile into their jeeps for the three-hour drive back to Quito. Unfortunately, in spite of much goodwill and massive expenditures of national and foreign funds, the majority of these programs failed, and little positive evidence of them remains today.

The Feria Educativa has a noticeably different approach. It enters a village only by invitation. Feria members -- themselves indigenous RDFs (men and women) -- arrive in traditional dress, play local music, sing songs in Quichua, and get people to dance and sing with them. For a few nights, the Feria is radio, television, stage and newspaper to people hungry for information and new perspectives on a world that can be seem hopelessly rigid and hostile to Indians. Often it is past midnight before the audience allows the Feria to finish. The songs are about historical events, the world of nature, love, festivals and ceremonies, death, planting and harvest, pride in being an Indian, the problems of alcoholism, domestic animals, favorite foods, religion, crime, and politics -- in other words, the entire human drama.

Only after trust is established do Feria members begin to encourage people to identify their most important problems. The Feria Educativa does not offer answers or promises of support for projects. The sociodramas and puppet shows typically sketch out a common problem: illiteracy, unresponsive or abusive authorities, discrimination against indigenous people in the cities, poverty, deforestation and erosion, or the lack of schools and teachers. Then, almost in mid performance, they halt abruptly and the floor is given to the people, many of whom have been commenting openly or talking to each other or laughing in recognition, at times in discomfort, throughout the presentation.

Sometimes a woman will speak out in favor of establishing a local weekly market, or a man will ask how a neighboring village was able to start a community bakery or plant a mountainside with trees. Often people will simply talk about the performance and how it resembles, or differs from, their own experiences. According to the Feria's strategy, this collective recognition of how a problem is rooted within the local reality is a prerequisite for building the resolve and summoning the social energy and creativity necessary for solution. The trick is to promote a raised consciousness on the part of the campesinos that prepares the ground for constructive future action, rather than to simply leave them more embittered and frustrated than before. Sometimes action results immediately; sometimes nothing happens. Usually the Feria's visit is the first step in a long process of reflection and planning, leading eventually to action.

The Feria's sociodramas are generally scripted, at least in outline, and rehearsed, although in performance the actors at times will improvise a sociodrama based on the particular problems of a given group. Often comments from the audience provoke direct answers from the actors -- and vice versa -- or even a departure from the script. On a number of occasions, members of the audience go beyond verbal participation in the drama literally to step into it. Feria members often encourage such participation. If no one steps forward spontaneously, they will put a microphone before a potential speaker or take someone by the hand and lead him or her on-stage. Usually there are roars of approval from the audience for the new actor, and the sociodrama takes a new direction, somewhat out of the hands of the Feria.

Other elements of the Feria's work, such as song, story, and dance, also demonstrate to campesinos the social value of their instinctive need to preserve their music, their festivals -- each with its characteristic dances and costumes -- their folktales and metaphoric riddles, and above all, the Guichua language. When the Feria was formed in 1974, there were only two campensino music groups in the province that promoted the playing of traditional music. By 1990 over 100 such groups were independently performing traditional music; many of them are also collecting and preserving it. At least 12 of these groups were formed by women. Helped by the Feria's promotional work, a number of RDFs working in the area have helped establish some 132 community bakeries, nearly 50 artisan-managed workshops, more than 145 community centers and to plant more than 200,000 trees in reforestation efforts. Such RDFs have been especially helpful in setting up literacy programs in over 1,000 training centers using local villagers as teachers.

Undeniably, one of the Feria's most important achievement has been the encouragement and enabling of a collective sense of ethnic pride and "can do" -- a sense that Indians in Chimborazo Province have a valuable culture and are capable of contributing to society as a whole. Indians are not as compliant and manipulable as they were in the past. They are more assertive, more questioning, and more skilled in dealing with government bureaucracies. Several of the RDFs found the local authorities were at first critical of the Feria's role in this process. Everybody recognizes that it will take some time to build bridges of understanding and cooperation between these two communities. But that is what cultural enhancement is all about.

Cultural Protection Among the Amish

The Amish is a strict Protestant sect, an offshoot of the Mennonites, who came to American from Switzerland in the late 1700s and early 1800s. The distinctive ethical feature of the sect is a strict interpretation of St Paul's injunction "be not conformed to this world" (Romans 12:2). Their response is to subject all the innovations of "the world" to rigorous scrutiny and, as a result, they generally make do without tractors, cars, telephones, and electrical appliances. Cultural criteria overrule economic ones. To them, consumption means fulfillment of needs rather than wants. The Amish clearly expresses the self-discipline necessary to preserve communities based on contrary values to consumerism. Although their lives may seem laborious and austere, they have a sense of community purpose and meaning and a social stability that are conspicuously absent in mainstream America. They are, in essence, a unique example of successful cultural resistance, pursuing a process of reflective dialogue suggested earlier as an important part of any stage three program of development.

Unexplained Movement toward Development

In the mid-1980s, I was involved in a USAID evaluation team, collecting data on barrio communities in rural Philippines. We attempted to collect data on infant mortality, income, illiteracy, incidents of different types of diseases, etc. In reviewing the data on some 347 villages, we noticed that one particular village was unique, for on all the indicators of development, they were two and three standard deviations above the norm of such rural communities. In conducting a follow-up case study, we quickly gained insights into this anomaly. It appears a young school teacher had decided to organize a school band, using traditional instruments and performing traditional songs. Over a period of time, this school band gained some notoriety and they were invited to play in fiestas in neighboring villages. Parents and village leaders from this village began to raise money to buy new instruments and a local mothers' club began sewing new costumes. A sense of pride and social energy was developed through this small school band, that went far beyond the mere teaching of music to its children. Community committees were established to clean-up the village, to start a health program, to invite agricultural extension workers into their community, etc. What started out as a cultural enhancement program, started by one young school teacher, emerged as a new perspective, a new sense of pride and identity, a new sense of purpose and dignity. This is the essence of cultural enhancement.

Conclusions

The projects described in this chapter are all based on the faith that if a fading cultural system can be restored, it will strengthen the capacity of the people to deal with the challenges that surround them. Charles Kleymeyer suggests in the conclusion of his most useful edited collection of case studies devoted to cultural enhancement that people interested in protecting and strengthening local cultures might consider the following action steps:

PVOs and NGOs interested in village development must be willing to allocate significant resources for the direct support of cultural expression activities. Such resources are best used in one of three ways: 1) the preservation perhaps even the "rescue" of some cultural forms which are on the verge of extinction through conscious efforts to collect, document and preserve such traditions through film, recordings, drawings and interviews; 2 the maintenance of on-going cultural forms through the support of community based activities which legitimize, reinforce and cherish such traditions; and finally 3) cultural "revitalization" which entails activities such as the recuperation of expressive forms that have been lost or are being lost, as well as efforts to use traditional forms in new ways and develop entirely new forms to express reality. This type of action (cultural re-creation) calls for appropriate ways to introduce change without undermining the core values of community identity.

Local RDFs must seek to provide other forms of support through intermediary institutions or associative networks. Yet there are dangers. Well intentioned attempts to "help" ethnic groups maintain their culture or use cultural expression for development may end up primarily benefiting outsiders, including commercial and political interests, academics, and funders themselves, ironically reinforcing old modes of paternalism and dependency. Often, the best that an outside organization can do is to find ways to enable grassroots cultural activists and their organizations to carry on their own work for their own purposes and on their own terms. One particularly effective way that RDFs might support cultural activities is to enable communities to form and strengthen informal networks and formal associations at the local, national, and international levels. Such coalitions facilitate those most closely involved in preservation, revitalization, and other activities in setting their own agendas, design their own strategies, and carry out their own efforts to support and enable one another.

Most important for PVOs and NGOs committed to cultural enhancement will be activities which seek to support and work with clearing houses structured to service cultural activist organizations in fundraising and networking. Many RDFs working to enhance a given culture are commonly handicapped by their remote locations and their inexperience in "grantsmanship." They would benefit from clearinghouses to put them in touch with sources of grant monies, bibliographical materials, data on similar projects, and other resources. Two existing organizations that are playing such roles are the Paris-based International Fund for the Promotion of Culture, an official body of UNESCO, and CULTURELINK, the Network of Networks for Research and Co-operation in Cultural Development, sponsored by UNESCO and the Council of Europe.

PVOs and NGOs at both the national and international levels must seek to assure that ethnic peoples control their cultural property rights. Many peoples have seen their cultural property expropriated freely over the past several centuries -- from traditional medicines, crafts, and food crops to songs, designs, and antiquities (not to mention land, water, and mineral rights). While such issues are not often addressed by people interested in development, it is time that such property rights be protected, so that outsiders and even individual insiders are not able to cash in on such property with no benefit to the wider community. A number of groups, the Kuna in Panama, the Taquile Islanders in Peru, are attempting to increase their economic and legal influence over local handicrafts and tourism. Nevertheless, in most cases there is no barrier to prevent the expropriation of culture and no system of copyrights to funnel profits back to indigenous groups. Official national and international bodies can call for respect and forbearance but are hard pressed to enforce it. This issue has special urgency in the case of indigenous peoples in endangered tropical forests. A considerable portion of the modern pharmacopoeia derives from the knowledge of flora and fauna embodied in the ethnoscience of native peoples, yet there is no payment for use of this intellectual property. If fair compensations were made, forest peoples would have a better chance of surviving and of protecting the habitat that still possesses untapped renewable resources.

Knowledge systems throughout the planet are disappearing. As explained by Darrell Posey in *Anthropology Today* in 1990: "For many years there have been warnings of the impending destruction of indigenous cultures and the implication of those losses for all of humanity. . . Medicinal plants, natural insecticides and repellents, fertility regulating drugs, edible plants, animal behavior, climatic and ecological seasonality, soils, forests and Savannah management, skin and body treatments -- these are just some of the categories of knowledge that can contribute to new strategies for ecologically and socially sound sustained development." The annual market value for medicines derived from medicinal plants discovered from indigenous peoples is $43 billion: less than one-hundredth of one per cent of the profits derived from those sources has ever been returned to those peoples.

Finally, special efforts are needed to broaden and strengthen processes leading to cultural pluralism. Building societies that are truly culturally pluralistic requires self-determination and self-governance by minority peoples to ensure their long-term cultural survival. It also requires efforts to increase inter group tolerance, respect for the civil rights of all ethnicities, and general knowledge and appreciation about the cultural roots, contributions and history of all groups in society. When characterized by autonomous participation and mutual tolerance, enhanced pluralism can lead to more workable democracy, improved internal and cross-border relations, and reductions in animosity and violence at the national and international levels. As we come to the end of this century, we are painfully aware that few of the many challenges we face have greater importance for human welfare and survival.[11]

The strategy of rural development defined in this book is based upon a set of important assumptions. First we want to shift the village community from relying on service delivery systems controlled by outsiders to becoming a resource acquisition system controlled by the villagers themselves. Responsible RDFs do not aim to work in a given area for a long period of time merely to make the villagers more dependent on the outsiders. All the activities of RDFs must be to help the villagers become empowered, independent and self-reliant. Cultural enhancement is an important part of the process of empowerment, networking and coalition building. From our experience, it is hoped that RDFs would be willing to work in a district for at least five years and during this period, make a serious effort to organize clusters of villages to pursue the basic principles of sustainable rural development. Let us now consider the broader issues of how such long-term programs might be organized, funded and supported over the next century.

---

[1] Gunnar Myrdal, *Asian Drama*, (New York: Twentieth Century Fund, 1968).
[2] Frantz Fanon, *The Wretched of the Earth*, (Translated from the French by Constance Farrington, New York, Grove Press, 1965).
[3] Charles David Kleymeyer, (ed.) *Cultural Expression & Grassroots Development: Cases From Latin American & the Caribbean*, (Boulder: Lynne Rienner, 1994), pp. xi..
[4] *Ibid.*, pp. 19-33.
[5] Marvin Harris, *Cows, Pigs, Wars and Witches: The Riddle of Culture* (NY: Vintage Books, 1974), p.141. He is a most powerful exponent of the view that culture and customs make practical sense.
[6] Ruth Benedict, *Patterns of Culture* (NY: Houghton Mifflin, 1934), p. 81.
[7] Elizabeth Fernea, *Guests of the Sheik: An Ethnography of an Iraqi Village* (New York: Anchor, 1965), p. 313.
[8] Asma El-Deer, *Women, Why Do You Weep?* (London: Zed Press, 1982), pp. 67-76.
[9] This case study is an edited version of an article: Brent Goff, "Reviving Crafts and Affirming Culture: From Grassroots Development to National Policy", *Grassroots Development*, 14 (1), 1991.

[10] This case study is an edited version of a chapter: by Charles D. Kleymeyer and Carlos Moreno, "The Feria Educativa: A Wellspring of Ideas and Cultural Pride," in Charles David Kleymeyer, (ed.) *Cultural Expression & Grassroots Development: Cases From Latin American & the Caribbean,* (Boulder: Lynne Rienner, 1994).

Chapter 16

Technical Assistance and Foreign Aid: Mistakes of the Past and Opportunities for the Future: Non Government Networking Organizations (NGNOs)

The time has come to consider a new vision of technical assistance and foreign aid, one that builds on the truly great ideals of some of our past leaders, but which redefines the character and meaning of such assistance in new terms, new goals, and new challenges. For many, foreign aid has been a "give away program" deemed necessary but only because of the challenges of the Cold War. Now that the threat of communism is over, the logical conclusion would be that foreign aid is no longer necessary. Equally common is the perception that our foreign aid has been a failure, that all we have done is support dictators and elites with our aid, that the common people, the truly needy, seldom received any benefit from our aid programs. While many might assume that foreign aid is no longer justifiable, given the demise of Russian communism, the thrust of this book must suggest otherwise. Certainly a number of other factors need to be considered before we come to that conclusion.

Section One
A New Threat to be Considered!

Clearly, it is time for the American people to consider the emergence of a new threat outlined specifically in this book, a threat that may have as many negative implications as the spread of communism had in the 1940s and 1950s. I should like to suggest that this new threat will continue on into the early decades of the 21st Century and it may have consequences as serious and dangerous as communism was in the past. This new threat is not based upon a threatening ideology nor a totalitarian dictatorship bent on world conquest. The threat I am describing tends to exacerbate the tragedies of malnutrition and hunger, sickness and poor health, illiteracy and social fragmentation, all of which lead to frustration, fanaticism, terrorism and violence. This expanding threat generates political instability, civil wars, domestic violence, threats to tourists and business people, even the world-wide spread of AIDs and other dangerous diseases. It is often associated with environmental degradation, soil erosion and increased dessertification, the burning and destruction of limited forest lands, and the pollution of streams and lakes. This new threat, is not some expanding ideology such as communism, it is the expanding world-wide phenomenon of extreme poverty, the inequitable and unjust distribution of food, resources and opportunities.

As was mentioned in an earlier chapter, the industrialized nations with roughly 20 percent of the world's population have access to over 80 percent of world's goods and services. The bottom 40 percent of the world's population has access to less than 15 percent of world's wealth and even worse, the bottom 20 percent (roughly one billion people) has access to less than 2 percent of the world's wealth, measured in Gross National Product (GNP) terms. The tragedy of these statistics is that the gap between the rich and poor is growing, not decreasing. The extremities of poverty are even worse today than they were two decades ago. The low-income countries contain nearly all of the world's chronic poor people. Throughout the world, according to the World Bank, more than 1.1 billion people live in chronic poverty, and of those, 630 million are "extremely poor," having an average annual per capita income of less than $275 (roughly $23 per month).

For many, this extreme gap between the haves and have-nots is both immoral and economically and politically very dangerous. Nations that ignore the lessons of history are condemned to repeat past mistakes. The general public and several leading members of Congress concluded in the early 20th Century that isolationism was the key to our security. It was argued that we should simply ignore the conflicts and problems of Europe and the rest of the World. It was not until Hitler had moved into Eastern Europe and the Japanese had bombed Pearl Harbor, that we woke up to the reality of our situation.

When we ignore the problems of world poverty with its accompanying violence, repression and misery, then we easily forget the killing fields of Cambodia, Rwanda and even Guatemala; when we ignore how a dictator in a far away place exploits his own people, violates basic human rights, begins to generate a nuclear capability that could plunge the whole planet into a war of massive destruction, then we will be forced to relive the expansionist policies of a Saddam Hussayn in Iraq; a Kim Sung in North Korea, or an Idi Amin in Uganda, over and over again; and when we ignore how extreme poverty and the lack of basic public health systems can lead to the spread some of the most dangerous diseases known to men, we will be forced to experience the spread of AIDs-like diseases on into the 21st Century.

Viewing the immense power of today's concentration of wealth, and the remoteness of most governments from their people, one may feel despair at the prospects of civil society being able to harness these forces to the common good. Indeed there is no certainty that they will be thus harnessed. The tragedy of world poverty may simply run its awful course. Since 1989, at least, there is proof positive in the popular revolutions in Eastern Europe and the Soviet Union, that civil society can overturn seemingly omnipotent despotic structures. All over the world various movements for peace, justice, gender and environment are organizing for human betterment. The stakes have never been so high and the outcome so uncertain, but there are legitimate, and inspiring, grounds for hope. Let us review what some of these trends might be.

Development and the Violation of Human Rights

One important part of the development equation must reflect the tragedy of ethnic and religious violence and political instability that characterizes so much of the less developed countries of the world. The great tragedies of Bosnia, Rwanda, Ethiopia, Somalia and Cambodia, etc., are all attributable to brutal civil conflict and social disintegration. The conflict between the blacks and the Arabs in Sudan, the Hutus and Tutsis in Rwanda and Burundi, between the Singalese and Tamils in Sri Lanka, the Kurds and the Iraqis in Iraq, the Latinos and the Indians in Guatemala, all reflect this problem. The costs have been staggering. The toll in human lives is compounded by the sterile economic investment in weapons and warfare, and the corresponding impoverishment of social and economic development policies. The environment is another victim, as war scars the earth with bombing and shelling; refugees fleeing conflict raze forests for firewood and shelter, and children are crippled and maned long after the conflict from the undiscovered land mines and non detonated bombs. Insecurity has stunted long-term economic planning, and international aid has been squandered on soldiers and the military establishment.

What is important to recognize is that civil conflict represents a deadly drag on development. A nation at war with itself is an unlikely candidate for sustained and secure growth, and for too long, too many nations of the LDCs have suffered from endemic conflict, often exacerbated by the developed nations vying for the opportunity to sell more weapons, more systems of destruction, to the very nations that are suffering the most from the tragedies of extreme poverty.

Equally tragic, is the reality that the processes of development themselves may be a potential source of conflict. Where development projects advance the interests of some groups to the disadvantage of others, they may serve to exacerbate social inequality. The least empowered groups, including the urban poor, landless agricultural workers, and indigenous peoples, often find that the price of economic growth for wealthier segments of the population, comes at their expense. In the Amazon region, for example, logging and ranching development has jeopardized the livelihood of indigenous Indian groups; and in Nigeria, the wealth generated by oil production has failed to reach the poorer tribal communities of that country where the oil was discovered. The tension resulting from such inequitable development can erupt and in these instances has erupted into sustained or sporadic armed conflict, setting back the cause of broad-based development even farther.

Section Two
A New Vision for Foreign Aid is Needed!

The vision I am suggesting must reflect these realities of world violence and terrorism, environmental degradation and extreme poverty. We are no longer able to live in isolation, our society is inextricably tied to what happens in the rest of the world: When millions of people on this planet live in extreme poverty, this is the breeding ground for political terrorism, domestic violence, the "killing fields" that destroy peaceful trade, exacerbate public health concerns, threaten tourism and business development, and generate environments where dictators and tyrants gain popular support. It seems to me that while the spread of communism was the great threat of my generation, the threat that my children and my children's children will face will be this extreme poverty, this spread of violence and terrorism, this inequitable distribution of wealth and resources. Yet, in the final analysis, we are not talking about simply distributing wealth, we are talking about distributing opportunity. These millions of poor families are not asking for a handout, they are asking for a handup. They do not need our relief as much as they need release -- release from their poverty, their illiteracy, their sickness and their lack of a fair chance at raising their children and living with some dignity and self-esteem. Foreign aid practices of the past have stimulate much disillusionment among our people. We resent the misuse of our tax dollars for projects and programs that are not sustainable, we are frustrated when we see development programs that benefit corrupt governments and help keep tyrants in power, and we resist our natural generosity, when we see money wasted on inappropriate technology and over-centralized systems of bureaucracy.

Today our commitment to foreign aid and development assistance has been guided by a series of strategic visions: (1) President Roosevelt argued that our international commitments were based upon the realization that economic autarchy and political repression during the decades after W.W.I were major sources of the Great Depression and W.W.II. (2) President Harry Trumen, in his inaugural address of 20 January 1949, proposed a "bold new program for making the benefits of scientific advances and industrial progress available for the improvement and growth of underdeveloped areas" (3) John F. Kennedy articulated a vision that "a more prosperous world would also be a more secure world." (4) in the early 1970s a new direction in foreign assistance was defended by members of the House Foreign Affairs Committee suggesting that foreign assistance should focus on basic human needs and human rights. Aid should be directed to achieving greater equity among peoples, both within and among countries -- to achieving political empowerment and improvement of the economic well-being of the poor majority in the poorest countries. (5) in recent years the concept of sustainable development has emerged. Its central theme is intergenerational equity -- "sustainable development is development that meets the needs of the present without compromising the ability of future generations to meet their own needs." This new vision of development assistance did not emerge from official levels -- neither from the administration nor Congress. It was advanced first by the international environmental community and later by a broad coalition of NGOs. It was initially greeted with cautious skepticism at official levels, but in recent years is becoming more legitimate.[1]

What is needed is a new sense of purpose and direction that would clarify why such aid-giving might be needed and appropriate. There is a great need to articulate a common vision of the relationship between U.S. assistance efforts and the kind of world Americans want to live in and the kind of world, they want their children to live in.

Recent History of Foreign Aid

Over the past several years, US development assistance programs have been in disarray. The bilateral development assistance budget had declined continuously in real terms since the mid-1980s. During the second Reagan administration, the easing of political tensions between the United States and the Soviet Union had contributed to a decline in the willingness of Congress to continue to sustain foreign assistance at the level funded in earlier years.

Earlier, in a series of conferences beginning in the Spring of 1986, which had been organized by Ralph H. Smuckler of Michigan State University and Robert J. Berg of the International Development Conference, a series of reports and discussions were developed to consider how foreign assistance might be restructured and reorganized in the 1990s. One of these reports argued that in the 1990s, U.S. development assistance should focus on "broadly based growth, an effective attack on poverty, and an end to the destruction of the environment." It urged that it is time to forge a more mature relationship with the Third World that would involve a shift away from the old idea of aid to a focus on mutual gain through cooperation. Development assistance should give priority to four areas: (1) the enhancement of physical well-being through health systems and population planning, (2) the development of sustainable agricultural systems of production of food, (3) the development of environmental programs and policies to protect natural resources and assure energy security, and (4) the implementation of sound urban and rural development policies. The study urged the separation of responsibility for development assistance from security-oriented strategic and military assistance. The agency envisaged in the report would, however, have a much broader mandate for economic cooperation than the present USAID.

One of the most significant reports in the recent efforts to redefine what our foreign assistance program should be like was the report of an Independent Group on the Future of U.S. Development Cooperation. This Independent Group's report, growing out of a series of seminars organized by the Rockefeller Foundation and the Overseas Development Council, argued that U.S. development assistance efforts ought to be fundamentally restructured and focused around the goal of sustainable development. By sustainable development the group meant "growth that brings with it the alleviation of poverty and preservation of the environment for successive generations in a context of government accountability and social justice consistent with the aspiration of all members of a society."[2]

To accomplish this objective, the Independent Group recommended the replacement of AID by a U.S. Sustainable Development Cooperation Agency (SDCA). The new agency should emphasize a series of sectoral policy and program priorities: (1) investing in people, including employment creation, education, health promotion, and family planning; (2) protecting the earth, including environmental management, agricultural production, energy production, forestry and fisheries programs, and biological diversity; and (3) strengthening the institutions of free societies, including assistance in building accountability in government, strengthening of the capacities of non-governmental and civic organizations, and protection of the rights of the disadvantaged.

While one can easily agree with the agenda established by the Independent Group, The Bread for the World, an inter-denominational assistance interest group, voiced its concern that the emphasis given to natural resource and environmental issues by the Independent Group, would divert assistance resources from the most basic problems faced by the poor people in poor countries. The Bread for the World, suggested, that whatever the agency for development assistance might be called, that the central focus should be on: (1) improving livelihoods -- creating and enhancing opportunities for poor people to increase their earning capacity and quality of life and (2) meeting basic human needs -- expanding investments in health, access to safe and adequate supplies of food and water, education, and shelter.

In recent years, some form of consensus among a number of reports and conferences appear to be emerging, generally suggesting that USAID needs to be reformed, redefined and restructured, that the four areas of assistance (development assistance, humanitarian assistance, political or strategic assistance, and military assistance) should be administered as separate programs. Most agree that the reorganized USAID agency should be responsible only for development assistance.

When J. Brian Atwood was confirmed as USAID administrator in May 1993, he identified growing populations, mass migrations, political repression, ethnic conflict, environmental degradation, and a worsening global economy as core issues with which U.S. foreign policy must be concerned. He emphasized that the overall goal of U.S. development assistance must be sustainable development.

In my opinion, our foreign aid program needs to be redefined to emphasis economic cooperation rather than economic assistance. US assistance efforts should focus largely on the high pay-off areas of human capital development and of technical and institutional change. My preference would be to keep the present name United States Agency for International Development (USAID), but to give it a new autonomy, a new structure and a new role. Both the State Department and Department of Defense should continue to develop bilateral agreements with key nations of the world who for diplomatic or security reasons will continue to receive assistance (technical, military and strategic). In contrast, USAID should have a separate budget, independent of these strategic considerations, and allow it to focus on what it can do best, provide technical assistance at the macro-level and encourage local institutional development at the micro-level in the countries needing our support and encouragement.

The Macro-emphasis would support and encourage the exchange of knowledge and technology among all nations, especially in the areas of agriculture, health, population, micro credit and environment. It would also include cooperation in the areas of economic reform, societal democratization and increased pluralism, policy analysis and administrative reform, and program implementation. In my opinion much of this macro-approach to assistance should largely be subcontracted to universities, research institutes, and the sectoral departments and agencies such as Agriculture, Health, Education and Welfare; Environmental Protection; and the National Institute of Standards and Technology, all agencies within our present system capable of providing much needed technical support and organizational reforms.

The Micro-level approach would emphasis institutional development and humanitarian concerns for the poor at the local level in the poorest countries. USAID's role in the micro-level emphasis would clearly distinguish between disaster relief functions that might require food and medical aid for short-term crises and the longer-term activities needed to institutionalize grassroots efforts at poverty alleviation. In my opinion, much of this micro-level emphasis should be contracted out to Non government Organizations(NGOs), Private Voluntary Organizations (PVOs) and private companies and consulting firms on a competitive basis.[3] Such funds must not be seen as entitlements or welfare payments to the poor. A whole new philosophy of grassroots development based on the three stage process of development defined in this book, including: community development, local resource mobilization, local leadership training and support, the basic empowerment and strengthening of local institutions capable of solving their own problems and linking to broader national and international sources of help, must be conceptualized, operationalized and internalized by the development assistance community.

The growing perception that private aid groups are better able to identify needs and deliver help has persuaded the US government to increase the proportion of aid delivered through NGOs from 17 percent in 1992 to 30 percent in 1995 and to a projected 40 percent in 1996.[4] Nor has the attractiveness of NGOs been lost on private organizations and individuals, who continue generously to support voluntary development work. The OECD counted over 2,500 NGOs in Northern countries in 1990 (up from 1,500 in 1980) and countless counterparts in Southern localities.[5] The rising non government tide is best reflected by the NGO presence at several UN conferences (1992 Earth Summit in Rio de Janeiro and the 1995 Social Summit in Copenhagen) where voluntary organizations played a role as prominent as governments', giving voice to the grass-roots interests they represent and earned the ear of national policy makers and the international media.

While non governmental efforts are not a panacea, they offer an efficient and people-centered development alternative to large government and multilateral projects, and constitute a direct channel for constructive aid and communication between concerned individuals of the more developed nations of the North and the economically impoverished people of the South.

In reflecting how our nation ought to confront world poverty, we need to consider three propositions: First we need to understand that much of our past foreign aid giving was far more successful than our mass media and general public impressions might suggest. Second, we can and must give far more than we are presently giving if the challenges of this new threat of world poverty are to be confronted. Third, we have learned a great deal in the past three decades about what strategies and interventions have been most successful and also how the strategies and interventions of development assistance ought to be structured in order to have the maximum impact possible on the poorest of the poor of this planet.

Foreign Aid More of a Success than Widely Believed!

It is important that the considerable accomplishments of two generations of development be fairly evaluated. Televised images in the first half of the 1990s have left too many Americans with the perception that the countries of the developing world are hopelessly poverty-stricken and conflict-ridden. From Main Street, USA, to the floor of the Senate, the shibboleth that aid is invariably squandered and that our programs are no more than "money down a rat hole," has been invoked to undermine support for development assistance. In reality, however, the record of foreign assistance and development discloses important successes: In little more than a generation, average real incomes in the Third World have more than doubled; child death rates have been reduced by more than half; malnutrition rates have tumbled by over 30 percent; life expectancy has increased by about a third; and the percentage of rural families with access to safe water has risen from less than 10 percent to more than 60 percent. [6] Literacy rates are up 33 percent in the last 25 years, and primary school enrollment has tripled in that period. Indeed, virtually every index of human development discloses dramatic gains for human well-being across the Third World. Much of this improvement can be directly attributed to the support and direction of international donor agencies. Various world-wide programs, sponsored and encouraged by United Nations agencies, organized and implemented by many national technical assistance organizations, and funded and allocated by the thousands of Non Government Organizations (NGOs) throughout the world, have had a very positive and cumulative impact on many aspects of human existence.

The progress of the past forty years, as impressive as it might be, must still be considered within a set of questions concerning what progress might have been possible if a different set of strategies, interventions and programs were to have been implemented during this same period of time. Thus while we of the West can take some pride in the progress made, it is perhaps more important to reflect on what still needs to be done, what mistakes were made in the past and how best to confront the still staggering consequences of extreme poverty that characterizes the lives of nearly two billion people in the world today.

We Can and Must Give More than We are Presently Giving!

Foreign aid as a percentage of our Gross National Product GNP has been dropping significantly over the past several decades. At the present time, 19 countries out of the 21 industrialized nations of the world give a greater percentage of their GNP for development assistance than we do in the United States. In relative terms, Norway has long been the biggest donor. Since 1981 the Norwegian people have been willing to give over 1.2 percent of their GNP to spend on development assistance for the poorest nations of the world. This is a percentage of their GNP that is much greater than what the United States has been willing to give. We clearly could and probably would give more if we, as a people, were more assured that such aid would truly benefit the poorest of the poor.

Aid programs, of course, are motivated by various, sometimes competing, influences, of which poverty reduction is but one. National security is still a powerful motivator. One-quarter of the US $21 billion foreign aid budget consists of military assistance. Areas considered strategically important, such as the Middle East, Eastern Europe, the former Soviet Union and more recently South Africa, have benefited from US aid disproportionate to their development needs. When the military and technical assistance is subtracted from the foreign aid budget, it leaves less that one half of one percent of the federal budget (substantially less than $1 billion) for economic development assistance to the poorest countries of Africa, Asia, and Latin America.

Much of the foreign aid and technical assistance that we have given, while it has proven very useful for many less developed nations, also serves our own self- interest as much or more than the needs of the poorer nations. A significant percentage of all of the aid given by the Northern (more developed nations -- MDCs) is tied to the purchase of the donor nation's goods and services, so that the wealth sent abroad is guaranteed to pay dividends back at home. The less developed countries (LDCs) are required to buy goods and services from the richer countries that gave foreign aid in the first place. For example, some $12 billion annually is given for "technical assistance" -- advice, training, and development project design work -- of which 90 percent is spent for the salaries of Western experts and consultants. Seen in its most skeptical light, these developed nation aid programs might best be seen as a system of elaborate subsidies for the domestic development industries of the giving-nations. Still other donor nations, probably the most aggressive example would be Japan, structure their development assistance to ensure that it goes primarily to countries that have the most potential markets for their domestic exports.

Even where the impulse behind assistance is humanitarian, results on these grounds have been erratic. The standard canard, that aid is no more than "poor people in rich countries paying taxes to provide aid to the rich people in poor countries," has a measure of truth in it. Recent studies of the US assistance program show that over $250 per recipient of US aid was sent to relatively middle-income Third World countries but less than $1 per person was earmarked for the poorest countries. For many of us, it is inconceivable that over 60 percent of all US foreign aid goes to two countries: Israel and Egypt. While we may acknowledge the importance of maintaining the peace between Egypt and Israel, it is tragic that such huge amounts of foreign aid should benefit these two countries.

Nearly two-thirds of the world's poorest people live in some ten countries and yet they receive but one-third of world assistance. Still, worse, within donor countries, aid-supported services seldom reach the neediest. Analysts attribute these spending patterns to the priorities of recipient governments, which often labor under political pressure to satisfy urban populations over their poorer rural counterparts, and may favor showy capital improvement projects like dams or hospitals over less glamorous poverty-reduction activities in the countryside. Donor governments, however, must bear responsibility for the fact that LDCs with large military budgets receive more aid than their pacific counterparts, as national security interests are used to justify the underwriting of large military budgets.

Perhaps in response to the perceived failure of official aid to meet its humanitarian mission, perhaps more in response to competing pressures on domestic agendas, and partly because of the end of the cold war, all of these things have reduced the wealthier nations' interest in subsidizing the often unstable political regimes found in LDCs. Consequently the political commitment to global aid is on the wane in most MDCs. Throughout the 1970s and early 1980s, the official development assistance disbursed by industrialized countries increased by some 25 percent in real terms, but growth slowed sharply in the late 1980s and early 1990s; and by 1993, the net flow of assistance to developing countries fell to $56 billion, down from $61 billion the year before. US development engagements abroad has followed the international trend: American assistance to sub-Saharan Africa fell by almost half a billion dollars between 1985 and 1992. Budget cuts in 1994 hit the poorest parts of the US development portfolio hardest, as USAID closed 8 of its 35 African missions. And, in response to strong domestic pressure to cut assistance, the US announced plans in April 1995 to cut by nearly half the nation's annual pledge of overseas food aid, which had remained unchanged for two decades.

The portrait of international assistance in the mid-1990s is not all bleak. First, even as the US government moves to slash overseas funding, polls strongly suggest that the American public remains more generous than their representatives and that current hostility to assistance springs from misconception rather than indifference. According to polls taken in 1993 and 1994, average Americans mistakenly believed that the US government was allocating 20 percent or more of the federal budget on foreign assistance; while the real figure was roughly 1 percent, and much less than half of that budget goes for development aid administered by USAID. Asked to indicate the amount that the US government should allocate for foreign aid, the average American suggested that the appropriate US investment in international aid should be about 5 percent -- or five times the current outlays for foreign aid. Obviously, there is both wide misunderstanding as to how much we are spending, but also a large reservoir of humanitarian support within the American people that remains untapped in the United States. If the United States were to give one percent of its budget to deal with the tremendous problems of world poverty, we would still be giving less than a number of nations in Europe. Such spending would have the great potential to under gird a whole new North-South partnership for poverty alleviation and rural development.

We Have Learned a Great Deal About What Works and What does not Work in Development

We have learned a great deal in the past three decades about how development assistance ought to be structured in order to have the maximum impact possible on the poorest of the poor of this planet. The discourse of development aid, including the catalogue of success stories described throughout this book, is too often interpreted to suggest that development is something that is imposed upon the poor. In fact, it is people of the less developed countries of the South, working in cooperation with various development organizations in the North that are the true repositories of development expertise; and these success stories are theirs, not ours. Better evaluation, coordination, and above all, greater appreciation for the dynamics and issues of local experience are necessary preconditions for the more effective utilization of development resources.

An insightful critique of international aid has noticed that such changes will require: "a fundamental change in the posture of the aid community as a whole toward the poor, which must be reflected in a responsive approach to their organized initiatives. Implicit in this approach is not only a genuine respect for the capacity of the poor to manage their own development, but, perhaps more importantly, an appreciation for their understanding of their own circumstances, their knowledge of external constraints and internal capabilities, their creativity and their ability to define appropriate development paths for their immediate and wider communities."[7]

Development assistance, and even crisis relief, cannot succeed without the participation of community-based indigenous organizations and individuals. With their help, important efficiencies have been discovered and costly mistakes are much more apt to be avoided. The central insight -- that effective development assistance demands popular, community involvement -- lies behind the increased role for NGOs in the overall development equation and justifies optimism that the next generation of foreign aid will yield still better results than those just past.

Recent History of NGOs

Over the past decade, NGOs have played an increasingly important role in the development assistance process. NGOs had gained a reputation for innovation, for promoting local participation, and for reaching the poor.[8] In the 1980s, major donors such as the US Agency for International Development (USAID) and the World Bank, turned increasingly to NGOs as flexible and less expensive instruments for their development activities.[9] In 1984, some 2,200 NGOs from the developed countries (MDCs) utilized approximately $4 billion in assisting an estimated 100 million people in the LDCs. This represented more than a threefold increase in expenditures since the mid-1970s. The NGO resource contribution coming largely from private donors and the general public soon surpassed 10 percent of the combined bilateral and multilateral foreign aid budgets of the MDCs and nearly 20 percent of that total when the services contributed by voluntary agencies were included.[10]

Able to work directly at the community level, which the larger assistance agencies can reach only indirectly, many NGOs argued they were in a better position to ascertain local needs and priorities, base programs on local input, transfer technical know-how more appropriate to a given setting, and to organize or strengthen local institutions. At their best they were seen as responsive to local needs, more sensitive to local cultures, supportive of the truly poor, builders of self-reliance, flexible and innovative, and participatory through the project cycle,

In reality, the NGO record has been uneven. While many studies have concluded that aid channeled to and through NGOs generally do reach those in need, others, were questioning their efficacy. Many argued that there was a huge gap between their rhetoric and their practice. For example, most NGOs talked about popular participation, but in the actual process of project identification and planning, there was little evidence that communities were actually involved, that little effort was given to help organize and mobilize local communities to be prepared to participate in the implementation and evaluation of projects, and finally that many NGOs simply implemented pre-planned programs with little effort to assess their relevance or acceptability to the community being served. Equally apparent was the tendency for such NGOs to work with communities that were close to urban centers, to ignore the poorest of the poor and the more isolated rural communities.

An OECD report published in 1990 showed that in 1988 over 6.5 billion dollars in NGO support were granted to LDCs. It should be noted that 75 percent, i.e., the lion's share of the assistance NGOs were receiving, was channeled through only 200 organizations.[11] In recent years a number of governments and multilateral agencies are starting to emphasize directly supporting local NGOs, instead of going through the larger NGOs organized in Europe and the United States. The governments of Canada and Sweden, but also those of Norway and the Netherlands are leading this trend. Within the United Nations family, a number of agencies have embarked on a course of cooperation with indigenous NGOs for the purpose of planning, implementing and evaluating projects and programs. For example, the UNDP Division for Non-Government Organizations was established in December 1986, with the intention of implementing a "major policy thrust towards community-based grassroots approaches in development and toward expanding cooperation with NGOs." Currently, UNDP seeks to emphasize a policy dialogue, information exchanges and implementing programs related to the strengthening of indigenous NGOs.

Many of these new NGOs, are generally founded by local people. Their aim of self-sufficiency includes the financial aspects of development and they are very wary of the imposition of external agendas, are quite aware of the dangers of fostering strong ties with the larger Western-based NGOs, and thus tend strongly to reject most financial support from abroad. Many of these smaller NGOs have developed several surprising forms of self-financing. The number of indigenous NGOs has skyrocketed in the past ten years. In India some 12,000 local NGOs have been formed in recent years, some 7,500 in Bangladesh, over 1,000 in Brazil. Other countries experiencing impressive NGO expansion include: Chile, Bolivia, Ecuador, Senegal, Ghana, and the Philippines.

This emphasis on indigenous NGOs, emerging locally in the less developed countries as a new set of key actors and potentially far more effective for implementing effective development activities, is a relatively new phenomenon. Many are beginning to see these new indigenous NGOs as being far more effective in initiating long-term, more sustainable forms of development. This belief that the locally based NGOs are better situated to work for more meaningful political networking and greater democratization; and to establish significant administrative and management linkages with outside sources of funding, influence and support, can be seen in much of the development literature of the 1990s.[12]

Section Three
New Perspective on How NGOs Should be Structured

David Korten, in his path breaking analysis of development alternatives for the 21st Century, suggests that NGOs have gone through a series of changes over time, reflecting what he calls different generations of NGO activity. First generation NGOs were concerned with relief and welfare: focusing upon the immediate needs of people facing famine, drought or flood. Most of their activities emphasized short-term emergency relief efforts, with the NGO being active and the beneficiaries being passive. What was not understood was the tendency for such relief and welfare activities to provide short-term help without considering the long-term consequences of these approaches. Careful consideration of these activities demonstrated how such NGOs were dealing with symptoms and ignoring the more fundamental causes of world poverty.

Second Generation NGOs tend to engage in community development activities, emphasizing village level programs of self-help in health, literacy, water and agriculture. The interventions implemented implied a kind of partnership between the NGO and the community. While such activities sought to introduce change and development into the local areas, they were almost never sustainable and seldom were structured to confront the broader political and economic constraints for long-term development. In contrast to the village level approach implied in Second Generation Approaches, Third Generation type NGOs emerged in the 1980s to stimulate efforts to pursue policy reforms, greater democratization and administrative decentralization, and through greater national-level efforts to implement institutional and structural changes. Such activities sought to stimulate greater public awareness and elite commitment to the need for political and economic reform if development was to be sustainable and equitable.

While Third Generation NGOs sought changes in specific policies and institutions, working largely through national and international systems of political influence and interest group lobbying, Korten argues that a broader set of activities is needed, transnational in scope, international in focus and resting upon the activities of what he calls Fourth Generation NGOs that seek to stimulate and support voluntary mass movements committed to the Alternative Development Paradigm that I outlined in Chapter Four. Over the past decades a number of mass movements have been established to raise the world community's consciousness concerning, the need to curtail nuclear testing, the need to make people aware of global warming, dessertification, and deforestation, the need to organize an International Planned Parenthood Federation in the wake of an unacceptable level of population growth in many areas of the world, the need to sensitize the world community to the problems of gender inequality through the efforts of various human rights and women's issue groups. Thus the Fourth Generation NGOs would seek to mobilize the world's citizenry to the terrible challenge of world poverty, seeking to encourage and stimulate mass movements, organized through voluntary community, regional, national and international networks of concerned citizens. As Korten argues, "the job of the Fourth generation [NGO] is to coalesce and energize self-managing networks over which it has no control whatever. This must be achieved primarily through the power of ideas, values and communication links." [13]

I owe a great deal of gratitude to David Korten for his insightful assessment of the types of NGOs that will be needed into the 21st Century. His book outlines in some detail the ways in which private citizens might become involved in the activities of NGOs committed to poverty alleviation. As we, including our representatives and government officials, reflect on how financial resources might best be used to deal with the problems of poverty, it should be clear that a significant portion of our federal budget, allocated for foreign aid, needs to be earmarked for the work of NGOs willing to sponsor and work with grassroots organizations and networks.

It is my contention that before we can expect Third and Fourth Generation NGOs to perform their roles in this process, they will need to be supported, encouraged and allowed to function independent of any government system. This, of course, does not mean that evaluations and accountability of resources given would not be expected. It would mean that the challenge of world poverty is going to require the combined efforts of our governments, our corporations, our private voluntary organizations, and individual citizens all working together. If we have learned anything in the past three decades, it is that local, more decentralized, voluntary efforts are absolutely vital in any process of national development and that a significant share of our foreign aid dollars must be allocated to strengthen and institutionalize these self-help, local initiatives. NGOs, structured to strengthen local institution building, committed to creating self-sustaining local resource mobilization activities, organized to develop networks of collaborative program implementation in which both private and public sources of funding are integrated, and finally established to reinforce and support mass movements of private citizens, seeking to reform and improve the political and economic systems that presently need changing if the problems outlined in this book are to be confronted appropriately.

While all four generations of NGO activity still have relevance for the present situation, it should be clear that there is still little known about how these different generations of NGOs are related and how they each in their own way support and facilitate the movement from the early stages of trust building and awareness, through the second stage of capacity building and problem solving, into the third stage of local institution building and empowerment. The growth and influence of mass movements committed to this new Alternative Development Paradigm must all start with individuals, building trust and commitment, increasing capacity and learning, forming local organizations and networks of influence. This is what development is all about and this why this book has been written.

If the three stage process of rural development defined in this book is to be implemented, it will require the creation, funding and long-term support of local NGOs willing to send full-time, highly skilled and dedicated RDFs into the villages and rural communities where the poorest of the poor are residing, It will require the creation of district level networks of local institutions, willing to mobilize much of their own resources, utilizing local problem solving groups, cooperatives, clubs and associations, to initiate their own processes of service delivery activities. It will also require systems of linkage and collaboration between these networks of local institutions at the district level to provincial, national and international sources of technical and financial help. As these linkage mechanisms are institutionalized and formalized into self-sustaining systems of political and economic influence, the third stage of rural development associated with community empowerment and democratization will gradually help create political and economic institutions that demand accountability, protection of human rights, concern for the environment and the establishment of a more equitable society.

The creation of these networks of local institutions and community leaders, these linkage systems of collaboration and mutual support between local communities and public and private agencies, organizations and groups along with these processes of community empowerment have the potential to stimulate mass movements of citizen volunteers who organize themselves to confront and challenge the problems of the environment, the tragedies of extreme poverty and the senseless violation of human rights and communal violence that characterizes so many of the LDCs of this world.

What are the Options Available?

It might be appropriate to suggest that NGOs can be classified by considering a set of specific characteristics that clearly distinguish the different kinds of NGOs that are presently working in the field of development: three indicators of the relationship between the NGO and the neighborhood, community or village; two indicators of the relationship of the NGO with the government; and three indicators of the type of services or resources being offered.

First, **Time Orientation** (1) NGO mostly deals in disaster relief (limited term generally 3-6 months), (2) mostly in technical assistance (short term usually 1-3 years), or (3) mostly in local institution building/empowerment activities (long term, 5-10 years).

Second, **Policy Orientation** (1) the NGO agrees to support and encourage Government Policy, (2) the NGO is neutral concerning Government Policies, or (3) the NGO seeks changes and reform in governmental policy (policy concerns may include administrative reform efforts, budgetary allocation questions, greater democratization and human rights issues).

Third: **Financial Orientation** (1) NGO provides all the resources for the project, (2) NGO seeks a partnership in which both the NGO and local community members mobilize some of the resources (3) NGO seeks to create a network/Linkage system in which resources are mobilized through the joint efforts of local community institutions, outside government agencies, various other NGOs, and other private sector sources of help.

Fourth: **Implementation Orientation**, (1) NGO works mostly at the national level, implementing nation wide programs through a centralized system of administration (2) NGO works mostly at the individual community level, implementing grassroots projects in individual communities, neighborhoods and villages or (3) NGO works mostly at the sub national level, supporting networks and linkages between clusters of villages, local government agencies, and a variety of NGOs and other sources of support, generally at the provincial or district level.

Fifth: **Program Focus Orientation**, (1) The NGO's program is narrowly focused generally in one sector: (disaster relief, agriculture, literacy, health, micro-credit, etc.), (2) NGO's program is broadly focused generally seeking to integrate a number of sectors (combining agriculture, health, literacy, micro-credit, etc. into one program), or (3) NGO's program is open-ended, allowing the individual communities to determine the focus and emphasis of the activities and programs developed through processes of empowerment and coalition building.

Sixth: **Facilitation Orientation**, (1) NGO representative is a sector specialist, an agronomist, public health expert, specialist in micro-credit, etc., (2) NGO representative is a generalist, works mostly in the area of community development, helping an individual community to organize itself to become more self-reliant, or (3) NGO representative is a network facilitator, organizing community associations that can be linked to a district or provincial level system of program implementation, links these communities to local government agencies, various NGOs willing to work in their areas, and other private sector sources of help.

Seventh: **Local Indigenous NGO Orientation**, (1) the NGO tends to ignore indigenous NGOs, preferring to implement programs through their own administrative system, (2) the NGO works with indigenous NGOs, creating a partnership, providing the local NGO with resources, personnel and other support, or (3) the NGO not only works with an indigenous NGO in setting up programs, but seeks to emphasis making the local NGO independent and sustainable, able to function autonomously in replicating their programs in other areas.

Utilizing the kinds of criteria of classification just mentioned, I should like to identify a new type of NGO that is beginning to play a significant role in rural development: the linkage/networking and empowerment type of NGO, (1) that has a long-term time orientation agreeing to work in a rural area or district for at least five years, (2) that actively encourages local resource mobilization through networks of collaboration, integrating both public and private sources of support, (3) that works mostly at the sub national level, supporting networks and linkages between clusters of villages, local government agencies, including various national and international NGOs willing to provide resources on terms determined and established by the local communities rather than by the donors, (4) that utilizes a program focus that is open-ended, allowing the individual communities to identify the programs and strategies that they want to implement, (5) that employs representatives (RDFs) that are network facilitators, generalists, able to organize community associations that can be linked to a number of district or provincial systems of program implementation, and (6) that is deeply committed to working with local indigenous NGOs, not only helping them set up programs, but also making them self-sustainable and independent of outsiders. Such an NGO focuses more on their ability to create sustainable systems of development through various networks of government agencies, national and international NGOs, and other organizations, public and private, that support long term change and reform in the political environment and long-term economic and social improvements in the local grassroots areas of society.

Section Four
What is a Non government Networking Organization (NGNO) Approach?

I should like to suggest that USAID seriously consider allocating significant portions of their aid and support for NGOs willing to implement what we have been defining as a Community Empowerment and Linkage/Networking approach. I would suggest that we use the term Non-Government Networking Organization (NGNOs) as a separate category of NGOs in order to distinguish the few NGOs that are focusing on a formal networking strategy with a commitment to structure their activities in ways that establish networking/linkage building systems at the rural district level. NGNOs are committed to supporting local community/local institution building activities at the grassroots level. In an attempt to operationalize the term NGNO, a preliminary set of characteristics might include: (1) a strong commitment to supporting and strengthening local problem solving groups, institutions, cooperatives, and activities located at the community grassroots level. (2) a strong commitment to rely heavily on local leadership, local decision-making, local autonomy, and providing villagers with a great deal of freedom to determine their own needs, their own program emphases, and their own timetables and schedules. (3) a strong commitment to provide some initial financial help (not necessarily in the form of money), but in the form of project start-up supplies, training materials, basic tools and equipment, but never so much that the local people become dependent on the resources given. (4) an up front commitment to strengthen local resource mobilization, both as a way of ensuring that the activities being implemented will be sustainable, but equally important, that local organizations will develop the skill, the confidence and the ability to become self-reliant in the long-run; (5) the outside support organization (NGNO) provides facilitative help and training in group and local leadership organizing skills, consciousness-raising opportunities, project planning and implementation training that encourages self-reliance, and social, economic and political autonomy. (6) NGNOs are especially committed to integrating, supporting and helping to institutionalize the many small, indigenous NGOs emerging in the districts and provinces of the country, giving them training, financial and management support as they seek to become self-funding, self-managing and independent of outside larger NGOs. Finally (7) an NGNO seeks to help organize links and networks of mutually beneficial contacts and long-term support systems that will remain in place after the outside NGNO leaves a particular district or region.

It is this last characteristic of the NGNO approach that needs to be clarified and emphasized. NGOs of the past have generally worked within two almost mutually exclusive mind-sets: (1) the top down, highly centralized model which seeks to help the disadvantaged of the world by offering them pre-determined, outside funded plans and programs that reflect what the outsider considers the most appropriate. The outsider is the helper, the local people are the beneficiaries, the outsiders, because of their training and experience, often assume that they know what is best for the villagers. The villagers have so many problems and disadvantages that they will be grateful for whatever the outsider might give them. (2) Another mind-set emphasizes the grassroots approach or the single village approach, insisting that villagers must be protected from the harmful influences of the outside world, must be given limited resources that are needed to solve their most pressing problems. This approach tends to reject central government help, insisting that government-support seldom benefits the poor, and often causes more problems that it solves. Interestingly, both approaches are widely used in the business of development and technical assistance and both of them are based upon a common set of assumptions: (a) The outsiders really know best how to help the local communities, (b) the local communities are too poor to mobilize any of their own resources and thus they must rely on outside resources if they are to be helped. (c) local communities need outsiders to define their problems, identify solutions, and fund the projects to solve these problems.

The approach suggested in the NGNO model rejects these three assumptions and argues for a very different mindset. (a) the disadvantaged communities of the world have been surviving without outsider help for centuries, and thus know a great deal about survival and self-reliance. Their local knowledge, experience, traditions and indigenous institutions are a resource that needs to be developed and supported. (b) very few outsiders are aware of the amount of local resources that are available, that can be mobilized once the community is committed to a course of action that is meaningful, meets clearly understood needs and reflects traditional ways of doing things, and (c) long-term sustainability does require that local communities are gradually integrated into the broader society through institutional linkages and mechanisms that promote mutually beneficial contacts, relationships and associations. Many NGOs that work at the national level often fail to implement meaningful programs at the village level. Other NGOs that focus on the village level seldom implement projects that are sustainable. While both national-focused and village-focused NGOs do have a role to play in development programs, I am suggesting that a more appropriate focus is at the sub national level, where clusters of villages linked to district level political systems have the greatest probability of strengthening local leadership, stimulating local resource mobilization, and eventually being linked and integrated into local government systems and national and international NGO support systems without destroying the local initiative and sense of accountability that is stimulated by the sub national/district level approach.

It would be hoped that people will see the advantages of this third type of NGO: (1) It can serve as a funding channel from donor agencies to grassroots needs, but at a level that is more reflective of the local systems capacity to utilize such resources in a non-dependency inducing way (What I am calling the Absorptive Capacity Issue). (2) It can establish mechanisms for linking community participants to facilitate the sharing of ideas and information on key issues, the strengthening of local problem solving skills, and building confidence and awareness for local communities in ways that help them begin to take ownership and responsibility for the solving of their own problems (What I am calling the Problem Ownership Issue). (3) It can help to build indigenous capacities for learning, documenting, and sharing among other NGOs and donor agencies working in the districts or provinces where the program is being implemented, and can help to empower local communities to contact and confront such NGOs and donor agencies to supplement and encourage local efforts and activities organized to solve local problems. (What I am calling the Empowerment Issue.)

The NGNO strategy seeks to initiate participatory development and to redefine the concepts of participation and leadership in terms relevant to the local situation. Whether in political theory or in the practice of rural development, participation is hard to define. Experience suggests that there are many forms of participation, yet in terms of the NGNO model it requires that local people are intimately involved, that the agenda, the options considered and the processes used to determine goals, methods, strategies and commitments ensure that all the people feel involved, that their opinions are not only valued but seriously considered, that the decision making process reflects some form of consensus building that integrates and unifies rather than fragments and divides the community. The type and form of the actions taken must be decided upon by the membership collectively.

The objective of a participatory approach is to strengthen the membership's confidence in their own capacities, and to develop leadership that is accountable to and reflective of the disadvantage people being targeted. The local leaders must have the status and the confidence of the people (people must trust them and acknowledge their leadership as legitimate and proper), local leaders must have skills in project design and implementation, and must have the self-confidence to take responsibility for their actions and be willing to take some risks in initiating something new. Such leadership, especially among the poorest of the poor is hard to come by, needs a fairly long-term process of training and encouragement from an effective RDFs who are supported by this NGNO process. The development of such capacities and skills are best institutionalized through the process of problem-solving group training outlined in chapter nine.

One example of a NGNO that is seeking to establish a district-level system of community empowerment and linkage/network building approach is CHOICE, which I have been involved with for nearly 15 years. The approach of CHOICE is best described as a process of working with villagers to help them acquire the motivation, confidence, status and skills necessary to identify their problems and needs, press for their own interests with governmental authorities and other donor supported activities, and thus eventually to assume responsibility for decision-making in the implementation of self-help projects. CHOICE seeks to emphasize a five dimension approach, emphasizing health, literacy, income generation, ecology and the enhancement of the local culture. Full-time rural development facilitators (RDFs) are assigned to a rural district for 3-5 years, with the explicit goal of putting themselves out of work in that rural district as soon as possible.

The key emphasis is on building local village problem-solving groups that eventually begin a networking process with other villages and communities; and the empowering of such clusters of problem solving groups to contact and network with various NGOs and government agencies willing and able to engage in a cooperative effort in one or more of the five dimensions being emphasized by the community itself. The value of this approach is the tendency for villagers to change from their traditional activities and behaviors to a more critical and self-reflect process of thinking and problem solving. This, in turn, involves both appropriate technology transfer and an increase in villager awareness and confidence, but also helps demonstrate the value of cooperative ventures in literacy, health, credit acquisition, more productive methods of agriculture, alternative ways of increasing income, and the value of networking with potential allies and support groups available to the provincial, national, even international levels.

Another element in this district-focused empowerment model of development is the linking and supplementing of community resources with external resources. Local resource mobilization is a key factor in local project success and particularly for the sustainability of benefit flows. Resource commitments from local people may be in cash or in kind and may be generated in a variety of ways, ranging from user fees for services provided, to the establishment of some enterprise specifically devoted to raising funds for a local program in health, education or cultural enhancement. What is important is that the local village participants control how these local resources are mobilized, allocated and used.

CHOICE has often found it appropriate to formalize resource commitments with a contract negotiated between the communities and indigenous NGOs and outside funding sources. Such a contract takes community inputs seriously and provides increased local leverage. Of course, negotiation may go well beyond resource inputs to the setting of project targets, establishing a schedule of implementation and pay-back, and the outline of specific implementation responsibilities. The benefits of such contracts linking local communities and some NGNO with host governments and donors include: linking local action to national priorities, insuring greater technical acceptability, and providing needed administrative and financial support. This must be done in ways that retain local choice, stimulate local involvement and deal seriously with local potential. Such NGNOs can play important roles as intermediaries in this process. Let us quote from a CHOICE field report outlining the basic strategy of the community empowerment and linkage/network building approach initiated in Guatemala.

Some Preliminary Efforts in the NGNO Approach
El Chol Area of Guatemala

"In the Fall of 1994 two RDFs were assigned to the El Chol area (roughly 60 miles north of Guatemala City) for roughly 18 months. This area which includes approximately 10 major villages and nearly 50 smaller hamlets was classified by government statistics as both isolated (no paved roads to El Chol) and disadvantaged (the level of poverty is far above the average of the country). The RDFs lived in the village of Ojo de Agua, roughly four miles outside the district capitol of El Chol. Before the RDFs were able to purchase a vehicle, the RDFs generally walked to El Chol 2-3 times a month for supplies and to make telephone calls. During the rainy season the road was nearly impassable to vehicles and there was no bus service to Ojo de Agua. The RDFs living conditions were modest to say the least, (two rooms, no electricity, no indoor water or toilet facilities), their rent was roughly $5.00 per month. From interviews, observations and my general assessment of the situation, the RDFs were able to accomplish a great deal of trust building with the local communities, establishing good rapport with the local government officials and building a network of contacts with PVOs and NGOs that are presently operating in Guatemala.

Examples of their success

1. In the village of Ojo de Agua, there are 3-4 hamlets. This village has had the reputation of being very poor, (the soil is very rocky and of poor quality), generally uncooperative with the local government, and historically, the various hamlets in the village have been unwilling to work together on any common project which might have benefited the entire community. Over the past 18 months, the RDFs have sought to identify a project that all the villagers might agree upon and thus work together. Up until just recently, they appeared to have had little if any success. When the RDFs convinced some of the villagers that a group of gringos was willing to come to work with them on the condition that the villagers themselves would identify a project and would be willing to work on the

project themselves, representatives from all the hamlets started meeting with the RDFs to organize some type of cooperative project. It was finally agreed that the old school in their village could be renovated to be a community center, with one of the rooms to be used as a small health clinic. Because of past vandalism in the area, the villagers all agreed that a wall was needed around the new community center. It was this project in which a CHOICE expedition participated. The project was a huge success. Representatives of all the hamlets worked during the entire week, but what was most important, this project demonstrated to the villagers that they could work together. At the end of the week, an evening of eating (the village women prepared tortillas), dancing, singing, and general intermingling was a great success.

2. Potable water in the village of El Chol is a very serious problem. Some water projects have been completed in the past, but most are inoperative and clearly need repairs and expansion. The RDFs started visiting with the Department of Water Works in Guatemala City nearly a year ago, trying to convince them that the El Chol area desperately needed help. At first, they were told that no funds were available, that there was already a long list of applicants from other areas. The RDFs then convinced some of the villagers to go to Guatemala City themselves to present a petition that their water system be repaired and expanded. The villagers were very hesitant and seemed fearful of contacting a government agency. With much discussion and persuasion over several months, a few village leaders agreed to go. In the Fall of 1995, the village was informed that their village had been put on the list for repairs in 1996. There is no question that the RDFs were largely responsible for this change of events. One of the key roles for our RDFs in the field is to help local people gain the confidence and social skills needed to help them take more responsibility for their own lives. While the CHOICE expedition was in El Chol in March 1996, a delegation from the Water Department came out to project site (obviously they were curious to see gringos living in a Guatemalan village), and announced to village that $120,000 had been set aside to repair and expand the water system in four of the ten villages in the El Chol district. This is a dramatic example of why RDFs willing to live and work in the rural areas of a country is so important.

3. Regenerative Agriculture: Most of farm land in El Chol is of poor quality, very rocky and located on steep, marginal hillsides. Yields have always been very poor, and the farmers barely produce enough to subsist. Their diet generally consists of beans and corn with occasionally some vegetables and fruits to supplement their meals. One of the RDFs convinced a few farmers to go with him to participate in a one week regenerative agriculture training course sponsored by the GMRR (an affiliate of the Jimmy Yen organization). During this course, the farmers were introduced to organic farming, learning how to put nutrients back into the soil, how to develop compost piles and other nature fertilizers that were both ecologically better for the soil but also much cheaper to the farmers than

traditional chemical fertilizers. While the RDF had no formal training in agriculture, he also attended the training course, along side the villagers, in the use of this technology. The RDF's willingness to start his own little garden demonstrated to the farmers that they too could do this. If a "dumb" gringo with no experience in farming could do this, surely they could do it. The RDF spent days and days working directly with the farmers in their own fields. He sought to understand local farming methods and what it really means to grow the food needed for subsistence. After the first year, several farmers who had agreed to use this regenerative technology, obtained significant increases in their yields and now several other farmers in the village have agreed to try this system this next year.

4. One of the RDFs began working directly with the women in this village. She had been holding weekly training session on primary health work, encouraging women to understand the concepts presented in the book *Where There Is No Doctor*. Teaching women about oral rehydration to deal with diarrhea, the importance of nutritious food for their children, the value of having their children vaccinated, and other health related activities, This RDF has had a significant impact on the women of this village. She was able to recruit 4-5 village women to become village health workers. Networking with a number of NGOs in Guatemala, she was instrumental in bringing several visiting instructors to this village, giving more advanced training in basic health care. Such training never would have been available in this village, if it had not been for the RDF. Far more significant has been efforts in working with the district nurse in El Chol. Together they have identified and recruited 30 women for all the ten villages in El Chol, and with the support of various NGOs, it is hoped that a series of training sessions will eventually be organized. Because of the RDF's input on the importance of building sustainable health care programs in this district, the women are being taught to charge some fees for the services they perform, helping them to see that if they accept free medicine and give it away, there is no way that medicine in the future would be available for these village health workers. Even if the villagers only pay a portion of the cost of medicine, they are, nevertheless, being taught a valuable principle about sustainability.

5. The RDFs have been in contact with FINCA, an urban based program in Guatemala, organizing women's micro-credit programs. John Hatch, the president, has agreed to allow women from El Chol to receive training from the FINCA staff, to support the RDFs in these efforts to help establish income-generating projects in the El Chol area. The RDFs were very excited about the possibility of setting up a micro-credit system in El Chol. With the support of John Hatch's organization, this could be a reality during the next several years. One woman mentioned that with a small loan of $50 she would be able to start a small business that would increase her income from less than 50 cents a day to over $1.00 a day.

6. In meeting with the Mayor of El Chol, I was impressed with how he described the work of the two RDFs. He said to me: "It is obvious that CHOICE is very different from most NGOs who come to El Chol. Most outsiders bring us free clothing, free food, medicine, and other gifts and after they leave we are still the same as before. The CHOICE RDFs do not bring us gifts they bring us hope, they bring their time and effort in helping us to help ourselves. I wish El Chol had twenty couples like these two RDFs. They give us hope, they teach us how to organize ourselves, how to get other organizations to come to El Chol to support our own efforts. I understand that CHOICE has very little resources to give, but what CHOICE brings us is far more important than any material gift, what the RDFs have given us is not money or free gifts, what they give is their time, their willingness to help us help ourselves!" He mentioned to me that many other districts in the area have now heard of CHOICE and are wondering when we will be sending rural development facilitators (RDFs) into their areas."[14]

A Process of Sustainable Village Development

At this point it is time to summarize the lessons learned from this book and to reflect on what role an RDF can play in initiating sustainable rural development. The focus of this book has been on the rural areas, both because this is where most of the really disadvantaged of this planet still live and secondly because effective rural development must be seen as one of the key foundations of any successful national development strategy. Also, it should be clear as implied by the title of this book and as was noted in the case studies of Unit Two and Unit Four, that one person working with local communities can make a difference. This phrase might seem trite and even unrealistic in a world dominated by huge donor agencies, expanding multinational corporations and missive centralized bureaucracies, but the evidence of this study suggests that individuals working together can bring about change, can preserve and strengthen cultures, and can develop solutions to problems in ways that are meaningful and appropriate.

As we conclude this discussion, let us for a moment focus on the four lessons learned. In Unit One of this book, we learned that there are serious problems and issues that all people should be concerned about and working in rural areas is a significant part of any process designed to confront the tragedies of poverty and underdevelopment In Unit Two, we learned that while the problems seem almost overwhelming, that individuals working on their own and in conjunction with others have been able to organize groups of people to challenge these problems in small and quiet but still in very significant ways. In Unit Three, we sought to operationalize the process of rural development implied in the three stages of rural development: trust building, local capacity building and local institution building pursued through a process of empowerment. Specific training and practical field experience will be needed before RDFs will be ready to introduce the three stage process defined. In Unit Four of this book, we reviewed in some detail a set of strategies, interventions and approaches that have proven useful in implementing projects in the five policy areas of rural development: literacy, health, income generation, protecting the local environment and enhancing and strengthening the local culture.

Sustainable Village Development: The Ultimate Goal of Rural Development
As a final observation, let us consider the ultimate focus of this book as one of village community development -- but village development that is sustainable over time. Sustainable Village Development (VSD) must be seen as a mosaic of reinforcing activities, a process of synergism that reflects more than the sum of its parts. In the final analysis Sustainable Village Development(SVD) is a process in which disadvantaged people organize themselves to overcome the obstacles to their social, cultural, political and economic well-being.

In focusing on the total village community, the RDF comes to appreciate the importance of how all aspects of the society are inter-related and that introduction of change in one dimension of rural development requires some changes in the other dimensions. An effective RDF must be sensitive to these inter-relationships and will be constantly thinking of how he or she can be certain that the various projects being implemented will be sustained after the RDF leaves. Below are the five principles of village sustainability that helps to ensure that the long-term goals of integration will be implemented as communities seek to pursue the three stages of rural development.

1. The Creation of a Common Sense of Community. It is important that the RDF operates within a clearly delimited geographical area. When the area involves too much diversity or too much distance between people, it is very difficult to create a common identity and sense of community. This is important if the RDF hopes to stimulate a sustainable process of village development. An RDF cannot spend too much time helping a cluster of village communities, usually at a district level, to perceive themselves as a unified whole with common problems and needing to work on common solutions.

2. Active Encouragement of Local Leadership. Long-term sustainability requires the identification, recruitment, training and support of local leaders in the various activities identified in the five dimensions of rural development. Each project area: (education, health, income enhancement through agriculture and small scale enterprise development, cultural enhancement, and protecting the environment) should be approached through the stimulation of village committees committed to dealing with these separate activities. The establishment of problem solving groups is an excellent way of identifying formal and informal leaders and giving them training in problem identification and solution implementation. Remember the 12 steps of problem solving group development mentioned above.

3. Broad Participation of all the People Sharing Equally in the Benefits of the Projects. Great effort will be needed to involve all groups, clans, families of the community. Sustainability requires that there be active involvement from all the people in the decisions being made, in the implementation of the projects agreed upon, and in the distribution of benefits from the projects developed. Over and over again we can find examples in the literature of how many small projects depended on broadly defined participation. The emergence of neighborhood groups, a village health committee, a woman's club, a farmer's marketing cooperative, a young people's sports club -- all tend to succeed -- not so much because of one individual's efforts but because the members pulled together using their common abilities and feeling a mutual responsibility for reaching the goal. Such activities will be sustainable to the extent that the benefits are equally shared by all the people participating in the project.

4. Moving from a Service Delivery System to a Resource Acquisition System. Most rural development programs are structured to provide services and resources made available by outsiders. The capacity building phase of rural development requires that RDFs and local village leaders begin to build linkages with local and national government agencies, national and international donors and other organizations that may have resources. This linkage building process is crucial if funding of projects are to continue after the RDF leaves the village. A resource acquisition system also includes developing resources in the community itself through community owned income-generating activities, collection of donations from the wealthier villagers, charging fees for the use of services provided, and other resource mobilization strategies.

5. Create Key Community Symbols. Special efforts will be needed to create specific links between the projects being implemented and the local culture. Communities need social reminders of the decisions they have made. Projects become sustainable when they provide not only the services needed but also a certain pride and *esprit de corps* within the communities as a whole. It is important that key cultural symbols are developed which bring a new sense of identity and meaning into these rural districts. The use of important traditions, sacred values and rituals, humor, games and sports, and other highly visible symbols of the unique characteristics of these rural areas are absolutely essential if the new projects are be internalized and made long-term. Without the creation of such culturally relevant symbols, the work and effort of the RDF will soon be forgotten and little of what he or she did in the district of focus will be sustained over time.

The Impact of Sustainable Village Development

Sustainable village development (SVD) is based upon a system of interventions that goes beyond simple economic and material well-being. This type of strategy seeks to achieve social and cultural objectives as well. Because sustainable village development (SVD) assumes that economic change must be built upon a solid social and cultural foundation, this strategy includes among its goals, for example, building collective confidence and self-respect, fostering a positive group identity, particularly if the group's members are from the most disadvantaged of a given society. The results of this strategy are often intangible: for example, improved problem solving skills, better communication skills among villagers, more effective use of group meetings, the development of local leaders to motivate villagers to work together on a common problem, increase sense of pride in the history and traditions of the village and a greater awareness of civil rights, government programs and land and water rights presently available. These are not attributes that are readily measurable or easy to document.

Too many outside donors want tangible results for the dollars they give, thus insisting that some concrete building or project activity be implemented that can be seen or measured in concrete terms. Such tangible results often circumvent the process of sustainable village development (SVD) by encouraging the outsider (RDF) to force or coerce the villagers to complete a project within the budget timeline of the donor agency, generally within only one or two years. When such projects are forced, the results will be the result of the RDFs' efforts not the efforts of villagers. Again, this problem can best be solved when the RDF is funded by some kind of Endowment Fund program that ensures that long-term resources will be available -- preferably for at least 5-10 years. Many outside-induced programs generally define poverty and development in relatively narrow terms, emphasizing material ends and imported technology and will generally downplay basic human needs such as self-esteem, a strong identity, group cohesiveness, creativity, and free expression. Programs that attend only to material factors by, for instance, increasing the production of cash crops for export often miss the point as to what brings about lasting improvements in a group's capacity to develop. These programs also frequently miss the point as to what people in poverty feel they need. When people lack dignity, self-esteem, and group solidarity, they can feel culturally and socially impoverished, which can perpetuate their being disadvantaged in a material sense.

Remember the long-term goal of sustainable village development (SVD) is to move through the stages of trust-building, capacity-building, and finally local institution building and empowerment. Within this strategy, empowerment and democratization replace humanitarian charity and the short-term treatment of the symptoms of poverty. Improved organizational and problem solving capacities are crucial for each community, including the formation of mutually supportive coalitions and networks, even the possibility of mass movements with like-minded communities and large groups of people working for long-term change and reform.

It is important to see how SVD requires a variety of different activities. And while it must begin with an appreciation for the local cultures of these disadvantaged communities and must seek to strengthen and reinforce local social energy through the enhancement of the traditional culture, it must be understood that this emphasis on culture is no panacea and will generally will not be enough to ensure that the processes started by the RDF will be sustainable. A culture-based approach must go hand in hand with other approaches that encourage people to achieve empowerment by strengthening organizations and coalitions; increased productivity by forming cooperative enterprises; heighten individual and group capacity through consciousness-raising and non formal education; or sustainable agricultural production through increased environmental sensibility. This is the reason for the importance of seeing the process of sustainable village development in holistic terms in which all of the five dimensions of rural development must be integrated over time. In the final chapter of this book we have sought to reflect on the ways in which foreign aid and technical assistance might be better organized into the 21st Century to have a maximum impact on the tragedies of world poverty and second we have sought to identify the special role that NGOs can play in implementing an effective program of sustainable development.

Final Conclusions

A Community Empowerment and District Linkage and Networking Approach to development based upon these principles of Sustainable Village Development (SVD) in no way addresses all of the main issues that face the world economy, but it does provide a promising approach, structured to initiate a set of interventions needed if the extremes of world poverty are to be confronted. Rejecting both the well-funded top down, centralized bureaucracy approach of many national governments and international donor agencies and perhaps the more culturally sensitive, but much less sustainable grassroots, single village approach, the district level approach seeks to build a gradual restructuring of society, in which a more equitable, pluralistic society, open to the needs and interests of a broader spectrum of the rural population are considered.

Much of the optimism that characterized the development literature of the late 1940s on through to the disillusionment of the 1980s and early 1990s, suggests that the time has come for some new, fresh thinking on how development programs might be implemented. The Western biased theoretical and practical shortcomings of the established models of both capitalist and Marxist thinkers are today so apparent, that many are seeking a broader, more flexible vision of development, capable of addressing the diverse realities of the less developed countries of this world.

Tendencies toward grand theorization, which is often intellectually stimulating and conceptually appealing, have proven incapable of dealing with the divergent constraints and opportunities available in the complex interplay of competing local, national, and international factors. Too often, the development process is artificially fragmented and compartmentalized to fit the areas of specialization, research methods, and theoretical frameworks of individual disciplines found in most major universities. As a result, many experts have failed to take advantage of ideas and methods found in other disciplines as well as from a variety of non-academic sources found in the local traditions and cultural wisdom of the common people of this planet. This bias for Western dominated thinking about development, ignores the views, wishes, and values of LDC peoples themselves.

The lessons of the past twenty years suggest that the processes, strategies, and interventions most apt to stimulate a self-sustainable approach to development must pay closer attention to a number of factors including: the historical legacy of colonialism that has dominated in many LDCs, to the sociocultural factors that give meaning and self-esteem to local people, and especially to the overarching structural conditions that reinforce economic inequality, social injustice and human rights violations. For this reason, very little of the theoretical material found in the literature of development is of any immediate use to local practitioners (RDFs) of development in the field. Unfortunately, too many practical development projects continue to make the same kinds of mistakes, being unwilling to approach the situation from the perspectives of the local people most involved in the process of development.

The one lesson that has come from this book, hopefully is that development is about people, about their strengthens, weaknesses, about their feelings, hopes and dreams. And while the structural constraints of exploiting local elites, dominating regional middlemen, and powerful national and international economic interests, often appear determining in most local settings, such predictions, such dominating systems of exploitation, greed, and violence, are not inevitable nor impervious to human will, agency and reflective thought. As was stated earlier, a model of development that ignores this capacity in the human spirit to reflect, to challenge, to organize, to change such structures overtime is incapable of reflecting the realities of world history. Progress requires more awareness of the ways that perceptions will constrict, even distort, what we see, experience and understand, filtering out potentially important factors that cannot be comfortably accommodated in most Western systems of development thought. Many of the realities of the world today that influence development processes are based upon the subjective impressions, feeling, and perceptions that are not neatly included in the rational, more positivist models of development

While the overarching systems of authoritarian control, economic exploitation and social intolerance cannot be ignored, they are not necessarily inevitable nor determing, as long as the reflective and organizing skills of people are recognized, reinforced and allowed to flower over time. The process being presented is by definition open-ended, never the consequence of a single cultural perspective, nor the inevitable result of any one coalition of interests, resources or perspectives. This model is not naive to the realities of social and economic inequalities or to the political cultural systems of human rights violations, but it does seek to approach such systems and such realities through a process of local problem solving, a set of local institution and district linkage-building activities, and a long-term commitment to popular empowerment and coalition-building that potentially can challenge the major systems of exploitation and inequities over time. A clear explanation of the various building blocks upon which significant mass movements for change can be developed is established upon a set of epistemological assumptions that respect both the determining factors of structure and power relationships, but also the open-ended factors of human agency and critical reflection. Upon these assumptions rests the processes of the District Networking Approach outlined in this Chapter and implied in the activities and roles that an RDF can play in the different stages of rural development. This approach hopefully will be a model or foundation upon which a broader, more comprehensive understanding of development processes will be built.

The quintessential argument of this book is that *One Can Make A Difference.* This book is filled with examples of people who have and are making a difference. What this world needs are hundreds and thousands of people like: Jimmy Yen, Ahmad al-Naggar, Muhammad Yunus, Mother Teresa, Wangari Maathai, Chico Mendes, A. T. Ariyaratne, Stan and Mari Thekaekara and hundreds of others unmentioned. While such people are the heart and soul of what is needed, the greater challenge is to form organizations, movements, networks and systems of actions that are sustainable, relevant and appropriate for the needs of specific communities. Such activities will build and formalize the processes of rural development and strengthen and institutionalize the ways in which these processes might impact appropriately on the great challenges of world poverty, ecological degradation, and political instability.

What I am arguing is that people who can make a difference are most apt to emerge and become self-sustaining not by working only at the national or provincial capital level or contrarily in some isolated village, but better, by developing their skills and capacity for intervention at the district level, at the level where clusters of villages can be integrated and linked to the broader system without destroying their own autonomy, their own sense of community, initiative and innovation. At this level, innovators and risk-takers are more apt to emerge as they work at a level that is generally freer from the demands of the central bureaucracy and the machinations of national politics, but also broad enough to provide for some economies of scale for program development and also diverse enough to field test a number of different strategies and models of intervention in a variety of different communities.

It is my conclusion that NGNOs have as one of their major functions, the identification, the recruitment and the support of future Jimmy Yens and Mother Teresas. This is what the future of rural development is about, this is the way in which both the foreign aid resources of our government and the generous donations of private citizens and organizations can best ensure that the processes of sustainable development will be implemented. Jimmy Yen used to say, a journey of one thousand miles must begin with the first step. One step at a time, one village at a time, one district at a time, this is the process by which rural development strategies and programs will be implemented.

---

[1] World Commission on Environment and Development, Our Common future (New York: Oxford University Press, 1987); Al Gore, Earth in the Balance: Ecology and the Human Spirit (Boston: Houghton MIfflin, 1992); and U.S. Agency for International Development, Strategies for Sustainable Development (Washington: USAID, March 1994).

[2] Independent Group on the Future of US Development Cooperation, *Reinventing Foreign AID: White Paper on US Development Cooperation in a New Democratic Era* (Washington: Overseas Development Council, December, 1992).

[3] Peter J. Davies, President of the American Council for Voluntary International Action (InterAction), in a presentation to the US Congress, House Select Committee on Hunger, suggested that a separate agency, which he called the Center for Voluntary Cooperation in Development (CVCD), should be established to implement this type of micro-approach that I am suggesting. I see no reason to establish another government agency, especially when USAID has functioned reasonably well over the past 30 years. See: US Congress, House Select Committee on Hunger, *Role of Private Voluntary Organizations and the US Foreign Assistance Program: Hearings* (Washington: USGPO, 1989), pp. 15-18, 122-40.

[4] Barbara Crosette, "Gore Says U.S. Will Shift More Foreign Aid to Private Groups," *New York Times*, 13 March 1995, A8.

[5] For example, one expert counts some 25,000 NGOs in a single Indian state. See *The Economist*, 7 May 1994, 20.

[6] See: Jonathan Power, "Our Views of the Third World is Warped," *Los Angeles Times*, 7 November 1993, M8.

[7] Stephen Hellenger et al., *Aid for Just Development: Report on the Future of Foreign Assistance* (1988).

[8] Judith Tendler, "Turning Private Voluntary Organizations into Development Agencies, "AID Program Evaluation Discussion Paper No. 12 (Washington DC: USAID, 1982).

[9] Samuel Paul and Arturo Israel (Eds.) *Non governmental Organizations and the World Bank: Cooperation for Development* (Washing, DC: The World Bank, 1991) and USAID, Development and the National Interest: US economic Assistance into the 21st Century (Washington, DC: USAID, 1989).

[10] Van der Heijden, *Development Impact*, pp. 1-4.

[11] OECD, Directory of Non-Government Organizations in OECD Member Countries, (Paris, 1990).

[12] Michael Bratton, "The Politics of Government-NGO Relations in Africa, World Development, Vol. 17, No.4 (1989); David L. Brown and David C. Korten, "Working More Effectively with Non governmental Organizations in Paul and Israel, op. cit., Fisher, op. cit.; and Thomas F. Carroll, *Intermediary NGOs: The Supporting Link in Grassroots Development* (West Hartford, CT: Kumarian Press, 1992

[13] David C. Korten, *Getting to the 21st Century: Voluntary Action and the Global Agenda*, (West Hartford, Connecticut: Kumarian Press, 1990), p. 127.

[14] James B. Mayfield, Field Notes, (CHOICE files, May 15, 1996).

Index

ACCORD, 168-75
Acid rain, 427
Action research, 393-94
Adolescence, 196
Adulthood, 197-99
Agriculture 389-93
  world, 389-390; traditional, 390-92
  modern, 391-92; large scale, 392
  peasant, 392-93
AIDS, 18
al-Naggar, 4
Appiko movement, 443-44
Appropriate technology, 177-78

Basic health care, 379-80
Basic needs, 105
Beliefs and attitudes, 252
Bread for the World, 478
Bretton Woods Conference, 77

Career in development, 183
  motives, 184-87
Capacity building, 267-72
Childhood, 194-96
Chipko movement, 441-42
CHOICE, 114-18
  micro-credit, 410-12; networking, 94-496; rural hospital outreach, 377-78
Civil disobedience, 148-49
Clitoridectomy, 461-62
Coalition building, 299, 315-77
Colonialism, 57
Community service, 206-14
Community unity, 62
  autonomy, 277; empowerment, 501;
  forestry, 438-39
Cooperatives, 406-08
Creativity, 456-57

Credit, local 409-11
  basic principles, 414-15;
  subsidized, 41314
  See also micro-credit
Crop rotation, 397-98
Cultural enhancement, 334, 463-65
  contrasting views, 452; creativity
  and innovation, 456-57; pluralism
  457-58
Culture, understanding, 212-13
  assumptions, 248-49; awareness,
  254-57; dialoguing, 258-65, 333-34;
  negative consequences, 458-59;
  persistence, 462-63; primary health
  care, 458-59

Deforestation, 24, 56, 422, 434-44
Delegated powers, 276-77
Dependency theory, 62, 90-93
Desertification, 423
Development,
  alternative, 96-98; definition, 424-25
  human rights violations, 475;
  paradigms, 85-97; political economy,
  85-97; role of culture, 450-54,
Development careers,
  common myths, 230-31
Dialoguing, cultural, 258-69, 451
Diarrhea, 15-16

Earthworms, 398
Education, 130-31, 155-56
  central government, 330-31
  primary education, 327-30
  program flexibility, 338-39; self-initiated, 338;
  village community, 330-31
Egypt, 3-4, 135-46

Empowerment, 112-13, 122, 299-303, 337-38
  coalition building, 315-16; community level, 304-05; individual level, 303-4; linkage building, 307-8; process, 305
Endowment fund, 119
Environment, 21-22, 418-19
  case studies, 433-44; contrasting approaches, 427, protection of, 425-26
Epistemology, 237-42
Eric Erickson, 192-99
Expeditions, 114-15
Exploitation, 278-79

Facilitator model, 270
Fieldwork, 214-18
Food production, trends, 22-23
Foreign aid programs, 481-83
  some successes, 480; recent trends, 476
Four C's, 189
Freire, Paulos, 34

Gandhi, 3, 424
General systems theory, 308
Gini Coefficient, 36-37
GNP, 48, 66
Grameen bank, 1067
Green belt movement, 439-40
Green house effect, 418-22

Group identity/solidarity, 455

Harris tadaro, 75
Harold Domar, 71
Health, 11-20
  China 133-34; leadership, 385-86; needs assessment, 384-85, organization, 386; resource mobilization, 387
Hospital outreach program, 377-78
Human development index, 45-48
Human rights violations, 475
Hundred village program 154-55

Hunger, 11-12

IIRR, 430
Illiteracy, 19, 325-26
Immunization, 362
Imperialism, 88-89
Income enhancement, 405-07
Indigenous management 179
Inequality, 32-39
Infancy, 193
Infant mortality, 13-14
Interdependency, 95-96, 291-93
Internships, 115-16, 224-30
Interpersonal skills, 281-84

Kolb, David, 204-06
Korten, David, 83-84
Kuznets "inverted u", 70-71

Leadership, rural 295, 385-86
Learning style, 204-06
Lenin, 89-90
Lewis, Arthur model, 75
Literacy efforts, 339-45
Livelihood, 131-32
Local culture enhancement, 448-50
Local dialects, 277-78
Local government, 277
Local institution building, 105, 299-300

Maison Familias rurales, 341
Malnutrition, 12,16, 361-62
Marketing systems, 408-09
Marshal Plan, 68
Marx, Karl, 87
McNamara, Robert, 77
Medicine, traditional, 366-68
  modern, 380
Micro-credit, stages, 411
  problems/constraints, 413
Modernization theory, 86-87

Index 507

Moral development, 208-10

Needs assessment, 384
Neem tree, 403-04
Networking, 106, 179-80, 299, 379
Non formal education, 327
Non Government Organizations (NGOs)
   classification, 488-89; first generation, 485-86, second generation, 486; third generation, 487, fourth generation, 488
   networking, 490-93
Nutrition, 12

OPEC, 78
Openness, 289-90
Organic farming, 396-401
   earthworms, 398; fertilizers, 398-99
   pesticides, 399, weed control, 399
Ozone layer, 422

Paraprofessionals, 368-69
Participation
   challenges, 277-78; health, 383-87;
   research, 371-72; typology, 274-77
Participatory Rural Appraisal, 429
Peasant agriculture, 392-93
Plague, 18
Planning, effective, 268-69
Pluralism, 457-58
Point four program, 68-69
Policy definition, 319
Polio plus, 351
Political instability, 24-25, 57, 63
Political strategy, 319-20
Population, 25-31
   contrasting views, 28-30
   trends, 26
Poverty
   definitions, 42-43; explanations, 52-53;
   extreme, 473-75; global perspective, 47;
   measuring, 46-51
Power, realities, 213-14, 276

PQLI, 48
Primary education, 327
Primary health care
   combination strategy, 354-55;
   horizontal/vertical 352-53;
   local culture, 369-70
   north-south paradigm, 35051
   paraprofessional, 368
Problem solving, 121, 284-94, 296-98

Rapid rural appraisal, 429
Realization, 290-91
Resource mobilization, 387
Rural development
   career levels, 201-02;
   three stages, 108-09, 119-22
Rural development facilitator (RDF)
   agriculture, 401-03; attributes, 188-90; confronting, 283; culturally skilled 251-53; empowerment, 305-07;
   environmental protection, 428-33;
   health care, 381-82; interpersonal skills, 190-92; professional status, 318-20; rural transformation, 315-18
Rural district approach, 310-14
Rural hospital outreach, 377-79
Rural leadership, 295-96
Rustow, Walt, 70

Sanitation, 360
Sarvodaya, 147-54
Self-disclosure, 249
Self-government, 134
Self-reliance, 177
Soil erosion, 23-4, 417
Small scale enterprise, 406-7
Social energy, 453-54
Social learning theory, 310
Specie extinction, 422
Spirulina, 402-3
Stage one of rural development
   agriculture, 393-94;

cultural enhancement, 454, 458
education, 334-37;
environment, 428-30
income generation, 411
Stage two of rural development
  agriculture, 394
  cultural enhancement, 454, 458
  education, 334-37
  environment, 430-32
  income generation, 411-12
Stage three of rural development
  agriculture, 395
  cultural enhancement, 455, 458-59
  education, 337-38
  environment, 432-33
  income generation, 412
Structural adjustment, 81
Subsistence cycle, 396-401,
  poor, 410-11
Supervising interns, 227-30
Sustainable development
  economic dimension, 419-20
  environmental dimension, 421-22
  human dimension, 420-21
Sustainable village development, 497-500
Sustainability
  poor, 410-11; health, 362-63, 381

Take-off stage, 70-71
Teacher-initiated education, 345-47
Technical assistance, 112
Technology, local, 404-5
Technology transfer, 104
Ten basic needs, 158
Time, assumptions, 249
Ting Hsien, 128-29
Tolstoy farm, 149
Toxic waste, 423
Traditional agriculture, 391-93
Traditional medicine, 366-67, 380
Trust building, 120, 250, 282, 288-92, 333-34

Unemployment 20
UNICEF, 15

Values, educational, 210-11
  role of values, 243-46
  western vs eastern, 248
  family, 249
Village
  bank; community education, 330-32;
  competencies, 278-80;
  development, 497-99;
  income development, 405-9;
  problems solving groups, 284-94;
Village community health care 357-58
  basic principles, 378-79

Water
  depletion, 423; sanitation, 16-17
witchcraft, 459-60
Women
  agriculture, 400-01; credit, 412-15;
  role of, 412-15

Yen, James, 125

Zambia case study, 345-47

DATE DUE